MARATHON

Also by Jules Witcover

Eighty-Five Days: The Last Campaign of Robert Kennedy (1969)
The Resurrection of Richard Nixon (1970)
White Knight: The Rise of Spiro Agnew (1972)
A Heartbeat Away: The Investigation and Resignation of
    Vice President Spiro T. Agnew (1974) *(with Richard M. Cohen)*

MARATHON
The Pursuit of the Presidency
1972-1976

Jules Witcover

THE VIKING PRESS   NEW YORK

Copyright © Jules Witcover, 1977
All rights reserved

First published in 1977 by The Viking Press
625 Madison Avenue, New York, N.Y. 10022

Published simultaneously in Canada by
Penguin Books Canada Limited

LIBRARY OF CONGRESS CATALOGING IN PUBLICATION DATA
Witcover, Jules.
  Marathon: the pursuit of the Presidency, 1972–1976.

  Includes index.
1. Presidents—United States—Election—1976.
2. United States—Politics and government—1969–1974.
3. United States—Politics and government—1974–1977.
I. Title.
E868.W57   329'.023'730925   77–4387
ISBN 0–670–45461–3

Printed in the United States of America

Set in videocomp Times Roman

To Marilyn, Sabe, and family

I turned me to another thing, and I saw that under the sun, the race is not to the swift, nor the battle to the strong, nor bread to the wise, nor riches to the learned, nor favor to the skillful; but time and chance in all.

Ecclesiastes 9:11.

Contents

Preface

There ought to be, by any reckoning, something inspiring about a free people of more than 200 million electing their leader. With the franchise a mockery at best in many countries, and with the domestic and global role of the modern American President so immense, the quadrennial exercise of selection might be expected to occasion a massive outpouring at the ballot box. There was a time, in the adolescent years of the American Republic, when this was so. In 1840, 80 per cent of an electorate of 2.4 million turned out to choose William H. Harrison, the Whig candidate, over President Martin Van Buren, the Democrat. And in 1860, 81 per cent of an electorate of 4.7 million went to the polls in the victory of Abraham Lincoln of the new Republican Party over Democrats Stephen A. Douglas and John C. Breckinridge, and John Bell of the Constitutional Union Party. One hundred years later, however, only 62.8 per cent of 102.7 million Americans of voting age took the time to cast ballots in the critical election of 1960 in which John F. Kennedy entered the White House by a margin of one-half of one vote a precinct over Richard M. Nixon. Eight years later, when Nixon finally attained the presidency in a similarly narrow victory over Hubert H. Humphrey, only 60.9 per cent of 120 million Americans of voting age turned out. And finally, in 1972 when Nixon won a landslide re-election over George S. McGovern, for every American of voting age who bothered to go to the polls (only 55.4 per cent), roughly speaking one stayed home.

In the course of the fourteen tempestuous years between Kennedy's victory and Nixon's resignation, a gnawing public suspicion that the political system somehow did not work was hardened into conviction by acts of national violence, political assassination, deception, and corruption at the highest levels of power. Contrary to what John Kennedy in 1960 and his brother Robert in 1968 had so earnestly preached—that "one man can make a difference"—the voters seemed to believe that no politician could be a vehicle for real progress, for the collective good. Or, worse than that, that there were no honest, altruistic public officials any longer.

In the 1974 congressional elections, with Nixon deposed after the long nightmare of Watergate, the voter turnout fell to an abysmal 38 per cent;

a postelection survey by Decision-Making Information, a California based political-polling and research organization, indicated that for all the emphasis on voter education as the answer to political apathy, the informed citizen wasn't voting either. A leading Republican polling analyst, Lance Tarrance, suggested the survey pointed to the failure of voter education. But Patrick Caddell, a Democratic pollster from Boston, disagreed. What the survey showed, he said, was that voter education did indeed work; informed voters perceived correctly that politicians by and large were *not* making a difference or, in light of the Watergate scandal and all its sordid ramifications, that they could not be trusted, and those voters were telling the politicians so by staying home on Election Day.

In 1976 a survey on nonvoters for the Committee for the Study of the American Electorate by pollster Peter Hart found corroboration of the low esteem in which the political system is held. In a rating of the confidence that people placed in thirteen major American institutions, the two political parties were ranked at the bottom. And 55 per cent of nearly 1500 individuals participating in lengthy interviews said they did not vote because they agreed that "it doesn't make any difference who is elected, because things never seem to work right." On the credibility of candidates, the result was even more negative: 68 per cent said they didn't vote because "candidates say one thing and then do another." Also, 61 per cent thought "quite a few of the people running the government in Washington are a little crooked"; 57 per cent thought they could trust the federal government to do what was right "only some of the time"; 62 per cent thought it was "pretty much run by a few big interests."

In this climate of public apathy at best and public disillusionment at worst the 1976 campaign for the presidency began. It is convenient to talk about "the political season" as if it were like the baseball season—starting with early-spring training and a round of exhibition games, moving into the regular season, and culminating in a World Series. But in truth there is no political season; the struggle for the presidency never stops. On the November night in 1972 when Richard Nixon was re-elected, political forces already were in process that shaped the battle for the White House in 1976, and politicians were assessing them, adjusting their own demeanor to them, positioning themselves.

The horserace analogy has been much overworked in politics—the presidential sweepstakes and the winter-book favorite and all that—but in this one sense it remains apropos: the astute and ambitious politician always looks ahead; he acts today with his eye and his mind on tomorrow and next year and the year after that; he knows that the only thing predictable in presidential politics is that the unpredictable will happen, and so he positions himself to be able to take quick and optimum advantage of any break that comes his way. The prudent White House aspirant closes no doors behind him; he "keeps his options open," and in doing so he is very much like a jockey in the early going, trying to move ahead but always keeping the opposition in his peripheral vision, gauging his relative position, ready to exploit an unexpected opening in the pack, meanwhile pacing his mount for the long haul.

In order to begin to understand what a White House aspirant puts into his reach for power, and what it takes out of him, it is necessary to accept that running for President is no one-year crash effort, but a way of life extending over a number of years. The exercise is no romantic odyssey, at the end of which the winner emerges bright and shining and ennobled by the experience. It is a grueling, debilitating, and often dehumanizing ordeal that exacts an extravagant price not only for winning but also for the mere running and losing. The individual candidate and his family and friends all pay the price in varying measure, and so, importantly, does the country. The voters are bored, soured, outraged, numbed, disaffected by the long procession of public statements, charges and countercharges, newspaper photographs and television film of seemingly nonstop campaigners at endless factory gates on endless frigid mornings. They wish it would all go away, at least for a while. But it does not go away; within days after the election of a President, the fires of ambition in other politicians, banked only fleetingly, are flickering again; the course ahead is surveyed, the potential opposition for next time is scanned and assessed, the jockeying proceeds apace. That is how the seizing of power is attempted in the United States, and it is done in close quarters; lofty purpose, private fortunes and personal dreams all are bumped and jostled in the process, and as often as not, bruised or even crippled. So it is not surprising that the national consciousness and the national interest also are bruised and even crippled en route, until a great disenchantment approaching bitterness blankets the public attitude toward the whole punishing business.

Yet, for all that, there has been no swelling demand, in or out of politics, that this excessively exacting ordeal be somehow civilized. Proposals in Congress to revamp the presidential primary system, a marathon obstacle course that consumes time, money, and humans like some insatiable furnace, have gotten nowhere; the individual with his eye on the White House must persevere or quit. Nearly all stick it out as long as money, physical endurance, and emotional stability last and the dream of success is not overwhelmed by the reality of failure. When a realist like Senator Walter F. Mondale of Minnesota, after more than a year of actively "exploring" his chances, recognized in November 1974 that the price was more than he was willing to pay, he dropped out. But when he did so, and said candidly that the price was too high, his admission came as a shock; in the American glorification of the presidency, no price is supposed to be excessive for its attainment. Mondale, in announcing his withdrawal, expressed the common belief that a candidate should be "willing to go through fire" to become President. And less than two years later, he agreed after all to take his share of the heat as his party's vice-presidential nominee. Never mind that the principal survivor of the campaign brimstone may emerge badly scarred by the experience, to the detriment of his capacity for later public service; the mythology requires that the aspirant wants the presidency so much he can taste it. Like the Roman gladiators, the American candidate for President must be ready to give all, and risk all, at the whim of the crowd. That some lose and live to fight another day is more a tribute to their durability and unquenchable ambition than any evidence of a merciful system. An election year does not go by without the dashing of great expectations, the arrest of promising careers, and even the destruction of personal lives, from the candidate himself to members of his immediate and campaign families. The reach is high and the fall long.

Why, then, do any of them try it, and why so many in 1976? Part of the reason, on the Democratic side at least, was that for the first time the federal treasury, thanks to a new campaign reform, was picking up roughly half of the cost of running. But, aside from that factor, the prize is worth the effort beyond all caviling: the power to do good, to preserve peace, to unleash the energies of a huge bureaucracy; above all, to be the leader of the people. The same drive that initiates the first campaign handshake for whatever lower office propels and sustains these ofttimes egocentric, sometimes masochistic men and women to undertake the most arduous test in politics. Some, like Hubert Humphrey, run with zest and joy, and seem unable to stop at the end of the longest day, so filled with the experience do they become. Others, like Edmund S. Muskie, in 1972, trudge through the daily schedule like Bogart tugging the lifeboat from the *African Queen* on a rope behind him, waist-high in polluted waters with leeches mercilessly fastened to him and sucking away. But the common inducement is power, its exercise, and the accouterments thereof.

This is the story of that quest for power by ordeal in 1976; of what it did to the candidates, to their families and friends, to their campaign workers, to the press that dogged their footsteps, to the political parties and, finally, to the country itself. A campaign for the presidency is an endurance test to be sure, but it is as well a contest of wills, strategies, and, above all, the interaction of people. It is also, in part at least, a running statement on the condition of the country, on the issues that do or should command its attention; on the problems that face it, as perceived by the professional politicians who strive, by addressing those issues and offering solutions to those problems, to seize leadership through the democratic process. And so, in sum, this is a story about where America found itself leading up to and through the presidential election year of 1976, about the individuals who struggled, won, and lost, about the changes they wrought, about their failures and what those failures suggest about them and the country, two hundred years after its birth.

Acknowledgments

One morning over breakfast at the Republican National Convention in Kansas City, one of the better press secretaries of the 1976 or any other campaign, Peter Kaye of the President Ford Committee, was telling me about the strain of it all. "It's a cumulative effect," he said. "From January into August, it was just one crisis after another—one primary, one convention state, one bunch of uncommitted delegates. You're really worn out. I know I was flatter than hell. That's a god-damned long campaign. I remember coming back from Missouri: at the airport in Springfield, I ran into Mike Deaver of the Reagan campaign and another guy, and we got to talking. They were saying how tired they were, how they'd never been to a movie, how they just hadn't had any life for six or seven months, and how wearing it was. Suddenly I could sympathize; I felt the same way. You're a fraternity of lost souls in a campaign this long; the reporters too. I'd never been in anything this long. All of a sudden you've run out of things to say against the other guy, and about your guy. But you have to go through it all in another state, when you're exhausted—physically, mentally, and every other way."

Without this fraternity of lost souls, whose members run into the thousands in the huge business of electing a President and reporting about it, anyone attempting to chronicle the quest for the presidency would himself be a lost soul. The fraternity, however, engenders a sense of shared experience and interdependence through the long months, and its members are an immense resource for one who undertakes such a task; to my great fortune, a willing and generous resource.

Politicians and members of the press are supposed to be, and by and large regard themselves to be, in an adversary relationship. The one group strives to elect a President, the other labors to find how they are doing it and why. Yet because they are all embarked on the same adventure every four years, they become like fellow passengers on a ship, thrown together for a long voyage on which there is no alternative to peaceful coexistence. There are arguments and disagreements and dissembling and distorting on both sides, to be sure. But the common experience fosters a mutual candor and trust that is indispensable to one who seeks to put down whatever he can learn about what happened, and why it happened, on this quadrennial political journey.

To Presidents Carter and Ford, who took time to examine with me the great adventure in which they were the featured participants, I am indebted first of all. And then to these members of the fraternity of lost souls, the losers—Birch Bayh, Jerry Brown, Frank Church, Fred Harris, Henry Jackson, Ronald Reagan, Terry Sanford, Milton Shapp, Sargent Shriver, Morris Udall, and George Wallace;

Also, Peter Bourne, Chris Brown, Landon Butler, Patrick Caddell, Rex Granum, Hamilton Jordan, Charles Kirbo, Tim Kraft, Dick Moe, Frank Moore, Jody Powell, Jerry Rafshoon, Betty Rainwater, Greg Schneiders, Phil Wise, and Andrew Young of the Carter-Mondale campaign;

Doug Bailey, Jim Baker, Bo Callaway, Dick Cheney, John Deardourff, Bob Dole, Mike Duval, Bill Greener, Peter Kaye, Ron Nessen, Brent Scowcroft, Stu Spencer, Bob Teeter, and Kim Wells of the Ford-Dole campaign;

Jeff Bell, Charlie Black, David Keene, Jim Lake, Lyn Nofziger, Richard Schweiker, John Sears, and Dick Wirthlin of the Reagan-Schweiker campaign;

John Gabusi, Tom Kiley, Stanley Kurz, John Marttila, Bob Neuman, Jack Quinn, Paul Tully, and Stewart Udall of the Udall campaign;

Mike Casey, Brian Corcoran, Bob Keefe, and Ben Wattenberg of the Jackson campaign;

Mike Bleicher, Fred Droz, Dick Murphy, Jim Rosapepe, and Barbara Shailor of the Harris campaign;

Mickey Kantor of the Shriver and Jerry Brown campaigns;

Mickey Griffin and Charles Snider of the Wallace campaign;

Bill Wise of the Bayh campaign; and

Dick Drayne of the Shriver campaign.

Also, to these members of the media: Ken Bode, Dick Bradlee, David Broder, Lou Cannon, John Chancellor, Dick Cohen, Walter Cronkite, Lester Crystal, Joe Daughen, Helen Dewar, Jim Dickenson, Sam Donaldson, Max Frankel, Jack Germond, Bill Greider, Bob Healy, Myra McPherson, Margaret Mayer, Walter Mears, Warren Mitofsky, Charles Mohr, Susan Morrison, Jim Naughton, Don Oliver, Tom Ottenad, Jim Perry, Marty Plissner, Ed Rabel, Sam Roberts, Bob Scheer, Marty Schram, Jerry terHorst, John Thompson, Bob Turner, Ed Walsh, Curtis Wilkie, and Jim Wooten.

And to these others in the political community: Sam Brown, Hy Cannoli, Curtis Gans, Judy Green, Hugh Gregg, Hubert Humphrey, Jacob

Javits, Jim Karayn, Drew Lewis, Charles Percy, Clarke Reed, Alex Seith, Mark Shields, Bob Shrum, Mark Siegel, Bob Squier, and John Tower.

I would like to thank also Larry Fox, Ed Goodpaster, and Harry Rosenfeld, my immediate editors at *The Washington Post* during the campaign; my wife Marian and daughter Julie for valuable assistance in collating much research material; my editors at The Viking Press, Elisabeth Sifton and Georgette Felix, for painstaking, intelligent, and constructive editing; and my agent, David Obst.

Finally, no such account of a long political campaign could be written without the help of countless campaign workers in primary and caucus states across the country, and the reporters who write of their activities. They know who they are, and I know who they are, and I thank them greatly.

Jules Witcover

Washington, D. C.
February 19, 1977

part I

**THE
END
OF THE
MARATHON**

1. The Ultimate Media Event

It was three o'clock in the morning on the East Coast. About two hours earlier, the last voters in Alaska and Hawaii had cast their ballots. All through the long night, in the curious way of American presidential elections in the Age of Television, the two principals—Gerald Rudolph Ford, Jr., the Republican, the President of the United States, and James Earl Carter, Jr., the Democrat, the challenger—had been remote, unseen figures, glued, as millions of ordinary Americans were, to the television screen.

Jerry Ford was in the family quarters on the second floor of the White House with his wife, Betty, his daughter Susan, his sons Jack, Mike, and Steve, and his running mate, Senator Robert Dole of Kansas, and his wife, Liddy. Present as well was a rather large contingent of Grand Rapids friends, and others—campaign companions and political associates (including, somewhat incongruously, the liberal senator Jacob Javits, from New York, whose judgment Ford particularly valued). The millions who had viewed Ford's election campaign through its televised commercials could have recognized at once two star surrogates: the ex-baseball player and now television personality Joe Garagiola, and singer Pearl Bailey. They and others had shared with the First Family a buffet of beef stroganoff and shrimp creole and were now settled in, digesting a long diet of televised election news. Four television sets were turned on in three locations—one in the main living room at the far end of the building, overlooking the West Wing; two in the President's small study adjacent to the master bedroom just off the living room; one about halfway down the main second-floor corridor that runs east from the living area, where chairs were set in a wide semicircle around the monitor. The President sat for a time with one group in one room, then strolled on to the next and the next, talking easily with his friends as he watched. Betty Ford did the same, sitting for a while on the floor with her arms around Pearl Bailey as the tension mounted.

The Republican candidate had known he was facing an uphill struggle. Richard Cheney, his chief of staff; James Baker, his campaign manager; Stuart Spencer, his chief political strategist; and Bob Teeter, his pollster, had come to the Oval Office earlier in the evening with network "exit" polls —taken as voters left polling places in key precincts around the country. NBC showed him trailing badly; CBS had him trailing narrowly; but no breakout of likely electoral-vote apportionment was included, and people were hopeful. The President had been forewarned that Carter could be expected to build up an early lead in the South, and that his own strength would grow as returns came in from the Midwest and West. And so he and his friends followed the results with nervous anticipation, knowing always the dimensions of the political miracle they sought. "We're still going to win this thing," he told his family and friends.

At the same hour, in the Capitol Suite on the fifteenth floor of the Omni International Hotel in Atlanta, a markedly subdued Jimmy Carter sat in shirt sleeves before a trio of television sets, each tuned to one of the three networks. With him were his wife, Rosalynn, his daughter Amy, and his sons Jack, Jeff, and Chip; also, Charles Kirbo, his close friend and senior adviser; Hamilton Jordan, his campaign manager; Jody Powell, his press secretary; Pat Caddell, his pollster; Jerry Rafshoon, his advertising specialist; and other aides, their wives, and children. The Secret Service had cordoned off the fifteenth floor, and the Carter political family moved around the corridor and adjacent rooms in a continuing buzz of excitement. Insiders drifted through Carter's suite, talking, often ignoring both the candidate and the television sets, sometimes standing in his line of vision and requiring him to ask that they move so he could watch. He would make the request quietly, courteously, behaving for all the world in the manner of a tolerant, loving father in a roomful of boisterous children. He sat with outward serenity, sometimes holding hands with his wife in that overtly affectionate way that had become a trademark for him—and an awkward embarrassment to hardened politicians outside the tight personal and political family circle that now enveloped him.

Carter, too, had been briefed, by Caddell, on the NBC and CBS "exit" polls at the start of the long evening. They had run down all the states, noting those that constituted his expected base—214 of the 270 electoral votes he needed—and those in the toss-up category, totaling 170 electoral votes. Then, as the night wore on, the Democratic candidate sat, with what Jordan later called "an air of inevitability," absorbed by television's tracking of the returns. As his electoral vote mounted, Carter worked the telephone like any old pol, thanking prominent supporters around the country—Mayor Richard J. Daley in Chicago foremost among them—and seeking their informed reading of the progress in their states. (Daley told him early he was holding out the vote tallies for a thousand heavily Democratic Chicago precincts, in the event Carter needed a late surge to withstand downstate Illinois Republican strength; Carter eventually did need these votes, and more. Ultimately, for all of Daley's efforts, he lost the state.)

To arrive at this momentous night, each candidate had been obliged to travel an incredible, arduous route; for Jerry Ford, up from a dead end as House minority leader to the vice-presidency and then the presidency in rapid succession; for Jimmy Carter, up from a single obscure term as governor of Georgia; for both, survival after enduring an unprecedented calendar of thirty presidential primaries against stiff competition. But they, too, were reduced to being spectators now.

In this critical political hour, the mechanics and the sheer power of mass communications in contemporary America dictated that the two candidates surrender the spotlight to the barons of Election Night: to the famous network commentators and analysts in New York's television centers reporting the state-by-state returns and sifting out their meaning for the millions of Americans who awaited the results. The largest share of this vast audience—30 per cent—was tuned to the man judged in public-opinion polls to be the single most trusted individual of all Americans, Walter Cronkite, of CBS News. Cronkite, a sincere and warm-hearted man of sixty, even-handed yet inquisitive, with the instincts and enterprise of a good reporter, reigned in Studio 41 on West Fifty-seventh Street, Manhattan, over a stable of old and new television stars—Eric Sevareid, Mike Wallace, Roger Mudd, Dan Rather, Bill Moyers, Leslie Stahl—whose names and faces had become as familiar to most Americans as those of the candidates themselves. The second-largest audience—28 per cent—was watching the NBC News team, headed by John Chancellor, a relaxed, engaging man of wit and intelligence who still haunted the political beat as time allowed, and David Brinkley, whose dour humor had become an Election Night fixture. They were assisted in Studio 8H at 30 Rockefeller Plaza by the "Today" host, Tom Brokaw, a former White House correspondent, and Catherine Mackin, a solid, experienced political reporter. In third place, with 18 per cent of the audience,[1] was the rejuvenated ABC News team of Barbara Walters, the "Today" show hostess graduated to anchorwoman status, Harry Reasoner, a comfortable old shoe of broadcasting, and the veteran analyst Howard K. Smith.

Celebrity brings authority in this country, and when any of these commentators spoke of how Ford or Carter was faring in the East, South, Midwest, or West, the audience listened as if these expert communicators were themselves the official election tabulators. Indeed, the networks' elabo-

---

1. The remaining 26 per cent was tuned to public broadcasting or local independent channels.

rate polling mechanisms geared to key precincts enabled the "decision desk" at each to "project" a winner in each of the fifty states; this precipitated an internetwork competition that made America a nation of channel-switchers throughout the long night. Even in selecting a President, the name of the game in the television business was ratings: the network that could suggest it knew more about what was going on, and could say first and with certainty who the winner would be, would presumably seize and hold the largest audience.

Behind the mystery of the television projections was a complex judgmental system deeply steeped in statistics and computer calculations. At NBC, the analysis proceeded on two tracks. One was in the hands of Richard Scammon, former director of the U.S. Census Bureau and a voter-analysis expert. A huge man in both height and girth, Scammon, with a full case of iced soft drinks at his feet, off camera range, checked incoming results to determine whether normal trends were holding and, from such information, sought to project statewide votes. The second NBC track, manned by statisticians, was based on more extensive raw-vote data and mathematical computations. In order for NBC to call a state, it was necessary that the two tracks reach the same conclusion.

At CBS, there was no Scammon. Instead, three separate teams of statisticians pored over raw election results and sample precincts, under the over-all direction of Warren Mitofsky, another Census Bureau alumnus. Minute by minute, correspondents in the studio received updates on monitors built into their desks, but they were required to await Mitofsky's judgment on when a state could be called for Ford or Carter.

At ABC, three decision desks functioned under John Thompson at a private computer center in Middlebury, Connecticut, with direct relays to Studio TV One on West Sixty-sixth Street. At each desk were four experts: an ABC newsman, a political scientist, a sampling statistician, and a mathematician. Using sample precinct data and the raw vote from the National Election Service (NES) that was available to all the networks, all four had to agree before they made a state projection to Thompson, who then phoned it in to Walter Pfister, an ABC special-events vice president at the Manhattan studio.

Projecting the winner by such arrangements was only the first part of television's task, for it needed a swift, accurate, and effective way to convey the result to the viewing public. To achieve this end, each network had a new electronic device to produce instantaneous graphics. The push of a button flashed on the television screen a printed report of any state, the projected winner, the percentage of the vote in, and the number of electoral votes won. NBC's machine, called Chyron,[2] is a complex data bank that can be programed to receive data and produce a display on demand. With this device, which Chancellor likens to "an electronic filing cabinet," it is no longer necessary to keep the old-fashioned ceiling-to-floor tote boards with postings by hand that were so slow and confusing in earlier years. From a glass-enclosed control room, NBC's Election Night producer, Lester Crystal, directed a futuristic wonderland of gadgetry and internal telecommunications, coordinating Chyron with reports and commentary. And on a large electronic map of the United States, which at Chancellor's suggestion had been assembled by the network's visual-aide geniuses, states lit up in red as they went for Carter, in blue as they went for Ford. It proved to be the most arresting way of transmitting the results offered by any of the networks on this night. (Those watching on black-and-white sets saw the states in light gray for Carter, dark gray for Ford.)

As soon as their Election Night coverage went on the air at 6:30 o'clock, all three networks called Kentucky for Carter and Indiana for Ford. Then, with Kansas, Nebraska, and Connecticut early exceptions for the President, they ticked off a string of Eastern and Southern states for Carter: Massachusetts and Rhode Island to West Virginia, North Carolina, and Tennessee, down to Florida and over to Alabama, a crescent of electoral votes tumbling to the peanut farmer from Georgia whose very candidacy was a signal that first-class political citizenship had finally come to Dixie. Not since the 1848 election of General Zachary Taylor, a Louisiana planter and hero of the Mexican War, had a man of the Deep South won the presidency without benefit of incumbency. Carter's regional appeal, and his pull among Southern blacks especially, enabled him to build a clear lead as the early returns came in. All the television barons agreed in their projections (though there were sharp discrepancies in the time they called certain states), and all held out on two other Southern states—Virginia and Mississippi. But already Carter had done something for the Democrats that had not been achieved since the New Deal days of Franklin D. Roosevelt: he had established a firm Southern base on which to construct victory; it was a return to the Solid South after its near-demolition by the war-hero candidacies of Dwight D. Eisenhower and then by the "Southern strategies" of Barry Goldwater and Richard Nixon.

In the Atlanta hotel suite, confidence and buoyancy quickly built up,

2. Named for Chiron, of Greek mythology; leader of the centaurs and chief instructor of the gods, who was wounded by Hercules, became immortal, and went off to become the constellation Sagittarius. A duplication in license filing required the spelling change.

and Carter's aides let out whoops of joy as the results came in. At the White House, President Ford watched the figures mounting against him, bit on the stem of his pipe, and dug in for what his aides assured him would be an even longer night.

After the first rush of Southern and Eastern support for Carter, however, the President began a comeback, depicted vividly on the NBC electronic map as one after another the Plains and Rocky Mountains states were posted for Ford in bright blue: first Kansas, Dole's home state, at 8:41, then Nebraska, Colorado, Utah, Idaho, Wyoming. Dial-twisters picked up other Ford states awarded by the rival networks around the same time: New Hampshire and Vermont, Montana, North and South Dakota. On the second floor of the White House, the mood gradually shifted from glum to mildly hopeful as the Ford states flashed on. "Go blue!" yelled the President exuberantly, an old football player and still a fan, thrusting his arm up, fist clenched, like a cheerleader.

As expected, the election battleground was the northern industrial belt running from New York west through New Jersey, Pennsylvania, Ohio, Michigan, and Illinois. These six states together had 157 electoral votes, well over half the 270 needed for a majority and election. Along with Texas and California, they constituted the Big Eight in the strategists' calculations in both the Ford and Carter camps; everyone seemed to agree that the President, bucking the Solid South, would have to win five or six of the eight. Late-reporting California looked good for the President, but with Texas leaning to Carter, Ford would have to win four of the industrial-belt six to have a chance.

By midnight, the reporting had slowed. Returns from the industrial north were close, but the networks were wary about awarding so many electoral votes with anything less than certainty. Half a dozen smaller states were similarly tight. The American people wanted to know who their next leader would be, but above all they did not want to be misinformed. Yet CBS prematurely declared Carter the winner in Oregon at 12:02, and Cronkite, somewhat embarrassedly, at 2:58, had to pull back and list the state again as uncertain. (It finally went to Ford.)

In Carter's suite Hamilton Jordan, confident from the start, viewed the delay with trepidation. "When I saw the ten or twelve states that were out, it occurred to me that the thing could slip away from us," he recalled later. "I could see the possibility of us losing every one of those states. Then the stuff we began to hear was bad. The first [partial] results from Hawaii, which were incorrect, were bad. That scared the hell out of me. Too many of them were close. Jimmy called Daley and he said we'd gotten a good vote in Chicago and if Jimmy did as well downstate as he thought he would, it should be enough. But still there was that gnawing feeling that there was a lot out and everything was close. I think Jimmy thought like we did, that the thing was going to be over earlier. But if he was deeply concerned or worried, he didn't show it." Jordan called staff members into a bedroom to hash over returns, and more phone calls for information were made to key states. But that was about all anybody could do: no action could be taken to affect the outcome.

As the night wore on, more and more people arrived in the Democratic candidate's suite, and it became harder and harder for him to watch the returns. Martin Luther King, Sr.—"Daddy" King—and Coretta King, widow of his son, came by, and a host of others who could not be turned away. To escape the noise, Jordan and Carter went into Carter's bedroom to review the numbers. Jordan showed his boss what was out, and Carter smiled.

"It looks like we've got a lot of loose ends," he said.

Caddell, taking soundings by phone around the country, reported again to Carter: he was going to lose New Jersey, and the situation was confused in New York. Carter phoned Mayor Abraham Beame in New York City, and Beame assured him the city would deliver a large enough margin to carry the state. When Caddell told Carter he was about to carry Pennsylvania, Carter asked, "What's the margin in Philadelphia?" It was about 260,000, his pollster reported. Mayor Rizzo, whom Carter had painted as a villain in the Pennsylvania primary in April but who had since come aboard, had said of Philadelphia's vote, "Whatever it is, it'll be enough." Carter now laughed, and said, "Well, he promised me three hundred thousand, but we'll take it."

With Pennsylvania, the big states at last began to fall: New York to Carter, Michigan to Ford. Illinois and Ohio remained tight. In Atlanta, local exuberance hampered the flow of good news to Carter's suite. The local television stations repeatedly switched from the networks to the World Congress Center downstairs in the Omni for interviews with the Georgia faithful, who were waiting by the thousands for their Jimmy's election. At one point Rafshoon, on the phone to Bill Moyers, an old friend, asked, "What do you know about Pennsylvania?"

"We called Pennsylvania a half-hour ago," the CBS man replied.

By now, Iowa, Oklahoma, and Arizona had come in for the President and Virginia appeared to be his by a narrow margin. Carter watched the Virginia returns closely. He had hoped to sweep the entire South, and as the Old Dominion seemed to slip away, he told Caddell he was thinking of "moving the Mason-Dixon Line south, below Virginia." But Louisiana had gone for Carter as well as Missouri. His late trip to New Orleans had paid off, Carter said, as had his tardy endorsement by Louisiana's flamboyant Governor Edwin W. Edwards.

Now it was after 2 A.M., and the networks all had Carter only a handful of electoral votes away from victory: NBC and CBS gave Carter 261 and ABC gave him 257. The first two were saying that the key undecided states were Hawaii, with four electoral votes, and Mississippi, with seven; ABC had already projected Carter the winner in Mississippi but was still holding out on Wisconsin (eleven electoral votes) and Hawaii. To most television viewers, then, it came down to Hawaii and Mississippi. If Carter could win both, he would be the next President of the United States.

All along, traditionally Democratic Hawaii had been considered a sure thing for Carter, but he and his aides had been given a turn earlier when CBS reported Ford ahead with 99 per cent of the vote in. What the report really meant was that 99 per cent of Hawaii's precincts had reported their results up to mid-day, as is the practice there. "We got nervous," Rafshoon recalled later. "We called out to Hawaii and found out it was the one state that gave incomplete returns. It meant nothing. They told us, 'Don't worry about it. The outer islands aren't in.' 'Oh, Jeez,' I said, 'One of those islands is a leper colony, and we never said anything for the lepers.' "

Shortly after 2:30 A.M., NBC moved Hawaii into the Carter column, giving him 265 electoral votes—five short of election. Now Mississippi's seven were the key. At 2:57 A.M., United Press International in New York fired off a message that said: "FLASH: WASHINGTON—CARTER WINS PRESIDENCY." It was passed on to the network barons, but each looked warily to the decision desks to make the final call. At NBC the same conclusion was flashing through the statistical computers. Roy Wetzel on the decision desk, after conferring with Scammon, called Crystal in the control room with the word: NBC was giving Carter Mississippi—and the presidency. The time was 3:26 A.M. Up in Connecticut, similar calculations on the ABC decision desk were moving that network to a similar judgment. The results from Wisconsin and Hawaii were finally deemed sufficient to make a call.

At CBS, meanwhile, the network of the dependable Cronkite was being especially cautious. Mitofsky at the decision desk, having already been obliged to pull back on Oregon—faulty data from reporting counties had produced an erroneous projection for Carter—did not want to make a second bad call. And so, as Cronkite visibly fumed, he waited for more numbers. Later, however, Cronkite defended the caution of the CBS decision-makers. "We don't have the capacity to second-guess our analysts, nor should we," he said, "I don't see this as a race. Obviously we'd like to be right and be first, but that's not the name of the game."

NBC and ABC were now ready to go with the news, but a procedural matter blocked them both. Each had cut away from the network program to allow local stations to give area-election updates, according to standard procedure for each half-hour. And ABC's Pfister told Reasoner and Walters their decision desk was projecting Carter the winner on the basis of Wisconsin and Hawaii, and to get ready. Crystal got on a phone to Chancellor and Brinkley, who were off-camera. "Okay," he said, "right after the local break we're calling Carter for President because we're projecting Mississippi for Carter. John, you do it."

But then a quirk did ABC in. NBC had only one state, Mississippi, to program into all its electronic gadgetry, but ABC had two. On top of that, ABC had assigned each of its three principals—Walters, Reasoner, and Smith—seventeen states to keep track of; when a state's total vote was projected for Carter or Ford, the disclosure was to be made on the air by the one responsible for that state. It so happened that Wisconsin was one of Reasoner's states and Hawaii was one of Walters'.

At 3:30, with the networks back on, Crystal at NBC telephoned Chancellor. "John, will you call it, please?" he said. Then he told the technician operating the Chyron: "Put it up." On an internal holding screen, the words "Carter Elected" appeared instantly. Next, he called another technician sitting at the controls behind the electronic map. "We're calling Mississippi for Carter," he said. "Get ready to flash it red."

As Crystal spoke, Chancellor looked into the camera—enduring butterflies in his stomach, he confessed later—and announced: "And nine and one-half hours after the polls began to close today, we now have a projected winner in the presidential election. NBC News projects James Earl Carter of the state of Georgia, elected President of the United States." Crystal pushed a button and "Carter Elected" appeared on the network screen, followed by the electronic map with Mississippi flashing first in white, then solid red. The spread of crimson, from New York and Pennsylvania into and across the South, told the story.

At ABC, meanwhile, Reasoner was cued in to project Carter the winner in Wisconsin, and then Walters gave him Hawaii and the election —only seconds behind NBC. And at CBS, Cronkite continued to stew, for another fifteen minutes, until Mitofsky could satisfy himself that the figures were right.

In Atlanta, somebody handed a pink phone slip to Frank Moore, Carter's southern regional man in the primaries, and later his liaison with Congress. Governor Cliff Finch of Mississippi had called. Moore picked up a phone and called back.

"Frank," Finch said, "did you hear the good news about Mississippi?"

"No," Moore replied.

"You know the big Gulf counties that always go Republican? Well, they're coming in for—"

Moore broke in: "Wait a minute," he said. "Don't tell me, tell Jimmy." And he handed the phone to Carter.

At that moment, 3:31 A.M., Chancellor came on the NBC screen with his pronouncement. Carter listened to Finch and to Chancellor simultaneously. "Cliff," he said, "it just came over television. Mississippi just put me over. I love every one of you."

To the end, the candidate who professed a special intimacy with the voters had no hesitancy about using that old-fashioned word reflecting deep affection. Few would have argued with his choice.

The suite burst into a chorus of rebel yells. Aides shouted, "We did it! We did it!" and embraced each other. Carter smiled, throwing up one arm in a gesture of ultimate triumph, then grabbed his wife and hugged her, then his children in turn. Jody Powell, who had traveled the long road with him from the now-distant, lonely beginning, walked over with his wife, Nan, and started to shake Carter's hand. Then, emotionally, the two men embraced, tears in their eyes. At once a crowd of aides and well-wishers rushed around the winner; the children of Rafshoon and other aides broke through and were hugged by him. Scores of insiders crowded into the suite, pressing toward the man who had just achieved the political feat he had insisted steadfastly all along he would.

At the White House, the defeated President had not waited to learn the official verdict. His chief of staff, Cheney, and his pollster, Teeter, had gone up to the second floor shortly before 3 A.M. to go over the numbers with him. They suggested that the three of them step into a small side room for privacy, and the President agreed, asking Senator Javits to join them. Teeter gave the President the bad news: it was unlikely he could win, but it was still possible; the outcome would turn on whether he could take Ohio and one other state that seemed to be going for Carter, like Hawaii or Mississippi.

Ford was tired and had completely lost his voice during the last few days of the campaign grind. He raspingly asked Teeter to tell the others. So, with Ford sitting to one side, the pollster ran through the pessimistic numbers again. The group took the report gravely, and the President rose and said good night.

Shortly before, Ron Nessen, the press secretary, in his office on the first floor had spied the UPI bulletin. He tore it off the wire, scribbled "Based on Mississippi" on it, and took it to Cheney's office. Not finding him there, Nessen went to the second floor. "As I got off the elevator," he recalled later, "I walked off and into the central hall, and the President was standing right there. I had the copy in my hand. He is a great massager of arms and squeezer of shoulders. He squeezed my arm and said, 'I'm going to bed. If I'm going to be worth a damn tomorrow, I'd better go to bed.' I did not show him the wire copy. I did not tell him that the UPI had given Carter the election." The President walked down to the television area in the corridor, bid good night to some of his guests, kissed Pearl Bailey, and walked off to his bedroom. Within a very few minutes, everyone was gone. Nessen could not be sure, but he believed that Ford had retired "without knowing that the networks had given it to Carter." It was not until nearly ten o'clock that morning, after one final review of the returns, that President Ford was told he had been defeated, and dispatched a congratulatory telegram to Carter.

Now, at last, the election "year"—the great quadrennial exercise of selecting a new national leader—was over. But for the candidates and many others it had been much longer than a year. Even before the re-election of Richard Nixon in 1972 Jimmy Carter had set his sights on the White House; in the intervening time he had taken on and survived an exhausting competition from a dozen contenders. On the Republican side, Ford had begun to think about and position himself for a term in his own right almost immediately after his succession, and he had spent much of his abbreviated tenure in the White House trying first to discourage Ronald Reagan from challenging him for the GOP nomination and then beating back that challenge.

While Ford's ascendancy to the White House over the politically prostrate forms of Agnew and Nixon was unprecedentedly bizarre, Carter's rise from obscurity was perhaps even more incredible. If there were two personal ingredients that fueled his success, they were his durability despite the punishment that the American political system inflicts on its seekers after power, and his comprehension and use of the national media—television especially—in capitalizing on that system. He had campaigned in the face of public incredulity, even ridicule, visiting small towns and cities large and small espousing the seemingly ludicrous proposition that the country should put itself into the hands of a peanut-farming one-term former governor of a Deep South state. At first he had been a novelty, worth a feature story in local newspapers, but few national reporters paid any attention to him. His grass-roots diligence, however, and his conviction that the people were looking for a fresh face, took hold. They brought him early success in Iowa, where the 1976 delegate-selection process began, and with it the national press and television coverage that until then had not been his. Almost at once it gave him national recognition as no other political unknown had enjoyed it in American political history. Though within a few days of his election he was to rail against what he saw as fickleness, sensationalism, and unfairness in television's reporting of *his* campaign, and a concomitant softness toward the incumbent, who had campaigned for weeks from a White House sanctuary, Carter acknowledged that television had been his savior. For all the frenetic comings and goings of his twenty-two months on the stump, most American voters had their only look at Jimmy Carter, and Jerry Ford, on their television screens. The three televised debates in which they engaged in September and October, coupled with a blitz of paid television commercials in behalf of both candidates, had elevated television as never before to the major instrument of communication with the voters. It was fitting, therefore, that the reigning television barons had presided over the climactic act of Carter's long odyssey, and had been the vehicle for conveying the news of his victory to the nation and to him, amid his excited, chattering fellow Georgians in a hotel room in Atlanta.

For Carter and his associates, for Ford and his entourage, and for all those hundreds of staff aides and journalists who had made the long physical and emotional trek with the two men to this final night, it was a vivid break with the past—simply to sit back and watch the conclusion unfold on a television screen. For all of them, the campaign had been a grinding flesh-and-blood affair, full of airplane flights, airport rallies, live bands and cheering and handshakes and speeches, plant gates and factory assembly lines, shopping centers jam-packed with humanity. Still, for most Americans, watching the campaign's climax on television was merely a continuation of what had gone before. The campaigners often lost sight of this fact, but for the great majority of voters, the presidential campaign *was* what they saw on television—the brief snatches of film on the morning- and evening-news shows, the debates, and, especially at the end, the paid commercials that cascaded down on them.

That had been the case at least since the election of John F. Kennedy in 1960, but it was particularly so in 1976 for one important reason: Carter and Ford were the first to run under a new campaign finance law that channeled the presidential campaign into the television studio and America's living rooms as never before, and off the streets of the nation. The law provided $21.8 million from the federal treasury to each of the two major-party candidates, but required that they raise or spend no more. This amount was roughly one-third of what it had cost to re-elect Richard Nixon four years earlier against an ineffectual, politically wounded opponent. Determined to achieve the maximum possible voter-contact within this spending ceiling, each camp in 1976 budgeted about half the federal subsidy for the media, and nearly all of that amount for paid television. As a result, costly grass-roots politics—organizing in the field, distributing campaign literature, buttons, bumper stickers, manning telephone "boiler rooms," hiring political workers (fortified in large cities with "street money" to encourage voting)—was severely cut back. State, county, and big-city campaign headquarters that in past years had been beehives of activity, sending ripples of enthusiasm, commitment, and volunteer involvement out into the community, were crippled for lack of funds.

The presentation of the candidates by way of television would have been acceptable, indeed even laudable, if television had functioned as a mirror of the actual campaign. But this was not the case. First of all, in all the paid commercials, the contenders predictably sought always to put their best foot forward, and while distortion and deception were not particular problems, exaggeration nearly always was. It is, of course, the essence of paid advertising to put any product, including a candidate, in the best possible light and, as well, to exaggerate the shortcomings of the opposition. But the public is not always equipped to discriminate fact from fancy.

Beyond this, the political strategists had mastered the art of fashioning a campaign to entice television cameras with visual exercises that presented their candidates most advantageously. The television era has brought with it the notion of the "media event"—a staged encounter with a visual gimmick, which cameramen and television reporters could not seem to resist —and by 1976 media events were dominating the candidates' daily schedules. Engineering "free media" became the highest political art form. Getting the candidate on the network evening news was the *sine qua non* of each day's plan; everything else revolved around that objective. The bare arithmetics of campaigning in the television era—obtaining street crowds numbering tens of thousands at the very most, with perhaps a hundred or so actually shaking the candidate's hand, as opposed to the millions watching Cronkite or Chancellor or Walters—was overwhelmingly persuasive.

It could be said, indeed, that by 1976 television had very nearly crowded out the old-style meet-the-people campaigning, or at the very least had intruded itself so completely as to have destroyed its naturalness. Crowds at an airport fence often worked as hard to capture the eye or hand of a well-known television reporter, or to be filmed by his cameraman, as they did to shake hands with or catch a glimpse of the candidate. This ever-growing focus on television by candidate and public alike inevitably diminished the importance and the possibility of direct voter-contact in the general election; the introduction of strict limits on campaign spending, starving grass-roots politics, dealt such contact an even greater blow. The name of the game had been mass-media "exposure"; now this threatened to become virtually the whole game.

In this scheme of things, it was not altogether inappropriate that Election Night in America should have become in some ways the greatest media event of them all. The voting results were real, certainly, but the trappings—the colored, flashing electronic maps and the spinning numbers and the projections of state-by-state victory and defeat—somehow became in themselves the election. CBS "gave" Carter Oregon, then took it back, while the country—the candidates anxiously in their suites and the voters in their living rooms—watched, marveled, and, concerning the projections especially, wondered.

This ordination-by-television of the 39th President of the United States —not simply a hyped-up presentation of Election Night results but also the medium's dominant influence on actual campaigning and on what most voters ever saw of it—gave in many ways a distorted view of the process of presidential selection in the bicentennial year of 1976. Yet perhaps nothing better illustrated the vast changes wrought in the conduct of politics in America than the development of television as the prism through which the public perception of the process was filtered. It was certainly a very far cry from the elitist exercise of the franchise envisioned by the nation's Founding Fathers.

part II

*HOW
WE
GOT
HERE*

2. From Elitist to Mass Politics

Had the Founding Fathers somehow been able to witness the presidential election of 1976, they would have been astonished at the spectacle. An unelected President blatantly using the trappings and aura of the White House to keep himself in office, entertaining convention delegates at state dinners, and campaigning frenetically across the country—that was something they would not have begun to understand. Nor would they have made much sense out of an obscure peanut farmer stumping tirelessly through some thirty presidential primaries, bypassing the elder statesmen of his own party, winning its nomination in convention, and unceremoniously ousting the incumbent.

The Founding Fathers would also have been astonished by any single aspect of the process. The political parties themselves would have been baffling. So would have been the primary elections held in various states to select convention delegates, and for that matter the great national conventions to choose the party nominees. Nor would they have comprehended the popular franchise itself, the reality of millions of average Americans walking into polling booths to express their will on who would be their President. All these elements of the political system that seem basic today —the parties, the primaries, the conventions, and the popular vote—were nonexistent at the nation's birth.

Presidential politics in America today is in fact exactly contrary to what the writers of the Constitution envisioned in 1787. Then they saw the choice of a President essentially as an elitist exercise of the franchise by the few propertied, white men who were involved in the legislative process in the states or in the new federal government. The intent was the selection of prominent, high-minded men of demonstrated achievement and worth by a narrow band of their peers.

The development of the present system occurred, Topsy-like, over the next two hundred years, devoid of any master plan. While extending the franchise and refining the practice of politics to meet the demands of a growing population and nation, the Republic evolved a procedural maze that engendered abuses, mischief, and corruption along with the broader expression of the public will. What Gerald Ford and Jimmy Carter endured in 1976, and a weary, surfeited nation with them, was the product of that random evolution, an exercise in self-government so remarkable and yet so convoluted and frustrating that nearly half of everyone who might have voted did not bother to do so.

How did we get here? The language of the Constitution that started it all was clear enough, albeit broad and vague: Article II, Section One, said, "The Executive power shall be vested in a President of the United States of America. He shall hold his office during the term of four years. . . . Each State shall appoint, in such manner as the Legislature thereof may direct, a number of electors. . . ." That was in 1787; in the course of the next year George Washington became the unanimous choice of the sixty-nine presidential electors from ten states then participating. Every four years thereafter, without exception, the exercise has been repeated, in time of war and peace, of domestic tranquillity and turmoil, of prosperity and depression.

The electoral college they established survives, but its original objective has long since been obscured. It was conceived, Alexander Hamilton wrote in *The 68th Federalist,* so that the choice of a President would be made by "a small number of persons, selected by their fellow-citizens from the general mass, [who] will be most likely to possess the information and discernment requisite to such complicated investigations." They would be individuals "most capable of analyzing the qualities adapted to the station" under circumstances "favorable to a deliberation and to a judicious combination of all the reasons and inducements which were proper to govern their choice." This approach would tend to eliminate "tumult and disorder," Hamilton wrote, as well as "cabal, intrigue and corruption," and would be "much less apt to convulse the community with any extraordinary or violent movements than the [direct] choice of one who was himself to be the final object of the public wishes." Indeed, since it was expected that few candidates, after the universally approved Washington, would ever obtain a majority in the electoral college, the authors of the system fully anticipated that a second step would apply: selection of the President and Vice President by the House of Representatives.

The selection process, of course, has long since moved out of this elitist cocoon of dispassion originally constructed for it. By the nature of political competition, it has—ironically—plunged into just the sort of tumult and disorder, cabal, intrigue and corruption that Hamilton said the Founding Fathers wished to avoid. The sheltered electoral college has become an anachronism, and the House has been called on to decide only three elections, choosing Thomas Jefferson over Aaron Burr in 1800; John Quincy Adams over Andrew Jackson in 1824, and arbitrating the dispute between Rutherford B. Hayes and Samuel J. Tilden in Hayes's favor in 1896. The original, supposedly antiseptic system has been compromised by an incredibly grueling and expensive competition for public support, subject to the most intense pressures, conducted in an atmosphere of carnival on the grandest scale.

From the earliest days when Washington had to be prevailed upon to stand and, when persuaded, adopted a posture of strict noninvolvement in the election, hunger for national power has produced candidates of insatiable political appetite and unbridled determination to satisfy it. And at least until the enactment of the new campaign finance reform law in 1974, they had been equipped with an unrestricted arsenal of political resources with which to achieve their ends. The re-election campaign of Richard Nixon in 1972 embodied more discovered corruption and manipulation than any other in that long period. Nixon managed by cunning and the protective shield of his office to insulate himself from all the tumult of the 1972 campaign, only to be brought down by postelection revelations of his campaign's, and his administration's, venality. But for the principal loser in that same campaign and others who earlier in the year sought the Democratic nomination against him, the demanding experience of seeking the presidency was nothing short of trial by ordeal; an ordeal made worse by overt attempts to sabotage their campaigns.

All the Democratic candidates labored under an even greater abuse—the tyranny of the system as a whole. The subsequent reform law sought with some success to alleviate the tyranny, and the financial provisions played an important role in Jimmy Carter's remarkable emergence as a serious presidential contender in late 1975. But the length of the presidential election campaign, the tremendous cost of it, the confusion and demands of so many primary elections conducted under as many different sets of rules, made the undertaking a sort of madness.

Some of the historical development seems in retrospect unavoidable, including the basic establishment early in the Republic of the party system, growing out of the relatively gentle and discreet sparrings of the Federalists of Adams and Hamilton and the Republicans (only later called Democrats) of Jefferson and Madison. Their competition brushed aside George Washington's warning against parties in his farewell address of 1796: "The spirit of party . . . serves always to distract the public councils and enfeeble the public administration. It agitates the community with ill-founded jealousies and false alarms; kindles the animosity of one part against another; foments occasionally riot and insurrection. . . . A fire not to be quenched, it demands a uniform vigilance to prevent its bursting into a flame, lest, instead of warming, it should consume." Washington, despite his warning, in a sense blinded the Founding Fathers to the inevitability of a party system; he was so obvious a choice for the presidency that he had no competition, and hence no party mechanism was required to advance his cause.

At the outset the party framework was regional—the commerce and industry-oriented Federalists of New England coalescing behind Adams, the agrarian-minded advocates of decentralized government in the South behind Jefferson, and states were mostly one-party. But the Federalists' very regionalism, marked by their opposition to the War of 1812, contributed to their demise. They soon were replaced, out of an alliance of John Quincy Adams of Massachusetts and Henry Clay of Kentucky, by the National Republicans, advocating a strong centralized government and banking system. The Jeffersonians, now led by Andrew Jackson, John C. Calhoun and Martin Van Buren, perforce switched their own formal name from Republicans to Democratic Republicans or simply Democrats, still hewing to the Jeffersonian emphasis on individual and states' rights. In short order, the new Democrats merchandised themselves as the party of the people, or even of the poor, labeling the National Republicans at the same time as the party of commerce and banking, of the business interests and, in convenient shorthand, the rich. Some refinements were still to come—including the short and stormy life of the Whig Party, and the emergence of what we know today as the Republican Party—but here for the first time were the clear outlines of the two-party system as it has come down to the present day. With it, too, came political clubs and committees at the local, state, and national levels to undertake campaign rallies, parades, and, most significant of all, fund-raising, which blossomed under Jackson's popular appeal and Van Buren's professional political skills.

The selection of party nominees for national office at the same time evolved from an informal system of congressional caucuses and state legislative caucuses, the latter often choosing favorite sons, to the holding of national conventions. As early as 1812 the waning Federalists conducted the semblance of a national convention in New York, when sixty-four delegates from eleven states tried but fell short of nominating DeWitt Clinton for President. By 1832 three parties, the National Republicans, the Jeffersonian Democrats, and the Anti-Masons, all selected their nominees in national conventions. It was not until the turn of the twentieth century that the system of state presidential primaries was to emerge as a major force in nominee selection.

It was some time, too, before the tradition of aloof candidacy set by Washington was shattered. Surrogate speakers carried the fight well into the nineteenth century; the famed Lincoln-Douglas debates were in a senatorial, not a presidential campaign—though Douglas as the Democratic nominee in 1860 did finally take to the stump extensively. Still, the practice was frowned on until the advent of the primaries, which eventually made personal campaigning unavoidable.

The development of the party system was also marked in the early 1800s by a broadening of the electorate. Many states lifted property ownership as a requirement to vote; only two states, South Carolina and Delaware, continued to choose their presidential electors in the state legislatures rather than by some form of direct popular vote. The expansion of the electorate in turn encouraged more extensive and sophisticated party organization, a refinement of state nominating conventions, and, inevitably, regular national conventions every four years.

The emergence of the Whig Party in 1834 out of the remnants of the National Republicans in a coalition of fallen-away Jacksonians and Anti-Masons, signaled a growing awareness that only an effective reaching-out to the mass electorate could win elections. Sectionalism as a trademark of party was passé, and what has come to be called the second American party system—Democrats against Whigs—was national in scope in a union now expanded to twenty-six states. The parties continued to try to "stand for something"—to carry an easy-fix label to the mass of voters—but henceforth there was something for everybody in each party. The Democrats continued to cast themselves as the party of the people, of individual and states' rights; the Whigs as the party of commerce and industry, of the propertied, of national development, and a strong central banking system. But it was opposition to the Jackson coalition on a variety of grounds, not the least of which was the desire to beat it, that gave the new Whig Party its heterogeneity.

The Whigs were slow learners about the ways of party politics, eschewing a national convention and winding up with three presidential candidates who were easy prey to Van Buren in 1836. But they learned well. Four years later, in what has been called the "Image Campaign," they got behind William Henry Harrison, a general of modest reputation, and merchandised him into a national hero with slogans, symbols, and all the trappings of "charisma" that later became standard props in presidential campaigning. Now the party pols and pros were taking over; songs, floats, campaign clubs flourished as the Harrison and Van Buren forces beat the precincts for crowds in what came to be known as "militia" campaigning. The result was a record 80.2-per-cent voter turnout; presidential selection by elitism was already well buried.

Greater public participation in turn encouraged greater competition within the parties for the right to be the party standard-bearer. In 1844 the first of the truly dramatic "smoke-filled-room" conventions brought out former Governor James Knox Polk of Tennessee as a compromise Democratic candidate on the ninth ballot; in 1852 forty-nine ballots were taken before Franklin Pierce was nominated by the Democrats, and fifty-two before the Whigs chose General Winfield Scott. When Pierce won, he gave the Democrats victory in five of the seven presidential contests since Jackson's triumph of 1828 had effectively launched the party. But the Whigs, after barely twenty years in existence, were now impossibly split on the slavery issue and finished as a force.

But this same slavery issue gave birth to the modern Republican Party and the two-party alignment as we now know it. With the ambitious Democratic Senator Stephen A. Douglas fanning the issue, antislavery leaders met in Ripon, Wisconsin, in Jackson, Michigan, and other northern states; the new party was on its way—a conglomerate of these forces with a strong base of northeastern and western supporters of the dying Whig Party. Antislavery proved a strong recruiter in competition with the so-called Know-Nothing Party for the Whig remnants; the Republicans from the start emerged as ideologically motivated and zealous in their opposition to the Democrats. They accused the Pierce administration of "murders, robberies and arson" in the slavery struggle, and in their first try for the presidency ran a respectable second with John C. Fremont, carrying eleven of the sixteen northern states. The Republicans' swift emergence as a party of zealous sectionalism struck trepidation in the hearts of Southern political leaders, making talk of secession commonplace. The third American party system was in being, confirmed in the next election by the selection of Abraham Lincoln, aided by a North-South split over slavery that produced two Democratic nominees, Douglas and John C. Breckenridge.

The two-party system, like the nation itself, survived the Civil War but in weakened state, with the Democrats particularly debilitated. And surviving too was the electoral college, reduced to a kind of countinghouse for the popular mandate, straining the popular vote through an anachronistic funnel of regionalism. In 1876 the electoral college barely functioned in the disputed election between Tilden, the Democrat, and Hayes, the Republican. Tilden led Hayes by about 250,000 popular votes, but disputed electors in four states threw the issue to Congress. Tilden needed only a single vote for an electoral college majority and Hayes needed twenty; after much maneuvering and investigation that ultimately produced evidence of fraud and corruption on both sides, Hayes received his twenty and the election. And the electoral college stood.

There was by this time, in fact, little inclination to meddle with the election process in any way. The power-wielders maneuvered in advance of and during the conventions and picked their men. Then they mobilized party organizations at the state and local levels, dunned money from wealthy supporters, and dispatched printed propaganda and surrogate speakers around the country while—as still was the custom—the nominees mostly sat home, wrote letters, received visitors, and kept their mouths shut. Those few who ventured onto the stump usually had cause to regret it. Seven days before the election of 1884, for example, James G. Blaine, the Republican nominee, met with several hundred clergymen in a New York hotel and was welcomed by Dr. Samuel D. Burchard, pastor of the Murray Hill Presbyterian Church. "We are Republicans," Burchard told Blaine and the crowd, "and don't propose to leave our party and identify ourselves with the party whose antecedents have been Rum, Romanism, and Rebellion." A stenographer working for the Democrats conveyed this remark to party leaders, who quickly spread it to Catholics and Blaine was undone.

Still, with the electorate ever expanding, and the ever-increasing number of newspapers focused on politics, the tradition of the stay-at-home candidate was bound to wither, regardless of the risks demonstrated by Blaine's misfortune. The appearance of the silver-tongued William Jennings Bryan in the cause of free silver in 1896 shattered that tradition entirely; he traveled eighteen thousand miles conveying his electric message—"You shall not crucify mankind upon a cross of gold"—to crowds at railroad depots all day and into the middle of the night.

Bryan was a theatrical success, but his opponent, William McKinley, chose to stick to his own front porch in Canton, Ohio, luring the party faithful and the press to hear him finesse free silver as "cheap money" and Bryan along with it. "I might just as well put up a trapeze on my front lawn and compete with some professional athlete," he said when Mark Hanna, his manager, urged him to take the stump and go out speaking against Bryan. "I have to think when I speak." Bryan was colorful, but he was unsettling too, and the pull of safe, traditional party voting proved more comforting than all his oratory, and he lost. He tried again to stump his way into the White House against McKinley in 1900, leading Charles Francis Adams to write of him: "He is in one sense scripturally formidable, for he is unquestionably armed with the jawbone of an ass. He can talk longer, and say less, than any man in Christendom. . . . A talking machine, he can set his mouth in action, and go away and leave it, sure that it will not stop until he returns."

There would not, of course, always be a Bryan to act as a catalyst for active campaign competition, though it may have seemed at the time that Bryan would run forever. As the Great Commoner was undertaking his marathon pursuit of the presidency, a major structural development in the nominating process was taking shape; ironically it might have been used to great advantage by Bryan had it matured sufficiently in his time. That was the emergence, out of a Progressive rebellion against party-boss rule in the big cities and states, of new methods to bring grass-roots voter preference to bear on the process. They took two principal forms: direct popular election of delegates to the national conventions, and direct presidential preference primaries.

No other development more severely or more effectively shook the system of nominee selection in the twentieth century; the presidential primary, for selection of delegates or nominee preference or a combination of the two, became in time the dominant feature of preconvention presidential politics, seizing candidates previously sheltered from public exposure and thrusting them into the pit of open, exhausting, punishing competition. In time, the candidate who remained on his front porch while the opposition worked the primary hustings usually did so at great political peril; rather, he was most often forced by competition or lured by the opportunity for public endorsement into trial by primary, a trial that by 1976 had become, indisputably, trial by ordeal, so extensively had the presidential-primary system grown.

The best evidence indicates that this critical development began in Florida in 1901, when the state legislature enacted an optional primary law, permitting state or local party officials to select any party nominee by primary, including national convention delegates. Four years later, under the prodding of Robert M. LaFollette, Sr., the Progressive-dominated legislature in Wisconsin passed a law specifically providing for direct election of national-convention delegates. LaFollette and the Progressives had been shut out at the 1904 Republican convention, an old-guard delegation having been seated in their place. A year later, in 1906, Pennsylvania's legislature inched toward the direct presidential primary, passing a law providing direct delegate selection with the option that a candidate for delegate could have printed next to his own name the name of the presidential candidate he supported. Finally, in 1910, Oregon voters, acting on an initiative advanced by another Progressive, Senator Jonathan Bourne, approved the nation's first unadulterated presidential-preference primary. It provided for popular selection of presidential candidates and for election of delegates legally pledged to support the preference-primary winner; the law remains in effect to this day, and is regarded still as the model of the "pure" presidential primary.

Direct voter involvement in the nominating process had considerable and immediate appeal; by 1912, twelve states had adopted primary laws providing presidential preference or direct election of convention delegates, or both. Three others gave state parties the option of turning to the voters to pick their convention delegates. The rapid spread of primaries was a favorable trend for Theodore Roosevelt, one of the most formidable street campaigners in American political history. Now an ex-President seeking a return to power and determined to move his party toward social reform, Roosevelt recognized that his own chance for nomination was to demonstrate such overwhelming support in the primaries that the party regulars in charge of the convention would be persuaded to shunt William H. Taft aside in his favor.

In a string of state primaries marked by bitter personal invective and raucous behavior on both sides, Roosevelt tried to storm the establishment. He won important primaries in about a dozen states and entered the convention clearly as the people's choice. But the Republican National Committee, in Taft's hands, controlled the convention. It awarded Taft 235 of 254 contested delegates and Taft won the nomination easily on the first ballot. The Roosevelt forces bolted and shortly thereafter formed a new Progressive Party with Roosevelt as its standard-bearer. But while running ahead of Taft he succeeded only in splitting what probably would have been a Republican majority and delivering the election to the Democrat, Woodrow Wilson. Nevertheless, 1912 emphatically demonstrated the importance of the primaries as a yardstick of popular support and as a means, however unsuccessful in this case, of challenging the established party machinery.

The 1912 experience was a spur to the development of presidential primaries. By 1916 some twenty-six states had passed primary laws—this amid the Progressive drive for reform, along with frequent state enactment of provisions for initiative, referendum, and recall procedures, all aimed at holding office seekers and officeholders more accountable to the voter. However, political realities and World War I arrested the trend toward primaries before it had hardly begun. The high cost to participating states, declining voter participation, and a disinclination of leading candidates to risk running in primaries all led to their disuse. By 1935 eight of the twenty-six states had repealed their primary laws. Nomination by bossism filled the void, most notably in 1920, when Warren G. Harding, after doing poorly in two primaries, won out in the most famous smoke-filled room convention, and in 1924, when John W. Davis was nominated in a 103-ballot convention at Madison Square Garden.

Though professional politicians looked with disfavor on the primary because it took decision-making out of their hands, certain factors were conspiring against closed politics, notably the election of Franklin D. Roosevelt in 1932. While he campaigned in no primaries himself that year and left most of the autumn whistlestopping to President Herbert Hoover, Roosevelt made heavy and effective use of radio and, in the process, brought a new dimension to voter persuasion. Also the growth of social-welfare government under FDR gradually diminished the role of big-city bosses as the exclusive dispensers of public largesse and, in consequence, their power in the country and within their own parties. Presidential aspirants with little traditional organization support turned in time to the primary once more as a device to demonstrate their popular appeal.

In many cases at first, that decision backfired, with the primary only demonstrating a candidate's popular weakness. Wendell L. Willkie, having been nominated by the Republicans in 1940 without entering any primaries, resorted to that route four years later and was quickly eliminated. But in 1944, and again in 1948, competitive primaries played a critical role in the selection of Thomas E. Dewey as the Republican nominee over Governor Harold E. Stassen, General Douglas MacArthur and Senator Robert A. Taft.

In 1952 the growing effectiveness of a strong primary showing was demonstrated emphatically by Democratic Senator Estes Kefauver of Tennessee, who plunged into the New Hampshire primary against absentee President Harry S Truman and in a whirlwind handshaking campaign beat him by about four thousand votes. Truman called primaries "eyewash" but less than three weeks after this defeat he announced he would not seek re-election. Kefauver was not popular in the party, however, and he was bypassed for the nomination in favor of Governor Adlai E. Stevenson of Illinois, who had entered no primaries. On the Republican side, though the issue was decided in a bitter convention fight, General Eisenhower, an unknown political quantity, first displayed his voter appeal with a New Hampshire victory, rallying his forces for a successful battle with Taft.

That battle was seen by a rapt nation over television, which was just coming of age as a communicator of public events. In short order, television revolutionized politics and politicking in America, drawing candidate and voter alike, like some giant magnet, determining the shape and content of the presidential debate, increasing the costs of gaining the presidency, and, ultimately, elevating the matter of money to a desperate, savage, destructive necessity.

By now the competitive primary was an integral part of the presidential-election process, and more and more states adopted it. Stevenson slugged it out with Kefauver in the 1956 primaries and won; John F. Kennedy, in 1960, proved himself to doubting party leaders by defeating Senator Hubert Humphrey in Wisconsin and West Virginia; in 1964, after having lost in New Hampshire and Oregon, Senator Barry Goldwater nailed down the Republican nomination with a narrow primary victory over Governor Nelson A. Rockefeller in California.

In 1960 a series of four debates between presidential candidates

Kennedy and Nixon highlighted feverish personal campaigning by both men; indeed, in the first encounter Kennedy's more forceful presentation and image—that was a word in vogue in the television era—was thought to have been the critical element in his victory. But candidates shied away from the debates for the next sixteen years, so unpredictably influential were they considered to be in their naked spontaneity. Television became instead a purchased vehicle for putting over the candidate as his managers wished the electorate to see him, and it was a vehicle that sent campaign budgets skyrocketing. In 1964 the Goldwater forces bragged they had raised and spent more money for their candidate than any earlier presidential campaign effort—$12 million. In 1968, under master money-raiser Maurice Stans, the campaign of Richard Nixon by Stans's own reckoning almost tripled that total—$34 million.

Also adding to the cost, and the complexity, of running for President was public-opinion polling, now considered an indispensable tool for the campaign manager. Surveys to determine not only who was ahead, and by how much, but also what issues and attitudes were on the voters' minds and why, were taken by professional samplers and analysts, and again at considerable expense. They served as a flashlight into the dark unknown where votes were mined; no serious candidate who wanted to survive the long tunnel of primary competition would venture forward without them.

In 1968 as in 1952 the primary was an effective device in unseating an incumbent President. Senator Eugene J. McCarthy of Minnesota scored a psychological victory with a near-miss against President Lyndon B. Johnson in New Hampshire, and Johnson bowed out soon after. Senator Robert F. Kennedy meanwhile had launched an eighty-five-day blitz for the Democratic nomination, running in six primaries, winning five of them, and heading toward a likely nomination when he was murdered. In the Republican Party, Nixon was utilizing a string of uncontested primaries, paid television commercials and his incredible campaign budget to dispel the impression that he could not win. He drove his chief competitor, George Romney, out even before the first primary and was nominated easily.

Finally, in 1972, George McGovern, limping along at 5 per cent in the national public-opinion polls before the first primary, ran an unexpectedly close second to the front-runner, Senator Muskie in New Hampshire, beat the field in Wisconsin and Massachusetts, edged Humphrey in California's showdown winner-take-all primary and captured the Democratic nomination on the first ballot. This demonstration of grass-roots organization overwhelmed the traditional party establishment. Organization, and— money. That second ingredient became more and more important.

In the course of 189 years, then, the presidential selection process had

changed vastly—from the choosing of Washington, uncontested, with no
party apparatus or campaign and with the candidate playing no active role,
to the multimillion-dollar business of public-opinion shaping, extensive and
bitter combat in primaries, paid professional campaign managers, high-
powered solicitation of money, and heavy personal involvement of the
candidate. Campaigning for the presidency had become not so much the
ventilation of issues or even of personality as it was a contest of techniques,
of devices, of sophisticated highwaymanship exercised through muscle-
bound political organizations and made possible by huge amounts of ready
cash. When Republican-sponsored burglars broke into the Democratic National Committee headquarters at the Watergate, they were demonstrating
no more than the latest wrinkle in the no-stone-unturned *modus operandi*
that came to govern the quest for victory conducted by Richard Nixon and
his associates and—though to a vastly lesser extent—by other presidential
aspirants.

Something, obviously, had to be done. And Congress, pressured by the
public outrage against the excesses of Watergate, finally acted. In 1974 it
hammered out a series of sweeping amendments to an existing but hereto-
fore largely ineffectual Fair Campaign Practices Act, and tried above all else
to control the raising and spending of money in presidential campaigns. In
the 1972 campaign one man alone—Chicago insurance executive W. Clement Stone—had given more than $3 million to Nixon's re-election bid, and
others had given hundreds of thousands of dollars to various candidates.
The new amendments struck hard at such "fat cats"—imposing a ceiling
of $25,000 on contributions by any individual in a campaign, and a limit
of $1000 by that individual to any one candidate. Furthermore, it limited
any political committee to giving no more than $5000 to any one candidate,
and it imposed strict reporting requirements on presidential candidates
concerning how much money they raised and spent—where it came from
and where it went. A ceiling that in 1976 amounted to $10.9 million in
expenses, plus nearly $2.2 million more for fund-raising, was placed on each
candidate in pre-convention campaigning. In presidential primaries, no
candidate could spend more than 2 cents per voting-age person in any state,
with a minimum of $200,000 ($218,200 in New Hampshire, for instance,
and nearly $2.6 million in California).

Under the law, a six-member Federal Election Commission was established, the composition of which eventually was to be a major headache, and
an inhibition to the flow of federal funds to the candidates at a critical time
during the 1976 primaries. A foe of the whole scheme, Democratic Representative Wayne Hays of Ohio, chairman of the House Administration
Committee with jurisdiction over the legislation, insisted that Congress and

not the President retain control over the Commission. Consequently, it was agreed that the House and Senate leadership each appoint two members to the body, and the President the remaining two. The Commission was given both investigatory powers, clearly within the legislative prerogative, and the oversight and monitoring of the law, clearly executive functions. Many warned that its composition and duties violated the separation of federal governmental powers, but Hays demanded his way. And Wayne Hays, an arbitrary, arrogant bully, always had his way—another fact that ultimately was to spice the 1976 political scene, in a manner wholly unforeseen.

This sweeping legislation immediately came under challenge: by some of the more prominent fat cats; by civil libertarians who claimed the limitation on individual contributions undercut First Amendment guarantees of free speech and petition; by independent candidates like Eugene McCarthy, who charged discrimination in a law that unconstitutionally perpetuated the two-party system. But the courts, taking note of the excesses that had culminated in Watergate, said the need to eliminate the demonstrated evils of unchecked spending took precedence. Later, some modifications were made, after an adverse Supreme Court decision affected some parts of the law, but for the 1976 election, the principal elements governed—with ramifications probably far beyond what its authors had anticipated.

Reforms within the parties too, and especially within the Democratic Party, had a major effect on the 1976 campaign. The Democrats, having liberalized their delegate-selection process to the point where many regular-party functionaries and leaders had been shut out of the 1972 convention, rolled back somewhat on requirements for representation to minority groups. But new machinery to make sure state parties took "affirmative action" to have minority representation in their convention delegations made for a record proliferation of primaries. It was easier to throw the delegate-selection process to the voters than to maneuver in state party caucuses and conventions and risk challenges on grounds of discrimination later. By 1976 some thirty states and the District of Columbia had passed some kind of presidential primary law, creating an interminable and incredibly expensive obstacle course for the candidates. And further complicating the picture on the Democratic side was a party decision to rule out winner-take-all primaries and permit proportional allocation of delegates according to primary results—a system that seemed all but certain to inhibit any one candidate from getting the required majority of national-convention delegates, and assuring a brokered convention.

Still, into this demanding marathon run there poured a small army of presidential challengers on the Democratic side, and an overt challenger to the sitting President on the Republican side. The system under the new law appeared to benefit the well-heeled and the incumbent, but the public-financing provisions were supposed to be an equalizer. It was every candidate for himself; anyone foolhardy enough to venture a prediction on how it would all turn out just did not understand the complexities and imponderables now legislated into any already bewildering competition.

Entering 1976, the basic Constitutional structure—states choosing individual presidential electors who in turn choose the President—remained unchanged. But within that framework had grown a maddeningly intricate mechanism, developed ostensibly to extend the franchise more directly to the people. In the process, a punishing procedural maze was established that brought candidate and public alike to the point of exhaustion and frustration. Everyone said something had to be done about the system beyond the financing of the campaigns, and from time to time, some members of Congress introduced modifying legislation. But Congress ignored all such proposals. The 1976 campaign was obliged to proceed using Rube Goldberg political machinery. It seemed, to some, to be masochism on a national scale. But that was the way it would have to be for all those who chose to seek the American presidency in the bicentennial year.

part III

**JOCKEYING
FOR
POSITION:
THE REPUBLICANS**

3. The Serendipitous Gerald Ford

On Sunday morning, June 18, 1972, House Minority Leader Gerald R. Ford, Jr., went to the front door of his modest home in Alexandria, Virginia, and picked up his copy of *The Washington Post.* There, on page one, he learned that only hours earlier a band of wiretappers and political second-story men had broken into the Democratic National Committee headquarters at the Watergate complex. He had no reason to suspect that the incident would set in motion the most bizarre political developments in the nation's history, culminating in his elevation to the presidency of the United States. He was a modest man of modest ambitions, who after nearly twenty-four years in the House of Representatives hoped but did not really expect that he might yet become Speaker. The chances of his Republican Party capturing the House and putting him in charge were slim. Even the anticipated solid re-election of Richard M. Nixon in November was unlikely to bring in enough GOP House seats to wrest control from the Democrats.

That indeed proved to be the case, and in 1973, as he embarked on his twenty-fifth year in Congress, Jerry Ford seriously contemplated retiring. He had discussed the step with his wife, and she had favored it, and so as the new year unfolded and the specter of Watergate spread over Nixon's administration like a shroud, he was more the dismayed partisan observer than a personally interested principal.

So it was too, on June 7, 1973, when *The Wall Street Journal* and *The Washington Post* reported that Vice President Spiro T. Agnew was under investigation in connection with a kickback scandal that had occurred when he was a county executive and governor in Maryland. Through the summer, as Agnew fought for his political life, Ford remained the loyal Republican soldier. When the Vice President, staring down the barrel of Justice Department prosecution, turned to the House of Representatives and asked that it conduct its own investigation, among those with whom he consulted was the sympathetic minority leader. But Ford was powerless to initiate such a diversionary inquiry; only Speaker Carl Albert could do so, and he was a loyal Democrat, not in the least interested in giving Agnew an alternative to prosecution. And so Agnew, after much thrashing about, finally succumbed to the best deal he could strike—resignation in exchange for his freedom. Elliot L. Richardson, then the attorney general and fearful that Richard Nixon was on the edge of physical or mental collapse or both, was determined above all else to clear the line of succession to the presidency; to make certain the moment would not come when a suspected felon might suddenly ascend to the office. He hammered out the deal and Agnew plea-bargained to save his skin, agreeing to plead *nolo contendere* to a single count of tax evasion (although Justice had him on much more) in return for a suspended sentence. On October 10, 1973, Agnew submitted his resignation—moments before facing a federal judge in Baltimore. As of 2:05 P.M., the United States had no Vice President.

Gerald Ford was at that moment sitting at the minority leadership table in the House of Representatives. A Michigan colleague, Elford (Al) Cederberg, in the private members' lobby off the floor, spied a bulletin coming over the news wire, ripped it from the machine, and rushed onto the House floor. Ford, like the rest, was stunned but still had no reason to suspect it would have any immediate effect on his life, let alone be the cause for a radical change.

The shock of Agnew's resignation, coming while he was still maintaining a public posture of defiance, stunned Washington and the American people, but the search for a successor had to begin at once. Under the new Twenty-fifth Amendment, Congress had to confirm the President's choice, and Nixon, ever motivated by self-preservation, was in no mood for a fight with the men and women who would also sit as prosecutors and jury in his own impeachment, if it came to that. Nor did he want someone whose political attractiveness and ability were so outstanding as to make his own impeachment more palatable in Congress. Loyal, commonplace Jerry Ford clearly filled the bill. His House Republican colleagues drew up a petition recommending him to Nixon and the beleaguered President willingly yielded. (Ford loved to tell audiences later how he got the news. When the fateful phone call came from Nixon, young Susan Ford was using the only Ford phone with an extension, and Ford had to take it on a single line. So when Nixon urged that Ford put his wife Betty on an extension to hear what he was going to say, Ford had to interrupt and ask, "Mr. President, would you mind hanging up and calling on the other line?")

Ford sailed through his confirmation hearings, displaying an openness and candor seldom seen in the Nixon administration. In nearly two months of congressional investigation and grilling, not only did he survive but he improved his favorable position with his Capitol Hill colleagues. William Greider of *The Washington Post,* among the nation's most perceptive and fairest reporters, wrote of his confirmation: "The more they thought about Jerry Ford, the more they thought of him."

Joining an administration already on the skids was considered at the time the sort of thing only a political lightweight, or a good party soldier, would do. Washington was still inclined to believe that Nixon would beat the rap, and the vice-presidency was regarded as a pleasant way for Jerry Ford to end his political career, to be a footnote in American history. Speculation that selecting a Vice President on this occasion could well mean selecting the next President was either disbelieved or disregarded: Washington men and women could not yet bring themselves to accept the idea that a President could or would be impeached or otherwise deposed.

In the White House itself, that disbelief hung on through the early months of 1974. Sitting behind his desk in the Oval Office, Nixon himself was reported by *Newsweek* in May to have asked Nelson Rockefeller with amused contempt: "Can you imagine Jerry Ford sitting in this chair?" (Rockefeller later denied to Ford that Nixon had made the remark. But to those who knew Nixon's capacity for contempt, the observation had the ring of believability to it.)

Ford, for his part, did not allow himself to entertain that prospect until very late. Instead, like a child who will not give up on Santa Claus, he held fast to an expressed belief in his President's innocence. Perhaps there was little else he could do under the circumstances, but there was more to it than that; Ford was grateful to Nixon for having selected him, and although he and Nixon were not close friends—their personal styles could not have been more different—they were fellow Republicans, both fiercely partisan. The difference was that Nixon, for all his fawning attempts to veil it, hated Democrats with a passion, while Ford was remarkably free of malice. "I have many adversaries," he liked to say, "but no enemies." Still, as the circle closed on the Watergate cover-up schemers, and the men in the Oval Office took the position that a conspiracy of liberals in the Democratic Party and the press was doing Nixon in, Ford could sympathize with him. And so, at a time when it might have been politically prudent to keep his mouth shut, the new Vice President stood in the front rank with the Republicans who insisted that the emperor was not naked.

Ford's behavior in the vice-presidency was an important signal of the manner in which he would deal with Nixon once he himself reached the presidency. Not until Nixon's administration was on the verge of collapse did Ford adhere to the pleadings of his friends and agree that silence was called for. Occasionally he would allow himself a criticism of the White House's editing of the Watergate tape transcripts or its refusal to turn over additional tapes to the House Judiciary Committee. But he held firm to the conviction that Nixon was "innocent of any impeachable offense"—a notably limited exoneration—and he waited.

Some time in early July, however, some of Ford's old and trusted friends, led by Philip Buchen (eventually his White House counsel), began to look into the problems he would encounter if the presidency were suddenly thrust upon him. Without informing Ford, lest he tell them to desist, they met privately several times at the home of William G. Whyte, Washington representative and a vice president of the United States Steel Corporation. The group also included Senator Robert P. Griffin of Michigan, former White House aide Bryce Harlow, former Secretary of Defense Melvin R. Laird, and a former Republican House leader, John W. Byrnes of Wisconsin. As the House Judiciary Committee moved ever closer to impeachment of Nixon, Ford absented himself more and more from Washington, transparently getting an early start on the November congressional elections, touring the country to speak at Republican fund-raising affairs, and holding the clammy hand of a sick party. Just ten days before the roof finally fell in, Ford sat in shirt sleeves aboard *Air Force Two* on a postmidnight flight back to Washington from a West Coast swing, and discussed what lay ahead. He was relaxed and cordial, puffing on his pipe, but he pointedly did not want to talk about the growing likelihood of his becoming President. It was as if even to talk about it would be an act of disloyalty to Nixon. Still he could not avoid thinking about the prospect, because the evidence that the presidency was advancing on him was everywhere: the Secret Service contingent was increased and especially alert; the traveling press corps had swelled, as well as the crowds that greeted him along the way (with signs that called him "President Ford"); local politicians elbowed each other to get next to him and offer him their help, a sure sign of approaching power.

Sure, he said in that late-night chat, he was aware that Republican friends felt he was hurting himself when he proclaimed Nixon's innocence, however narrowly. But Nixon had told him face-to-face that he was innocent of the charges against him, and until he was convinced that Nixon was lying, that was good enough. The Vice President said he sincerely believed that the Judiciary Committee hadn't made a sufficient case against Nixon, and although he wasn't kidding himself about the gravity of the political situation, he was not going to abandon the man. But why did he feel obliged to go beyond that, attacking some of Nixon's Democratic accusers on the committee? Was he not aware that he might soon have to take over the leadership of a deeply wounded and split country that would need above all a healing hand in the presidency? Certainly, Ford replied, but having spoken up for Nixon, he could not suddenly fall silent or dodge the issue, for that would be taken as abandonment. For the time being he would address himself to doing what he could, to helping the party in its time of travail.

A few weeks earlier, Ford had been a luncheon guest of *The Washington Post,* on the day, in fact, when the Supreme Court ruled that Nixon had to produce tapes being subpoenaed by the House Judiciary Committee. Ford frankly did not know, even at that late hour, what Nixon would do in response, though just before coming to lunch he had been on the phone to San Clemente. Then, and in subsequent discussions, it was clear that Ford for all his loyalty was not remotely on the inside of the strategies to save the Nixon presidency. As we flew back to Washington that night, while Nixon remained in office, I reminded him of that open, friendly lunch, and how it contrasted with Nixon's relationship to the press. Ford acknowledged the difference, deplored Nixon's way with reporters, and vowed that in any Ford presidency things would be different. But he was very careful to say nothing directly critical of Nixon, and he forbade me to use any observations he had made about how he would function in the White House. He was sorry for the man, and he could not hide it. "One senses," I wrote in *The Washington Post* at the time, "a sense of personal sympathy, even compassion, toward Mr. Nixon that transcends Mr. Ford's best political self-interest." And that sympathy, nurtured through the few but agonizing months of his own vice-presidency, held in it the seeds of an attitude that was to harm severely the early moments of the Ford presidency and, eventually, the prospects of Ford's election in his own right in 1976.[1]

On the weekend before the complete collapse of the Nixon presidency, Ford went to Mississippi and Louisiana, still expressing his belief in Nixon's innocence. But meantime some key fellow Republicans, notably his old Michigan colleague, the Senate Minority Whip Robert Griffin, had learned of the critically important tape recording in which Nixon admitted complicity in the Watergate cover-up only six days after the break-in. The game was over. The word was flashed to Ford, who on his return to Washington issued a terse statement saying it would serve no useful purpose for him to

1. That same night aboard *Air Force Two,* I asked Bob Hartmann, Ford's chief of staff as Vice President and later a White House aide, the same question as to why Ford was attacking Democrats on the Judiciary Committee when conciliation would seem to be the prudent course. Hartmann noted that these same Democrats had voted against Ford's confirmation as Vice President, and their action "really hurt him, because he really believes they opposed him out of pure partisanship, not on the facts. Sometimes," Hartmann observed, with a remark that seemed almost to foresee Ford's later pardon of Nixon, "politicians don't do the smart thing, even when they know what it is. Sometimes they just do what they want to do, or what they feel they have to do."

continue discussing the matter of Nixon's impeachment. That night, he called in his transition team to get to work. Four days later he was President of the United States.

Gerald Ford, like Lyndon Johnson before him, came to the presidency with a rare opportunity. The country was in a state of shock and turmoil, and although the people did not know much about him and were disillusioned by what had gone before, they were clearly willing to extend to him their hope and good will. For all the expressed skepticism of the American people, a strain of basic confidence and belief in their political system exists from which any new President may draw and on which he can build. Johnson perceived this resource in November 1963 when he assumed the presidency from the late John F. Kennedy; he subordinated his own personality and called on the national good will, rallying the people to "let us continue" what had gone on before. Ford was not in quite so advantageous a position; he could hardly ask the public to continue what had gone on under Nixon. But so hungry were Americans for a break with the past— not just Nixon but also the last dissembling years of Johnson—that they were ready to respond to any sign that at last they had a President who was open, candid, honest: any President, some even said, who was "normal," who was not paranoiac about the enemies, real and imagined, dedicated to his fall.

As a man who might satisfy this public longing, Jerry Ford was almost perfect. He was nothing if not "normal." He had the look of a strapping steel worker, dressed—even overdressed—in his one slightly noisy Sunday suit. He spoke haltingly and plainly; reporters found that they could speed up his voice on their tape recorders and still hear the words distinctly. Best of all, he spoke frankly, and he was not afraid to laugh at himself. It was as though the presidency suddenly had been given back to the people. That Ford's politics were not far removed from Nixon's in any important respect, and that he was himself a politician with a survivability record of a quarter of a century, were facts lost or at least temporarily overlooked in the euphoria of a return to normalcy in the White House.

As deftly as Johnson had grasped the national mood in 1963 and launched his own unexpected presidency on the fuel of public good will in adversity, Ford in his own way made the most of the disenchantment and national exhaustion of August 1974. On the night of August 9, after watching Nixon announce on television his intention to resign the next day, Ford walked out of the living room of his Alexandria, Virginia, home and promised, before a battery of microphones and television lights, that he would govern in "a spirit of cooperation" with Congress and the people. The next morning, after Nixon had left the White House in a final emotional farewell that convinced onlookers the country had survived a close call, Ford took the oath of office and immediately set out to grasp his opportunity. Calmly, reassuringly, he told the country that "our long national nightmare is over" and, in a conciliatory speech that he labeled "just a little straight talk among friends," spoke the words the nation wanted to hear: "I believe that truth is the glue that holds government together, and not only government but civilization itself. That bond, though strained, is unbroken at home and abroad. In all my public and private acts as your President, I expect to follow my instincts of openness and candor, with full confidence that honesty is always the best policy in the end."

He was particularly aware of the importance of such a policy, he said, because he knew he was the first President not elected by the people. "If you have not chosen me by secret ballot," he said, "neither have I gained office by secret promises. I have not campaigned either for the presidency or the vice-presidency. I have not subscribed to any partisan platform, I am indebted to no man and to only one woman, my dear wife, Betty, as I begin the most difficult job in the world."

It was an auspicious and confidence-building start. Gerald Ford asked the American people to take him at his word, and they did. For the first four weeks of his administration, a sense of relief swept over the deep gloom that had shrouded the federal city and the nation through the last dark year of the Nixon reign. There was something very refreshing about this natural and open man, after five years of the self-conscious, awkward, posturing Nixon, so taken with the trappings of high office. For several days after taking the oath, Ford continued to live in his house at 514 Crown View Drive in Alexandria. He would come out early in the morning on his way to the Oval Office like any other Washington commuter—except that now the street was always lined with reporters and neighborhood gawkers, and heavily guarded by Secret Service and local police. He would walk down his short driveway or over the brief lawn, exchange pleasantries with the reporters, answer a few questions, and climb into the black presidential limousine for the short ride across the Potomac. It would be the same in reverse at night, and the seeming absence of haste or desire to move into the White House, that residence of power and elegance, was becoming to Jerry Ford too.

I remember going in the presidential motorcade as part of the press pool from the Alexandria house to Capitol Hill several nights after Ford's swearing in, and standing on the floor of the House of Representatives as he strode, for the first time as President, into this old chamber that held such long and cherished memories for him. It was like the return of an old football hero; Republicans and Democrats rose from their seats and cheered him; old colleagues rushed up to shake his hand as he moved down the aisle from the rear to the well of the House. And positioned just above me, in the VIP gallery, were Betty Ford, the Ford children, and, standing erect and impassive, applauding almost automatically, White House chief of staff General Alexander M. Haig, Jr. It was Haig who had largely orchestrated Nixon's resignation, who had alerted Ford of his imminent ascendancy, and who now stood in the American version of the royal box, in a sense applauding his own deft achievement of presidential transition, never contemplated in quite that way by the Founding Fathers. The Haig presence and manner suddenly were a bit unnerving, if not frightening. In the climate of Watergate, nothing was impossible, not even a bloodless presidential coup engineered by an army general, a man who had gravitated to the very right hand of one President and who, when that President fell, saw to a swift removal of the body and a ready replacement, maintaining at the same time his own proximity and influence. But the disarming openness of Jerry Ford did not permit such thoughts to endure for long. Here, at last, the country had a regular guy as President.

At times now, Washington seemed absolutely buoyant with the normalcy of Jerry Ford; there were jokes in the White House again, and good-natured ribbing among reporters, staff aides, and the President himself. His first act after taking the oath had been to come into the press room, the site of bitterness and adversity during the Nixon years, to introduce his new press secretary, a respected reporter named Jerry terHorst of the *Detroit News,* and his new press policy of openness and candor. There was hope that Ford's good will and honesty might enable Americans to believe in their leaders again.

Within four weeks that hope was painfully shattered by a single act that spent the full treasury of public confidence Jerry Ford's first statements and actions had so rapidly collected. On Sunday morning, September 8, as much of the nation had its attention riveted on one of the "great" publicity stunts of the century—Evel Knievel's rocketed-motorcycle leap of the Grand Canyon—Ford suddenly announced an unconditional pardon for Nixon. He informed—but did not consult—only a handful of associates. In a stroke, the President of "openness and candor" who was "indebted to no man," by acting in secret in a critical matter going to the very core of public trust, damaged his greatest strength: his own credibility. "As we are a nation under God, so am I sworn to uphold our laws with the help of God," Ford said in a sudden television appearance. "And I have sought such guidance and searched my own conscience with special diligence to determine the right thing for me to do with respect to my predecessor in this place, Richard Nixon, and his loyal wife and family. Theirs is an American tragedy in which we all have played a part. It could go on and on and on, or someone must write an end to it. I have concluded that only I can do that, and if I can, I must." Nixon as a former President instead of enjoying equal treatment under the law "would be cruelly and excessively penalized either in preserving the presumption of his innocence or in obtaining a speedy determination of his guilt in order to repay a legal debt to society," Ford said. And the country could not stand such a drawn-out ordeal. "My conscience tells me, clearly and certainly, that I cannot prolong the bad dreams that continue to reopen a chapter that is closed. My conscience tells me that only I, as President, have the constitutional power to seal this book. My conscience tells me it is my duty, not only to proclaim domestic tranquillity but to use every means that I have to insure it."

The reaction was equally swift and decisive. TerHorst, whose conduct as press secretary had quickly restored confidence in an office that had hit bottom under Nixon's spokesman, Ronald Ziegler, did not learn of the decision until he found himself, on the night before, at a meeting in the Oval Office to discuss its implementation. As the others—Ford, Buchen, Haig, Hartmann, White House aide Jack Marsh, and Benton Becker, a lawyer brought in to negotiate with Nixon in San Clemente—began to discuss what needed to be done, dismay and anger grew in terHorst. He said nothing then. But after the meeting he went home and, when some guests had left, told his wife and then sat down and wrote his letter of resignation. The next morning, after arranging for Ford's televised statement, terHorst went to the Oval Office and handed the letter to the President, telling him he could not in conscience support the decision or speak for it. For nearly an hour Ford tried to dissuade him, telling his press secretary he thought the pardon was the right thing to do. TerHorst dejectedly said good-by.

His resignation made him an instant hero; letters and telegrams poured in to him from citizens around the country who were appalled not only by the pardon itself but by what it seemed to say about a new President in whom they had placed their trust. The obvious conclusion was immediately drawn: that Ford had struck a deal to gain the presidency, that he had agreed before assuming office to pardon Nixon if he would step aside. Ford flatly denied it, and even took the near-unprecedented step of appearing before the House Judiciary Committee to testify on the matter. But a public twice burned had moved from skeptical to cynical. Ford's early popularity plummeted; the great storehouse of good will that had been his for the taking was emptied as rapidly as it had been filled. He was "just another politician," voters told a *Washington Post* survey team the week after the pardon, and they would treat him accordingly.

For all of Ford's protestations that he had acted for the good of the country, to get its attention off Nixon and Watergate and on to more pressing problems, the harm had been done. It did not matter that at the time no proof was uncovered of any deal, and that there had been ample warning of an eventual pardon in Ford's earlier sympathetic attitude toward Nixon. Jerry Ford had come in selling honesty and candor, and in the view of millions the national elixir had turned out to be more water and syrup.[2]

Ford's early political troubles could be clearly charted from that point. Economic and energy woes worsened with every passing month and were unimproved by the halfway concessions of a President chained to Republican economic dogma; this situation combined with the aftertaste of Watergate and the Nixon pardon to produce a catastrophic off-year election result for Ford and the GOP in November 1974. The Democrats strengthened their control of Congress with a pickup of forty-nine House seats and five in the Senate plus four governorships, giving them power bases in eight of the ten largest states. It was music to the ears of the bumper crop of Democratic presidential hopefuls already sprouting, and a knell of impending political doom to Ford, who already had declared his intention to seek a full term in 1976.

Ford's own efforts to salvage something for the Republicans in the 1974 elections had only revealed his shortcomings on the stump. He raced around the country warning of a "veto-proof Congress"—one in which the Democrats could recklessly override his efforts to stem their spending orgies. Substantial Democratic gains were mounted, but still Ford resorted to the veto as his major legislative device. And, in early 1975, he resumed campaigning in an obvious effort to pin a "do-nothing" label on the Democratic Congress, after the fashion of the man whom he increasingly and openly admired, Harry S Truman. As Ford's popularity plunged in the national-opinion polls—43 per cent of voters disapproved of his leadership in the Gallup Poll in February—so did public respect for him. And reflecting that mood, the press joined in the carping. For example, Ford's inability to pronounce difficult words, and some not so difficult, was immediately seized upon as a measure of his brainpower. In a speech in Atlanta, in early February, he stumbled an inordinate number of times in a speech on his energy proposals before getting out the word "geothermal" correctly. A

2. In December 1975 *Washington Post* reporters Bob Woodward and Carl Bernstein reported that Ford had in fact pardoned Nixon "after hearing urgent pleas from the former President's top aides that he be spared the threat of criminal prosecution." See below, pp. 89–90.

tape of the speech became an overnight box-office hit in the White House press room.

Later in February, during the Lincoln Day congressional recess, Ford went to Topeka to speak to the Kansas legislature, seeking support for his economic/energy program. He told the predominantly Republican legislature that "ever since I was a youngster, I have had a special feeling for Kansas, because Kansas is where Dorothy lived before she went to visit the wonderful land of Oz, where all kinds of strange, whimsical, and unexpected things happened." But, he said, "I'm beginning to think that if strange, whimsical, and unexpected things were what Dorothy was really interested in, she wouldn't have gone to Oz. She would have come to Washington." Mention of the nation's capital, always a favorite Republican target, triggered the sought-after laughter and applause, but it also set the press corps traveling with Ford to thinking. The President was not unlike the Wizard of Oz himself, sitting behind a screen, turning wheels, and sending up great puffs of smoke signifying nothing. Soon the reporters addressed themselves to the time-honored after-hours relaxation of their trade, the writing of a parody. To the tune of the song sung by Ray Bolger as the Scarecrow in that all-time favorite movie, it went:

> I could while away the hours
> Reflecting on my powers,
> As we go down the drain.
> I could spend like Rockefeller,
> I could talk like Walter Heller,
> If I only had a brain.

> I could overcome inflation,
> Put gas in every station,
> And we would feel no pain.
> I could make the Arabs cower,
> I could be an Eisenhower,
> If I only had a brain.

> Oh, gee, if I could be
> Like Truman in his prime;
> Salty speeches whipping Congress into line,
> Say "geothermal"—the first time.

> I could hold down grocery prices,
> Wipe out the oil crisis,
> Solve problems with no strain.
> I could do a lot of thinkin',
> I could be another Lincoln,
> If I only had a brain.

It was in such a public climate—of disillusionment deteriorating into ridicule—that Jerry Ford in the spring of 1975 prepared for the campaign of 1976 that would determine whether the people wanted him to be their President. And within this public atmosphere two other factors, one personal and one political, cast a shadow over 1976 for him.

The first was the health of his wife, Betty. In late September 1974 she was hospitalized because of a cancerous growth in her breast. She underwent a radical mastectomy, and although the operation was declared a success and Mrs. Ford soon resumed many public White House activities, the history of such operations was uneven; there remained constant speculation about whether her husband would run again if her condition worsened.

The second consideration was a growing unrest among conservative Republicans fueled by three Ford actions—his selection of Nelson Rockefeller to be his Vice President, his modest amnesty offer to Vietnam draft evaders, and his resort to a heavy budget deficit in the face of the twin problems of inflation and recession. After an abortive "Whip Inflation Now" campaign in late 1974 (symbolized by red-and-white "WIN" buttons that soon became a favorite comedians' prop), Ford yielded to Democratic pressures and reality: he shifted his efforts to fighting recession, which required a tax cut and other efforts to stimulate the economy and to check steadily mounting unemployment.

At a Conservative Political Action Conference in Washington, sponsored by the American Conservative Union and Young Americans for Freedom in February 1975, talk flourished among the five hundred delegates of a third-party effort behind retired Governor Ronald Reagan of California, who already was working what he liked to call "the mashed-potato circuit," pocketing an average of $3500 a speech and preaching the gospel of the conservative True Believer. Both Reagan and Senator James L. Buckley of New York talked the idea down, urging instead a greater conservative effort to assert authority within the GOP to bring the Ford administration to its senses. "Is it a third party we need," Reagan asked, "or is it a new and revitalized second party, raising a banner of no pale pastels, but bold colors which makes it unmistakably clear where we stand on all of the issues troubling the people? Americans are hungry to feel once again a sense of mission and greatness." Most of the delegates would have gladly fallen in behind Reagan had he announced his candidacy then and there. Instead, because he continued to play coy, the conference voted to create a thirteen-member committee, with Senator Jesse A. Helms, Jr., of North Carolina as the chairman, to look into the possibilities of a third-party presidential effort.

A couple of weeks later, at a weekend meeting called by Buckley in the Eastern Shore town of St. Michaels, Maryland, more than two dozen Republican conservatives served notice on Ford. They would not "be taken for granted," they said, and were looking forward to an "open" Republican convention, despite the presence of an incumbent President of their party. They said they wouldn't endorse or oppose any candidate "at this time," but the gesture was a clear warning to Ford that his nomination in 1976 would by no means be automatic.

At the same time, a new group was formed calling itself the Conservative Caucus, organized by Howard Phillips, Nixon's ruthless executioner of the federal antipoverty agency, and financed with the professional fund-raising help of Richard Viguerie, a right-wing direct-mail magician who helped Governor George Wallace of Alabama raise $1.7 million in 1974. The group was building the framework for a third-party effort for either Reagan or Wallace that would be a threat to Ford's chances in the fall of 1976. "I believe both of them are going to be denied their party's nomination," Phillips said in April, "and I believe they could come together to run for the presidency."

Finally, if Ford were challenged from the right, then he also might be challenged from the left, where the likes of Illinois Senator Charles H. Percy had already done the standard "exploration" of candidacy during the last Nixon months and was ready to make his own bid if the field were thrown open. And of course there was the ageless Rockefeller, who before being selected by Ford to be Vice President had resigned as governor of New York to prepare for his third "final" bid for the presidency. As long as Ford remained in the running and Rockefeller was Vice President, Rockefeller could not move. But a decision by the President to settle for Nixon's unexpired term would certainly propel Rockefeller into the race, too.

Throughout the spring of 1975 rumors persisted that Ford would—despite his repeated denials—step aside for Rockefeller in the end. But if that thought ever crossed Ford's mind, the clamor from the Republican right dispelled it. Rockefeller, for all his efforts in his last years as governor of New York to move to the right and hence become more acceptable in the national party that had always repulsed him, remained an anathema to party conservatives. In late February, presiding over the Senate, Rockefeller had done himself in. He sought to cut off the parliamentary inquiry of a conservative Democrat, James B. Allen of Alabama, in order to expedite a vote on a move to liberalize the Senate's antifilibuster rule. At once, fellow Republicans on the right climbed all over him in the most open and humiliating fashion. Barry Goldwater, a long-time Rockefeller archfoe, told him that Senate rules required the presiding officer to recognize any senator who asked. When Rockefeller quoted the relevant passage from the Senate rules that said he had discretionary power to ignore a parliamentary inquiry at the start of a roll call, his response only triggered more criticism: legality wasn't the question; senatorial courtesy was. Carl T. Curtis of Nebraska, one of the Senate's moldiest mossbacks and chairman of its Republican Conference, charged that Rockefeller had "no responsibility or authority to assume a role of expediting the business of the Senate or preventing the use of dilatory tactics."

Rockefeller finally apologized to Allen and to the Senate. He was, he said obsequiously, "a servant of the Senate." But the harm was done, and it rubbed off on Ford, too. His supporters in the Senate were openly critical of the fact that the Vice President apparently had been left on his own, without White House instructions, in favoring the Senate gag-rule reformers over the conservatives. "Here we are trying to defend the President against bills he doesn't want," a Republican senator told *The Washington Star*'s Martha Angle, "and we're being denied the most valuable tool available."

It's probably fair to say, given the hostility with which the GOP conservatives regarded Rockefeller, that had this episode not happened, something else would have been seized upon as a rationale for a get-Rockefeller drive on the right. As pressure for Rockefeller's removal from the 1976 ticket began to build, it became abundantly clear that Ford would never be able to will the Republican presidential nomination to his Vice President, if he decided not to run himself. And with Reagan traveling widely among the GOP faithful and being warmly received everywhere, it became equally clear that a Ford withdrawal from the 1976 race would invite Reagan to seize the nomination without a serious fight.

Ford's decision to run was made easier by virtue of an event that suddenly lifted the gloom surrounding his chances of success. The development began to unfold half a world away on May 12, in the Gulf of Siam. Southeast Asia had been the arena for the United States' most shattering and humiliating foreign-policy defeat: the fall of South Vietnam at the end of March, amid a desperate evacuation of Americans and South Vietnamese clients, including the bizarre sight of evacuees frantically climbing to the roof of the American embassy in Saigon to board helicopters. At home, the abject failure of the American intervention in Vietnam struck at the national consciousness—and the national pride. Ford, seemingly blind to the realities of the lost situation, pressed Congress for more emergency aid when it was perfectly clear such aid could not turn the tide, and when it was equally clear that Congress had no stomach for prolonging the inevitable. For all the rhetoric to the contrary, Uncle Sam—and Gerald Ford— had his tail between his legs. The spectacle was not pleasant for Americans who for so long had proudly proclaimed that their country "has never lost a war."

On top of the loss of South Vietnam came a swift conclusion to the war in neighboring Cambodia, with the United States again supporting the losing side. Already the debate was heated between hawks and doves: what did it all mean to America's role in the world? Could the United States stand idly by in Southeast Asia letting allies go under, and retain its credibility when it pledged resistance elsewhere to military or Communist takeover? Was America's word, the hawks liked to ask, worth nothing? In this climate of national self-doubt, embarrassment, and feistiness, Ford was presented with a dramatic opportunity to display American muscle and resolve. For reasons still not entirely or satisfactorily explained, on May 12 the victorious Khmer Rouge had intercepted and seized an American merchant ship, the *Mayaguez,* and its crew of forty, and held them in the port of Sihanoukville. Ford, faced with the first genuine foreign-policy crisis of his administration, summoned the National Security Council, which proceeded to kill a fly with a cannon. The President approved a military plan to recapture the ship and save the crew, a plan that involved both daring and brute force, including heavy air strikes against Cambodian mainland installations. A Marine rescue mission against the island of Tang was carried out, and both ship and crew were eventually recovered (though a later General Accounting Office report said most of the U.S. crew was not on the island at the time). The news was both electrifying and exhilarating to Americans whose patriotism was badly in need of strengthening. Ford overnight was transformed into a man of guts and action; never mind that the eventual loss of American lives in the mission exceeded the number saved, or that the international diplomatic community was horrified when the American giant resorted to force so quickly and massively against a small country. Jerry Ford might be a nice, easygoing guy personally, but he was no pushover when American rights, lives, or self-respect were at stake.

Along with the *Mayaguez* decision, one other important development worked in Ford's favor: the long recession/inflation that had bogged down the economy appeared to be bottoming out at last. Though unemployment remained frighteningly high, big industry was showing signs of snapping out of the doldrums, and price increases seemed to be tapering off. Democrats like Hubert Humphrey agreed that the economic trend was all-important for 1976. Ford did not have to right the economy or solve all its problems; if there was evidence that things were just getting better, it would be difficult to make political hay on the economic issue.

Finally, through a series of vetoes that were upheld, Ford worked himself into a position where he could paint the Democratic-controlled Congress as a squabbling, ineffective body of irresponsibles. It mattered little that the Democrats genuinely regarded his proposals to deal with the economy, with the energy crisis, and with other critical issues as inadequate, and that government by veto was essentially negative government. The pollsters were abroad in the land and they were bringing back a consistent finding: the voting public, as never before, was fed up with government and disbelieved that it could be an effective vehicle for providing a better national life. The Ronald Reagan–George Wallace theme of get-the-government-off-our-backs was playing in Peoria, and Jerry Ford, as he had done all his life as a congressman, was singing it too. His chances to win a full presidential term in his own right appeared to be brightening.

4. Ford the Candidate

Through the first half of 1975 the political thinkers at the White House devoted much time to talking themselves out of the reality of Ronald Reagan as a 1976 presidential candidate. They told other Republicans they didn't believe Reagan would really run, and for a time some of them encouraged talk that Rockefeller would be dropped from the ticket, in the hope Reagan would be enticed to hold off in anticipation of being given the second spot. That master games-player and Ford intimate, former Secretary of Defense Melvin Laird, floated the notion in early May that an "open convention" should be held on the matter of a Vice President. "I think the frustrations and some of the pent-up feelings that some members of the party have will be used up to some extent in the fight for the vice-presidential nomination," Laird said. Barry Goldwater chimed in with the suggestion that Rockefeller "might make a fine secretary of state" in the next Ford administration. It was clearly a tactic to draw right-wing heat and competition away from Ford himself, but neither Reagan nor his political lieutenants took the bait.

A group of influential conservatives, led by Senators Buckley of New York, Helms of North Carolina, and James A. McClure of Idaho, met on Capitol Hill and, without endorsing Reagan, proposed in early June "that as neither the President nor the Vice President was elected to office, it would be in the best interest of the Republican Party and of the country for the 1976 presidential and vice-presidential nominations to be sought and won in an open convention. . . . The merits of the current administration must be judged in 1976 by delegates pledged only to support the principles of their party. The President can ask for no more—and he deserves no less."

This and similar signs of an impending Reagan candidacy generated small ripples of concern among Ford's political advisers. They pressed him to start planning for his own campaign so as to discourage Reagan. So, without formally declaring his candidacy, in mid-June he appointed Dean Burch, Goldwater's choice as Republican National Chairman for his disastrous 1964 campaign, later chairman of the Federal Communications Commission and a Nixon White House political aide, to establish a planning group; he also sent a letter to the new Federal Election Commission authorizing the group to raise money for his nomination. But if this activity, too, was intended to scare Reagan off, it was a waste of time.

In an obvious gesture to conciliate the GOP right wing, and Republicans in the South particularly, Ford selected another old Nixon lieutenant of 1968 who luckily had not been involved in the 1972 campaign, Secretary of the Army Howard H. (Bo) Callaway, a former Georgia congressman, to take over as campaign manager. The choice seemed on the surface a shrewd one: Callaway was a Southerner and a card-carrying conservative who knew the party's right-wing geography without a road map; he was independently wealthy and could take the job; Ford had known him in the House, liked him personally, and they had a good, direct relationship. Overlooked or at least shunted aside in all this was the fact Callaway was a man who had never run a national political campaign, and he was working with a candidate who had never run in one. In 1966 he had been the GOP's hope to become the first Republican governor in the South since Alfred A. Taylor in Tennessee in 1923, running against segregationist Lester G. Maddox. National party leaders had considered his candidacy their best shot in years, and Callaway in fact outpolled Maddox in the popular vote, but he failed to win a majority, and when the election was thrown into the Democratic-controlled state legislature, he lost. Worse, Callaway's performance in the 1968 campaign had been, in the judgment of insiders, disastrous. As Nixon's Southern coordinator, he had told the Mississippi Republican Convention that Wallace should be brought into the Republican Party—giving Rockefeller an opportunity to paint the Nixon campaign as racist. Callaway defensively contended he had merely said that since Wallace as a third-party candidate also wanted to beat the Democrats, "maybe we can even get [him] on our side, because that's where he ought to be." Rockefeller wanted Nixon to repudiate Callaway, but Nixon brushed aside the demand, disavowed Wallace, and suggested that Callaway "may be subject to misunderstanding." Still, Nixon and John N. Mitchell, who was running his campaign, did not dismiss the episode. Callaway was regarded as a lightweight in Nixon's inner circle, and Mitchell wanted him fired, but Nixon, even then unable to come to grips with such personnel confrontations, held off. Callaway was shunted aside for the rest of the campaign, however, and lost his chance to become a member of Nixon's cabinet, as he had hoped.

That history had apparently been lost by June 1975 when Ford began shopping around for someone to run his campaign. Callaway had made a good record as secretary of the army in the difficult period after abandonment of the draft, and had built a reputation in Washington as a man of candor—precisely what the Ford campaign needed after Watergate. Callaway eagerly accepted the assignment.

Finally, on July 8, speaking from the Oval Office, President Ford declared his candidacy. He vowed he would run an "open and above-board campaign," stressed his incumbency by giving his duties as President first priority, but also vowed to involve himself actively in the campaign. Nixon in 1972 had run for President from the Oval Office, treating the nomination and election campaign as a bothersome intrusion; later, after Watergate, he publicly blamed much of the disaster on his failure to play a more active role in his own campaign, instead of leaving it to the bumblers. That would not happen in Ford's campaign: Ford pledged he would run in compliance with "the letter and the spirit" of the new campaign reform law, and after Watergate he and his associates knew it had better be that way.

Ford recruited David Packard as his finance chairman, a former deputy secretary of defense under Nixon who was chief executive officer of the Hewlett-Packard Corporation in Palo Alto, California. In little more than a month Packard announced he had raised about $600,000 for the President's campaign and had easily qualified for federal matching money under the new law. The Ford campaign and Packard were determined scrupulously to avoid any comparison with Maurice Stans's fund-raising machine of 1968 and 1972, a core element in the whole Watergate mess. Any danger of such a comparison however proved to be slim, whether on grounds of ethics or efficiency. Packard's operation, while free of the strong-arm methods Stans had used to induce corporate executives to contribute to Nixon, was likewise free of Stans's effectiveness. Over the next three months Packard failed to bring the total to even $1 million and thoughts of nobly rejecting the federal money were quietly abandoned.

Callaway, meanwhile, determined to get off on the right foot, instead stuffed it in his mouth at the very start. The morning after the President's announcement of candidacy, he held an open house at the temporary headquarters of the President Ford Committee, an office several blocks from the White House. For more than two hours, he sipped coffee with visiting reporters and conducted what amounted to a floating press conference. A single topic—the future of Nelson Rockefeller—was raised and dealt with repeatedly, until there were as many variations to Callaway's answers as there were reporters, always a dangerous public-relations situation in a political campaign. The committee, Callaway took pains to emphasize, was a vehicle for nominating Ford, not Ford and Rockefeller, and the group's name expressed that fact. This was not unusual at all: in 1956 Dwight D. Eisenhower, a candidate for re-election, did not say Nixon would be his running mate again until just before the Republican convention; in 1972 Nixon declared in January and did not reanoint Agnew until shortly before the GOP convention in August. Ford's declaration of candidacy, however, was made against the backdrop of his political agents' efforts to keep Reagan out of the race. It was suggested unofficially, in fact, that Reagan might be Ford's running mate. The reporters bored in on Callaway: why were Ford and Callaway failing to say anything about Rockefeller? Why were color photographs mounted on the walls of the Ford committee headquarters showing Ford only, never Rockefeller? Did this mean Rockefeller was expendable? Ford himself had nourished such speculation a few weeks earlier when he expressed his personal preference for Rockefeller in 1976, but so worded the statement as to suggest to many that he intended to leave the matter to the Republican convention—an open invitation to the party's conservatives to turn it into a shooting gallery against Rockefeller. "Both of us in these coming months will be submitting ourselves to the will of the delegates at the Republican National Convention," Ford said. "I am confident both of us can convince the delegates that individually and as a team we should both be nominated." Callaway, however, was clearly saying now that so far as he was concerned, Ford and Rockefeller were not running as a team. He bluntly gave the reason: "A lot of Reagan people are not supporters of Rockefeller, and I want it clear to them that we want their support [for Ford] whether they support Rockefeller or not."

Rockefeller, all too aware of Ford's strategy to co-opt the party's right wing from Reagan, said he fully agreed that the President should run on his own. He knew full well that his own candidacy for the vice-presidency depended on Ford's nomination. Even in the event Reagan failed to defeat Ford in the primaries and take the nomination, a strong showing by him would be a signal to Ford that his candidacy against a Democratic nominee would need shoring up on the right. And the obvious way of achieving that end would be to dump Rockefeller.

Despite White House denials that the President wanted Rockefeller off the ticket and was using Callaway as his hit man, speculation to that effect flared up again later in July when Callaway, at a meeting with reporters, volunteered that Rockefeller was his "Number-one problem." "You and I both know that if Rockefeller took himself out," Callaway said, "it would help with the nomination." As a matter of fact, he suggested, it might be Ford's "best judgment" that he needed "a younger man." Rockefeller would be sixty-eight at the time of inauguration to a full term as Vice President, Callaway said, perhaps too old to make use of the incumbency advantage for the Republicans and be the logical successor in 1980. "We're hearing that a lot," the campaign manager reported.

Again it looked as if the skids were being greased for Rockefeller. Liberal GOP senators, both before and after receiving phone calls from the vexed Vice President, criticized Callaway and asked Ford to throttle him.

The campaign manager's remarks, said Senator Javits, an old Rockefeller ally, were "a great disservice to the President." Dumping Rockefeller, he said, would "endanger the President's support from the whole centrist bloc in the country." And Senate Minority Leader Hugh Scott of Pennsylvania dispatched a terse note to presidential aide Donald H. Rumsfeld that asked: "Is Callaway managing Reagan's campaign, or Ford's?" Over at Reagan's unofficial campaign headquarters, his managers conceded happily that they could not have done a better job themselves. Reagan himself, in Raleigh, North Carolina, where he was speaking at a fund-raiser for Senator Helms, added his bit by accusing Callaway of subjecting his good friend Nelson to "shoddy treatment." Said Reagan, with crocodile tears flowing, "It's embarrassing, it must be, for a man who has served his country in a number of capacities for many years to now be held up as if he were at auction."

The next morning, Rockefeller was on the phone to Callaway, furious. Rockefeller said he agreed that it was wise for Ford to run on his own, but Callaway had gone too far. "Bo," Rocky told him, "we had an agreement [on downplaying Rockefeller], but it didn't include calling me the number-one problem." Rockefeller also talked to the President and came away saying he was more relaxed than ever about his relations with Ford. That was what he *said*, anyway.

On July 20, Callaway, at a breakfast meeting with reporters, turned away all questions concerning the matter. He denied he had been "muzzled" and would concede only that he had received some "general advice" to cool off the anti-Rockefeller talk. Two days later, with the same group, Rockefeller, while insisting he still had no quarrel with Callaway, blamed the man's inexperience in national politics for the whole flap. In his zest to woo Reagan supporters in Dixie, Rockefeller said, Callaway had gotten carried away and failed to make clear he was reporting Southern sentiment, not his own. Bo had not appreciated the sophistication and "creative imagination" of the veteran reporters with whom he had been speaking, Rocky said wryly.

For the time being, it appeared that Callaway had been told to lay off. But the message to conservatives—that Rockefeller, if necessary, was expendable—had been delivered.

At any rate, what to do with or about Rockefeller was, at this juncture, a secondary concern for Ford's campaign. The first priority was cutting Reagan off at the ankles before he could make real headway.[1] Ford's aides,

1. A Gallup Poll of Republicans and Independents in late June, after Ford had declared and the Reagan committee was registered, gave Ford 41 per cent, Reagan 20 per cent, in a field of ten prospective candidates. In a two-man matchoff, the results were: Ford 61 per cent, Reagan 33 per cent, undecided 6 per cent.

and in some instances the President himself, began calling Republican leaders around the country for support. Four state party committees responded almost at once with endorsements—Michigan, Ohio, Pennsylvania, and New York—and others followed suit shortly. In California, a major effort was undertaken, with considerable early success, to take advantage of Reagan's foot-dragging. Paul Haerle of San Francisco, once Reagan's appointments secretary and now GOP state chairman, endorsed the President; so did a long list of one-time state officials or businessmen and money-raisers associated with Reagan, the most notable of whom was Henry Salvatori.

During his summer vacation in Vail, Colorado, the President made political forays into Midwest and Western states, preaching the conservative gospel in an obvious attempt to stop Reagan in his tracks and to dissuade him from the 1976 competition.[2] Illustrative was a hard-line speech to the American Legion's annual convention in Minneapolis in which Ford defended his policy of détente with the Soviet Union but warned the Russians, with whom he had just completed talks on strategic arms limitations in Helsinki, that he was prepared to ask Congress to spend $2 billion to $3 billion more on strategic weapons unless further agreements were reached. And when Southern Republican state chairmen met in Wrightsville Beach, North Carolina, in late August, Callaway and other Ford lieutenants lobbied aggressively against efforts made in behalf of the still formally unannounced Reagan. Whether the Dixie state chairmen liked it or not, Callaway told them, Reagan couldn't win enough delegates in the primaries to beat Ford; a major fight for the nomination could split the GOP and invite a third-party effort. Rather than oppose Ford, who was not so different from Reagan ideologically, the best way to affect the party platform was to get on the Ford team. And as for Rockefeller, that would be up to the convention.

At the same time, at Ford's urging, Rockefeller began speaking around the country, particularly in the South, to boost his own stock and make it easier for the President to keep him on—*if* the anti-Rockefeller clamor from the right could be stemmed or finessed. In Mobile, Alabama, and Columbia,

---

2. The President's travels caused a controversy over assignment of the costs under the new campaign finance law. The White House shunted the expenses for political trips to the Republican National Committee, on the grounds that Ford was giving his speeches to fatten local and state Republican campaign treasuries and not in the course of his own presidential campaign. Democrats immediately charged that this was a violation of the new law, and they appealed to the Federal Election Commission, but to no avail. The commission ruled the procedure valid and said Ford did not have to assign his travel costs to his own election effort until he began campaigning on his own behalf. The decision enabled Ford to leave his own campaign treasury virtually untapped until the start of 1976.

South Carolina, Rockefeller characteristically threw himself wholeheartedly into the effort to, in his own words, "prove to them I don't have horns." The one-time leader of liberal Republicanism, who in nearly sixteen years in New York had used the tools of state government and state bond issues as no other governor ever had to build schools, hospitals, and the most expensive welfare rolls in the nation, called for a return to balanced budgets "at all levels of government." He said, rather incredibly, that he regretted his role in the growth of social-welfare programs in the 1960s and that welfare programs should be revamped to make certain that "cheats . . . who don't belong on the rolls don't benefit." It was a startling performance, but his Dixie brethren, who had long memories, were not moved. Edgar Weldon, Alabama's Republican chairman, met privately with Rockefeller in Mobile and came out saying he still preferred a younger running mate for Ford. He didn't see, Weldon observed, how Rockefeller could "become totally acceptable to the South, not after eleven years"—an obvious reference to Rockefeller's 1964 opposition to hero Barry Goldwater. Weldon noted, however, that Rockefeller now sounded surprisingly like Governor George Wallace, who had addressed the same meeting. Wallace's press secretary, Billy Joe Camp, told reporters: "We lost a speech in the office the other afternoon and now we know where it went."

Rockefeller was trying, but the pressure was mounting against him. During his Southern swing, the Gallup Poll reported that a survey of Republicans in early August found 44 per cent preferred Reagan as the President's running mate, to 40 per cent for Rockefeller, with the South as well as the Far West going strongly for the former California governor. Still, the President appeared to be holding firm. In late August he told a television interviewer in Newport, Rhode Island, that Rockefeller "has exceeded any expectations that I have had. He has done a superb job. He has been a good teammate. I don't dump good teammates."

But Ford clearly had a problem with conservative Republicans, and Rockefeller was not the only cause. Potential trouble now came from a totally unexpected source—the First Lady. Betty Ford, asked on CBS's "Sixty Minutes" what she would do if her eighteen-year-old daughter came to her and told her she was having an affair, said cheerfully, "Well, I wouldn't be surprised. I think she's a perfectly normal human being, like all young girls. If she wanted to continue it, I would certainly counsel and advise her on the subject. And I'd want to know pretty much about the young man that she was planning to have the affair with—whether it was a worthwhile encounter, or whether it was going to be one of those—She's pretty young to start affairs."

Before the interview was over, Mrs. Ford had supported the Supreme

Court in legalizing abortion to "bring it out of the backwoods and put it in the hospitals where it belongs"; she had compared marijuana experimentation by the young with taking "your first beer or your first cigarette"; she had suggested that premarital sex might cut the divorce rate. It was, by any standard, a mouthful for the First Lady of the nation.

Predictably, the traditionalists attacked her with unfettered zeal. Typical was a telegram that Arthur S. Howatt, chairman of the Quakers, shot off to the White House: "We wish to protest against any such statement and to deplore the views of that kind as being contrary to the good standards of American society in which chastity outside of marriage is approved." Howatt warned Ford that his failure "to uphold high ethical and moral standards before the people of America . . . would have an adverse political effect on you."

President Ford, accustomed to the tribulations of living with an independent, outspoken wife, tried to shrug off the whole thing, observing he had never tried to muzzle her in the past and wasn't going to start now.

But in some conservative quarters the President's hands-off attitude only compounded Betty Ford's sin of bitter-truth-saying. In Manchester, New Hampshire, the publisher of the ultra-right-wing *Union-Leader,* William Loeb, wrote a signed page-one editorial entitled "A Disgrace to the White House" that took both Fords to task. "The immorality of Mrs. Ford's remarks is almost exceeded by their utter stupidity," Loeb wrote. "Involving any prominent individual, this would be a disgusting spectacle. Coming from the First Lady in the White House, it disgraces the nation itself. . . . President Ford showed his own lack of guts by saying he had long ago given up commenting on Mrs. Ford's radio interviews. What kind of husband is that? As President of the United States, he should be the moral leader of the nation. He is not in the position of an ordinary husband making the best of his wife's foolish and stupid remarks. . . . It is up to him to take a moral stand. He should repudiate what Mrs. Ford said."

The episode was one of those totally extraneous intrusions into the serious political dialogue, but conservatives tend to be moralists, so there was no telling what Betty Ford's frankness had cost her husband in his continuing effort to appease them, and for that matter to court the electorate at large as the nation's first unelected President.

In the job of selling himself to the voters, Ford embarked, shortly after Labor Day, on a routine two-day trip to the West Coast. Before it was over, the nation was treated to yet another bizarre illustration of the unpredictability of American presidential politics. After giving well-attended and well-received speeches in Seattle and Portland, the President arrived on *Air Force One* in Sacramento for a speech to the California legislature on September 5. He attended a large breakfast of area businessmen and growers, then set out on foot from his hotel to the state capitol just across the street. It was a day of bright sunshine and good cheer. Thick crowds lined his way and Ford walked easily, as was his custom, waving and shaking hands with well-wishers standing behind a restraining rope. He was about halfway toward the capitol when he walked by a young woman wearing a deep-red gown with matching bandana. As he went by, she reached under the gown, quickly withdrew a .45-caliber Army Colt automatic from a leg holster and tried to point it at him. Just then the President looked back and saw, as he described it later, "a hand coming up behind several others in the front row, and obviously there was a gun in that hand." A Secret Service agent walking just behind him, Larry Buendorf, grabbed the young woman's hand holding the gun (cutting himself on the gun in the process), pushed her back into the crowd and down, then disarmed and quickly handcuffed her.

This all happened so swiftly, so silently, and so unspectacularly that few realized how close the President had come to assassination. I was walking about ten feet to Ford's right and just a step or two behind him, when I saw him turn from his handshaking, look down briefly, then turn ahead and permit himself to be hustled off by two Secret Service agents, each holding him by an arm. He seemed befuddled at first, but his face displayed no emotion, no panic, just a grimness, as more agents flocked around him, shielding him with their own bodies as they looked in all directions and led him into the building. I heard Ron Pontius, the agent-in-charge, call out, "Forty-five!"—the kind of handgun the girl held—and "Let's go!" as he and other agents moved forward, as if he were calling signals for an oft-rehearsed drill. No guns were drawn; the only indication to bewildered onlookers that something was amiss was the sudden scurrying of television cameramen and photographers backpedaling frantically to keep the fast-stepping President in focus.

Other cameramen captured the scene and preserved a good record of the twenty-six-year-old Lynette Alice Fromme, a member of the Charles Manson mass-murder "family," a short, mousy-looking woman, who kept explaining to her captors, as they led her away, "It didn't go off, fellas." Later, examination of the gun determined that although four bullets were in the clip, there was none in the firing chamber. Fromme contended she had never intended to shoot the President, only to draw attention to the plight of Manson, imprisoned in San Quentin Federal Penitentiary. But the presence of live bullets in the clip was enough for a grand jury. She was indicted on a charge of attempting to kill the President. In November she was convicted and in December was sentenced to life imprisonment, the maximum penalty provided.

"It didn't go off, fellas." One must wonder what the course of American political history would have been had Lee Harvey Oswald been apprehended after a similar misfiring in Dallas in 1973, or Sirhan Sirhan in Los Angeles in 1968, or Arthur Bremer in Laurel, Maryland, in 1972. Or, more to the point for the politics of 1976 and beyond, one must wonder what would have happened had Fromme's effort not failed. As it was, the attempt on the President's life only stiffened Ford's resolve, not only to seek a full term in his own right, but also to campaign for it openly, even defiantly. The incident in Sacramento, Ford said afterward, "under no circumstances will prevent me or preclude me from contacting the American people as I travel from one state to another. I'm going to continue to have that personal contact with the American people. In my judgment it's vital for an American President to see the American people and I intend to carry it on."

True to his word, within the week, on September 11, Ford had an opportunity to demonstrate he meant what he said. In the final days of a special Senate election in New Hampshire, he put on an incredible display. Republican Louis C. Wyman, held to a virtual standoff by Democrat John A. Durkin the previous November in an election that ultimately required a rerun, called on the President for help, and Wyman got it—in spades. For eleven hours Ford toured the southern tier of New Hampshire, from Keene to Portsmouth, repeatedly jumping from his open limousine, plunging into crowds and shaking outstretched hands. It was as if he was determined by excess to show he had not been intimidated by the Sacramento episode.[3] Stopping in fourteen towns and at several other points along the way, he would take a microphone attached to a loudspeaker system plugged into the front fenders of the black presidential limousine, stand on the car's runner, an easy target for a would-be assassin, and speak at length to the impressively large and enthusiastic crowds that turned out along the route. Secret Service agents, including Buendorf, his protector in Sacramento, were at Ford's side constantly, scanning the crowds, rooftops, and office windows at each stop. Security seemed to be no greater than usual, with one exception. Although nothing was said about it by Ford or anyone else in his party,

---

3. In yet another example of the most bizzare editorial writing in the country, William Loeb, on the morning of Ford's arrival, urged the good people of New Hampshire to set themselves up as a kind of mass vigilante committee to protect the President "in view of the complete incompetence of the Secret Service."

you could see at close range that he was wearing some kind of protective vest under his white shirt. The shirt fit more snugly than usual, and just above his belt on either side was a small fastening device. The White House and the agents would not confirm that the President was wearing a bullet-proof vest, but there was no doubt about it.

The motorcade through New Hampshire was notable not simply as a test of Ford's courage. Here was a man presiding over a people who were suffering from high unemployment, high prices, and general economic malaise, yet the voters of New Hampshire turned out in remarkably large numbers to greet him. He was there to speak for Wyman, but one saw only a few Wyman campaign signs. Clearly, it was a bipartisan turnout, and this made Ford's aides buoyant. If there was to be a challenge from Reagan, the first battleground very likely would be the New Hampshire primary, and this outpouring was a good sign for Ford there.

Or so it seemed. Five days after Ford's visit, however, New Hampshire's voters went to the polls and resoundingly rejected the President's candidate. In the towns where Ford had campaigned for him—Republican areas that had shown serious slippage in the earlier Wyman-Durkin election —Wyman picked up 994 more votes than he had received the previous November, but Durkin in the same towns gained an additional 8088. In Portsmouth, where the citizenry had waited for nearly two hours to greet and cheer Ford in a town-center mob scene reminiscent of the final days of a presidential campaign, Wyman lost to Durkin by more than two to one. For politicians and political reporters alike, the vote was an eloquent reminder that crowds are a poor barometer of political popularity, or of one man's ability to translate his own appeal into votes for someone else. And for Ford's campaign planners especially, Wyman's failure in the end generated apprehension about New Hampshire as the site of a Ford-Reagan test of strength.

Despite the failure of Ford's day-long motorcade in Wyman's behalf, he continued his almost frenzied round of speaking tours. The next week he was in St. Louis (where police said they spied but did not catch a man with a gun in the hall where Ford was to speak) and Dallas (where the Secret Service has been particularly jittery about presidential visits since John Kennedy was assassinated there in 1963). And the third week of September he went back to California in another transparent effort to demonstrate his strength in Reagan's own back yard. He spoke in Los Angeles and, on September 22, in San Francisco, continuing to fulfill his pledge that he would not be deterred from going out among the people, and he even discarded the bullet-proof vest, which he found too warm and uncomfortable. He did, however, adhere in San Francisco to the Secret

Service's recommendation that he stay out of street crowds. The only street appearance scheduled was perhaps six strides from the side lobby of the St. Francis Hotel to the presidential limousine, after doing a television interview in a private room. Only six strides, but that was enough.

Ford came down the hotel elevator with his assistant, Donald Rumsfeld; his television adviser, Robert Meade; and several Secret Service agents. They walked through a small marble vestibule and past a pair of glass doors into a sidewalk area cordoned off by police sawhorses. Across the street, a crowd of about three thousand persons was waiting behind restraining ropes, and as Ford saw them, he waved and said, "Hi!" It was a typically cool and crisp San Francisco mid-afternoon. At that instant, a stout, matronly looking woman standing in the crowd about thirty-five or forty feet from the President with her right hand thrust the barrel of a .38 caliber Smith & Wesson revolver between the heads of two other onlookers. Steadying her right wrist with her left hand, she fired a single shot. The nightmare of Dallas, of Memphis and Los Angeles, Laurel and Sacramento, was with the American people again.

The shot missed President Ford, and the bullet hit the pavement and ricocheted weakly against a cab driver standing nearby, so weakly that it did not even penetrate his clothing. Ford, just a step or two from the limousine, looked in the direction of the sound, stunned for a split second. Then, on firmly stated orders from a Secret Service agent, he quickly crouched down against the side of the car. Other agents and Rumsfeld huddled around him, shielding his body. George McManus, a reporter from Station KCBS in San Francisco, caught the terrifying moment on his tape recorder: first the shot cracking, then his own voice: "Oh, my God! Oh, my God! There's been a shot! There's been a shot! We don't know if anyone's been hurt!"

At this instant, in the crowd across the street, a former Marine veteran of Vietnam named Oliver Sipple reached over and hit the outstretched arm holding the gun. Police officers immediately closed in and knocked the woman down. (She was later identified as Sara Jane Moore, forty-five, a member of a militant prisoners' rights group.) As they handcuffed her and dragged her into the hotel others in the crowd screamed, "Get her! Get her!"

By now, Ford had climbed into the back seat of the limousine, crouched on the floor with Rumsfeld and two agents shielding him, and been borne off toward San Francisco International Airport, where *Air Force One* was waiting to take him back to Washington. Betty Ford, who had been staying with friends in Monterey, was flying to the same airport when the shooting occurred. She boarded *Air Force One* before her husband and, una‧ware of what had happened, greeted him by asking: "Did you have a good time?"

As in Sacramento, the President was still determined not to be deterred from freedom of movement. The moment he was back in Washington, he called the television networks to the White House and around midnight broadcast a statement. "The American people," he said, "expect—and I approve of it—a dialogue between them and their President or other public officials. And if we can't have that opportunity to talk with one another, something has gone wrong in our society." He promised to "stand tall and strong" against intimidations.

Yet there was much more than Ford's courage at stake. The stability of the American government demanded that the President exercise more prudence during his travels. Much was written and said about the importance of enabling the people to see their chief executive, particularly their first unelected chief executive, and especially so after the trauma of Richard Nixon, who had so studiously insulated himself from them, except under the most controlled and contrived circumstances. Many people, including Ford himself, felt that a visible, open, and gregarious President was required to help deliver the country from that trauma. And so Ford continued to travel. He had announced, for good or ill, that he considered himself obliged to campaign actively in the presidential primaries in 1976, though no recent sitting President had felt compelled to do so. Between the shot in San Francisco and Election Day in November 1976 he knew he would have to go out among the people if he hoped to become President in his own right. And by now it was abundantly clear that he would have to turn back a serious challenge within his own party, a circumstance that would not allow him the luxury of isolation.

Still, Callaway, other Ford political lieutenants, and the President himself did not abandon their efforts to get Reagan to stay out. Callaway had old Reagan friends in California call the former governor and point out that Ford was picking up strength all across the country; in competing against him, Reagan was running the risk, as one of them said, "of becoming the Harold Stassen of 1976." But by mid-September, after the special election in New Hampshire, Reagan's willingness to run that risk began to sink in. On the very day Wyman was beaten by Durkin at the polls, Richard Mastrangelo, a close aide to Elliot Richardson in his days as attorney general, was sent into New Hampshire by Callaway to take soundings on the makings of a Ford organization there. Governor Meldrim Thomson already had the conservatives tied up for Reagan, but the state GOP was split deeply between the right wing and a moderate-liberal faction. Mastrangelo went to two of that faction's leaders, former Governor Walter R.

Peterson and Republican National Committeeman Robert Bass, and began to put together a group that would work for the President.

Before the first snow fell in New England, the battle lines were already drawn among Republicans in New Hampshire. Still, many people around the country could not grasp the idea that Ronald Reagan was really going to challenge the President, and many more could not begin to entertain the idea that he could be successful. "The notion that Ronald Reagan can get the Republican nomination away from Ford," James B. Reston wrote in *The New York Times* in early September, "is patently ridiculous unless you suspect the Republicans of suicidal tendencies." There was plenty of history, of course, to feed just such a suspicion, most notably the GOP's voluntary walking of the plank behind Barry Goldwater in 1964. In that year, the conservatives controlling the nominating machinery were determined first of all to seize control of the party from the hated Eastern liberals as represented by Nelson Rockefeller; and they had no trouble persuading themselves that by offering the American electorate "a choice, not an echo" —"no pale pastels," as Reagan would put it twelve years later—they could capture the country as well. They succeeded in the first objective, then failed abysmally in the second. Now, approaching 1976, they were still in control of the party, with the liberals in greater disarray and retreat than ever before, their old field general, Rockefeller, having conspicuously defected. What was so farfetched about the party that so loved Ronald Reagan giving him its presidential nomination? Sure, Jerry Ford was in the White House, and he had always been regarded as a conservative. But he was Nixon's choice, not the choice of the party out around the country. And for all his conservative rhetoric and use of the veto against the Democratic Congress, he was presiding over a federal budget out of balance by a colossal $66.5 billion. Moreover, he was not the kind of leader to stir passions, to excite the voters, to give life to the old GOP ideology. As a political leader, he was, in fact, a sort of present-day version of the old Ronald Reagan, the movie actor whom everybody liked but who always lost the girl to Errol Flynn. And now there was a new Ronald Reagan—the former two-term governor of the nation's largest state, a winner.

Yet as 1975 wound down, the invincibility of the incumbent—a notion shattered in the 1968 demise of Lyndon Johnson—still survived in the minds of millions of Americans. It would fall to the good people of New Hampshire, who had tumbled Humpty Dumpty from the wall only eight years earlier, to attempt the feat again for those who might not have been paying attention, or who had forgotten.

5. *Ronald Reagan Begins to Stir*

One afternoon in early spring, 1974, when Ronald Reagan was in his last of eight years as governor of California, a staff aide from Sacramento named Robert Walker, accompanied by James Lake, head of Reagan's office in Washington, paid a call on a young lawyer at the firm of Gadsby & Hannah on Pennsylvania Avenue, just half a block from the White House. The lawyer was John P. Sears III, thirty-four years old, a shrewd political tactician of subdued ideology who had masterminded Richard Nixon's impressive delegate search in 1967 and 1968. Sears had been Nixon's political adviser for a short time in 1969, before being undone by the then Attorney General John Mitchell, who disliked his influence with the new President.

Walker was an old friend of Sears. Together they had helped establish and run the first national Nixon for President office in 1967 just a few doors down from Gadsby & Hannah's present location. Now Walker wanted to try out an idea on Sears: What did he think of Reagan running for President? The Californian had nearly eight years of heavy governmental experience and was immensely popular in the Republican Party; Richard Nixon not only could not succeed himself but was on the Watergate ropes, presumably in no position to dictate the party's choice in 1976; Spiro Agnew was out of the picture and of course his successor, Jerry Ford, was no threat. Sears mulled over the idea in his office and later at the Black Angus across the street, where the three men had retired for a few drinks and more talk. "Yeah," Lake recalls Sears finally saying, "Reagan could do that. He could be the nominee."

More conversation went on between Sears and Lake in Washington and by phone with Walker in Sacramento in subsequent weeks. Reagan himself was saying nothing about his presidential ambitions, but key personal aides like Mike Deaver were assuring Lake and the other plotters that when the time came the decision would be "yes." In May Sears and Lake went to Los Angeles to meet with the California insiders—Walker, Deaver, Ed Meese, Jim Jenkins, Peter Hannaford, Lyn Nofziger. One other non-Californian was present, a man considered then to be of vital importance to the whole endeavor, a man who could be instrumental in bringing not only his state but his entire region into the Reagan column at the 1976 Republican National Convention: Clarke Reed, the Republican chairman of Mississippi and head of the influential and conservative Southern Republican State Chairmen's Association. Reed, a fast-talking, silver-haired political poker player who incongruously offset a sometimes almost indecipherable Southern drawl with the parlance of a street hipster, liked Reagan. He liked the hell out of him; he liked Reagan's complete and unabashed commitment to old-fashioned conservatism and his ability to verbalize it. For Clarke Reed, though every inch an opportunist, was also an ideological conservative to his core. He wanted very much to be in on the take-off of this effort to seize the nomination for a True Believer like Reagan, and subsequently to put him in the White House.

The meeting began in a suite at the Beverly Wilshire Hotel, continued over lunch, and then the group repaired to Reagan's home in Pacific Palisades, just west of Beverly Hills, where they were joined by Reagan and a collection of his old financial backers including Holmes Tuttle, Justin Dart, and David Packard (later to be Ford's first campaign finance chairman). Meese summarized the morning's discussion and the general agreement that Reagan should run, but that the effort would have to be contingent on Nixon's remaining as President through 1976. Reagan then suggested that each person in the room say whether he agreed, and why. Everybody agreed until Reagan got to Sears, whom he had met only once or twice before. One who was in the room recalls Sears's response, in paraphrase, this way: "I think it can be done, I think it should be done; the party needs it, the country needs it; but I disagree that Nixon has to stay as President. In fact, Nixon will be gone in six months." This last remark held Reagan's attention. "Jerry Ford can't cut the mustard, he's not perceived as a leader; he can't lead the Congress or the country. He will be vulnerable and we can beat him. He will not be seen as a true incumbent; you have as much support around the country as he has. We can challenge him successfully in New Hampshire." Lake, sitting next to Sears, agreed with him, but he was the only other one.

Reagan himself seemed intrigued but not persuaded. A man of orthodox, loyalist impulses, he had trouble buying the idea that Nixon would not finish his term, and that even if he did not, it would be right and proper to challenge his successor. But it was clear that he was impressed with Sears's level-headed, unemotional appraisal of the state of Republican politics, and especially his prediction—unexpected from an old Nixon loyalist and friend—that Nixon would not survive the Watergate ordeal. When the dramatic events of the summer of 1974 proved Sears to be right, Reagan's confidence in him rose even higher.

Through 1974 and into 1975 there were more meetings, mostly just to take stock of Nixon's resignation and Ford's ascendancy, and in these sessions Sears's leadership emerged more clearly. "You can't be in a meeting with John Sears present, discussing national politics," an insider said, "when it's not clear to everybody in the room that the guy who knows the most, is the most articulate about it, and has the strategies and concepts about how you get from Point A to Point B, is John Sears. It was an almost natural evolution."

Sears was as different on the surface as he could be from the sixty-four-year-old seemingly gregarious but insulated Reagan. Sears had a deceptively shy outer crust that camouflaged a biting humor and political toughness and skepticism. Also, his appreciation of and affinity with members of the Washington press corps set him apart from most of the political operatives around both Nixon and Reagan. Where many of the paranoid Nixon types looked upon reporters as the enemy, to be warded off at every turn, Sears saw them as an essential and unavoidable element in the drama of electing a President, and as valuable source material. He drank and socialized with them (it was a prime reason Mitchell purged him), told them what he could without jeopardizing his candidate, took them into his confidence, and won theirs in return. He had long felt that not only Nixon but H. R. (Bob) Haldeman, John D. Ehrlichman, and the other principal architects of Nixon's success and downfall had seriously erred in shutting off the press, in not using its readings of public concern as an early-warning system.

Nixon's crash, though it had occurred nearly five years after Sears's departure from the White House, had nevertheless been a severe personal blow to the young lawyer. The leader of the Kennedy for President forces in a mock convention at Notre Dame in 1960, Sears had met Nixon in New York as a young member of the Nixon, Mudge law firm. He had been impressed with Nixon's political savvy and durability, and taken with his strange vulnerability. Unlike others around Nixon, Sears saw the man's weaknesses as well as his strengths, but believed that the latter would prevail. He saw something else in Nixon too: an incredible single-mindedness about the mechanics of getting elected that seemed to push aside ideology. When Nixon was elected with his considerable help in 1968, Sears went to the White House aware that the President-elect was a man who in his intense effort and concentration on getting there had no real idea of what he wanted to do on arrival. I remember Sears, then in his late twenties, telling me shortly after Nixon's inauguration that a brutal fight was going on within the highest levels of the new administration "for Nixon's soul." On his left, Sears said, Nixon's old crony Robert Finch was trying to pull the President toward a socially activist administration, while on his right,

John Mitchell was pulling him in the opposite direction, toward social-welfare retrenchment and doctrinaire conservatism. Sears favored Finch's tilt, but that was not his undoing so much as was his openness (with the press particularly) in the fortress that Mitchell was trying, quite successfully, to make of the administration and the White House. Mitchell moved ruthlessly against his critics, and he especially resented anyone who had known Nixon longer than he had—particularly one so young. So Sears had to go.

The young lawyer left the White House without any surface display of resentment. He had many friends who stayed on; he remained in touch with them and, occasionally, with Nixon. Very early he saw the trouble signs—the risky moves that polarized the country, the attacks on the press, the insulation of Nixon from the realities around him. When Watergate occurred, there was no one in the White House who could get to Nixon with counsel contrary to the stonewall, cover-up advice of Haldeman, Ehrlichman, et al. Later, indeed when it was too late, Nixon would telephone Sears and ask for counsel and commiseration; Sears often felt that if he had still been in the White House he might have saved Nixon. The prospect ate at him, made him restless, and whetted his appetite for one more presidential campaign. But this time he did not want to be a mere technician who would help engineer victory and then be cast aside. This time he wanted to run the show, to be in a position afterward to affect the new administration and the politics of his party. To the astonishment of his friends in the press, he began to take a look at Ronald Reagan.

Reagan was probably not the kind of candidate Sears would have picked had he had a wide choice. But in the reality of the party and the time, it was Ford or Reagan, and Sears knew he would never be in command in a Ford campaign. The President's men, well aware of Sears's performance for Nixon in 1968—and of Reagan's interest in him—in fact offered him a White House job in 1974 dispensing patronage, looking toward a political role in the 1976 campaign, but apparently not full control. "I'd had enough of being in the White House with eighty-five guys hanging around," he said later. That, Sears judged, was the formula for frustration. He knew enough about the inner workings of the White House to have no illusions that under such an arrangement he would have the access to and influence over the President he believed were necessary to succeed. Beyond that, he had seen Jerry Ford the campaigner at work in 1970 and had found him ineffective; he knew that Ford's only real political strength was his incumbency, and that too was flawed by the circumstances under which he had attained it. One or two early failures in the primaries, Sears reasoned, and Republicans everywhere would be going over the side. In that circumstance, the obvious beneficiary would be the one man in the picture who preached the True Faith of Conservatism. Sears reasoned that Reagan would not have to be inhibited by the fact Ford was a sitting President, because of the way Ford had arrived at the White House. Loyalty in the GOP, Sears told me over a long lunch at Harvey's in early June as he agonized over his personal decision, was loyalty to conservative principles, not to any one man— particularly when that man was perceived, rightly or not, as less than a pure conservative.

To Sears, a Reagan nomination was, in the political jargon, do-able. Yet he was troubled about an alliance with Reagan because as a pragmatic political operative he did not want to be tagged as an ultra-ideologue of the right; he did not want Reagan's right-wing label to rub off on himself. And, beyond that, Sears's association with members of the Washington political press corps was more to him than a marriage of convenience; he wanted them to understand and accept his move to Reagan. Reagan, he told me earnestly, was not the lightweight many in the press saw him to be. He had learned a lot being governor of California for eight years, and he was a listener, Sears said, recalling long conversations with Reagan about politics, about national goals, about where the society was going and should go, about ethics and religion in politics. Most important, Reagan was malleable: the man could be educated on the issues, and could be moved more to the center of the political spectrum if handled correctly. As an actor, Sears said frankly, Reagan was accustomed to direction; he could keep the True Believers in the ranks while altering his rhetoric to broaden his appeal. It was, to say the least, an optimistic outlook, but Sears obviously needed to believe that he could succeed in this remaking of Ronald Reagan if he were going to undertake direction of his candidacy and live with himself and his friends. It would be a service to the country, he rationalized, if he could harness Reagan's appeal to constructive goals and give the nation a Presi- dent they could believe in. The people, he said, were basically in agreement with Reagan in their disenchantment with the government. What was needed was to get the harsh edge off Reagan's pitch, to show some capacity for compassion in the man, without giving way to the old liberal litany of the welfare state. The Sears plan for Ronald Reagan was a big order, but Sears was of a frame of mind that could accept the challenge only on those ambitious terms.

In that endeavor, Reagan himself proved to be a hurdle. The patriotism the man wore so transparently on his sleeve really did seem to beat intensely in his breast as well; he seemed to aides sincerely to want the new President, Jerry Ford, to be successful. "Sears convinced the rest of us that Ford would be unsuccessful," one of them told me later, "but Reagan really was reluctant. He didn't have that burning, that gut desire to be President that Jimmy Carter or Richard Nixon has. He was always present when we had these meetings, but he wasn't dying to do it." Because of this attitude, the meetings were not so much to discuss plans as "to massage him, to massage everybody a little," Jim Lake said. Sears, Lake, Walker, and Nofziger were gung-ho to go, but most of the others, inexperienced in national politics, uncertain about how to proceed, and intimidated by the scope of the problem, took refuge in talk and more talk.

Ed Meese, Reagan's top staff man, was a very methodical, careful type and he had severe reservations. "John's constant, plaintive cry," Lake said, "was, 'You've got to make up your mind to do it. It doesn't do any good to sit around and discuss what Ford's going to do and whether Ford's going to be successful or not. We've got to make up our mind to do it, and go do it.' They all wanted to do it, but it was a scary enterprise, and they'd never done it." While Walker prodded the others to get started, Sears and Lake champed at the bit. Finally, near the end of 1974, Walker took matters into his own hands. He traveled to Washington and told Sears and Lake he wanted to start a national committee right away, announce it, and get going. Walker and Sears went to New York to talk to banker and Republican fat-cat Jeremiah Milbank and William Rusher, the ultraconservative publisher of *The National Review*. Afterward, Rusher took it upon himself to check with Reagan, and Reagan was furious. He was still deliberating, just starting to get his lucrative radio show on the boards, and an early candidacy would certainly squelch it. Walker nearly was fired as a result.

Matters chugged along like that until mid-spring, when Reagan, at a meeting in Los Angeles, confessed his increasing disillusion with Ford's leadership and said he was willing to run. He held off, though, on the timing. In June, Sears—weary of overblown meetings with too much debate and no action—flew to San Francisco to talk to Nofziger, Deaver, and Hannaford. The latter two, closest to Reagan in his last years as governor, agreed that it was time to form a national Reagan for President committee. The die was cast: Sears returned to Washington, and Nofziger, after closing his public-relations firm in Sacramento, soon joined him. Working at first out of a small office in Sears's law firm, they started sending out the word to conservatives around the country.

A prime order of business was finding a prestigious, credible front man for the Reagan effort. Shortly before, during a low-key Reagan visit to Washington, Sears had arranged a private dinner for Reagan and Senator Paul Laxalt of Nevada in Reagan's suite at the Madison Hotel. Laxalt had urged Reagan to run, to give Republicans a choice, and subsequently Sears decided Laxalt was the man he wanted. It so happened that Senate Minority

Leader Hugh Scott had circulated a resolution of support for Ford among Republican senators, and Laxalt hadn't signed. He seemed a good prospect. Accompanied by Lake, Sears went to Laxalt's Capitol Hill office to bag him.

Lake, in unvarnished admiration, recounts his recollection of the conversation between Laxalt and Sears:

"John, how are you?"

"Paul, this is Jim Lake."

"Jimmy, how are you? Good to meet you."

"How's it going, Paul?"

"Oh, that crazy Hugh Scott. Trying to get all these senators lined up. That's just the wrong thing to do. I told him, 'Hugh, I've never gotten involved in a primary contest in my life, and I don't expect to start now.' "

Sears took this in stone-faced, and cheerfully discussed the foibles of Hugh Scott. Lake asked himself what they were doing there and how quickly they could beat a strategic retreat. Then the dialogue continued:

"Well, John, what can I do for you?"

"Well, Paul, we've talked before, and I wanted to let you know we're going to do it, form a committee."

"Ah, that's terrific. That's a great idea. Who's going to run it?"

"Well, we thought you'd give us some ideas." Sears laid out the qualifications he was seeking—well regarded, articulate, attractive, all the things Laxalt was. "Frankly, we're having a time picking the right guy."

"Well, I think you're going about it in the right way, John. Let me think."

Laxalt and Sears then methodically went through all the prominent Republican governors, mayors, and senators. Each time Laxalt named one, Sears would come up with an obvious objection. Finally he said:

"Well, there *is* a guy."

"Yeah, who is it?"

"The Senator from Nevada."

"Oh, no, no."

Laxalt did not commit himself that day, but as Lake and Sears walked out of his office, Lake said, "You nailed him. He's on the hook." And he was. "He had the worm in his mouth," Lake said later. Sears advised Reagan, who called Laxalt. Laxalt wanted assurances that Reagan would indeed run, and was told that unless the committee's soundings produced a negative reaction, he would go. That was good enough for Laxalt. He was aboard.

In California, some of the old money men like Tuttle and Dart, also party loyalists, didn't want Reagan to run, but Sears talked to them, too, and eventually they came around. Reagan's wife, Nancy, painted in some quarters as a kind of West Coast Dragon Lady, was protective of her husband and didn't want him to make a fool of himself, but she was quickly convinced he had a serious chance and was generally supportive thereafter.

Through all this, Reagan continued to deny that he had decided to run, but that was all part of a carefully devised plan to keep him out of a premature confrontation with Ford. Sears wanted to let more time pass to determine what the real issues of the 1976 campaign would be, and to prepare Reagan carefully to cope well with them. Also, if Reagan did not formally declare his candidacy, he could continue to do his syndicated radio show, by then being bought by about 230 stations around the country, without subjecting those stations to the Federal Communications Commission's provision that requires granting equal time to candidates for public office. And he could continue as well his lucrative weekly column in nearly 200 newspapers.[1]

And so, on July 15, with Reagan still diligently working "the mashed-potato circuit," simply "exploring the possibility of running," Sears trotted out the front men for the Reagan campaign—Laxalt plus an unimpressive pair of burned-out right-wingers, former Governor Louie B. Nunn of Kentucky, and retired antediluvian Representative H. R. Gross of Iowa, like Reagan an old radio broadcaster (who in fact once worked with "Dutch" on a station in Waterloo, Iowa). This would be, Laxalt said, the Citizens for Reagan Committee. "We're not saying President Ford is not doing a good job," Laxalt explained, walking a thin line between loyalty to the incumbent and a direct challenge to his future tenure. "We feel he is. But Governor Reagan could do a better job, because he is totally independent of the federal government scene." The voters "want a change in the direction of government. They want to be left alone. They want the federal government off their backs." And he was not at all certain that Ford, who had spent twenty-five years in Washington, could produce that change.

The formation of the Reagan committee did not exactly set Washington or the country on fire. Reagan's own seeming indecision tended to dampen the effect, but that was all right with Sears: he had a lot of spade-work to do, and it could be best done out of the glare of national publicity. Within two weeks of the announcement he and Lake went to New Hampshire and met with its two key conservatives—Governor Meldrim Thomson

1. A few days before Reagan went to New Hampshire to campaign for Louis Wyman, I accompanied him to a private recording studio in Los Angeles (ironically at the corner of Hollywood and Vine, where imbedded in gold stars in the sidewalk are the names of many of Reagan's old co-stars). There, in less than an hour, he recorded about ten three-minute commentaries, enough to tide him over until he returned from his impending speaking tour in the East and South. The head of the studio, Harry O'Connor, told me the Reagan commentaries would gross $500,000 if they ran a full year.

and William Loeb, the eccentric, heavy-handed but crafty publisher of the Manchester *Union-Leader,* the only statewide daily newspaper. Both immediately pledged their support, but Sears and Lake soon determined that with Thomson particularly, an embrace too publicly fervent could be the kiss of political death. The Republican Party in New Hampshire was deeply split over his leadership, his personality, his idiosyncracies. After all, a man who had once proposed issuing atomic weapons to members of the National Guard was bound to be somewhat controversial. The immediate problem, therefore, was somehow to corral Thomson's support without the undue, conspicuous presence of his body; to get and keep him on Reagan's side but not out front, and further to find somebody who would give the Reagan effort a more moderate image.

In this endeavor, Thomson was at first a quite willing partner. In their first meeting with him, at breakfast at Thomson's house, he volunteered that it would be a good idea to get someone else as chairman because he had his own re-election to worry about. Both Thomson and Loeb suggested that former Governor Hugh Gregg, a moderate and former Rockefeller backer, might be the right man. Sears was surprised to hear these two Neanderthals propose Gregg, and to learn that he might indeed be available.

It took a while for Sears and Lake to contact Gregg, who did a lot of business in Canada and was up there often. Finally they arranged to stop by Gregg's house in Nashua one Sunday night in late August on their way to Concord from Boston. En route, they got lost and arrived only after midnight, with Sears's young son, Jimmy, asleep in the back seat of the car. "It was the well-oiled Reagan campaign pulling into New Hampshire," Lake recalled. At first Sears asked only that Gregg become "part of the team"; Gregg made it clear he did not want to be associated with any campaign in which Thomson was the boss.

At the same time, it turned out, Gregg was dealing with the Ford forces to play a leading, or *the* leading, role in *his* New Hampshire campaign. The night before Ford arrived for his day-long motorcade with Louis Wyman, Reagan was the centerpiece of a major rally at the Manchester Armory. True Believers packed the place and cheered themselves hoarse for Reagan and his standard anti-Washington, no-pale-pastels-for-the-GOP sermon: he strode down the center aisle of the armory through a wild scene of jumping women and flashing Instamatics, his movie-star-turned-governor appeal undeniable. Gregg, in the crowd, was impressed. The next morning, he had coffee with the would-be candidate, then left to join Ford in Wyman's motorcade.

At a lunch stop in Amherst, former Senator Norris Cotton took Gregg off into a woodshed where he introduced him to the President as one of the two people Cotton had recommended to be state campaign chairman (the other was Representative James C. Cleveland, the eventual chairman). According to Gregg, Ford told him: "I'd be pleased to have you head up my campaign." Gregg accepted, conditional only on working out details. Donald Rumsfeld, then the President's chief of staff, was called in and said he would have Bo Callaway get in touch with Gregg. But, according to Gregg, Rumsfeld never bothered. For the next couple of weeks, as Sears and Lake continued to woo Gregg by phone, he waited for the call from the White House. Finally Gregg told Cotton he had decided to throw in his lot with the Reagan people, who were more professional and seemed really to want him. Cotton, apologetic, asked Gregg to hold off a few more days while he got things straightened out.

A few days later Gregg's phone rang. Callaway was calling from Los Angeles. "I've just heard about this thing and I understand you're upset," he said. "What's the problem?"

Gregg said there was no problem; he had just decided to go with Reagan.

Callaway phoned the White House and was back to Gregg again: the President wanted him, but not necessarily as chairman.

That did it. Gregg met with Lake at the New Hampshire Highway Hotel in Concord and began to put together a Reagan steering committee. Gregg's acquisition proved to be a critical element in Reagan's eventual strong showing in New Hampshire, for he was an extremely hard worker whose knowledge of state politics was invaluable.[2]

Because the fifteen-member steering committee included a number of moderates, Sears and Lake feared they might still run into "the Thomson problem"—that the governor's friends around the state might put up a squawk. So they went to the governor's son and chief aide, Peter, and told him about their concerns. "Well," Peter Thomson said, "you know the Governor is leaving next week for Israel." It was a stroke of luck; the committee could be announced while he was out of the country, thus minimizing the possibility of a backlash. On October 5, a crisp early-fall day, Thomson held a press conference in his office in Concord. He was sorry he would be abroad when the Reagan committee was named, he said, but he supported it.

The Reagan people had indeed finessed "the Thomson problem." Reagan, in a well-publicized letter to Gregg, underlined the strategy. He called Thomson "a good personal friend," but added that the governor "knows

---

2. Ford campaign officials disputed Gregg's version of what happened. They denied he ever had flatly been offered the chairmanship.

and agrees I should not be looking to him to put your organization together and make it function. He agrees that your committee must be able independently to develop as an organization on my behalf which will assure a victory. Finally, and I'm sure you will agree with this, any campaign for the Presidency must reflect my philosophy, my views and my proposals for leading our nation." The committee, with Gregg as chairman, included two other very prominent middle-road Republicans: Stewart Lamprey, former Speaker of the State House of Representatives and chairman of Nixon's 1968 campaign in the state, and David Gosselin, a former state chairman. Lamprey particularly was a surprise and valuable recruit. Sears had worked closely with him in 1968, when Nixon humiliated George Romney in New Hampshire, and Lamprey was among the most astute Republican politicians in New Hampshire. He had compiled and computerized a list of Republican voters that gave Sears an organizing tool that no other candidate ever had in this small state (160,000 registered Republicans).[3] Nearly five months before the primary itself, and more than a month before an official declaration of candidacy, Ronald Reagan's campaign was off and running in the Granite State.

For all the public show of harmony among his supporters, however, "the Thomson problem" was not yet solved, nor would it ever be entirely. When Meldrim Thomson returned from Israel, he ran smack into editorials in the Concord *Monitor,* the thinking man's alternative to the Manchester *Union-Leader,* and other papers observing in effect that Reagan had shoved the governor into a closet and thrown away the key. "His ego was really bruised," one insider said later. "Any slight or perceived slight sent him into a rage. He told us: 'You people have really embarrassed me. You put my worst enemy on the committee [Sam Tamposi, a long-time foe], you signed a contract with Stewart Lamprey. You've done it to me for the last time. You're going to make me honorary chairman, and when Reagan comes in again, I'm going to be with him.' "

That solution, of course, was impossible: Hugh Gregg for one would not stand for it, and Reagan simply could not afford to have that close an association with Thomson. It turned out, however, that Thomson had reasons other than ego for his concern about the Reagan steering committee. He was fearful that it would pick the Reagan delegates to the national convention, and his faction would be short-suited. Sears finally assured him he would have a majority on the committee and a majority of convention delegates. Still, Thomson insisted on campaigning with Reagan and eventu-

3. The enterprising Lamprey, covering his bet, later also sold use of his list to the Ford campaign.

ally did, for one day, but the joint appearance was confined to Manchester and suburbs—clearly conservative "Thomson Country," where the association would not hurt.

By this time Ronald Reagan's public indecision was a charade, a façade behind which money was being raised and planning done. After his quick visit to New Hampshire to speak for Wyman, he and Sears came away persuaded more than ever that he had nothing to lose and everything to gain in taking on Ford in the primary there. And Wyman's loss to Durkin drew little negative reaction in the press about Reagan, they noted; he was not, after all, the President, and he had made only one speech, compared to Ford's day-long motorcade and speechmaking, which had managed, in spite of the very large crowds, chiefly to underscore the weakness of his political coattails. The unelected President, as Sears had insisted all along, was ripe for the taking.

6. Ford Faces Reality

Ronald Reagan's ploy of neutralizing Governor Thomson in New Hampshire, and other signs of his campaign activity, finally began to stir the Ford camp. Despite brave talk from the White House that Bo Callaway's forays into the South and the President's own trips to California were blunting the Reagan challenge, the contrary began to dawn on even the most wishful of thinkers there. While Callaway was out around the country exhorting party conservatives to embrace the President and forget Reagan, Sears and Company were getting a jump in organizing in key states, Florida as well as New Hampshire.

Lee Nunn, a long-time GOP organizer and fund-raiser who had been finance vice chairman in the 1972 Nixon campaign, was nominally in charge of organizing the states for Ford, but he groused about the job, complaining he could get neither money nor authorization from the gallivanting Callaway to proceed at the necessary pace. Also, White House political types felt, the absence of a solid, experienced technician as a full-time deputy to Callaway frustrated progress and efficiency. "Bo is a good front man," one White House aide said at the time, "but we need a mechanic over there. If we don't get one, Reagan is going to give us fits."

Callaway was, indeed, a front man in more ways than one. President Ford's assistant, Donald Rumsfeld, was officially designated White House liaison with the election committee, and he proceeded to dominate the important decision-making. But as Ford's day-to-day chief lieutenant and traffic cop, he already had his hands full, and many decisions fell between the cracks. The urgency that Reagan's activities should have generated was muted by the continuing belief among Rumsfeld, Melvin Laird, and other Ford advisers that Reagan wouldn't run or could be kept out of the race, and by Callaway's efforts to make that hope a reality. His dump-Rockefeller intimations, and the excessive focus on it, were part and parcel of the diversion. And from Callaway's perspective, the White House—especially Ford himself—was not giving sufficient or serious attention to the task of winning the nomination. Right after the Republican loss of the special Senate election in New Hampshire Callaway told me that the President was being much too casual about Reagan—an observation that surely would have surprised people in the White House, and in the country, who felt Ford was spending entirely too much time, and risking physical danger to boot, in his repeated treks to Reagan's California.

For Callaway's part, he tried to run an effective operation but simply wasn't up to it. Nuts-and-bolts politicking went by the boards while he held weekly staff meetings that started with old-fashioned pep talks about how much the country needed Gerald Ford. He would go around the table asking each subordinate to report to the others about what was happening in his area of interest. "It was like show and tell," one of the inner circle said later. "One day I was going to bring in a frog, but I decided against it." Mimi Austin, Callaway's personal aide, exerted power beyond her position, authority, or experience, and others on the staff were in over their heads. Leo Thorsness was typical, a one-time prisoner of war in Vietnam who had run unsuccessfully against George McGovern in South Dakota's senatorial race in 1974. His job was touching bases with Republican congressmen and senators and gathering intelligence about their leanings. A memo from Thorsness to Callaway would report that the subject "is solidly with the President" and thought he was a great man. The memos read like a high-school civics student's report of a visit to Capitol Hill. Callaway too was an inveterate writer of memos for the record, full of gung-ho: "I talked to Jim Gardner in North Carolina. He said that Jerry Ford is tremendous. He is very closely associated with him and he likes him very much. . . . He says that the main thing happening in North Carolina is a party split between Helms and Holshouser and that will get bitter. He says he hates to see this. . . . He's going to think for a few days and get in touch with me. He sounded like there is a good chance that he will join our team. He says if he does join the team he wants to get active, not only in North Carolina but in surrounding states."

Beyond Callaway's memo-pushing, the Ford committee finally began to move in early October with the addition to the staff of two politically-wise Californians, Stuart Spencer and Peter Kaye. Spencer, a veteran political consultant, in partnership with Bill Roberts had run Rockefeller's near-successful primary campaign in California in 1964 and Reagan's two successful gubernatorial races in 1966 and 1970. Kaye was a long-time California newspaperman who was highly regarded by his colleagues; Spencer admired his directness and critical mind, but eventually they were Kaye's undoing. He believed in a policy that is not widely adhered to in politics, especially not in his party—to be totally honest with reporters. And in that policy he had a willing but not always deft ally in Callaway, who was determined after the Watergate experience not to preside over a latter-day version of CREEP, the scandalous airtight Nixon committee of 1972. But some of Callaway's associates didn't seem to get the picture. Austin came into Kaye's office one day and said, "Peter, do you think we ought to have a shredder?"

"What?"

"Do you think we ought to have a shredder?"

Kaye, dumbfounded, quickly answered in the negative. A paper shredder was a symbol of Watergate days, the last thing the Ford committee needed.

Shortly afterward, James Naughton of *The New York Times* got wind of this exchange and wrote about it. Kaye overheard two campaign workers talking about Naughton's article.

"Did you see the shredder story?" one asked.

"Yeah," said the other. "Do you think that's a shredder in our office?"

Kaye, unbelieving, walked into the office in question, and sure enough, there sat a "tall thing with claws," as he described it. "Either that goddamned thing goes, or I do," he shouted. The shredder, ordered by a zealous efficiency expert in the headquarters, was carted out and Kaye stayed.

Spencer's arrival, and Kaye's, marked a turning point in the Ford effort. Spencer had limited experience in national politics, but he was an extremely able professional. He came in as political director and, when Nunn left in a huff, also took over the organizing task and gave the committee a strong nuts-and-bolts performance, which it had lacked. As an ex-Reagan ally Spencer recognized both the strengths and the weaknesses of his fellow Californian and had a special zeal to beat back his challenge, which he knew to be real.

"We didn't have a national plan," he said later. "I made the assumption that Reagan was going to run when I came here. I tried to build a base in California to discourage him, and we went heavily into the first two primary states and organized them, the basic assumption being Reagan had to win New Hampshire and Florida to get in the ball game. Conversely, if the President lost New Hampshire, it was over with. We put a national organization together basically to block Reagan early so he couldn't get off the ground."

The day after Hugh Gregg was named Reagan's campaign chairman in New Hampshire, Spencer was in the state with Representative Cleveland, now the chairman of the Ford committee there. At last, the people responsible for seeing to the President's nomination were waking up to reality, were starting to deal with Reagan as a live challenger rather than some political bogeyman who could be willed away.

Ford, who liked to compare himself with Harry Truman, demonstrated the old Truman trait of loyalty to a fault, however, as he extravagantly defended Callaway and continued to insist all was well at his bumbling campaign committee. But all was far from well. Callaway was still moving slowly in organizing the states, and on top of that he was having a running argument with David Packard, the California industrialist who had signed on as finance chairman.

Packard, a fund-raiser of the old school who insisted on autonomy, tried to run the money arm of the campaign from his home in Palo Alto, taking the old route of exhorting fat cats, despite the new campaign law. He had set as his objective the raising, by the end of 1975, of the full $10 million permitted a candidate in the preconvention period, then had scaled it down to $5 million, and failed abysmally in both objectives. By the end of October he had raised only $956,585, and over 60 per cent of that was in contributions of more than $250, hence not eligible for federal matching money. He was adamantly opposed to a direct-mail effort, although that approach—best-suited to garnering small contributions—seemed made to order for an incumbent President with high public recognition. Although a direct-mail drive eventually was launched, much valuable "prospecting" time was lost—the taking of sample mailings to identify reliable givers for subsequent mailings. Callaway tried to bring Packard's operation under his own, and the two were on a collision course.

In mid-October Packard came to Washington to complain directly at the White House to Rumsfeld and Hartmann. They temporarily smoothed Packard's feathers, and he told me in a telephone interview at the time that, although he "sometimes gets puffed up" with frustration at the job, "I've made a commitment to the President and I'm going to keep it unless he wants to get somebody else." But two weeks later Packard was out and Ford's election committee was in a shambles.

Yet that fiasco was a mere ripple in the President's sea of troubles.

For some time President Ford had been at odds with his secretary of defense, James R. Schlesinger, whose hard line toward the Soviet Union often clashed with Secretary of State Henry A. Kissinger's policy of détente. In a Byzantine plot that unfolded in early November the President decided to jettison Schlesinger and replace him with Rumsfeld. (Richard Cheney, Rumsfeld's assistant, a solid, cautious man with little national political experience but good instincts and sound judgment in people, became the new White House chief of staff and contact for the President Ford Committee. Cheney's elevation was a happy development in the President's campaign, for he and Spencer became a cordial and effective team.) Kissinger, made to look the heavy, lost his second hat as the President's national security adviser, that job conveniently going to his pliant deputy, General Brent Scowcroft. As described later, the maneuver was intended to get rid of Schlesinger in such a way that Schlesinger's conservative defenders could take solace in Kissinger's "downgrading." Kissinger, of course, was no more downgraded than Rumsfeld was; he continued to run the nation's foreign policy as if it were his own, which indeed it was.

While Ford was at it, he resolved also to get rid of another problem child, William E. Colby, director of the Central Intelligence Agency, who had, in Ford's view, been too cooperative with Congress in its investigation into the CIA. Colby was replaced by another Ford favorite, George Bush, brought back from Peking where he had been the U.S. representative to the People's Republic of China. And finally, Elliot Richardson was returned from the Court of St. James's to become secretary of commerce.

These moves took on added significance in light of still another, even more dramatic development. A day before the ax fell on Schlesinger and Colby, Nelson Rockefeller informed Ford, abruptly, that he had decided he did not want to be considered for the 1976 ticket. This decision had been brewing for some time; for months Rockefeller had tried to accommodate himself to the political views and the climate of Ford's administration—to the point of making an ass of himself. Ever since Bo Callaway had fingered him as a liability to the ticket, he had been fighting a rear-guard action within the Republican Party, and losing. No matter what he said—and he willingly ate a king-sized portion of political crow on those fence-mending trips into the South—he remained an anathema to party conservatives. Rockefeller liked to call them "a minority of a minority" but he knew, or should have known better. They, not he, were where the Republican Party was; to them, he would always be the stand-offish, arrogant New Yorker who thought he knew more than the rest of them, who thought he could buy anything he wanted. They had not forgotten 1964, when Rockefeller had turned his back on the beloved Barry Goldwater. Since then the liberal bloc of the GOP had shrunk to insignificance, and he had shrunk from it in a rather clumsy, obvious attempt to get right with the party that so abhorred him. Politically, he was as bankrupt as the City of New York.

Ford was confronted with what was clearly a windfall, and he did not attempt to dissuade his Vice President. He was, if the truth were known, glad to be rid of him. In his pell-mell determination to out-Reagan Reagan on the right, he could not afford the albatross that was Nelson Rockefeller, but having selected him at the outset, he could not publicly repudiate him, either. And so Rockefeller's offer to jump before he was pushed was a welcome one, and a recognition of the political realities.

The mechanics of the move, however, were troublesome. Plans were laid for Rockefeller to put his head on the block first, and for Schlesinger and Colby to follow two days later. But *Newsweek* got hold of the news about Schlesinger, and Ford felt obliged to make public the whole package in one swoop. Inevitably, it was written that Rockefeller had pulled out in pique over Kissinger's "downgrading," an interpretation that endowed Rockefeller with an excess of compassion for his old friend Henry that was hardly warranted by the facts of the case. Ford, in a bravado "I am the President" press conference worthy of a Nixon in his most trapped mien, dissembled his way through by insisting there was nothing personal in Schlesinger's and Colby's dismissals and that he simply wanted his "own team" after fifteen months of Nixon holdovers. "That's the way I wanted it. That's the way it is," he said. Under sharp questioning about why Rockefeller was leaving the ticket, he had the gall to say that a totally vacuous letter that the Vice President had written, expressing his desire to be included out in 1976, spoke for itself.

Here for the first time was the new Gerald Ford—no more Mr. Nice Guy. In opting to demonstrate a new toughness, Ford was risking one of his strengths, indeed one of his few strengths—his personal warmth and integrity. Yet the whole episode showed Gerald Ford coming apart at the seams, perhaps not even realizing it. A nation uninspired by Ford's performance in office but lulled to some degree by his easygoing, friendly style, was seeing him as an activist President, and the image was poor. He was, there was no other word for it, a bumbler. Here he was trying to woo the right wing and dumping one of its heroes, Schlesinger; then trying to cover it by taking one of Kissinger's jobs away but giving it to Kissinger's trusted deputy. (In an interview on NBC's "Meet the Press," he acknowledged that "a growing tension" within his administration involving Schlesinger and Colby had motivated him, but he allowed himself this bit of candor only after reiterating that his earlier explanation had been the "simple truth" and had concealed "no hidden motives" or "devious actions." So much for the newfound credibility in the White House.) Well, at least the withdrawal of Rockefeller was an unvarnished plus, at least for the time being.

That move was a bombshell. When Reagan, who was campaigning in Florida though still pretending to be undecided to run, was informed by a local television reporter, his face dropped; he was, he said, "astonished," and he looked it. At first Reagan said he thought Rockefeller's pull-out enhanced Ford's chances to be nominated, but in due course the Reagan campaign line, from Sears, was established: that Rockefeller on or off the ticket didn't matter; Ford was the issue, and Reagan intended to run against him, with or without Rocky.

On November 3, Rockefeller finally held a press conference to explain why he had acted. He was through, it seemed, dissembling about Callaway: "It [Rockefeller's presence on the ticket] is a subject of concern to those who are responsible for the President's campaign and nomination. It is just not worth it. . . . I came down here to help [the President] in connection with solving problems, not dealing with party squabbles. Therefore I eliminated myself and therefore I eliminated the issue which was the basis of a lot of the squabble."

But all that was history. On the more critical and interesting subject of the political future, Rockefeller was his old cantankerously evasive self. Some reporters in the audience, ever mindful of his unquenchable presidential ambition, suspected that he might be making a tactical withdrawal so as to position himself for a possible later re-entry as a full-blown presidential candidate. They remembered his divisive, all-out drive in 1964 and how in 1960 and 1968 he had conducted on-again, off-again flirtations with the Republican nomination process. Now he was asked: If Ford were to be driven out in the early primaries, would he, Rockefeller, consider running?

"That is a speculation that I have not made," the Vice President said. "I think he will be nominated. History has clearly indicated that the incumbent President is nominated by his party and I have no speculations on the subject." Rockefeller was always great for the sweeping statement, whether supported by the facts or not. In recent history, of course, primary setbacks in New Hampshire suffered by Harry Truman in 1948 and Lyndon Johnson in 1968 had helped to persuade incumbents to withdraw.

He was pressed further: he wouldn't rule out running under *some* circumstances?

Rockefeller: "Absolutely no speculations on this subject." Another reporter persisted: "People, I am afraid, are not going to believe now that you are not running for President. You have been running for President since 1958. You were asked before what you were going to do in the subsequent election. I wonder if you would explain to people how you see yourself with respect to your long-time quest for the presidency." Rockefeller attempted to turn the question aside with a gag. "I have to say I am closer to it right now than I ever have been," he said, grinning, proud of himself. That one got laughs, but the reporter pressed on. Was he going to stop there? Could he say flatly he wasn't seeking the presidency? Rockefeller: "Listen, I wouldn't have accepted the vice-presidency if I hadn't been willing to take the presidency should, God forbid, something happen to the

President. So I am not going to kid you that I came down here with no thought of the presidency in mind. But I have no plans beyond what I have said." Well, he had categorically and unequivocally removed himself from consideration for the vice-presidency. Why couldn't he give the same categorical answer about the presidency? Rockefeller: "Then what would I do if anything happened to the President? Resign?" So it was possible he would consider the presidency if something happened to Ford? Rockefeller: "How can I avoid it? When you accept the vice-presidency—that is the whole point of having a Vice President, should anything happen to the President." But in the sense that the President might be defeated in the primaries? Rockefeller: "I haven't given any consideration to it."

Rough translation: In the heart and mind of Nelson Aldrich Rockefeller, all things were still possible.[1]

On other fronts, more political trouble was brewing for President Ford. The first was from the right, in the person of former Secretary of the Treasury John B. Connally. Fresh from his acquittal on federal charges that he had accepted an illegal gift, the former Texas governor was the beneficiary of a Salute to John Connally dinner in Houston that netted more than $400,000. With the money, he established a group called Vital Issues for America to bankroll an extensive speaking tour, and on CBS News' "Face the Nation" in mid-October hinted at the game he intended to play. President Ford, he said, would have to show more leadership if he hoped to be nominated and elected in 1976. Traveling around the country trying to dissuade Reagan from running was "basically a political mistake," and Connally predicted a "horserace" between his two fellow Republicans in which he just "might" run as a favorite-son candidate in Texas. The message was clear; let Gerald Ford slip to one knee in the early primaries and John Connally would be bounding into the ring to challenge Ronald Reagan.

As for his indictment and trial, Connally baldly insisted it was politically beneficial: "I don't think the indictment hurt me one bit. As a matter of fact, it helped me. . . . I was innocent before it started and the jury said I was innocent. The jury said, 'Not guilty.' How does that hurt you? I don't

---

1. A month later, at a private meeting of Southern Republican state chairmen in Houston, Rockefeller demonstrated his national political sophistication anew. Trying, in his fashion, to rally the troops for Ford, he accused them of wasting time complaining instead of working. At one point, according to Jack W. Germond of *The Washington Star,* he told them, "You got me out, you sons of bitches, now get off your ass."

know why everybody assumes . . . this might hurt me. Since when have you become guilty on indictment? The presumption is one of innocence." Connally had been accused of a lot of things in his day, but never innocence, at least in politics.

The other prospective bit of trouble for Ford came from the left, or what passes for the left in the Republican Party. Senator Charles (Mac) Mathias of Maryland, in a speech at the National Press Club in late October, had expressed deep concern that "President Ford's fascination with a very real threat on his right is limiting debate among Republicans," and he had suggested that he himself might seek the party's presidential nomination. Warning that a conservative nominee would make the Republicans "the Whigs of 1976," Mathias said he might run as a liberal Republican in the Massachusetts primary. To enter the race in New Hampshire, he said, might tip the scales against Ford and in Reagan's favor, and "whatever you do, you don't want to make a bad situation worse, so maybe you have to wait beyond New Hampshire." Members of the liberal Senate Republican "Wednesday Club" also were discussing the idea of fielding an alternative to Ford to combat what they called his "drift to the right" under pressure from Reagan. Speculation centered on Senator Howard H. Baker, Jr., of Tennessee, himself a moderate conservative and not a Wednesday Club member, but considered electable. And so, two months before the election year even began, the incumbent but unelected President was being pulled in both directions by his own party.

Ford, for his part, reacted like a man under siege. At a party fundraising rally at the Boston airport on November 7, he unexpectedly announced that he would enter every 1976 primary. "We're going to go right down to the wire in the convention in Kansas City and win there," he said. The announcement caught his own strategists by surprise, but it did not take a political genius to guess what he was up to: Ford was trying to counter the prognosticators' judgment that two straight primary defeats in New Hampshire and Florida would finish him off. By declaring he would enter all the primaries, Ford was trying to change the press' perception of the primaries as an elimination contest to a view of the entire primary period as the battleground. But the perception remained unchanged, and, as matters turned out, to Ford's advantage.

Ford's strategists, however, had no intention of permitting the incumbent President to race around the countryside like a candidate for assemblyman. Already, there had been loud complaints from influential backers that Ford was diminishing the currency of the presidency by his frenetic fundraising gambols in behalf of the party. What he had to do, a steering committee of GOP wise men said, was to stop gallivanting, stay home, and be President. So it was not surprising that the morning after Ford's Boston outburst of campaign enthusiasm, both the White House and his campaign headquarters issued statements saying the President had not meant he would actually *campaign* in every primary, only that he would *enter.* "I wouldn't count on him doing a whole lot of primary campaigning," said Ron Nessen. "I would expect him to spend most of his time being President and to let people judge him on his record. He will not be sloshing around in the snow in New Hampshire every week." His record in office, Nessen said, is "what really is going to persuade people. . . . "

That seemed true enough. But was it wise for the President to pin his chances on public confidence in Gerald-Ford-in-the-White-House? Unemployment was still high, the economy was still a mess, inflation was still a problem, the Schlesinger-Colby shakeup was a black eye to conservatives, the New York City fiscal crisis was developing into a no-win political situation, controversial bills—on energy, a tax cut, common-situs picketing —were moving to his desk, laden with political woe. For all the public exposure and maneuverability, the presidency brought with it a mountain of hard decisions, most of them, it seemed, with more political risk than benefit. When he was doing well in office, fine; but when he wasn't, Ford might fall heir to all the disaffection toward big-government Washington that he himself often mentioned—rather tortuously, since he had been a Washington creature for so long.

Jerry Ford took office making note himself of the significance of being the nation's first unelected President, but as he put on and began to enjoy the trappings of presidential power, he seemed often to lose sight of his special circumstances. The voters didn't, however. At first, his hominess, his old-shoe quality, was charming, endearing, especially in a man they felt they could trust. But as he floundered in office, his folksiness came to be a kind of trademark for bumbling good intentions. The old Lyndon Johnson gag that "Jerry Ford can't chew gum and walk at the same time" did not die easily; in fact, it flourished against a backdrop of repeated personal pratfalls, until an image sometimes approaching buffoonry, or oafishness, attached itself to the man. And it was not simply a television image. Those reporters who got closest to him became accustomed to an easily triggered horselaugh of vaudevillian proportions. His mispronunciation of words was commonplace; some in the White House press corps dubbed him "President Turkey," and accused him of "trying to sew up the klutz vote."

Above all, there were what came to be known as "the incidents." Jerry Ford seemed to be especially vulnerable to physical "incidents." The two most prominent, and unfunny, were of course the attempted shootings in Sacramento and San Francisco. But before and after them, an almost incredible string of personal mishaps plagued the President. Disembarking from *Air Force One,* he tripped and nearly fell down the steps; taking his customary laps in his swimming pool, he apparently miscalculated and crashed into the end, cutting his head; climbing aboard the presidential helicopter, he sometimes bumped his head, until a Marine was assigned to insert rubber cushioning above the entry hatch prior to the President's arrival, and to remove it after he was safely aboard. Greeting a crowd at Westover Air Force Base in Springfield, Massachusetts, Ford suddenly "bent his head forward and groaned," the Associated Press reported, and first accounts said that a boy had stuck him in the head with the sharp point of a small American flag. Secret Service agents in fact converged on the boy and knocked the flag from his hands. A few hours later the wire services sent through a correction: the President had not been poked in the head by a flag, after all; actually, he had tripped over the outstretched leg of a woman in a wheelchair! It seemed to go on and on like that. In his speech as well, Ford seemed to have inordinate difficulty; like the time he toasted President Anwar Sadat of Egypt and "the people of Israel" as guests gasped and reporters listening over a public-address system in an anteroom chortled. And with each comic reference, Lyndon Johnson's old line came back to haunt him. Concerning another Johnson line—that Ford had played too much football without a helmet—the press room's new version was, "He can't even play President without a helmet."

All this was good for laughs, but in time it was no longer a laughing matter. In politics, perception counts for as much as reality, sometimes more; what a public official is to the voter is more often than not what he seems to be. That is why so much emphasis is placed on public image, and why so often a sow's ear can be sold as a silk purse. But the negative also works; a negative perception can take hold, and politicians especially have always been vulnerable to the dangers of negative public perception. Often a single episode will be seized on by press and public to epitomize all the reasons people have disliked someone, until it becomes a kind of trademark. Usually, the episode is a public and typical incident that after several similar unhappy experiences serves to distill a negative attitude in the public mind.

Take Robert Kennedy's reputation as being a "ruthless" man. As campaign manager and trouble shooter for his brother the candidate and President, Bobby was a tough nay-sayer, and a number of stories fed that image of him. When, in February 1968, he decided to seek the Democratic presidential nomination, declaring his candidacy shortly after Eugene McCarthy had scored a psychological victory over President Johnson in the New Hampshire primary, his reputation as a "ruthless" politician seemed for many to say it all. It did not matter that Kennedy was a man capable of great individual compassion, generosity, and kindness, in fact a man of uncommon shyness and gentleness in many personal dealings with others. He was "ruthless" and that was that, regardless of any transformation he may have undergone. Throughout his brief and tragic campaign for the nomination, Kennedy was haunted by this identification, to the point that it may well have been an element in his only defeat, to McCarthy in Oregon a week before his death.

A similar fate befell George Romney, the governor of Michigan who, after a resounding re-election in November 1966, was rated the front-runner for the Republican nomination in 1968. A man of inordinate determination, Romney had as well inordinate difficulty expressing himself clearly and consistently, especially on the then-burning issue of Vietnam. He seemed for all his attempts to explain himself to be digging himself into an ever deeper hole, until the idea set in that George Romney was a kind of oafish plodder. He would say one thing, then another, then insist he had been saying the same thing, almost, all along. (Jack Germond threatened at one point to have a special key installed on his portable typewriter that at a single touch would print: "Romney later explained. . . .") The culmination—not the beginning, importantly—came when he acknowledged on a television talk show in Detroit that American generals in Vietnam had "brainwashed" him. The word seemed to say it all about George Romney, and he never recovered from the damage that remark did him. Never mind that there was substantial truth to what he was saying—that not only he but many other American officials had been sold a bill of goods by lying and/or dissembling brass in Saigon; from Romney, the remark was a confession of stupidity, and the perception of him as a stupid man suddenly had a convenient, easily remembered negative peg. Romney, already slipping, hit the skids thereafter. Anything he did that reinforced the perception became front-page news, like the day during the New Hampshire primary when he walked into a duckpin bowling alley to shake hands and decided to try his luck: he failed to knock down all ten pins with the allotted three balls, so kept going—teeth gritted, jaw set, in full view of reporters and network cameras, until he knocked over the tenth pin—thirty-four balls later! It didn't matter that Romney later produced a plan for reducing the American presence in that country and turning the fighting over to the South Vietnamese that later became the cornerstone of the policy of the man who defeated him. He remained the clown who had been "brainwashed."

There are many other examples of the destructiveness of negative perception, however fair or unfair. Nixon himself struggled nearly all of his career against the notion of him as "Tricky Dick." "Would you buy a used car from this man?" the Democrats asked, and the question seemed to sum up all there was negative to say about him. It was a triumph for Nixon and for his perception-oriented political and media managers that they were able to overcome for so long the destructiveness of a broadly held negative public perception.

Jerry Ford, unfortunately, had neither the cunning nor the talent to overcome what came to be the press and public view of him as a well-meaning bumbler. He was not a devious man, and his openness increased his vulnerability. He liked people, liked to be out among them, liked to respond spontaneously to events and to whim. None of these things were a fair measure of the man's intelligence, or his seriousness, or his diligence, which were considerable, but they were ingredients in the public's perception of him. When, on a trip to Hartford, a motorist crashed his car into the White House limousine bearing the President, there was concern about inadequate Secret Service precautions. But, the public was bound to ask, was Ford especially vulnerable to mishap? Rich Little, the impersonator of political figures, asked to "do" the President, stepped back from his microphone, then, without saying a word, proceeded in full stride to walk up to and into it. The comprehending audience roared. News photographers took to snapping pictures of Ford as he got tangled up in the leashes of his family's two dogs when he tried to board the presidential helicopter with them. It was all very unfair, and yet for many people it seemed typical. Ford as President seemed always to be getting tangled up: with Congress, over a tax cut, energy legislation, aid to New York City; with his party, over Nelson Rockefeller, Bo Callaway, his whole campaign; with his own administration, over Schlesinger and Colby and Kissinger; with the press, over his dissembling about Schlesinger; with the public, over his excessive traveling, and his insistence that things were getting better, when people out of work or bedeviled by high prices knew otherwise. Pat Oliphant, the *Washington Star*'s brilliantly biting editorial cartoonist, summed up Ford's dilemma by illustrating him on skis at the very edge of a snow-covered mountain, with a group of security agents, also on skis, behind him, kneeling in the snow, hands clasped in prayer. He is turning to them and saying: "Personally, I think you're carrying this no-confidence thing a bit too far." Taking the buffoon image to its ultimate, Oliphant had the letters "R" and "L" printed boldly on Ford's right and left ski gloves and boots, kiddie style.

Ford's confidence factor received no boost, either, in mid-December when the *Washington Post*'s two Watergate bloodhounds, Bob Woodward and Carl Bernstein, just completing their book on the last hundred days of the Nixon administration, reported that Ford, contrary to his testimony to Congress, had pardoned Nixon "after hearing urgent pleas from the former President's top aides that he be spared the threat of criminal prosecution." Quoting "reliable sources," they said Ford had given General Haig a private assurance the pardon would be granted ten days before that action was taken. The two reporters said Leonard Garment, former counsel to Nixon in the White House, had written an "impassioned" memo to Ford urging the pardon and warning that if it were not granted, Nixon might take his own life. Though Ford himself may not have seen the memo, they wrote, Haig used its argument in his talks with Ford. Woodward and Bernstein noted that Ford in testifying on the pardon before the House Judiciary Committee in October 1974 had said at no time after he became President had the subject of a Nixon pardon been "raised by the former President or by anyone representing him," nor had anyone made such a recommendation to Ford. Haig acknowledged he had talked to Ford about the pardon, but the White House stiffly denied any wrongdoing. The timing was particularly unfortunate for Ford; he most certainly needed no additional shaking of public confidence in him right then.

Ford's dilemma also took some tangible forms, not the least of which was a money crisis. After much thrashing about, his campaign finally came up with a replacement for David Packard as finance chairman, Robert Mosbacher, a Houston wildcat oil man with millions of his own—not precisely the image Ford needed at this juncture. Mosbacher was candid; in his first day on the job he acknowledged to reporters that he would have to "either get more money or curtail our campaign." Ford's organization, building toward the primaries, was spending a good deal more each week than it was taking in, he said. Whereas Packard had once talked of raising the legal limit of $10 million by the end of 1975, Mosbacher now reported that only $1.25 million had been raised and about a million of it was already spent. Ford's campaign would accept the federal subsidy provided under the new campaign finance law, and would have to hustle for the rest. In the past, incumbent Presidents did not have to hustle all that much. But the day when one could brazenly strong-arm defense and other government contractors for contributions was over. And Gerald Ford, the nation's first unelected President and cartoon-certified bumbler and clown, was not proving to be much of a magnet.

Still, it was hard for many to imagine that an incumbent President could be denied his party's nomination. James Reston, on November 20, the morning when Ronald Reagan announced his candidacy formally in Washington, wrote: "The astonishing thing is that this amusing but frivolous Reagan fantasy is taken so seriously by the news media and particularly by the President. It makes a lot of news, but it doesn't make much sense."

So it seemed, in the conventional wisdom of American politics, 1975. But 1976 was not a year of conventional wisdom, as Gerald Ford was painfully to learn.

7. Reagan Plunges In

For Ronald Reagan, the easy waiting game that had lasted through most of 1975, the luxury of sitting back and letting Jerry Ford take all the heat, was over. On the morning of Thursday, November 20, he strode before a battery of microphones and television cameras at the National Press Club and staked out his position as the Gentleman Caller of Republican politics, the outsider with clean hands, the savior come to Washington to purify the waters. The fact that his formal declaration rated live television coverage was in itself a measure of his clout. "Our nation's capital," he said, "has become the seat of a buddy system that functions for its own benefit —increasingly insensitive to the needs of the American worker who supports it with his taxes. Today it is difficult to find leaders who are independent of the forces that have brought us our problems—the Congress, the bureaucracy, the lobbyists, big business and big labor."

Reagan did not list Gerald Ford as a member of the buddy system, but the intent was clear. Nor would he single out his opponent for any other criticism. Instead, as he had done in his two gubernatorial campaigns, Reagan pledged to honor California's "Eleventh Commandment" that said "Thou shalt not speak ill of any fellow Republican." It was a transparently cute device, but Reagan invoked it with a perfectly straight face. For upwards of an hour he fielded, or sidestepped, a barrage of questions from the Washington press corps, supposedly the most aggressive in the country, and departed unscathed.

As in his many Sacramento press conferences as governor, Reagan demonstrated a talent for answering the easy questions with great verve and detail, and for finessing the tough ones. As theater the performance was excellent; as information it left much to be desired. Few seemed to notice, but the few who did spotted a Reagan trait that bore further watching. When pinned down for specifics, he would wriggle off by claiming insufficient information. He could not make specific criticisms of the defense budget, he said in Washington, because he didn't have the necessary classified information about the Russians' military budget on which to make a comparison. He didn't have the figures on the New York fiscal crisis, either, and when asked about revelations of the FBI's investigations into the personal life of Martin Luther King, Jr.—reported in the previous day's papers —he said blithely that he hadn't read this morning's papers. But Reagan was not one to willingly repeat error. When the questions came up at subsequent press conferences, he had more specific answers.

From Washington, Reagan and his party, with a phalanx of reporters, boarded a chartered jet for Miami and a swift, two-day swing into the four early primary states that was pure media event.[1] With John Sears in charge, the tried-and-true old Nixon devices were employed deftly to assure "optimum candidate exposure" under maximum conditions of control: a very limited number of well-planned events, scheduled at places and at times to facilitate local or network evening news coverage; a well-fed and professionally serviced press contingent; above all, a relaxed and well-rested candidate. To these Nixonian staples was added one un-Nixonian element: a candidate accessible to press interrogation. On the plane itself, Reagan stayed in the first-class cabin with his wife, Nancy, and his staff, thumbing through his speech cards and taking it easy. He made the all but obligatory stroll back to the press compartment for about twenty minutes of casual banter, but he did not permit himself to be drawn into heavy discussion. At each stop, however, unlike Nixon, Reagan held a full-fledged press conference where he fielded all questions from both local reporters and the traveling press. In 1968 and 1972 Nixon had avoided such pitfalls of spontaneity like the plague; an inquiring reporter was for Nixon a loaded bomb, likely to explode in his face at any moment, and hence to be shunned except in the most controlled of circumstances. But Reagan, a man of much more confident temperament and on-camera skills, thrived in the press-conference format. He was a master at saying everything and nothing; he had the retentive mind of the actor, and the actor's ability to speak with conviction, whether he meant it or not.

These talents also enabled Reagan's campaign managers to use him to great advantage in freewheeling public forums. In 1968, in New Hampshire, Nixon had literally sneaked out on the accompanying press and had conducted staged town-meeting–type sessions with selected local citizens for taping and later television use; in November 1975, on the night before his declaration of candidacy, Reagan confidently stood before about a thousand New Hampshirites and took all questions, friendly and hostile, for nearly an hour. That he again dodged some of the tough ones or, more often, filibustered them to death with unrevealing circumlocutions, did not de-

1. At the very first stop, at a Ramada Inn near the Miami airport, a young man threw Reagan's entourage and the crowd of well-wishers into a turmoil by pointing what proved to be a plastic toy gun at him. The man was wrestled to the ground and seized by Secret Service agents, and Reagan, with aplomb, resumed campaigning.

stroy the image of openness and candor he projected to the crowd. Joe Napolitan, the Democratic pollster and media consultant, once told me that he rated politicians' effectiveness on television by turning off the sound and just watching the picture, and this was one test Ronnie Reagan could pass resoundingly. Afterward, fully three-fourths of the crowd waited in line for up to forty-five minutes to file past him and shake his hand. In this exercise, too, he was the polished performer; taking not only the person's hand in his, but his or her eyes with his own, holding the contact until the other person's glance fell away. Anyone who saw him at the Sheraton-Wayfarer Hotel in Bedford, New Hampshire, that night, had to be convinced that Jerry Ford was going to have his hands full with Mr. Reagan.

Reagan's style and confidence went back well beyond his days as a Warner Brothers film star, back to his years as a radio sportscaster on Station WHO in Des Moines. There, it was his lot to simulate for Iowa baseball fans the play-by-play of all Chicago Cubs home games, taking arid, monosyllabic reports from a wire-service ticker and transforming them by his own wit and imagination into a lively account of the game. Back in Des Moines for the station's anniversary dinner in 1974, Reagan described himself describing a ball game: "You say, if there's a stall [in the telegraphic report], 'He shakes off the sign, gets back down off the mound, rubs his hand on the resin bag . . . back up on the mound getting the sign again. Out of the windup, here comes the pitch! There it goes! A hard-hit ground ball. Second baseman going over after the ball, makes a one-hand stab, comes up, almost falling down, throws *just* in time for the out!' " Once during a big game, he said, with the Cardinals' Dizzy Dean pitching to the Cubs' Billy Jurges, the ticker stopped in mid-pitch. "I had a pitch on the way to the plate," he said. "There's only one thing you can do that doesn't get in the scorebook. I had him foul it off. . . . I just couldn't say to that audience in the ninth inning, 'We've lost our service. We're going to give you a brief interlude of transcribed music.' So I said, 'Diz Dean'—I slowed him down a little, I had him use the resin bag a lot and I had him shake off signs— lengthy windup, finally let go with another pitch, and he fouled that one off to the right. And then he fouled one off back of the stands. And then he fouled one off back of third base and I described the fight between the two kids trying to get the ball. Then he fouled one off that just missed a home run by a foot." Finally, in the nick of time, the wire resumed. "I started another ball on the way to the plate, grabbed the wire and it said: 'Jurges popped out on the first ball pitched.' "

Reagan's talent for harmless fiction still served him well, and he demonstrated it most notably on the third stop of his opening campaign swing, at an airport press conference in Charlotte, North Carolina. Pressed on his views on desegregation by reporters in the state that had witnessed the first effective lunch-counter sit-in demonstrations, Reagan took a hard-line posture against any kind of demonstration. He opposed both violent and nonviolent illegal protest because, he said, "There can never be any justification for breaking the law." Asked whether he thought blacks in the South needed to demonstrate to get the right to vote, Reagan gave forth with the following incredible stream-of-consciousness reply:

". . . I happen to be of a generation where I think the first change began. . . . I have often stated publicly that the great tragedy was then that we didn't even know that we had a racial problem. It wasn't even recognized. But our generation, and I take great pride in this, were the ones who first of all recognized and then began doing something about it.

"I have called attention to the fact that when I was a sports announcer, broadcasting major-league baseball, most Americans have forgotten, that at that time the opening lines of the official baseball guide read, 'Baseball is a game for Caucasian gentlemen,' and in organized baseball no one but Caucasians were allowed. Well, there were many of us when I was broadcasting, sportswriters, sportscasters, myself included, began editorializing about what a ridiculous thing this was and why it should be changed. And one day it was changed. When the first bombs were dropped on Pearl Harbor, there was great segregation in the armed forces. In World War II, this was corrected. It was corrected largely under the leadership of generals in the Pacific like MacArthur, and General Eisenhower, C-in-C in the European theater, and in the navy.

"One great story that I think of, the time that reveals a change that was occurring, [was] when the Japanese dropped the bombs on Pearl Harbor, there was a Negro sailor whose total duties involved kitchen-type duties—cooking and so forth—who cradled a machine gun in his arms, which is not an easy thing to do, stood on the pier blazing away at Japanese airplanes that were coming down and strafing him, and that was all changed. And we went on with those developments."

What? Surely Ronald Reagan was not saying that a black sailor at Pearl Harbor, by the act of firing a machine gun at the enemy, had ended segregation in America's armed forces? But that was what he said, though President Truman—not MacArthur, not Eisenhower—had ordered desegregation of the armed forces in 1948, seven years after Pearl Harbor. As for the reference to Reagan's pioneering efforts to end the color line in baseball, it was not until 1947, ten years after Reagan had left the Des Moines station for Hollywood, that Jackie Robinson became the first black player to compete in the major leagues. Nor has anyone been able to find Reagan's line, "Baseball is a game for Caucasian gentlemen," in the *Official Baseball*

Guide. Joe Marcin, editor of the guide, looked for it fruitlessly when asked to substantiate Reagan's claim.

This kind of response showed that while Ronald Reagan was one hell of a political performer, he had his vulnerabilities, and one could expect the press to zero in on them now that he was a declared presidential candidate. Hanging over his candidacy, indeed, was a perception of him as potentially destructive as the image of well-intentioned bumbler was to Ford: the perception of Reagan as "another Barry Goldwater," a tall-in-the-saddle conservative cowboy who in his ideological purity would pull whatever trigger or push whatever button to protect the homeland and extend the true political faith. The "Goldwater problem" had surfaced briefly when Reagan had spoken at the New Hampshire town meeting on November 19. He had been asked about Senator Percy's remark that day that Reagan was guilty of "simplistic thinking" and that his candidacy would lead to a crushing defeat for the Republican Party in 1976. How did he plan, the questioner wanted to know, to accommodate the moderate wing of the party?

"When they talk about the moderate wing of the Republican Party," Reagan replied, "and intimate some of us are out of the mainstream, we're over on one side or the other, you know, sometimes I think moderation should be taken in moderation." The audience laughed and applauded. Among the press, however, and for some in the Reagan entourage, a red flag went up. They remembered the chilling words Goldwater had uttered in accepting the Republican nomination in San Francisco in 1964: "Extremism in the defense of liberty is no vice. Moderation in the pursuit of justice is no virtue." Goldwater had let those words settle in, and the public had taken them as confirmation of his extremism.

Reagan, in a somewhat similar spot, now handled the situation more astutely: "If you're lying on the operating table and the man is standing there with the scalpel in his hand," he said, smiling, "I'd like to know he has more than a moderately successful record." More laughs, more applause, and the "Goldwater problem" was on the run. Reagan then routed it, arguing that Republicans "keep giving each other political saliva tests to find out where we stand in the party" instead of looking at the record. And his own record in California, he insisted, would show he had been an effective, and not extreme, governor. He had hired more minority citizens for executive and policy-making jobs than any previous governor, he said; he had reduced the state mental-hospital population from 26,500 to 7000 by adequately funding county mental-health clinics; he had increased state support of local public schools to a record; he had reformed welfare, cutting 400,000 names from the rolls but boosting aid to the genuinely needy.

"Maybe Senator Percy will tell me," he concluded, "what is immoderate about those things that we did." Even more applause. So much for the "Goldwater problem" that night.

The next day, en route to Los Angeles on the last leg of the tour, I sat with Reagan and discussed the same matter. He turned out to have an interesting view of Goldwater not as an incorrigible Neanderthal but, rather, as a man who in 1964 had been ahead of his time. "There's no question," Reagan said, "Goldwater tried to tell us some things that maybe eleven years ago we weren't ready to hear. We still were wrapped in the New Deal syndrome of believing that government could do all these things for us. I insist Barry Goldwater never was defeated on the basis of his philosophy. The opposition, aided and abetted by Republican opponents in the primaries—which makes me so strong in my Eleventh Commandment belief—created a straw man, and what the people really voted against was a false image of a dangerous radical. All they could see was a great big thumb over the nuclear button, and they never got acquainted with the real Barry Goldwater until long after, and today it is hard to find a man who is more widely respected in government than Barry Goldwater. . . . He was possibly a little ahead of his time. There's one thing for someone to hear him and say, 'Hey, I believe what he said,' but it's even more effective for the person that ignored him, who believed the false image, who never bothered to listen to what he said, who now a few years later, turns around, looks back, and says, 'Hey, I should have paid attention to him.' This person is probably even stronger now in his conviction than the original person."

But what of Goldwater's notorious *gaffes* in the 1964 campaign, such as his proposal to put social security on a voluntary basis and his suggestion that the Tennessee Valley Authority be turned over to private enterprise? "The funny thing is," Reagan answered, "in the speech that I made about him [in 1964] which was so well received, I said some of the same things. It is also true Barry has a blunt, forthright way of speaking. People who know him well understand him and love him for it. Today, we look at what he was trying to tell us about social security. We know now by actuarial standards it's two and a quarter trillion dollars out of alignment. And Barry did not mean to dismantle it or anything, but Barry had a way of saying the blunt thing first and then nobody stuck around to hear the qualifying remarks. He'd say, 'Now look, I don't mean to take Social Security away from any of the people who are now getting it, and we must fix the program so that those people are still taken care of.' But he had already lost most of them with his first scare line."

As a speaker himself, Reagan said, he had learned from Goldwater's unhappy experience: "I've always believed that you say the qualifier first.

If you say, 'Now look, let's make it plain; the first priority must be that no one who is depending on that for their nonearning years should have it taken away from him, or have it endangered. It is endangered today by the shape that it is in.' So you then can go on and say, 'Now, the program is out of balance. Down the line someplace, can come a very great tragedy of finding that the cupboard is bare. Before that happens, let's fix Social Security.' "

With or without a "qualifier" to take the curse off, Reagan revealed himself in this interview to be an only slightly updated, albeit smoother, Barry Goldwater. Take, for instance, the controversial issue of welfare, whose public rolls he sharply reduced as governor of California: "In your paper," he said, "you print a story, a human-interest story, of some individual who doesn't come under any particular government program but has had a calamity. Let us say it is one of the great emergency illnesses or accidents in which his earnings will never begin to pay for what has to be paid for. And you print the story from a human-interest angle. Before you can get the second edition out, the people who have read the paper rally around and the next thing you know, a committee has been formed to help this individual. Now, I am not suggesting that we stop welfare tomorrow. *So, having qualified with that,* let me say, I just have faith in the American people that, if through some set of circumstances welfare did disappear tomorrow, no one would miss a meal. The people in this country, in every community all over, would get together, form emergency committees, and take up the slack. Those are the kind of people they are." Just why, in a country in which thousands of people still go to bed hungry each night, despite a welfare program, such community action has not occurred, Reagan did not say.

This conversation about the "Goldwater problem" was a clear indication of things to come in Reagan's campaign. Before long, in New Hampshire and Tennessee, Reagan would be saying some very Goldwater-like things on such subjects as social security and TVA, and paying a heavy political price for it.

As Reagan spoke on the plane, he opened a briefcase on his lap and thumbed through a stack of four-by-six index cards with abbreviated phrases printed on them in block letters. Together, they constituted what was known in Reagan's entourage as "The Speech"—the stock message of conservatism he had been delivering to audiences ever since he first started public speaking. Honed over the years 1954–62, when he hosted the "General Electric Theater" on television and toured the country speaking to a quarter of a million employees at 135 GE plants, The Speech was a marvel of theme-and-variation. Each card bore a thought, in Reagan's own shorthand, and by shuffling them and putting them in different patterns, he was able to build a cohesive, natural talk that was a little different each time. As he went on he added and subtracted phrases, ideas, clever one-liners. Shunning a formal text, Reagan depended on the index cards for his flow, maintaining at the same time an extemporaneous feeling that won audiences over. A delegator of tasks in other areas, Reagan kept construction of The Speech to himself. One of his former aides, discussing the phenomenon with my *Washington Post* colleague Richard M. Cohen, offered this description of Reagan the speechwriter in action:

"I've seen it a hundred times. Say we were flying back East to do a speech. We would put him in a seat and just forget about him. He would work with a felt-tip pen. From his briefcase he would take two cards out of the Cincinnati speech and one card out of the Cleveland speech and two from some other speech, and that would be his next speech. You could take the cards and put them down on the typewriter and it's nothing. It's incomplete sentences. He would continue to work until he got to the hotel. He'd rest, take a shower, and work on the cards. He'd get into the elevator and work on the cards again. He'd go to a staging area and work the cards some more. He wants to do well. He wants to be perfect."

Writing The Speech was more than an exercise for Reagan. It was, in the strictest sense, a self-education, the formative element over the years in his political thinking. He started out as a New Deal Democrat, "a very emotional New Dealer" inspired by Franklin D. Roosevelt. "I still believe," he told me, "when he was first inaugurated, yes, if he didn't do anything else, he gave back to the people of this country their courage. His line 'We have nothing to fear but fear itself' was one that can be repeated many times in many circumstances. [But] I now have to look back and see that the panaceas that were offered didn't solve the problems."

Reagan began believing, he said, that "there were more elements in the private sector that probably could be better handled by government. But I began to discern some cracks in the wall after the war, or during the war when I was an adjutant of an air base [in Los Angeles] and dealt with bureaucracy. When I came back from the military to the picture business in time for that big attempt on the part of the Communists by way of the infiltration of some of our unions to take over the picture industry, I again saw a side of liberalism, of which I thought I was a member. I had liberal friends who could not see any threat from the left. Always it was only from the right. Early on, I was on the mashed-potato circuit. I began to see discrimination against our industry and I'd speak on that subject. Then the subject gradually broadened to what I saw as government interference and government growth that was limiting freedom, not just in our industry but in other industries as well. And eventually what happened to me was, because I always did my own speeches and I always did the research for them, I just woke up to the realization one day that I had been going out and helping elect the people who had been causing the things I was now criticizing. So it wasn't any case of some mentor or someone coming in and talking me out of it. I did it with my own speeches."

And now he had talked himself into the thick of the 1976 Republican presidential race.

On the day Reagan flew from New Hampshire to North Carolina and Illinois to Los Angeles, the pollster George Gallup began sending his interviewers out among the voters. Three weeks later, after careful tabulation, startling news resulted: Reagan, trailing Ford by 23 percentage points a month earlier as the presidential preference of Republicans, had surged ahead, 40 to 32 per cent—an unprecedented one-month gain of 31 percentage points! He also picked up among independents—from a 20–26 deficit in October to a 27–25 lead. The effect of this news was immediate and devastating, especially among knowledgeable politicians who had been sensing that such a development might occur. The polling had taken place during and after Reagan's first heavily publicized swing as a candidate, but it would have been a mistake to attribute the mammoth switch to that alone. Other pollsters and interviewing reporters around the country had been picking up everywhere the increasingly negative perception of Ford; he was, people were saying more and more, a nice guy who was in over his head. Now, at last, Republicans were being given a choice, an option, and, as far as they could tell, a responsible one. Ronnie Reagan was an old actor, sure, a movie and television performer, but he also had been governor of the nation's largest state; he was a believable alternative to the bumbler in the White House.

To remain believable was now the task confronting Reagan. For all his assurances that he was not just another Barry Goldwater, the differences were essentially stylistic, not substantive. On the issues that romanced right-wing hearts and appalled the left, Reagan was every bit as conservative as Goldwater: abortion is murder; pot is poison; permissiveness breeds crime; welfare "chiselers" crowd the public rolls; détente with the Russians is dangerous. Still, in the Republican Party whose nomination Reagan was now seeking, these positions hardly ever raised an eyebrow.

In Reagan, Sears had the great advantage of having an experienced professional speaker, and one who would listen to and take advice. In the opposition camp, the situation was very different: a campaign manager and a candidate who in their inexperience and rigidity played blind-leading-the-blind much of the time. An example of this unhappy combination was

Callaway's and Ford's handling of the important conference of Southern Republicans in Houston in mid-December, the last major party gathering before the election year. GOP governors, senators, congressmen, state and county chairmen, and state legislators met to talk politics in general and the presidential campaign in particular. Reagan and another 1976 prospect, Connally, both addressed the group, but Ford, for some unfathomable reason, elected to stay in Washington and sent Callaway instead. The decision was a double disaster: the Dixie Republicans resented the presidential snub, and Callaway only compounded the injury. "I just think that when [Reagan] says he's Sir Galahad on a white horse, and he's the wonderful guy that just lowered taxes and cut back things, that's just not true," Callaway said. "All of the major people" in California Republican politics were backing Ford, he went on, because Reagan's "rhetoric was great and his performance was poor."

Callaway's remarks, in a press conference even before Reagan had spoken, were met with dismay and even anger among Southerners for whom Reagan had always been a special favorite. In a meeting with Callaway the night before, Governor James Holshouser and others had sought to dissuade the campaign manager from attacking Reagan, but he had gone ahead anyway. Some of them, disposed to going along with an incumbent President as long as they could, now had second thoughts.

Here it was December, with the election year just about to begin, and already there was disarray in the Ford campaign and candidacy. Seemingly oblivious to it all, the President and his family went off to Vail, Colorado, for Christmas and skiing—despite some staff protests that the situation required him to stay in Washington and keep up the working-President image. In a few days, the photos from Vail began to hit front pages around the country, showing the President, laughing heartily, on his back in the snow. Everybody takes a spill on the slopes now and then. "It Happens to the Best of Skiers," the *New York Times* caption said. Readers chuckled. Good old Jerry Ford.

Still, Jerry Ford was after all the President, and his political team had been strengthened with the addition of Spencer and Kaye and the expansion of Cheney's role. In politics as in sports, the ball often takes unpredictable bounces. In a way, Ford's troubles proved to be an advantage; once the reality and seriousness of Reagan's challenge in New Hampshire became clear, the President surprisingly and incongruously was cast as the underdog in the minds of many voters.

It is always helpful to run from a posture of low expectations, a truism that was being graphically illustrated at the very same time on the Democratic side by the little-known farmer-businessman from Georgia, Jimmy

Carter. While Gerald Ford and Ronald Reagan were settling into the New Hampshire starting gate, Carter and a much larger field of Democratic contenders were already locked in a competition that scarcely could have been foreseen four years earlier. Then, the Democratic Party, humiliated in the landslide defeat of George McGovern, was looking, without great enthusiasm, to the politically scarred Senator Edward Kennedy of Massachusetts somehow to resurrect its national fortunes. But even back then, in 1972, the fires of ambition were burning determinedly in Jimmy Carter, with fateful consequence for himself, his party, and the country.

part IV

**JOCKEYING
FOR
POSITION:
THE DEMOCRATS**

8. The Stirrings of Jimmy Carter

During the second week of July 1972, while the convention forces of George McGovern were single-mindedly nailing down the Democratic presidential nomination, close associates of the freshman governor of Georgia, a relatively obscure fellow named James Earl Carter, Jr., who in the ostentatiously folksy Southern way called himself Jimmy, set out on a preposterous mission. After conferring with Carter, and with his approval, they determined they would try to make him McGovern's running mate. What made the enterprise preposterous was not simply the fact that Jimmy Carter was a mere one-time governor from nowhere. Carter, at a National Governors' Conference in Houston only weeks before, had been a conspicuous leader in a last-ditch stop-McGovern effort. He was against McGovern, he said, because he was convinced the South Dakotan could not win. Why, then, one might have asked, would he want to join McGovern's ticket?

To ask the question was to confess total ignorance of Jimmy Carter. Ever since he had left his family's peanut farm in Plains, a movie-façade of a sleepy south Georgia town, to go to Annapolis in 1943, he had been a climber. He had put in eleven years in the navy, becoming an officer on a nuclear submarine, and when he quit to try his hand in politics, he reportedly told an associate he would have become chief of naval operations, the nation's number-one sailor, had he decided to stay on.

Back in Georgia to take over the family's peanut business after his father's death, Carter was beaten narrowly in his first bid for state senator in 1962. Convinced he had lost fraudulently, he sought out a south Georgia country lawyer named Charles Kirbo and persuaded him to take on his case. Kirbo won it; Carter was in the Georgia Senate and on his way. In 1966 Carter ran for governor, lost, and immediately began campaigning for another try in 1970. For four years he worked the state like a migrant worker hustling for harvest work, putting in a regular day at the family's peanut plant, then driving to all corners of Georgia to speak and meet voters. No invitation was too small or too distant to turn down. A young graduate student at Emory University named Joseph E. Powell, Jr., called Jody, saw Carter's potential and signed up, and the two men traveled the length and breadth of the state from 1970 on. They hit every town and county courthouse they could find, Jimmy working the local pols and hangers-on, Jody scribbling down the names of anyone who offered to help. Coming from nowhere, Carter beat prestigious former Governor Carl Sanders in a Democratic runoff.

Once in office Carter became known as one of the "New South" breed of governors who looked squarely down the shotgun barrel of racial segregation. "The time for racial discrimination is over," Carter said in his inaugural address, though he had posed as friendly to segregationists George Wallace and Lester Maddox during his campaign and even identified himself as "basically a redneck." But he was a one-term governor by Georgia law, and he knew political history; he knew how John F. Kennedy's bid for the 1956 Democratic vice-presidential nomination, although unsuccessful, had paid great dividends in public awareness. And so, when several of his Atlanta aides approached him during the 1972 Democratic convention with the idea that he ought to bid for the number-two spot on the national ticket, Carter was receptive. Jerry Rafshoon, his media adviser, says he first broached the subject at a convention party in Miami Beach. "Let me ask you," Rafshoon said, "would you be interested in Vice President?" Carter replied, "Why not?"

Rafshoon had in his possession polls that had been taken in conjunction with David Gambrell's Senate campaign. Gambrell knew that to win in Georgia he would have to put as much distance as he could between himself and McGovern, and, in the hope of finding ways to mitigate McGovern's negative effect in Georgia, the pollster William Hamilton had been asked to survey whether McGovern would be more acceptable with Carter as his running mate. To nobody's surprise, the answer was yes.

Armed with Hamilton's poll findings, Rafshoon and Hamilton Jordan, Carter's executive secretary at the time, set off to make the case to the McGovern people. "The most degrading thing," Rafshoon recalled later, "was Hamilton and me standing outside trying to get an audience with Pat Caddell." Caddell was McGovern's wet-behind-the-ears pollster, only twenty-two years old and still a Harvard undergraduate; he later became Carter's poll-taker and analyst, working for Jordan and with Rafshoon. "We could never get in to see him," Rafshoon recalled. "He wanted to see us but he was busy and all that. The scene is, we're sitting outside, trying to get on the main floor at the Doral Hotel, the nineteenth floor, and we had been waiting for an hour on the floor below, where they kept the turkeys. The holding room." Only the intercession of Alan Baron, a liberal activist who had met Jordan and Rafshoon as a promoter for Senators

Harold E. Hughes of Iowa and Ed Muskie and was then working for McGovern, got them up to the nineteenth floor.[1]

"We spent about three minutes with Caddell," Rafshoon recalled. "He said, 'Yeah, yeah, it looks good. Oh, yeah, I'm going to make a recommendation.' He said later he recommended a Southerner. I think he recommended Reubin Askew. He thought we were crazy."

Next they tried Bill Dougherty, then South Dakota's lieutenant-governor and an amiable interference-runner for McGovern, in the Doral coffee shop. Rafshoon's recollection was that "he was saying things like, 'Well, will Carter back us on the California challenge?' 'No.' 'Will he come out for a pro-busing plank?' 'No.' Our idea was, You give the nomination to somebody who has supported McGovern, you've made a big mistake. Because you won't have a ticket that's very viable."

It was an education for the two young Georgians. "We came out of there realizing that as much as we knew about Jimmy Carter and thought he had a good national image, the national politicians didn't take him seriously, and didn't take us seriously," Rafshoon said. "I remember walking back from the convention the night McGovern was nominated, and Hamilton and I are saying, 'Why can't Jimmy run for President? He's not going to run for the Senate. And four years from now we certainly aren't going to go around here trying to curry favor with somebody [asking] to put an ex-Georgia governor on as Vice President.' "

A day or two later Jordan was sitting on the beach with Dr. Peter Bourne, a psychiatrist who had worked with Carter's wife, Rosalynn, on mental-health and drug-abuse problems and later headed the Georgia drug-abuse program. The same basic discussion ensued: Why not Jimmy for President next time? (The subject had come up once directly with Carter. In July 1971, just a year earlier, he and Bourne were returning from a congressional hearing when Bourne asked him, "Have you ever thought about running for President?" Carter replied: "No, I haven't, but if I did, here's what I would do. I'd run for four years, the same way I ran for Governor.")

Shortly afterward Bourne sat down and wrote a ten-page memorandum to Carter outlining why he should run and how he could win. The memo noted first that reforms had changed the control of the Democratic Party. "The old politicians who think that once McGovern is defeated, it will be politics as usual are dead wrong and do not understand the social

1. Ironically, Baron was fired by McGovern in 1976 for operating too openly as a leader of a stop-Carter effort.

forces at work in the country," Bourne wrote. McGovern was not a Goldwater, who was a throwback; McGovern was where the party was heading.

"National political power has become increasingly issue-oriented," he continued, and added in an observation that certainly would have tickled Carter-watchers in 1976: "Particularly in 1976 I believe the electorate will support candidates not for whom they represent but because they have taken a clear decisive position on the right issues. . . . The people who will win the big prizes are going to be increasingly the people who are willing to take risks, particularly in terms of hazarding existing power bases. One can take the moderate and compromise positions on issues and remain a successful, respected, secure politician, but one will not get the big apples." Four years later Carter would take risks all right, notably by competing in all the primaries. But taking clear-cut issue positions was never his cutting edge.

Bourne's memo was amiss in other respects too. He identified John D. (Jay) Rockefeller IV, then running for governor of West Virginia, as "someone to watch" as a potential rival, but Rockefeller's star fell quickly when he lost that race. Still, in important ways the memo was on target. Bourne said Carter had not hurt himself in bidding for the vice-presidential nomination since he had not openly campaigned for it, and if he got an early start on 1976 and made a full commitment, he might succeed. He urged Carter to develop expertise in key areas such as health care and the environment (Carter did neither) so that he could "capitalize on your greatest asset—your personal charm." It would have seemed to an outsider at the time this obscure governor's charm was a slender reed on which to build a presidential candidacy. But it proved, to nearly everyone's amazement, a surprisingly strong one. "What is critical," Bourne concluded, "is the psychological and emotional decision to take the risk and to run for the Presidency to win, whatever the eventual outcome might be."

Bourne's memo was the first tangible ingredient in the Carter saga. As he wrote it, McGovern's campaign was already unraveling, and events were occurring that would contribute notably to the party's turning to a fresh face in 1976. On the very day Bourne's memo went to Carter, Missouri Senator Thomas F. Eagleton stood with McGovern before a press conference in Custer, South Dakota, and told the world that he had been treated for mental illness. Then and there the Democratic ticket was a lost cause.

Back in Atlanta after the convention, four of Carter's stalwarts—Jordan, Bourne, Rafshoon, and Landon Butler, an Atlanta lawyer who also worked for the governor—held a series of meetings in Jordan's apartment. They decided finally to approach Carter personally. After two years in the governor's office and seeing the big-name national politicians at governors' conferences and the convention, Jordan recalled later, reaching for the presidency with Carter didn't seem all that preposterous. "Granted we don't know much about this national stuff," Jordan told his colleagues, "but Carter's smarter than most of these guys and we can all be smarter than most of these guys around them."

Carter by now had received and digested Bourne's memo, but had said nothing. Everybody seemed gun-shy about talking straight out about such an undertaking. But finally Jordan took the first step. "I told Jimmy one day," he recalled, " 'I want to bring a few of us out to talk to you about the future.' " That was the way he put it: about the future.

So one night in late September 1972 the four trooped out to the Governor's Mansion. "Governor," Jordan said, "we've come to tell you what you're going to do with your future. We don't know how to say it other than to say, we think you can be President." Carter, Bourne remembers, just smiled.

"I can't tell you how difficult it was to talk about," Jordan recalls of that moment. "There we were, in Atlanta, Georgia, in the Governor's Mansion in 1972. The general election hadn't even taken place. We all knew it looked kind of preposterous. But we were serious about it. It was hard to say it. I can remember I didn't make a very good presentation. It was hard to really talk about. It was almost embarrassing. I kind of sneaked up on it. It was obvious he was two or three steps ahead of us. It was obvious that this thought was not original with us. It was not an idea we had to force upon him."

For about six hours the aides and Carter discussed the pros and cons of the idea, and the political climate in the country. From the first, they and Carter hit on the attractiveness of an unconventional campaign. Rafshoon remembers "Jimmy saying, 'How do I run? As a farmer, a nonofficeholder? A Georgian? Do you see any negatives there?' But what the conventional wisdom perceived as negative was all positive, because everything he had to do had to be against conventional wisdom."

The men all agreed that the times offered a unique opportunity for a man of Carter's background. "With the Vietnam war coming to a close," Jordan recalls saying, "domestic problems and issues were apt to be a more important consideration, the problem-solving ability of the American government was very much in question, and someone outside of Washington and outside the Senate, a governor who had proved that problems could be dealt with effectively by the state, could win. I thought one of the things that was manifested in the McGovern campaign was the real need for moral leadership in the country, for somebody to stand up and tell the American people to do the things that were unpopular, a feeling that if politicians dealt more openly with the electorate that they would respond well." McGovern "had understood and projected this moral leadership," Jordan said, "but at the same time not seeming presidential, not seeming competent."

Rafshoon recalls that Carter was noncommittal after that first meeting, and asked Jordan to incorporate in a memo all the major points raised during the discussion. "I don't believe he said go," Rafshoon says. "I think he took it all in. But we knew. I remember Ham and I walking out and saying, 'The son of a bitch, he wants it.' "

Carter himself says he had already thought of the possibility, even before the meeting or Bourne's memo, and had discussed it with his wife. "It was hard for us to talk about the prospect at first. It was all very tentative and somewhat embarrassing. We never used the word 'President' for the first three or four months, because it was kind of presumptuous. . . . We tried to assess the inventory, everything that existed in the way of an asset or a problem, including financial requirements, the fact that I was not in office, I was from a little town, the fact that I was not in Washington, the fact that I was not well known, the fact that I had no power base, and so forth. We enumerated all those problems and tried to figure how we could either minimize the problem or make an asset out of it."

Shortly after the meeting Rafshoon sent Carter a memo about how other people perceived him. "I talked about the negatives and the positives, and the negatives were positives; I turned it around," Rafshoon recalled. "Hamilton made up his memo, and I made up a little flip-chart presentation. . . . We got one of our artists to write out the different points."

Jordan, after more meetings with his co-conspirators, drew up a document more than fifty pages long, dated November 4, 1972, in which he talked obscurely of "a national effort"—"like running for national president of the March of Dimes," Jordan said later, still laughing at the audacity of it. "This memorandum," Jordan at the advanced age of twenty-seven wrote to Carter, "is an attempt to set forth in a logical fashion some specific thoughts and recommendations on your national effort." It is worth quoting from at some length for the light it sheds not only on Jordan's prescience but for what it conveys about the sense of purpose in Carter's inner circle.

The first topic was George Wallace. "In my opinion," Jordan wrote, "a serious national effort by George Wallace in 1976 would [changed to "could" in 1974 by Jordan] pre-empt your candidacy. Hopefully he will not run for President in 1976 and your candidacy should be an effort to encompass and expand on the Wallace constituency and populist philosophy by being a better qualified and more responsible alternative to George Wallace. Because George Wallace is a fighter and a scrapper, I would expect that

George Wallace has a dream, however unrealistic, of complete recovery and a successful campaign for President. A recent article relates that President Nixon sent Wallace a copy of the film *Sunrise at Campobello,* the story of Franklin Roosevelt's successful struggle to overcome his physical handicaps and his subsequent election to the presidency.

"Because Governor Wallace's mental attitude and motivations can play a significant part in his physical recovery, I suspect that his staff, family and physicians have not attempted to dampen his hopes for the future, although they must realize that another presidential campaign is a remote possibility. At some point in the future, Wallace will have to come to grips with his physical limitations as relates to his own political future. Unless the information provided the news media has been completely erroneous, George Wallace will be crippled or paralyzed for the balance of his life. The point that I would make here is that although another Wallace candidacy is unlikely, and probably would be discouraged by his wife and friends, George Wallace today probably has every intention of running and winning in 1976 to prove himself and vindicate his philosophy."

Jordan then wrote: "It is my guess that George Wallace resents you a little, as we used him effectively and beneficially in our campaign but refused to nominate him at the Democratic convention. We should make every effort to court Wallace and gain his friendship and trust. If he cannot and does not choose to run in 1976, I doubt that he will sit it out. I would hope that you might gain his support if he saw in your candidacy an extension and continuation of his earlier efforts. This may be too much to hope for but it is an opportunity that cannot be disregarded."

(Jordan's acknowledgment that Carter had played footsie with Wallace in Carter's own 1970 gubernatorial campaign was at odds with Carter's later public denial that he ever had embraced Wallace or his ideas.)

Dealing with Kennedy was the next priority item. Kennedy could win the nomination easily, Jordan suggested, but would have a much tougher time in the general election. "Perhaps the strongest feeling in this country today," he wrote, "is the general distrust of government and politicians at all levels. The desire and thirst for strong moral leadership in this nation was not satisfied with the election of Richard Nixon. It is my contention that this desire will grow in four more years of the Nixon administration. For this reason I believe it would be very difficult for Senator Kennedy to win a national election, as the unanswered questions of Chappaquiddick run contrary to this national desire for trust and morality in government. Time solves a lot of problems but the memory of the Chappaquiddick incident is still fresh in the minds of a majority of American people as indicated in recent polls."

Not only Chappaquiddick but a general "anti-Kennedy feeling" worked against the senator, Jordan wrote. "You may be sure that in two decades of American politics, the Kennedy family has run over and alienated a lot of people." There were other reasons that made it plausible that Kennedy would not run, including his family responsibilities and problems and the real threat to his life if he did. Nevertheless, Jordan wrote, it would be prudent to assume that Kennedy would be a candidate in 1976, "the front-runner and strong favorite." Jordan mentioned this possibility not to discourage Carter from running but to enable him to face it and even turn it to his advantage. If he couldn't beat Kennedy, maybe he could become his running mate.

"I'm of the opinion that Kennedy probably would like to see someone from the South other than Wallace make a national effort. He knows that he cannot depend on the Southern states for any initial support for the nomination and would rather have someone like yourself to deal with than with George Wallace. He would have hopes of encompassing your candidacy and effort by putting you on the ticket or involving you in his administration, but he could not risk doing this with Wallace. At any rate, I would place a high priority on an early meeting with Kennedy and a discussion on the future of the party and your intention to play an active role in the 1976 elections."

In this very first memo, Jordan observed that "it is likely that once again the Democratic nominee will be selected in the state primaries; for this reason it is not too early to begin thinking about [them]." He listed the prospective primary dates and pointed out that "the New Hampshire and Florida primaries provide a unique opportunity for you to demonstrate your abilities and strengths as a candidate in an early stage of the campaign." He cited New Hampshire as a pitfall for front-runners (Johnson in 1968, Muskie in 1972) and a windfall for dark horses (McCarthy in 1968, McGovern in 1972); small, rural, independent, "given to the kind of campaign effort that you and your family are capable of waging . . . your farmer, businessman, military, religious, conservative background would be well received there. It is not too early to begin to make some contacts with people there, learn something about the state, and be looking for an appropriate opportunity to make a major speech or address there."

Florida, shortly afterward, "affords an excellent opportunity to build on a good showing in New Hampshire," Jordan wrote. He named two people—Bill France, operator of the Daytona Beach Speedway and one of Wallace's strongest backers (he eventually was again in 1976), and Sylvan H. Meyer, then editor of *Miami News*, who should be wooed.

Jordan did not minimize the scope of the audacious undertaking. He observed Carter had been a small fish at the national convention, and he cited the failure of Washington Senator Henry M. Jackson to gain public recognition despite his greater prominence. "National recognition and acceptance by the people and the party leadership is not easily achieved and is the result of a meticulous and concerted effort over an extended period of time."

For all the need to expand public recognition of him, however, the overriding need was to keep Carter's national plans secret for the time being. Essential to any political future for Carter was the prevention of a comeback in Georgia of Lester Maddox. This overtly segregationist restaurateur, in stepping down from the governorship after his single term, had run for and won the lieutenant-governorship, and he was a plague to Carter. If Carter were to be taken seriously on the national scene, it would not do for Maddox to bounce back and succeed him in the Governor's Mansion for a nonconsecutive term, reducing Carter to a mere interlude in the reign of redneckism in Georgia. Carter had a successor ready: Bert Lance, who had been state highway commissioner. Jordan recommended that to avoid having it look as if Carter, in backing Lance, was simply trying to protect his home base for a national campaign, Lance should quit the Georgia highway job and set an independent course. Until that was achieved, he wrote, it would be best to say nothing about Carter's running for President.[2]

Nonetheless, the task of developing national recognition of Carter would have to start. "Stories in *The New York Times* and *Washington Post* do not just happen but have to be carefully planned and planted," Jordan wrote. He submitted a list of nationally known writers "who you know or need to know," and advised: "You can find ample excuse for contacting them, writing them a note complimenting them on an article or column and asking that they come to see you when convenient. Some people like Tom Wicker or Mrs. Katharine Graham are significant enough to spend an evening or leisurely weekend with." Others listed included James Reston and Max Frankel of *The New York Times,* Jack Nelson of the *Los Angeles Times,* Garry Wills (spelled Willis in the memo), David Broder of *The Washington Post;* the columnists William S. White, William Buckley, Bill Moyers, Robert Novak, and Rowland Evans; and magazine writers Marshall Frady, John Fischer, and Willie Morris. In all, eighteen names were listed on a sheet with forty numbered spaces, the rest blank—a measure of the campaign manager's own limited knowledge of the media heavyweights.

But if Jordan did not know all the players, he was well aware of their

2. Lance eventually lost the gubernatorial primary, but to George Busbee, not Maddox. In 1977 Lance became President Carter's director of the Office of Management and Budget.

potential. "Like it or not," he wrote, "there exists an Eastern liberal news establishment which has tremendous influence in this country all out of proportion to its actual audience. The views of this small group of opinion-makers and the papers they represent are noted and imitated by other columnists and newspapers throughout the country and the world. Their recognition and acceptance of your candidacy as a viable force with some chance of success could establish you as a serious contender worthy of the financial support of major party contributors. They could have an equally adverse effect, dismissing your effort as being regional or an attempt to secure the second spot on the ticket."

Carter was not without some advantage here, Jordan noted. "Fortunately, a disproportionate number of these opinion-makers are Southerners by birth and tradition and harbor a strong subconscious desire to see the South move beyond the George Wallace era and assert itself as a region and as a people in the political mainstream of this country. It is my contention that they would be fascinated by the prospect of your candidacy and treat it seriously through the first several primaries." Jordan proposed that Don Carter, the governor's cousin, now editor of the Lexington, Kentucky, *Herald,* invite Wicker and Frankel to spend a weekend fishing on Cumberland Island.

The memo then laid out this basic strategy—a rough outline of what was to happen three and a half years later:

"1. Demonstrate in the first primaries your strength as a candidate. This means a strong surprise showing in New Hampshire and a victory in Florida.[3]

"2. Establish that you are not a regional candidate by winning early primaries in medium-size states outside the south, such as Rhode Island and Wisconsin.[4]

"3. Select one of the large industrial and traditionally Democratic states which has an early primary to confront all major opponents and establish yourself as a major contender. Pennsylvania and Ohio would be possibilities.[5]

"4. Demonstrate consistent strength in all primaries entered."[6]

Finally, while he was still governor, Jordan recommended, Carter should establish Georgia trade missions abroad "for the purpose of travel-

3. Carter won both in 1976.
4. Carter won in Wisconsin, but he ran behind an uncommitted slate in Rhode Island, which eventually held a late primary.
5. Pennsylvania eventually was a "middle" primary (April 27) and Ohio one of the last (June 8). Carter carried both.
6. Carter won eighteen of thirty and did not experience a primary night without a victory somewhere.

ing to each of the continents of the world."[7] Later, when Carter went public with his campaign and he was asked about his lack of foreign-policy experience, he was fond of ticking off all the places he had been in connection with Georgia's trade missions. "I've been to Paris, France, Bonn, Germany, Brussels, Belgium, Tokyo, Japan, São Paulo, Brazil," et cetera, et cetera. He would always give the name of the country as well as the city, like a Georgia country boy mentioning the far-off places of his dreams. One could never be certain whether Carter did this guilelessly, or whether it was a clever way of reminding listeners that for all his world travels he *was* essentially a Georgia country boy. At a candidate's dinner in Manchester, New Hampshire, in the fall of 1975, I kiddingly noted to him in a private conversation that Wallace was about to go to Europe for the first time, and I suggested that as the anti-Wallace candidate he might have to run off there too, in self-defense. "No," he replied without smiling, "in the last two years, I've been to Paris, France, Bonn, Germany, Brussels, Belgium. . . ."

(On a later visit to New Hampshire, we were trooping through a heavy snow in Berlin, to the north, and I said to him, "So you wanted to run for President, did you?" He smiled and said, "Oh, I thought I'd try it for a few primaries and see what happened." We both laughed. So far, so good. "This heavy snow is not new to me," he said. "We had it when I lived in Schenectady, New York, where I worked at the nuclear reactor plant as a nuclear physicist." And he proceeded to recite his qualifications as a scientist. I had been covering him as a reporter for nearly a year by that time, and well knew his credentials.)

Hamilton Jordan's memo became a sort of blueprint for the still-secret Carter candidacy. In January 1973 Carter launched his effort, though not explicitly, with a speech before the National Press Club in Washington in which he outlined his visions for the country. Andrew Young, then an outsider but later a member of Carter's inner group, was sitting at the head table. As Carter spoke, he jotted something on a slip of paper and passed it to Peter Bourne. It said: "I'll be damned if he isn't running for President." Every few weeks throughout 1973 and 1974 the inner circle—Jordan, Bourne, Rafshoon, Butler, Powell, Kirbo, and Robert Lipshutz, an At-

7. An indication of where Carter stood on foreign policy at the time were suggestions in Jordan's memo that he include former Secretary of State Dean Rusk, a fellow Georgian, in his inner circle of campaign advisers and "ask him to assume responsibility for educating you on foreign affairs and develop a continuing program that would include regular briefings, a reading list, and establish an informal task force."

lanta lawyer and political fund-raiser—met with the governor to discuss progress and political developments. During the time remaining in Carter's term, maximum use was made of the governorship as both a forum and a magnet for drawing in the influential, the prestigious, the informed. Atlanta is America's third largest convention city. Prominent national politicians, business and labor leaders, journalists, college professors with particular expertise who went there found themselves invited to the mansion for discussions with Carter. The purpose was twofold: to get him better known and at the same time to extend his familiarity with and knowledge of a broad range of subjects, as befitted a presidential candidate.

Out-of-state reporters from prominent newspapers who encountered Carter anywhere were likely to receive invitations to come to the mansion. One Washington political reporter talked about his daughters with Carter on an airplane trip and shortly afterward one of the girls received a package of authentic Indian arrowheads that Carter had dug up on his Plains farm —and a handwritten note.

Through all this period, the basic premise was that the 1976 Democratic race would be a three-cornered affair. According to Carter, "For two years we made all our plans based on George Wallace and Ted Kennedy being my opponents. I think most of the candidates who finally came forward would never have come forward had Kennedy stayed in the race. I would have."

"The one thing we sensed that the rest of the country didn't know," Landon Butler said later, "was that George Wallace was through and Jimmy could beat him. And we sensed that if a respectable Southerner could beat him that would be seen as a service in itself." And Kennedy would keep the size of the field down, Jody Powell reasoned. "We figured there would be very few others who would have the guts to get in," he said. "The idea was to make a fast start against Kennedy and Wallace, to run respectably against Kennedy in New Hampshire and maybe beat Wallace in Florida. We felt Kennedy would be held accountable against a strong campaigner in New Hampshire and New Hampshire would provide momentum for Florida."

The notion that Jimmy Carter could beat either Wallace or Kennedy anywhere was, of course, considered ludicrous by nearly everyone who had ever heard of Carter, and outside of Georgia that meant practically nobody. From time to time his name surfaced in stories about the New South governors or he would pop up at a National Governors' Conference, always the diligent, nongolfing, noncardplaying, minimally-drinking loner. In the gubernatorial fraternity, in which the ability to relax is a powerful requisite for acceptance, Jimmy Carter was just a bit too conscientious—some said devious—for his brethren. Carter's fellow governors were down on him, too, for introducing resolutions such as one that expressed the belief that the Watergate affair did not touch the presidency and Nixon. It was being circulated at a governors' meeting in Ohio on the day Nixon fired Haldeman and Ehrlichman, and was withdrawn. Also, some governors remembered how Carter had solicited their support for Governor Reubin Askew of Florida to be chairman of the National Governors' Conference and then switched his own support to someone else. He was, in their view, definitely not one of the boys.

So, for all his efforts to build public recognition, Carter was still a relative unknown in 1973, even within the activist political community of his own party. He was a lame-duck governor in what was widely and often disdainfully regarded a backwater region and if his extravagant scheme was to have any chance at all, he had to reach out. In early March of 1973 a serendipitous encounter occurred. Robert S. Strauss, just recently installed as the Democratic National Committee chairman, was in Atlanta to give a speech. Carter, naturally, invited him out to the mansion. As Strauss recalls it, he, Carter, and Charles Kirbo were sitting on the porch before dinner sipping drinks when Carter volunteered that he wanted to help the party in the 1974 campaign, since state law prevented him from seeking re-election. Strauss told him he hoped to involve the national committee more directly than ever before in electing Democratic governors, senators, and congressmen. The job and the man came together, and in a few days Strauss and Carter were working out the details whereby Carter would run the committee's 1974 campaign drive. In May Jordan left Carter's guber-natorial staff and moved to Washington to be executive director of the effort —Carter's eyes and ears at the national committee.

Carter's new job really was not much, and Strauss didn't think he was giving anything much to him; Carter was not a particular favorite of his. But Carter made the most of it. The post provided an entree for him to labor leaders, political consultants, and liberal special-interest representatives in agriculture, education, consumerism, and other areas who met regularly at the national committee to consider political matters. At a series of six regional seminars in 1973 Carter and Jordan met state party leaders from all over the country and offered themselves as the instruments of national party assistance. "If it hadn't been for that," Jody Powell said later, "no-body would have known Jimmy."

Through all of this Carter deftly downplayed his presidential plans to make certain his offers of help would not be thought self-serving. "We basically decided that the best thing to do," Powell said later, "was to provide as vivid a contrast as we could, to provide a genuine service for the candidates, and to bend over backward to make sure none of them felt we were doing them a big favor by being there. We wanted to do whatever they wanted done." And wherever they went, Jimmy shook hands and made friends and Jordan or Powell jotted down names—by the hundreds. After a trip, Carter would follow up by phone or letter, saying how glad he was to have met his new friends. "There was nothing unusual about it," Mark Siegel, executive director of the Democratic National Committee, told my colleague, David Broder. "Except for the care with which it was done and the extraordinary personal involvement on the Governor's part. He must have spent a fortune in the last two years on flowers. At every wedding, birth, and funeral in a Democratic family, there were flowers and a card from Jimmy."

More important in the long run were Carter's contacts not with local party power-brokers but with the young, experienced party activists in the thirty-two states he visited. These were to become the foot soldiers of his presidential campaign army.

Keeping his long-range intentions secret was not, of course, hard to do at the time. The notion of Jimmy Carter running for President was absurd on its face; beyond that, Democrats continued to expect that in the end Kennedy would agree to run and would be nominated routinely. But so far as Carter was concerned, it really didn't matter what Kennedy did. He, Jimmy Carter, was already seeking the presidency and was laying plans to bring Kennedy's political star crashing if the young and dashing New Englander decided after all to attempt to reinstate the family dynasty in the White House.

9. The "Inevitability" of Teddy Kennedy

Ever since the November day in Dallas in 1963 when John F. Kennedy was gunned down, there had been a sense of inevitability in the Democratic Party: somehow, it was believed, that which violence had wrested from the American royal family of the 1960s would be restored. In the frenetic and tragic presidential campaign of Robert Kennedy, in 1968, that prospect flared briefly and then was brutally snuffed out. Yet the sense of inevitability survived, was perhaps even enhanced by the horror of the two political murders, and the peculiar code of destiny and daring that gripped the royal family. The youngest brother, Senator Edward M. Kennedy (Teddy), spoke soon after Robert's death of his determination to "pick up a fallen standard," and although he declined to do so as a presidential candidate in 1968, the expectation was that a third Kennedy bid for the White House was only a matter of time.

On the night of July 19, 1969, the idea of a Kennedy restoration suffered still another severe jolt. Teddy Kennedy, after a drinking party on Chappaquiddick Island at Martha's Vineyard, plunged his car into a pond with a twenty-eight-year-old woman, Mary Jo Kopechne, at his side. He escaped, but she perished under circumstances that raised questions of the sort that politicians can seldom survive: why was he, a married man, there at all with a single woman, and why had he not saved her? An overnight delay in reporting the tragedy, and then a bizarre explanation delivered only after an interminable period of consultation with the family's most experienced image-shapers, compounded the damage. Many oracles of presidential politics intoned that the episode was fatal to the Kennedy restoration, and indeed it persuaded the young senator to withdraw from contention for the next Democratic nomination. But by the time 1972 came, it was clear that the sense of inevitability remained; had Ted Kennedy wanted the nomination, most thought it could have been his. And with the disastrous defeat of George McGovern that year, 1973 saw a seemingly inexorable drift in the party back to the dream of another Kennedy candidacy, with all the political magic it promised.

Through the first half of 1974, as the sickness of Watergate eroded the Nixon presidency and eventually destroyed it, the prospect of a Kennedy return to power grew, in spite of Chappaquiddick. Many doubted he could be elected, but few questioned that he could be nominated. The Democratic Party was leaderless; it was a stable of old plowhorses and untested colts; and as long as Ted Kennedy was present, no one dared move boldly toward the nomination. National polls showed him far ahead of all prospective contenders; local and state Democratic politicians who came to Washington for party meetings and other affairs adopted an attitude of resignation about a Kennedy candidacy in 1976. They shared doubts about the man's electability, but accepted the inevitability of his nomination if he wanted it. And Kennedy, for his part, kept his own counsel; he was, if nothing else, an experienced and astute wielder of political power who maintained his options and in the process preserved his influence. He was a rare Kennedy, legislation-oriented, who reveled in his Senate service, and he knew he could command more forums for his objectives as a prospective presidential candidate. Beyond that, as long as he left his future political course open, potential competitors would be immobilized or at least seriously restricted.

Some others—Senators Henry M. Jackson of Washington, Walter F. Mondale of Minnesota, Lloyd M. Bentsen of Texas, and Congressman Morris K. Udall of Arizona—started probing the presidential prospects, but they always had Kennedy in their peripheral vision. Gamblers all, they bet on his withdrawal, and in the meanwhile positioned themselves to run hard and effectively if fortune so willed.

The first signs were that Kennedy would run. In mid-September 1974 he embarked on a trip to California that had all the earmarks of a political sounding expedition. In two small chartered planes—one for himself, his aides, and local politicians, one for a contingent of Washington-based political reporters who went along to be in on the take-off of a presidential campaign—Kennedy spent a long and nostalgic Saturday going from Los Angeles to San Francisco, speaking for local Democratic candidates and picking up the threads of old Kennedy connections. In the bright, breezy afternoon, his plane landed at Monterey, where just eight years earlier, in 1966, his brother Robert had generated a mob scene when he appeared there in a futile rescue mission for Governor Edmund G. (Pat) Brown, who was trying to stave off a movie star-turned-politician named Ronald Reagan. Californians on that earlier occasion had turned out festively to see the brother of a martyred President; the crowd was so thick and emotional that a small girl was nearly crushed against the airport fence; Robert Kennedy had had to stop speaking, implore the crowd to get back, then reach down and extricate the child himself. Now, on the occasion of Ted Kennedy's visit, the crowd was smaller and its enthusiasm more controlled, and there was one other distinction: the Democratic gubernatorial candidate, Edmund G. (Jerry) Brown, Jr., son of Pat, was not present; he saw fit to campaign elsewhere, to do without the Kennedy magic.

That suited Ted Kennedy fine; he considered young Jerry Brown nothing special. But Brown's absence said something about the ambivalence of the Kennedy appeal after Chappaquiddick. Kennedy himself seemed to have doubts, to be going through the motions, and he lacked the usual zest that had marked his campaigning in earlier years. Accompanying reporters probed his intentions, but came away with little more than the usual half-sentences of indecision—with one exception. Previously Kennedy had been saying he would make his decision known by mid-1975; now he said he would announce his intentions by the end of the year or early in the next, and that when he did make up his mind, he'd say so. As he spoke, on his small chartered plane headed toward San Francisco, he seemed distracted, uncomfortable. But for a man who had nearly lost his life in a small plane several years earlier, this behavior seemed natural to the rest of us in the cabin. We did not know then, but learned later, that he had already decided —or had traveled 99 per cent in the process of deciding—against running.

Some months earlier Kennedy had begun a personal soul-searching, shared by a few close aides and friends. Personal matters dominated his agonizing, though Chappaquiddick also continued to weigh on his mind as a political consideration. On July 4 he had gone to Decatur, Alabama, for a controversial appearance with Governor George Wallace. The visit, made to demonstrate Kennedy's willingness and ability to be a conciliatory force within the party, generated an avalanche of unfavorable mail. That was no surprise, considering the antagonism toward Wallace among liberals who were the mainstay of Kennedy's constituency. What was startling was the fact that the mail referred so often to Chappaquiddick. People had not forgotten; and the slightest stirring that suggested a Kennedy presidential candidacy flushed out their animosity. The issue remained, submerged but potent.

Even more difficult were the personal matters. In addition to trying to play a father role to the thirteen children of his brothers John and Robert, his own son, Teddy, Jr., had been stricken with cancer in 1973 and had lost his right leg. The boy needed continuing treatment and therapy, and his father involved himself personally in both. On top of that, Kennedy's wife, Joan, beset by this concern and other emotional traumas stemming from the demands and stresses imposed on the wife of a famous public man in a famous family, had a drinking problem. Attempts to deal with the problem at private sanitoria in Connecticut and California without public knowledge proved futile; the word was out. "He wasn't going to leave her," one insider said, "but she couldn't take a campaign like that. He knew it wouldn't work publicly, and, besides, he wanted to spare her." A man with these troubles in his own family and home life would be hard-pressed to conduct the kind of single-minded campaign required to win the presidency. That, in the view of some insiders, was the single most important inhibition.

Finally there was the matter of which few spoke but all thought in considering the candidacy of a third Kennedy: possible assassination. The man's two older brothers, controversial figures in a country infected with hate and irrationality in its politics, had been removed from the public scene by the exercise of the franchise of violence; enough madmen were at large, not to mention an abundance of easily acquired firearms, to assume that someone, somewhere, would try to make it three. Two men who had failed to make something of their own lives, Lee Harvey Oswald and Sirhan Bishara Sirhan, had won a place in history as the killers of John and Robert Kennedy; the temptation to be the instrument assuring the end of the Kennedy political dynasty, to finish off the last of the Kennedy brothers, might be too great for some one of the unreasoning haters, of the deranged, to resist. Ted Kennedy understood this prospect better than anyone else. In 1972 he had persuaded himself that he could campaign safely for George McGovern because he was not himself reaching for power; he reasoned to close friends that it was only when he sought power in his own right that the threat of assassination would be present. It was a questionable theory at best, attributing as it did rational conduct to irrational human beings. But friends said this rationale did sustain him after 1968, and especially in 1972, when he plunged into crowds with his usual abandon in behalf of McGovern.

Kennedy had, in fact, avoided public appearances for a brief time after Robert Kennedy's death. In the spring of 1969, on the first anniversary of the assassination of Martin Luther King, Jr., Kennedy was invited to accompany Coretta King in a public memorial walk around the block of the Memphis motel where King was shot. The exercise had trouble written all over it, and Kennedy asked two aides, David Burke and his press secretary, Richard Drayne, to find out more about it. One day when they were walking down a Senate corridor with him, he asked: "Well, what's gonna happen down there?"

"They're going to meet at the church," one of his companions told him, "walk around past the motel and back to the church."

"Well," Kennedy said, smiling, "if I go, next year they're going to have to walk around the block twice."

It was the first time the aides could remember Kennedy laughing about the threats to his life, and in the end he did go to Memphis. Thereafter,

Burke and Drayne would kid Kennedy, saying that whenever they were in public with him, they wished he would wear a large placard with an X on it, and they suggested as they walked on each side of him they might carry signs with arrows pointing inward.

At bottom, however, the matter was no joke, and they all knew it. Threats were intermittent; once, in 1970 or 1971, a death plot was inadvertently uncovered by a police officer in northern Virginia when he picked up a phone and as a result of crossed wires overheard two people talking about it. As was customary in such cases, plainclothes police were assigned to Kennedy. He was advised only that there had been another threat and authorities were taking precautions. In this instance, attempts to trace the call were fruitless and nothing ever came of it. In Kennedy's Senate office, a special buzzer to the Senate police was installed under the desk of his receptionist, Melody McElligott, but it never had to be used.

"It's quite a thing for a man to ponder," one of Kennedy's close advisers observed bluntly once as we were discussing the options the third Kennedy faced. "You know your two brothers have had their heads blown off, and out there somewhere there's probably somebody waiting to do the same to you. When you put it in those terms you can understand why he might be reluctant to run."

This consideration also was paramount in the minds of the rest of the Kennedy family. Eleven years after Oswald had abruptly terminated their personal, idyllic world of Camelot, they continued to nurture the memories and the myths of that happy time. They guarded the public images of the slain President and his driven, melancholy brother against all critics, imposing whatever social penalties they could upon any who transgressed.

I remember a touchy discussion on the patio of Hickory Hill, Ethel Kennedy's home in McLean, Virginia, with Eunice Kennedy Shriver and Lemoyne Billings, John Kennedy's college roommate, shortly after the publication of Ben Bradlee's personal recollections of the late President, *Conversations with Kennedy.* Both were irate over references in the book to Kennedy's use of profanity.

"In more than twenty years I never heard him utter a word of profanity," Billings said, a recollection that was just a bit too much, even for his sister.

"Well, I wouldn't say *that,*" Eunice remarked, "but certainly not anything *filthy.*"

Eunice then went on to deplore what she called Bradlee's "betrayal" of a personal relationship, of a trusting friendship that gave him access to the President in unguarded moments. She could not understand, she said, how Bradlee, who had been Washington bureau chief of *Newsweek* and Kennedy's neighbor in 1960 (later he became executive editor of *The Washington Post*), could have done such a thing.

In sum the Kennedys had become a kind of royal family in exile, awaiting in their Washington and Cape Cod homes an eventual return to the political summit from which they had been so brutally banished on the tragic day in Dallas. They wanted the promise of John and Robert Kennedy to be realized and fulfilled in Edward Kennedy; they were a family of strivers, of achievers, in whose vocabulary there was no word for quitting. But in spite of all that, they were tragedy-prone and they knew it; they had suffered as much as any prominent political family in modern history, anywhere; they had lost enough and the odds were too high now. The consensus, however reluctantly, was that Teddy should not run.

One weekend late in August 1974 Kennedy phoned David Burke, who had been his administrative assistant and was still a close personal and political adviser, and asked him to fly up to Hyannis Port from New York, where Burke was now a successful executive for the Dreyfus Fund. For several hours they discussed the political and family situations. Kennedy was strongly inclined to declare himself out of contention, and Burke personally agreed. But in the manner of political game-planning, Burke assumed the role of devil's advocate, playing out all the considerations on the other side. Any way they looked at the matter the answer was the same: under the circumstances, Kennedy could not run. The decision was communicated to the family and close friends at a Labor Day weekend gathering in Hyannis Port.

All that was left now was the timing; when he should say so. It was Kennedy's hope that he could delay until after the 1974 elections, the better to use his position as a potential candidate to help Democrats in congressional races. He set off on the California trip a few weeks later with this timetable in mind, but discovered that the trip was being interpreted almost entirely in terms of his own 1976 ambitions. Pressed by the reporters from Washington, some of them long-time associates and friends, he found himself extremely uncomfortable dissembling with them, telling them he hadn't made up his mind. When he returned, he resolved that there was no sense delaying any longer. A week later he acted. At a press conference at the Parker House in Boston on September 23, with Joan at his side, the third Kennedy brother made a final effort to clear the air once and for all, and to open the field for those others who would seek the 1976 Democratic presidential nomination.

"From the campaigns of my brothers before me," he said, "I know that seeking the nation's highest office demands a candidate's undivided attention and his deepest personal commitment. If any candidate is unable to make that commitment, he does a disservice to his country and to his party by undertaking the effort. My primary responsibilities are at home. It has become quite apparent to me that I would be unable to make a full commitment to a campaign for the presidency. I simply cannot do that to my wife and children and the other members of the family."

This last reference, oblique as it was, acknowledged the special problems in Kennedy's personal life that dictated his decision. He called the decision not to run "firm, final, and unconditional," and said there were "absolutely no circumstances or event that will alter the decision." General Sherman had not been more categorical. "I will not accept the nomination," Kennedy said. "I will not accept a draft. I will oppose any effort to place my name in nomination in any state or at the national convention, and I will oppose any effort to promote my candidacy in any other way." He was speaking out now, he said, "in order to ease the apprehensions within my family about the possibility of my candidacy, as well as to clarify the situation within my party."

Kennedy's decision did indeed throw the race for the Democratic presidential nomination wide open. Ambitious men, needing little more than their personal appraisals of the competition to persuade themselves of their own merits, looked around and asked themselves the perennial question: "Why not me?" And the answer came back, as it usually does: "Why not, indeed?" The question was asked with renewed zest and answered with even greater conviction after the 1974 fall elections, which gave the Democrats control of thirty-six state houses, solid majorities in both houses of Congress, and the kind of political base about which any national candidate dreams. One 1976 hopeful, Democratic Governor John J. Gilligan of Ohio, was rudely upset in his bid for re-election by former Republican Governor James A. Rhodes and banished to the side lines, but others were born, at least in the minds of the handicappers: the new governors of California and New York, Jerry Brown and former Representative Hugh Carey; former astronaut John Glenn, now a senator in Ohio, and Governor Dale Bumpers of Arkansas, also elected to the Senate. Of these only Brown eventually made an overt bid for the nomination; they were newcomers struggling to acquaint themselves with their new responsibilities and determined to demonstrate their diligence to the people who voted them into office. Still, they were now political forces to be watched, especially with Kennedy out and the prospects thereby increased for a multiballot convention in 1976 and, just possibly, a deadlock and a return to nomination-by-power-broker.

Kennedy's withdrawal was at first viewed as a boon to two undeclared candidates, Jackson of Washington, the old New Dealer and middle-roader who had been Kennedy's chief competitor for the support of organized labor, and Mondale of Minnesota, a progressive generally regarded as the most acceptable alternative to Kennedy among party liberals. But in both cases the appraisal was faulty. Jackson soon found himself in conflict with AFL-CIO President George Meany over his support of a U.S.-Soviet Union trade bill that Meany regarded as a threat to domestic jobs, and labor's support, delivery of which was questionable under any circumstances in this era of the independent-minded voter, was no more in Jackson's pocket now than it had been before. As for Mondale, he was unable to raise much money after a year of "exploring" a candidacy, and with the financial situation not notably improved by Kennedy's withdrawal, he abruptly quit two weeks after the 1974 fall elections, observing, "Basically I found I did not have the overwhelming desire to be President which is essential for the kind of campaign that is required." In a perhaps unwitting but scathing commentary on the ordeal the American system imposes on its would-be leaders, he added: "I don't think anyone should be President who is not willing to go through fire."

Mondale's decision to bow out even before the race had begun, and after having spent $100,000 in the preliminaries, was a genuine shocker in the political community, and to no one more than myself. I had last encountered Mondale in early February 1974, waiting for dawn and the first flight out of the Johnstown, Pennsylvania, airport to Pittsburgh. Then, I had never seen a prospective candidate—with the exception of his fellow Minnesotan and mentor, Hubert Humphrey—who seemed to have more zest for running and determination to see it through. He had made a speech the night before in behalf of a Democratic congressional candidate in the first special election of the post-Watergate period, had talked politics with Pennsylvania labor leaders, caught a few hours' sleep, and was up and ready for another big day of prospecting. He had in tow an old Humphrey henchman who knew the labor crowd, Stan Bregman, to run interference for him, and Bregman's presence underlined his seriousness at that time. Mondale was not going to run simply as a liberal darling; he would be reaching out to the party's middle, riding on Humphrey's credentials and contacts as well as his own, with Humphrey's blessing. We climbed aboard a small commuter plane and Mondale spoke nonstop to Pittsburgh about the task ahead of him. My subsequent story in *The Washington Post* indicated how convincing he had been in painting himself as a candidate "willing to go through fire." It said:

"As the small plane flew over the grays and browns of the early morning Pennsylvania countryside, Mondale sat hunched forward in the cabin and spoke with the kind of enthusiasm that infects men of ambition.

It would be a long, tough road, but he was convinced this was the right time to travel it. Politicians looked for a man with 'a hard edge,' and he thought he had that too, and he had to find a way to demonstrate that. . . ."

Yet, nine months later, Fritz Mondale was out of it. The "hard edge" he was certain he possessed had in that time melted away in the heat of the ordeal. He couldn't face, he said subsequently, spending another whole year "sleeping in Holiday Inns." And that, of course, was only shorthand for all the other burdens that would-be candidates without broad national recognition had to accept: meals on the run, except for long boring political dinners with pedestrian food at best; small talk at endless receptions with glad-handers, groupies, phonies, con men; not to mention separation from family, and loneliness, even when surrounded by people. Politicians are supposed to be inured to all these, of course, and especially the latter considerations. In fact, many are not.

At any rate, Mondale's decision came as a surprise to nearly everyone if only because it occurred at precisely the time one might have expected him to plunge in even deeper. The day of Kennedy's withdrawal two months earlier, Mondale's men had begun an active solicitation of Kennedy supporters and money sources, with some expectation that the void would bring both interest and campaign funds his way. It didn't happen, and that disappointment, as much as any other factor, may have dictated his decision.

With both Kennedy and Mondale out by the fall of 1974, a gaping hole suddenly existed in the Democratic Party's presidential picture. Into it, in due time, a dozen candidates would jump, none of them sufficiently known or liked to draw to himself the kind of special support that would separate him from the pack.[1] Eight were considered liberals:

• Representative Morris K. Udall of Arizona, fifty-two, a tall and witty former professional basketball player seeking among other things to capitalize on the new esteem of the House generated by the Nixon impeachment hearings.

• Former Governor Terry Sanford of North Carolina, fifty-seven, gentlemanly president of Duke University, convinced he could reason Wallace supporters to his side.

• Former Senator Fred R. Harris of Oklahoma, forty-four, an earthy, barrel-chested new radical with a folksy populist pitch and a quick mind,

---

1. State Senator Julian Bond of Georgia, one of the most appealing black politicians in America, who had been nominated at the 1972 convention for Vice President before he had reached the constitutional age of thirty-five, entered the lists briefly but soon bowed out for lack of funds. Senator Robert C. Byrd of West Virginia also declared his intent to seek the nomination but drew back to an unproductive favorite-son posture.

offering himself as a kind of thinking man's George Wallace without racism.

• Governor Milton J. Shapp of Pennsylvania, sixty-two, a low-key former cable-television executive with the look of a persecuted nebbish, who had compiled a good liberal record in two terms but as a Jew was bucking one of the great remaining political bugaboos for the presidency.

• Senator Birch E. Bayh, Jr., of Indiana, forty-six, a shrewd and ambitious politician with strong labor support and a deceptive veneer of country-boyish looks and backslapping cordiality.

• R. Sargent Shriver, Jr., fifty-nine, husband of Eunice Kennedy Shriver, brother-in-law of Ted Kennedy, former Peace Corps and antipoverty director, ambassador to Paris and 1972 stand-in for Thomas Eagleton as the Democratic vice-presidential nominee.

• Senator Frank Church of Idaho, fifty, a stocky, boyish-looking foreign policy specialist.

• Governor Edmund G. Brown, Jr., at thirty-six the freshest of new faces, preaching the politics of skepticism and diminished expectations.

Occupying the center were two middle-road senators veering to the right: Henry M. Jackson of Washington, sixty-two, veteran of thirty-five years in Congress and recognized expert in the fields of energy, national defense, and conservation, now free of the onus of having supported the Vietnam war, support that had hurt his 1972 candidacy; and Lloyd M. Bentsen, Jr., of Texas, fifty-three, rich and antiseptically handsome, with a desire to be President and little else on the record in his two years in the Senate to recommend him for the job.

There was also former Governor Jimmy Carter of Georgia, fifty, a soft-talking, evangelistic-sounding peanut farmer with a reputation for administrative efficiency and a New South rhetoric on racial problems; he defied ideological categorizing.

And, finally, off on the right by himself, George C. Wallace—fifty-five, crippled, confined to a wheelchair, hard of hearing, totally inexperienced in foreign policy—but still the nation's tuning fork of discontent in a year when cacophony seemed the dominant theme of middle-class America.

Several obvious factors encouraged this proliferation of Democratic candidates. First and most obvious was the vacuum on the left. Another was the seeming vulnerability of the Republican opposition after Watergate, its congressional losses, the low state of the economy, and Ford's poor early showing. Also, there was, on the surface at least, a growing Democratic unity, constructed with Band-Aids and Scotch Tape by the party's national chairman, Robert Strauss, at an unprecedented mid-term convention in Kansas City one month after the off-year elections. It was a tenuous unity, to be sure, but the basis for some optimism among the faithful. And, finally, there was the new campaign-finance reform law, enacted in 1974 to be effective at the start of 1975, containing myriad provisions whose intent was to equalize opportunity among the candidates and destroy the dominating influence of the traditional big-money givers. Provision for a federal subsidy matching restricted private contributions made it seem, at first blush, that just about anyone could now run for President.

Most of the then-undeclared candidates flocked to the mini-convention in December 1974, to woo party activists. The prime purpose of the meeting was to approve a new party charter and delegate-selection rules. While reaffirming the basic structure of the national and state committees, with a nominating national convention at the end of the long presidential-primary road, the charter codified reforms designed to keep the party open to broad grass-roots participation. The 1972 convention, in which blacks, youth, women and other previously underrepresented groups were required to be included in all state delegations, had gone too far for most party regulars, and so did a requirement that all delegates be elected—including governors and other important state and national party leaders. Because some of these leaders had hitched their trip to the convention to the wrong horse—usually Muskie—they found themselves sitting out the convention at home, or at best in the galleries in Miami Beach. Even McGovern, the beneficiary as well as a prime author of these reforms, acknowledged afterward they had bucked party orthodoxy and pragmatism excessively. This time, the states were given the option of selecting one quarter of their delegates through the party apparatus, thus assuring most state party leaders a free ride to future conventions. In a deadlocked, eventually "brokered" convention, the presence of these experienced and influential political and party officeholders could be crucial to the outcome.

The matter of representation for minorities and women was not so easily disposed of. The commission appointed to write the party charter, chaired by Terry Sanford, failed to resolve the issue, and four separate approaches were submitted to the mini-convention. The reformers—party liberals, blacks, women, and a growing group of independent-minded union leaders fed up with the orthodoxy of George Meany and his political director, Alexander Barkan—wanted the strongest assurances of full participation in selecting the nominating-convention delegates. Meany, Barkan, and their conservative traditionalist allies argued just as strongly that "quotas" had produced chaos at the 1972 convention and disaster thereafter, and that there could be none for the future, not even implied ones. Any delegate-selection procedure that could bring on a challenge on grounds of a state delegation's composition, this group argued, would persuade state committees to observe quotas in building their delegations so as to avoid such a challenge at the convention or before. Fine, said the reformers: that was what the issue was all about.

At a meeting of the Democratic governors at Hilton Head, South Carolina, in advance of the mini-convention, the governors had taken it upon themselves to recommend a solution: a separate party commission headed by Baltimore Councilwoman Barbara Mikulski had approved antidiscrimination language for the 1976 convention only. It barred "mandatory quotas" but required each state to adopt and implement a plan of "affirmative action" to assure full participation in the delegate-selection process. Meany and Company had fought the Mikulski commission bitterly, and Barkan was outraged (no woman scorned could touch the fierce-visaged Barkan in the heat of "betrayal") when he learned that the governors had voted to urge that the mini-convention adopt Mikulski's approach for inclusion in the permanent party charter. Strauss, a card-carrying compromiser who was determined to achieve unity—or, failing that, the outward appearances of unity—had knuckled under to the governors and then proclaimed the setback a victory.

It was in this atmosphere of distrust that the issue was drawn in Kansas City. Barkan knew he was beaten even before the mini-convention opened, and he made clear to me, driving in from the airport on the first day, that he was about through with intramural politics. Let the Democrats pick their nominees, he said, and the AFL-CIO would then decide whether to support them or not. Strauss was well aware of Barkan's grousing. But he ignored it, purposefully steered the mini-convention past a series of minor obstacles, eventually satisfied the women and blacks, and got out of Kansas City with a semblance of unity that he could then proclaim, in his fashion, an intra-party love affair.

As 1974 ended, the impact of the new campaign-finance reform law was the major question mark. Indeed, shortly after the law's effective date of January 1, 1975, it came under broad challenge from liberals and conservatives alike as an unconstitutional abridgment of freedom of speech and the right to petition for redress of grievances. But a lower court upheld its main provisions, and the contest for money and supporters went forward through 1975 under its limitations. The candidates, most of them making an unprecedented early start in order to qualify for a federal subsidy, had no choice but to conduct their campaigns in accordance with the law as passed and see what would happen as the issue moved toward the Supreme Court. For politicians with visions of the White House, raising $5000 in chunks of $250 in twenty separate states—only 400 contributions—was an irresistible lure. At the outset, the law seemed indeed to be a great equalizer, an invitation for those individuals without a Maurice Stans to muscle the big money, and indeed with the Stans approach outlawed, to get into the race. But the new law also tossed presidential politics into uncharted waters —for the candidates, for the political scientists, for the political writers following the candidates, and for the public. Understanding the law and drawing a strategy best designed to capitalize on its provisions became a prime campaign exercise. Some advance calculating could be done, but whether the law would work out in reality as it was supposed to in theory had to await developments within the dynamics of the campaign itself. And over the whole picture was the court suit: if part or all of the law was thrown out, the guaranteed confusion inherent in a complex and untried law would escalate to chaos. The prospect was disconcerting, but the quest for the White House does not permit or often harbor timidity. By the fall of 1974 the uncharted waters were already full of ambitious men, undaunted by that or any other uncertainty.

10. Carter Adjusts His Plans

Of all the 1976 Democratic hopefuls, only one—Jimmy Carter—could be said to have been somewhat let down by Kennedy's decision not to be a candidate. He alone had predicated a 1976 campaign not on the possibility that Kennedy would stay out, but—brazen as it seemed at the time—in the hope that he would get in, keeping all the other ambitious Democrats on the side lines.

Jody Powell later confessed to having been initially "dismayed" by Kennedy's decision, but in the long run the proliferation of liberal candidates it set loose could be beneficial to Carter, as his savvy young strategists quickly realized.

One immediate effect of Kennedy's withdrawal was a flurry of meetings in the Carter camp and a decision that Carter would have to advance his declaration of candidacy, or at least get the word out privately to important Democrats. Because it was a keystone of the strategy to present him as a progressive alternative to Wallace, others who might lay claim to that position had to be headed off. In this category, clearly, were two "New South" governors who had been mentioned more prominently than he as presidential prospects—Reubin Askew of Florida, who had no use for Carter, and Dale Bumpers of Arkansas, who appeared well on his way to a seat in the U. S. Senate. And, it was also imperative to squash Georgia's "little Wallace"—Lester Maddox—in his bid to return to the governorship. The defeat of Lester Maddox continued to be essential to the early Carter strategy, as a minimal confirmation of Carter's influence in the New South.

In a confidential memo dated August 4, 1974, Hamilton Jordan had noted that Bert Lance, Carter's personal choice to succeed himself, had been defeated by House Majority Leader George Busbee, and now, Jordan contended, it was essential that Carter support Busbee. "If there's a runoff," Jordan warned, "you can be sure that David Broder and other nationally prominent columnists and reporters will be through here to cover [it]. I think it is critically important that the national press know you are working quietly and effectively behind the scenes to defeat Lester Maddox. When it is all over, hopefully the news stories will read that the progressive administration of Jimmy Carter and his political organization in Georgia were major factors in Lester Maddox's defeat." But Jordan knew that Carter would have to keep his own presidential plans out of the gubernatorial race. "If you tell David Broder your plans," Jordan wrote, "there are too many risks involved in terms that he will write and the way the outcome might be interpreted."

So the early presidential-campaign planning went forward covertly, with Carter's customary careful attention to detail. A full four months before the Democratic mini-convention, for example, Jordan drew up a battle plan and submitted it to Carter. Lists of delegates were obtained and profiles sketched of them, for use by Carter personally and by well-positioned aides. In his August 1974 memo Jordan had said, "We will give Joel Solomon, the young man from Tennessee who worked for us at the DNC and is a delegate to the conference, profiles on fifteen to twenty other young delegates. His job will be to seek out these young delegates, get to know them, talk to them about Jimmy Carter, and maybe get those who respond favorably together to talk with you. Bebe Smith[1] would be assigned to people she met and knew in the McGovern campaign. Jesse Hill [a prominent Atlanta black leader] would contact blacks, et cetera. I think it is absolutely essential that we organize and take this approach if we hope to make the best use of our friends who go to Kansas City."

Kennedy's decision to withdraw had accelerated Carter's timetable, but a month before Kennedy bowed out Carter's staff was still drawing up plans in an atmosphere and context that might have suggested to an outsider the strategy for another sneak attack on Pearl Harbor. They compiled lists of individuals in different categories who were to be notified in advance, and when. One group, Jordan wrote in a memo to Carter, would consist of people "who will be complimented to be told personally of your plans and who cannot use knowledge of your plans against you." This group included John C. West, then governor of South Carolina, and Morris Dees, a direct-mail expert whom Jordan hoped to recruit. A second group was made up of those who were politically "significant who you know and who are friendly to you but are not likely to respond to being told of your plans with a pledge of support"; this included Alexander Barkan, of the AFL-CIO's Committee on Political Education (COPE); Senate Majority Leader Mike Mansfield, Mrs. Graham of *The Washington Post,* House Speaker Carl Albert, and New York State Democratic leader Joseph Crangle. Plans were also made to send a mailing to all members of Congress, governors, members of the Democratic National Committee, state party chairmen, eight

---

1. An Americus, Georgia, liberal who, after a falling out with Jordan, left the Carter campaign and eventually became a supporter of Morris Udall.

thousand contributors in Georgia, and six thousand from another list. An outline of the announcement statement itself was proposed by Jordan that included Carter's concept of the presidency, suitably dressed up with historical references for intellectuals in the audience. "It is important," Jordan wrote, "that your speech reflect an appreciation and understanding of American history and contain some quotes and references to great men and women whose attitudes toward politics and government service reflect your own."

Jordan's memo—and remember this was written in August 1974, before Kennedy withdrew—emphasized that Carter's declaration of candidacy must state categorically that "you are totally committed to the race and will run against anyone anywhere; you will run against Wallace in the South and Kennedy in New England." He even specified when and where the announcement should be made: the week after the mini-convention at the National Press Club in Washington.

Carter's job as chairman of the DNC's drive to elect more congressmen would be the framework of his preannouncment activity. "For example," Jordan wrote, "you are scheduled to make a speech in September before a religious group in Peoria, Illinois, at a breakfast. We have generated a couple of good invitations for you to participate in two congressional campaigns and Bob Lipshutz's cousin may host a reception for you. We will continue to look for opportunities such as this one that we can expand on so as to take full advantage of your trips," especially into primary states.

Kennedy's pullout a month after this memo was written required a new look at the realities. Knocking off Wallace was still the centerpiece of the strategy, but now the Georgians had to gear themselves for the longer haul. In yet another memo, Jordan in early fall exhibited again his remarkable political perspicacity. He outlined a carefully conceived formula for allocating the campaign's resources—money, time, and staff effort—according to each of the fifty states, all through 1975 and 1976 up to the national convention. This plan was called "percentage of effort targeting." Jordan's memo said: "In a national campaign to win the Democratic nomination for President, there are three major factors to be considered: the relative size of the states and their delegations to the Democratic National Convention; the sequence of the primaries and the sequence of the delegate-selection process in the nonprimary states; and our own campaign strategy. Two of these factors are constant: size and sequence. Only one is variable: our campaign strategy. This memorandum is an attempt to account for these factors and reconcile them through development of a formula that will guide us in the allocation of the major resources of our campaign."

At the time of writing, Jordan noted, 75 per cent of the 1976 delegates would be selected in primaries, and twenty-three states were planning to select delegates by caucus. "The lessons here are quite obvious," he wrote. "Most of the delegates to the 1976 convention will be selected by primary and that percentage is only likely to increase. . . . The sequence or chronological order of primaries are important for obvious reasons. Good or poor showings can have a profound and irrevocable impact on succeeding primaries and a candidate's abilities to raise funds and recruit workers. The press shows an exaggerated interest in the early primaries as they represent the first confrontation between candidates, their contrasting strategies and styles, which the press has been writing and speculating about for two years. We would do well to understand the very special and powerful role the press plays in interpreting the primary results for the rest of the nation. What is actually accomplished in the New Hampshire primary is less important than how the press interprets it for the nation. Handled properly, a defeat can be interpreted as a holding action and a mediocre showing as a victory. [We] remember the McGovern and McCarthy campaigns of 1972 and 1968 as victories when in fact they ran second to Muskie and Johnson.

"The sequence of the selection of delegates in the nonprimary states is important but more as a test of organizational ability than a test of the candidates and their campaigns. The initial delegate-selections will generate some news stories and will be important, but in the long run they will take a back seat to the coverage of the primaries, and will be significant in relation to the number of delegates selected and its impact on the delegate totals of the various candidates.

"I have made the arbitrary judgment that the sequence of the primaries and the strategy of the campaign combined are as important factors as is the size of the state delegates. Consequently, for the purpose of this exercise I have translated the 3071 delegates to the national convention [later reduced to 3008] into points. In the equation which is developed, each delegate equals one point. Using this as a base and point of comparison, I have assigned a sequence factor of 1569 points, on the premise that sequence of the primaries is one-half as important as the size factor. As 73 per cent of the convention delegates are selected by primary, I have allocated 73 per cent of the 1569 points—1144—to the primary states, 27 per cent—425— to the nonprimary states."

Jordan then proceeded to allocate sequence points to the various key states: New Hampshire, the first primary, 150; Florida (expected then to be the second but eventually the fourth), 125; Illinois (eventually the fifth) 100; and so on. Iowa, the first caucus state, was given 40 points.

Jordan continued: "The strategy factor is one-half as important as the size factor. Consequently the strategy factor is assigned a numerical factor of 1550, approximately half the number of delegates—1320 points allocated to primary states and 230 to the nonprimary." Thus, though the importance of Iowa as the first caucus state and the first genuine test of strength was not overlooked , the focus in the Carter strategy at this juncture was on the primaries. "The prospect of a crowded field, coupled with the new proportional representation rule, does not permit much flexibility in the early primaries," he wrote. Then came this key observation: "No serious candidate will have the luxury of picking and choosing among the early primaries. To propose such a strategy would cost that candidate delegate votes and increase the possibility of being lost in the crowd. I think we have to assume that everybody will be running in the first five or six primaries. The crowded field enhances the possibility of several inconclusive primaries, with four or five candidates separated by only a few percentage points. Such a muddled picture will not continue long, as the press will begin to make 'winners' of some and 'losers' of others. The intense press coverage which naturally focuses on the early primaries plus the decent time intervals which separate the March and mid-April primaries dictates a serious effort in all the first five primaries."[2]

The depth of Jordan's strategy went far beyond what the unsuspecting public might imagine from a man they perceived essentially as a stop-Wallace candidate. Jordan took note of this factor, too: "Our public strategy would probably be that Florida was the first and real test of the Carter campaign and that New Hampshire would just be a warmup," he wrote. "In fact, a strong surprise in New Hampshire should be our goal, which would have a tremendous impact on successive primaries. Our minimal goals in these early primaries would be to gain acceptance as a serious and viable candidate, demonstrate that Wallace is vulnerable and that Carter can appeal to the Wallace constituency, and show through our candidate and campaign a contrasting style and appeal. A minimal goal would dictate at least a second-place showing in New Hampshire and Florida, and respectable showings in Wisconsin, Rhode Island, and Illinois. Our maximum goals, which I think are highly attainable, would be win New Hampshire and/or Florida outright, make strong showings in the other early primary states, and beat Wallace."

2. At the time this was written, the first five were expected to be New Hampshire, Florida, Illinois, Wisconsin, and Rhode Island. Massachusetts, Vermont, North Carolina, and New York subsequently moved their dates up and Rhode Island moved its date back.

Jordan went on to discuss what then were scheduled to be the middle primaries, and although the sequence turned out to be somewhat different, his analysis is worth quoting for its expression of the immense confidence that characterized Carter's campaign from the very outset:

"Late April and early May primaries will dictate difficult and strategic decisions on the allocations of resources. Lack of funds and time will restrict us from running a personal campaign in every state. Hopefully, good press in the early primaries will have solved some of our name-recognition problem and given Jimmy Carter some depth to his new national image. Nevertheless, there will be ten primaries in two weeks. If by this point we have knocked Wallace off and led the field in a primary or two, we will be in a strong position to raise funds and enter them all. The results of the first primaries are not likely to be so conclusive and we will be in a position of making some tough decisions that could win or lose the Democratic nomination. In my allocation of points I have assumed that Wallace will be damaged at this point but still viable, and we would focus our efforts on Alabama, Pennsylvania, and Indiana [Carter won the latter two], which would be better states to confront him in than Ohio, District of Columbia, and Massachusetts [Carter won the first two of these as well]. If we survive that ordeal, the next three states—Tennessee, North Carolina, and Nebraska [again, Carter won the first two]—would be ideal for us to take on anybody and everybody."

Because the dates of the nonprimary states' caucuses had not yet been fixed, Jordan arbitrarily assigned each one ten strategy points, with the proviso that the allocation would be reviewed later, which it was.

New Hampshire and Florida were rated even, each being allocated 125 strategy points. Illinois and Wisconsin were next, with 90 each. Finally Jordan made an over-all allocation of "percentage of effort" for each state, combining the factors of timing of primary or caucus, delegate strength, and the special Carter strategy of going after Wallace. Under this formula, Illinois was assigned the largest percentage of effort—5.8 per cent of the total—with Florida, the first and prime anti-Wallace target state, and California, the nation's richest delegate prize—second with 5.5 per cent. New York, the second largest, was next with 5.4 per cent, and little New Hampshire next, with 4.8 per cent. Later, as primary dates were switched and the importance of the early caucuses was appreciated more, the allocations were adjusted.

The withdrawal of Teddy Kennedy had required, for Carter, some modifications in thinking and planning. But because it had been his intent always to take Kennedy on, Kennedy's pullback was not really a milestone in the Carter campaign. The same could not be said for the horde of liberals whose plans or at least hopes for success were tied inextricably to what Kennedy did. His announcement inevitably produced a stampede among them. And the swiftest was the old professional basketball player familiar with the fast break, Mo Udall.

11. The Rush to Fill the Liberal Void

There was something faintly out of character for Representative Morris K. Udall of Arizona to put himself forward, as he did in late November 1974, as the first formally declared candidate for the 1976 Democratic presidential nomination. Though he was a very tall—six feet, five inches—and imposing man, there was about him a distinct quality of deference; he was a man slow to anger, slow to become visibly aroused, a contemplative man who liked to sort things out before leaping. Nor did he find it easy to blow his own horn; he was given to veiling his seriousness behind a mien of witticism; indeed, some of his critics suggested that he permitted his good humor to create an impression of frivolity. It was not that he was some rapid-fire stand-up comic; it was, rather, that he was so self-deprecating, and often self-deprecatingly funny, that the substance of the man sometimes had trouble getting through. But given Udall's basic reluctance to brag about himself, it was perhaps inevitable that he would fall back on keeping the mood light. None of his aides was surprised, for example, when he warmed up audiences by telling about the day he walked into a barbershop in Keene, New Hampshire, and shook hands with the man in the first chair. "I said, 'Hi, I'm Mo Udall, and I'm running for President.' And he said to me, 'Yeah, I know. We were just laughing about it.' "

For all that, Mo Udall was dead-serious about the presidency. More than a score of his House Democratic colleagues had urged him to take the step, and he well knew, from McGovern's experience, that an early start was imperative. And so, only two days after Fritz Mondale withdrew, he went to Bedford, New Hampshire, and declared he would run in that state's primary in the winter of 1976. Udall portrayed himself not only as that much-desired commodity in post-Watergate politics, the fresh face, but also as a fresh thinker, a maverick of sorts. The very fact that he sought the presidency from the House of Representatives—the bleachers of Washington power politics—in itself set him aside from the pack. He hoped, and the House colleagues who supported him hoped as well, that the impressively responsible performance of the House Judiciary Committee in the impeachment inquiry against Richard Nixon had created a new public acceptability for a congressional candidate.

In this sense Mo Udall *was* a different kind of presidential candidate. But in other important ways he was as traditional as the New Hampshire primary. In 1972 he had been an early and avid supporter of Muskie's candidacy, and while he had a much more easygoing personality than Muskie's, and was not given to private or even occasionally public temper flare-ups and crankiness, he did share one Muskie trait: he exhibited a caution, a prudence in politics that to the very liberals he sought to enlist seemed often a lack of conviction or commitment. Like Muskie, Udall wanted to build a broad constituency in the party and in the country, one that could deliver him the nomination and then the presidency itself. He was well aware of George McGovern's experience in 1972, when McGovern established himself as the point man of Democratic liberals in the primaries, only to fail in the general campaign because he ran from too narrow a national base. His attempts to broaden that base had been astutely exploited by the Nixon forces, who spotlighted and magnified every shift in his posture, succeeding in the end in portraying him as a sail-trimming radical bowing to expediency. Udall was determined not to fall into that trap; he would run in the primaries on the same issues and generate the same public perception of himself as he would convey in the general election if nominated.

The trouble with that approach, however, is that activist, left-of-center Democrats want their Daniel to stick his head in the lion's mouth. They believe that the Democratic Party must clearly define and advocate progressive positions. Like their counterpart power-wielders in the Republican Party, the conservatives who consider that their party should be the vehicle for communicating the True Faith, liberal Democrats also hold that such ideological purism is the route to political success: the winner must offer a choice, not an echo—in the phrase popularized, and proved so fallible, in Goldwater's campaign of 1964. That approach, appealing to those who believe elections are won on issues and that they are demonstrably right on issues, would have more validity in a politically polarized country. Then, the voter would be obliged to make clear-cut choices. But in the real world of grays, of shadows and overlaps and contradictions, the candidate who can seem not all things to all men, but most to most, is the likely winner. Thus, in each major party, the cagey aspirant for the presidential nomination must try to appeal to, or at least mollify, the ideologues who are the most energetic and often the most influential in nomination politics, taking care not to paint himself into a corner from which he cannot escape in the general-election campaign among an electorate of nonideologues. In 1972

Muskie failed in the first task because his eye was too much on positioning himself for the fall campaign, and McGovern failed in the fall campaign because he had succeeded too well, too visibly, in the first undertaking. (Nixon, by contrast, walked the tightrope skillfully in both 1968 and 1972.) Udall, a Muskie disciple with an eye to recent Democratic history, hoped to avoid both Muskie's and McGovern's miscalculations.

A force in the politics of 1974–75, however, was pulling, or in Udall's case pushing, Democratic candidates out of conciliation and into contention, and that force was George Wallace. Wallace, for all his shortcomings, still seemed to appeal to a considerable segment of the national electorate, and a temperate seeker after the Democratic nomination was not of a mind to alienate that segment by castigating its hero. But any candidate of the left who hoped to win the nomination could ignore Wallace only at his own peril; in liberal eyes, Alabama's governor was not simply wrong or unqualified but a menace, a racist demagogue, an inflamer of passions and prejudices who disregarded the progressive objectives that had marked the history of the Democratic Party since the New Deal. The candidate who took Wallace on and disposed of him as a serious competitor or spoiler might well earn the blessing and support of the left wing that had muscled Lyndon Johnson aside in 1968, might have coalesced around Robert Kennedy that same year, and had won the nomination for McGovern in 1972.

Udall hoped at the outset to finesse this dilemma. In New Hampshire he said he was offering himself as a candidate who might be able to "bring the party back together again," while at the same time taking courteous aim at the Wallace constituency. He would make his appeal to "the working man and woman in America," he said. "We've got to give them more hope, a feeling of participation in this country, and we've got to find ways of meeting the needs of ordinary Americans." In subsequent months, however, "the Wallace problem" gnawed at Udall, and eventually he had to face it more openly and squarely.

In early 1975, at a dinner meeting with a group of Washington-based reporters at the home of Loye Miller, now of the Chicago *Sun Times,* Udall's plight as a liberal *and* a pragmatic politician became painfully obvious. Settling his long and wiry frame into an armchair, he nursed a scotch and water and fielded repeated questions about Wallace. Was Wallace a demagogue? Well . . . If he thought so, why not say so? Well . . . Would he have Wallace on his ticket? If not, why not say so? Udall tried patiently to explain, then and through dinner, that he saw no need to go out of his way to antagonize any segment of the electorate. He would run his campaign and let Wallace run his. The voters would decide. Muskie had seriously erred, Udall said, in calling Wallace a "demagogue of the worst kind" after Wallace trounced him and the rest of the field in the 1972 Florida primary. That statement was an unnecessary dig at Wallace's constituency and he was not going to make that mistake. But still the questions came. Was Wallace a racist? If so, why not say so? In the end, the harried candidate reluctantly acknowledged that he couldn't run on the same ticket with Wallace, but he wasn't going to throw rocks at him either.

This interrogation by a group of political reporters who had been out around the country and had some feel for what was going on made a strong impression on Udall. He began to worry more about "the Wallace problem," his aides later acknowledged, or more exactly about how the press and liberal circles viewed his handling of it. At breakfast with another group of reporters several weeks later, Udall was still playing it cozy, but not confidently. Wallace, he said, was "asking the right questions but didn't have any answers." That idea, that Wallace had put his finger on the root causes of national discontent but wasn't equipped to do anything about them, soon became a litany with Udall and other anti-Wallace candidates.

(By this time four other candidates were officially in the race—Carter, Harris, Bentsen, and Jackson. The first two acknowledged "the Wallace problem"; the second two tried to ignore it. Carter, running clearly as a Southern alternative to Wallace, obviously did not need to belabor the point. Harris, who for more than four years had been espousing a "new populism" that sought to strip Wallace's constituency away, worked the same side of the political street, but more aggressively and bombastically than the low-key Carter. Bentsen and Jackson, however, knowing they could never get the Democratic left wing to support them anyway, said little about Wallace, hoping that if and when the Alabama governor went under, they would inherit large segments of his constituency).

The second formal Democratic entrant was Jimmy Carter. He announced his candidacy on December 12, 1974, in Atlanta and Washington, but by then of course his campaign was already in high gear. The week before, he had worked the state delegations at the Kansas City mini-convention as if he were at the national convention itself, and he did so with a straightforwardness that took on special appeal in this post-Watergate year. Whereas in the past candidates had traveled almost clandestinely from one state to another, meeting in secret with the power-wielders, Carter, for example, sat in Room 2318 of the Holiday Inn and made his pitch to the New Hampshire delegation while anybody who cared to drifted in and out through an open door. He told his small audience of perhaps fifteen people he recognized how important their state's primary was in establishing a foothold for any presidential candidate, and he pledged, more than fifteen months in advance, to enter it.

But his openness notwithstanding, Carter from the very outset was hard to figure. The first question that came to mind about him was not what kind of President he would make or what he would do if he were President, but what on earth ever persuaded him that he was presidential material in the first place. At dinner with the same group of political writers in Washington who had grilled Udall on Wallace, Carter confessed that he first got the idea when Hubert Humphrey and George McGovern visited Georgia. The old "Why not me?" syndrome worked on him, he acknowledged. A pleasant, conscientious man, he was possessed of a quiet self-confidence that could be almost irritating in its stolidness. He declared himself to be a voracious reader, and he told the reporters he could and did digest several books a week in preparation for the presidency, or simply to broaden his mind. Perhaps unwittingly—but probably not—he painted himself as a sort of Dixie Abe Lincoln, reading not by a log cabin's blazing fireplace but by the bedside light in countless motel rooms in cities and towns all across America. Five and a half days on the road, one and a half at home in Plains with his family: that was Carter's regimen for the next year and a half.

Carter was often ingratiating on this particular night, so soft-spoken that one sometimes had to lean forward to hear him. (He seemed to do exceptionally well in small groups; newspaper editors whom he visited as he traveled around the country were invariably impressed by him.) His modest style and imperturbable confidence suggested that here was a man unrattled by the scope of his undertaking and by the challenges he would have to embrace if he were successful. But behind this self-assurance the assembled reporters also saw a man who seemed seriously out of tune with the rest of the country concerning the role the United States ought to play in the real world of power politics. This dinner was on April 2, 1975, just weeks before the final fall of the government and army of South Vietnam, and the debacle was easily predictable. But he told the dinner group that American military aid should continue to flow to South Vietnam for a year, and he predicted that the Saigon government would stand for at least that long. It seemed clear that Carter continued to be attuned to old Cold War thinking long rejected by his party's left.[1] By the time Carter had to undergo

---

1. Much later, on March 16, 1976, in an interview with me at the home of Dr. Peter Bourne in Washington, Carter denied he had advocated continuing such aid to Saigon for a year. He said, "I did say I was in favor of adequate aid to the Saigon government to get our troops out safely, but I never had any inclination to continue support beyond that point." The reporters present that night all had a different recollection.

more widespread public and press scrutiny, however, the Vietnam war was behind the country and he tried to finesse the whole matter by saying he had called in 1971 for American withdrawal, avoiding mention of his earlier support of U.S. policy. He failed to point out his call for withdrawal was not based on a stated belief that American intervention in Vietnam was wrong, but that "since we are not going to do what it takes to win, it is time to come home."

Running against Wallace, Carter knew, would not be enough to overcome the difficulties faced by a Southerner seeking the presidency. He would take Wallace on in the Florida primary, to be sure, but meanwhile he would attempt to construct a nationwide constituency that could enable him really to capitalize on a Florida victory over Wallace. Throughout 1975 he labored at this task diligently and effectively; he raised enough money to qualify for federal matching funds, impressed old and new politicians with his soft sell, and, most important, built a grass-roots organization in every section of the country.

Fred Harris, in contrast, was the epitome of the hard sell. By all odds a more formidable public speaker than either Udall or Carter, he seemed in both his approach to issues and his style better equipped to take on Wallace on his own ground. A small-town Oklahoma boy who never stopped talking like one (though he could), Harris was equal parts brilliant, friendly, shrewd, impulsive, folksy, aggressive, and ambitious. No, make that at least two parts ambitious. A southwestern Sammy Glick sans malice, he was the classic young man in a hurry: elected a state senator at the age of twenty-six; ran a close race for governor of Oklahoma at thirty-two; elected to the U.S. Senate at thirty-three to an unexpired term; re-elected for a full six-year term at thirty-five; co-chairman of Hubert Humphrey's campaign for the Democratic presidential nomination in 1968, at thirty-seven; Democratic National Chairman at thirty-eight. His alliance with Humphrey marked him as an orthodox pol taking the orthodox route to power—but it turned out to be the wrong route, and for one reason: Vietnam. As the American people soured on the Vietnam war, the minority opposition to the war that had labored and lost at the 1968 convention became the majority. Harris claimed later that he had opposed American involvement in Vietnam as early as 1967 and had tried with others to move then Vice President Humphrey into open opposition (and thus into a clean break with Lyndon Johnson) before and at the 1968 convention. But among the early political infantrymen in the effort to end the war, Harris was considered a water carrier at best, and so patently ambitious that his motives on whatever issue were always suspect. Also, his service of little more than a year as head of the Democratic National Committee made him few friends; he was considered a poor administrator and insensitive to the needs and problems of the Democratic governors. On the orthodox track of national Democratic politics, Fred Harris had come to the end of the line by 1970, at the tender age of thirty-nine.

There then occurred what can only be called the radicalization of Fred Harris. The timing is in dispute, because Harris himself contends that his liberal-left views long predated the 1970s. But the fact was the perception of Harris in the political community and among the press changed sharply at this juncture. He spoke increasingly against the Vietnam war and, even more notably, began to embrace what he called "the new populism"—radical tax reform, all-out war on privilege for the rich and big business, massive public-service employment.

Whatever the explanation for his political metamorphosis, Harris's outspoken radical views by 1972 had cast a shadow over his chances for Senate re-election in 1972. Facing a tough primary challenge and then a race against incumbent Republican Governor Dewey Bartlett after it, Harris opted to take a giant leap and run for President. He and his activist wife, LaDonna, a Comanche who later became head of Americans for Indian Opportunity, found themselves an angel, a New York investor named Herb Allen. They chartered a campaign plane in the summer of 1971 and took off on a pell-mell, one-way trip to oblivion. Running on a slogan—"No More Bullshit"—that delighted campus youth but soured the squares, the short and giddy presidential campaign of Fred Harris crash-landed about six weeks after it had begun, when Allen confronted him with a bare campaign cupboard.

The setback only convinced Harris the more that his new commitment as a reformer, focusing on the inequities of income distribution in the country, was right for him. For more than a year he dabbled in a tax-reform lobby called New Populist Action that also got nowhere ("Take the rich off welfare" was one of its better slogans, aiming at tax loopholes for the wealthy and big business). He wrote a book entitled *The New Populism* and worked on a novel. Fred Harris had no reverse gear; it was always full ahead with him, and no looking back. Through the years of the Watergate trials and the Nixon slide, he tapped in to the public discontent and awareness of the climate of special privilege in Washington, and carried his message to campuses, to reformist labor unions, and to farm groups. He and LaDonna worked the lecture circuit to sustain themselves and the message that Harris now embraced evangelistically. As he did so, he seemed in appearance and style to become even more the country boy, as "ain't" and "cain't" peppered his Oklahoma twang more than ever before. There was no denying he had the common touch. Workingmen, white and black, liked his shirt-sleeve, tie-at-half-mast, I've-been-there-myself approach, and men and women alike liked LaDonna, attractive, open, and just as persuasive. In Fred Harris the Democrats indeed had a George Wallace without racism, at a time when many Americans seemed, according to the polls at least, to want just that.

And of course that was exactly what Harris wanted liberal party leaders and voters to think. But it was not easy to persuade them, since they had long memories. They remembered all too well Fred Harris the young hustler who lined up with Humphrey when he could have joined McCarthy or Bob Kennedy in 1968; they remembered Democratic National Chairman Fred Harris, trying to run that job with one hand and be a senator with the other and always looking down the road for the next political opportunity. And they remembered his abysmal stab at the presidential nomination in 1971. "I knew Fred Harris," one party liberal put it in a memorable phrase, "before he was a virgin."

But the Harrises were nothing if not persistent. During an early foray into New Hampshire in December 1974 I arranged to meet them in the little town of Windham in the state's southeast corner, at the home of Bill and Janet Fredette, two early recruits. The Fredettes, a pair of involved liberal Democrats—she a social worker who first heard Harris speak at a welfare conference, he a returned full-time college student at the age of thirty-eight —were putting the Harrises up in their old, white frame house, full of New England history and charm. When I arrived, the undeclared candidate and his wife were returning from Keene, and it was past midnight when they careened up in a magenta-colored jeep, bundled against the December cold, pulled their own luggage from the back, and trudged into the house. In the living room, warmed by a blazing fire of white birch logs, they set their bags down, shed their overcoats, and went directly to the fire, where LaDonna rubbed her hands briskly and Fred warmed the seat of his pants, both grinning like two kids on a Dartmouth winter carnival weekend.

They talked enthusiastically about the crowd that had turned out in another private home to hear them and to sign cards pledging free time to the Harris campaign. After a while, LaDonna went into the kitchen and returned with drinks for us, as Bill Fredette set out cold meats, cheese, and rolls. And that was how it went, the campaign of the populist candidate: low-budget, high-enthusiasm, living off the land guerrilla-style.

The next morning, over bacon, eggs, and coffee at the Fredettes' dining-room table, the Harrises joked about how different it would be eating breakfast at the White House. Fred regaled Fredette with reminiscences of his early days campaigning as a state senator, including his first big trip to

New York, wherein he and an Oklahoma crony got sandbagged into buying a couple of bottles of watered-down champagne for table "hostesses" who sat with them. It wasn't every day that an average family in New Hampshire had such conversational fare, from such guests. The word got around, and the Harrises never had to worry where they were going to sleep when they went to any corner of the state.

The same approach was employed elsewhere as Harris's campaign developed in key primary and caucus states during 1975. Part of the idea was simply to save money, but it also had a psychological purpose. By staying in private homes, using borrowed cars, eschewing high-priced media experts and paid television, the Harrises were putting credibility into their "people's campaign."

The trouble for Harris was that he wasn't the only Democratic candidate who had hit upon this grass-roots *modus operandi.* Jimmy Carter used it with just as much diligence and—it turned out—considerably more credibility. An irony in the whole thing was that Harris, unwittingly, had drawn up a blueprint for Carter's eventual success in the early going. In a four-page memorandum written in conjunction with his wife and Jim Hightower of Texas, his campaign manager, the previous June (1974), Harris might have been planning Jimmy Carter's campaign: "No limousines and drivers for the candidate. He must campaign like other people live. Buses. Public transportation. Coffee in homes. Personal contact. Staying in people's homes. No campaign jet and big staffs. These will not be gimmicks: they will be financial necessities. One enthusiastic volunteer, with a clear understanding of the theme, style, basic assumptions, and strategy of the campaign is worth three lukewarm, paid workers. If the campaign starts paying people, other than for a small central office, there will be no end to the paying; people won't volunteer to do the same work for nothing that other people are paid to do. People with no experience, if they understand the nature of the campaign and come to it with enthusiasm, can be taught the necessary skills—press, radio, canvassing, organization. Most of them must be able to live off the land or their own resources, in order to do so. Don't worry about selling the national press and political officials and observers in advance on the 'viability' or 'credibility' of the candidacy. For months, while the national polls are bad, this will require a lot of faith, nerve, and patience on the part of the candidate and his supporters. Prove viability. Prove it in New Hampshire. . . . Set up skeletal crews in primary and nonprimary states throughout the country. But concentrate, first, on New Hampshire. Build a door-to-door, person-to-person, iceberg organization in New Hampshire. . . . The strength of the campaign will only become visible in the last days before the New Hampshire primary, just when the national press and political officials and observers are beginning to get really interested in what's happening."

Only in the dimensions of his confidence did Harris differ from the audacious Carter: "The candidate does not have to run No. 1 in the New Hampshire primary," he wrote, "because the 'conventional wisdom' of the national press and political officials and observers will be that he will not make a showing there. . . . Twenty-five per cent in New Hampshire will probably be enough in 1976. Running in the top three will probably do it." After running in the top two or three in Wisconsin, "showing that New Hampshire was no fluke," Harris wrote, "the candidate then goes 'national' —not because the national press and political officials and observers say so, but because the people of Wisconsin say so."

In Harris's case, however, the people of New Hampshire were destined to deliver a quite different message, and those in Wisconsin in effect were never really asked for theirs.

Another failed 1972 candidate hoping to resurrect himself at the expense of Wallace was Terry Sanford. Now the president of Duke University, he seemed more college president than political candidate; distinguished in a down-country way, he was in a sense like one of those bonus players in professional baseball or football who never was able to live up to the expectations laid out for him by others. He had tried to stop Wallace in the North Carolina primary in 1972, counting on the enlightened spirit of the New South to carry the day, but starting late, and not viewed as a serious national candidate, he was soundly beaten, Wallace winning 50 per cent of the vote to 37 per cent for Sanford. Once considered the Democratic Party's bright new hope for the South and sometimes mentioned as a prospective running mate for John Kennedy in 1964, Governor Sanford had led North Carolina through the difficult days of the early 1960s, the days of lunch-counter sit-ins and bullheaded "massive resistance" to racial integration in other southern states. In those days, his voice was one of quiet reason, and now he tried to employ that same weapon to bring not only North Carolina but the rest of the South and blue-collar America to their political senses. Personable and politically astute at close range, Sanford lost something on the stump, and his invocations in 1975–76 of his record on civil rights fifteen years earlier, with pointed references to the New Frontier, only reinforced the impression that he was a politician of the past.

Sanford, a man of fifty-seven who looked older and distinctly grandfatherly, knew that for him, North Carolina was critical. He had to beat Wallace there, or it was all over for him. In announcing his candidacy in May 1975 Sanford faced that reality squarely. "We might as well shoot it out at high noon," he told me at the National Press Club a few minutes after he had formally entered, "and if we can't cut it there, get out." Allies were already at work in the North Carolina legislature to move the state's primary date ahead a month, to give Sanford an early crack at Wallace. Having personally lobbied for retention of the primary against anti-Wallaceites who had wanted to kill it, Wallace himself was in no position to stay out. Sanford's strategists hoped to persuade other liberal candidates to bypass North Carolina so that he could run one-on-one against the Alabamian.

In many ways, Wallace was the perfect foil for Sanford. Where Wallace was coarse and bombastic, Sanford was courteous and benign. His record as governor from 1961 to 1965 was in striking contrast to Wallace's in Alabama, where he had practiced open defiance of the federally imposed desegregation at the University of Alabama. It was Sanford's plan to compare his own record in the same time and place with Wallace's, facing the same problems and atmosphere. He would appeal to Southern voters to demonstrate that their region had matured on the issue of race relations.

As 1975 wore on, three more Democrats registered campaign committees with the Federal Election Commission. It was clearer and clearer that the days of waiting to declare until the start of a presidential election year were over. To qualify for federal matching money by raising funds from an increasingly disenchanted and politically apathetic public, one had to run early and long.

In June Governor Milton Shapp of Pennsylvania chose the platform of the National Governors' Conference in New Orleans—as usual an orgy of excessive food, drink, and rhetoric—to announce his intention to join the pack. Not his candidacy, mind you, just his intention to be a candidate. A mild, soft-spoken man with the faintly bedraggled look of a door-to-door salesman who hasn't met his quota for the month, Shapp immediately encountered a credibility gap. Although no other governor was offering himself as a candidate, and the conference itself was almost totally devoid of news, Shapp had such trouble attracting press attention that his aides were reduced to soliciting individual reporters on major newspapers to have breakfast or lunch with him. As the two-time governor of a major industrial state, Shapp might have expected to be taken seriously, but his style cooled all ardor, even interest.

The governor professed to be undismayed and undeterred by this lack of reception, noting that he had encountered the same ho-hum reaction when he first ran for governor of Pennsylvania in 1956 and won the Democratic nomination (but lost the election). He was a solid liberal with an excellent record as a self-made businessman, a pioneer in the cable-television industry, and as the administrator of the state. His handling of a massive truckers' strike in 1974 that had threatened to cripple the state had marked him as a patient, tough, and shrewd negotiator. But he was, as Jack Germond of *The Washington Star* noted, "about as charismatic as a head cold." In late September 1975 Shapp formally announced his candidacy with all the fanfare of a wetback sneaking across the Texas border at midnight. "The last thing American people need is another smiling politician or spellbinding orator spewing rhetoric," he said, and he certainly wasn't talking about himself. He was nothing if not candid: as President he would pursue full employment by pumping federal tax money into the public sector, not worrying about the national debt. New jobs would mean new taxpayers and a cut in welfare rolls. "Money is just a tool to increase wealth," he said. But hardly anyone was listening.[2]

In contrast to Shapp's quiet entry into the race, the kickoff campaign of the one Democrat most qualified among the 1975 pack as a celebrity— Sargent Shriver, the 1972 vice-presidential nominee—was accomplished with the subtlety and smoothness of a final scene in a Marx Brothers movie. Shriver, to his unending chagrin, had always been cast as understudy to his younger but more famous brother-in-law, Teddy Kennedy. It was understood within the family and without that only with Teddy out of presidential contention could Sarge even begin to think about getting in. And so, after taking soundings among his friends, Shriver paid a call on his brother-in-law at Teddy's Senate office on June 4. Shriver contended later that he had gone there primarily to urge Teddy to reconsider his decision against running. In traveling around the country, Shriver said he had told Kennedy, he had found a strong consensus among Democrats that the field of men offering themselves for the nomination was unsatisfactory, that Teddy was still the candidate they wanted. But when Kennedy reiterated his determination not to be a candidate, Shriver then said he was thinking about running himself.

A few days later, *The Washington Star*'s James Dickenson broke the story of this meeting, along with reports that he had been taking political soundings and was about to enter the race. Publication on page one, under the headline " 'All Engines Go' for Shriver Bid for Presidency," intruded on and upset Shriver's timetable. He was vacationing and fishing in Florida, and attempts to reach him were at first unavailing. His aides insisted to me, as I tried to follow up my rival paper's story, that Shriver had made no decision. So to straighten out the mystery, I took a cab to Capitol Hill and

2. Most long-shot candidates are asked whether they're really running for Vice President. Shapp, on announcing, was asked if he was "really running for secretary of transportation"!

asked Kennedy directly about the meeting with his brother-in-law.

Between appointments in his office, Kennedy dealt with my questions with wry amusement. Shriver's own lack of enthusiasm and commitment to Robert Kennedy's presidential bid in 1968[3] had not been forgotten by the Family of Long Memories, and Teddy, while not disposed to stand in Sarge's way, wasn't about to become his campaign manager either.

"What did Sarge say to you when he came up here to see you?" I asked Kennedy. "And what did you say to him?"

"He told me he was going to run," Kennedy replied without equivocation, "and I wished him well." The senator from Massachusetts had the slightest grin on his face as he spoke.

"Well," I asked him, "if Benito Mussolini walked in here and told you he was going to run, would you wish him well?"

Kennedy laughed, and then, grinning broadly this time, said, "If he was married to my sister!"

Barely six weeks later, on July 15, a Shriver for President Committee, organized under the direction of former Deputy Secretary of Defense Cyrus R. Vance, an old Kennedy/Johnson administration associate, was registered with the Federal Election Commission. Shriver authorized it to raise money for him, though he was still saying he had not decided whether he would run. In his coyness, he had unwittingly gotten off to a comic start on a campaign that, while openly ridiculed by most politicians and members of the press, deserved to be taken as seriously as any of the others. For one thing, Shriver, with or without Kennedy family assistance, had mounted an impressive record running the Peace Corps, the Office of Economic Opportunity, the American Embassy in Paris, and in the party vineyards as the replacement on the 1972 ticket for Tom Eagleton. True, Shriver had never won elective office, but he was a seasoned and zestful campaigner, perhaps the only easily recognizable "celebrity" in the pack, the only one who could walk into a political reception and get all the hands out of the shrimp tray to shake his. He was, in fact, a kind of white-shoe Hubert Humphrey.

Sarge Shriver was not, to say the least, a shrinking violet. On Septem-

---

3. In March 1968, when Robert Kennedy decided to run, for reasons of keeping the family peace he invited Shriver into the campaign. At the time, Shriver was about to go to Paris as ambassador to France for President Johnson—soon to be Kennedy's public foe and long his private adversary, as Shriver, still serving in Johnson's administration after most other Kennedy loyalists had left, well knew. At a somewhat uneasy breakfast meeting at Hickory Hill, Bob Kennedy offered Shriver a campaign job. Shriver said he would have to think it over. Later in the day he phoned and said he was going to Paris. To the Kennedys, the decision meant that Shriver had weighed Bobby's chances and found them wanting.

ber 20, when he finally made his formal entry into the race at a press conference in the ballroom of the Mayflower Hotel in Washington, he unabashedly invoked the Kennedy family name and the yearning for a return to Camelot as a principal rationale for supporting him. With Eunice and his sister-in-law Ethel Kennedy at his side, with old Kennedy and Shriver faithful hanging from the rafters, he said of the late President who was his brother-in-law, "His legacy awaits the leader who can claim it. I intend to claim that legacy not for myself alone but for the family who first brought it into being; the millions who joyfully entered public life with him and the millions of people throughout the world . . . for whom the memory of John Kennedy is an inspiration and a lifting of the heart." This conclusion to his declaration of candidacy was not in Shriver's prepared text, and its boldness in donning the polical mantle of the family surprised those who knew that some Kennedy family members frowned on Shriver's presidential ambitions. But now that Teddy Kennedy had unequivocally removed himself from consideration, Shriver was going all out.

In a sense, it was only simple justice that Shriver should have invoked the Kennedy legacy as his own. For as long as he had been mentioned as a presidential prospect, he had labored—and would continue to labor— under the public perception that he was merely a stalking horse for his brother-in-law. Just as his old family friend Ben Smith had warmed the Senate seat from Massachusetts vacated by President-elect John Kennedy in 1960 until Teddy was old enough and positioned to run for it in 1962, so it was assumed by many that a Shriver candidacy would simply hold the Kennedy constituency from the onslaughts of other liberal Democratic aspirants until such time as Ted Kennedy was ready to claim it for himself. Asked at the press conference whether he would step aside if Kennedy did in fact change his mind and enter the race, Shriver, unsmiling, shot back, "Somebody said, 'Wouldn't everybody?' " It was "a source of sadness" to him that his brother-in-law did not choose to run, he said, but "we ought to take him at his word, let him alone and get on with the business of selecting the candidate." But the stalking-horse problem was destined to plague Shriver throughout his forlorn candidacy.

The last liberal candidate to make his intentions known in 1975 was, in some ways, the left-of-center Democrat with the best combination of political credentials—organizational ability and support and personal campaign magnetism—Senator Birch Bayh of Indiana. At forty-seven, Bayh was a seasoned campaigner elected to the Senate three times over tough Republican opponents in a state generally regarded as a conservative Republican bastion. Bayh, blue-eyed, boyishly handsome with a Tom Sawyer style to go with his physical attributes, parlayed his gee-whiz, aw-gosh politicking into a position in the Senate from which he built a record of achievement that often was obscured by the very barefoot-boy image he projected. As chairman of a judiciary subcommittee on constitutional amendments he became the chief architect of the Twenty-fifth Amendment that determined selection of a Vice President in the event of a vacancy (ironically, the vehicle for ascencion to the presidency of the man, Gerald Ford, Bayh now sought to displace). He also was a chief sponsor of the Equal Rights Amendment, and that fact won him the support of women's groups the country over, as well as the (predominantly female) opposition of ERA foes. Finally, also within judiciary, Bayh claimed leadership of the successful fights against the Supreme Court nominations of Clement F. Haynsworth, Jr., of South Carolina in 1969 and G. Harrold Carswell of Florida in 1970, two stinging defeats to Richard Nixon's effort to make the Court more conservative—and to make political hay in Dixie.

Bayh had begun a presidential candidacy in 1971 (under the political direction of Robert Keefe, who in 1975 ran Jackson's campaign), and, strong with both orthodox and reformist labor, he had been given an outside chance for the nomination. But his wife, Marvella, then the stereotype of the ambitious woman behind the ambitious man, was hospitalized with breast cancer, and he was obliged to drop out. Afterward, according to Bayh associates, Mrs. Bayh as a result of her experience came away with a new outlook on life. She felt she had her own life to lead and, if the truth were known, became resentful about the career for her husband that earlier she had pushed so singlemindedly. "How much does a person have to give?" she asked one of her husband's aides when the time came to consider another presidential race, shortly after Bayh had survived another tough re-election campaign in the fall of 1974. "I've given enough." She started a television show of her own in Washington and became very active in volunteer work against cancer. "She decided her life was going to be her life," this insider said later. "She was going to do some of the things that she felt were important to her. Most of her life, she felt, she was helping him serve the public, and life was too short."

For this and other reasons, Bayh dragged his feet on making a firm decision, and on starting to build an organization, through most of 1975. His press secretary and chief political staff adviser, Bill Wise, in December 1974 had written him a memo telling him that if he wanted to be President, 1976 was his year and why. But there was no response. He was exhausted from the 1974 campaign, in which he barely beat then Mayor Richard Lugar of Indianapolis, and he wasn't convinced the field was open. Finally, when he was persuaded that "nobody really was putting it together," Wise said later, he agreed to start organizing. In early August a Bayh committee registered with the Federal Election Commission. But by this time all the other candidates who were contenders in the first phase of the 1976 competition were already in the field, busy raising money and signing up the experienced political hands. Birch Bayh was late getting out of the gate, and the political and psychological pressures that such a circumstance engendered took their toll. "It took me a long time to come to grips with doing it," Bayh said retrospectively, long after Carter's nomination. "Marvella was not excited about it, but she went along with it. Once I made a decision I put in twenty-hour days." But in 1976, against Carter and the liberal field, even that would prove not to be enough.

In the third week of October 1975, on his farm in Shirkieville, Indiana, Bayh officially took the plunge. For sheer corn, the scene rivaled anything Bayh had ever done in the past, and it was a perfect beginning for his heavy-on-the-trappings, light-on-the substance campaign. He arrived with Marvella and spent nearly thirty minutes pushing through the assembled crowd of hayshakers. Billed as a little courtesy visit by Bayh with his rural neighbors before going to Indianapolis for his formal announcement in the state capitol, the Shirkieville caper was a full-blown media event, complete with a red-and-white tent, under which the candidate aw-shucksed his way into the presidential race. "Those of you who know me longest here know," he said with a straight face, "I've never had a burning desire to be President of the United States. . . . I felt closer to my God and I felt more fulfilled out in these fields than anything else I've done."[4] Then a motorcade whisked Bayh and the assembled press corps east for about an hour's drive to Indianapolis, where he pledged to "restore moral leadership to the White House." The prime polyester candidate was now in the race and the campaign could go forward, assured that not a cliché would be left unspoken or an opportunity for the banal left untapped.

Even before the early 1976 field on the left was completed with the formal candidacy of Bayh, the Democratic Party's liberal activists set about trying to sort out the applicants, well aware that failure to do so would diminish the impact of any liberal candidate in the 1976 primaries. Under the leadership of Representative Donald Fraser of Minnesota, chairman of Americans for Democratic Action, the liberals—essentially ADA and the labor reformers who had been active and effective at the Kansas City mini-convention—held a series of regional conferences in the fall of 1975, to which all the declared or prospective candidates were invited. In the first,

---

4. A few weeks later, at a dinner meeting with political reporters, Bayh was needled unmercifully about his "closer to God" remark. He insisted it had been genuine, but said that on reflection it probably had been a mistake to say it and he wouldn't say it again—"at least to guys like you."

in Minneapolis, Harris the populist evangelist elicited the most emotional response, making war on corporate America. But the negative lesson of the candidacy of George McGovern was not lost on the liberal True Believers. Ideas and rhetoric to the left of mainstream American politics, they had learned painfully, inspire too few voters for success in a general election, and are too vulnerable to attack. And so, though they liked Fred Harris, most did not take him seriously, and they combed the rest of the field for a more acceptable, palatable alternative. The process continued in subsequent weekend conferences in Springfield, Massachusetts, Atlanta, Baltimore, and Los Angeles, and in a Democratic National Committee issues forum in Louisville, all without tangible result in winnowing the field.

Thus, all knew as 1976 approached that a survival of the fittest lay ahead for the members of the liberal pack. Unless one of them could emerge in the early caucuses and primaries, liberal party strength would be dissipated among them, providing an opening for some other, less liberal or even conservative, candidate. It was a disconcerting prospect, but one that nevertheless did not in the slightest diminish the liberal competition.

12. The Field on the Right

In the Democratic Party particularly, attempts to categorize politicians as liberal and conservative nearly always encounter protest. Old New Deal liberals especially, whose constancy convinces them they are entitled to the label as much as they ever were, balk at any other characterization. But because the party's left has moved steadily further out on the ideological spectrum, or perhaps because the center itself has shifted on a wide range of issues, it has become fashionable to refer to these old liberals as moderates or even, alas, conservatives.

One so labeled was Senator Henry (Scoop) Jackson. In twelve years in the House and twenty-two in the Senate, he had been a loyal workhorse of the New Deal, and not surprisingly the name "conservative" bugged the hell out of him. Yet when contrasted with the likes of Udall, Harris, Shriver, Bayh, Sanford, and Shapp, it was inevitable and not altogether unjustified that he was so identified. And in that context, against this overpopulated field on the left, Jackson came in 1975 to be regarded the chief candidate of the right, or at least the middle-right. By his experience in Congress, leadership on critical issues, organization and fund-raising capability, Jackson met the orthodox definition of the front-runner. He had been voted Most Effective Senator by a congressional study group working under Ralph Nader. As chairman of the Senate Interior Committee and the Senate Permanent Investigations Subcommittee, he had status and the wherewithal to extract maximum publicity from major issues that came before his forums. On paper, Scoop Jackson had nearly everything going for him. A confusing array of candidates competed to the left of him, and they were likely, in their competition for the liberal mantle, to diminish the chances for solidarity behind the eventual survivor. On the right, there was Wallace, whose image as an extremist—a Harris survey in May 1975 found—was on the rise again after having lessened in the wake of the attempt on his life in 1972 and his consequent courageous personal struggle to survive. And competing with Jackson for the middle was only the freshman senator from Texas, Lloyd Bentsen, who was widely regarded to be running for President merely in the hope of being nominated for the vice-presidency. Also, Jackson in four years had climbed in terms of voter recognition, from 29 per cent in the Gallup Poll in 1971 to 74 per cent in the Harris Survey by 1975.

To achieve such progress, Jackson had started early, planned well, and worked hard. For at least a year before his formal announcement of candidacy on February 6, 1975, he had been taking careful aim on 1976. With his Senate administrative assistant and chief political adviser, Sterling Munro, in charge, Jackson through most of 1974 had traveled the standard old-line Democratic circuit—organized labor, the American Jewish community, veterans organizations—and projected himself as the kind of solid citizen who would bring the party back to sanity after the far-out ideological orgy of the McGovern campaign. Without missing a single important Senate vote and only a handful of minor ones, Jackson prospected on weeknights and weekends among all those old Democratic leaders who felt they had been shunted aside by the "crazies" of the McGovern effort.

At the same time, he embarked on an extremely diligent fund-raising drive designed eventually to free him of that time-consuming and onerous chore in the election year itself. In July 1974 an "exploratory" group, called the Jackson Planning Committee, was created, with leased offices just a few blocks from Jackson's Senate office. The first important staff aide hired was not a political strategist but a professional director of political fund-raising named Richard Kline. Kline is a Californian who in 1972 was Muskie's prime planner for fund-raising. Kline established a battle plan whereby small groups of backers from major cities would come to Washington for private, unpublicized meetings with Jackson in his Senate office. The as-yet-undeclared candidate would personally brief them on his campaign plans and money needs, and they would return to their home cities to get the nucleus of a Jackson organization going. Periodically, private fund-raising dinners in each of the cities were held, with Jackson flying in for the night, making a short speech about his objectives, and socializing. During 1974 the Senate version of the campaign-finance bill under consideration had a maximum individual contribution limit of $3000, and Jackson adopted that figure. Drawing heavily on the Jewish community on the basis of his long-held and vigorously expressed support of Israel, Jackson raised $1,130,728 before the new law, with its lower limit of $1000, became effective at the start of 1975.

That campaign war chest gave Jackson a mighty jump on all the other presidential aspirants—except Wallace, who had an even better money-generating system going for him (which will be discussed shortly). While the others were struggling to get their campaigns started, Jackson was well along the way to raising the money he anticipated he would need, and all through 1975 his emphasis continued to be on fund-raising. Jackson qualified for federal matching funds in December 1975, at the same time as

Wallace, and—with Kline methodically organizing the country, identifying, instructing, and assisting money-raisers—he was able to launch a costly but effective direct-mail effort. These mailings, along with the highly successful dinners in key cities, enabled Jackson to enter 1976 believing he had virtually no money worries. That belief, unfortunately, proved in time to be without basis.

In vote-getting, too, the Jackson organization appeared to be sound. At the end of 1974 Jackson signed on Robert Keefe, then executive director of the Democratic National Committee, to be the political brains of his organization. Keefe, who had run Birch Bayh's aborted presidential campaign in 1971, had strong AFL-CIO connections and in fact was a key tactician in the Committee on Political Education's 1972 drive to elect labor delegates to the Democratic National Convention; choosing not to support any one candidate, COPE instructed its forces to back whoever appeared strongest in any area, the idea being that in a crunch, or stalemate, labor delegates, regardless of whom they were originally pledged to, would come together and help nominate labor's choice at that time. The fact that this strategy failed miserably in 1972 did not diminish Keefe's reputation as a tough political operator. (Just before the 1972 convention, Keefe also became importantly involved in the cabal of bad losers—Humphrey, Muskie, Jackson—who ganged up on McGovern and nearly stole a large share of the California delegation that he had won in a then authorized winner-take-all primary.) A burly, cigar-chomping pol of the old school in his early forties, Keefe was not known for finesse; he was a give-no-quarter money player.

Keefe oversaw the careful, slow building of a political organization, based on all the old Democratic Party power sources—labor, big-city and state leaders. Important figures who had supported Humphrey and Muskie in 1972 were particular Jackson targets in 1975. Like Muskie's campaign of 1972, Jackson's started out looking like a winner—well financed, well organized, with a prominent candidate who had a strong record of accomplishment in Congress.

There was, however, one big question mark, and that was Scoop Jackson himself. For all his experience, and his diligence, and his earnestness, he did not seem to touch people. He impressed them, yes, but he seldom warmed them, seldom made them laugh, seldom made them feel he was someone they would like to have as a friend, or even simply get to know better. He was cordial enough, a ready handshaker and easy smiler, but there was in him at the same time an awkwardness, a sense that inside himself he was ill at ease in the rituals of politics. He seemed so intense, whether in pursuit of facts, or in the interrogation of a witness before his committee, or in the defense of a position, that he could not enjoy himself. He was not exactly humorless, but his humor seemed almost stingy; it never really intruded on his single-minded preoccupation with an issue or argument before him. And he was not a man to appreciate humor; attempts to pull his leg or needle him would more often than not go over his head. He was above all else convinced he was right, and determined to bring the world around to the same conviction—by wearing the world out with his perseverance, if nothing else.

One of his best friends in Seattle, lamenting Jackson's obvious difficulty in warming the press and public, told me this story to illustrate the problem:

The chairman of the board of a well-known dog-food manufacturing company called in his directors, sat them around a long table and, somberly, said to them:

"Gentlemen, we make the best dog food. We use the best ingredients. We have the best container. We have the most attractive label. Why doesn't it sell?"

There was silence in the board room for several minutes, and then a solitary voice was heard at the far end of the table:

"Dogs don't like it."

In all this, Scoop Jackson was very much like another political figure who brought the same impressive but personally antiseptic recomendations for the presidency—Richard Nixon. Like Nixon, Jackson was a workaholic, a man who immersed himself in issue exploration and discussion as if it were a sanctuary, protecting him from the discomfort of casual discourse from which others might draw relaxation. Like Nixon, Jackson was poor at small talk; one most often came away from close-in exposure to him with a sense of relief, like a small boy leaving the dentist's office. It wasn't that he inflicted pain or discomfort, but rather that being around him was usually so stiff and awkward that you would rather be somewhere else. Like Nixon, Jackson had flat and expressionless eyes that gave him a look of cold calculation. Not the shifty look of Nixon—who was so ill at ease and untrusting in the presence of a relative stranger, or of any member of the hated press, that he constantly stole peeks at his interlocutor to gauge what the reaction to him might be—but the look of the hard sell. Jackson on or off the stump fervently peddled his world view—of friends and enemies, of exploiters and exploited, of the Cold War and the New Deal. If the world, and his own country, had gone crazy all around him, he stood firm in the assurance that he still knew who his country's friends and enemies were. If he was distant, it seemed to be because he was preoccupied; the world was a place in which to accomplish goals, not a place for meaningless self-indulgence. That too was a Nixon trademark (though Nixon found plenty of time for, and developed considerable interest in, self-indulgence once he attained his objective).

It was not surprising that one discerned these similarities between Scoop Jackson and Richard Nixon. Their humble origins, austere child-hoods, and adolescence in home environments of strict religious and paren-tal discipline turned each of them out as a no-nonsense striver. As a kid, Jackson won a prize for delivering 74,880 copies of the Everett, Washing-ton, *Herald* "without a single complaint for nondelivery." With a school-teacher-sister's help, he worked his way through the University of Washing-ton, then served briefly as a welfare caseworker, got elected county prosecuting attorney and promptly drove the whorehouses and slot ma-chines out of the rough timber-mill town where his Norwegian-born parents had settled. "It's the Norwegian thing," Jerry Hoeck, an old friend, once told me. "It's drummed into them. You work hard, you build something, your hopes are all pinned to your children. His father was like that. Scoop never had outside interests."

Some professed to see another Nixon-like trait, too. William Prochnau, coauthor of a Jackson biography, liked to recall the time he asked Jackson, who is under five-feet-ten inches, how tall he was. "About six feet," he said Jackson answered. Prochnau went on: "This is the same kind of *macho,* tough-boy stuff behind the scenes that the Nixon tapes revealed. In private, he puts on an air of being one of the boys, slightly salty in his speech, but it comes off unreal. It's all really frightening. I see a lot of psychological things involving his manhood—the military stuff, the toughness toward the Russians."

But there were, certainly, marked differences between Jackson and Nixon. Jackson's public and private lives were impeccable and if he was not exactly one of the boys, he was far more comfortable with strange people, including reporters.

If the two men differed in political background, the difference came only later in life. Nixon had a meteoric rise in politics before losing elections for the presidency and governor of California in successive campaigns. Jackson had a slower but still unbroken string of political successes, never losing an election as he compiled thirty-four years in Congress and winning as much as 85 per cent of the Washington state vote. But then in his first bid for the Democratic presidential nomination in 1972, he had failed miserably, electing in a fool's errand to contest the Florida primary against George Wallace, where he was widely perceived as trying to out-Wallace Wallace on the stormy school-busing issue, and he ran a poor third. He fared even worse a few weeks later, running fifth in the Wisconsin primary, and was through. On the stump outside of his home state, he was dull as dishwater and a whiner to boot, giving way, as his campaign slipped, to carping at his liberal opponents. Not only did he fail to make friends in the electorate; he succeeded in making enemies in the party, to the point that liberals disregarded his New Deal origins and liberal voting record on domestic issues, and painted him as a warmongering conservative; they talked of a walkout if Jackson somehow were nominated in 1976.

But just as Nixon had done after his 1962 gubernatorial defeat in California, Jackson after 1972 took stock in his typically deliberate and thorough way. He concluded that he had not organized early or well enough; that he had not picked his battlegrounds wisely enough; that he had not worked hard enough within the party and among its money-givers. And so, like Nixon in 1967 and 1968, Jackson as early as 1974 set out to create a political operation as fail-safe as could be achieved. With American troop involvement in Vietnam at an end, that sticky issue for him within the party was removed.[1] And with the Middle East oil holdup of the Western countries and the ensuing energy crisis, Jackson's prime issues—support of Israel against the Arab world, U.S. energy independence through development of alternative sources of power, a strong national defense with a suspicious eye to détente with the Russians—were on the nation's front burner. From his positions of power and initiative as chairman of two Senate committees and as a member of the Armed Services Committee, he thrust himself into the forefront of nearly every major issue, foreign and domestic, in which there was any significant political capital. In January 1974, as long lines outside gas stations gave vivid expression to the energy crisis, Jackson called executives of major oil companies onto the carpet and read them out for their excessive profits—this in the full glare of network television. The oil men squealed like stuck pigs, and a number of Jackson's colleagues squirmed at what they thought to be a flight into demagoguery as he bullied his witnesses in a theatrical affair that was sometimes all too reminiscent of Jackson's old foe, Joseph R. McCarthy.

In foreign policy, Jackson came to be regarded as a sort of Democratic secretary of state, jousting regularly with Henry Kissinger over détente and over American dealings with the Russians, especially in the Middle East. In December 1974, when the Russians suddenly declined to go forward with new trade agreements, the Ford administration and some other senators blamed Jackson's earlier insistence on freer emigration for Soviet Jews—the Jackson amendment to the U.S.-Soviet trade bill—as a congressionally

1. A champion of national defense spending and of the armed forces, Jackson had been an unyielding advocate of aid to South Vietnam. But in 1975 he joined the congressional forces that rejected President Ford's request for an eleventh-hour transfusion to the dying regime of Nguyen Van Thieu, which Jackson now called "repressive."

imposed condition. But on balance, the issues and events were going Jackson's way.

Still, the major question for Scoop Jackson remained: could he sell himself in the primaries? It all came down to that: for all the money, organization, and expertise he had assembled, he had to demonstrate that he could succeed in 1976 where he had failed so completely in 1972. He had to demonstrate that he was, after all, a winner. Nixon in 1968 had faced just such a test, with just as many doubters after his 1960 and 1962 setbacks. He had passed it impressively on the strength of a finely honed and financed organization, his ability to sell himself, and the weakness of the opposition in the Republican Party. The only difference was that Nixon's opposition had been limited—first Romney and then Rockefeller and Reagan, and none of them effective—and Jackson's was broad. But most of that opposition was bunched on the left, where there was the potential for divisiveness and resultant ineffectiveness. There were only two others Jackson had to worry about: Bentsen seemed to offer little threat at all; Wallace of course was a headache, but not only for Jackson. And, oh yes, there was also that fellow Carter, floating somewhere between the left and the right.[2]

Lloyd Bentsen's candidacy was, at face value, an exercise in supreme egoism. He had been in the Senate for only four years, in which time he had said or done nothing that might have singled him out as a presidential prospect. He had earlier served a similarly unspectacular six years in the House of Representatives, then had returned to Texas and a highly successful career in the insurance business, before taking on and beating Ralph Yarborough in the Democratic primary, and Nixon's favorite, George Bush, in the general election in 1970.

Perhaps Bentsen's best recommendation was that he looked and sounded like a President straight out of Central Casting. Tall, trim, always tanned, with an easy, ingratiating smile and a cordial manner, Bentsen went to more than thirty states during 1974, trying to convert his personal magnetism, and his generalized pitch as a politician-businessman who could

---

2. In the summer of 1975, as the Democratic field grew ever larger, Jackson's strategists labored to find some way to pull him out of the pack. They came up with what they thought was a novel idea: have Jackson select and announce his running mate even before the 1976 campaign started, and have the two run as a team. The scheme was presented to Jackson and he was intrigued, though concerned about the cost of having to finance two campaigns. If he were going to do it, he told his chief aides, it could only be with someone with whom he felt comfortable.

The idea kicked around for some time, and in the early fall Jackson finally decided on Ed Muskie. He could help Jackson with the liberals and Jackson could get along with him. Arnold Picker, a major Muskie financial backer in 1972 now working for Jackson's candidacy, was the intermediary, and the two senators eventually discussed the matter. After due deliberation, Muskie declined, and Jackson abandoned the whole plan. "Scoop wasn't going to shop around," Bob Keefe said later. "There never was a second pass at anybody."

best cope with the nation's sagging economy, into a realistic candidacy. He had made little impact on the polls at the time of his formal announcement on February 17, 1975, and he made little more in the ten months before the primary competition began. A large Texas fund-raiser in 1974, which produced $350,000, kept him going through that year, and thereafter he labored to build a broader financial base so that he could escape being labeled as a regional candidate. By early 1975 he had raised $1 million (mostly from fellow Texans), more than any other Democrat except Wallace and Jackson, and he qualified easily by year's end for federal matching funds. But politically and psychologically he was on the defensive from the start: about being a Texan; about being a long-time ally of Lyndon Johnson; about being a freshman senator with no legislative achievements; about being rich, and comporting himself as such while campaigning as a Democrat committed to helping the poor and unemployed. (At the Kansas City mini-convention, Bentsen had laid on a huge cocktail party/reception that cost $8000 and served mainly as a reminder of the spending that had marked pre-Watergate politics and had led to the new campaign-reform law. Bentsen had to minimize his Texas fat-cat image if he wanted to broaden his support within the party and the electorate, and this party, which looked much more expensive than the Bentsen campaign owned up to, did nothing toward that end.) While some of the other Democratic hopefuls tried to find ways to achieve "issue identification" with the voters, Bentsen struggled throughout 1975 without achieving any kind of personal identification (in introductions his name sometimes came out "Floyd Bensten," or worse). He seemed little more than a middle-road alternative to Jackson, or a ticket-balancer for a northern liberal presidential nominee.

By early October 1975 Bentsen was obliged openly to trim his objectives. Pulling away from a national strategy—a move that cost him his campaign manager, Ben Palumbo—Bentsen announced he would concentrate on pockets of strength in eight or ten states; he was counting on a stalemated convention that might turn to him. He would run, for example, in upstate New York and downstate Illinois, but not in the liberal bastions of New York City and Chicago; in rural Michigan and Pennsylvania but not in Detroit and Philadelphia; in a string of southern and border states and of course in Texas. If he could demonstrate some support in the North, he contended, and come into the convention with four hundred or five hundred delegates, he would have a chance. Thus, even before the first caucus or primary vote was cast, Bentsen by his own definition had been relegated to the status of a fall-back candidate.

George Wallace, by contrast, seemed to pose a direct and serious threat to Jackson on the right, just as he had done in 1972. Since the nightmare of the assassination attempt against him in a Laurel, Maryland, shopping center in May 1972, Wallace had waged a painful but awe-inspiring fight for his life that, in the process, had also resurrected his political prospects. Confined to a wheelchair, shaking off periods of deep depression, the spunky bantam rooster of American politics underwent rigorous physical rehabilitation that eventually enabled him to stand with the aid of a special brace. Each morning through the dark years of 1972 and 1973 Wallace spent hours lifting himself with his arms in a special device, strengthening his upper torso. As he stood on legs devoid of any feeling, he would cradle a telephone and talk nonstop to political associates around the state and beyond. As ever, he was a man of insatiable political appetite and personal drive. Favored newsmen around Montgomery, and some not favored, became accustomed to receiving his calls, to listening to his monologues about his personal trials, the politics of the state and nation, and his possible role in them. He had always been a driven man, hooked on power as only a man with a limited education and a gnawing inferiority complex could be. Now his handicap compounded his concentration and his drive; if anything, he became more single-minded. His physical comeback, though precarious, demonstrated to him what he could achieve, and it brought him new public acceptance as well as the solicitation of his peers. Teddy Kennedy himself came to Alabama to pay tribute to him, and when Wallace, with the help of his brace, stood unassisted before the throng of proud sons and daughters of Dixie under the bright, hot summer sun, Kennedy along with the rest applauded loud and long. He was what Baltimore's dynamic city councilwoman Barbara Mikulski liked to call "a power junkie," and nothing short of a physical or mental relapse was going to stop him from forcing all those national politicians who used to sneer at him and ridicule him to do business with George Wallace.

Long before Wallace's recovery had reached the stage in 1974 at which anyone outside his own entourage could seriously consider him a realistic prospect for the 1976 presidential race, the machinery to make such a race possible was already gearing up. Wallace had by now run for President three times—in the Democratic primaries of 1964, in which he surprised the nation by receiving a third or more of the vote in Wisconsin, Indiana, and Maryland; as a third-party candidate in 1968, receiving 10 million votes, or 13 per cent of the total; and in the Democratic primaries of 1972, in which he collected the largest popular vote in the preconvention period, up to the time of the attempt on his life. And even before he had made up his mind that he would survive to run again, the power-seekers around him had willed it. I remember well the hot May 1972 night when he was shot, keeping vigil inside the hospital in Silver Spring, Maryland, and watching members of Wallace's entourage bustle through the corridors, shocked and excited. Decked out in their bright-red sports jackets with "Wallace" emblazoned over the breast pocket, they alternated between cursing out the as yet unidentified "they" who had gotten their leader, and almost gleefully anticipating the political future. When word came down that the lengthy surgery on Wallace had been successful and he would live, I heard one Wallaceite turn to another and say, "Now we got a candidate!"

Through those first uncertain months when Wallace's life hung in the balance, his political agents held together the organization known simply as "the Wallace Campaign," and steps were taken to assure the faithful that their man had not surrendered his ambitions to his infirmity. The Wallace newsletter, central to his operation, reported steady progress on his health that did not always square with the assessment of neutral observers in Alabama, and soon the first essential ingredient in a 1976 campaign—the collection of money—was being planned. Richard Viguerie, a Washington professional fund-raiser with dedication to right-wing politics, took on Wallace's account. In eighteen months he raised $2 million by direct mail and spent about that much doing so. But the important fact was that he was "prospecting"—testing various direct-mail lists, filtering out dependable contributors, and building a special Wallace list that eventually totaled some six hundred thousand names. From this list, Wallace eventually was able to raise $6.9 million.

At the headquarters of the Wallace Campaign on the top two floors of a downtown Montgomery office building, six bonded women labored in a special room every day, emptying checks and cash from as many as five thousand envelopes daily, sorting them into piles, and shipping them off to the bank. With the Wallace newsletter, which kept the governor's message of discontent flowing to Middle America, went collection envelopes indicating desired date of return, as if the recipients were tithing to their church. The comparison was not far off: to these hundreds of thousands, George Wallace was their preacher, their evangelist, and his recovery from the jaws of death only confirmed their conviction that he was as well their anointed political savior.

Viguerie's operation carefully computerized all contributions, keeping track of how much each individual gave. The computer flagged any gift that put the giver over the $1000 maximum permitted under the new law, and a letter was quickly dispatched with a reimbursement of the excess, thanking the faithful supporter. (Of all the candidates, Wallace probably benefited most from the new law. Contributions he received were nearly all below the $250 figure that qualified for federal matching funds, and easily met the requirement of raising $5000 in small donations in each of twenty states.

This money-raising operation was impressive, but not surprising. He had always been able to generate cash, even in the leaner days when plastic-looking young girls passed plastic buckets through the crowds at his speeches. What was more notable was the development of a Wallace organization throughout the country, taking dead aim on delegate-selection at the 1976 Democratic convention. While Wallace underwent his daily physical exercises, his political aides set about educating themselves about then-changing party regulations as to how to qualify to be a delegate. Mickey Griffin, a bright and tenacious twenty-seven-year-old who was Wallace's representative on the executive committee of the Democratic National Committee, spent much time in Washington and around the country, learning the various state procedures for getting to the national convention.

These procedures also appeared to benefit Wallace. Some thirty states and the District of Columbia elected to hold presidential primaries in 1976, and this was the delegate-selection process most attractive to him, as one who sought the nomination over the heads of party leaders. Limited by his confinement to a wheelchair, Wallace from the start planned heavy use of television. His staff prepared a video-taped presentation in which Wallace, seated at his desk in Montgomery, urged supporters to become delegates for him or to help others do so. Young aides equipped with portable video-tape projectors then set off to major cities all over the country, showing the film in hotel meeting rooms to supporters garnered from the direct-mail list, explaining to them in detail what they had to do to become Wallace delegates. This attention to local recruitment and organization was new to a Wallace campaign, and it expressed a new seriousness and determination.

Griffin sat in his Montgomery office in April 1975, gleefully anticipating the 1976 primaries. "Bear Bryant [the Alabama football coach] used to call it schedule luck," he said, poring over a tentative list of primary dates. "Well, we got schedule luck in '76. There's not a single place where we can't do exceptionally well, even if the Governor doesn't go in there. It's not only what we do in this period but what the others do. Who's going to beat us in these places? . . . This is the fold-up period, and we feel maybe nobody will be left but us after it."

That was bold talk, and what it got down to was a belief that the governor would be not simply a troublemaker for the other candidates in 1976 but the presidential nominee—possibly on the first ballot! Griffin leaned back, looked at a wall map with pins in the primary states, and spelled out the reason for his high optimism. First, five "Wallace states" that had not had primaries in 1972 would have them in 1976—Alabama, Mississippi, Georgia, Louisiana, and Arkansas. Second, the schedule strung together between March and May a host of states in which Wallace had fared exceptionally well in 1972: Florida (he trounced the field there), Wisconsin (he was a surprising second with little effort), Pennsylvania (second, after one night's visit), Indiana (second, only a whisker behind Humphrey), Tennessee (first), North Carolina (first), Maryland (first), Michigan (first).

Griffin and Wallace's campaign manager, a forty-three-year-old former pilot and home-builder named Charles Snider, labored under no illusions that their man could be nominated by anything short of a display of political muscle. Their goal was 1505 delegates—a majority—though Griffin said he could foresee the circumstance whereby Wallace might make a deal with somebody like Jackson, at either end of the ticket. The consensus in Montgomery seemed to be that Wallace would settle for the second spot on the Democratic ticket, but was prepared to run as a third-party candidate again if turned away altogether. "I'm running as a Democrat," Wallace himself told me in his office at the Capitol, "but I'm not ruling anything out." Snider speculated that a Wallace-Reagan or Reagan-Wallace ticket was not out of the question. "They do have things in common," he told me, smiling.

Toward this possible end, Viguerie while raising money for Wallace also was doing the same for a new right-wing group called the Conservative Caucus, headquartered in the same building where Viguerie had his office in Falls Church, Virginia, a Washington suburb. Masterminded by Howard Phillips, given a contract by the Nixon administration in 1973 to rub out the Office of Economic Opportunity, the Conservative Caucus sought to create units in all 435 congressional districts to raise the prime issues of the right. Not coincidentally, these units would come together in convention shortly after the Democratic convention in 1976 and, Phillips allowed, conceivably might select a presidential candidate. His preference was Reagan, but he said he could live with Wallace, and so could Viguerie, avowing the death of the Republican Party as irreparably tainted by Watergate and Nixon.

It was as a Democrat, however, that Wallace posed the initial problem to the broad field of hopefuls within the party. By the time the nation's governors met in New Orleans in the second week of June 1975, "Get Wallace" had become the favorite game. Not only liberals, but such Southern governors as William Waller of Mississippi and Edwin Edwards of Louisiana, who saw him as a threat to their own home-base dominance, publicly questioned his ability to campaign or serve in the presidency. Wendell Anderson of Minnesota said, "I am not going to support any candidate who is not willing to commit himself in advance to the nominee

sight unseen. . . . Governor Wallace's track record on party loyalty is zero."
Reubin Askew agreed. Wallace replied with typical aplomb: "I wonder if
all these national leaders want to say that they will support me if I am the
nominee. I don't know that I ought to take a loyalty oath when a lot of the
leaders of the party say they can't support me."

It was a situation that delighted the tough little Alabamian. A day or
two after the governors' conference began, two other reporters and I were
interviewing Wallace in his suite at the Fairmont Hotel. As he sat in his
wheelchair, twisting a long cigar in the fingers of his left hand, we asked
him about the growing stop-Wallace phenomenon, and specifically Terry
Sanford's overtly anti-Wallace candidacy.

"You want to write down my reaction to that?" Wallace inquired.

"Yes, sir, I've got my pad out," his interrogator said, holding his pencil
at the ready and looking down at his pad.

Wallace yawned. The reporter didn't see the reaction, and, when he
heard nothing, finally looked up quizzically.

"I yawned," the governor told him, amused. "I just yawn at all this
business."

No one in American political life can better convey contempt for the
opposition than George Wallace. He knew that he was becoming the prime
target of the other Democrats because they feared his real or potential
strength, and because they recognized that his head on a platter would bring
a great bounty in support from grateful party leaders, especially on the left.
"They're stepping up the interest in beating me," Wallace said, "and I
haven't even announced yet. I must have some support out there. . . .
Everybody's attacking me. Everybody's kicking my dog."

And so they were. Basking in the spotlight, and running ahead of all
other Democrats in the Gallup Poll, Wallace delayed a planned formal
announcement of candidacy, sat back, puffed on his cigar, and let the others
go at it.[3] He would remain in Montgomery, attend to the business of
Alabama, and await the time when he could take his case to the voters, to
what he called "the great, gutsy middle class" of Americans, ignored and
misunderstood by all politicians save himself.

Through all this, Wallace's health continued to be a matter of constant
discussion, rumor, and—for those who most feared his political potential
—wishful thinking. Reports that Wallace was periodically in the throes of
deep depression, contemplating a decision to bypass the 1976 election cam-

---

3. At the end of March 1975 Wallace, according to the Gallup Poll, was the first choice for
the presidential nomination of 22 per cent of Democrats. Humphrey, not a declared candidate,
was second with 16 per cent, and Jackson third with only 13 per cent.

paign altogether, emanated regularly from Montgomery. Other candidates like Udall and Sanford asked aloud whether the governor could stand the rigors of the campaign. In July, when he suffered a broken leg while being moved about in his wheelchair, Sanford speculated that Wallace might skip the Democratic primaries and run only in the general campaign as a third-party candidate again. But Wallace's own actions and words belied such a strategy. "We have a movement in this country," he told the people of North Carolina, appealing to them to preserve the primary in their state, "to remove the average man, the tobacco workers, the textile workers, to remove the truck driver and beautician and the barber and the waitress and the little businessman and farmer from the process of having a voice in the nomination for the presidency of the United States." The argument worked, the legislature backed down about repealing the primary, and so did others in Louisiana and Tennessee, where he also made the same pitch in person. The exercise was a prime example of why other Democrats viewed Wallace with such trepidation. Once again George Wallace was taking on "the establishment," "the hierarchy," on behalf of the folks, undeterred by the gang-up tactics used against him.

Still, Wallace was apparently reluctant at times. Before his declaration, he held a large meeting in Montgomery of all his leading backers from around the country. He sat them around a large table and for an hour or more asked each in turn what he should do. They all said, of course, that he had to run. Finally his brother, Gerald, more aggressively concluded, "God damn, George! You gotta do it!" Wallace listened as his brother ranted on for a few more minutes. "Gerald," he said, "why don't you go out and get your ass shot at, get bricks thrown at you, with your wife at one end of the country and you at the other. You give me your list of girls you see at all the bars in town, and I'll stay here." The meeting broke up without Wallace's committing himself.

As Wallace's threat was viewed more seriously, his actual political beliefs came under closer scrutiny. In March 1975 he had been visited by a delegation of foreign journalists, and two months later a transcript of his freewheeling monologue on the state of U.S. relations with its old World War II adversaries, Germany and Japan, made its way into the hands of *The Washington Post*. "I think we were fighting the wrong people, maybe, in World War II," Wallace suggested at one point, and later he told a Japanese correspondent that "I wish we'd been on the same side in World War II." The *Post*'s story—which ran these two comments together and drew a rebuke from the paper's own ombudsman as denying Wallace a fair shake—precipitated a controversy that focused public attention anew on his lack of foreign-policy experience. This and other Wallace monologues on the subject demonstrated once again he was a simplistic and unreconstructed Cold Warrior (at one point he suggested that in its excessive concern over totalitarianism, the West had given communism a free ride to global power). As ever, though, Wallace brushed off the criticism and continued to preach and practice the politics of negativism, employing the old tactic of a strong offense as the best defense.[4]

Still, he was sensitive to his shortcomings on foreign policy. And in mid-October he set off on a six-country, two-week tour of Europe, his very first. Aboard a chartered British jet, Wallace traveled to meet British Prime Minister Harold Wilson and the Tory leader Margaret Thatcher, Belgian Prime Minister Leo Tindemans, Italian President Giovanni Leone and Premier Aldo Moro, West German Foreign Minister Hans-Dietrich Genscher and French Minister of Industry Michel d'Ornano—but he was pointedly snubbed by West German Chancellor Helmut Schmidt, French President Valéry Giscard d'Estaing and Pope Paul VI. (Wallace, ever resourceful, dismissed the snubs by acknowledging the protocol—they were all heads of state and he wasn't.)

It was perhaps the strangest overseas odyssey made by a prominent American politician. He permitted no reporters to accompany him—begging, without justification, lack of space on his plane. But he did find space, however, for a number of old cronies, including two men linked to the John Birch Society who at first were billed as "foreign-policy advisers" but later, when their identities became known, as just old friends along for the ride.

Throughout, Wallace was on his best behavior, careful not to make a slip that would cause him to be embarrassed. "I hope I don't commit any foxpaws in Europe," he was overheard saying to a friend as he left a Brussels hotel. And he tried hard to be a gracious visitor—as in Belgium, which he described as "this fine small country, which has sent a number of people to Alabama."

During and after the trip Wallace declined to discuss the substance of any of his talks in detail. "What's good for Western Europe is good for the United States and vice versa," he said repeatedly to questions. He acknowledged at one point that his talks were "mainly courtesy calls" and that a major reason he was in Europe was simply to be able to say he had been there. "So many of you folks have written that Wallace never was abroad,"

---

4. Wallace's habit of turning criticism around was no better illustrated than in his response when liberal Democratic hopefuls began assailing his record in Alabama, focusing on such matters as its regressive tax structure and near-bottom rating in public education. Coming at a time when New York City was facing a fiscal crisis, Wallace observed, "The City of New York has taken the advice of *The New York Times* all these years and has finally gone completely broke. The least thing you can say about Alabama is that we're not about to close down."

he told one reporter. "Well, I've been abroad now. That's the main thing I'll say [when I return], that I've been abroad now." There was, as well, the idea of showing Wallace-in-wheelchair touring the capitals of Europe without flagging in health—to underline his ability to campaign and, if elected to the presidency, to serve. In other words, the whole trip was a Grand Tour in public relations.

The surprising thing was how little Wallace seemed to enjoy the experience. When he was back home, I went down to Montgomery to interview him, and I asked how Europe impressed him. "I've seen Europe on television," he told me, "and thousands of Europeans, so really it was nothing new to me. You can learn as much about going abroad by watching and reading news, and reading books and stories and publications, as you can by seeing some concrete walls, a few automobiles in traffic jams and some scenery."

Unable to believe that Europe had so little effect on a man seeing the Continent for the first time at the age of fifty-six, Tom Ottenad of the *St. Louis Post-Dispatch* and I tried in every way we could think of to get him to talk more. But it was like pulling teeth, and he kept reverting to American matters. When I asked him how he felt when he saw the infamous Berlin Wall, he said it convinced him "we live under the best system right here." What about the food, the sights, the languages? No response. An aide allowed that Wallace and his wife, Cornelia, had slipped off with several Secret Service agents for "a romantic little dinner" at Maxim's and reported later that the highlight was—being recognized by Christina Onassis. Wallace summed it all up when I asked him whether he had gone to determine whether he had the strength to run for President. "I was more interested in showing you," he replied. "I already knew."

The trip was, nevertheless, a milestone on Wallace's road to candidacy. A little while earlier Snider had prepared a detailed black book crammed with information on what had been done to organize and finance Wallace's 1976 national campaign, down to the names and addresses of individuals ready to run for nearly two thousand convention-delegate seats in the primary states. Wallace read the book while he was in Europe, and on his return to Montgomery he gave the final go-ahead. "The governor said to me," Snider confided, " 'I'm sitting here in this wheelchair. I'm not going to run unless I've got a chance to be elected President of the United States.' " The black book was persuasive.

And so, on November 12, at a press conference at the Governor's Mansion Motel in Montgomery, the Little Judge made it official. A large exhibition hall was used, with a wide door to the outside that permitted Wallace's car to drive directly in, so he would have to be pushed in his wheelchair only a short distance to the speaker's podium, which was bedecked with fresh flowers. The announcement was timed for live television and Wallace was armed with a long text, which, predictably, he discarded as soon as he was on the air. In its place, he launched into his patented harangue, pledging to wrest the Democratic Party from the "ultra-liberal, exotic left-wing few" who had seized it. The prime issue was "the survival and salvation of the middle class," and he called on "average Americans" to join him in "a political revolution of the ballot box in the primaries in 1976." Addressing the question of his fitness to campaign, he said with voice rising that he was in "excellent" health and "able to campaign actively and I do not care what they say." The faithful packed into the hall cheered at this, and when a reporter asked Wallace whether he would submit to a medical examination conducted by a special board, many in the crowd booed. Wallace didn't hear the question, and his wife, Cornelia, sitting at his side, repeated it to him in an audible whisper. Then, adding her own two cents, she complained: "It's an insult to your own physicians." Wallace took up the cue. "When you talk about independent doctors," he said, "it's really an insult to some of the best in the country." But he added, "If all the other candidates want to submit to this board, I'll consider it. But my health is all right. In fact, people ask me, do I get tired? I'll tell you what I get tired of. I get tired of you asking me about my health."

The announcement event was full of hokum, as Wallace events always were. Willie Murphy of Cleveland, president of the Hard Hats of America, was on hand to present a construction helmet to Wallace, and a band whooped up the crowds before and after the speaking. The trappings were the same as always, but behind them was a craftier Wallace, a better-organized Wallace, a more positive-sounding Wallace. Gone was the 1972 slogan "Send Them a Message." In its place was the 1976 version: "Trust the People."[5] But the essential ingredient remained the man himself, stirring emotions and dissatisfactions with his provocative oratory.

Wallace thus became the tenth declared Democratic candidate, and the last of 1975. Until the state caucus and primary competition actually began in 1976, the American voters at large generally ignored the entire business.

5. Cornelia Wallace added a homey touch to her husband's campaign at Christmastime when she sent holiday greetings to three hundred thousand folks on the Wallace mailing list, suggesting what they could give George for Christmas: money. "I think the most wonderful gift for my husband would be to know he will have the money he needs for a successful presidential campaign in 1976," she wrote. He was going to have a big television bill in the coming year, she noted, adding: "If only this heavy financial burden could be eased by Christmas, George would have a wonderful relaxing and worry-free holiday. I don't want to suggest what amount you should send as a gift. Let your heart decide in this most joyous of seasons." Sure enough, joyous hearts coughed up some $140,000 to make Wallace's Christmas merry, according to his campaign reports.

They were disillusioned with politics, and the aftertaste of Watergate was still with them. But *aficionados* observed it all with a kind of morbid fascination—waiting to see which of the gladiators would be devoured first, and how.

Of these onlookers, none had a greater interest than three men of the past—Humphrey, Muskie, and McGovern. If all the active combatants managed to do each other in, then the party might once again examine this pack of old warhorses to find a standard-bearer. This prospect was a forlorn one, but the theory of a brokered convention was still at large. Hard as it may have been for the rational mind to comprehend, flickers of hope still lived in these three oft-pummeled political breasts, as we shall see.

13. Wishful Thinkers

All through 1975, the unlucky triumvirate of George Mc-Govern, Edmund Muskie, and Hubert Humphrey remained in a holding pattern of availability. They harbored no great expectations but allowed themselves moments of daydreaming—especially when asked, as they often were.

The three were, in a sense, a hapless trio of burned-out national power-seekers. McGovern, after a remarkable campaign in which he parlayed the flaming issue of Vietnam and a dedicated band of young organizers and ideologues into the 1972 Democratic nomination, was perhaps the most politically scarred. His mishandling of the selection and then discarding of Tom Eagleton as his running mate and his inability to satisfactorily explain the Demogrant plan helped Richard Nixon avoid any real campaign accounting for Watergate, and buried him. All those regular Democrats who had contributed to the depth of his defeat by refusing to support him now treated him as some sort of political leper, ridiculing both the man and his positions, and using his defeat as justification to turn the party away from the many valid social-welfare reforms he advocated. The circumstance made McGovern, who was an introspective but often stubborn man, a brooding figure on Capitol Hill thereafter. For all the vindication that the Watergate revelations later brought him, he resisted the temptation to say —as he could have—that he had told the country in the 1972 campaign what sort of man Nixon was. He held his tongue, took the ridicule and—sometimes—seethed.

Muskie, also somewhat humiliated by a 1972 performance in which he was rated the odds-on favorite, only to be brought down by McGovern and by his own inability to develop any deep, committed political base, seemed to settle back more easily into the Senate routine. Muskie was a detail man; the life of the Senate committee was more conducive to his life-style than the dawn-to-midnight harried existence of the campaigner. Yet he too felt that 1972 had dealt him some bad cards. His own campaign had been the subject of sabotage by Nixon dirty-tricks agents, and he felt he had been unfairly painted as the front-runner, thereby raising unrealistic expectations for his candidacy. And so as 1976 approached, he too inevitably gave some thought to a second try. As was typical of him, he would never say straight out that he yearned after the presidency or would reach for it again, but he had been smitten by Potomac Fever once, and there has never been any sure immunization against the bug.

Humphrey, of the three, had gotten closest to the White House and had, for all his own shortcomings and setbacks, maintained the esteem of his party. He too had been disappointed by his failure to be nominated in 1972, after having come so close to election in 1968, but the eternal torch of Athens had nothing on Hubert Humphrey. He had more bounce and comeback in him than a rubber ball; there was something in the man that depression and defeat simply could not conquer, or even suppress for long. Those who did not know him well might have supposed that his buoyancy, his good cheer, his indestructability of spirit was an act, but it was not. Hubert Humphrey could no more stay down than a cork could sink; it seemed at times as if he had helium in his lungs, not just the mere air breathed by other mortals. And at the end of 1975 he did not kid himself about his chances, but he didn't quite turn up his nose at the prospect that his party might turn to him again. He wasn't going after it; he was having a grand time in the Senate. But he wasn't running away from it either.

McGovern, somewhat disdainful of the active candidates, had told me in February 1975 that he thought he could put his 1972 coalition together again, although it would be more difficult without the issue of Vietnam as a touchstone. If the party turned to him, he said, he would not make the mistake of trying to broaden his base to the point of alienating his original support. Unity in the Democratic Party was neither desirable at any cost nor even possible, given its ideological spectrum and splits. "I would try to stay with a clearly defined position," he said in his Senate office, "and go after the Independents and Republicans, without trying to unite all Democrats. I don't think it's possible to unite the Democratic Party around questions that are meaningful in terms of what the country needs. You'll always alienate forces within the party. I think there's a majority coalition out there. Maybe I backed off my positions too much in the general election. I should have stuck with the thousand-dollar welfare proposal."

Muskie, the very next day, said that he too had made a mistake in 1972 in trying to reach out to a new constituency—in his case what he called the party's New Left—and had "caught hell from my labor friends, my regular party friends." But he thought the party could be unified, with Vietnam stilled and economics a burning topic. "I don't see any great issue dividing the party right now," he said. "Nothing that has the divisive impact of the war. The Democratic Party almost always unifies around economic issues. Economic issues always give people an excuse to get together." Still, he remained the supreme procrastinator. "I think it is essential that I meet my commitment to the people of Maine," he said, looking ahead to a Senate re-election campaign in 1976. (And he had just taken on the chairmanship of a new Senate budget committee that would make great demands on him.)

Humphrey, bouncing back after his 1975 surgery and throwing himself with customary vigor into his Senate duties, said that he had had enough of racing around the country. "I'm so sick of asking people for money for political campaigns," he said. "I want to vomit every time I think of it." He noted with mock dismay that "my timing has always been off." Under the new campaign-reform law, pursuing fat cats for large contributions was out. But for all that, Humphrey made it clear what would happen if his party's call came: "If that happened to me," he said, brightening, "I wouldn't say no. I'd say, 'Let's go, boys. Let's get this show on the road.' "

Humphrey said he didn't believe there would be a stalemated convention. The primaries had a way of shaking out a candidate, he said, and it would probably happen in 1976 too. McGovern and Muskie didn't necessarily agree, except on one thing—each said he thought in such a circumstance the party would turn with least contention to Humphrey.

By the summer of 1975, with the stalemate theory still current, that same consensus seemed to be emerging amongst all shades of Democrats. McGovern held several meetings with his 1972 aides, and each time they put a damper on his reviving presidential ambitions. As for Muskie, he still had no taste for the effort, only for the prize. If there was to be a fall-back candidate, it would be Humphrey. Liberals who could not abide Humphrey in 1968 and even less in 1972 were looking at him, absent Vietnam, with a kind of nostalgic forgiveness, even fondness. "We could do worse than old Hubert," one of them told me, and that sentiment was echoed repeatedly as summer approached. One morning in late July, as I was walking across the Capitol Plaza, I spied Humphrey—jaunty in a bright plaid sport jacket and burgundy slacks—accompanied by Bill Connell, his old 1968 and 1972 campaign lieutenant. I caught up and told them what I had been hearing. "We were just talking about that," Humphrey said, smiling happily. "Can you beat it? After all I've done to get it. What was the name of that old show —*How to Succeed in Business without Really Trying.* That's it. Well, there's only one thing to do"—and the Humphrey jaw jutted out now—"you do your job and stick to it." Hubert Humphrey, like a ghost from the past, his emotional batteries recharged, at sixty-four only two years older than the incumbent President, was ready and waiting.

As summer and then fall passed, it was heard again and again: "We could do worse than Hubert." By late October he had moved ahead of Wallace in the Gallup Poll as the first choice among Democrats. Quietly,

Humphrey started to settle $925,000 in 1972 campaign debts for as little as three or four cents on a dollar; friends established a special Triple H Committee to pay off the debt, and they were obviously looking ahead to a 1976 campaign—though as the party nominee Humphrey would be entitled to $21.8 million in federal money after the convention. At the annual AFL-CIO convention, Humphrey was cheered and mobbed as if he were a Kennedy in the old days; it came to be known as the "Humphrey Phenomenon," and he deftly and coolly nursed it.

One afternoon in late October I had lunch with him in the Senate Dining Room in the Capitol, and on the way over from his office and in the private dining room itself, he was implored repeatedly: "Senator, why don't you run for President again?" He was tickled by it all, yet the irony was not lost on him. "It's like everything got backward in my life," he said. "At a time when the money-raising would be the least difficult because of the public financing, and when there seems to be more support and the issues are best made for me, I find myself personally not wanting to make that challenge. It just doesn't sound like Hubert Humphrey, but that's the way it is."

That attitude on Humphrey's part suited the active candidates just fine. The first primary in New Hampshire was still more than four months off, but they were raring to go. On the day in early October when Governor Thomson was cooperatively putting himself on the side lines of Reagan's campaign by leaving for Israel, six of the Democratic presidential aspirants dutifully trooped into Manchester.

They held press conferences, visited local schools and civic clubs through the day and then took part in a showcase reception and dinner thrown by the state Democratic committee. Each of them—Udall, Carter, Shriver, Bayh, Harris, and Shapp—was allotted ten minutes to show his stuff, and each, as expected, took much more. Billed as the "official" kickoff of the 1976 Democratic primary campaign, all those present treated the evening as such, vying oratorically to best the field, like a bunch of high-school sophomores in a debating contest.

Shriver, just back from a candidates' obligatory pre-election-year trip to Moscow, presented himself as some sort of special emissary from the Kremlin, telling of his person-to-person conversations with the Russian mighty, hinting that he had broken new ground in arms-limitation negotiations, and even reporting he had won concessions for worship by Catholics in the Soviet Union with the prospective appointment of a French-American priest from New England. It was an extremely ill-timed, everything-but-the-kitchen-sink pitch, and the campaign-wise New Hampshirites recognized it for that. Bayh served up his customary country-boy-with-a-dream speech, the Jack-Kennedy-of-the-Midwest gambit, and it seemed to go over, with the young in the audience especially. Carter, too, delivered one of his better speech-sermons, drawing with the quiet warmth of his message a sharp and impressive contrast to Shriver's shrill hucksterism. As it often did when he spoke, a strange calm came over the audience as he talked of America's basic goodness, a decency only temporarily obscured by the debasings perpetuated by Nixon, Agnew, et al. He was applauded only at the end, and then almost as if the act of clapping intruded into the prevailing mood. His essentially nonideological and inspirational message was both theatrical and tactical—though the tactic of almost imperceptibly splitting himself off from the liberal field was not yet generally appreciated.

When the night of speechmaking was over, only one thing was clear: the struggle for the liberal heart of the Democratic Party would have to be fought out in scores of these forums before any one candidate emerged. So diffused was the effect of their presence, that, in fact, one couldn't be sure that a liberal consensus would result at all. Accordingly, the "Humphrey Phenomenon" tenaciously held on. (Before the year was out, at least two unauthorized Humphrey campaigns were under way. One, organized by a New Hampshire sales promoter, asked for a write-in vote in the New Hampshire primary; another, more serious, put together by Democratic Representative Paul Simon of Illinois, undertook to rally other congressmen behind a Humphrey draft at the convention.)

No one was more distressed about this situation than George McGovern. A couple of weeks before the large National Democratic Issues Convention in Louisville, McGovern's secretary called me and said the senator would like me to join him for lunch at the Capitol. When I arrived at his office, it became clear after a few moments of conversation that the party's 1972 standard-bearer, for all his disavowals of candidacy, was still champing for another try. In a speech in Ames, Iowa, a few weeks earlier, he had strongly urged the assembled candidates not to mistake his own 1972 defeat, for which he personally assumed total responsibility, as a repudiation by the voters of legitimate, still valid liberal objectives. And on the flight back to Washington from Iowa the next morning, he and I talked briefly about the speeches made by other candidates in Ames. McGovern was unconvinced that they were saying the right things; it was hard for him to acknowledge openly that he thought he was still best qualified to bring the liberal agenda before the American people, but that was clearly how he felt.

As we rode from his office in the Senate subway to the private Senate Dining Room, it came tumbling out. He was determined, McGovern said, to maintain his voice and views in the party, and the best way, obviously, was to be the party's nominee. But how could he even reach for it? First of all, he had pledged, during his difficult campaign for re-election to the Senate in 1974, that he would not seek the presidency again. Second, all those people who had worked for him faithfully and with dedication in 1972 and who were still his supporters had signed on with other candidates, in the belief that he would not run. How could he put them through the personal anguish of breaking away and joining him again, and, indeed, how many of them could or would?

We took seats at a table in a far corner of the dining room and McGovern laid out the alternatives. If he jumped into the primaries now, he would not only put the squeeze on his old supporters but antagonize the other active candidates and shatter any hope of party unity. Yet it plainly pained him that his old friend Hubert, with whom he had now reached an accommodation of sorts and whom he plainly admired as a campaigner, might become the automatic beneficiary of a preconvention stalemate. It was George McGovern, not Hubert Humphrey, who had been right on the war, right on the criminality of Richard Nixon, whose administration he had repeatedly called "the most corrupt in American history." And the party activists who would be the driving force of the state caucuses and primaries would be largely old McGovernites, not Humphreyites. The party convention, he reasoned, would be peopled with McGovernites for Udall, for Shriver, for Harris, for Bayh, and so on. If each group could not get its own man, wouldn't they just as likely opt for George McGovern as for a man they had ardently opposed in 1972?

The problem was, McGovern said, how to position himself as the alternative to Humphrey at such a convention. As a reporter I was not in the business of advising politicians, but I confirmed his own view that competing with the declared candidates in the primaries was suicidal. Perhaps the most he could do was project himself outside the primary competition as an alternative voice to Humphrey's in the party. To that end, McGovern told me, he was planning another speech somewhat like the one he had made in Iowa, in which again he would call on the declared candidates to face up courageously to the liberal agenda. That seemed to me, I told him, the best he could do under the circumstances.

As we finished lunch, and later as we walked back to his Senate office, McGovern reflected on the unhappy circumstances that had led to his overwhelming defeat in 1972. He had been buried, after all, under an avalanche of dirty political money, the most massive bankroll ever raised and spent in an American political campaign. Not to mention the Nixon dirty tricks. People weren't aware of all that at the time, he said, but they were aware now, and wherever he went, they exhorted him to run again. He tried not to be affected by such personal encounters, but it wasn't easy.

We recalled his early days in New Hampshire in 1970 and 1971 when he practically had to pay people to listen to him; there was one breakfast meeting in Dover at which five people showed up, and he sat with them at one end of a horseshoe-table arrangement and discussed the country's problems for the appointed hour. Things had changed since then; now he was readily recognized everywhere. It was hard to turn his back on all that, hard to resist picking up the pieces and trying one more time. Especially when Humphrey, who had been so wrong on so many issues for so long, seemed to be positioned to have the big prize fall in his lap.

We were back in McGovern's Senate office now, and he seemed not to want to break away. He asked me to sit down; he wanted to tell me something, off the record (only now, after the 1976 campaign is over, has he lifted the prohibition).

A few months earlier, he had been out in the Midwest and had received a call from Humphrey, asking him and his wife, Eleanor, to stop off at the Humphrey home in Waverly, Minnesota. They went, and had a good day's talk about the past and present. They got to reflecting about how their individual paths had crossed and intersected, and how, ironically, each of them had been victims of Richard Nixon—Humphrey in 1968, McGovern in 1972. Except for a handful of votes in 1968, and for all the Watergate shenanigans in 1972, each might have been President. Instead, each lost and the Democratic Party was badly damaged. It would be appropriate if somehow they could now be the architects of party unity, which both men said they wanted above all else. Suddenly McGovern had a brainstorm. Why, he asked Humphrey, didn't they run as a team in 1976? Humphrey for President, McGovern for Vice President? The assignments were McGovern's idea—a realistic assessment of the existing power equation and likely public acceptance. McGovern was serious, and Humphrey pronounced the idea "interesting." Nothing more was said that day, and on the morrow the McGoverns departed. Later a local reporter interviewed Humphrey; his article reported only that Humphrey had quoted McGovern as encouraging him to seek the presidency! Not a word about the proposed Humphrey-McGovern ticket.

But it was clear that the idea still intrigued McGovern. Humphrey, after all, would be sixty-six if sworn in as President in 1977. And McGovern would be fifty-five, still relatively young, and he knew full well how important the vice-presidency had become as a stepping stone to higher office. Our luncheon conversation was over now, and I left persuaded that McGovern was resolved that the waiting game was the only one for him, either until the convention turned to him or until Humphrey himself turned to him as a running mate.

I was not prepared, however, for *how* McGovern would play the game. At the Louisville issues convention in late November, attention was seized not by any of the candidates but by a demonstration outside the hall by local people protesting school busing. Court-ordered transportation of children to schools outside their home districts in order to achieve racial integration was a hotly debated issue all over America, and in Louisville, a raging controversy. While most of the candidates fell over each other to avoid getting involved, McGovern was prepared to hit the issue head-on. He asked all the Democratic candidates to support court-ordered school deseg-regation by busing "openly and plainly." And a candidate who "perjured" himself by promising to stop busing, McGovern said, could expect his active opposition. "Any candidate who says or implies that by supporting him the voters can stop the buses will prove as President to be either a liar or a violator of the Constitution," McGovern proclaimed.

He was obviously trying to stake out the most categorical liberal position on busing, but this position also amounted to an outright attack on Jackson and Carter, both of whom criticized busing and advocated compromise. Jackson thought that busing had failed in its aim to achieve integration, and he warned, "We'd better be intellectually honest about this subject, or the Democratic Party will go down to defeat next year." For once, he was more in tune with the party liberals than McGovern. Nobody wanted to touch the busing issue with a ten-foot pole, especially not with the specter of George Wallace down the road. McGovern succeeded only in isolating himself even more.

Beyond all these actual and potential Democratic candidates there remained one other major political figure long identified with the Democratic Party whose ambitions and reading of the American political climate had to be considered in the 1976 equation. He was Eugene McCarthy. Disillusioned with his party, and with the orthodox presidential politics he had pursued with considerable success in 1968 until elbowed aside by Robert Kennedy, McCarthy had given up his Senate seat, toyed for a while with the notion of running for the House of Representatives, then instead became a book editor, wrote poetry, and gave lectures. Perhaps one of the few real political philosophers among America's active, vote-seeking politicians, McCarthy brooded long over the function and performance, in both the constitutional and the practical senses, of the two major parties. The Founding Fathers had made no provision in the Constitution for political parties or for primary elections and national conventions. The President and Vice President were to be selected by electors chosen by the state legislators (or, later, by popular vote)—a collection of the United States' wise men, as it were, who in their wisdom would choose Presidents and Vice

Presidents of genuine stature and ability. The emergence of the parties, however, undermined and eventually scuttled this concept, replacing it with fierce political competition by ambitious men who actively sought these high offices. It was McCarthy's notion to try to turn the selection process back to the simpler and theoretically purer approach. His objective was not, of course, entirely altruistic; he would be that individual of genuine stature and ability for whom the electors of 1976 would vote in the electoral college.

Forecasting a large multicandidate field that would create disarray in his old Democratic Party, and regarding the Republican Party as a wounded minority body, McCarthy set about enlisting individuals in many states to run as independent electors committed to him. He knew that the public seemed to be disenchanted with the two major parties and with politics-as-usual, and he hoped that after the conventions they would seize the alternative he would offer in the general election. He saw the electoral college as no mere formality, no mere paper concept, but as a living body that would be forced by necessity actually to meet or at least communicate among its members and deliberate on the selection of a President and Vice President. The law provides only that electors in their respective states forward their votes to the seat of national government to be counted; thus, there is not an actual "meeting" of the full electoral college; McCarthy's scheme would have had such a meeting take place in the event no candidate had a majority as a result of the election itself. The electors would then deal among themselves, producing a majority for one candidate, obviating the necessity of turning the matter over to the House of Representatives, as the Constitution provides when the electoral college cannot produce a winner. In the Democratic-controlled House, theoretically at least, an independent candidate such as McCarthy would have little chance against the Democrat in what could expected to be a straight party-line vote. But there was always the possibility that the Republicans would prefer to make a deal with an independent in the electoral college rather than face sure defeat and selection of a Democrat in the House. And, finally, there was also the prospect of Wallace as still another independent controlling electoral votes. Such an eventuality would compound the confusion, and perhaps increase the willingness of both Democratic and Republican electors to deal with some other alternative to Wallace.

It was a long shot, to be sure, but Gene McCarthy had a track record of some note as a long shot. Accused in the past of campaigning in a sometimes lackadaisical, sometimes mystical, nearly always aloof manner, McCarthy applied himself with unusual energy and discipline to this independent candidacy. All during 1975 he toured the college-campus circuit, tapping into the remnants of his 1968 movement and trying to expand it by the sheer force of his engaging personality and the novelty of his approach. To those who remembered his valiant effort that forced Lyndon Johnson to the side lines in 1968 and for a time brought the Vietnam war into focus as a campaign issue, McCarthy was received as a sort of weathered folk-hero; to those younger people who had only read of him, he was a curio of history, rehashing his 1968 line, yet it was remarkably pertinent to 1975–76, a tribute to the man's political prescience. From his earlier ridicule and warnings of Lyndon Johnson's imperial presidency he adapted effortlessly to the excesses of the Nixon presidency, and the other themes required even less adjustment: the need to reduce a bloated military establishment and contain its dangerous control over society; the need to put a clamp on the activities of secret intelligence agencies; the need to govern our consumption of resources and to funnel more of them into a fight to arrest poverty; the need to bring foreign policy in line with American idealism, to restore confidence in the United States at home and abroad.

He was, in most ways, the same Gene McCarthy who had been amusing and often vexing other politicians, political writers, his own supporters, and the public at large for decades. As no other figure campaigning for high public office, he remained his own man, who marched to his own drummer, and tolerated only those who might want to march along or just observe. I accompanied him in mid-April 1975 on a swing through northern Illinois and his home state of Minnesota, and remember best one night at Oakton Community College, north of Chicago. He was speaking to a campus writers' group in a makeshift hall under a long, high galvanized-tin roof, when a downpour of rain suddenly pelted the roof so heavily that McCarthy could barely be heard. He droned on, oblivious to the interruption, until one of his hosts, sitting behind him on the speakers' platform, walked over to suggest that perhaps he ought to stop until the rain let up. McCarthy, in the midst of a disquisition on his own poetry-writing, demurred. "It's all right," he said with a wry smile, "I can hear."

That was the quintessential McCarthy. Yet, for all that, he did extend himself in this new presidential effort in ways that were not in keeping with the curiously limited commitment that had so perplexed and even outraged his supporters in the past. He continued to say, as he had in 1968, that he was "willing" to be President rather than "wanting" to be President, convinced as he was that excessive zeal in the pursuit of the White House was uncomely and dangerous—a conviction reinforced and vindicated by the example of Richard Nixon. But he demonstrated by his actions and by an almost uncharacteristic patience that he was embarked on an undertaking of importance to him. Returning to Chicago that same night from Oakton, a young student from Northwestern had hitched a ride with us. He was considering working for McCarthy but was uncertain about McCarthy's positions on issues of concern to him, and wanted clarification. In 1968 such a petitioner would probably have been brushed aside or shunted to an aide. But now there were no aides. McCarthy, his long legs and frame stuffed into the front seat of a tiny Volkswagen next to a volunteer driver, sat huddled and vulnerable. He looked straight ahead as the car drove over wet, late-night roads, with the young man from Northwestern at my side in the back seat, hunched toward McCarthy's ear. How did he stand on abortion? On amnesty for draft resisters? On Ford's pardon of Nixon? One after another the questions came, without the slightest deference to this man who had helped drive a President from office and who had given a nation a new awareness about the unpopular war it was fighting. McCarthy, still looking ahead, answered curtly, politely at first, but then with an edge of resentment. There were long, uncomfortable silences, but the student perservered, and McCarthy, for all his testiness, replied to the very last question.

When the student at last was deposited at his residence on the Northwestern campus, it was a cool leave-taking, without commitment given or asked. After he was gone, McCarthy turned to his driver and said, "Let's have a rule from now on. No more questions after eleven o'clock at night." But he had answered them, and he went on answering many hundreds more like them, under similar uncomfortable, even demeaning, circumstances. This might be Gene McCarthy's last shot at history, and he was not going to skimp on it.

And so, as 1976 approached, the field of competitors for the primacy held by Gerald Ford through two monumental accidents of politics and human failing—the deposing of Spiro Agnew and Richard Nixon—was remarkably large and varied. The prospect was for chaos; a chaos compounded by the new campaign-finance law—untested, its provisions not well understood by an electorate that had in any case apparently tuned out, its effect uncertain, its meaning unclear even among scholars who examined it and politicians who tried to make the most of it or, at the very least, to survive under it.

part V

**THE
DELEGATE
HUNT:
THE DEMOCRATS**

14. Skirmishing

The actual competition for delegates to the 1976 party conventions began first on the Democratic side, crowded as it was with candidates seeking some early circumstance to break loose from the pack in
public recognition and support. A month before 1975 was over, some of the
Democrats were already actively contesting for delegate backing, whereas
the two Republican contenders, Gerald Ford and Ronald Reagan, awaited
1976's first primary, in New Hampshire, to commit themselves to the same
task.

Even before the battle was joined by Jimmy Carter in Iowa, looking
toward the first delegate-selecting precinct caucuses of 1976, the first real
test of strength took place in New York. There, the late-starting Birch Bayh,
hoping to compensate for the earlier organization-building of Mo Udall in
New Hampshire and elsewhere, focused his prime attention and resources
on winning the endorsement of New York's New Democratic Coalition. At
a statewide convention in early December, the NDC would select its own
candidates to run in the April primary that would in turn choose the bulk
of the New York delegation to the Democratic National Convention in July.
The NDC, a collection of some 112 liberal reform Democratic clubs all
across New York State, was an outgrowth of the effort to merge the forces
of Gene McCarthy and Robert Kennedy after Kennedy's death in 1968.
The coalition had endorsed McGovern in 1972 but its record on picking
winners for state offices was spotty at best. Still, the NDC endorsement was
an important prize because it gave a candidate manpower for the primary
race itself,[1] and a psychological upper hand. Bayh hoped to muddy the
waters among the liberal candidates in the early caucus and primary tests
and then deliver a knockout blow to them in the New York primary on
April 6, using the NDC endorsement as a strong base. With it, he might

1. Under New York law, delegate candidates for the party national convention were to run
in each of the state's thirty-nine congressional districts without any identification as to preferred presidential candidate; the arrangement would put a premium on organization, because
voters would have to be educated about whom they were voting for. Also, for delegates to be
filed, the state required upward of 100,000 signatures on petitions, a mammoth task in which
NDC manpower could be essential.

also influence Governor Hugh Carey and his state party chairman, Patrick Cunningham, not to form an alliance with Jackson, who was expected to do well in New York, or to back an uncommitted slate of delegates that would enhance the governor's negotiating power at the national convention and possibly win him a place on the ticket.

In this New York effort, Bayh had as a principal ally Robert Abrams, president of the borough of the Bronx, and an important liberal politician. Abrams focused on the NDC endorsement as a means of catching up organizationally in New York, and all through November and into early December, Bayh beat a steady path to the Empire State, working the reform clubs avidly. On the stump he was an embarrassing, unmitigated cornball; he bathed his listeners in platitudes and shamefacedly stole ideas and even phrases from his opponents. Still, audiences seemed to be taken with him. He hammered away at his own "electability" and the theme that he could unite the party: "Birch Bayh: The One Candidate for President Who Can Put It All Together."

Other candidates, notably Harris and Udall, also hustled for NDC endorsement, but not nearly so tenaciously, and their efforts soon became essentially stop-Bayh drives. A quirk in NDC rules encouraged them: to win statewide endorsement, a candidate had to receive 60 per cent of the assembly's votes under a procedure that discarded candidates as they fell below a minimum percentage.

The NDC assembly, held at Stuyvesant High School in lower Manhattan on December 6, had all the trappings of a political convention. Harris and Bayh enthusiasts packed the galleries and cheered their candidates, who during the day held forth in hospitality "suites" in classrooms, serving New York delicatessen specialties—hot dogs from Nathan's on Coney Island in Bayh's, bologna and cheese sandwiches in Harris's, bagels in Udall's. When the voting began, Abrams dispatched his lieutenants to the various delegations; with each ballot, as lesser candidates fell away, Bayh crept up on the magic figure, but Harris hung on, until the two faced off in a sixth and final ballot. Delegations were permitted to split their votes down to the decimal point, and when the final results were in, Bayh had 59.974 per cent, to 30.21 per cent for Harris and the rest voting "no endorsement." One delegate asked to switch, but was denied permission, and the coalition adjourned without endorsing anyone.

Bayh put the best face he could on the outcome. "Whenever you can defeat your nearest rival two to one, you have a lot of supporters out there," he said. "I hope we can lose this well in every other election I'm in." His near-miss demonstrated at least that he had a capacity for polishing up the old politics: party leadership endorsement (Abrams) plus strong labor support. But he had mortgaged a lot of money and time in the NDC drive, and he would suffer accordingly in the first delegate fights in 1976. Harris, for his part, said his showing kept his candidacy on schedule, building from nothing in the early tests.

Udall's forces rejoiced that Bayh's bid for the NDC endorsement had been blocked, but Udall didn't escape unscathed himself. He had done some early politicking among the New York reform clubs, whose positions on the issues might have been expected to make him a logical consensus choice. But by running consistently behind Harris, and eventually being eliminated, Udall reinforced the idea that he was the Ed Muskie of 1976—a candidate smack in the middle, with no appreciable constituency of his own. Even the electability pitch he had been making earlier was being undermined by Bayh, who seemed to fare much better with labor. (Udall had once voted against repeal of state right-to-work laws, and this fact was a continuing source of trouble to him.) Still, when the final vote was announced, there were cheers and much backslapping from the Udall contingent in the auditorium balcony; after all the months of preparation, there seemed to be a great need for emotional release, even in such a nebulous "victory."

The next day, in Worcester, Massachusetts, a similar test took place before another liberal reform group, the Massachusetts Citizens for Participation in Political Action (CPPAX). Bayh made no serious effort here, in part because his operatives had been discovered reproducing CPPAX membership application blanks for use by his partisans, a move that was legal but that many thought unethical, and the attendant publicity had forced him to back off. CPPAX was to be a major forum for Udall, but the late entry of a group supporting Senator Frank Church of Idaho, not yet a declared candidate, cut deeply into his support. For endorsement, a candidate needed two-thirds of the total vote, and nobody came close. Harris, continuing his surprisingly strong organizational showing, finished first with 38.7 per cent, to 25.7 for Udall and 23.7 for Church. Like the NDC balloting, the vote was significant chiefly for its demonstration of the lack of consensus in liberal ranks.

Frank Church, who had been hanging back from presidential politics, ostensibly because his time was occupied with the chairmanship of the Senate committee investigating the CIA and other intelligence agencies, in mid-December finally approved formation of an "exploratory" campaign committee whose initial focus was to be on Massachusetts, where about sixty draft-Church committees already existed.

Church, who had once been the Senate's youngest member, and still looked it nineteen years later, was largely an unknown quantity as a national candidate. As one of the early critics of the Vietnam war, and now as a senatorial sleuth into the excesses of the intelligence community, he certainly had the right credentials to capture the hearts of many party liberals. But he was a Westerner, and an opponent of gun control, and though a genial and smiling man, he was too studious, too straight-laced, for the clubhouse politicians to warm to him. He would have to make it on his brainpower, and that would take considerable public exposure. He declined to enter the competition personally, however, until he had completed his investigatory responsibilities, and that fact undercut his chances. It was not until the next March 18 that he would formally enter the race.

Another prospect, Senator Adlai E. Stevenson III, had been advanced as a glorified favorite-son candidate in Illinois by Chicago's Mayor Richard J. Daley simply as a device for Daley to control the Illinois delegation. But Stevenson, after entertaining the idea for months, finally balked, in the process assailing the system. "A candidacy today," he said, "triggers a thousand skirmishes, a welter of endless, draining detail. It plunges the candidate into a morass of unintelligible regulations and dervish-like activity, all largely beyond his control and comprehension." With such an oversized field, "the press is beleaguered and spread too thin. Commentators gauge the viability of candidates by the most superficial devices: the size of campaign bankrolls or the volume of applause at joint appearances." And television, he said, "offers episodes and spectacles, and the citizen is hard put to fathom their significance. I think I can give more to the national debate without the distrust and distractions a candidacy would entail." He did, however, agree to head a slate of Daley delegates in the Illinois primary. Stevenson was not missed. The field was ridiculously overcrowded as it was.

On the right, while there were no such preliminary overt sparrings for support as in New York and Massachusetts, important decisions were being made. Foremost of these were the deliberations in Jackson's camp about whether or not he should run in the New Hampshire primary. Jackson had been in the state a number of times, and the generally orthodox, even conservative, flavor of the Democratic Party there seemed good for him. In 1972, after toying with the prospect, he had decided instead to make his first major effort in Florida, where he along with everyone else ran into the Wallace buzzsaw. Some in his campaign, including the author-speechwriter-polemicist Ben Wattenberg, thought that had been a mistake in 1972 and would be a mistake again in 1976.

But Jackson labored under the specter of his past failures, and the image that had developed of him as an efficient, effective, but dull and uninspiring senator. "We really thought that given the peculiar circumstances of Henry Jackson," said Bob Keefe, his campaign manager, "we had to *win* someplace. He had come out of the 1972 thing with the reputation that he couldn't win. We felt that the most devastating thing would be to run someplace and lose. So we had to look for a place he could win. We were never able to attract the quality and quantity of people in New Hampshire to make it look like a winning possibility."

Actually Jackson had hoped to make his first big push in New York, but as other states like Massachusetts moved the dates of their primaries forward, he saw he would have to get involved earlier or be accused of ducking. Massachusetts, with its reputation as the most liberal state in the union, at first blush seemed even more suicidal than New Hampshire. But there, in the March 2 primary, all the liberals would be competing against each other, theoretically leaving Jackson an opening on the right. He could present himself as a more reasonable alternative to Wallace, especially among the thousands of Bostonians who felt caught in the middle of that city's festering school-busing controversy. And so he decided to skip New Hampshire and run in Massachusetts.

Jackson himself later expressed the belief that he had erred in staying out of New Hampshire. "I think in retrospect it was wrong," he said in an interview in his Senate office after Carter's election. "There was a feeling [among my staff] that New Hampshire as a psychological media state was overwhelming, that it was New Hampshire or bust. We had great debates about that. The problem we were up against was that Carter had a strategy of appearing to go everywhere. We felt that by trying to go everywhere, you could end up nowhere. It was our feeling that the choice was Massachusetts; it was the kind of state that would provide the kind of acceleration in the campaign effort that would more than offset not going into New Hampshire. Also, New Hampshire involved a long, tedious, one-on-one type of campaign, whereas Massachusetts did not. . . . If we had gone all-out in New Hampshire, I think we could have won, because we had a good media campaign going in Massachusetts, and with it you could hit New Hampshire."

George Wallace made a similar decision to stay out of New Hampshire and to enter Massachusetts. His campaign manager, Charles Snider, in late 1975 urged him to stay out of both New England primaries and concentrate on kicking off his campaign with a victory in Florida, as he had in 1972. But Wallace liked the notion of going up north and sticking it to the Yankees in their own back yard, and wild horses couldn't keep him from doing so. Eventually, the narrowness of the Florida vote and all it meant to Carter's candidacy triggered a lot of second-guessing in Wallace's camp about the wisdom of that northern foray.

But Wallace was always one to exercise complete tactical independence from the other candidates. Except for Carter, they were, if the truth were known, scared stiff of him as a political force, for all their brave talk about dealing with him. And he knew it. He had nothing but contempt for the pack of them.

He demonstrated that contempt in a typical gesture at a meeting of Democratic governors at the Mayflower Hotel in Washington in December, where all ten then-declared candidates, including Wallace, were invited to discuss their candidacies and to field questions, and where all ten dutifully appeared. Wallace was tenth on the list, and when he showed up for a private lunch with his colleagues in advance of his scheduled appearance as a candidate that afternoon, he casually informed them he didn't think he'd be by later; so, if anybody wanted to ask him anything he was available then and there, at lunch. Of course, that was not the planned format, and Wallace knew it. Other governors, including Philip W. Noel of Rhode Island, chairman of the Democratic Governors' Conference, urged him to reconsider, saying it would look bad in the press if he failed to take his regular turn, but he was adamant. Later, in his suite at the Washington Hilton, he told me: "To go over there and get up and talk, and then have a bunch of folks that ain't never going to vote for you, have them interrogating you? Hell. Why do I want to let a bunch of governors, ain't any of them for you, and they're all hostile to you, they get you before the public and interrogate you. Let me interrogate them. . . . I told them, yeah, I'd be here. When I got over there, I got to the luncheon and I said, 'Listen, gentlemen, to save time . . . I don't want to prolong this thing. A few of you want to stay. Most of you want to go.' I said, 'Let me just say what I want to say now, just say hello to you, and I'm here. That's the main thing, all of us are here.' Two or three of them got up and said, 'Well, Governor, I think the press will note it if you don't do it.' And I said, 'Well, what if they do note it?' " And later, in a meeting with a group of reporters, Wallace said he felt he could better spend his time talking to waiters in the hotel, who might vote for him. What had he done during the time he was supposed to be addressing the governors? "I was reading the funnies, I guess, or maybe I was looking at TV," he replied. "Yeah, TV, that was it."

For George Wallace, the rules always were made to be broken. He was always the wild card in the deck, and there was nothing to do but to proceed with the game, under the rules, and deal with the wild card as best as could be managed.

But if Wallace was generally perceived as a threat by the other candidates, the confident Carter, as we have seen, viewed him as an opportunity. A long-shot candidacy such as Carter's required a high-risk strategy and the achievement of surprises. The early caucuses and the New Hampshire primary would give him a chance to make a sudden, unpredicted impact on the national consciousness, but a confrontation with Wallace in Florida had been projected since 1972 as the critical make-or-break exercise. Carter repeatedly went back to Florida—twenty-five times before 1976. Rosalynn did the same, and other friends and relatives from south Georgia made sorties into the northern panhandle region that until then had been indisputably Wallace country. Carter knew that if he could rid the Democratic Party of the pesky Wallace, liberals, blacks, and other Southern Democrats weary of being perceived in the Wallace image would all be in his debt.

One technical cloud hung over the bicentennial year election as it approached. The Supreme Court, which had been expected to rule on the new campaign-finance-reform law before 1976, instead held off, leaving the candidates and the voters in limbo about the rules governing the raising and spending of campaign money. Plaintiffs Eugene McCarthy, James Buckley, et al., sought an injunction against the federal payment of matching funds to the qualifying candidates, but the Court, by a four-to-four vote, refused to grant it, and the Federal Election Commission proceeded to make the first installments.

A year after the act went into effect, all the candidates who had declared for their party nomination were still in the race, able to take their case to the voters in at least the early caucuses and primaries. The law had many flaws, no doubt, but its basic objective had been met. The voters would have a wide choice in the challenging party, and some choice even in the party of the incumbent. Now, after all the preliminaries, all the private maneuverings and public debates, the selection of the presidential nominees at last was going before the people.

15. Early Caucuses

One day in late February 1975 Jimmy Carter and his side-kick, Jody Powell, had motored over from Nebraska into Iowa for a testimonial dinner for Marie Jahn in Le Mars, just north of Sioux City. Mrs. Jahn was retiring after thirty-eight years as Plymouth County recorder and Carter, just retired himself as governor of Georgia, was the guest speaker. It was small potatoes, but the only speaking engagement Carter could wrangle. "I think," Powell said later, "they may have asked a couple of other people first." Harold Brady, host of the affair, was more specific. He told Jim Flansburg, a political writer of the *Des Moines Register* and *Tribune:* "We wanted someone of national prominence—and relatively inexpensive." For his labors, Carter was declared Le Mars' Citizen of the Day by local radio station owner Paul Olson and was given his payola: a free car wash, a movie pass, and a coupon for a free pizza.

After his speech, Carter circulated through the crowd shaking hands as Jody, notebook in hand, jotted down the names and addresses of well-wishers. By now this routine was a well-practiced one; Jimmy and Jody had been constant traveling companions since early 1970. In the early days during Jimmy's second gubernatorial try, they would drive several hours, switching off at the wheel, from one small town in Georgia to another (on long hauls, one would sleep while the other drove). While they drove they would do a critique of Jimmy's performance at the previous stop and talk Georgia politics, and chat about their families, and religion.

It was a time for getting to know each other, for building a friendship and a working relationship rare in politics between an older and a younger man. It was considerably more than a father-son thing, because Powell came to be as much counselor as protégé. He had voted for Carter in 1966 in his first, unsuccessful gubernatorial bid, after having shaken the candidate's hand at a shopping center. But they did not really get together until the fall of 1969, when Powell wrote Carter a letter discussing the need for a rebirth of the Democratic Party in the South as an alternative to the development of an independent, Wallace force. Carter replied with a long letter, and the weekend before Christmas invited Powell to join a small group (also including Ham Jordan and Jerry Rafshoon) to Plains to discuss his next campaign. Powell was then twenty-six years old. He signed on shortly afterward, and their long solitary hours together on the highways and back roads of Georgia strengthened the ties between them.

Powell told Carter about his dismissal from the Air Force Academy (just before Christmas in his senior year, after turning himself in under the honor system during a final examination in military history); Carter said it didn't matter to him. Carter told Powell of his own personal concerns: of his worry over a tumor his wife, Rosalynn, had contracted, from which she recovered.

The idea of running for President developed much later. For Powell, the visits to the Governor's Mansion in Atlanta of two 1972 presidential contenders, McGovern and Humphrey, were persuasive. If *they* were presidential timber, then so was Carter. On McGovern's visit, one of the senator's aides had the preposterous notion of wanting a McGovern banner flown from the dome of the state capitol. He was going to the Georgia secretary of state to seek permission when Powell stopped him and saved everybody an embarrassing scene. "That kind of gave me the idea that national campaigns are basically like any other campaigns—screwed up," Powell told me in Iowa, and inevitably the notion arose that Carter should make a try. "I don't think we underestimated what a long shot it was," Powell said, "but we saw how it could be done. We could see, at least in our own minds, that if we did this and this and this in a row, you could win the thing. We got ourselves psychologically to say this was how you could do it. If anything happened out of our control, so be it."

Powell recalled flying back to Atlanta with Carter after that first Iowa trip in early 1975 and reading a front-page report by Flansburg in the *Des Moines Register.* Flansburg was impressed with Carter, and said so in print. Noting Carter's flat-out promise that he would "never tell a lie," Flansburg wrote: "If there weren't believers, there were certainly those who were persuaded on the basis of one speech to seriously consider the candidacy of Carter. Indeed, seldom has a candidate without a fabled name made such a fast and favorable impression on Iowans." Powell showed the story to Carter and the two talked about Iowa's potential, and the good reception he had just received. "We were looking for a place to go in the caucus states," Powell said. "We were seeing if we could find a place to surprise before New Hampshire, and the people of Iowa seemed to be our kind of folks. Once we became convinced we had a good shot, Iowa became the place."

Powell quickly seized upon the importance of local coverage in the Carter kind of campaign. "At that point, the *Des Moines Register* became more important than *The Washington Post,*" he said later. "The only coverage you get at that stage is local. We might not have known much about anything else, but we did know local media." So while other candidates may have fretted about a lack of national coverage, Powell realized that the large Democratic field in 1975–76 would dilute national coverage for everyone. "Where we were perceptive," he said, "was we knew not only that we couldn't get you [the national press] but the others couldn't get you either." This was one reason it was decided that headquarters could remain in Atlanta rather than being moved up to an expensive Washington office. "With Kennedy out, a lot of things would start tumbling," Powell said. "The field would be bunched up and nobody would break out of this pack in 1975. We didn't need a big Washington office; nobody could afford to cover it so nobody would get a jump."

The Iowans' response to Carter's first foray was a bit of a surprise to the candidate and his press aide. Several weeks before, Jordan had phoned Democratic State Chairman Tom Whitney, and Whitney told him, according to Jordan: "You really ought to forget about Iowa. It's not your kind of state." But it was not Jimmy Carter's nature to forget *any* state. "We realized from the outset," said Jordan much later, "that what we were going to do was very unconventional—a man running for office who had no forum, who was not an incumbent, who was not from the traditional breeding ground of American politics, who was a Southerner. We were going to have to prove ourselves early, and the early primaries and even the caucuses were going to have a disproportionate amount of influence in the media." This approach made sense for another reason: it fit right in with the way Carter did things. "Jimmy's nature is to run a total effort everywhere," Jordan went on. "When he ran for governor in '66 and lost, and then decided to run in '70, a lot of people, myself included, tried to [dissuade him and] talk him into running for lieutenant-governor or commissioner of agriculture. I went over to see him in '67 or '68 and I said, 'Jimmy, you should be the governor, but you know, this guy Carl Sanders just can't be defeated.' And he told me in his living room, 'If I don't get but two votes, mine and yours, I'm going to run for governor.' He made that same kind of total commitment to the presidential campaign. And that kind of commitment does not allow you to say, 'Well, we may not run in these ten or fifteen states. . . .'

"I felt like there was going to be an overreaction to the new rules of the Democratic Party, that people were going to pick and choose, to shape strategies that presumed a brokered convention. We shaped a strategy that presumed there was *not* going to be a brokered convention. We felt like other candidates, particularly the ones who had duties and responsibilities in Washington, were going to have to say, 'Well, there are fifty states; we're going to focus on these twenty.' Because Jimmy was a tremendous, full-time campaigner, we could spend a little time on the states they had written off and do well there, plus also contest them for their priority states. I never remember a meeting where it was even discussed which states we were going to run in and which states we were going to skip. Circumstances dictated that we were going to run everywhere."

A great irony about the Carter strategy is that it was essentially the same one that Muskie had used in 1972, and that had helped to bring him down. But there were at least two notable differences: Carter had much greater determination and a stronger affinity for campaigning, and he did so in an atmosphere of low expectations. He was neither discouraged by small crowds and long hours nor was early public indifference particularly bad for him. Muskie had acted as if he were already the party's nominee and a great deal was expected of him; Jimmy Carter ran as the longest of long shots, and whatever favorable reaction he generated was gravy.

Over the next eleven months Carter returned to Iowa seven times. Tim Kraft, a New Mexico party organizer and state committee official whom Carter had met and recruited during the 1974 congressional campaign, was made the campaign's Plains states coordinator, and he advanced several of the trips. Each time, he became more convinced that Iowa was a golden opportunity. Jordan and he began scouting around for somebody who could take on the state full time, and when no one else could be found, Kraft agreed to do it himself. "We felt the sequence of the primaries and the new federal-election law would make winners out of some candidates and losers out of others," Jordan said, "and candidate attrition would take place very early." But little time was wasted on speculation. "There are things in a political campaign you can control and things you can't. You can't control issues and events and who your opponents are, or what they do or what they say about you. The things you *can* control are your own organization, your own fund-raising. Because of Jimmy's commitment to the thing we never spent a lot of psychic energy worrying about who we were ultimately going to face."

So, while other candidates and prospective candidates concentrated most of their pre-election year energies on minor liberal skirmishes in the East or on New Hampshire, Carter zeroed in early on Iowa. He combined an easy, warm, personal style with an icy, resolute determination, a kind of soft-sell evangelism that won adherents across the ideological spectrum. There was almost a hypnotic quality to his stump technique. He spoke very softly, in a rush of words that obliged his audiences to listen closely. In all he said, he punctuated his remarks with frequent ingratiating smiles and expressions of affection. The word "love," awkward coming from the mouth of the commonplace politician, was used by Carter as if it were a natural neighborly embrace, with baffling effect. "I want a government," he would intone to his rapt audiences in a quiet, deliberate cadence, "that is as good, and honest, and decent, and truthful, and fair, and competent, and idealistic, and compassionate, and as filled with love as are the American people." He recited this sequence almost as if it were his personal rosary, and, in crowd after crowd, it worked. Then, having given the assembled this layman's benediction, he would descend among them, smiling benignly, this peanut-farmer Billy Graham, and put his hands upon them, and in the process commit them thoroughly. From these personal political baptisms came a small army of dedicated supporters who defied ideological classification, united in their conviction that "Jimmy"—everybody called him that —would restore harmony, and peace, and honesty, and decency, and compassion, and, yes, love, to government.

In August 1975, five months before the Iowa voting, Tim Kraft decided he should move full time into the state. He discussed Iowa's importance again with Jordan, who agreed but asked him to write a strong memo that Jordan could use to win support from others in Atlanta for the necessary resources. "Build yourself a case," Jordan told him. In the memo, dated August 28, 1975, Kraft wrote: "It is past time that we began to devote to Iowa the money and manpower that that crucial state requires. You are aware of the media/political significance of Iowa's January 19 precinct caucuses. . . . JC has indicated very strongly that he does not want to finish second to any candidate. We'd better get going. . . . We'll solicit money but it [the Iowa campaign] can't pay for itself. Money can't buy the kind of press we'll get if JC finishes first in the precinct caucuses. . . . [It has been argued] that there are only X amount of materials for fifty states and, accordingly, they must be rationed. Set up a priority, then, and ration Montana, Vermont, or somewhere else. But don't tell me that Iowa, Oklahoma [also an early caucus state], New Hampshire, and Florida should be treated like any of the other forty-six states."

Kraft's memo did the trick, and by Labor Day of 1975 he was living in Iowa, implementing the campaign plan.

A short, mustachioed fellow with the look of a cocky desperado about him, Kraft had helped engineer the election of New Mexico's Governor Jerry Apodaca, and he knew the business of grass-roots organizing. He too had been won over by Carter's political evangelism. Carter dealt with Kraft, as he did with most others, on an intensively personal level: that was a big part of his effectiveness; he would listen long, no matter who was talking to him, important politician or crackpot on the street. That was an almost missionary quality: no soul was not worth saving, nor beyond redemption, if only Carter persisted. And so persist he did, almost with a vengeance and, beyond that, with an unshakable conviction of right. "As the Father knoweth me, even so know I the Father: and I lay down my life for the sheep. And other sheep I have, which are not of this fold: them also I must bring, and they shall hear my voice; and there shall be one fold, *and* one shepherd." (John 10: 15–16).

Carter's opponents in Iowa soon found that the Good Shepherd was going to be no pushover. Kraft worked the state like a local precinct, visiting 110 cities and towns between Carter's own visits, which were marked not only by speaking engagements but casual drop-bys in the middle of nowhere. He would call on a farmer in the morning, talk for a while, stay for lunch, then come by again a few weeks later. If the farmer wasn't home, he would leave a handwritten note pinned to the front door that said: "Just dropped by to say hello. Jimmy." Many such visits were followed by telephone calls or notes of thanks. And as Carter and his wife and children pursued this retail campaigning, Kraft shrewdly studied the state caucus machinery.

At the summer's end, an opportunity presented itself that was in a sense the first tangible Carter triumph, and first solid evidence of his diligent thoroughness. Iowa is gifted with one of the most progressive and professional Democratic Party organizations in the country. The state's Democrats have always prided themselves in being in the forefront of reform, and in Tom Whitney they had a young and ambitious chairman who saw the potential for national attention in the 1976 political calendar. Well in advance of the first precinct caucuses of 1976, scheduled for January 19, Whitney and his committee laid plans for delegate selection in accordance with the new and complex national party rules. So complex were they, in fact, that dry-run caucuses were scheduled around the state to familiarize Democrats with the system and to encourage participation. It was decided that it would be good publicity to conduct a straw poll on presidential preferences in conjunction with these practice caucuses. Kraft, seizing on this development, quietly but efficiently mobilized his growing forces to generate a show of strength for Carter that would be noticed by the national press—and, he hoped, by the nation's public as well, far in advance of the New Hampshire primary.

"I worked in a white heat just to get a steering committee named by that time," Kraft recalled later. "I sent out a mailing of six hundred or seven hundred county leaders in the party and came up with a list of nineteen fairly impressive people on a state steering committee." He put out a press release, but the *Des Moines Register* buried the story. It was important, however, that Democrats around the state hear about the names Carter had corralled before they attended the dry-run caucuses. They included James Schaben, the unsuccessful 1974 gubernatorial nominee; Edris (Soapy) Owens, retired state president of the United Auto Workers; and James Maloney, auditor of Polk County (Des Moines). So Kraft alerted all the steering committee members to attend their own precinct meetings, spread the word, and vote for Carter in the straw poll. There wasn't much to pull together, but at this earliest stage it was enough. Carter polled 9.9 per cent of 5762 persons voting—more than any other active candidate achieved. Shriver was second with 8.7 per cent and Bayh third with 8.1 per cent. About 34 per cent said they were uncommitted.

It was by all odds an insignificant gauge of over-all Democratic strength in Iowa, but it was the only show in town—the only hard bit of political information looking to the 1976 Democratic race available for the press and television to latch on to, and it made news in Iowa, especially because the "winner" was an obscure one-term former governor from a Deep South state who had no business making any splash at all there. As the other candidates moved into Iowa—Harris, Udall, Jackson, then Bayh and Shriver—they seldom found a place where the velvet pitch of Jimmy Carter had not been heard or conveyed by proxy by his growing legion of workers. Iowa had the makings of a trap, but it was not one easily resisted, because along with the Carter invasion came, eventually, the media invasion as well, offering a prize no 1976 hopeful could resist.

The media's seizing upon Iowa, though it chose only 47 of 3008 delegates to the Democratic National Convention, was both understandable and defensible. In 1972 the rise of George McGovern's barely detected grass-roots efforts at the precinct level had been overlooked for a considerable time by the major newspapers and the television networks; their focus was squarely on Muskie as he collected big-name endorsements en route, nearly everyone thought, to a routine first-ballot nomination. Not even McGovern's show of strength in Iowa shook that perception, and only in retrospect was it realized that something significant had been building for McGovern out in the country. Through the early going, he was mired among the also-rans in the Gallup and other public-opinion polls, not moving up until his primary campaign successes. For their romance with Muskie, the press and television paid heavy alimony after 1972 in terms of their reputation for clairvoyance, let alone clear thinking and assessment of evidence at hand. Some reporters, to their credit, had recognized and chronicled early the Muskie slide and McGovern climb, but this time around, in 1976, if there were going to be early signals, the fourth estate was going to be on the scene en masse to catch them.

The Iowa straw poll had sneaked up on most of the press, but it had served to alert most political reporters of the state's importance as an early line on the 1976 contenders. The next important event did not go unnoticed.

In late October the state Democratic Party held a large Jefferson-Jackson Day fund-raising affair at Iowa State University in Ames, just north of Des Moines, to which all the prospective presidential candidates were invited. The affair had all the trappings of a political convention, with booths set up at the back of the arena for each of the hopefuls, and time set aside before and after each speech for the candidates themselves to man the booths, shake hands, and answer questions. Kraft drew an early bead on this affair too. The *Des Moines Register* and *Tribune* had decided to poll all those who attended the dinner and Kraft did his best to pack the hall. The other candidates' staffs either failed to grasp the psychological impact promised by the poll or could not get supporters out in sufficient numbers. The Harris campaign, for instance, observing that its backers were among the common folk and could not afford the price of admission, made only a modest effort. Bayh's forces depended on labor to come through for them and were disappointed. The result was predictable—a clear-cut victory for Carter, with 23 per cent of 1094 respondents, for the largest share.

Tim Kraft's effort had been audacious and thorough. He had sent out three memos to all Carter workers, friends, and supporters advising them of the showcase opportunity the dinner presented, and the plans for a poll. Pick-up points for the trip to Ames were arranged and information about bus and car transportation dispensed. Though the dinner was expensive—$50 a couple—Tom Whitney confided to Kraft that Democrats would be admitted to balcony seats for $2 apiece. Kraft, in a memo, passed the word that the two bucks "gets you everything but the chicken dinner." And he suggested that "one probably could drift down from the balcony onto the floor and vote" in the poll. (This guerrilla tactic was foiled initially when the *Register* distributed the ballots at the door to full-paying guests, but some of the Carter two-dollar types infiltrated anyway, slipping down to the floor and appropriating ballots along with box suppers of fried chicken. Nothing was left to chance. In the same memo to Carter supporters, Kraft wrote: "Have the bumper sticker on whatever you drive to Ames; slap it on the chartered bus if need be. There's usually a reporter who polls the parking lot and throws in a sentence about it. Bring whatever extras you have; we may need them for the [straw] hats.") At the auditorium, Rosa-lynn Carter went into the balcony handing out oversized Carter buttons to people in the first rows, an easy focus for the television cameras. She and Neil Hamilton, an Iowa State student on the steering committee, "must have put on three hundred of these buttons, all in the front row," Kraft recalled. "We knew the thing was going to be covered. Politics is theater. We planned for that."

All of America's major newspapers immediately perceived this first solid sign of Carter's strength in Iowa. In *The New York Times,* for example, political writer R. W. (Johnny) Apple, Jr., wrote that Carter "appears to have taken a surprising but solid lead" in Iowa's delegate race. "Whether he can maintain his early lead here when the contest switches from opinion leaders to rank-and-file voters is unclear," he went on, but "what is evident is that Mr. Carter, working from Atlanta rather than Washington, has made dramatic progress while attention was focused on the scramble for liberal primacy" among Udall, Bayh, Harris, and Shriver. Nearly three months before the first caucuses of 1976, Carter had grabbed the media spotlight. In one sense, it was what he and his campaign had labored for in obscurity for three years. But some feared it had come too soon. "It was not an unmixed blessing," Jody Powell said later. "It tipped our hand. We never had a chance to surprise anyone after that." The Ames poll did in fact establish Carter as the man to watch, and in that sense raised expectations about him, raising at the same time the level of performance he would have to achieve in the January precinct-voting to impress the media. Impress the media: that was the name of the game now, and some people—chiefly those who were having trouble doing so—didn't like it.

When the press and the networks began to descend on Des Moines right after New Year's Day, one lament was heard repeatedly: Iowa, it went, was no more than a "media event"—the overblowing of an insignificant early phase of the delegate-selection process, for the purpose of satisfying the need for hard news after all the months of vapid preliminaries. Iowans themselves weren't excited about the whole business—barely 11 per cent of the state's Democrats eventually participated in the caucus—but the national media elevated the caucuses to a bogus extravaganza. So said the complainers. One unhappy Udall worker later stated in *The Washington Post* that the candidates themselves and the issues were lost in the efforts to draw press attention, and in the reporters' determination to draw significance from an insignificant exercise. "The reality of a presidential campaign," he wrote in a woeful misunderstanding of the dynamics of the system, "is the delegate count, but no significant number of delegates will be selected until March" (in the Massachusetts primary, presumably). The fact is that the reality in the early going of a presidential campaign is *not* the delegate-count at all. The reality at the beginning stage is the psychological impact of the results—the perception by press, public, and contending politicians of what has happened. Because the candidates themselves act on that perception—adjusting their campaigns to meet criticisms about perceived shortcomings—the perception becomes the reality. Hamilton Jordan and his associates grasped this truth early and acted on it repeatedly.

The performances and reactions of the four most important candidates in the Iowa caucuses—Carter, Bayh, Harris, and Udall—attest to this point. Going into the caucuses, Carter had already moved from being a surprisingly strong prospect to the odds-on favorite who had to win or be judged to have peaked and slipped. Reporters did not pull this viewpoint out of a hat, as their critics were wont to suggest. Tom Whitney, who presided over the caucus process with admirable neutrality, drew the same conclusion in advance of the voting. "If Carter doesn't win here," he told me in his Des Moines headquarters, "there isn't any other thing you can judge than that there has been some slippage. Carter can't finish lower than second or he's finished." And then he added, "The press will write that, and some will write that he should have finished higher."

Within his Washington headquarters, a debate raged over whether Mo Udall should be in Iowa at all—a debate that was to have tremendous ramifications for the whole Udall campaign. Almost from the outset, Udall's first campaign manager, John Gabusi, a veteran congressional staff aide, had discouraged Udall's entry into Iowa. When others argued that the press in 1976 was going to make Iowa the "new New Hampshire," Gabusi countered that no matter what the media said or did, the New Hampshire primary would still be the first real election, and hence would retain its importance. Through early 1975 Udall's campaign had sent organizers first into New Hampshire, then into Wisconsin, Massachusetts, and California, but not into Iowa. Rick Stearns, who had been McGovern's chief delegate-counter in 1972, conferred with Gabusi and contended that if Udall were to go into Iowa at all, he would have do so in the spring of 1975 to be effective. Gabusi agreed, and so Iowa was virtually ignored through the summer.

For personal reasons, Gabusi left the campaign in the end of September. He recommended that Jack Quinn, a young political aide, be made political director and that Stewart Udall ("Stewdall," in the campaign's jargon, in contrast with "Modall"), who was nominally the campaign chairman, take a more active role, rather than simply being a private counselor to his brother. But Stew Udall did not take hold, and Quinn moved into the breach.

The argument resurfaced about Iowa. Quinn agreed that the Iowa precinct caucuses in mid-January would steal a march on the New Hampshire primary as the opening round in the liberal elimination contest, and he sent three field organizers into the state to work with two experienced

Iowans, Norma Matthews and Cliff Larsen, a former state chairman.

A few weeks after the Ames dinner, another more general poll by the *Des Moines Register* and *Tribune* underscored the fact that Udall still was an unknown in Iowa. Quinn was concerned. He dispatched Stearns and Ken Bode, a young veteran of liberal Democratic wars who was soon to become a writer for *The New Republic,* to Iowa in late November to take a fresh reading. They returned split in their assessment: Stearns still believed it was too late to do much; Bode argued, in a long memo, that "the state is up for grabs," and urged a step-up in both radio and television commercials and Mo Udall's presence in the state. "Iowa justifies the expense," he wrote. "It will be covered like the first primary always has been in the national press. If we can emerge as the clear liberal choice in Iowa, the payoffs in New Hampshire will be enormous."

Other important figures in the campaign—Stew Udall and Terry Bracy, one of Mo Udall's congressional aides—openly disagreed with the plan to compete in Iowa. They said it made no sense to plunge in so late, just because others, like Bayh, were going in, and particularly made no sense to use expensive media and costly candidate travel—both wholesale political devices—in a retail political situation, which the precinct caucuses indisputably were. Getting people to the polls was fairly simple, and could be done with radio and television appeals; getting them to spend a night at some neighbor's home for actual discussion of a candidate's merits was quite another matter.

The fight grew more heated between Quinn on one side and Stew Udall and Bracy on the other. Memos were fired back and forth, usually via the candidate himself, into December. Quinn wrote to the candidate: "What can we hope to get in Iowa? Realistically, I think we keep the field muddled, as our floor operation did at the NDC. We force up the stakes in New Hampshire and, to a lesser extent, Massachusetts. We play the only game in town in early January and at the same time begin to allocate matching revenues to New Hampshire and, particularly, Massachusetts. At bottom, I believe we cannot risk helping someone else win Iowa [presumably Bayh] by staying out, leaving us after a strong New Hampshire showing with a Mexican standoff going into Massachusetts. We must, I think, do our part to keep Iowa muddled and make New Hampshire all the more critical."

Finally a showdown meeting was held among the combatants and Mo Udall himself, who finally committed himself to spending ten days in January and, according to one campaign aide, about $80,000. He rented a bus and toured the state more in the style of a primary-election campaigner seeking to turn out the vote than of a contestant in a caucus state trying to motivate the few party activists who determine precinct caucuses. And so, what had been a bad situation to start with became even worse.

Four days before the Iowa vote, the columnist Joseph Kraft wrote that Udall was indeed in so much trouble that if he "lags badly here, the pressure will be on him to get out of the race." Never mind that simultaneously Udall was building an effective organization in New Hampshire and Massachusetts. To avert disaster Udall finally turned to extensive television advertising to try to bridge the gap between him and Carter, but this resort to television was in itself an acknowledgment of organizational failure.

In his room at the Ramada Inn in Dubuque early one morning, several days before the Iowa caucuses, Udall sprawled in a chair and talked frankly about the outlook. He underscored his own understanding of the importance of perception in politics, and how it can become the reality. "I think my campaign is catching on and doing well *in other states,*" he said, "and we expect to *survive* here." Survive. That was hardly the way for a candidate to be talking more than a month before the first primary in New Hampshire. But the word accurately reflected Udall's state of mind—and the reality of his political situation. Failure to do passably in Iowa would send the temperature soaring in the psychological pressure cooker, and he knew it.

A great irony in Udall's entry in Iowa to muddle the picture, and prevent Bayh from jumping to the forefront of the liberal pack, was the fact that Bayh himself had entered Iowa to hold Udall back. "The reason we went in," Bill Wise, Bayh's press aide, said later, "was to block Udall and the start he had in New Hampshire." Thus, by withdrawing from Iowa Udall could have frustrated Bayh's effort.

Bayh, though he began to campaign in Iowa rather late, suffered the pitfall of excessive expectations, and largely through his own blundering. He plunged into the state, trying hard with personal campaigning and labor support of questionable deliverability to close the gap with Carter. Declaring himself the "electable" candidate on whom most Democrats could agree, Bayh thus made it essential to win—or surrender the argument of his electability. On the final weekend, he bused in a flock of young Indiana supporters to go door-to-door for him—a step that must be done much earlier if it is to be effective (time is needed to screen out nonsupporters and "leaners"). And in the excitement of the closing hours, his lieutenants let their enthusiasm get the best of their judgment. A straw poll at a large gathering of most of the candidates in Sioux City—a labor stronghold—on the Sunday before the vote showed Bayh comfortably ahead, 36.3 per cent to 28.8 per cent for Carter. Dick Sykes, Bayh's young Iowa campaign coordinator, told me it was just a question of whether there was still enough time to "overtake Carter." A comment like that had the effect of raising expectations, when Bayh's real objective in Iowa had been not to beat

Carter, whom he did not see as an immediate competitor, but to deal with Udall, Shriver, and Harris. But now Bayh's people were saying he was in a horserace with Carter, and they would have to bear the psychological burden of it.

Harris, by contrast, though he had gone to Iowa more frequently even than Carter and was one of the big spenders there, approached the caucuses more cautiously. Because so little was expected of him, he had everything to gain and very little to lose. Just as Bayh was expected to do well because he was supposedly "electable," Harris was by all odds considered "unelectable" because of his positions on the corporate structure of America, which were perceived as too far out of the mainstream of Democratic politics. But his diligent volunteer organizing team milked the high intensity of his support for its maximum yield.

The two other active candidates in the field were also not expected to do well. Jackson made a rather feeble attempt to mobilize the Iowa Jewish community, and Shriver hoped to cull a respectable showing in the Catholic strongholds of Dubuque and Carroll County. But in neither case were the stakes high, because the expectations were so low. (Shriver's high name recognition did not turn out to be much help. The Kennedy clan and its long list of old political and social associates who had turned out in droves for his declaration of candidacy were in short supply in Iowa. Sarge had been given a great bon-voyage party at the pier; now, as he sailed off, most of them stood on the dock and waved.)

A highly vocal, highly visible segment of the Catholic vote, in Iowa as elsewhere, was the so-called right-to-life movement—the fervent foes of abortion who have been seeking a constitutional amendment to bar all abortion and thus negate the Supreme Court ruling that a woman and her doctor have the unrestricted right to end her pregnancy in its first three months. Each of the six active candidates in Iowa was confronted by "pro-lifers" who demanded to know whether he would support such a constitutional amendment. None would. A few, notably both Shriver and Carter, expressed their unequivocal opposition to abortion as a matter of personal or religious conviction, but there appeared to be little to choose between them—that is, until Carter, in response to a question from a local Catholic newspaper, offered that under certain circumstances he might accept "a national statute" restricting abortion. Also, according to the columnists Rowland Evans and Robert Novak, Carter, when asked by a young "pro-life" woman whether he would support a constitutional amendment uniformly applying to all states the antiabortion ban in a Georgia law voided by the Supreme Court, "whispered" (their word) that "under certain circumstances I would." These observations managed to convey to pro-life adherents the notion that Carter was more favorably disposed to their point of view than any of the other candidates; so much so, in fact, that in some Catholic churches priests spoke of Carter as the preferred candidate on the issue of abortion. Carter, pressed by reporters for clarification, said he opposed a constitutional amendment but would favor any law, not in conflict with the Supreme Court decision, that would restrict abortions through better planned parenthood, availability of contraceptive devices, and improved adoption procedures. All these were measures favored by all the candidates but—significantly—not enunciated in just this way.

Evans and Novak subsequently reported that Carter's intentional ambiguity on abortion had "made the difference between first and second place" in Iowa by undercutting the only Catholic candidate, Shriver, with Catholic voters. They reported that when Democratic National Committeeman Don O'Brien, Shriver's in-state manager, convinced Monsignor Frank Brady of Sioux City that Carter was trying to work both sides of the abortion issue, Monsignor Brady had checked Atlanta and been surprised to learn that Carter indeed opposed an antiabortion constitutional amendment. When he went on local television to denounce Carter, his action came too late.

Carter's handling of the abortion issue in Iowa was a signal of things to come. He would display a talent for being on two sides of an issue that both dismayed and frustrated his opponents. In a political society accustomed to having its leading figures neatly compartmentalized as liberals and conservatives, Carter defied such categorizing. Why should a candidate be liberal or conservative down the line, he argued, when most of the American people were not? In his intensifying battle with the media over his unwillingness to be pigeonholed or, indeed, pinned down on any detail concerning his major proposals, he dismissed the insistence on clear-cut responses by saying that reporters asked him "frivolous" questions that the public really didn't care about.

Typical was his response to inquiries about one of his major campaign promises: to cut the federal bureaucracy from 1900 agencies to 200, just as he had reduced Georgia's 300 state agencies to 22 during his gubernatorial term. In Sioux City, about a week before the Iowa caucuses, a local reporter asked him to specify which federal agencies he would abolish. He replied that it was "impossible to say now" because he hadn't been able to take a close enough look. Later, when I pressed him on it, he remained adamant to the point of mild irritation. "I may set up a task force after the convention," he said as we flew across the state in his small chartered plane. "I'm not being evasive. People have common sense. They don't expect me to have all the answers. Reagan has been making the mistake by getting tied to a specific commitment. I have some ideas. For instance, there are forty-two federal agencies in education. I don't know now which could be cut. It would just be conjectural. It would just be a guess on my part."

Later, in Vermont, New Hampshire, and the interview at Peter Bourne's in Washington, I tried other tacks, all unavailing. In Washington, when I asked him why he didn't set up a task force to look into one specific area as a pilot example of how his reorganization would work, he told me that his staff and others "have been working on an analysis for, I'd say, about a year," but he was unable or unwilling to be more specific. The forty-two education agencies could be cut to two, he told me on another occasion. Which two? He couldn't say. "I know the techniques that must be used," he said, "and also the difficulties involved to make guesses about what will be the form of the government three years from now. That's something I don't care to do." Why not? Because it was just a matter of press curiosity; the public couldn't have cared less, and he wasn't going to permit himself to be hung up on it. "I think that most voters have enough judgment to know that a candidate for President can't spell out the form of government that's going to exist three years after the candidate is in office, after a complete analysis of what the structure of the government is and ought to be," he argued.

This confidence in his ability to convince the public, without being specific, to get the public to trust him on the details, was at the core of Carter's campaign style and strategy, and of his attitude toward the press. From the beginning, in Iowa, his campaign was oriented to the individual voter; the premise was that if he could ignite a spark with the people, the press would have to come around. Supporters once made remained supporters, because they were not simply supporters made, but friends made. And not only Carter engaged in this Good Shepherd exercise; his wife, Rosalynn, his sons, and his sister, Ruth Stapleton, a sexy blond mother who was also a professional evangelist, all worked Iowa like some foreign mission whose natives had not found salvation, but only needed to hear the word.

Carter's campaign in Iowa and other early caucus and primary states was patterned rather interestingly on something called "the pioneer mission," in which Carter was involved in 1967, after his first and unsuccessful race for governor against Lester Maddox. As he told me later, his church in Plains, Georgia, leased long-distance telephone lines and, in conjunction with a small Baptist college in Pennsylvania, proceeded to identify families in several northern towns that were without religion. "They hired WATS lines they could use at night," Carter said. "And they called and identified one hundred families in this little community of about eleven thousand people, and in none of those families was there a Christian. They didn't have any church affiliation. We didn't want to go up and proselyte people who had other religious beliefs, so we went up there with the names and addresses of these people on cards, and we stayed there until we visited every one of those families. And we witnessed to them about our Christian faith and when we left, we had organized a new church."

In Iowa and subsequent 1976 political battlegrounds, Jimmy Carter not only witnessed to voters about his Christian faith but about his faith in the nation and the American people. And when he left, he had organized his own church of political believers, thoroughly committed to him, willing to work with a zest and dedication approaching his own. And like a missionary so convinced of the Word that he was confident his new church would stand against all manner of secular pressures, Jimmy Carter openly disdained the demands of the infidel press that he speak in specifics, that he say exactly what his general proposals would do, would cost. He asked of voters the same "leap of faith" that is at the core of religious belief, and to a remarkable degree they gave it to him.

Carter's approach also took at face value the belief, fallen into disfavor during the Nixon years, that a campaign for the presidency is and should be an educational process, not only for the voter but for the candidate himself. I have noted elsewhere[1] that John F. Kennedy first came upon the full meaning of the toll taken on human beings in coal-mining when visiting mines in West Virginia as he campaigned there in 1960, and the searing experience colored not only his candidacy but later his presidency. Richard Nixon, on the other hand, in 1968 so insulated himself that he failed to grasp the burning intensity of the protests against Vietnam and against racial prejudice in the land. What I said then about Nixon could never have been said about Carter in 1976: "In the most antiseptic, controlled campaign in American history, he was a candidate in a glass booth. . . . It was difficult for a candidate who had been so effectively sealed off from genuine dialogue with the public, and from debate with his opponents, to grasp the depth of the public passions . . . and the resoluteness of those who disagreed with him. . . . One of the striking things about Richard Nixon all along his determined road back was that he seemed so often to be traveling it by helicopter—hovering above, studying the route, but never absorbing anything emotionally from the pilgrimage. In public, he seemed often to be a spectator in his own drama, or at best the guest of honor in a series of testimonials. Spontaneity was avoided like a Viet Cong land mine. And in his constant courting of the presidential image, there never was the harried, loose-necktie image of the personally involved, seeking campaigner that

1. *The Resurrection of Richard Nixon* (New York, 1969), pp. 463–64.

often adds a humanizing element to his quest, and warms the voter to the candidate."

At a time when much was written about the punishing demands imposed on candidates by the nominating system, Carter told voters it was his pleasure, his joy, to be among them, learning from them. This was something new—a candidate telling voters that the madness he was enduring to be elected President was not madness at all, but a cherished opportunity to learn—about them and about the country. He was not the first candidate to talk this way, but the same words in the mouths of the likes of Lyndon Johnson and Richard Nixon were a transparent ploy. Johnson in his last embattled days as President would go off to a totally insulated military base, shake a few hands, make a chest-thumping speech, and return saying he had talked to The People. And Nixon was forever inventing little old ladies in crowds whom only he seemed to see and hear, who posed questions undetected by accompanying reporters that he would proceed to answer in his most self-serving manner: "And she asked me, 'Mr. Nixon,' she said, 'why do you say that?' And I answered, 'Madam, I say that because . . .' "

But Jimmy Carter did in fact talk to the people, often at great length. It was forever a source of frustration for his staff that this man who insisted always on being on time—in order not to give offense or, putting it positively, to show he cared—would stop in a crowd and start a dialogue with anyone who asked him a question. He would respond fully, and then ask, "Have I answered your question?" Perhaps more than any other campaigner in recent times, Carter could truly say that he was out among the people, conversing with them, and learning from them. And this self-education was perhaps an element in his steadfast conviction that categorical answers were not always the best, that people did not always come down squarely on one side or another of an issue, but often had mixed views. He campaigned with almost a haughty confidence that what the press saw as dissemblance on issues would be understood as reasonableness and common sense by voters, who themselves seldom saw things in clear black and white. In Iowa, he talked about what 260 days on the road in 1975 had done for him: "I feel better than I did a year ago. I'm relaxed and confident. I'm a lot more sure of myself. I know a lot more about this country than I would have if I hadn't been to Sioux City three times, or to Florida for twenty-five days."

It is of course not uncommon for a candidate to learn about the country if he really throws himself into the campaign, and among the people. Some, like John Kennedy in West Virginia, see experiences in human deprivation and difficulty that have been foreign to their own experience. Others, who may be exposed to voters en masse but because of pressures of time, safety measures, or sheer campaigning chaos, cannot engage in lengthy dialogues, nevertheless draw impressions of an intensity of feeling or concern. Such was the case with Robert Kennedy, with whom the voters associated more often than not by grabbing for his hand or his cufflinks and shirt buttons in scenes bordering on hysteria. Yet he, too, for all his personal shyness, like Carter, seemed to hunger for personal contact with the voters. On many occasions in 1968 he would try to go off, with young voters particularly, for long conversations about politics and the state of the nation and world. He wanted everyone on his side, especially the young, and he went to considerable lengths to woo them. (It was one of his enduring disappointments that so many antiwar youth were for Gene McCarthy in 1968, a man not of their generation, and against him as an interloper.)

As the 1976 campaign wore on, Carter was often compared to John Kennedy—many even said they saw a physical resemblance between the two men—but it was Robert Kennedy he increasingly reminded me of, in this constant striving to get an indefinable something going with the electorate. Robert Kennedy was too reserved a man, too hard-bitten a politician, too angry at the war and Lyndon Johnson to talk to Americans as unabashedly as Carter did about love. But he also spoke urgently about the need to bring the country back to its principles, about how those principles should guide the nation's foreign policy, not be mocked by it, and how we needed once again to be able to be proud of our country. Later on in 1976, when Carter became the focus for large emotional crowds, when he would shed his jacket and wade into them in his shirt sleeves, Robert Kennedy would come to mind again—a small man, wiry yet durable, in his privateness somehow an unlikely beneficiary of such adulation, but capable of generating a rare electricity between himself and the public. Sally Quinn of *The Washington Post* said in a profile of Carter: "The conventional image of a sexy man is one who is hard on the outside and soft on the inside. Carter is just the opposite." Robert Kennedy had been classicly a man hard on the outside but soft on the inside, yet even in that, his Irish playfulness often softened the hard outside shell—particularly in the years after his brother's death, when his own reaching out and the events of the day worked changes on his brooding personality. In family background, education, experience, political and social milieus, the Jimmy Carter of 1976 and the Robert Kennedy of 1968 were miles apart. Yet in the determination of each to build a communication of intense feeling and commitment with the voters of America by throwing himself unsparingly into the effort, they were not that far removed.

(Later, after his election, Carter and I talked about Robert Kennedy in a conversation in the Oval Office. "I never met Bobby Kennedy," the President said. "When he was campaigning in 1968, there was a little girl working for him as a volunteer, from Albany, Georgia. When Bobby Kennedy was assassinated, the next night this girl, whom I had never seen in my life, called me on the phone. She said that a week or two before that, when Kennedy was campaigning in some state, she was hanging around the outside of his hotel door just hoping to get a glimpse of him. He came home to the hotel at night, tired, and had a whole bunch of staff folks with him. He saw these two high-school girls standing there, and they told him they had been volunteers for him. He invited them in—there were several staff folks around the room—and she asked him who from Georgia he knew. He said, 'Well, the only one I can think of right now who I know is supporting me is Jimmy Carter and his family.' She was crying on the phone, and said, 'I just wanted you to know Bobby said that, now that he's been killed.' " Carter said his mother "has practically worshiped the Kennedys for a long time," and had told him about Robert Kennedy's memorably emotional speech about his late brother John at the 1964 Democratic convention, at which she was an alternate delegate. "She was our connection with them," he said.)

Other presidential candidates—notably Harris, Udall, Bayh, and Shriver—also went out among the people, striving to build a sense of personal association. Harris appealed to the restless young voter, radical- ized by the Vietnam war and by dislike of the glaring economic inequities in American society, but he always seemed more the head of some rag-tag, blue-jeaned cult of the disaffected than a political statesman able to lead all segments of society. Udall on the stump as in private was gracious and witty, yet he somehow failed to transmit certainty about where he was going. Bayh was simply an old-fashioned pol operating behind an eager- youth façade, and his attempts to be taken as a heavyweight offered a glaring contrast with his glad-handing style. And Shriver, for all his impres- sive record and a penchant while campaigning for dressing like an enlisted man, had an air of an aristocrat out among the field hands for the day, trying his damnedest to extend *noblesse oblige*. Only Carter seemed in the early going to achieve personal closeness with an appreciable segment of the electorate he encountered.

On the night of January 19 the Carter mission paid off. In 2530 individual precinct caucuses in Iowa, in schoolrooms, church basements, libraries, and private living rooms, Democrats gathered to start the process that led to the national convention of 3008 delegates in New York's Madison Square Garden in July. I attended Des Moines precinct No. 59, in the basement recreation room of the Simpson United Methodist Church. There, thirty-five Democrats out of nine hundred thirty-seven registered in the precinct, one of the city's two largest, showed up to select seven delegates to the county convention. The precinct chairman, a thirty-year-old Des Moines lawyer named Pat Payton, explained the rules: the participants would form smaller caucuses of their own in various corners of the room according to candidate preference—the Carter people at one table, the Jackson people at another, the uncommitted people over in a corner, and so on. To elect a county delegate, a candidate would have to claim at least 15 per cent of the precinct caucus vote, or in this case, roughly five votes. If the backers of a given candidate failed to achieve that 15 per cent, they would be allowed to recaucus and join another candidate's group. While a crowd of costumed round dancers pranced obliviously on the floor above—a crowd larger than those gathered in the basement for the important business of electing a President—Payton gave the word to start. Twelve of the thirty-five made a Carter group; eight sat with the undecideds, and eight for Jackson; four joined a Harris caucus and three a Bayh; Udall, Shriver, and Wallace were shut out.

Payton, counting heads, told the Harris and Bayh caucuses that they each had failed to achieve 15 per cent of the total but could join another group. Of these seven, one Harris person moved over to the Carter table, one joined the uncommitteds, and two threw in with the three Bayh people, just enough to qualify him at 15 per cent. So Carter, with thirteen votes, was entitled to three of the precinct's seven delegates; the uncommitted caucus of nine, to two delegates; Jackson with eight and Bayh with five to one each.

Most of the Carter people said they had met the candidate personally or one of his family, and they liked his style. The Harris person who switched to Carter, Rick Hoenig, a twenty-seven-year-old employee of a local oil company, told me, "I really couldn't make up my mind which one I wanted. I prefer Harris on most things. I didn't want to say undecided. And I like Carter's sincerity, and maybe I sense there's support for the man here." Was he saying he liked to be with a winner? "Yes, in a sense," he said, in a response that would be heard from many a Carter voter in the year ahead. "I guess that's what I'm here for."

All over Iowa that night, that experience was being repeated. At the Des Moines Hilton, just across from the airport, the Democratic State

Committee and the national press corps gathered to compile and report about 1976's first hard vote for the presidency.[2] So novel was the presence of such television luminaries as Roger Mudd of CBS that State Chairman Tom Whitney peddled admission just to watch. And from the very first posting it was clear that it would be Jimmy Carter's night, the first of many. Shortly after midnight, with nearly 40 per cent of the precincts reporting, Carter had 34 per cent of the total. He ultimately slipped to just under 28 per cent, trailing the uncommitted slate, which had about 37 per cent, but he still maintained a margin of more than two to one over his next rival, Bayh. The final vote was Carter 27.6 per cent, Bayh 13.1 per cent, Harris 9.9 per cent, Udall 5.9 per cent, Shriver 3.3 per cent, and the rest undecided or split among other candidates.

Carter was in bed in New York, at the apartment of Howard Samuels, a former Democratic gubernatorial hopeful, when Powell phoned him at about 2 A.M. with the news. Greg Schneiders, Carter's efficient and outspoken personal aide, a twenty-nine-year-old former Washington restaurant and bar operator, took the call and summoned the candidate, who talked to Tim Kraft. Carter had been discussing with him where he would go, and now he told Kraft: "I guess we won't have to send you to Alaska now." Then he unceremoniously went back to bed.

Carter the next day was modest in victory. "I think just one state's results out of fifty is certainly a premature basis on which to predicate who is and who isn't a front-runner in the final election," he said. Fred Harris, who with about 10 per cent finished a surprising third, was not so modest. "Iowa started the winnowing-out process," he said, "and we've been winnowed in."

While nobody dropped out as a direct result of Iowa, four days later the 1976 campaign did have its first casualty. Terry Sanford, unable to extend his candidacy beyond his home state and hurting for money, announced at a press conference at Duke University that he was bowing out. "The ordeal of running a political campaign from a nonpolitical position is tougher than I anticipated," he conceded. He had continued as president of Duke through the end of 1975, and the job had been more inhibiting than he expected. But that was only part of his problem. He was a voice out of the past in a year in which voters seemed to be looking for new voices. Most of his money had come from North Carolina, and he had woefully under-

---

2. The precinct caucuses were just the first of four steps in Iowa's delegate-selection process. The delegates chosen that night went to county conventions, where they in turn selected delegates to the party's six congressional district caucuses and a state convention on May 29. In the end, Carter won 25 delegates, to 20 for Udall, 1 for Brown, and 1 for Kennedy.

estimated the task of fund-raising under the new campaign-finance law. By stepping aside, Sanford opened the way for another Wallace-Carter confrontation in North Carolina two weeks after the Florida primary.

The second caucus test, in Mississippi, brought the first measure of George Wallace's strength and his ability to function in a delegate-selection system. With his premium on organization, Wallace had been expected to bypass most caucus states and focus on the primaries, where retail politics—going directly to the voters with the candidate—figured to be effective. But Mississippi always had been one of his strongest states outside Alabama, and so, weeks in advance of the voting, the Wallace campaign sent in a twenty-five-year-old veteran of the 1972 Muskie campaign, Steve St. Amand, to organize for the precinct caucuses. Four other Democrats chose to contest Wallace: Carter, hoping to parlay his Iowa victory into an early upset over him; Shriver, attempting to tap his support in the state's black community, built in his days as head of the War on Poverty; Harris, making only a mild effort to demonstrate black *and* white voter support in the Deep South; and Bentsen, spending an estimated $25,000 in media. None could match the Alabamian. With professional skill and thoroughness, St. Amand reached down to the precinct level and tapped the support that had given Wallace 63 per cent of Mississippi's vote as a third-party candidate in 1968. It was no contest: Wallace 44 per cent, Carter 14 per cent, Shriver 12 per cent, Bentsen 1.6 per cent, Harris 1.1 per cent, uncommitted 27 per cent. "We got the word out that this is it," St. Amand later told Jim Dickenson of *The Washington Star.* "We told them that if they didn't vote for him now, there wouldn't be any way they could vote for him next November."

For Carter, the Mississippi result was mildly disappointing. I was traveling with him that day in Vermont, and before the first results were available, Carter was expressing optimism that he would surprise Wallace. At about 4 o'clock in the afternoon, Greg Schneiders heard the bad news at a radio station while Carter was cutting a tape. Walking to the next stop, Schneiders told him, "We're not going to win it and we're probably going to lose pretty badly." But it was still early, he said, attempting to console Carter, and it wasn't important.

"I know," Carter replied, "but I hate to lose anything."

The big loser in Mississippi was Bentsen, who was humiliated, for all his considerable effort. Everyone but the Texan with the fixed, radiant smile knew he was a goner, but he determined to take another stab at it in the next contested caucus state, Oklahoma, two weeks later.[3]

Oklahoma, never a major part of the presidential sweepstakes, took on early importance in the Democratic elimination contest because of Fred Harris. Usually a native son is so strong in his home state that no one dares challenge him; in Harris's case, his personal political history—moving from being a protégé of the oil companies as a state senator to one of their prime foes as a corporation-busting populist crusader—made him a marked man. And in his eight years in the Senate and four more out of it, Harris had become a transplanted Washingtonian; he not only neglected to mend fences, but seemed to chop them down in a headlong rush into left-wing politics that Oklahomans saw as unvarnished radicalism. It was said that Fred Harris had made his first abortive try for the Democratic presidential nomination because he knew he would be defeated for re-election to the Senate that year; Harris denied it, but the evidence was strong in support of the thesis. In any event, running in the Oklahoma caucuses was the last thing Harris wanted to do, since it was a no-win proposition: if he survived, that would be what he should have done; if he lost, the political community would say he couldn't even carry his home state, so why should he be considered a serious candidate? Yet he reasoned he could not very well duck Oklahoma, and so Harris committed himself to a big effort there, though the voting came only two weeks before the New Hampshire primary on which he was pegging so much.

Carter, as he had in Iowa, but with not quite the same degree of thoroughness or amount of time, had done a good job of organizing in Oklahoma. He had patiently wooed the state's Democratic governor, David Boren, and while Boren chose to work in behalf of an uncommitted bloc, the courtship yielded at least moral support. Boren said publicly he was "leaning" to Carter, and at the same time he was outspokenly against Harris.[4] Bentsen, hoping to gain supporters because he was a Texas neighbor who could help Oklahomans in the White House, enlisted much of the old Democratic county courthouse crowd in Speaker Carl Albert's "Little Dixie" district and other rural strongholds. Finally, a week or so before the

---

3. With a sharp eye to the psychology of the campaign, Carter had given himself another boost three days after Mississippi by winning forty-four of ninety-six votes in the city of Portland, Maine, when it caucused for votes to Maine's delegate-selecting convention, in the start of that state's month-long precinct-caucus process. No other candidate even tried, but the showing, and strength elsewhere in Maine throughout the month, enabled Carter to add that state's name to the string of early successes he was later so fond of ticking off in nearly every one of his speeches. Jordan said of this windfall later: "We couldn't believe we would not be challenged in Maine. All we did was have three hundred people in Portland on a Sunday. I was amazed other people were skipping so much."

4. Less than six weeks after the Oklahoma vote, Boren—seeing the Carter's bandwagon beginning to roll—became the first Democratic governor to endorse him.

voting, St. Amand arrived to try to pull off a repetition of his Mississippi surprise for Wallace.

From start to finish, the issue was Fred Harris—the old and the new —with Harris rather uncomfortably trying to salvage something from both. With most of the vote expected to go uncommitted, a quite small percentage could carry the day over Carter and Bentsen, and so he reached back to all his old supporters around the state, plus a small hard core of liberals, and hung on for dear life. The effort put a severe strain on his volunteer organization and cut into what proved to be a flagging campaign operation in New Hampshire.

Only the fact that Harris's top staff people appreciated the media importance of Oklahoma saved the day for him, at least temporarily. Knowing full well that defeat would be a severe psychological setback, they set up an elaborate internal system for reporting the results on caucus day. Oklahoma itself, and the state party, had no effective apparatus for reporting what in the past had not been a very important caucus; Bill Crain, the executive director of the Oklahoma Democratic State Committee, arranged to have precincts from Oklahoma and Tulsa counties, the state's two largest, phone in returns to his office. But for other results he had to rely on a combination of sources—local newspapers, county chairmen, and the individual campaigns.

Of all the reporting systems, Harris's was the most productive. On caucus night its results were fed to Crain, keeping Harris in the running, although Carter maintained a narrow but steady lead most of the night. Sometime before midnight, however, Harris began to catch up, with his staff picking up reports of Harris strength here and there and feeding them to Crain (he had no personal love for the Harris campaign but acknowledged their effective fact-gathering). Over and over reporters computed the candidates' percentages on a hand calculator and when Crain finally closed down for the night, under a barrage of favorable Harris figures from his own headquarters, Carter and Harris were close to a flat-out tie: Carter 20.27 per cent of the delegates chosen for county conventions, Harris 19.84 per cent, and most of the rest uncommitted. That was close enough for the newspapers and television to call it a tie. "Carter, Harris Lead in Oklahoma" was *The Washington Post* headline the next morning. The Harris camp's vigilance had bought a day's time for their candidate, and it had taken the edge off what the media might have billed as a Carter victory.

The next morning, the Harris supporters got an early start, determined to nail down at least a media victory, if not a real one. Even before Harris held a "victory" press conference in his Oklahoma City headquarters, one of his national field coordinators, Barbara Shailor, got on the phone to all the county chairmen who had not reported the previous night. On the very first call she made, she came up with a gain of forty-two Harris delegates. As she continued calling and found more Harris (as well as Carter) support, David MacDonald, Harris's Oklahoma coordinator, and Frank Greer, his press aide, rushed over to the state committee headquarters to get some action. Crain began posting additional figures, some called in by county chairmen on their own, but most delivered by MacDonald and Greer, who hovered over the tote board as he added the new figures. The state committee was arriving for a Sunday afternoon meeting, and Crain finally decided to shut down the board. He was not all that interested in the precise results, for he knew that with such a large uncommitted bloc the eventual national delegation would be very different from what the apparent Carter-Harris tie at the precinct level suggested. MacDonald looked at the board, and saw that Harris was trailing by two; he called Shailor, and she promptly came up with another reported precinct in which Harris had a three-vote edge over Carter. MacDonald told this to Crain, who was bugged good and proper by now at this pestering by the Harris camp. But, mumbling to himself, he posted the vote and closed down the board. The tally that stood until the official results were in nearly a week later read: Harris, 19.889 per cent, Carter, 19.871 per cent—a margin of a single delegate to the county conventions. The next day's headline in *The Washington Post* said: "Harris Tied with Carter in Oklahoma." About a week later, when the official results showed Harris actually to have lost to Carter by 1.5 per cent, attention had shifted to other events. The New Hampshire primary was now in full swing and the final Oklahoma figures were given short shrift. "The Great Oklahoma Steal" by the Harris staff had worked. *The Washington Post,* which had played the first two stories of Harris's "tie" on page one, relegated the official results to a few paragraphs in a political wrap-up story well inside the paper.

As for Carter, he was a psychological winner no matter what the exact numbers were. He had first tied, then beaten a native son on his home ground, and no amount of explaining that Fred Harris was no longer an Oklahoman could diminish that fact. There was, in Oklahoma, one indisputable loser, however. Bentsen, trailing badly with 12 per cent in a state in which he had committed lots of time and money, threw in the towel a few days after the Oklahoma caucuses, reducing his campaign to a favorite-son effort in Texas. His had been the most conspicuously ostentatious and ineffectual of all the early candidacies. Going into the race, he had to cope with the question of why a freshman senator with no notable legislative record behind him thought he was qualified to be President. Going out, he still had not coped with it. Meanwhile, the others pressed on.[5]

The political prize in the early caucuses of 1976 was not delegates but acceptance—by the media, by other the politicians, and to a lesser extent, by the public—of the seriousness of the candidacies. Carter's victories in Iowa, Oklahoma, and Maine did not remove all the doubts about him, to be sure; and the precinct caucuses were, accurately speaking, only preliminaries. But he could not now be easily dismissed, and as everyone headed for the early New England primaries, they weren't snickering at Jimmy Carter any more. What Arthur J. Hadley has called "the invisible primary" —all the preprimary events leading up to New Hampshire—had already significantly shaped the politics of 1976.

One other development, however, that took place in the week between the Mississippi and Oklahoma caucuses cast a long shadow over the unfolding election year. On January 30, the Supreme Court handed down its decision on the broad challenge by Senator James Buckley of New York, former Senator Eugene McCarthy, and others to the constitutionality of the Federal Election Campaign Act as amended in 1974. The Court upheld the whole public-financing arrangement on which most of the candidates pinned their hopes to compete on a par with the field, and the political community generally breathed a sigh of relief. But it was a premature response.

The Court at the same time found by an 8–0 vote that the manner of appointment of the Federal Election Commission, charged with investigating violations and otherwise monitoring the law, rendered it unconstitutional. As critics had warned, the Court ruled that the appointment of four members of the commission by Congress and only two by the President, when the body exercised clearly executive powers, constituted an encroachment on the executive branch by the legislative. The approach taken would have been satisfactory, the Court held, as long as the commission's role was limited to functions "of an investigative and informative nature . . . which Congress might delegate to one of its committees." But because the commission also was vested with significant executive duties in overseeing enforcement of the law, the scheme violated the Constitution unless all six members were appointed by the President.

Realizing the chaos the decision could cause in the midst of the ap-

5. Ironically, Carter at the outset thought Bentsen would survive the early primaries to be his main challenger for the nomination. "At the very beginning I thought it would be Bentsen," Carter told me long afterward. "He had a good start in New Jersey, Virginia, Oklahoma, Tennessee, South Carolina. But he didn't have his heart in it. He didn't make an all-out nationwide effort, and he faded."

proaching presidential campaign, the Court accorded "de facto validity" to all past acts and rulings of the commission. It also provided a thirty-day stay of judgment, during which the commission could continue to function as it had, including dispensing earned federal matching funds to the candidates, and during which Congress could reconstitute the commission to conform with the Court's decision. But matters would prove not so simple to resolve. Before Congress would revamp the commission and a dilatory President Ford finally approve the action, most candidacies would undergo a severe, if not altogether destructive, financial drought as they struggled to get through the long and costly string of primaries.

Concerning other features of the act, the Court upheld the $1000 limitation on what any person could give to any one presidential candidate, the $5000 limit on a political committee's contribution to a single candidate, and the ceiling of $25,000 on total contributions to all candidates by any one person. But it struck down a $1000 limit on what an independent committee or group could spend entirely on its own in support of a candidate, and it found that while a limit on contributions was constitutional, a candidate could spend as much as he wanted—provided he raised it himself within the contributions ceiling. Any presidential candidate accepting public financing, however—all of them at this stage—did have to abide by the national and state-by-state expenditure limits tied to that provision.

The Court also let stand the law's treatment of minor parties and minor-party and independent candidates like McCarthy. It pointedly found that the public-financing approach did not deny equal protection of the laws; Congress' requirement that a candidate produce "some preliminary showing of a significant modicum of support" to qualify for a federal subsidy was a legitimate exercise of legislative discretion, the Court said; the absence of such a requirement "would not only make it easy to raid the United States Treasury, [but] would also artificially foster the proliferation of splinter parties."

The immediate need was to put the Federal Election Commission back together in a way that would satisfy the Court, and the most obvious way was to rewrite the legislation to enable the President to appoint all six members. But Representative Wayne Hays, who didn't want the commission in the first place, immediately announced he would introduce a bill to do away with it, rather than revamp it. Supporters of the law said they would sponsor their own revisions, but the commission chairman, Thomas B. Curtis, was glum about the temporary stay. "It's hard for me to believe something as complicated could be straightened out in thirty days," he said. And he was so right.

Over the next month the presidential candidates' finance chairmen and accountants, fearful that it could not be done, hastened to complete and submit records of the private contributions they had received; it was vital that they collect as much in matching funds as possible before the commission's power to disburse money ran out. The real squeeze would not be felt for some weeks to come, because commitments were already made for the first primaries. But the knowledge that the federal subsidy could abruptly end if the commission's life and powers were not extended was now a Damocles sword over all the presidential aspirants as they moved into those early primaries, starting with New Hampshire.

16. One-on-One Politics in New Hampshire

The New Hampshire primary has been much maligned by those who see no justification in permitting a handful of voters—443,500 registrants, of whom only 48 per cent actually voted in 1976—to have so much to say about the fortunes of the American presidency. New Hampshire is said to be too small, too remote, too atypical to be seriously regarded as a national political barometer. Except for an uncommonly small percentage of blacks, however, New Hampshire is not all that unlike many other states. Contrary to the impression given by picture postcards of snowy covered bridges and white church steeples, the state is heavily industrial, and growing more so each year as plants and blue-collar workers push northward from Boston and the eastern Massachusetts complex. From Manchester and Nashua south and over to the seacoast, where most of the state's population works and lives, New Hampshire hums with the rhythms of machine and manual labor, and with considerable white-collar energy as well.

For the well-financed, well-known political candidate, New Hampshire can be a pesky, troublesome preliminary, an intrusion that must be tolerated —or dodged—before committing one's resources to the mass-media salesmanship of larger, more cosmopolitan states. But to the long shot, to the candidate with little money or celebrity, New Hampshire is the great equalizer. It is ideal for the candidate who is trying to launch a campaign on a shoestring, because it is a place where time and energy can effectively overcome lack of money. The candidate who starts early enough can have an impact more effective than any contender with a last-hour television blitz, and the impact is magnified by the national media attention focused on the year's first primary.

Because New Hampshire is small it is ideal for low-budget retail campaigning—knocking on doors, touring plants and shopping centers, being seen on the cheap, with a fair chance of contacting many voters directly or through canvassing supporters. There is no statewide television, which further reduces costs, unless a candidate wants to buy time over Boston television. In the past, that practice was eschewed by most candidates, but in 1976, with Massachusetts conducting the second primary a week later than New Hampshire, candidates could "buy Boston" and allocate most of the cost to their Massachusetts campaigns.

Also, candidates hungry for national exposure find a rich lode in the Granite State; for more than a month before the primary, most hotels in Manchester and Concord, a twenty-minute drive to the north, are booked solid, mainly with representatives, famous and little-known, of the news media. The New Hampshire primary has become as much a staple in the national political diet as national conventions, election day in November, or a President's inauguration. It is big business for the state. In addition, veteran political reporters like New Hampshire because they know all the players in presidential politics down through the years, and the state is so manageable. One can bed down in Manchester for several weeks and travel to most parts of the state and back in a day. It is like going to spring training camp for a major-league baseball player. Here is the place where rookies on the make and veterans trying to prove they have one more season in them test themselves before smaller crowds than they will encounter later down the road.

If one of the purposes of the new campaign-reform legislation was to open the system to more competition, and to take the decision away from the money men and give it to voters, then the New Hampshire primary served that purpose well. The large field attracted by its cost-effective appeal was untidy and undoubtedly raised the premium on an already small number of votes cast—30 per cent proved enough to "win." But the alternative —starting the winnowing-out process in one of the large industrial states —would have made money the winnower. If the long primary trail of 1976 had started in New York or Ohio or even Massachusetts, it is questionable whether any but the well-heeled candidates could really have competed.

There is something inherently sound about a flock of would-be Presidents, some well known and some not, wooing a constituency whose roots are so deeply entrenched in the early history of the nation. The tradition of the town meeting in New Hampshire is a lasting reminder of our political origins and the American allegiance to grass-roots participation in the governance of our society. Braving bitter cold and snow at factory gates on frigid mornings admittedly is no measure of a person's intellectual ability to lead the nation. But in a time when memory of the imperial presidencies of Lyndon Johnson and Richard Nixon was still fresh, it was not a bad idea to see the candidate go directly to the people to ask for their mandate; not bad for the people, and not bad for the candidate.

In New Hampshire, a diligent vote-seeker can make his presence felt to an unusually high percentage of the electorate, and the experience can tell him things about the United States and its citizens that are not conveyed by the practice of wholesale politics in some arid television studio or anti-septic motorcade through a jammed inner-city noontime crowd. Politicians are individuals with their antennae out; the candidate who lives on a steady diet of genuine exposure to and discourse with the voters, as Jimmy Carter and Morris Udall did in 1976, can come away with a profound and invaluable sense of what the country is, what it wants and needs, and what it is likely to accept in leadership. As well as any other state, New Hampshire throws candidate and voter together.

In advance of the New Hampshire primary, much had been written and said about how its importance would be diminished in 1976. Politicians proclaimed that the Iowa caucuses were the "new New Hampshire." And the decision of Massachusetts, which would be selecting 104 Democratic convention delegates, to move its primary date forward to only a week after New Hampshire's vote was said to assure that the Granite State, which was selecting only seventeen national convention delegates, would be overshadowed. Neither proved to be the case. The Iowa experience had only generated more interest in New Hampshire, and it received the full national spotlight throughout February; Massachusetts was shunted aside.

The beneficiary of these circumstances once again was Jimmy Carter. He came into New Hampshire as the man to beat, and in spite of his early successes he remained enough of a novelty to catch the imagination of voters and the press alike. Again as in Iowa, he had the luxury of running against a highly competitive liberal field—Udall, Bayh, Harris, and Shriver —and the same advantages of an early start and a solid grass-roots organization. This time, it was true, expectations were high, but Carter had the wherewithal to contend with the pressure brought to bear on him.

Carter had been in New Hampshire repeatedly over the previous year. At the beginning, heavy mailings from his young state coordinator, Chris Brown, would roust out only five or six people to meet him, but slowly a cadre of workers was built. There had been lean days, with Carter slipping in and out of New England almost unnoticed. One day, driving to his Concord headquarters, the driver got lost and Carter wound up in Massachusetts. He called his headquarters from a pay phone, told Brown to cancel the next few events on his schedule, then turned to his driver and said, "Can you find the headquarters?" It was no serious indictment to be accused of being unable to find it. The office was located up a very long flight of stairs in a building on a side street, one floor below a gymnasium, where basketball players pounded up and down the court all day, to the constant distraction of the Carter volunteers. In the next-door room, an indoor golf course, with picturesque fairways and greens flashed on a screen, attracted winter duffers who thwacked away as the Carterites busied themselves trying to elect a President.

But with the reports of Carter's successes in Iowa and neighboring Maine, it was hard for anyone to ignore him. Interest and contributions picked up. And the publicity attendant on those early Carter victories assured him of special radio, television, and press coverage. For any little-known candidate, the customary motorcade is the candidate's car, perhaps with an enterprising reporter stuffed into the back seat alongside him, and a staff aide or two up front. That was how it was for most of the pack in New Hampshire. But in Carter's case a chartered bus now followed him, carrying his large press contingent. By such signs are winners and prospective winners gauged.

Yet if Carter embarked on the nation's first primary test with distinct advantages, he now carried with him the burdens of success as well. The candidates he had thrashed in Iowa were already scrambling for survival, and they tried, predictably, to find ways not only to advance their own candidacies but also to pull Carter back into the pack. They were, however, handicapped by two circumstances. First, they were functioning in the aftermath of Watergate, when press and public were especially watchful against a reintroduction of political dirty tricks, and when the candidates themselves were mindful of the injustice and the likely boomerang effect of political foul play—or even of excessive rhetoric. Second, they were dealing in Jimmy Carter with a man conspicuously difficult to corner on the issues. Carter was both unpredictable and inconsistent in terms of ideological orthodoxy. In most matters of civil rights, Carter was clearly liberal; in most matters of economics, clearly conservative. Beyond that, he was often both liberal and conservative on a number of issues—such as abortion, for example. He was against a constitutional amendment to ban it, yet he was personally opposed to it and would favor other measures to restrict its use. On a range of issues, he showed all the elusiveness of a scatback. In time, that very slipperiness would become one of the most effective issues against him—the "fuzziness issue"—but it took his foes, and the press, months to fully identify it and brand it for more effective tracking.

One fairly early attempt to nail Carter in the media, an article in *Harper's Magazine,* was notable chiefly for the uncommonly strong squawks it produced from Carter and his staff. The piece, by a young writer named Steven Brill, who earlier had cut up Wallace and Jackson in articles of uneven accuracy, hit Carter's propensity for overclaiming, cutting corners, and managing to come down on more than one side of a range of issues. It nit-picked here and there but also credited Carter with being a good governor and a "hard-working, smart politician," and gave a fair picture of the Carter soft-soap stump style. In response, Jody Powell wrote an eleven-page rebuttal, in which he charged broad misquotation and distortion. The Carter political braintrust apparently feared that Brill's article could open the door to all manner of investigations of Carter and even closer press scrutiny and criticism, at a time he had really begun to move.

Even before this article, about which Carter was livid, he had made clear his dislike of the press. "To have this concentrated attention on myself and the other candidates by the press at this early stage is really extraordinary," he told me in late January, as we rode in his car to a party dinner in Brattleboro, Vermont. "I think that [it] possibly will make the press more demanding than they should be on final answers on complicated questions at the early stage of a campaign, when the accumulation of advisers and the detailed analysis of major programs are unavailable to the average candidate who doesn't yet have the stature and the time of the nominee himself. I'll just have to be frank in saying I don't know the answer to a question when the question is too demanding.

"I don't care how much I'm questioned, I don't care how much the reporters desire it," he went on, "there's absolutely no way to give a definitive answer. . . ." If he did not know the answer to something himself, he insisted, far from his reticence being a shortcoming, it was actually a virtue. "No matter how demanding people might be," he said, "it would be a very serious violation of *my word of honor* if I pretended to know those answers." Carter had a distinct way of converting his every act, even a refusal to give a plain answer to a plain question, into an act of political morality. This pretension in him often rankled, but he never hesitated to invoke it if it served his purpose.

Carter could, in fact, be quite intimidating in his usually humorless way with reporters. But this did not spare him the barbs of the boys in the press bus. By the time we got to New Hampshire, some reporters had already given birth and voice to a new song on the tune of "Jesus Loves Me":

Jimmy loves me, yes, I know,
Jody Powell tells me so.
In Catholic groups he comes on strong,
Unborn babes to him belong.
Oh, Jimmy loves me, yes, Jimmy loves me,
Oh, Jimmy loves me, 'cause Jody tells me so.

Such parody-writing was the frivolous side of a commitment by reporters and their news organizations to campaign coverage that was, for the main part, very serious, wearying, and uncommonly expensive. The average day for the average reporter on the campaign trail was at least as long as the candidate's, and usually longer—when you added on time to write and arrange for transmission of copy after the day's events. It was a lively and exciting way to earn a living, but repetitively boring, too. The reporters who covered the campaigns seldom had a day or weekend off through the long political season. But still, few of them would have gotten off before the last stop. It was a rare opportunity to see contemporary history and historymakers up close, and even to play a part in the experience of self-government.

Reporters on the campaign trail never talked about themselves in such lofty terms, of course; they had, and enjoyed, the image of being shabby little men in rumpled suits forever scribbling in their notepads, making wise-ass side comments as the candidates emoted, much to the consternation of more serious types in the audience. But for all this outward derision of the exercise, they were by and large deeply committed to the importance of the political system, and they tried to do their work fairly and well. Sometimes they suffered from myopia, and a few took themselves and their role too seriously for their own good or the good of their readers, but it was hard to be pompous for long on a press bus; the same biting wit that worked candidates over with such abiding relish would be turned inward on them. Besides, competitiveness in the reporting business does not permit anyone much time for self-congratulation; important scoops were rare and the level of competence among those who covered campaigns regularly was such that a reporter who beat the competition one day could expect to be beaten himself the next. "Beating the competition" was always an objective, but the most serious-minded on the press bus strove more to be perceptive, to put facts or a situation already known into more comprehensible or significant terms.

The public would be astounded if they really knew the resources that are put into covering a national political campaign by the major news-gathering organizations—especially in the later phases, when candidates crisscross the country in jet planes, charging the press passengers first-class fare plus a premium. There were two basic approaches to coverage in the primary period: "man-to-man," with one reporter covering one candidate wherever he went; and "zone," with one reporter being responsible for all the candidates who came into a given primary state.

On the Republican side, man-to-man was not difficult in 1976 because there were only two candidates and one of them was the President, who was covered full time anyway. But on the Democratic side, the prospect of assigning ten or more reporters to follow the candidates around required compromises. *The New York Times,* for instance, which employed a modified man-to-man coverage, elected to have one reporter keep an eye on two or more candidates. The paper's highly competent reporter Charles Mohr started out with responsibility for Bayh and Harris, and when both faded as serious prospects was shifted to Carter. But this approach was a luxury most news organizations could not afford. At *The Washington Post,* we opted for the zone approach for the early round of caucus and primary states, then put single reporters on the surviving candidates later, still covering the major primaries on a zone basis.

This kind of intensive coverage assured the candidates, and especially Carter as the front-runner and the new face, plenty of press criticism. But there was also growing criticism amongst the candidates themselves about how Carter handled substantive political issues. Udall complained to reporters one night, in his room at the Ramada Inn in Concord, that he could not understand how labor could support Carter when he refused "to fight for the union shop": Carter often said he would not push for repeal of the federal right-to-work law, although he would sign it as President if organized labor could get a repeal through Congress. And Bayh—who was trying to emphasize his own heavy political background with radio ads that said, "It takes a good politician to be a good President"—asked with a mixture of incredulity and exasperation: "How can a man who is a former governor and has been going around the country running for President say he isn't a politician?"

Carter was, indeed, a tough man to bring down in the open field, and he had an open field against the liberal pack—in New Hampshire as in Iowa. Beyond that, he simply worked harder than anybody else. He would be up at the crack of dawn to greet workers as they entered their factories, smiling, cordial, shaking hands and distributing his dark-green-and-white campaign folders. His wife and sons, and their wives, targeted the state in similar fashion.

Meanwhile Chris Brown was constructing a strong organization, and the Carter effort became pervasive and professional—an attractive, hard-working candidate up front, a legion of dedicated supporters behind. And unlike some other campaigns, Carter's attracted a good share of middle-aged individuals; in staid New Hampshire, the phenomenon of these solid citizens going from door to door, instead of the hordes of college kids who seemed to invade quadrennially, was yet another factor working in Carter's favor.

Carter's organization in New Hampshire was generally underrated, in the media's focus on a new political personality with a different style. Brown had a particularly difficult task because the typical Carter supporter was not an activist. Most of the usual "doers" were liberals attracted to Udall; Carter appealed more to blue-collar workers who were inured to the pleas of presidential hopefuls and did not like to get involved. So it took time. Jean Wallin, a former national committeewoman, signed on after the Kansas City mini-convention and became a central figure; another was Ellis Woodward, a quiet but effective young man who took over scheduling (he later moved on to other primaries for Carter). In January 1976 a planeload of Georgians flew into Manchester and proceeded to knock on doors for their "Jimmeh." The novel Southern accents beguiled many old Yankees, French- and Italian-Americans, and they took a closer look at the man from Georgia.

Udall, a Westerner, by contrast made little of his differences with the New Englanders. As in Iowa, he found himself in an identity bind: he didn't want to be perceived as another bland middle-of-the-road Ed Muskie, yet at the same time he wanted to avoid George McGovern's mantle. Oddly, his dismal showing in Iowa now worked somewhat in his favor: if he could pull off what now would be widely perceived as an upset over Carter, his campaign would be rehabilitated overnight.

Udall brought considerably more strength to his New Hampshire campaign than he had had in Iowa. It was woven together painstakingly and expertly by David Evans, a 1972 organizer for McGovern who hailed from Rhode Island, a man of great cordiality and precision, together with Maria Carrier, who had been the 1972 state coordinator for Muskie. By the time the bad news from Iowa struck, Udall's operations in New Hampshire were in place and functioning well. All through January Evans had fifty canvassers ringing doorbells somewhere every night, and by primary day nearly all Democratic homes had been canvassed and recanvassed to identify sure votes, "leaners," and undecideds, so that efforts could be made to turn out the identifiable Udall vote.

If there are two words that hold more political significance for the professional campaign manager than any other, they are probably "identification" and "turnout." Most of their effort, beyond the showcase display of the candidate, is devoted to these two objectives—identifying who your voters are and turning them out at the polls. The job is an ancient one in politics; in the days of the ward heeler, it was his business to know all the voters in his territory personally and to build a voting loyalty among them, often by way of the straightforward device of services, or even financial aid, rendered. The dollar bill slipped into an open hand or, only slightly more subtly, the family turkey delivered on Thanksgiving or Christmas, sealed the arrangement and helped perpetuate the reign of political bosses. With the breakdown of the boss system, not least by the growth of governmental social welfare at the federal level, the role of the ward heeler diminished or even vanished in most cities.

In its place has developed a more thorough, sometimes computerized system of voter identification and delivery. It was used with most notable results in the 1968 "children's crusade" of Eugene McCarthy, was refined in McGovern's campaign of 1972 and in 1976 became standard operating procedure for nearly all presidential candidates. The system works this way: voter registration or other comparable voter lists are taken and checked against telephone books for addresses and phone numbers. The lists are then reorganized in terms of voting precincts. Volunteers, armed with "walk lists" if they are going door-to-door or "call lists" if they are working the telephone, then proceed to make personal contact with the voters, engaging them in political conversation and eventually asking them their preference in the approaching election. The foot canvass, as doorbell ringing is called, is considered far superior to phone canvassing, but requires more volunteers. In a system that now has become standard in most campaigns, voters are given a rating of one through five: (1) Positive commitment to your candidate; (2) Leaning to your candidate; (3) Undecided; (4) Hostile to your candidate or committed to some other; (5) Not home, recently moved or otherwise not classifiable 1 through 4.

This canvassing code, once insider's stuff, has become so well known in the political community and among the press that long conversations are held wherever those interested in campaigns gather, using only the numbers: "Things look better. Our ones and twos are up forty per cent over last week," or: "We're recanvassing our threes and getting considerable movement to twos and some to ones."

By going back by foot or phone, the canvassers try to build their list of "ones" and "twos" as a master call list for election day. Then, throughout the day, these likely voters are visited or phoned and urged to go to the polls, with transportation provided for those without it.

In a primary state, much of the vote comes into the ballot booth "off the street"—meaning of its own volition. But the canvassing operation is intended to provide a dependable base, a core of solid support. Good canvassing and get-out-the-vote operations are believed to benefit the candidate especially in inclement weather, or in an election marked by general apathy.

The system is hardly foolproof: in New Hampshire in 1976, a huge undecided vote was charted in all the candidates' canvasses, with considerable movement from "threes" to "ones" and "twos" for most of them in the final days. These reports made everyone very optimistic, but the end results suggested that many canvassers were being misled. Perhaps the beleaguered New Hampshirites were asked so many times by so many canvassers that in the end they took the easiest course and told the callers what they wanted to hear.

On the final two weekends before the New Hampshire primary an estimated one thousand or more volunteer canvassers were in the streets. Bayh, for example, imported several hundred Indianans and gave each an instruction sheet that said: "This is it, folks. Effectively, this weekend represents our last large-scale contact with the New Hampshire electorate. . . . It is most important to understand that in New Hampshire, more so than in most states, personal contact is by far the most effective campaign device. Media is far less important. There is only one television station in the state; the bulk of the television comes out of Boston. Additionally, New Hampshire is an organizer's dream—there are only 116,000 registered Democrats in the entire state, with 85 per cent of those Democrats living in the population centers in which you will be canvassing. The people in this state are political pros in terms of campaign techniques, as most every technique known to the world of politics has been tried on these people at one time or another. The voters know precisely what we are doing. So does everyone else. We must tell you that the techniques that we are using are also being used by other campaigns as well. This is natural, as many of us had the same training ground—the McGovern campaign."

The other candidates also had impressive canvassing operations. Carter's campaign compiled 50,000 file cards bearing voters' phone numbers, and it hired National Telephone Advertisers of New York for $18,000 to conduct a phone canvass that ran simultaneously with a foot canvass. Udall's supporters had completed a canvass of 36,000 households in key areas early in February. After each visit, a personal letter was sent from canvasser to voter thanking him for his support or urging him (if he was a "two" or "three") to take a closer look at Udall. Late starters like Bayh were obliged to crash-canvass on weekends with volunteers who spent the whole day on the streets and several hours that same night preparing as many as a hundred handwritten notes apiece to voters they had contacted. "When they leave," Bill Wise, Bayh's press aide, told me in New Hampshire, "they're basket cases. That's why infusions are important. This just chews people up."

Organization was a great deal, but not everything. In retail politics, the candidate himself must bear a heavy burden. It was imperative for any candidate serious about New Hampshire (with the exception, of course, of the incumbent President) not simply to go there but to go there often, and to work the voters as if they were constituents in a precinct or neighborhood election.

In this undertaking, none of the other candidates could approach Carter, though they tried. Freed of the obligations of public office and self-sufficient financially in a pre-election year without legal impositions on spending, he was able, through 1975, to campaign with uncommon diligence.

A measure of that diligence came one day in the final week in New Hampshire. The morning broke overcast and gloomy, with a light snowfall that had all the signs of growing to blizzard proportions. The outlook was ominous. It so happened that Carter was scheduled to fly to Berlin (pronounced BURR-lin), the northernmost city in the state and an obligatory campaign stop because it has a heavy concentration of Democratic voters. Candidates often go there early to get it over with; Carter had gone there early and, as was his custom, was going there late as well (it was in fact to be his third trip to Berlin). Two De Haviland Twin Otters were chartered from Air New England, but as the traveling press corps gathered at the Manchester Airport the expectation was that the flight would surely be canceled. After some delays in locating and fueling the planes, however, they took off.

As we flew north, the weather turned progressively worse; heavier snow and winds conspired to make the flight into the White Mountains extremely nerve-racking. With white knuckles gripping armrests throughout the plane, Jim Wooten of *The New York Times,* the Sid Caesar of the press corps, soothed the assembled chickenhearted by shouting over the drone of the lumbering engines: "Your courage vill not go unrevahrded! The Führer himself vill soon be leafing Berlin!" But both planes finally landed at Berlin. Through it all, Jimmy Carter seemed unperturbed.

The first stop was St. Patrick's School, where Carter spoke to primary graders, giving them an only slightly scaled-down version of his standard "a government as filled with love as are the American people" sermon. He had great rapport with the kids, who listened to him just as attentively as their elders did. He wanted to bring the country peace, he told them, and honesty, and to make sure that everybody paid his fair share of taxes, and was treated equally by the government. "I want a government always to tell the truth," he said, softly. "What we need is for our government to be as good as our people. Wouldn't that be a great thing?" He beamed, and the children beamed back.

It occurred to me as Carter talked that he was not especially talking down to these children, but that his standard speech itself was a subtle exercise in talking down to an audience, adult or child. In one breath he could quote Reinhold Niebuhr that the legitimate goal of politics was to "establish justice in a sinful world," and in the next say that the country, the system, the people all were good, decent, honest, fair, et cetera, et cetera. Jimmy Carter did not treat children as adults; it was more that he treated children and adults alike, *like children,* enveloping them with his smile and his message of goodness and love that could overcome all adversity.

From the classroom, Carter went to a combination gymnasium-auditorium, where perhaps a hundred more seventh and eighth graders awaited him. These older children sat on the floor in a wide semicircle around him, and he played a guessing game with them—but with a political angle, as always. "How many of you have mothers who vote? Raise your hands." And they did. "How many of you have fathers who vote? Raise your hands." And they did. "Grandmothers? . . . Brothers? . . . Sisters?" And, finally, "Do you know what my name is?" A chorus of small voices shouted in unison: "Jimmy Carter!!" Grinning broadly, he then launched into his government-of-love sermon again. The children sat absolutely rapt as he spoke in a low, almost reverent voice. And when he said, simply, "Thank you very much. I love all of you," as he raised his arms high, out over their heads, an interesting thing happened. As if on cue, the children sprang to their feet and swarmed up to him. He reached down, picked up one and hugged her, set her down and picked up another, and on and on. Others clung to his legs and tried to scamper up into his reach. My colleague from *The Washington Star,* Jim Dickenson, shook his head with wonder. "Suffer the little children to come unto me," Dickenson said, and that's about how it was.

Like the line in the old song, "The rich get richer and the poor get children," Carter's early progress brought him trappings of success that in turn created an aura of even greater success. His was the first campaign on the Democratic side to command enough press attention not only to warrant the renting of a real press bus but also to hire a separate press plane when he hopped to the northern reaches of New Hampshire.

Udall, by contrast, limped along with a kind of pick-up team of reporters who would spend a day with him here or there, or make a stop or two. Like Carter, he visited all the ethnic clubs in Manchester and Nashua—the French-Canadian and the Polish-American and the Italian-American and all the other hyphenated-American drinking, cardplaying clubs. But more often than not, the television notables with him attracted more attention than he did. One night, in St. Stanislaus Hall in Nashua, he spent the better part of an hour walking up and down long aisles of bingo players who scarcely glanced up from arranging their cards to look at him—well before the night's games started and the first lucky number was called. It took a good-humored man to endure such nights, and Udall persevered in good humor.

Harris was in much the same boat, and it could also be said of him that he had good humor in abundance to sustain him. Happy-go-lucky by nature, Harris continued to tool around in a camper—by now it was his campaign trademark—whistling country songs and "Blues in the Night," and enjoying himself. A bombastic speaker, he got crowds stirred up about as much as anyone, but he was speaking to a narrow constituency, as was soon to be made clear. Like Carter, Harris had accurately gauged the importance of New Hampshire, as his 1974 memo attested. But he permitted himself to be lured elsewhere, and failed to build the cohesive grass-roots effort his memo called for. Eventually his campaign fell into the hands of assorted crazies, and his imported national staff could not save the sinking ship.

Shriver, for all his celebrity, just didn't have it as a campaigner, and the old Kennedy hands by and large looked the other way. Typical of his efforts was a visit he made to the New Hampshire Insurance Company in Manchester. He walked through office after office of young women sitting at drab desks doing all the things that are done in deathly quiet at insurance companies. "Hi. Sarge Shriver," he would say, handing each a campaign button, "there you are," as if he were bestowing a piece of candy at an orphanage. He was laboring to be taken as his own man, not just the Kennedy brother-in-law, but inquiries among the young women revealed that he wasn't even doing well in that department. Linda Miller, a twenty-three-year-old customer-service representative, said, "He's associated with the Kennedys. Isn't he Ethel Kennedy's brother? No? Joan Kennedy's brother? No? There's so many of them."

Of all the others, Bayh seemed to be doing best. Trying to make up for lost time, he grimly set about cleaning up his own act. That is, he tried to put his aw-shucks style on the back burner and come on as the Experienced Legislator, which his record substantiated but his cornball manner and boyish looks always blurred. To achieve this reformation, his campaign cooked up a special routine: a documentary film emphasizing Bayh's record in the Senate, which was shown at evening gatherings in high-school cafeterias and the like. When it was over and the lights were turned on, a local supporter holding a hand microphone with a long portable cord would stand in front of the screen and, like some Yankee Ed McMahon, proclaim: "Ladies and gentlemen, the next President of the United States, United States Senator Birch Bayh!" From the rear, wearing his dark-blue sincerity suit and a serious look, would stride the senator from Indiana. He would take the mike, let some of the cord out behind him, and then start roaming around the room, a political Johnny Carson on the "Tonight Show," talking up his experience. "Why Birch Bayh?" he would ask, in that maddening habit of calling himself by his full name, in the third person, and then proceed to tick off the "tough battles" he had fought in the Senate: opposition to the Haynsworth and Carswell Supreme Court nominations; extension of the voting-rights act; passage of constitutional amendments lowering the voting age to eighteen and revamping presidential succession. (One problem with this whole approach was that it reinforced Bayh's image as a Washington political creature, in a year when Jimmy Carter was making hay running against Washington. But he had no choice; if his experience was a vulnerability, it was also his underutilized strength.)

As each of the candidates thus went about vending his political wares, the press trooped dutifully behind, writing mostly about personalities, because in truth there did not seem to be a very great difference among the Democrats on the issues. But this perception was in error. On several key issues, basic differences existed between Carter and the field.

On a number of occasions in New Hampshire, for instance, Carter said, concerning his stated advocacy of full employment, that he was reluctant to use the public sector—the federal government and payroll—to provide jobs. Jobs should come out of the private sector; only as a very last resort should the government take up the slack, in such programs as youth labor, rural conservation and the like. In contrast, the other Democrats were calling for aggressive use of the government as employer of those who could not be absorbed by the private sector. This was an important difference of emphasis on the subject that all the polls indicated was of greatest concern to the voters—the economy and unemployment. Yet it did not come into focus in the New Hampshire primary at all.

Even when a member of the press did isolate a basic difference, it did not seem to catch on generally. David Broder, my colleague on *The Washington Post,* in a column more than three weeks before the New Hampshire vote, disclosed a letter written by Carter in 1971 to the National Right-to-Work Committee, an antiunion lobby that had fought against repeal of Section 14-B of the Taft-Hartley labor law permitting states to bar union-shop contracts. In it, Carter said: "I stated during my campaign [for Georgia governor in 1970] that I was not in favor of doing away with the right-to-work law, and that is a position I still maintain." Broder contrasted this statement with Carter's 1975–76 campaign response: "My position now is the same as in 1970, when I was running for governor. I told the labor representatives from Georgia that any time the repeal of the right-to-work law could be passed by the legislature, then I would sign it. That has always been my position since 1970. I would do the same as President." And with this comment by Carter to labor leaders: "I think that the major responsibility for repeal of 14-B rests with labor, and when you see if you can get it passed, I'll cooperate. . . . I would be glad to see 14-B, the right-to-work law repealed, but I think the major responsibility ought to fall on you."

Carter's position was clearly not at all the same as the unqualified promises made by Udall, Bayh, Harris, and Shriver to work aggressively for repeal of 14-B. Yet the news media made little mention of this basic difference—although these men were contenders in a party in which organized labor support was considered critical to success. This was so even when Udall specifically took out after Carter on 14-B. "He seems to be saying he doesn't believe in the union shop," Udall said, "but in the goodness of his heart will go along with labor." Udall, who had once voted against 14-B himself, was reluctant, however, to attack Carter publicly. And without a candidate who would take the fight to Carter publicly and specifically, the reporters continued to write and say that New Hampshire was a no-issues campaign with no differences separating the candidates. Harris, of course, running hard on a platform that included breaking up the major oil companies, public-service employment, and closing tax loopholes benefiting the rich, did put some distance between himself and the rest of the field. But the others proceeded to adopt many of his positions and even some of his appealing rhetoric, and then he too seemed one of the pack. It took a presidential aspirant who was not in the New Hampshire preferential primary, Henry Jackson, to bring Carter's differences on issues to the fore, in succeeding primaries in Massachusetts and Florida.

In any event, there was not much indication that the voters of New Hampshire were very much interested in issues: if the reporters who were dogging the candidates failed to see much difference in their positions, it was a lot to expect of the citizenry, which was watching the primary with less than maximum attention, to do so.

By election day, February 24, the broad assumption was that Carter would finish first again, with Udall having some chance to edge him, but the rest of the liberal field uncertain. Udall's forces, in anticipation of that result, said their objective was to lead the liberal field. Bayh, burned in Iowa by letting it become a Carter-Bayh race, practiced the art of low expectations, saying he hoped to finish third; Harris did the same; and Shriver, while frankly acknowledging he might run last, hoped for better.

Each of the candidates rented a hotel ballroom for election night, where supporters could watch the returns on television. But, after weeks on the campaign trail with the candidates, a large segment of the working press was obliged by the pressures of deadlines and the scope of the story on election night to pass up the scenes of greatest excitement and pathos in the candidates' headquarters. David Broder and I worked out of the NBC television studio in the convention center of the Sheraton-Wayfarer Hotel in Bedford, where a bank of typewriters and telephones was provided. As election-night fever spread, with all the hoopla, we followed the progress by watching numbers mount on an NBC tote board and straining to hear the periodic reports and commentary on the hushed set by NBC's John Chancellor and David Brinkley. Monitors were placed strategically around the studio, and behind Chancellor and Brinkley was a battery of computers and other complicated mechanical devices, all keyed to decipher the New Hampshire vote. The network's vote analysts, I. A. (Bud) Lewis and Richard Scammon, sat in swivel chairs before a panel of television monitors on which computer print-outs flashed to show how candidates were faring among different voting blocs and areas. It was here the decision would be made, based on results from preselected sample wards, to make the network's projection of a winner. (When reporters arrived early, they found monitors bearing the words "Shriver Wins" in large block letters—and knew they were watching only a test pattern.)

Being locked in a television studio while the flesh and blood of the campaign is responding to the climax outside is always a frustration of covering a presidential campaign. Sometimes the network would switch to a campaign headquarters in Manchester or Concord to pick up activity or a candidate's remarks, and we writing reporters would abandon our typewriters for a few minutes and watch hungrily, jotting down notes for our stories or just gawking, regretful that we were imprisoned in our own jobs at precisely the time of greatest emotion.

Carter and his wife were staying at the home of Cliff Ross, the Democratic city chairman for Manchester. Greg Schneiders and Ellis Woodward were there, and later they were joined by Jody Powell, Jerry Rafshoon, and Pat Caddell. When the final results were in, Carter had received nearly 30 per cent of the vote and thirteen convention delegates, to 24 per cent and four delegates for Udall—a clear-cut victory. He again was very low-key about it, and there was nothing that could be described as a celebration. Bayh meanwhile trailed with 16 per cent but ran ahead of Harris (11 per cent) and Shriver (9 per cent). The first three could all claim to have achieved some objective. But for the other two, especially Harris, who had drawn a very large crowd at a Sunday-night Arlo Guthrie concert and rally (of mostly his own people, it turned out), and had hoped to beat out Bayh, New Hampshire was the beginning of the end.

After the last deadlines at *The Washington Post* had been met, it was possible to go out into the city to pick over the bones of the night's revelry and dismay. Because to me the most surprising result had been the very poor showing by Harris, I went to his headquarters at the Holiday Inn at the northern end of Manchester. In the lobby, young Harris workers stood forlornly, as if shell-shocked, talking aimlessly to each other, drifting in and out of the motel bar. Jim Hightower, Harris's campaign manager, held court at a small round table, drinking beer with his fallen colleagues and trying to put the best face on things. "We won! We won!" He shouted preposterously, unable to explain away the jolting setback.

Upstairs, in rooms occupied by the Harris staff, key members of the campaign who had given the most to the effort sat around and drank. Frank Greer, Harris's youthful and eternally optimistic press aide, fiddled nervously with a radio, seeking the latest results, as if the sheer numbers mattered any more. Fred Droz, a friendly, efficient man who handled Harris's schedule, spoke matter-of-factly and without illusion about the severity of the setback. Barbara Shailor, who had helped to salvage a temporary tie for Harris in Oklahoma, sat on the edge of a bed sipping a drink, occasionally reassuring herself that this was not the end of the road. But Harris himself had predicated his getting early media recognition and all the attendant benefits on making a good show in the year's first primary. Failure to achieve it left him on the edge of extinction.

The scene that night at the Harris headquarters motel was particularly poignant because, of all the campaigns of 1976, this was the most zealous, most emotional, most sacrificial. For a year or more, many on the staff had worked without salary, had subsisted on a steady diet of peanut-butter and jelly sandwiches and whatever they could grub. They slept in shabby hotels, often four or more in a room, the niceties of social etiquette set aside in the realities of a shoestring campaign. Through it all, they remained inspired by their candidate and his populist issues. They all called him "Fred," even the youngest kids, and to some he became more important than the issues. In the early going, when hopes were bright that he could be the surprise of the 1976 campaign, they had functioned on a steady flow of adrenalin. The early successes in the reform club caucuses in New York and Massachusetts, the third-place showing in Iowa, and the virtual tie in Oklahoma all fed their enthusiasm and helped them go on. It was easy to sacrifice in a winning cause, but now, when the adrenalin suddenly drained away in the reality of unvarnished defeat, the plunge into despair was agonizing. Many of these young workers did not sleep that night; others drank themselves to sleep; still others gave way to the sleep of utter exhaustion, and woke the next morning with a gnawing understanding that a corner had been turned and only a miracle in Massachusetts could put them back on course.

Much later Mo Udall complained that both reporters and politicians, for all their insistence that they were not going to let little old New Hampshire be decisive again in 1976, had let it happen. He was particularly sensitive because he ran a good race there and *almost* won; had he won, of course, he would have seen the New Hampshire primary as an ideal political vehicle. As it was, he said after the fall election, "We were moving in New Hampshire. It was very clear those last ten days that it was coming down to Mo Udall and Carter. . . . If I had had eight more days of bowling alleys and ward walks and personal contact, we would have won New Hampshire. It was a miracle in a way, with all those liberal candidates, that I got as close to Carter, having the center and the right to himself."

New Hampshire not only gave Carter a major boost but also started with breath-taking swiftness the reduction of the once-crowded liberal field. Udall, the survivor, had two serious problems remaining, however. First, the losing liberals were behaving like so many beheaded chickens in a farmyard. They just kept staggering forward and around in circles, and this behavior threatened to deny him the full liberal vote he might be able to garner in Massachusetts and again in Wisconsin. Second, for all of Udall's focus on "clearing out the left," the media was not buying this theme. *Their* story was the success of Jimmy Carter. Never mind that the Democratic turnout in New Hampshire was less than 80,000 votes, and that he had collared only 23,000 of them, or that he had run against a field of four liberals in a conservative state. He had *won,* and that was enough to assure him the morning headlines and the lead placement on the morning television news shows. Unfortunately for Udall, it was becoming clear that the dynamics and media focus of the primaries would not allow him time to eliminate the opposition on the left if, in the process, he continued to run behind Carter.

The Georgian, for his part, was breezing ahead now. He was cocky and confident, and the Massachusetts primary, just one week off, looked exceedingly inviting.

17. Massachusetts: Enter Jackson and Wallace

One week into the primary season, and the political air was already filled with alibis. If Morris Udall had stayed out of Iowa, he would have won New Hampshire. . . . If Birch Bayh had not let himself be drawn into a competition with Jimmy Carter in Iowa, he might have beaten Udall in New Hampshire. . . . If Henry Jackson had entered New Hampshire, Carter would have lost. . . .

Only Carter among the competitors wasn't offering an alibi. He was crowing. The morning after his New Hampshire victory, February 25, he drove down to Boston and served notice he was going to take a shot at Massachusetts the next week. He was already on the ballot and had a modest effort going there, but, though the Massachusetts primary had 104 convention delegates at stake, it had been considered no more than a way station in his plans. The do-or-die Florida primary against George Wallace was only a week after, and Carter had to focus his attention on that central showdown.

But his back-to-back successes in Iowa and New Hampshire had opened the publicity floodgates, and Carter was intent on moving downriver quickly. For the first time, two other nonliberal candidates would be up against him, Jackson and George Wallace, but Carter was in a euphoric mood that brooked no timidity. "I have no fear about the other candidates," he told a press conference. "I'm not writing it [Massachusetts] off at all. We have enormous momentum and large numbers of volunteers coming in from New Hampshire, and I think I'll finish first, second, or third."

But Jimmy Carter did not expect to finish third. With good reports coming in from Florida, Pat Caddell said later, "we thought we could effect a triple killing [Iowa, New Hampshire, Massachusetts]." It suddenly occurred to the Carter strategists "that if you could blitz the thing before it ever got off the ground," the opposition could be routed. The thinking was not so much that Carter had to win Massachusetts, Caddell said, as to make sure nobody else built momentum from it. "The fear in Massachusetts was, 'Who would you allow to win by not going in there?' Certainly no one imagined that Scoop Jackson could win. I was afraid Wallace might win.

That would have killed the Southerners for us. Our second concern was that one of the liberals would emerge very strongly out of New Hampshire and Massachusetts. So Massachusetts became by definition whether you could take it to keep anybody else from getting it."

This victory, however, would have to be achieved on the fly, because Florida was so crucial. Carter said he would spend most of the week in the South and return to Massachusetts only on the Friday before the primary. In place of heavy personal campaigning—the prime ingredient of his success—plans were laid for extensive television advertising that would bring the Carter magic into living rooms across the state, rather than on street corners. (His campaign spent more money on television in Massachusetts than any one else's—$105,000, to $91,000 for Jackson, the second-highest television buyer.) To pull things together, Tim Kraft, the engineer of the Iowa victory, was shuttled in quickly by Hamilton Jordan.

It was a high roll of the dice, no doubt about it. Massachusetts had a reputation as the nation's most liberal state, the only one that had gone for George McGovern in 1972; Udall was well organized; Jackson and Wallace, who would be cutting into the moderate and conservative vote, had hefty bankrolls, and Jackson had much of organized labor to boot. It was a big order, but Carter was flying high.

Udall, a respectable second in New Hampshire, saw Massachusetts as a good opportunity to eliminate Bayh. As early as November, his lieutenants had been saying that, by the Massachusetts date, Udall would have to have wounded or knocked out Bayh and the others because the party's liberal wing could not support more than one candidate for long. "My best and most carefully thought-out judgment," Jack Quinn told Udall in a memo then, "is that you will be expected to 'score' by the time of this primary. . . . Bayh is gambling on our inability to capture the viable left-center position in the race before New York, where he could convincingly take it for himself. . . . [We must] prevent Bayh from surviving credibly until New York."

Bayh, forced by his late start to play catch-up politics, had poured his time and money into New York and then New Hampshire, and was indeed on the ropes. Running as the most electable of all the prospects, losing hurt him more than it did the others—particularly, a Udall operative noted later, "because the group around him were the real calculators," meaning some worked for him not out of any personal commitment to or strong belief in him, but strictly because they thought he could win. But Bayh's scheme of pushing himself as a "good politician" in a year of antipolitics, first proposed to him by Democratic busybody Alan Baron, had been a disaster. Shortly before the Massachusetts primary, a decision was made to scrap the ads that had Bayh saying "It takes a good politician to make a good President." Bill Wise began writing some new stuff, but time had run out on his boss. Bayh staggered into Massachusetts leaking from every pore; his labor supporters were already looking elsewhere.

The other liberals—Fred Harris, Sargent Shriver, and Milton Shapp, making his first feeble start—were also dead in the water. Several individuals in Harris's campaign, mindful of the jump Carter was getting, and settling on Udall as the most likely liberal survivor, began to talk among themselves about getting Harris to withdraw in favor of Mo Udall. But Jim Hightower, one of Harris's closest friends, who had worked out Harris's basic strategy with him nearly two years earlier, could not bring himself to do it. And so Harris hung on, his aides loyal but despairing. At one point that week, a Harris aide confided, "I can't tell you how much it hurts. It's like having a dead baby inside you waiting to be born."

Meanwhile, Jackson and Wallace had been active in Massachusetts for weeks. For the best part of a year Jackson had concentrated on New York, with its heavy and influential Jewish vote, as his first big-state hit, but that primary would not be until April 6. When Massachusetts moved its primary forward to March 2, the lure of its 104 delegates, and his staff's conviction that the state was not so liberal as its reputation suggested, persuaded Jackson to move in. "The feeling we had," Bob Keefe, Jackson's astute campaign manager, said, "was that it had a lot better potential for us than people suspected. There were too many delegates there for us to pass up. We had a lot of good vibes from people up there, and the demographics made it look like a good state for us." Also, Keefe noted, there was a large psychological advantage to be gained: "It was misperceived [as liberal] to our advantage." Jackson would be the thinking man's alternative to Wallace, the wild-talking Alabamian. Or so at least went the Jackson rationale.

Wallace, likewise, thought Massachusetts was a place to spring a surprise. Sitting behind his desk at the state capitol in Montgomery in late October, he had told Tom Ottenad and me, "I'm not supposed to win in Massachusetts. I don't care about busing or nothing else, I'm just not supposed to. All that propaganda against George Wallace. I'm not supposed to do well at all. But if my name's on the ballot there, and I do just fairly good, that'll shake 'em up just fairly good. I ain't supposed to get no votes in Massachusetts. You know that." For anyone familiar with the ways of George Wallace, a man who could teach a fox a few things about cunning, the remarks were tantamount to a declaration of entry into the Massachusetts primary.

Sure enough, when Wallace announced his candidacy on November 12, he said he would probably enter Massachusetts. Later, in another interview, he remarked, with the slightest trace of a grin, "If I do go up there, I ain't gonna say a word about busing." Pause. " 'Course, all them folks in Massachusetts know that if I'm President, there ain't gonna be any."

But Wallace went to Massachusetts over the strong and persistent objections of his campaign manager, Charles Snider. Snider knew that Florida was absolutely essential to the Wallace strategy, and two of his most important in-state leaders, Fitzhugh Powell of Jacksonville and Bill France, the Daytona International Speedway impresario, were reporting that Wallace was slipping. Wallace was needed down there, not fooling around in the northern bastion of liberalism. But Wallace remembered with relish his visits to New England in earlier campaigns, and he knew he could make mischief with the busing issue in Boston. Finally they struck a compromise: Wallace would dip his toe in the Massachusetts water and take a temperature reading. "He said," Snider recalled, " 'I'll go up there for a couple of days, maybe three days, and that's it. But we're on the ballot there, so let me go up there and see what happens.' It was his first endeavor in national politics since the day he was shot, and when he got there, he was overwhelmed." Wallace came back to Montgomery fascinated by the possibilities. That did it.

"Maybe he felt if he could kick off with a win in Massachusetts he would be back where he was in '72," Snider said ruefully. "It was a very bold move, and if he could have won, maybe he would have caught on again."

In any event, shortly after New Year's Day 1976, Wallace was making quick trips into the state. He talked about "freedom of choice" in busing children away from their neighborhoods—which was, of course, a formula for perpetuation of racial imbalance in the schools; he railed against "pointy-headed bureaucrats in Washington" deciding "what to do with your children"; he noted all the turmoil in the North over civil rights, and asked: "What is the most basic civil right? The right to walk in safety." It was the same old Wallace mumbo-jumbo, a hell of a good political show and, in the early weeks at least, it drew large crowds, especially around Boston and Springfield.

But while the words were the same and also the music—provided as always by the twanging electric guitar of Billy Grammer of the Grand Ole Opry and his white-shoed associates—there was a distinct and glaring difference this time around. George Wallace himself, who in early campaigns strutted around the platform snapping off salutes to the cheering, carousing faithful, was wheelchair-bound. In the past he had, with mincing steps, come into an arena like a robed prizefighter eager for the opening bell; now his very entrance reminded the audience immediately of his incapacity.

Exceedingly heavy security brooked no personal contact between candidate and voter, and no handshaking; the crowds were roped in as burly state police and Secret Service wheeled Wallace through the door closest to the platform. Everyone watched as Wallace and his wheelchair were lifted and placed behind a bullet-proof lectern, then locked in place so that he would not roll off. For a time he used a special metal brace that enabled him to raise himself on his lifeless legs to speak, his aides locking the legs in the contraption so he could stand. But it was a wearisome strain, and only emphasized Wallace's condition, and was abandoned.

The voice was still strong, the facial expressions still menacing, the sense of humor still biting and sardonic. And yet something was missing: the instinct of the finisher was gone. In the midst of his patented attack on the bureaucrats in Washington "who can't park a bicycle straight," his voice would trail off, and he would talk not about winning, but about "the folks of Massachusetts giving me a good vote." He had all the old stories, like the one about leading in the Maryland primary in 1964 until "they called in the head recapitulator and he recapitulated on me." But the fire was gone. Going to a Wallace rally was half like going—hard to face, but true—to a side show at a traveling circus, and people being the way they are, quite a few acknowledged they were there out of curiosity. Wallace seemed to sense this; he was a slasher, but there was a native good humor and horse sense to him, and he had been incredibly courageous through his long physical and emotional ordeal.

Yet in this first primary for him in 1976, Wallace was hopeful he was on the long road back. He got them up out of their chairs at a raucous rally in South Boston, a cauldron of antibusing sentiment, by blasting the "social experimenters" who favored "carrying little children from here to Kingdom Come," by telling the citizens of turbulent Southie how it was—"putting the hay down where the goats can get it," as he said.

Jackson, too, was unable to resist the busing issue. In an effort to draw to his own side the middle-class protest against Federal District Court Judge W. Arthur Garrity, Jr., who had ordered busing in Boston's school districts, Jackson came up with a plan. He proposed placing school-desegregation cases in the hands of three-judge panels—an obvious slap at Garrity—and he ran full-page newspaper ads that said: "I am against forced busing." But he was considered a johnny-come-lately to the cause: at a rally in a Charlestown Knights of Columbus Hall three weeks before the primary, antibusing hecklers disrupted his presentation and denounced his proposals as politically motivated. Still, he *was* a more credible candidate than Wallace; he was an experienced legislator and he was in demonstrable good health. Wallace was himself his own worst advertisement. Everywhere he went, he had to be lifted in and out of his wheelchair, and he had either to speak from it or to be laboriously, and very visibly, taken from it and propped up at the special lectern. He had underestimated this political handicap. "To be brutally frank with you," Snider told me once, "we thought it might be an asset."

It was not Wallace, however, whom the other contenders were worried about; it was the high-riding Carter. Something, some way, had to be found to slow him down.

That something, in fact, had already come but had been largely overlooked. On the night before the New Hampshire primary vote, February 23, the candidates had trooped down to Boston for the first of a series of presidential forums conducted by the League of Women Voters, similar to one that had been held in Manchester the week before. Some of the candidates looked forward to these evenings as a chance to get their views out on an equal footing with the others, but one who distinctly did not rejoice at the prospect was Carter. He was a loner, a one-on-one specialist, and he did not like to compete with others, to have them cramp his style. At such forums he was like W. C. Fields in the midst of some swindle turning to an inquisitive boy and, with a flutter of his hand, saying: "Beat it kid, you bother me!" Carter would sit stone-faced, distracted, wishing visibly for all the world that it would come to an end so he could get on with his own thing.

In the Boston forum, Carter was asked by a member of the audience whether his proposals for tax reform would include elimination of the personal income-tax deduction for interest payments on home mortgages— a refuge for millions of low- and middle-income homeowners. Carter replied: "I'll come out with a complete analysis of the tax system later on this year, I hope. But in general, I would say, along with the elimination of hundreds of other tax incentives, those would be among those that I would like to do away with."

Carter went on specifically to emphasize that the home-mortgage deduction would be only one of "a lot of others that would also be eliminated" as part of "a comprehensive, all-inclusive tax-reform bill." But the distinction was lost in the stampede to nail him. "I was totally amazed he took that position," Jackson said later, recalling the incident. "I think he intended to put it as a package, and homeowners would get a trade-off." He did indeed, and clearly said so, but that didn't stop Jackson from zeroing in on the one politically vulnerable point.

The next day, a *Boston Globe* reporter, Robert L. Turner, began calling the other candidates for their reaction. Not surprisingly, they expressed horror that Carter would single out middle-class America for such action, when the rich were avoiding millions in taxes through elaborate loopholes. Jackson, especially, took hold. "I disagree totally and completely with Jimmy Carter on this issue," Jackson said. "The mortgage-interest deduction is one of the few tax advantages that the average family gets."

On the next day, Thursday before the primary, three candidates in rapid order held press conferences in Boston and denounced Carter. Jackson led off, calling Carter's idea an "incredible" proposal that would cost the average Massachusetts family $600 a year in income taxes and threaten "the destruction of the working- and middle-class American family." Udall said: "I think he made a mistake. I think he would have a taxpayers' rebellion on his hands. I can't believe he's serious." And Bayh charged the move would undercut the chances for millions of Americans to buy better homes.

Carter's headquarters in Atlanta tried swiftly to counter the attacks. The idea, a spokesman said, "is one part of one over-all tax-reform proposal that Governor Carter is considering. If he adopts the proposal, the elimination of hundreds of tax incentives would be irrevocably tied to a drastic slash in the total tax rate. Low- and middle-income homeowners would actually pay less in taxes under this proposal than under the present wasteful and unfair system." And Jody Powell weighed in with the political counterattack: "Jackson, Bayh, and Udall are all good men but they are playing the usual brand of Washington politics. The typical Washington attitude is to find someone to attack when you need to get your name in the news. Whether you know what you're talking about or whether what you say is correct is not too important so long as you say it loudly and manage to look indignant."

Privately, Carter directed his displeasure as much at the *Boston Globe* as at any of his competitors. He was convinced the *Globe* was out to get him and had pursued the home-mortgage issue for that reason. When he returned to Boston on Friday for one last bit of campaigning, his foes were still trying to milk this so-called blunder. On the flight north, Powell, Schneiders, and Carter discussed what tack to take. Articles in the major papers said that the other candidates were ganging up in a stop-Carter effort, and it was agreed that the opposition probably looked bad to the public. "We all decided it was best for Jimmy to go up there and take the high road," Schneiders recalled. "It was our ongoing tactic to emphasize that the country didn't want bickering and divisiveness. Besides, we thought we were going to win Massachusetts. We thought we didn't need to get in there and mix it up."

Accordingly, Carter came into Boston turning the other cheek—in his fashion. He played the injured party to the hilt, and branded his critics as unpatriotic in the bargain. Without volunteering any comment on the substance of the attacks, he wrapped the mantle of statesmanship around himself and told an audience in Boston's historic Faneuil Hall: "I don't believe that the nation appreciates personal animosities and attacks among candidates hoping to be President of the American people." Such attacks, he suggested, "won't hurt me, but I'm afraid it might hurt the country. . . . One of the things that concerns the people . . . is the bickering, squabbling, hatred, and animosities, and blame handed back and forth in our great nation's capital in Washington. This is not good for our country. I want to be the next President of this country. I expect to be the next President. But that doesn't mean that I have to take my political success from personal hatred [and] attacks on the character or ability of my opponents. . . . [The people] have got enough judgment, enough common sense, and know me well enough so that these attacks will hurt the ones who make the attacks."

This exchange was noteworthy more for what it revealed about Carter than for the effect it had on the primary's outcome. The criticisms made by Jackson, Udall, and Bayh, though sharp, had been issue-oriented and well within the bounds of reasonable dialogue in a hard-fought political campaign. Yet Carter chose to soft-pedal the issue and to suggest that his critics were playing dirty politics at the expense—no less—of the nation's welfare. This kind of cheap device had been popularized by Joe McCarthy in the 1950s and by Richard Nixon more recently, and it infuriated his opponents.

Senator Bayh had also criticized Carter's refusal to work affirmatively for the repeal of 14-B, and in the question period at Faneuil Hall Carter reiterated his position. He said he was "not going to take the leadership in repeal of 14-B . . . I don't think it really makes any difference whether [the state right-to-work laws] are repealed or not." Bayh, armed with a transcript of these remarks, called another press conference to blast him, charging that textile, shoe, and other industries in unionized states like Massachusetts were losing tens of thousands of jobs to nonunion shops in the South. Whatever Carter cared to say, his opponents were finally dispelling the impression that this was a no-issue campaign.

All this focus on Carter obscured other things that were going on in the primary. One was Mo Udall's decision to hit harder at Wallace. Another was a money crisis that kept him from purchasing television time at a critical juncture. John Marttila and Tom Kiley, the Boston political consultants who were handling all media in Massachusetts for Udall, had focused on newspaper advertising as cheaper and sufficiently effective in the Bay State, which they knew well.[1] There was no money for polls either, but Marttila and Kiley were not too concerned because they thought they knew the terrain adequately. "We got this state wired," Kiley recalls saying at the time. They made much of Udall's endorsement by Archibald Cox, the Harvard law professor who had been the first special Watergate prosecutor fired by Nixon in the infamous Saturday Night Massacre of 1973; it was the first such political endorsement Cox had ever given. But it was uphill fighting. "There's a mean streak in Massachusetts," Marttila said later, trying to explain why Jackson and Wallace received support in a liberal state Udall might have been expected to win.

Jackson meanwhile was pouring money into old-fashioned field work to get out the vote, and touching all the political bases.[2] He hit the union halls (taking due note of Massachusetts' exceedingly high unemployment), the Boston waterfront, an Irish bar in Dorchester, and the appropriate number of ethnic clubs and synagogues. Jackson's image as a loser was still current, and so it came as a surprise when he began flatly to predict that he would win the primary. His polls were showing some gains for him, and he had decided he'd better invoke the power of positive thinking. "It was a risk worth taking," Keefe said later. "He thought he had to say that, to make sure that people who were for him would think they had an honest chance to be with a winner."

Carter's polls, at the same time, were encouraging *him* to be optimistic (although Caddell said afterward that late data did show Jackson closing in). Caddell and Rafshoon met Carter at the airport in Atlanta on March 1, the night before the vote, and Caddell told him, "I'm getting kind of nervous about Massachusetts. Jackson's really coming on." To which Carter replied, "I can't believe that. That defies everything I know about politics, that Jackson could win."   ·

1. In addition to the lower cost of newspaper advertising, there was a very practical reason for buying it: credit, which was not available in dealing with cash-on-the-barrelhead television stations. "It's much easier to float newspaper advertising," Marttila explained, "and let the campaign income catch up to you on a short-term basis. The broadcast media require certified checks. We had credit with the agencies. When we put an ad in the *Globe,* we were given five days to move our fund-raising around. Literally, there were two or three periods when we had no money in the bank but we were confident it was coming in. We could not buy television so we wound up buying newspapers."

2. Money continued to be a matter uppermost in the minds of all the candidates and their managers. On February 27 the Supreme Court gave Congress, which had been haggling over the legislation to reconstitute the Federal Election Commission, three more weeks to act, thus giving the commission that additional period to certify federal subsidies for the candidates. The new deadline was March 22. President Ford, who wanted a simple bill permitting him to choose all six members to the commission, urged Congress to act promptly, but he warned he might veto any bill that went beyond his wishes.

And so it was with high expectations in several quarters that primary day dawned—amid typical early March New England weather. It snowed, and snowed, and snowed. Caddell and Rafshoon were flying back to Boston in the late afternoon, and as they arrived at Logan Airport, Caddell took one look out the window and said, "Jerry, there went our lead." He knew that Carter's vote, based on momentum and little organization, was soft, and needed a decent off-the-street turnout.

By the time Caddell arrived at his apartment and could telephone his sources at the television networks, the bad news was already coming in. And by early evening it was clear that *some* dogs outside of Washington state liked Scoop Jackson's dog food, after all. The man who couldn't win, and certainly couldn't win in the most liberal state in the Union, had pulled it off.

Jackson's share of the total vote was nothing to write home about, only 23 per cent, but he ran 5 percentage points ahead of the runner-up—who was not Carter, but Udall. Wallace was one point behind Udall with 17 per cent and then—a distant and embarrassed fourth—was the hot candidate from Georgia, with 14 per cent. (Harris came next with 8 per cent, then Shriver with 7 per cent and Bayh—completely humiliated—with 5, just one point ahead of Ellen McCormack, the antiabortion candidate, who edged out the hapless Shapp.)

At the Copley Plaza, the Jackson and Bayh forces occupied large ballrooms just across the hotel lobby from each other. Had you been blindfolded and led into one or the other, you would have had no trouble, the moment the blindfold was removed, identifying which you were in. Jackson's was vintage old politics—an older crowd of well-dressed middle-class matrons whose hands had known dishwater, and their balding husbands in leisure suits made for younger men. They milled about, apprehensive at first, but when good news came, a festive air swept through the place. The world at large had not believed Scoop Jackson was a winner, and his followers themselves seemed to have difficulty coping with it. "CBS projects us the winner!" one man shouted to his wife, incredulously.

In a smaller room adjoining the ballroom, Jackson's strategists held forth—notably campaign manager Keefe, portly despite a fairly successful battle with his waistline, a big cigar clenched in his teeth; he looked right out of a movie about Tammany Hall in the old days.

"Win the big ones," he said, "that's been our strategy. Now *they've* got to catch *us.* There was one reason Scoop Jackson was not considered the guy to beat, and that was that they said he couldn't win. We proved Scoop Jackson can win. Now that bum rap is off. We can go on to win."

Jackson, in an understandable excess of enthusiasm, painted himself as the personification of the New Deal, Fair Deal, New Frontier, and Great Society rolled into one. "The essence of our victory is the fact we put together once again the grand coalition that elected Franklin D. Roosevelt, Harry Truman, John F. Kennedy, and Lyndon Johnson," he told his tumultuous supporters. And indeed Jackson did have a wide base, winning half of the state's twelve congressional districts—and winning despite the fact that Wallace took Boston.[3]

Across from the Jackson celebration, Bayh's ballroom looked like a big Jewish wedding reception after the groom had jilted the bride. Young preppy faces were stunned. Chris Spiro, minority leader in the New Hampshire House of Representatives, who had been Bayh's chairman in the Granite State the week before, shook his head in disbelief. A hard-rock group named The Sunrise, determined to go forward with a victory celebration, belted out a song called "Jubilation," but there was none. Birch Bayh of Indiana, as the senator liked to call himself, was, as they like to say in Boston, deader than Kelsey's nuts. The next day in New York, which was to have been his big breakthrough state, he withdrew from the 1976 presidential campaign, saying he "just got so tired of being everybody's second choice." At that, he was overreaching.

Udall, predictably, interpreted the vote in terms of the liberal elimination contest that he so badly wanted the press to focus on. The results "clearly established" him as the standard-bearer of the "progressive mainstream wing of the Democratic Party," he said. And Wallace, on the basis of early returns, said in Florida: "Whether they like it or not, I'm running second and they thought I would run last. Second is a victory as far I'm concerned." In playing the game of low expectations, Wallace had no peer.

The other "serious" candidates, Harris and Shriver, still hung on, but Shriver began meeting with his aides to decide whether to bail out now or hold on for one more try in Illinois two weeks hence.[4]

In Orlando, Florida, the Carters were unprepared for the blow. In the early evening Rosalynn had phoned Caddell. "What's happening?" she had wanted to know.

---

3. Wallace liked to crow thereafter about how "I carried Boston"—neglecting always to say he ran a weak third statewide.

4. Shriver continued to be a forlorn figure. One night, at a political gathering at a Chinese restaurant in Boston, his wife, Eunice Kennedy Shriver, sat in the audience as her brother Teddy spoke. He introduced her simply as "Eunice," and when he returned to the table she berated him. "You didn't even mention my last name," she said.

"It just looks bad," Caddell had told her. "My God, it's snowing like hell. This is not what we needed."

The Carters were awaiting the returns in a special television election center set up for the March 9 Florida primary on the fifteenth floor of a new Orlando bank. Ed Rabel, the CBS correspondent covering Carter, recalled: "They started bringing the returns in to him and telephone calls came in. He began stuttering. He just kept repeating, 'That's too bad, that's too bad,' to reporters. He was not really able to comprehend what had happened to him. I had not seen him quite so unglued before. . . . After a while he was able to compose himself, but he didn't want to talk."

Carter himself soon called Caddell, and Caddell repeated the news, advising him that paper ballots from New Bedford, Fall River, and the western part of the state were not yet in, and might improve the picture.

"What . . . happened?" he asked. (Caddell said later, "I can't describe the tone.")

"Jimmy, we just evaporated. The turnout was atrocious. Our vote just didn't turn out."

Carter was shaken. "He was really off-balance and upset," Caddell recalled. "He wasn't angry. He was stunned and disappointed, because he felt he was going to do well. I thought he was going to do well. Everything had been coming up sevens. But we should have known from Mississippi, that if you can't put the resources and the time in, it doesn't work."

Greg Schneiders, who was with Carter on nearly every primary election night, said of the scene: "I think he was unhappier that night than any night in the campaign. I could see a difference in his mood. He was not going to be consoled on the thing. He was not in any sense despairing or pessimistic on the future of the race, but he was clearly down. I tried to cheer him up by saying, 'Well, we must have done well in the western part of the state.' But he said, 'You get fourteen per cent of the vote, you haven't done well anywhere'—and he smiled."[5]

Looking back at that night, Carter told me, "I took it with a lot more equanimity than most of my family. We thought we were going to sneak up on everybody in Massachusetts. But we didn't have time to dwell on it. We were so obsessed with Florida."

"Obsessed" certainly was a fair word. For more than a year Carter had haunted Florida and was working the state zealously now, only a week before the long-awaited confrontation with Wallace in the South. But run-

---

5. It was some solace for Carter that he scored a comfortable victory over Shriver in the day's other and largely overlooked primary, in Vermont. On every primary election night he managed to win somewhere, thus at least partially offsetting his losses, and always picking up convention delegates.

ning behind Wallace in Massachusetts clearly was no help. Nor was a Jackson victory. "We all understood what the game was at that point," Caddell said. "That the whole thing, which twenty-four hours before had looked like it was about to be wrapped up, could fall apart within seven days. Now all of a sudden we had Jackson coming into Florida to cut us, and spend resources. We knew he couldn't win, but he could really screw us up. We could be out of the race for all intents and purposes. The forty-eight hours after Massachusetts were just horrendous. We were off base, our candidate was off stride, and we were facing the crisis of our lives."

18. The Demise of George Wallace

Thanks to the jet age, it's a simple thing—if you have the time and money—to climb aboard a plane in a snowstorm in Boston and about three hours later get off under a broiling sun in Miami. Many New Englanders, in fact, do just that in wintertime, especially people retired or well-off enough to escape the freezing northern climes for the hardest months. From other northeastern cities, and from numerous points in the Midwest, too, the old and the middle-aged and the young come to Florida every winter to get in from the cold. And over the years, many who have come to get warm stay to stay warm, in a state of balmy Januarys and Februarys, and a more casual pace and life-style. To be sure, Florida is no California, no vanguard of new and crazy ideas, always at the point of some social or cultural innovation. But it is an escapist environment, at least for those who can enjoy its semitropical atmosphere.

The political climate, too, is different from the North. Florida is in the South, but not in any typical sense is it a Southern state. The influx of sun-worshipers and of Cubans over the years has made it infinitely more cosmopolitan than any of its Dixie neighbors, especially in the cities— Miami, Miami Beach, Palm Beach, Fort Lauderdale, Tampa, Saint Petersburg. The immigrants have brought generally more moderate political views with them than have existed in the more rural expanses of the state, particularly across the northern Panhandle. There, politicians call it redneck country or, in recent years, Wallace country. The contrast between north and south Florida is obvious; the land of the good old boy and the land of the sharpie in the silk suit. Pensacola and Tallahassee and even Jacksonville to a degree remain country and Southern, languid in their pace and look; Miami and Miami Beach on the other hand have become sets for a massive movie out of Damon Runyon, complete with Broadway characters, high rollers, heavy Jewish accents, and an air of hustle everywhere.

Both north and south, though, Florida remains essentially a Democratic state, with pockets of Republicanism, especially on the Gulf Coast, in the retirement communities like Saint Petersburg and Sarasota. And it is a state only recently accustomed to the spectacle of presidential campaigning. Though the first primary law in the land was enacted by the

Florida legislature in 1901, the state did not join the post-World War II parade of active primary competition until 1972. Then, in a state of exuberance, the legislature tried for a time to steal from New Hampshire the honor of holding the nation's first primary; it finally settled for having the second, when New Hampshire predictably raised a fuss. In 1972, George Wallace routed all comers.

In 1976, Florida was holding the fourth primary, after New Hampshire, Vermont, and Massachusetts. But a challenge to Wallace from a Dixie neighbor, Jimmy Carter of Plains, Georgia, only ninety-five miles north of the Florida line as the crow flies, insured a start to heavy campaigning, and an invasion of television and other news people, right after New Year's Day. In fact, for candidates and the press alike, Boston-to-Miami became a shuttle run through the months of January and February, as the New England and Florida primaries vied for the time and attention of those seeking Democratic votes in both places, and of those who chronicled their activities for the reading and viewing public.

Wallace's campaign strategy had originally called for a rerun of 1972 —a fast start by scoring a big sweep in Florida. But the governor's fascination with Massachusetts had first drawn him north with less than impressive results. "After that we had to try to turn a third into a first," Charles Snider said later, "and so we went into Florida a loser." Not only that, but the Wallace campaign had spent a lot of money losing in Massachusetts. For one thing, it was not cheap to move around; his chartered jet plane had to be specially configured for him. Also, his polls indicated that in Florida Wallace was actually trailing Carter by about 12 percentage points. (That finding did not square with Caddell's polls for Carter, which showed a much closer race, particularly with Jackson in the picture.)

But Florida was especially hard to figure because the Democrats did not have much of a statewide party organization to begin with, Carter had diligently laid down his own structure, and Wallace had always managed to win handily without a strong formal organization. He was a one-man show, "like a rock star," said Phil Wise, Carter's young organizer in the state. "He comes in and fires people up"—or at least, that was what he used to do. In Carter, however, Wallace had to deal with a thoroughness, a tenacity that he had not encountered in a foe before.

Wise, who had moved to Florida to stay in June 1975, organized twenty of the sixty-nine counties that had about 80 per cent of the Democratic registration. "We looked for people who knew the Florida situation but had managed to remain unscarred," Wise said. "Experienced, but not having antagonized anyone." Carter toured the state periodically, and Wise geared up for a ten- to twelve-week winter campaign in 1976.

In November the state party decided to hold a bicentennial convention, and Wise learned two months in advance that a presidential preference poll would be taken, in part to attract some press attention. "We found out how delegates would be elected and we tried to get as many of our supporters as we had identified by then elected to the committees, so we could start with a strong base," Wise said. "It was just good politicking. At the convention, we had a list of all the delegates by county. We knew who they were, we knew what kind of background they had, what they were interested in. We appointed a whip within each delegation and for two days we just worked them. We had a hospitality suite and we just sat with them and talked with them, and took our own votes." By contrast, the Wallace people were doing nothing at all. "I don't think any [of them] realized it [the poll] was going to come up." The payoff was dramatic: 67 per cent of 1035 ballots were cast for Carter, only 6 per cent for Wallace. The result at first was noticed more in the national news media, "but in turn that helped us in the whole state. It came back full circle." The whole exercise also was helpful as "a dry run for our organization for the primary," he said.

Heavy door-to-door canvassing was started in December, and in January 1976 Jerry Rafshoon began intensive media advertising, especially in south Florida, where Carter was running poorly, and Jackson well, among both Jews and Catholics. The Carter ads hit Florida's living rooms at just about the time of the Iowa caucus and, according to Wise, the combination was telling. The canvassers reported that many voters had told them about how they had seen Carter on television, how impressed they were with his Iowa success, and how maybe he had a real chance after all. That was always a hurdle at the outset—Southerners had been accustomed for so long to having their own rejected at the national level that it was hard to believe that he could win. But now that was changing.

With all the liberals except Milton Shapp giving Florida and Wallace a wide berth, Carter was able to claim the anti-Wallace position for his own. While taking pains not to offend Wallace's supporters in Florida, he sent out a fund-raising newsletter that hit the Alabamian broadside: "Please help us win a victory in Florida and allow the Democratic Party to choose its presidential candidate in an arena free of demagoguery. . . . I need your help now to end once and for all the threat Wallace represents to our country." Recalling Wallace's 1972 slogan of protest, "Send Them a Message," Carter told Floridians that now for the first time Southerners had a real chance not simply to do that, but to "send them a President."

Wallace apparently was slow in realizing how much of a setback his physical condition—and the changed times—would be to his cause. His first Florida rally, in Orlando in mid-January, drew barely half the capacity of the city's three-thousand-seat auditorium, a hall he had filled with no difficulty in the past—and this in spite of the fact Wallace supporters were bused in from Daytona Beach and Tampa. Campaign aides attributed the low turnout to their lack of local newspaper and radio advertising—which had not been necessary to bring in the faithful in previous years. Thereafter, the campaign began to spend money on advertising, and produced turn-away audiences. Wallace started holding doubleheaders and even triple-headers—filling a hall for a speech, emptying it, and filling it again for another. But the halls were often smaller than the ones he had used in earlier years; security, for one thing, was easier to manage that way, and it was also better for morale.

Wallace's state of mind was always a consideration now, and the press' incessant focus on his health grated on him. A particularly heavy Florida schedule was laid on just to make the point that he could handle it, and he repeatedly took the opportunity to demonstrate his physical stamina and strength. Sooner or later during all my interviews with him after the 1972 shooting, he would thrust out his hand, say "Shake," squeeze my fingers until they ached, and ask, "Does that feel like I'm not in good physical condition?" There was nothing wrong with him, he would tell callers, "except I'm paralyzed."

The staff thought this big effort was having some positive effect when a mishap befell Wallace that undid it all, and then some. At the airport in Pensacola, Wallace was being carried aboard the plane by two state troopers when one of them caught his foot on a carpet runner and fell, letting Wallace land on top of him. The trooper in back, a burly type approaching three hundred pounds, fell on top of Wallace, wrenching the governor's knee severely. He was taken to a doctor's office, where the knee was placed in a cast. Though he continued campaigning and in fact did a doubleheader that night, the incident was widely reported by the television networks, with reporters standing in front of the doctor's office. Wallace was portrayed as an extremely brittle man—a characterization definitely not needed by one seeking the presidency.

Snider, for one, did not minimize the deleterious effect of the media's focus on Wallace's condition, nor of the need to win in Florida in spite of it. "If we lose to Jimmy Carter in Florida," he told Wallace, "we're through."

Although Wallace was Carter's main target in Florida, events and temperaments conspired to shift Carter's focus in the final week before the March 9 primary. Running fourth in Massachusetts was a bitter pill to swallow, and Jackson's victory especially. Jackson's decision to run state-wide in Florida, after first targeting only a few urban areas, had already complicated Carter's life, but when the senator began to attack Carter on the home-mortgage issue, things were going too far. Carter insisted he had made clear he would monkey with that tax only as part of a broad reform package whose net result would be lower taxes for the low- and middle-income American. But Jackson had kept alleging anyway that they would be victimized. Carter seethed.

The relationship between Jackson and Carter had been deteriorating ever since the Democratic convention of 1972, at which Carter had placed Jackson's name in nomination. The day after the Massachusetts primary, it hit rock bottom. At a press conference in Orlando Carter said in effect that he had lost to Jackson in Massachusetts because Jackson had run a racist campaign. Asked why he had not spoken out against busing there, he said: "I'm not in favor of mandatory busing, but to run my campaign on an antibusing issue is contrary to my basic nature. If I have to win by appealing to a basically negative, emotional issue which has connotations of racism, I don't intend to do it, myself. I don't want to win that kind of race." He didn't want his remarks interpreted as accusing Jackson of being a racist. "I didn't say Senator Jackson was a racist," he insisted. "I didn't say he wasn't, but I don't think he is a racist. He exploited an issue that has racist connotations."

For all of Carter's rather limp, halfhearted efforts to soften them, these remarks were not demonstrative of a politics of love and compassion. In his Faneuil Hall speech in Boston only five days earlier, he had turned the other cheek, but not now. The outburst in short order had the wire services buzzing. It seemed that Jimmy Carter, confronted with serious adversity for the first time in his onward-and-upward campaign, was losing his famous cool.

That day, Carter decided he wanted to cut some new anti-Jackson commercials for the last week in Florida. Rafshoon, Jordan, and Powell all were upset at the turn their candidate had taken, but he was unyielding. Rafshoon met Caddell in Washington and together they flew to Jacksonville, where Carter would cut the new tapes (in a studio usually used, unbeknown to Carter, to make pornographic movies). As Rafshoon, Caddell, and Carter went over the scripts, the candidate toughened up references to Jackson, in one instance changing a sentence that said Jackson was trying to distort his position on tax reform to say Jackson was talking against tax reform.

Caddell got Carter aside. "I said, 'What you did today was very intriguing on Jackson. Why did you do it?' He couldn't explain it to me. He could not verbalize it. He just said, 'I knew I could get away with it if I did it up here, and I wanted to say it.' I knew it was more than that.

"The next morning I was driving from Jacksonville to Orlando and in a press conference at a local station he was explaining on the air why it was important that the liberals, who made up ten per cent of the vote in the Florida primary, ought to vote for him to stop Wallace and Jackson. I suddenly realized why he attacked Jackson. He realized if he attacked Jackson on busing in north Florida he could get away with it, but that, secondly, what he was after was that ten per cent of the vote that was still sitting with those minor [liberal] candidates. He understood where he had to squeeze more margin out. He couldn't articulate it to me the night before. I don't think he had verbalized it in his own mind until that morning. His instincts were running ahead of his ability to verbalize. But he understood what the game was, which was he had to pull some more from that group to beat Wallace, with Jackson coming up in the polls as we suspected he would, and cutting us in south Florida. Sure enough, that was exactly what happened. We reduced enough of the liberal vote to beat Wallace. . . . It was a cold political decision."[1]

Carter kept on pounding at Jackson. In Ocala on Thursday, he said, "To build a campaign in a state like Massachusetts on an issue that's already divided the people, already created disharmony, sometimes even bloodshed, which is obviously a very emotional issue which has racial connotations, to me this is the wrong approach." And at the Tiger Bay Club in Tallahassee on Friday, after learning that more Jackson ads were criticizing him on the home-mortgage issue and also charging him with threatening national security with excessive defense cuts, Carter said, "I can't sit back and have one of my opponents deliberately and consistently make false statements about me. . . . He's been in Congress for thirty-five years. He's not a dishonest man, he's not a bad man, but he wants to be President so bad he's departed from his normal truthfulness." (Carter thus tried to underscore Jackson's long ties to Washington, thereby emphasizing his own posture as the out-

---

1. Udall, assessing his campaign after the election, said in retrospect: "I should have stayed in Florida; Reubin Askew said the election was decided when I decided not to go into Florida. . . . Clearly, I could have pulled enough votes away from Carter to give Wallace the win. . . . He would not have destroyed Wallace; Wallace would have haunted him in North Carolina and other places." Udall acknowledged he could have been hurt in Florida too, as the liberals had been in 1972. But his liberal supporters came to him and said the Carter people had convinced them it was essential to beat Wallace, and they would probably wind up being Udall delegates anyway. "It was a ticket good for this train only," Udall said, and in the end he bought it. "I felt pretty good about the decision. It not only made very good sense to me, avoiding the swamp that is Florida, the immense amount of money and time you would have to plow into it, but I didn't think that the party was really going to nominate Jimmy Carter. If Carter could be used as an engine to destroy Wallace, well, then, fine." Udall was beginning to wonder, though. When Leonard Woodcock, president of the United Auto Workers, told him the union was going to back Carter in Florida to beat Wallace, Udall told him, "Fine, but Carter isn't going to go back to Plains and grow peanuts."

sider.) One of the offending Jackson ads, placed in classified-advertising sections, was headed: "Wanted—Someone to Buy My House." It told of a mythical homeowner willing to sell his $39,000 house at a loss because Carter's tax reform would drive his taxes on the house up nearly $600 a year. It concluded: "Can Floridians afford the Carter tax reform?" But Carter's polls showed Jackson still cutting in, with the "favorables" on Carter slipping and the "unfavorables" going up.

Through all this, Carter was, in Caddell's words, "wiped out, exhausted." The top staffers conferred. "We all felt if we blew it in the last few days and lost Florida, it might be all over," Greg Schneiders said later. "We talked about keeping him in Florida over the weekend, but decided it wasn't worth the risk. He was tired, and getting testy. So we sent him home. Some of us were uneasy about the stridency of Jimmy's attack on Jackson, but we didn't question that there should be an attack. We had gone the high road in Massachusetts by not saying anything about anybody, and we got clobbered. The public didn't respond to him turning the other cheek." But now, obviously, the hard line wasn't helping either. When a candidate says or does anything that clashes with the image he has worked diligently to create about himself, he is bound to get into trouble, and the Good Shepherd did not make a very appealing hatemonger.

Carter went to Plains for a day, returning on Sunday afternoon rested and resolved to go easy on Jackson, to end the primary on a positive note. He was on his best behavior at a Tampa fish-fry, allowing himself only veiled jabs at the Washington establishment. Meanwhile, Jackson was in Miami Beach, mining the Jewish lode vigorously, even to the point of going to the beach to remind the middle-aged and elderly bikini-clad women and paunchy sun-worshiping old men that nobody stood guard over the interests of the State of Israel the way Scoop Jackson did. Wallace also campaigned, but now the Carter camp saw the fight in terms of holding off Jackson's rush rather than going after Wallace. If that case was not made by now, it never would be.

On election day, March 9, Carter flew into North Carolina to get a jump on that state's primary, two weeks hence. While he was there, in the late afternoon, Powell learned of some early CBS–*New York Times* exit polls indicating Carter had a twelve-point lead. By the time he arrived in Orlando, it was not official, but Carter felt confident. "He was very pleased, quietly emotional," Schneiders said later; but he was also not feeling well, running a temperature and enduring a cold. He joined his wife and family at the sprawling Carlton House, a modern new motel complex, to watch the returns on television. Before he arrived, shortly before eight o'clock, CBS News projected him the winner. Jordan, watching inside Room 1004, the

Carter suite, let out a rebel yell and hugged Betty Rainwater, a youngish schoolteacher who served as assistant press secretary. When Carter finally came in and was told how well it was going, he remarked, "It's hard to believe"—especially favorable returns from Tallahassee in the Panhandle. He and Rosalynn, with their daughter, Amy, sitting on the floor, settled onto the gold corduroy sofa and watched the three television sets, each tuned to a different network. The atmosphere was rather stiff, because Carter was supposed to do interviews with CBS and ABC and a tape with NBC, and there was much arranging of positions. But after the detour in New England, he was on track again. "We found out [in] Massachusetts," he said at one point, "that a success in one state does not necessarily carry over to another one. Now Scoop Jackson has found that out too."

When the final results were in, the dimensions of Carter's victory were broad-based but much less than the early returns had suggested: Carter 34 per cent, Wallace 31 per cent, Jackson 24 per cent, Shapp 2 per cent. Three days later, Shapp joined Bentsen, Sanford, and Bayh as Casualty No. 4, saying he was "just facing reality." A late start, he said, had made it impossible to become well-known enough and raise sufficient money under the new campaign-finance law.

Carter was very careful not to push Wallace out the door. Asked what he thought the Alabama governor's future was, Carter said it would be "whatever he decides it should be"; their next confrontation, in Illinois the following week, would provide "a much clearer test" of his strength.

But in fact Carter was already looking past Wallace to Jackson and Udall. He knew he could not compete with Jackson in the senator's next major test, in New York on April 6, and so he proceeded to attack the primary system that required filing by petition in each of New York's thirty-nine congressional districts. He blamed unnamed "political bosses" for making it so difficult, said they were aligned with Jackson, but he would fight the system anyway. He was, of course, trying to make sure he would be seen as an underdog in New York.

Carter also said he expected an intensified challenge from Udall, who "will certainly come in first in Wisconsin" on the same day as New York's primary. What he did not say was that he had already decided that an effort be made in Wisconsin to clear Udall out; Carter foot soldiers in Florida, led by Phil Wise, would be dispatched forthwith to Wisconsin to generate some kind of organization in the twenty-eight days remaining before the primary.

Wallace was in a union hall in Countryside, Illinois, a Chicago suburb, when the Florida results came in. He sought to put a positive face on them: coming in second was "a splendid vote" in a highly cosmopolitan state, and he said he was pressing on and would pick up "a flock of delegates" in Illinois the next week. But he knew his campaign was in deep trouble. Snider had warned him it would be so.

Jackson likewise sought to minimize the Florida vote, but the luck of the calendar was against him. His day in the sun had been very short: before he could reap the media harvest of Massachusetts, Scoop Jackson was a loser again. He had picked up twenty-one delegates to thirty-four for Carter and twenty-six for Wallace, but the press was not in a delegate-counting mood. Winning or losing primaries was still what captured headlines and network television coverage, and so Carter headed out of Florida the top dog once more. He was, after all, the man who had burst the George Wallace bubble in the South.

Winner or not, the next twenty-four hours were something of an ordeal for Carter. Though he still had his cold, he stayed up late watching returns and talking to aides. As he was getting undressed to go to bed some UAW officials came by, so he put his pants back on—but no shoes and socks—and went out to see them. His wife finally came out and retrieved him. With only a few hours sleep, he got up early the next morning to appear on the television morning-news shows and was extremely short-tempered, in spite of the very good things that had befallen him the night before. On the way to one of the studios he was told he had been scheduled to fly to New York the next Saturday night to be on CBS News' "Face the Nation." Ordinarily he might have been expected to gobble up this free nationwide exposure, but he had been planning to have Sunday off in Plains. Ed Rabel of CBS, who was in the car with Carter and Barry Jagoda, the candidate's television adviser, recalled the scene: "He was livid. He read Jagoda up one side and down the other, and would not let go. 'You always go ahead and schedule me without telling me,' he said. He kept going back at him, four or five times."

This ill temper turned out to be very bad news for one Important Carter Aide. After the television studio stops, Carter's entourage boarded a campaign plane for Illinois. Going along, ostensibly to interview the candidate, was Dr. Hunter S. Thompson, the distinguished national correspondent and sometimes resident physician of *Rolling Stone* magazine, a Carter booster and friend. An interview with the good but wholly unpredictable Dr. Thompson could be an emotional experience under any circumstance, and Carter had hoped to sleep en route to Illinois. Finally the matter was resolved by Carter sleeping half the way and talking to Thompson the other half, but according to Schneiders, Carter was irritable all day.

Thompson, for his part, was irate at receiving such short shrift. The Important Carter Aide in Orlando had promised him he would have the full flight with Carter. The irrepressible High Priest of Gonzo Journalism grabbed the first available flight back from Chicago to Orlando with blood in his eye. The I.C.A., forewarned that one of America's most menacing figures was en route to take his revenge, retreated in the better part of valor to a room in the headquarters motel. But Thompson was not to be put off. Using his superlative skills of journalistic inquiry, persuasion, and intimidation, he tracked down the incommunicado I.C.A. Pounding on his door and shouting obscenities that most others would scarcely utter but the prose laureate of Aspen was accustomed to write, Thompson demanded that the Important Carter Aide come out and face the music. The I.C.A., as they say in legal circles, stood mute. Whereupon his pursuer produced a large quantity of cigarette-lighter fluid, proceeded to douse the door, and set it aflame. The I.C.A. escaped to the safety of an adjoining room.

While the aide was thus protecting his life and limb, Carter was proceeding to harvest the ample benefit of his Florida victory in Illinois. Carefully avoiding any challenge to Mayor Daley's slate in Cook County, Carter in a quick foray into the state parlayed the growing national focus on him into another primary victory of surprising proportions, driving George Wallace closer to the edge and pushing Sargent Shriver out of the race altogether.

Daley's threatening presence, unwittingly, ran interference for Carter. Not wanting to confront Daley, especially after the 1972 Democratic reform debacle in which Daley had been denied a seat at the party's national convention, most of the competing candidates had decided to skip the Illinois primary. Jackson had made a pass at it, but when Senator Stevenson agreed to head the Daley slate he backed off, and so did Udall. Harris, while seeking 80 delegates of the 155 at stake, also soft-pedaled Illinois to concentrate on some more hopeful test, Wisconsin or Pennsylvania. Carter ran 85 delegates and said he would be happy to win 20; Wallace, hoping his blue-collar Yankee friends would revive his sinking candidacy, ran 122; Shriver, seeking Daley's endorsement, got no more than a hearing before the Cook County Democratic Committee, and was doomed from the start.

After only four days in Illinois and expenditures of just $130,000, Carter scored an astonishing victory, not only winning the nonbinding preference primary (or "beauty contest") as expected, but collaring fifty-five of the state's convention delegates, to eighty-five for the Daley-Stevenson slate. He got 48 per cent of the vote to 28 per cent for Wallace, 16 per cent for Shriver, and 8 per cent for Harris. It was a remarkable showing for the minimal effort made, and in the face of the Daley machine, which Carter clobbered downstate.

The closeness of the Florida race had enabled Wallace to brush aside any thoughts of bowing out then. In fact, he made a strong public commitment to go on, to bolster his sagging supporters, and Snider, knowing Wallace, knew he meant it. But even in advance of the Illinois vote, Snider had indications from his own polls that Wallace was in for a drubbing. He urged him to abandon Illinois and go on to North Carolina.

"We gonna lose that badly?" Wallace asked.

"Yes," Snider said.

"Well, what about North Carolina?"

"You're gonna lose North Carolina, too."

"Well, why leave here and go on?"

"To minimize the loss in North Carolina."

"You don't think we can pull it out in North Carolina?"

"Governor, if you've got any chance at all, you'd have to go now, like right now."

But Wallace had made commitments to the faithful and he did not want to go back on them. So he pressed on. Yet the thought of quitting was now planted in his mind. In an appearance on the ABC News show "Issues and Answers," Wallace said he would finish out his commitments this year and then his political career would be over. This was not very helpful in rallying the troops, but Wallace was capable of such bursts of damaging candor.

In North Carolina the next week, on March 23, it was a case of a candidacy openly falling apart, and once again the luck of the calendar worked for Carter. Not only did he come breezing in on the strength of his Florida triumph and Illinois romp but the North Carolina primary was the only show in town for three weeks. The next tests would not be until April 6, in Wisconsin and New York, and both of Carter's principal foes now, Jackson and Udall, were immobilized until then.

There had been one slight distraction in the closing days of the Illinois race: word from California that Governor Jerry Brown would, after considerable shadowboxing, seek the Democratic presidential nomination. Characteristically, he first broke the news in a casual conversation with four reporters in his Sacramento office: he would run as a favorite son in California's June 8 primary. Elaborating, however, he made clear he would run as a national candidate. Playing the mystic to the hilt, Brown said he expected his campaign "will begin to materialize in California and spread east if that is the will of the people." Carter had talked to Brown on the phone, expressed disappointment that he felt he had to run, but could not and tried not to do anything further about it. Brown was a problem to be dealt with later; Carter had his hands full running someplace nearly every week and coping with the active opposition.

The same was true of the announcement two days after the Illinois vote that Senator Frank Church, his obligations fulfilled as chairman of a Senate committee investigating American intelligence agencies, would also be a candidate, with his first primary test scheduled for Nebraska in May. Carter considered Church an attractive figure, but, like Brown, he was getting in too late to win the nomination outright; Brown and Church could be nominated only in convention horsetrading, Carter said afterward, and he was determined with his own success to make such strategies moot.

Deposing George Wallace once and for all was the immediate business, and indications were that North Carolina would be a propitious place to do so. Carter was winging in on that much ballyhooed commodity of the 1976 campaign, momentum, and a *Raleigh News and Observer* poll had him comfortably ahead—31.6 per cent to 20.9—over Wallace. The Carter effort was purring now, while the Wallace campaign was foundering. Some Carter days were better than others. One morning during the last week, Carter rose at a Winston-Salem motel and went to the nearby general aviation airport to start the day's campaigning. When he arrived, the plane was there but no traveling press corps and no press secretary. Meanwhile, over at the Greensboro regional airport, Jody Powell and two busloads of reporters arrived, but there was no plane and no candidate. Powell was at the wrong airport. He sheepishly phoned Carter, who would almost rather tell a lie than be late. Carter boarded the empty plane and was flown to the Greensboro airport—which obliged him to miss his first two stops of the day and gave Powell a severe case of guilt. The candidate was irritated no end. When the plane landed, Sally Quinn of *The Washington Post* got aboard, sat next to Carter and engaged him in conversation. Carter was eying the front of the plane. "Watch," he said to Quinn, "Jody will be the last to get on board." Sure enough, Powell waited until all reporters were on the plane before boarding. ("You can thank Sally for saving you," Quinn remembers hearing Carter tell Powell as he came down the aisle. "She's put me in a good mood.")

Meanwhile, Wallace sent out a call for Alabama state officials and general citizenry to come to North Carolina to help him. "We made a last-ditch, desperation effort," Snider said, "and we moved half the state of Alabama up there: volunteers, door-to-door people, legislators. We paid expenses, and it was very admirable on the part of the people of Alabama, but it didn't help. As a matter of fact, the polls showed it hurt us a little bit. We got into some desperate politicking."

Part of the desperation tactics was a head-on attack on Carter as a liberal of the George McGovern stripe—an accusation that surely would have amused Carter's liberal critics. Wallace called him "a warmed-over

McGovern" and as evidence of their ideological kinship named two former McGovern campaign aides now close to Carter—pollster Caddell (a native of Jacksonville, Florida) and fund-raiser Morris Dee (of Birmingham, Alabama!), both men known more as practical hired guns than for their liberalism. But, Wallace said, "these are ultra-liberals who do not think like the average North Carolinian."

Wallace also charged Carter had used him to garner conservative support when Carter ran for governor, and was violating his own pledge never to lie in denying it. "When Carl Sanders, his opponent and a former governor, twice tried to keep me from speaking in Georgia it created a great political furor," Wallace said in Charlotte. "Mr. Carter said not only would he not keep me out, he'd invite me in. I think that implies he'd support me. And on his way from the governors' conference on June 8, 1972, he told the *Atlanta Constitution* that a Democratic ticket of Hubert Humphrey with George Wallace as Vice President was acceptable to him and it would do well in the South. . . . Is that misleading you or telling the truth?"

Carter sought to explain away the allegations. He had indeed invited Wallace to speak in Georgia, he said, but only in defending his constitutional right to do so. And as for the Humphrey-Wallace ticket, Carter said he had been asked how it would fare in the South and he said he thought it would do well, but had not *advocated* it.

Wallace also took Carter to task for arranging to have a portrait of the late Dr. Martin Luther King, Jr., who Wallace dubbed a "communist-associated civil-rights agitator," hung in the state capitol in Atlanta. To that one, Carter gladly pleaded guilty before a crowd at Saint Augustine College, a predominantly black school in Raleigh. (Carter made a special effort to woo black college students and to stress his Southern connection to both white and black Dixie audiences. "Won't it be great to have a President who doesn't speak with an accent?" he liked to say, grinning.)

Wallace's attacks did not make a dent; the old lip-curling magic was just not working. On top of that, his entourage fell to bickering among themselves, and second-guessing. George should never have gone into Massachusetts and Illinois; the campaign was spending too much money on television, and on that airplane; the press and television were killing George, what with their cameras focused on that damned wheelchair. Some of Wallace's helpmates tried to turn his handicap into political advantage, but without notable finesse. Like Steve Sammos, his master of ceremonies, observing that his candidate might be "weak in the legs, but other candidates are weak in the head." And warning the others to watch out, "because Governor Wallace is at his best when he's backed into a corner."

At a small luncheon in Greensboro the day after his Illinois defeat, reporters asked Wallace whether he would quit if he lost in the North Carolina primary. "If I come in again in an airplane like I did in Raleigh last night in windy weather," he said, "that might make me quit." He smiled wryly as he said it, evoking laughter. But shortly afterward, asked the same question in a television interview in Durham, he referred again to the Raleigh landing, in which a first approach had to be aborted because of severe ground crosswinds. "Short of that," he said, he could think of nothing that would make him quit.

Those who did not know George Wallace well might have thought his reference to the airplane landing was just a convenient peg on which to hang his stated determination to stay in the race. But anyone who had ever flown with him knew that for all his personal courage, he hated and feared flying more than any other individual in public life. I had first flown with him in 1968, when he was running as an independent candidate for President in a beat-up old propeller-driven DC-6 chartered from Mohawk Airlines, a feeder line. Many a night was spent flying through darkness broken only by engine exhausts spewing blue flame, with Wallace glaring out of the window, gripping his chair with both hands and white-knuckling it. When he was like that, there was no distracting him. It was not unusual for him flatly to refuse to fly in rainy weather, even if cleared by the authorities. He flew because he knew he had to if he were to be an effective candidate, but he hated it with a passion and didn't care who knew it.

An hour or so after the Durham television interview, I was sitting across from him in the forward compartment of his chartered BAC-111 jet, a plush leather-and-teak appointed plane that carried up to eighty passengers in its commercial configuration but was converted, at great cost to the campaign, into a twenty-four-passenger flying living room, complete with the kind of deep sofas you sink into.[2] We were on our way from Greensboro to Asheville, a route that took us west across the Appalachian Mountains,

---

2. The Wallace campaign learned about the comforts, and the cost, of flying first-class from no less an authority than retired Air Force General and Chief of Staff Curtis LeMay, whose greatest political distinction was his testimonial to the harmlessness of atomic bombs on the occasion of Wallace's introduction of him as his running mate in 1968. Deploring that folks seemed "to have a phobia about nuclear weapons," LeMay assured reporters that while the land crabs at the Bikini testing site were "a little bit hot," the rats on the atoll were "bigger, fatter, and healthier than they ever were before."

As Wallace's running mate, according to Snider, the former Strategic Air Command boss refused to fly in the Lockheed Electra turbo-prop which had been leased for him. He insisted on a Boeing 727 pure jet.

"How much is that costing us?" Wallace, who flew in the Electra, asked Snider.

"About a hundred and twenty-seven thousand dollars a week, Governor," Snider said. "More per day than two Electras cost for a week."

"God damn," Wallace shot back, "he's either spending all our money or dropping atomic bombs."

a range of only modest height but subject in March to the kind of crosswinds that had plagued the plane's landing in Raleigh the night before. Wallace was having a late lunch, a tray of steak with potatoes, peas, and the ever-present bottle of ketchup, without which any steak consumed by the Governor of Alabama would have been a gastronomic Lady Godiva.[3] He ate ravenously—his one eating speed—and talked as he ate, interspersing bites with puffs on his cigar, ashes scattering indescriminately on steak, potatoes, peas and the table alike in the process. Beneath us, the rolling North Carolina countryside passed on a clear, bright, but windy day.

"How's life treating you?" I asked him.

"Oh, fine," he said. "Too much flyin' in windy weather."

"I hear you had a pretty sticky trip last night."

"Coming in, yeah."

"This is a pretty comfortable plane, though."

"Yeah, but it ain't when you have bad weather."

The ride was smooth so far and Wallace was quite relaxed, enjoying his steak as he talked, but keeping an eye on the window as the plane hummed toward Asheville, nestled in the foothills of the Appalachians. I turned to the business at hand.

"How are you feeling after Florida and Illinois? It's a new experience for you."

"You mean physically?"

"No, I mean just emotionally, about losing two primaries."

"I feel all right. I don't know how y'all feel."

"I remember talking to you, back six months, a year ago, about Carter, and you didn't seem to take him seriously. You think you've underestimated him?"

"There no use taking everybody seriously in the sense of worrying about their candidacy. They all have rights to run."

"But here's a candidate from the South who's going right after your base. He's running in every Southern state. You've never had to face that before. By going into a state yourself, you've usually kept the other candidates out. Nobody would compete. . . . What happens if you lose a couple of more states in the South?"

3. My colleague Jack Germond, who rates as the Galloping Gourmet of the political press corps, once endeared himself to Wallace for all time in this fashion: having lunch with Germond in the nondescript cafeteria at the state capitol in Montgomery, Wallace reached for the ketchup. But, catching Germond watching him, he stopped and withdrew his hand. He was sensitive to a line in Marshall Frady's book, *Wallace,* about his pouring ketchup on everything he ate. Whereupon Germond, putting his own reputation on the line, reached out, grabbed the bottle, and shook its oozing contents all over his own lunch. Wallace, beaming, grabbed the bottle himself and went to town. They were bosom-buddies ever after.

"Well, I found out I went into this campaign with a handicap that I didn't realize, and that was being in a wheelchair. . . . All I can do is keep going and show people like y'all and tell them. But I can assure y'all that if my health wasn't good I wouldn't be in this thing."

"Do you get as much kick out of campaigning as you used to?"

"Well, it's not as easy for me to get around in the crowds. I miss that part of it. . . . But you just have to plow straight ahead. . . . You just can't get in a wheelchair and go out in crowds. Roosevelt was in a wheelchair but that was before television. A lot of people didn't know he was in a wheelchair."

"Are you committed to go all the way to the convention?"

"If I come in any more landings like I did in Raleigh the other night—"

Finally, we were back to that. Wallace kept watching the passing countryside as he talked about how he had "paid a high price" for the country. Suddenly the plane lurched and dropped as if it were falling through a trap door.

"Damn," Wallace said. "I hope we can land all right." He looked out the window nervously again, then picked up his narrative: "I paid a high price— Hell, I don't want them to land this thing if they goin' to have to land in the same kind of weather. We comin' into these mountains, you know. . . . Sheesh."

Billy Joe Camp, his press secretary, leaned over. "Bumpy air," he said to his boss, hopefully.

"We got the same stuff in Raleigh," Wallace said, grimacing. "I don't want to be gamblin' on landing, now."

"I don't know what we got on the ground," Camp said, "but you can look out and see this layer of haze. As we came up through it, it was rough."

"That was rough all the way to the ground," Wallace said, still thinking of Raleigh. "If we got that kind of weather to land in like Raleigh, just hell, turn around and go to Birmingham."

I tried to help. "These mountains here make it tricky," I offered.

"Well, I know it does," Wallace said. "That makes it double tricky in March too."

Now long silences set in as he gazed with unfeigned misery out the window. He would try to continue the conversation, but he just could not concentrate on it: "I told the people I paid a high price— I just don't like to fool around landin' these things. . . . We goin' higher?"

Camp went into the pilot's cabin to get some information on the weather.

"What did he say?" Wallace asked anxiously the moment he emerged.

"We don't have any crosswinds going in. This is just turbulence out of the mountains, and that layer of haze. There's a wind blowing, but it's straight down the runway. It's not a crosswind."

Wallace was not comforted. "Yeah, but we gotta go across how many mountains?"

"We're within about fifteen or twenty miles of Asheville right now," Camp told him.

Wallace strained to see ahead. "Is it in a valley? Are they reportin' that from the— That came from Gus? Ol' Gus [the pilot]?"

Camp: "He said it's steady at two-zero. Twenty."

Wallace: "Twenty knots? God, that's—"

I tried to help again. "Beautiful country," I said. Wallace ignored me.

"He said no problems?" he asked Camp.

"That's what he's saying."

"Asheville's in a valley? I don't know whether we're gonna get over these mountains or not."

I tried again: "What mountains are these, do you know?"

Wallace (impatiently): "Appalachians. . . . Didn't you say you see Asheville?"

Camp: "Not yet, sir."

I thought I'd try the light touch. "Well," I said, "it could be raining."

Wallace did not appreciate the humor. "Except if it was rainin' to start with, we wouldn't be here."

It was getting really bumpy now, and Wallace was holding on for dear life. I tried getting another conversation going. "You know, my family comes from North Carolina, on my father's side."

Nothing. Except a slow whistling sound from the governor. "Sheesh."

At last, the plane was below the bumpy air and easing in for a landing. "It's smoothed out now," I said, relieved myself.

"Yeah," Wallace answered, his eyes still riveted on the window, "but we ain't down yet." Not until the wheels touched the runway and the plane came to a stop did he loosen his grip and take his eyes off the scenery.

Outside, at the airport gate, about a hundred Wallace admirers were waiting. Wallace was carried to a car at the foot of the ramp and driven over to them. The window of the back seat of the car was opened and he reached out and shook the well-wishers' hands as they filed by, one by one. George Wallace the campaigner was in his element again. The ordeal of the rough plane flight was behind him now and, as he had said he had to do, he just plowed straight ahead. Wallace's reactions on the plane were comical, yes, but they were at the same time genuine and a telling measure of his courage and determination, after all he had been through. He was headed for certain and humiliating defeat here in North Carolina, but he was not going to quit. It was his life, and he knew it.

The North Carolina primary was notable for one other development. Here, for the first time, Carter spoke out at length about the roots of his deep religiosity that unnerved so many non-Baptists and contributed to the sense of uncertainty and even strangeness about him. It was what Ham Jordan called irreverently but unabashedly the "weirdo factor," and it plagued Carter throughout the long election year.

It happened that while I was covering Carter in North Carolina, Myra McPherson, my able colleague on *The Washington Post*, was preparing a long article on Carter's sister, Ruth Stapleton, a professional faith healer who practiced what she called an "inner healing" ministry and was becoming the subject of increasing interest, not to say curiosity. Not the least reason, beyond her kinship with the presidential candidate, was the fact she was a striking blonde given to wearing eye shadow, gold rings in her pierced ears, and turtleneck sweaters; not your basic faith healer by any means.

In the course of an interview, Carter's sister told McPherson of a long conversation she had had with her brother in 1966 after his loss to Lester Maddox in his first race for governor. He was depressed, and walking in the woods with her, she recalled, he asked, "You and I are both Baptists, but what is it that you have that I haven't got?" She told him, "Jimmy, through my hurt and pain I finally got so bad off I had to forget everything I was. What it amounts to in religious terms is total commitment. I belong to Jesus, everything I am."

To which her brother replied, "Ruth, that's what I want."

Thereupon, Stapleton recalled, they reviewed the sacrifices he was willing to make—he could give up his money, his friends, even his family. "Then I asked, 'What about all political ambitions?' He said, 'Ruth! You know I want to be Governor. I would use it for the people.' I said, 'No, Jimmy.' But he really meant it and became connected with part-time religious work." He went to Pennsylvania and New York to do missionary work in the Baptist Church, she said, and had been a new man ever since. Stapleton also told McPherson that she recalled her brother crying during that conversation, saying he'd give up being President of the United States if he could have the feeling of peace she had, and that he had indeed dropped out of politics for about a year.

The story was so dramatic and so bound to be controversial that I was asked to check it out with Carter before the *Post* printed it. That night, on the way to a fund-raising reception in the home of a wealthy Carter supporter in Winston-Salem, I rode with Carter in his car and told him what his sister had related to McPherson. He said the story was "accurate, basically," but that rather than doing missionary work in the North for a full year, he had made periodic trips of a week or ten days on several occasions. He denied having cried, or having said he would give up his political ambitions. Yes, he and Ruth had "walked out in a pine orchard over on our farm" and talked about how he could achieve the same inner peace she had. His involvement in pioneer mission work resulted, he said, but he continued his politicking in Georgia. This was very easy to do, because no one knew him in the Northern states where he toiled as a Christian layman. "I was really getting to be well known in Georgia," he said, "and it was more convenient for me to go to do this kind of Christian work where I was not well known and nobody would recognize me."

Stapleton had also told McPherson that her brother, as governor, would often go off by himself and, not converse with God or hear a voice, but feel some kind of strength coming from his meditation. When I asked about that, Carter said, "I don't think that ought to be said in a mystical way. It's just a standard part of my life. When I have intense pressures on me, or difficult decisions to make, I habitually go off by myself. When I'm at home in Plains I go up and take a walk in the woods or in the field. And when I was in the Governor's office I had my own private room . . . and I would go back there and just say a prayer and, you know, think quietly about what ought to be done. There was no wave of revelation that came over me, no blinding flash of light or voices of God or anything. I just had a quiet feeling that was reassuring. But I wouldn't want it connoted as a mystical set of events. It's a typical experience among Christians."

Directly after our conversation, Carter went into the reception, where he addressed his supporters from a large patio. It was a balmy night. Someone in the crowd asked him about his commitment to Christ. Again he confirmed it, and then went on to say at length that he saw no conflict between the active practice of his faith and public service, and that in fact his strong faith was a reassurance to him in making decisions affecting the lives of millions of others. "I spent more time on my knees the four years I was Governor," he said, "in the seclusion of a little private room in the governor's office, than I did in all the rest of my life put together."

Carter touched on his mission work in the North and then said, "In early 1967 I had a profound religious experience that changed my life dramatically, and I recognized for the first time that I had lacked something very precious—a complete commitment to Christ, a presence of the Holy

Spirit in my life in a more profound and personal way, and since then I've had an inner peace and inner conviction and assurance that transformed my life for the better."

At a press conference the next day at Wake Forest, Carter was asked to elaborate on that "profound religious experience," but he declined to be more specific—other than to say it had to do with his "personal witnessing in states outside Georgia" with non-English-speaking people. "It was not a profound stroke or miracle," he said. "It wasn't a voice of God from heaven. It was not anything of that kind. It wasn't mysterious. . . . I don't feel I'm ordained by God to win an election or to be President of the United States. And I would be perfectly at ease if I won or lost. I don't intend to lose, but I don't think God is going to make me be President, by any means."

These observations brought to the forefront a sort of whispered issue concerning Carter that had bothered many people outside the South unfamiliar with the ways of the Baptist faith. It was not something specific, but rather a general uneasiness about this rather strange man who had strode boldly onto the political landscape, speaking unabashedly about love and compassion and being influenced in his conduct of public office by God's word and guidance. It is not clear whether it was only happenstance that Carter aired his views at such length that night, or whether he was concerned that Myra McPherson's story might introduce a potentially damaging or difficult element into the campaign and hence had to be dealt with forthrightly then. At any rate, his observations only served to create more talk about Carter's religiosity, especially outside the South.

In North Carolina, though, nothing could slow Carter down. On primary day he ran strongly in every part of the state, posting his first clear majority in a primary, with 54 per cent to 35 for Wallace. In the process he picked up 36 of 61 delegates at stake and was approaching 200 delegates solidly committed. He predicted he would arrive at the national convention in July with "maybe a thousand" of the 1505 needed for the nomination. He would not count Wallace out of contention, calling him "a very courageous, tough, persistent campaigner," but he knew Wallace was through.

The Alabamian, in Montgomery, offered no excuses but vowed he would remain a candidate if only to keep the others honest. But on March 22, with Congress still at an impasse, the Federal Election Commission's power to certify federal campaign subsidies lapsed, and Wallace, who once talked grandly of refusing the matching funds, was desperate. He cut out many of the frills of his campaign and opted for a strategy of paid radio and television appearances. Bill Grammer and Steve Sammos both were given their walking papers, and thereafter the Wallace campaign was never a factor. In an interview with B. Drummond Ayres, Jr., of *The New York Times,* Wallace summed up what he saw to be his problem with the voters: "All they see is the spokes on my wheelchair. The television catches every one. You've got a man standing up saying 'Big government is eating you up.' And you got a man in a wheelchair, all humped over, saying the same thing. It's hard to beat." A few days earlier he had put it another way: "I guess you could say that Arthur Bremer really messed me up politically with that gun."

That, of course, was part of it. But Wallace's themes had been pre-empted by others, and he had drunk from the cup once too often. He would never be President and everybody knew it. If his old followers wanted to send Washington a message of protest, Jimmy Carter served that function very well. They did, indeed, come to realize that in Carter they could send Washington not just a message, but a President.

19. The Bad Luck of Mo Udall

While Jimmy Carter was busy disposing of George Wallace, Morris Udall was preparing at last to bring a serious liberal presence into the Democratic equation. Having won his much-discussed liberal elimination contest without scoring a single caucus or primary victory, he hoped finally to have the party's left wing coalesce behind his candidacy. Much time had been spent—wasted, it might have been more accurate to say—trying to woo the prominent, card-carrying liberals who had helped to engineer McGovern's nomination in 1972, while taking care not to drive off the moderates. The result had been a kind of stillborn candidacy, with the most attractive human qualities of the man somehow diluted. Mo Udall emerged as neither ideologue nor humanist. Still, he had survived.

For Udall's long-awaited breakthrough, Wisconsin was both an obvious and an ideal battleground. Its liberal tradition went back to the days of Robert LaFollette, and had been reinforced by Eugene McCarthy's primary victory there over Lyndon Johnson in 1968 and McGovern's first 1972 success over Wallace, Jackson, Muskie, and Lindsay. Madison, home of the University of Wisconsin and a major anti-Vietnam war center in past years, remained a pocket of radical politics, with among other things a young radical mayor, Paul Soglin. If Mo Udall was at long last to have his day in the sun, Wisconsin certainly would be the place.

Well aware of this favorable political climate, Udall had begun working in Wisconsin in early 1975, and by March 1976 one might have expected him to be well entrenched for the April 6 primary. But Carter by then had generated such a head of steam that he was able to storm into Wisconsin and, with little more than his pick-up squad of workers from the Florida campaign, immediately eclipse Udall in the polls. An early survey by Peter Hart showed Udall trailing Carter, 17 per cent to 34, in a state where conventional wisdom would normally have reversed the figures. Two weeks before the primary Udall seemed perilously close to elimination. (Carter, of course, soft-pedaled the extent of his effort in Wisconsin the better to convey the impression that he was the underdog in the state, and thus to amplify the effect of an "upset" over Udall there.)

Ironically, there was a time when the Udall camp had feared the

Wisconsin primary might go to Udall by default. In February 1976 Jack Quinn noted in a memo that only Wallace and Harris among the opposition "are seriously working the state," and that while "your potential there is greater than that of any other state and a smashing victory is entirely conceivable," it would be wise to "be cautious and hope you have some opposition over whom to have a meaningful victory." Quinn's advice was to avoid spending too much time or money there: "If the opposition smells a clear Udall lead, they could pull the rug on you and leave the state on the pretense of its having a meaningless primary."

At the time that memo was written, there were other reasons for labeling the Wisconsin primary meaningless. The state has an "open" primary—meaning members of one party may cross over and vote in the primary of the other—and as such it was not an acceptable means for selecting delegates to the Democratic National Convention under the new party reforms. Thus it was to be reduced to a statement of preference only, with the sixty-eight delegates selected by state convention. But Governor Patrick J. Lucey, failing by a single vote to have the state legislature close the primary, appealed to the national party in early March to permit delegate-selection through the primary anyway.

Udall supporters, who saw Wisconsin as their best chance yet for a victory, launched an intensive lobbying effort with the party's Compliance Review Commission, charged with making sure the states selected their delegates in accordance with the party rules. The liberal machinists' and communications workers' unions, and Udall personally, talked with commission members. Ironically, the reformers who had been instrumental in creating the CRC were now asking it to bend the rules for them. One commission member, Mayor Kathryn Kirschbaum of Davenport, Iowa, was told by machinists in her city that they would oppose her in her own approaching primary if she didn't go along. She finally acceded, providing the deciding vote to permit Wisconsin to hold its traditional open primary, but she was defeated in her primary anyway. Mark Siegel, the executive director of the Democratic National Committee, was irate at the cave-in. "You don't let Louisiana have more shots at racial segregation," he said afterward, but because it was the reformers who wanted to buck the reforms, that apparently was okay.

The ruling immediately made the Wisconsin contest more attractive to Carter, so Udall did not have to worry after all about any lack of serious competition.

Udall had, in fact, been looking forward to an essentially one-on-one encounter with Carter. In Iowa, New Hampshire, and Massachusetts, it had been Carter against the liberal pack, and Udall had been obliged to split the vote on the left with three or four others. This time, though most of the other candidates—Wallace, Jackson, Shriver, Shapp, Bayh, Harris, McCormack, even Bentsen—remained on the ballot, only Carter and Udall were campaigning hard. But even now there was a complicating and potentially diluting element. On the same day as the Wisconsin primary, New York also would be selecting 206 of its 274 delegates in a state primary. Jackson was conceded to be the certain winner there, by virtue of his support among Jewish voters, important segments of labor, and much hard work. But the delegate prize was too great, under proportional representation, not to make some effort. And so Udall was faced with the prospect of having to split between the two states—a split of his time, of his staff, and, most important, of his limited financial resources. The lapsing of the FEC's power to pay out the federal subsidies left Udall unable to get his hands on $89,500, for which he had qualified, and his failure to win a primary was discouraging new contributors.

On top of all these difficulties, there was the matter of the health of Udall's campaign itself. Within it, disorder and a general lack of leadership or direction reigned. "We were routinely involved in squabbles over decision-making," Quinn acknowledged. "I look at the Carter campaign and I see it was run by a submarine commander who didn't tolerate that sort of crap." A game of musical chairs was played most of the time over the leadership, first between two members of Udall's congressional staff, John Gabusi and Terry Bracy. When that was more or less resolved, Gabusi quit for personal reasons and Quinn moved into the vacuum; then Quinn and Stewart Udall, the candidate's brother and general overseer of the campaign, fought; "Stewdall" thereupon recruited John Marttila and Tom Kiley of Boston to handle media-buying in the New England primaries, and they started to elbow their way in; through all this, Stan Kurz, a long-time Udall friend, held a tight rein on the purse strings as treasurer, exercising effective control over what could and could not be done. Kurz said he was given an initial mandate by Udall to be certain Udall did not go broke in the 1976 campaign, "but every time Mo smelled a little victory, he changed the mandate a little. But he kept telling me, 'You've got to protect me.'"

Stew Udall, in the words of one insider, functioned as "a free-floating safety," intercepting or batting down balls that came his way, especially if they represented spending in a campaign that had not spent wisely and was now supercautious. Kurz and Stew Udall had been appointed by the candidate as guardians of his financial solvency. "Mo had given me the assignment from the beginning," his brother said, "to see he didn't wind up in debt the rest of his life. I was the brakeman." This concern about throwing good money after bad, in the wake of the initial losses, quickly steered the campaign into a defensive posture. In the closing days before the Massachusetts primary, for example, about $15,000 that was destined for much-needed television time was summarily cut off, precipitating a shouting match between Marttila and Stew Udall, who had conveyed the decision. Marttila, livid, went to Mo and told him Kurz was "putting a knife into the heart of your campaign." But the money still was not forthcoming.

Marttila and his partner, Kiley, were by their own admission "aggressive"—hardball players in the extreme. They were used to going all out to win, to thinking big, to raising and spending large sums of money, and their style ran roughshod over Udall's relatively inexperienced operation. After the Massachusetts fiasco, Marttila resolved that he and Kiley would have to take over if Udall's campaign was ever going to be righted.

They went to Udall at the Sheraton-Boston on the day of the Massachusetts primary and laid it on him, in the presence of Stewart Udall and Quinn. According to Marttila, he ruled himself out as director, acknowledging he was now too controversial within the campaign, and urged that Kiley be put in charge.

The Udalls well understood that the campaign needed a stronger manager, and Quinn was the first to say so. Both Mo and Stew would often talk of finding the "gray eminence"—an individual of indisputable knowledge and stature in the political community, like Larry O'Brien—to take over. But O'Brien, now the commissioner of the National Basketball Association, was unavailable, and other such stars—who could put a public-relations luster on the campaign by their very presence, and also could run the thing —were hard to come by.

After hearing Marttila out, Udall asked him to come to a meeting of the full staff in Washington the following Saturday. Marttila went and sat in as Udall, in a kind of pep talk, disclosed his conviction that the campaign needed new leadership. He had just the man in mind, he said. Also invited was Mark Shields, another Bostonian, who had been instrumental in the election of John Gilligan as governor of Ohio in 1970 and had a good reputation as a political operator. To the astonishment of both Shields and Marttila, his good friend, Udall told the assembled troops that Shields was the man he wanted, and hoped he'd take the job. Udall did not know that Shields had promised his wife he would not become involved in any political campaign in 1976, and he told Udall as much in his office moments later. Shields also recommended Kiley for the job, and Udall agreed.

Kiley thereupon moved to Washington—"it was supposed to be for one month, until they found the gray eminence," he said later—and Quinn shifted to Wisconsin. Though Quinn himself was cooperative, many of his friends in the campaign were outraged, and some of them even called Kiley at home after midnight with threats: "We don't need pin-stripe suits run-ning this campaign. . . . We're gonna get you and Marttila. Jack Quinn's a better campaign manager than you could ever be." Quinn in the end helped quell the revolt.

Kiley had agreed to take over only on the condition that he would "get the checkbook"—handle the disbursement of funds. That ultimatum in turn produced an ultimatum from Kurz that if he had to give it over he would leave. More shouting matches, with the benign candidate squirming in the middle. "It was," Marttila said afterward, "the political equivalent of invad-ing Normandy on a daily basis." Finally Kurz kept the checkbook—and the hassling over money continued.

It was in this contentious climate that Mo Udall was trying to fashion his first primary victory in Wisconsin. On the first weekend in March, as Carter was coming out of his post-Massachusetts tailspin and preparing for Florida, Udall had been tempted, after Bayh's withdrawal, to shift his major effort to New York. Instead, it was decided to focus heavily on Wisconsin, while keeping a presence in New York and wooing Bayh's supporters. The national party's agreement to permit delegate-selection in the Wisconsin primary in large part dictated this decision. "We ought to make a maximum effort in Wisconsin," Quinn said then. "To the extent that involves scaling down our New York effort, we're prepared to do that."

But by mid-March Carter's Florida veterans under Phil Wise were settling in throughout Wisconsin. (En route from Orlando, Wise had stopped in Washington to be briefed on Wisconsin by Gene Pokorny, architect of McGovern's success there in 1972 and now one of Caddell's partners.) "It was just a total voter I.D. effort," Wise said later. "We put in as many phones as we could scrounge and we started going door-to-door with any kind of registration list we could find, so we could identify our voters and pull them on election day. We tried to do in three weeks there what we did in a twelve-week campaign in Florida. But by now we had the momentum thing. We were moving."

It was difficult for Udall to match that momentum, since from the point of view of the press he had been on the shelf since his second-place finish in Massachusetts, just when Carter was dominating the political headlines. Udall did receive a boost when the United Auto Workers, the Communications Workers of America, the American Federation of State, County, and Municipal Employees, and the Wisconsin Education Associa-tion all endorsed him in seven of Wisconsin's nine congressional districts. But that advantage was offset by the hiatus in the flow of the federal subsidy.

Carter and Udall themselves both made fast tracks for Wisconsin immediately after the North Carolina primary. Carter told reporters in

Milwaukee, "There's a high likelihood that unless Mr. Udall has a very strong showing in Wisconsin, it will be conclusive evidence that he cannot possibly win [the nomination]." Udall's own words underscored the difficulty he had confronting the Carter rush. Asked if he could beat Carter in Wisconsin, Udall said, "I don't know that I can. But Governor Carter is in for the fight of his life here. He'd like me to go off to the sidelines for a quiet funeral, but I'm not going to do it. I'm not going to fall over and play dead. I think the American people are entitled to a choice."[1]

Back at the Udall headquarters, with Kiley in the van, more positive thinking held sway. A Marttila-Kiley partner, David Thorne, undertook to raise $225,000, and the firm went about making heavy commitments for television time. According to Marttila and Kiley later, the money was coming in, but somewhat more slowly than projected. Kiley made outlays on the basis of the projections, using his firm's line of credit—meaning that Udall's campaign went into debt to it, pending the receipt of contributions raised by Thorne. In short order, the Udall campaign owed the firm $115,-000, some ten days before the Wisconsin primary.

At the same time, however, another Peter Hart poll came in, showing a dramatic shift; Udall had narrowed Carter's lead to four points, 34–30. Marttila and Kiley decided that another $35,000 was needed for television in the closing days. But because they were already carrying the campaign to the tune of $115,000, they felt that the campaign, or Mo Udall personally, would have to pick up this added expense. Together, they went to New York to see Kurz and Stewart Udall. They told them: "We've got some good news and some bad news. The good news is the campaign is now thirty-four to thirty; the bad news is that our checking account is down by a hundred and fifteen thousand dollars." Kurz and Stew balked. These high rollers were going to put poor Mo in debt for life, and get fat themselves in the process. They said no.[2]

---

1. Still on the ballot and campaigning in Wisconsin, but now reduced to a pathetic figure, was Wallace. In what surely was the depth of campaign "humor," a group of students at Madison greeted him wearing masks of Arthur Bremer, the Milwaukee man convicted of shooting him in 1972, and chanting: "Free Artie Bremer, give him another chance; he should have shot him in the head, instead he shot him in the pants." Governor Lucey publicly apologized for the incident.

On the same day, in a separate encounter, Senator Jackson was spat upon and heckled, and paper airplanes labeled "Boeing" and "SST" were thrown at him. Earlier, Carter also had been heckled at the University of Wisconsin, and peanuts had been tossed at him, rather playfully, as he spoke. "It's a good thing you didn't raise watermelons," Powell told him.

2. Kurz denied that Martilla ever informed him Udall had a chance to win in Wisconsin. "If he had told me, 'We just took a poll, it's neck-and-neck,' I would have come up with fifty thousand dollars," Kurz said. "In no way was I ever trying to do anything to stifle the campaign." But, he insisted, he never heard anything to make him optimistic. "I said to my wife, 'I hate to go out to Wisconsin, but I might as well be with Mo to wrap it up.'"

Marttila and Kiley thereupon phoned the candidate, who had been spending—until then—a quiet Sunday night at home in Virginia. Mo Udall was caught in the middle again. "What," he asked Kiley after hearing the dispute, "are you asking me to make my brother do?"

Kiley replied: "Mo, I want you to tell him to spend the money." The candidate's wife, Ella, who held much of the staff in minimum regard anyway, took the phone at one point and told the high rollers what she thought of their idea of hocking the family jewels for Wisconsin. What it seemed to get down to was whether Mo Udall was willing to borrow the necessary money, and was willing to so inform the twin guardians of the Mo Udall exchequer, Stew Udall and Kurz. At this point, apparently he was not, although in later primaries he did accept personal debt.

All this went forward, it should be noted, amid an atmosphere within the campaign of considerable mistrust of Marttila. "There was a feeling he had made a ton of money off the campaign," one insider said later, though Marttila argued that his willingness to go into debt himself and jeopardize the solvency of his company should have been evidence enough of good faith.

In any event, the next day, March 29, the candidate flew to New York and spent all afternoon on the phone at his headquarters, trying to raise the $35,000. Meanwhile, Marttila, Kiley, and Thorne continued to go at it with Kurz and Stew Udall. The desperate personal fund-raising was not going well, and somebody suggested that $35,000 be diverted from other efforts to buy media time, which was now rapidly slipping away because of approaching television deadlines.

Marttila met with the candidate again. "Mo," he said, "you're going to win Wisconsin, but we need the thirty-five thousand dollars."

Udall finally agreed to squeeze it out someplace, and although it was now too late to buy television for the final Tuesday, Wednesday, and Thursday, Marttila did manage to get it for Friday, Saturday, and Sunday. (Also lost in the shuffle was about $7000 for mailing 40,000 handwritten letters to western, rural Wisconsin—precisely the area that was to do Udall in late the following Tuesday night.)

The final days were a ratrace for Udall. While he was concentrating on Wisconsin, some of his best people were at work in New York, trying to take advantage of a late endorsement of Udall by the New Democratic Coalition in the New York primary and the active backing of former Bayh supporters and slates in various New York congressional districts. Using an old Convair turbo-prop that lumbered along at 220 miles an hour—a crawl in the jet age—he campaigned in one state during the day and then returned to the other at night, sleeping on a long sofa at the rear of the plane or killing time playing cards with reporters. (A favorite Udall gag was his imitation of Carter playing cards. When it came time for him to make a bid, he would say: "Four." Somebody would ask him: "Four what?" And he would reply, grinning: "Play the cards. I'll tell you later.") The polls from New York also were encouraging, but no money could be spared there; if Udall was to make a breakthrough, it would have to happen in Wisconsin. (The money situation became so tight that on the final Saturday Udall had to fly from Milwaukee to Washington by commercial flight because the campaign couldn't raise the funds to pay the cost of the charter for the trip.)

In the Wisconsin struggle with Carter, so critical to Udall, there was one other notable figure: the barely surviving Fred Harris. Harris, like Udall, had been looking to Wisconsin as the land of political opportunity. Early in the game, he had recruited one of the state's most effective organizers, Michael Bleicher, a political-science professor at the University of Wisconsin. Bleicher had been a charter member of McCarthy's 1968 campaign that carried the Wisconsin primary, and he committed himself enthusiastically to Harris. By the time of the 1976 primary a solid core group continued to work diligently for Harris in the state despite his setbacks in New Hampshire, Massachusetts, and Illinois. This group fully expected it would have the chance to give Harris a second life, and thus Bleicher and the others were dismayed to be told shortly after the Massachusetts debacle that Harris would be bypassing Wisconsin for lack of funds, and in order to give Udall a clear shot at Carter there.

Even before the Massachusetts primary, Harris's national staff had discussed getting out and even endorsing Udall, but the idea had been rejected out of hand. Ken Bode, who had been the Udall scout in Iowa, urged several aides individually to try to talk Harris into dropping out of Wisconsin and concentrating on Illinois, where Udall was not a viable contender and Harris would be the only serious liberal competing against Carter. The overtures, however, only angered the Harris aides, and nothing came of them.

But the realities of campaign financing were forcing Harris's hand. Federal matching funds were being jeopardized by congressional foot-dragging on the revised campaign-finance law, and the campaign had no money to put a field operation into Illinois. Harris was on the ballot there, however, so he campaigned virtually alone in the state, hoping for a respectable showing. He was, of course, drubbed, and rationality cried out for him to quit. Yet there was the matter of a residual and mounting debt, and the need to remain eligible for the federal match. While Harris was occupying himself fruitlessly in Illinois, his staff gathered in Washington to seek some sensible way out.

Going seriously into the New York primary was dismissed because it would have required huge funds, though Harris slates were on the ballot in many congressional districts. It was suggested at one point that Harris go after Udall in Wisconsin, making the case that Udall was an elitist liberal who could talk to the academics but not to the working people the way Harris the Populist could. Harris turned away the idea, saying he liked Udall, who was closer to him on the issues than any of the other candidates. Instead, it was decided, Harris would leave Wisconsin to Udall and leapfrog ahead into the Pennsylvania primary on April 27, which would give him ample time to regroup and make one more effort in a state that already had the earmarks of a showdown among the survivors.

Bleicher, in Wisconsin, was caught utterly by surprise by the decision, and he argued strenuously against it. "We had no idea he was going to do that," he recalled later. "I told him that probably was an error, because we had both the money and the people to make a strong effort. I told him he could win delegates under our proportional representation system, but not if he didn't campaign. But his mind was made up." A few days later Harris's steering committee in Wisconsin met, and because there was considerable opposition to backing Udall "and because we had a lot of politically inexperienced young people," Bleicher said, most decided to persevere for Harris anyway.

In mid-March, a skeleton crew of organizers was sent to Philadelphia to see what could be done for Harris in Pennsylvania. It soon became obvious that the answer was very little, especially with no money. Jim Hightower gave Harris the bad news in a meeting at the Benjamin Franklin Hotel on March 31, six days before the Wisconsin primary—on the very night Harris was opening his Pennsylvania headquarters there. Harris agreed that his presidential campaign was over, but the question was when the obituary should be published; remaining eligible for the federal subsidy was of central tactical importance. Only key members of the staff were told how bad matters were.

Two nights later the principal staff aides met with Fred and LaDonna Harris at their home in McLean, Virginia, to consider how to implement the decision to terminate the campaign. Harris was resigned to it, and in a lighthearted mood, and there was much discussion about how the federal match could be protected, since the campaign was deeply in debt. According to two participants, campaign scheduler Fred Droz and campaign administrator James Rosapepe, at one point one of the national field coordinators, Barbara Shailor, spoke up. She said it was necessary to put the Harris campaign in relationship to everything else going on. With the Wisconsin primary only four days away, it would be a crime to undercut

Udall there, since he was the closest of the candidates to Harris on the issues and needed all the help he could get to beat Carter. Rosapepe reported that Louis Granados, a pollster now working for Marttila who earlier had been with Harris, had told him a poll showed Udall within striking distance of Carter in Wisconsin. Harris should consider dropping out at once, Shailor suggested, or at least should go to Wisconsin and publicly endorse Udall, urging his own supporters to back him. "We could certainly give him a percentage point," she offered.

Others questioned why such a step should be taken. "Most of the Harris activists didn't want us to do it," Rosapepe recalled. "Jim Hightower said we shouldn't screw our own people. Our first commitment was to them." He and others contended it wouldn't make any difference if Harris pulled out, that there would be a percentage of Harris supporters in Wisconsin who would vote for him anyway. "The argument," Rosapepe said, "was, you're not going to accomplish anything except turn your back on the people who supported you for a year and a half." And doing nothing was the path of no action; it's always easier to do nothing than do something.

Also, Harris thought such an action would jeopardize his slates in New York, where his foremost union backer, George Hardy, president of the Service Employees' International Union, had committed his prestige to the campaign. For the next two days some proponents of immediate withdrawal worked to persuade Harris to extend Udall a lifeline in Wisconsin. Bleicher, advised of the idea, phoned Harris. "I told him it was very close between Udall and Carter," Bleicher recalled, "and he ought to make a clean break because it could make the difference and also because many of us would feel better, with many of our friends now with Udall." He too suggested that Harris come to Wisconsin and endorse Udall, but Harris said he could not do that. "George Hardy couldn't stand Udall and was pushing Fred not to do it," Bleicher said Harris told him. "Fred thought he would win some delegates in New York the same day, and he said he didn't want to be part of a stop-anybody movement."

What had happened was that Harris had taken to heart the suggestion that he endorse Udall, and had gone to Hardy, his major labor supporter. According to Richard Murphy, head of COPE for Hardy's union, "Hardy asked him to stay in. He was against Udall on 14-B [the right-to-work law Udall had once voted for in the House]. He asked Fred for one last favor, because our people were out on a limb in New York and we thought we might pick off one delegate." Harris said later that it wasn't just Hardy, but others in both New York and Wisconsin who insisted he stay in the race, telling him—"probably unrealistically"—he would win some delegates in each state.

Harris meanwhile was feeling pressure from other sources. Sam Brown, the state treasurer in Colorado and leader of McCarthy's "children's crusade," also called him, but to no avail. Optimistic plans to fly Harris to Madison Monday for a press conference with Udall never materialized. Harris would quit, but not until after the New York—and Wisconsin—primaries.

All this discussion went forward unbeknownst to Udall and his aides, nor were they ever told later of the efforts to get Harris to endorse Udall. Flying in Wisconsin with Udall on the final Friday, April 2, I asked him whether he had made any move to get Harris out in advance of next Tuesday's vote. He shook his head in resignation and said, "I don't think he'll ever get out."

And so, on primary day in Wisconsin, Bleicher loyally rallied his troops in Harris's behalf (spurred on by an unusually successful fund-raiser the Saturday night before at which $4000 was raised). And while this last-ditch get-out-the-vote effort was going forward, Harris was sitting in his Washington headquarters all day Tuesday, phoning his campaign managers in various states to inform them he was withdrawing from the race—but not until Thursday.

The significance of this little drama in the backwater campaign of one of the losers became all too clear in the early hours of Wednesday, as the final results of the Wisconsin primary dribbled in. It was, for the hapless Udall, agony enough without knowing about this other case of what-might-have-been. Election night had started with nervous optimism among some of his insiders.[3] Udall was routing Carter in the Second Congressional District, which includes Madison and the University of Wisconsin, by a margin of two to one; he was slightly ahead in the industrial cities of Racine and Kenosha; he was holding Carter even in blue-collar Milwaukee, a Wallace stronghold in past years. The optimism mounted, then burst into celebration as first ABC News and then NBC projected Udall as the winner. Here at last was the long-awaited breakthrough. Some aides counseled caution until CBS also called it, but the pressure and the elation mounted, so Udall finally went down among his joyous supporters at the Marc Plaza in Milwaukee and jubilantly talked about the good news. He said, claiming to be quoting Nelson Rockefeller (but it was really Sophie Tucker, the Last of the Red-Hot Mamas): " 'I've been rich and I've been poor, and believe me, rich is better.' It looks like we are winners tonight. How good it is!"

---

3. Not, notably, for his brother Stewart. Despite the late Hart Poll showing Udall closing fast, Stewart told me later, "I went out there to be with Mo to console him when he lost. I really didn't expect him to win."

But lagging behind was the rural vote in western Wisconsin, where paper ballots, more time-consuming to compute, were used. CBS's sample precincts indicated that the race between Udall and Carter could continue down to the last few thousand votes, and Warren Mitofsky, the CBS decision-maker, refused to make the call. Now the pendulum swung the other way. The rural vote started to come in for Carter.

"We hadn't had time to set up our own returns system," Phil Wise recalled, "so as the night went on we didn't know where the results were coming from, from the cities or the towns or the countryside." Carter, in a suite at the Pfister Hotel, was tense at the start, and for a time, as the outcome looked bleak, he, Jordan, Powell, and Wise discussed whether he ought to concede. "The feeling was it was too close, and we weren't sure what was still out," Wise said. "If it was the rural areas that were still out, that gap was going to close some, and we needed to wait and see."

At one point, Carter went to the hotel ballroom to thank his supporters, especially a large group of Georgians who had been campaigning for him in Wisconsin, and say it was too early to call the outcome. It had been a very hectic day and he was tired. While Wisconsin voted, he had used the day to go on to Indiana, site of another approaching primary, and he had gotten into a flap with the traveling press over some language he had used in an earlier newspaper interview. The words seemed innocuous enough to him; he had expressed his support for preserving the "ethnic purity" of urban neighborhoods. It seemed at the time to be no more than one of those reportorial one-day wonders, an issue to write about on a slow day, and he thought little more of it. Now, of course, hc was busy with the Wisconsin returns and with the routine election-night phone calls he always made to key political people around the state and the country.

"We were getting the results from CBS, which hadn't called yet," Wise continued. "Every two minutes their people were calling in with new precincts and new totals. Finally we passed Udall by about three hundred votes, and then it started increasing; it got to about a thousand votes with ninety-nine per cent of the precincts in. So we said, 'That's it,' and Jimmy went on down. Because we were getting the results a little faster than they were being projected on television, Jimmy had a little bit of surprise on his part when he was able to give the news. There was a happy group of Georgians there."

It was a great stroke of luck, because on this same night in New York, Carter was being dealt a sound defeat, running well behind both Jackson and Udall. Now, overshadowing that setback, was the drama of a "comeback" in Wisconsin—perceived as such only because two major television networks had prematurely announced a Udall victory. And, with the extraordinary good fortune that seems to befall winners, the fates again conspired to enable Carter to make the most of the situation. Powell, remembering his political history, picked up a phone and called the Milwaukee *Sentinel.* "It looks like this thing's turning around," he told one of the editors.

"Yeah, it sure does," the editor agreed.

"Did you go pretty hard on it the other way?" Powell asked.

"Yeah, we did."

"You just go on and say Udall won?"

"Yeah, I'm afraid so."

That was all Powell needed to know. He dispatched half a dozen aides to fan out around the paper's building—to the front, the truck loading dock, and other places where one of the first issues might be found. Then he went down into the hotel lobby and waited for an aide to return with the evidence. Not one came back with it. But just as Carter was coming down in the elevator, a stranger walked into the lobby carrying the paper. He recognized Powell, came up to him and said, "Hey! Have you seen this? Isn't it something?" And he held up the *Sentinel,* whose front page shouted: "Carter Upset by Udall." Powell thanked the man, took the newspaper, and hustled it over to Carter, who needed no instruction on what to do next. As television cameras focused on him and flashbulbs popped, he held the newspaper headline aloft, grinning his broadest grin. The next day, thousands of newspapers across the country featured the picture—an updated version of the famous Harry Truman photo displaying the Chicago *Tribune* headline on the night of the 1948 election reading: "Dewey Wins." Not only had Carter avoided defeat in a primary the polls had indicated he would win; he managed through sweet serendipity somehow to seem heroic in eking out the oft-beaten Mo Udall. In hard, cold numbers, that night was not a good one for Carter; a third-place finish in New York and a virtual standoff in Wisconsin. But in the world of public relations and media politics, it had seemed another ten-strike.

The next morning Udall told reporters in that wry humor that never forsook him: "You may amend my statement of last night and insert the word 'losers' where I had 'winners.' " He was, nevertheless, shaken by the turn of events, but by convincing himself that Wisconsin really was a tie, and by realizing he had indeed done surprisingly well in New York, he was able to go on. The final vote in Wisconsin, however, was heartbreaking: Carter 271,220, Udall 263,771, a margin of 7449 votes of 740,528 cast. The rest of the field was far behind, including Harris, who drew 8185 votes— more than enough to make Udall the winner if all those votes had gone to the Arizonan.

Asked much later whether he thought he would have won had Harris pulled out in advance of the Wisconsin vote, Udall said, "Oh, sure. There was an intensely loyal Harris cadre in Wisconsin. All he had to do was go to Madison and make a speech that he was for Udall, help him and vote for him. The number of votes he would have gotten would have been reduced by several thousand and I would have won Wisconsin. But to ask a guy who's built an organization and has tasted defeat to do this, it rarely happens. I don't blame him or have any hostility about it. It just seems to be the way life works. . . . But if I had pulled out Wisconsin, the Carter momentum would have been slowed; I would have been on the seventh of April a major candidate. Support would have flowed to me in Pennsylvania from all sorts of people who were still in doubt. County chairmen, labor leaders would have gone with me instead of Scoop Jackson. Pennsylvania was there; it's a momentum state; it's a state that sits back and waits to see what happens. There wasn't much enthusiasm for Jackson [there]. The labor people, the liberals wanted a winner, and I would have had the aura of a winner and would have either won Pennsylvania or would have beaten Jackson. I just had to come in second in Pennsylvania because the doubts about Carter were building then. I would have been the guy who had momentum; I would have carried Connecticut, would have carried Michigan, and so on. It would have had a steamroller effect."

Mike Bleicher did not share Udall's view that a Harris endorsement could have made the difference. "Udall would have needed ninety per cent of the Harris vote, and I don't think he would have gotten that," he said. "A lot of our people went to Carter as well as to Udall." Whether they would have done so after an explicit endorsement of Udall by Harris was, of course, a matter of conjecture.

There was also much post-morteming on what would have happened to Udall if the money for television in the last week been had made available, and if the postage had been spent for the final mailing to rural, western Wisconsin.

To Kurz and Stew Udall the issue was not just the money but also the arrangement whereby Marttila, Kiley, and Thorne first raised it, then placed the media buys, then reaped a nice profit. These Udall fiscal watchdogs didn't like it, and saw a clear conflict of interest. "We were running short," Stewart explained. "We had an argument, so they pulled the plug on Wisconsin television. They just stopped it for three days, just before the election." He would not go along with spending any more of his brother's money, he said, because "my assumption was we were going to lose. I had to operate on that assumption: that that was the end of the campaign and Mo would run into debt so deeply it would be a big burden on him. And that's this thing he had me charged with watching. That was what caused the controversy. But to say, in an election we lost by seven thousand votes, that had the television been on those extra two or three days, that would have made the difference—this was what Marttila, Quinn and these other people said, this was their simplistic explanation." The failure to send out the forty thousand handwritten letters to people canvassed in a western area was just as important, Stewart insisted. "Marttila and these guys," he said, "they make their fees off television. If you buy television they make a fee, if you buy postage they don't. They have a built-in bias."

But the Udall campaign did neither, he was reminded.

He sighed. "We didn't have the money to do a lot of things."

Well, whose decision was it not to spend the money on the letters?

"When you get down to decisions like this, they're made on whether there's money available or not, and there was no money available. Marttila and those fellows, their whole orientation is media; they want to put it all in; their job is to make you plunge. Even if we won and we were too far in debt, you couldn't have continued anyway."

Politics, however, is not a game of what-might-have-beens. The fact is that Harris did not get out in time, and he did not endorse Udall. The fact is that ABC and NBC declared Carter a loser in Wisconsin and thus magnified the dimensions of his very narrow victory. The fact is that that action reduced the effect of Udall's near-miss and in the process all but obliterated his strong showing in New York. Politics is a game of what actually happens, or, more precisely, what appears to have happened. And the way the night of April 6 looked to the American electorate was not that Carter had a very shaky evening, which by the statistical vote he did, but that he was a winner again; that the untrustworthy mass communicators had goofed but he had triumphed over them; that the gods were on his side. In politics as in poker, sometimes it's better to be lucky than good. April 6 turned out to be a very lucky night for Jimmy Carter, and another very unlucky one for Mo Udall.

20. The Demise of Scoop Jackson

From the very beginning of his candidacy, Henry Jackson had pointed to the New York primary as the place where it would all come together for him.

There had been some concern that Hugh Carey, the ambitious freshman governor, and his state party chairman, Patrick Cunningham, would try to hold New York's huge bloc of 274 electoral votes through a favorite-son candidacy, but political troubles at home eventually diminished that prospect. And so Scoop Jackson's forces moved resolutely to make New York the linchpin of his candidacy, to forge a winning effort out of their candidate's solid appeal among Jewish voters, the building trades and other conservative unions, and alliances with downstate Democratic leaders. The decision to enter and go all-out in Massachusetts had been a big gamble, and it had succeeded (though at great cost); Jackson's strong third-place showing in Florida had nearly upset Carter's central strategy. It might have been expected that Jackson would come into New York riding high.

But Scoop Jackson was the kind of politician who never seemed to ride high on the national scene. For all his dedication, for all his expertise, for all his campaign resources, he always seemed an intruder—a brash, single-minded guy who didn't belong, who didn't fit in, who had to knock doors down because they were so seldom flung open for him. He never seemed to get a break. The calendar of events moved too rapidly for him. The spotlight swung to the Wallace-Carter showdown in Florida before Jackson could enjoy the benefits of his surprise in Massachusetts. The networks gave him short shrift and the news magazines overlooked him for their covers the next weekend, preferring to feature Carter instead. "We came in and creamed the field," Mike Casey, Jackson's chief scheduler, said later. "But it was like shaking a bottle of stale champagne. The pop didn't come out." Then, when he got 24 per cent of the vote in Florida and scared hell out of Carter, the media trampled over him in their stampede to focus on the political tamer of the menace from Alabama. Jackson was on the side lines for two weeks while Carter rubbed it into Wallace in Illinois and North Carolina. And, finally, by blowing his own horn Jackson had succeeded in raising expectations about how he would do in New York, unnecessarily escalating the pressure on him.

In Massachusetts, Jackson's prediction of victory on the final weekend before the March 2 primary had been a calculated move to nudge fence-straddlers who liked him but didn't care to waste their vote on a loser. In the flush of that victory, however, Jackson had gone on to talk about winning a "landslide" in New York, about picking up a majority of the 206 delegates contested in it (the other 68 would be selected by party leaders later, in proportion to the primary vote). In doing so, he set up his performance as a target for the opposition and, more importantly in this case, for the media scorekeepers. Scoop Jackson had to perform to get the Democratic nomination, there could be no doubt about that. Much as with Birch Bayh, Jackson was a vehicle to hitch onto for a ride to power and influence, rather than a hero to his constitutents.

On the surface, it appeared that Jackson could not be hurt much in New York. Bayh was out. Udall had not gotten off the ground and had his hands full in Wisconsin. And Carter, though he was slated in a good number of congressional districts, had made clear he would not force a confrontation with Jackson in New York, preferring instead to snipe at the system of selecting delegates. By characterizing the system, not without some justification, as a tool of the state's Democratic bosses, Carter painted himself once again as the put-upon underdog fighting against almost insurmountable, entrenched forces. He was always at his whining best in that sort of situation, and he started singing his lament on March 9, the night of his Florida victory, looking a couple of moves ahead, like a good chess player. But if Jackson could not be hurt much in New York on April 6, neither could he be helped by anything short of the landslide he was so impolitic to have predicted. And almost from the start, developments conspired against him.

First of all, there was the primary system itself. It was, as Carter charged, a bosses' primary, in which convention-delegate candidates in thirty-nine separate congressional district elections were listed "blind"—that is, with no identification of the presidential candidate they preferred. That provision was considered to be of enormous advantage to entrenched local politicians whose names *were* known to the voters and who had a political apparatus to "educate" them about the presidential preference of their delegate candidates. It was thought to benefit well-heeled candidates, too, those who could afford expensive voter education. On both counts the old system seemed to give an edge to Jackson; he was cozy with many county chairmen and New York City leaders and, going into 1976, except for George Wallace, had the largest campaign treasury of all the candidates.

But events in February and early March had undercut Jackson's advantages. First, his decision to campaign in Massachusetts and Florida with extremely costly television and other media outlays threw his carefully projected budget completely out of whack. "We tried to play the futures market," one Jackson insider said. "We played to the limit on a roll of the bones that we'd win and it would be a catalyst for future fund-raising. But Florida got in the way. In Massachusetts, the polls were strong and we were like a dog in heat; good judgment gave way to emotion. The rhetoric all through 1974 and 1975 in our big fund-raising phase was, 'We're going to run a cost-effective campaign, we're going to budget back, starting with the convention and working back through the primaries; we're going to have a sophisticated cash flow.' Then we had that spending orgasm in Massachusetts and Florida, with malice aforethought." Second, the New York state legislature passed, and on March 11 Governor Carey signed, a law revising the primary to permit identification of convention-delegate candidates according to presidential preference—for 1976 only. The legislation was a result of considerable wheeling and dealing between Republican legislators who didn't want the switch, and liberal Democrats who did. Udall, now picking up most of Bayh's well-organized slates, suddenly found himself in the ball game, though still without resources and with heavy financial demands from Wisconsin.

A series of court challenges ensued whose objective was to reduce the number of slates eligible in each congressional district. Even before the law had been revised, in fact, Jackson's forces had started the maneuvering by making successful challenges that reduced the number of competing Wallace delegates to only 16 in three congressional districts, on grounds of flawed petitions required for ballot position. In the end Carter was knocked off the ballot in ten districts, leaving him with 141 delegate candidates; Jackson wound up with 184 on thirty-five district slates; Harris with 101 on twenty-one slates; and Udall with the largest number, 192, as a result of mergers with Bayh supporters, on thirty-seven slates. In addition, 218 individuals were running uncommitted, some of them considered good bets because they were or had the endorsement of local party barons. And, finally, in the Buffalo area, under the direction of Erie County party boss Joe Crangle, there were three uncommitted but undisguised slates loyal to Hubert Humphrey, and there were other unofficial Humphrey delegates scattered throughout the state—for a total of 47. All this confusion complicated Jackson's self-proclaimed task of winning a majority of the delegates at stake on primary day.

To achieve that goal, Jackson poured nearly $900,000 into New York —a moderate budget compared to past New York campaigns that had been unfettered by federal spending limits, but a fortune by 1976 standards.[1] New York, the television center of the nation, had always gobbled up huge sums of campaign money, but this time the restrictions virtually ruled out use of television in this costliest of markets. Jackson in the end spent only $50,000 on television, mostly upstate to counter heavy outlays there by Carter.

While Jackson was still striving for a psychological breakthrough that would oblige the media to take him seriously, and while Udall was looking for a primary victory *anywhere,* Carter was heavily into the business of delegate-collecting. Earlier in the campaign, when psychological triumphs were all-important, generating as they did free network and other coverage, he had excelled. By now, though, he had milked all the benefit he could expect from winning in smaller states with few delegates. He alone was moving on now to the straightforward matter of accumulating delegates, and it was beginning to dawn on the competition and the press that he alone had a strategy that could bring him a first-ballot nomination without horse-trading. He was in New York, for instance, not to beat Jackson but to take his share of delegates toward the majority of 1505 needed for nomination. Those who had dismissed Carter's run-in-every-primary strategy, or had even ridiculed it as a foolhardy rerun of Muskie's 1972 disaster, were beginning to appreciate its potential.

Carter's ability to move into selected areas of New York without having to worry unduly about being labeled a loser, and Udall's success in bringing Bayh's slates on board, combined to make Jackson's optimistic prediction extremely difficult to deliver on. Udall also picked up a belated endorsement from Americans for Democratic Action, and his own polls showed him gaining fast in New York as well as in Wisconsin. But it was a particularly vexing time for John Marttila, handling the New York end, hassling with Kurz and Stewart Udall over more money for television in Wisconsin, and feeling at the same time that a golden opportunity for a genuine upset over Jackson was being passed by in New York. In a liquid interview at an East Side Manhattan watering spot a week before the New York and Wisconsin primaries, Marttila took my notepad and scribbled the following in it: "On March 29, the Udall campaign closed the door on the nomination." Then he muttered, "A hundred thousand dollars. We're a hundred thousand away. April sixth could have been a dynamite day for us. The jig is up. We just couldn't pull it together enough to spend what we have to in New York. With a hundred thousand, we would have made a genuine impression in this state. We have great television of Mo for the

---

1. An example of how the Jackson campaign spent money: it employed professional phone banks at which "volunteers" were paid $2.30 an hour.

closing in Wisconsin, and it would have been great here, too." Without the final expenditure, Marttila warned of Jackson's potential: "A very fragile landslide may be allowed to happen." (Much later, Martilla confessed that his lament about a missed opportunity in New York, though true, was to a large degree a cover for his even deeper chagrin over the loss of critical television buys in Wisconsin, for lack of money.)

Jackson meanwhile campaigned tirelessly across the state, especially in New York City and its suburbs. This was a typical day: a speech at a conference on Soviet Jews in a Manhattan hotel; a meeting with the New York State United Teachers in Ossining, just up the Hudson; a fund-raising brunch in White Plains; a lunch with the Jewish Teachers Association in another Manhattan hotel; a reception in Flushing Meadows on Long Island; another one at Lido Beach; a return to the midtown Manhattan hotel for a Yeshiva of Flatbush reception; finally, an appearance at the state Democratic Legislative Campaign Committee's mock convention at Madison Square Garden. Through all this Jackson peddled himself without apology as the Jewish voter's best and most steadfast friend, taking pokes at Carter and Udall in the process. "It is the New Politics liberals who change, they who tarnish the liberal label and they who seek political refuge these days by deleting certain words from their political vocabularies [presumably a reference to Udall's declaration that henceforth he would call himself a "progressive," not a liberal]." Commenting on a magazine article that had suggested he was edging to the left for the benefit of New York's liberal constituency, Jackson said: "I never thought that I had edged to the right. It is not conservative to stand for freedom, as in the Jackson amendment [requiring freer emigration of Soviet Jewry as a condition of American trade]. It is not conservative to stand for freedom and morality in the Middle East and [to say] that Israel must survive. It is not conservative to think that freedom is so important that it's worth defending."

Jackson campaigned as doggedly as he campaigned humorlessly, but one other cloud still darkened his candidacy: the continuing availability of Hubert Humphrey. As Carter appeared to be breaking from the pack, Humphrey could not restrain himself from making pointed observations that sounded for all the world like stop-Carter rhetoric. Though such remarks brought Humphrey into immediate conflict with Carter, the greater political significance was that they kept him in the spotlight as an alternative to Jackson as the candidate of party regulars.

At a breakfast meeting with reporters in Washington two weeks before the New York and Wisconsin primaries, Humphrey unburdened himself. "Candidates who make an attack on Washington," he said, "are making an attack on government programs, on the poor, on blacks, on minorities, on the cities. It's a disguised new form of racism, a disguised new form of conservatism." And inasmuch as Hubert Humphrey was the personification of "Washington," the chief defender of programs for the poor, for blacks, for minorities, for the cities, it was clear that he was saying those attacks were directed at everything he stood for in public life. Humphrey denied he was referring to Carter, his party's conspicuously anti-Washington candidate. "I was primarily talking about Reagan and Ford," he said lamely, "I was not charging anybody with being a racist. . . . Jimmy Carter is no racist, there is nothing in his record to support that." But in the language of political in-fighting, Humphrey's message needed no translation; it was a reminder that anybody who talked against Washington could not be much of a Democrat. "You don't win many elections by going around repudiating your inheritance," he remarked on another occasion, as if to say: "Are you listening, Jimmy?"

Jimmy indeed was listening. From Madison, he replied that it was "a departure from rationality or from the truth" for Humphrey to see racism in his criticism of Washington. Maybe Humphrey was concerned, Carter said, "because some of the things that he was influential in passing fifteen or twenty or twenty-five years ago are challenged as being perhaps not perfect." These alibis didn't stop him from observing once again here in Wisconsin that Humphrey had the image of a loser and would be a weak candidate unless he entered the primaries.

A few days later Carter got in another shot at Humphrey. To reports (denied by Humphrey) that the Minnesotan was encouraging support for Udall in the Wisconsin primary as a means of keeping the door open for himself, Carter warned that "machinations" to stop his own nomination could produce a brokered convention of the kind that nominated Humphrey in 1968—and produced defeat and division from which "our party still hasn't entirely recovered." The remark was reminiscent of the one Carter had made in New Hampshire about Humphrey being a loser, about which he later said he had been misquoted, or misinterpreted, or misunderstood, or one of the other alibis he used to fall back on after sticking his love-coated needle into a foe. And although Jackson stood aside through these Carter-Humphrey exchanges, anything that reminded Democrats that old Hubert was still around and available was bad news for him. The availability of Humphrey worked only modestly against Jackson in New York, but a few weeks hence in Pennsylvania, it would be another story.

In New York, on primary night, once again the fates conspired to deny Jackson the national spotlight. When the results were in, it was clear that he had fallen short of his goal of getting a majority. Udall was running surprisingly strong, Carter nibbled away in selected districts (though not impressively), and Humphrey carried the uncommitted Buffalo delegates. The final votes and delegate apportionment were: Jackson, 38 per cent and 104 delegates; Udall 25.5 per cent and 70 delegates; Carter, 12.8 per cent and 35 delegates; uncommitted, 23.7 per cent and 65 delegates, of which about 10 were considered favorable to Jackson and 16 to noncandidate Humphrey.

The results were a jolt to morale in the Jackson campaign. "The 'victory' simply reinforced Jackson's weakness," Mike Casey said later. "It showed that all he had was the Jewish base, plus Donald Manes [the Queens borough president and Jackson's state chairman] delivering the Catholics in Queens. Anybody who looked and saw Jackson Country end at the Westchester border had to be disappointed. We got killed upstate. Jackson's victory in New York was akin to Muskie's victory in New Hampshire in 1972. If you just looked at the numbers, you'd say, 'Not bad,' but the same negative psychology was working: big expectations, publicly enunciated, then not realized."

At the same time, Jackson sustained another disappointment: his second victory in a major state was all but lost in the public excitement over Carter's "comeback" over Udall—heightened by the erroneous premature predictions on the ABC and NBC networks—in Wisconsin that same night. "We got hit by a freak twice," Bob Keefe complained later (the first was Carter's victory in Florida eclipsing Jackson's in Massachusetts).[2] Thus, though Carter ran an unimpressive third in New York and barely pulled out a victory over Udall in Wisconsin, where not long before he had held a 2–1 lead in the polls, he was still perceived as the candidate on the move. Jackson was given hardly any boost at all, and Udall survived for a least another round.

That test round was in Pennsylvania on April 27, three weeks later— quickly recognized as a showdown primary, where Jackson could be expected to make his optimum effort. Governor Milton Shapp had hoped to have most of the state's 171 delegates behind him going into the national convention, but when he dropped out of the race he released his delegate candidates. Some ran as favorable to Jackson and some ran uncommitted, but Shapp himself took a walk. Though he more or less directed his state organization to support Jackson, his heart wasn't in it: just before the primary he left for Germany to try to recruit industry for Pennsylvania.

In this organization-minded Democratic state and orthodox labor

---

2. Jackson himself later blamed all his troubles on the networks' conscious decision to downplay the New York primary. He cited as evidence the fact two of them did their election-night broadcasts on April 6 from Milwaukee, rather than New York.

stronghold, however, the AFL-CIO's COPE was one of the most potent forces in Democratic politics, and it was outspokenly friendly to Jackson. And by now, he desperately needed all-out labor support. The one great advantage he was supposed to have in 1976 was money, but the spending sprees in Massachusetts and Florida, followed by New York, had all but wiped out that advantage. Of a $6-million campaign chest—$4.5 million raised by his organization and $1.5 million in matching funds from the feds —only $100,000 remained for Pennsylvania. Emergency measures were necessary.

Central to Jackson's fund-raising program had been the idea of keeping the candidate free of any obligations to raise money himself after 1975. One of the reasons Richard Nixon had been so effective in 1968 was that Maurice Stans had assumed the full burden of fund-raising. But now, in Pennsylvania, with federal matching funds still being held up while Congress and President Ford fenced, Jackson found himself scrounging along with the other candidates. Twice in the days following the New York primary, he was obliged to phone potential givers.

At the same time, Jackson's industrious chief fund-raiser, Dick Kline, who had constructed the financial cushion that had enabled the campaign to throw money at the Massachusetts and Florida primaries, was shunted aside. Kline was a deliberate money-raiser, a planner of fund-raising dinners and receptions that took time. He himself had no money; he was a technician, with yearnings, some in Jackson's campaign said, to get more involved in political decision-making. And so he was replaced by an expert fund-raising "hit man"—a personal solicitor of large contributions named Hershey Gold, from Los Angeles. Gold, himself a member in good standing of the nation's community of political fat cats, was an arm-twister with intimate connections among those with the most twistable arms in politics. Kline, putting it in a genteel way, said, "We have to go after more of the peer group people." S. Harrison (Sonny) Dogole, a Philadelphia security-systems executive who headed Jackson's fund-raising in Pennsylvania, was more direct: "Dick's forte was in getting fund-raising events. Hershey is more of a dynamo who does fund-raising himself. He creates a ripple effect. People give to people, not necessarily to causes."

Meanwhile Jackson's Pennsylvania campaign hung by its thumbs. One day I was interviewing Al Allen, Jackson's northeastern Pennsylvania coordinator. "We have no budget," he was telling me. "We spend as we get it." Just then Allen's phone rang. It was an offer of volunteer help from a group of young people from out of state, but it only distressed him. "Please tell these people we cannot put them up," Allen told his caller, plaintively. "We cannot feed them. It just ain't there. . . . I don't want them misled. That's worse than not having them here at all."

Such incidents underscored Jackson's dependence on labor in Pennsylvania. But labor seemed the strongest possible reed for him to grasp there. A state with a heavily ethnic, blue-collar population of traditional, orthodox Democratic voters, Pennsylvania had gone for Kennedy in 1960, for Johnson in 1964, and for Humphrey in 1968 and in the 1972 Democratic primary. It was widely known as "a Humphrey state"; nobody would have been much surprised if powerful labor leaders like Mike Johnson, until recently boss of the state AFL-CIO's COPE operation, and Ed Toohey, head of Philadelphia's AFL-CIO Council, had had the initials "HHH" tatooed on their chests. But Humphrey was not a candidate in Pennsylvania, so Jackson, with his solid labor record, had every right to expect he would be the inheritor of all this support, especially against Carter and Udall.

Or did he? Humphrey, it was true, had remained on the side lines so far. During the New York primary, he had canceled a visit to the Buffalo area at Jackson's rather frantic request lest he overtly spur Joe Crangle's effort to elect "uncommitted" delegates in his behalf. But he was never far from sight, and he could read the political tea leaves. Two days after the New York and Wisconsin primaries Humphrey breezed into Pittsburgh to address the state AFL-CIO, and their reception left no doubt where their hearts lay. In an early-morning appearance he stirred two thousand sleepy delegates with one of his patented, open-ended incantations to all the touchstone liberal issues. "We want Hubert! We want Hubert!" the awakened labor delegates chanted over and over again, desisting only when he shouted back: "You've always had me. You've been my strength, my inspiration." When the chant erupted again later, he cut it off with a pregnant admonition: "Never mind that now. We'll get around to that later."

Jackson clung to the hope that Pennsylvania labor, while loving Hubert, would climb in bed with him. But the signals of a Humphrey renascence were everywhere. The Gallup Poll in mid-April showed the actively campaigning Carter barely edging the inactive Humphrey among Democrats, 32 per cent to 31, with Jackson slipping to 6 per cent from 15 in early March. Also, two Midwestern Democratic congressmen, Paul Simon of Illinois and Bob Bergland of Minnesota, disclosed that with or without Humphrey's permission they were opening a draft-Humphrey headquarters. The effort was temporarily short-circuited by Federal Election Commission requirements of candidate approval, but it nevertheless underscored the existing sentiment for Humphrey to jump in. A story in *The*

Washington Post by Victor Cohn, a medical writer, reported that Humphrey had been treated with "a widely used anti-cancer drug to prevent spread of a chronic bladder condition his doctors say could be pre-cancerous." But even that story did not stem the talk of his presidential candidacy. In a panel discussion before a national group of editors in Washington, Humphrey simply shunted the report aside.

On April 11, the first Sunday after the New York and Wisconsin primaries, a group of major Pennsylvania labor leaders led by Jim Mahoney, Mike Johnson's newly installed successor as head of the state COPE, met with key Jackson campaign operatives, including Bob Keefe, in the Harrisburg office of State Democratic Chairman Harvey Thiemann. Advance word was leaked to Joseph Daughen, the knowledgeable political reporter of the Philadelphia *Bulletin,* that the meeting was being called to organize a stop-Carter effort with labor as the core force, ostensibly for Jackson's benefit, but at the same time looking past Jackson to Humphrey. "The labor movement won the state for Humphrey in 1968 and we won the primary for him in 1972," one of the participants told Daughen, "and now we've got to beat Carter. There is an alliance, it does exist, and the fact that we're going to help Jackson gives him a chance to win here." But at the same time, this labor insider said, as far as Pennsylvania labor was concerned, they were working toward the possibility that the nominee would eventually be Humphrey, their first choice. "They're all Humphrey people," he said. "They may be on the Shapp slate or the Jackson slate, but if they had their druthers, they'd all be for Hubert." Whether Jackson liked it or not, labor looked upon him as a stalking horse for Humphrey. After all, his state co-chairmen, Philadelphia City Councilman Lou Johanson and Fayette County Democratic Chairman Fred Lebder, had both been key Humphrey people in 1972; Dogole was Humphrey's 1972 national finance chairman and one of his closest friends; former Governor George Leader, honorary state chairman for Jackson, had held the same post for Humphrey in 1972.

The stalking-horse tag, used frequently by Carter now to describe Jackson, irritated Jackson no end. But Dogole saw nothing wrong with it. "It may be a plus for Scoop," he told me. "If Jackson's a stalking horse, voting for Jackson may be the best way to get Humphrey." Dogole himself was committed to stick out the campaign with Jackson, but he remained a Humphrey man through and through. He acknowledged he had cleared his support for Jackson with Humphrey, and his office was a testimonial to his fealty to the Minnesotan; the walls were covered with pictures of Sonny and Hubert at Pennsylvania Democratic bashes over the years.

So the stalking-horse image remained and grew. The day before he was to appear at a statewide Labor for Jackson press conference with the candidate, Ed Toohey told Daughen: "In my personal judgment, and the judgment of most of the people I know in the labor movement, Hubert Humphrey is the overwhelming favorite and is so because we believe he's the most electable person in the Democratic Party." Jackson was "the best announced candidate," but Humphrey had "cultivated the labor movement for twenty years. He calls when he comes to town. Even if he's only on the line a minute, he'll call and say, 'How are you?' I couldn't remember the number of times he's come here for us." Such praise, Toohey offered lamely, "does not mean to detract from Senator Jackson. You can't find a nicer guy than Jackson." As ringing endorsements go, that one certainly was not memorable.

Toohey's observations understandably threw Jackson on the defensive. One of the first questions to him at the next day's press conference was what he thought of Toohey's remarks. He replied by blaming all the stalking-horse talk on Carter as a diversionary tactic in anticipation of defeat. "He's built up a straw man," Jackson said. "There's never been a meeting, speaking only for myself, to stop Carter. I've never gotten together with anyone, directly or indirectly, to stop Carter." Well, what about his agents? "I don't know what my agents said," he stammered. "Oh, they had a meeting in Harrisburg to support Jackson. That was very open."

Several state labor leaders broke in to say they were 100 per cent for Scoop Jackson, and Mahoney capped the endorsements by assuring Jackson that "the state of Pennsylvania has a very sophisticated labor movement. It's one that has commitment and one that has organization. I think when you see what happens next Tuesday, you'll know that we've been out there. Historically, the labor movement has always gotten started in the last week. We find that if we start too early, things dissipate themselves. We're organized, we know how to put a drive on. We're stretch runners." As for all the talk about labor leadership being unable to deliver the rank-and-file, Mahoney said, "In at least seven out of ten times, our people vote *according to what we tell them the facts are.*" The room erupted in laughter, to Mahoney's exasperation. "What's wrong with the facts?" he wanted to know.

But one irrefutable fact was that labor had gotten a very late start in Pennsylvania, and the enthusiasm for Jackson simply was not there. Toohey, on the weekend before the primary, told Bob Kaiser of *The Washington Post* that it was "going to be very difficult" to get the labor vote out for Jackson because of the late start, and because of labor apathy. In 1972, he recalled, "we had four months' lead time [for Humphrey] so we had everything running with high efficiency." But this year, the membership was "so cynical and so fed up, it will be a test of whether or not we can get them out to vote." Another labor official confessed: "I wish we had two more weeks to go. It's going to be tough." Jackson himself began to hedge on an earlier claim to victory in both the delegate race and the "beauty contest," conceding Carter might beat him in the latter. "But," he insisted, "the name of the game is delegates."[3] That fact, of course, Carter well knew, and he was playing the game diligently.

Carter, sensing a political kill in Pennsylvania, had sent Tim Kraft to Philadelphia in mid-March, well before the New York and Wisconsin primaries. Together with a political novice, Jack Sullivan, a Philadelphia-area manufacturer's representative and one-time Annapolis classmate of Carter's, he quickly fielded an organization with twenty-two offices around the state. (Sullivan and another novice, Howard Lupovitz, had started a skeletal effort in late 1975.) More than a hundred Georgians and Floridians were brought in for neighborhood canvassing, and were housed by Carter delegate-candidates. It was the Iowa and Florida experiences all over again, but accelerated by necessity and bolstered by a hard-campaigning Carter. Deftly casting himself once again as the victim of plots and superior forces, Carter talked darkly of a "tight-knit effort" by the opposing candidates to stop him—as usual without specifying the conspirators. Mayor Frank Rizzo of Philadelphia, Carter observed in his benign way, had supported President Nixon and now was a Jackson backer. He labeled Rizzo a "machine politician" and "boss" (compared to Pittsburgh Mayor Peter Flaherty, a Carter supporter, who was a "leader") and said at one point, "I can't imagine Rizzo endorsing anyone without some sort of trade or arrangement." (Carter's lack of enthusiasm was encouraged, it turned out, by one of his campaign polls showing that three out of four Pennsylvanians had a low opinion of the mayor. If Carter was going to suffer at Rizzo's hands in Philadelphia, he wanted to make sure there would be some positive trade-off elsewhere.)

Meanwhile Carter took steps to assure that he had adequate funds for a strong media effort in Pennsylvania. He arranged to borrow heavily, including $100,000 against his personal assets—a tactic now permitted by the Supreme Court's ruling, which lifted restrictions on how much of a candidate's financial resources he could put into his own campaign. Neither Jackson nor Udall had similar personal wealth, so they were stymied on this front, although Udall borrowed what he could.

---

3. If Jackson knew the name of the game, he had some horrible problems with identifying the players. In Pittsburgh, touring an Italian-American neighborhood with Governor Ella Grassso of Connecticut, he walked out of a small grocery, turned, and said: *"Muchas gracias!"*

For Udall, lack of money was only one of many problems. Two days before the New York and Wisconsin primaries, Marttila informed him that he and Kiley were bowing out of the campaign. The decision came as a terrible shock to Udall. "The one time the campaign really hummed," he said later, "was through that Massachusetts primary. Young Kiley was in charge. For the first time here was a guy who had all the strings in his hands and was playing them right, had the confidence of people and was really moving. I was just stunned when Marttila came to me and said they were so deeply involved in other campaigns that he could no longer continue. I don't think they really wanted to pull out. I think they wanted to be begged, and that I should have begged them, because Kiley really had it under control. It hurt; I don't know whether it was the difference between victory and defeat. Marttila was a red flag to a lot of my people. A lot of them regretted him coming in and taking over, yet he and his organization were strong and they knew where they were going. When Kiley left us at a critical point, it was tough to replace him." (Another Udall aide suggested that the campaign's debt to the Marttila firm precipitated the split. Some were unhappy, he said, about Marttila buying media time and drawing commissions on the purchases, and because after Wisconsin and New York "we couldn't afford Marttila.")

Udall did have one thing going for him in Pennsylvania, but it did not amount to much any longer: he was finally the only liberal in the Democratic field. On April 8, two days after Udall's narrow loss in Wisconsin, Fred Harris bowed out. As all the preceding casualties had done, he blamed his demise on lack of money and television exposure. He did well enough in early caucuses, he said, but not well enough to claim victory, yet not poorly enough to admit defeat. "We didn't know what to call it," he concluded, "so we just decided to call it quits."

Udall, on hearing this news, asked only that Harris's supporters "take a close, a searching look at my positions on the issues he has championed." That restrained pitch summed up one of Udall's major problems. Tom Kiley talked about it with obvious affection much later. "As is inevitably the case in discussing the Udall campaign, you come back to Mo," he said. "The nature of Mo Udall is he does not have a sense for the jugular. His immediate instinct following New Hampshire was not, 'Let's squeeze Sargent Shriver out of the race for Massachusetts.' It was to call up Sarge and commiserate with him. Those qualities that make me such a fond admirer of Mo Udall also limited his effectiveness. I was there when he called Shriver after Illinois with the ostensible purpose of getting Shriver's immediate support. He said, 'Gee, Sarge, how you doing? I guess you need a vacation, huh? I sure feel bad. You think you might see your way clear, kinda, to maybe, supporting me, somewhere down the line?' He's just too polite a guy." Kiley thought for a moment, then added: "Carter would have gotten those guys out, fast."

Though Udall and Jackson faced the most obvious difficulties in Pennsylvania, Carter was not without his troubles. And it was in Pennsylvania that he had to face the repercussions of a flap that he had hoped would be no more than a one-day wonder, but that almost overnight burgeoned into the first major *gaffe* of the 1976 campaign.

The whole business started obscurely enough in an airplane interview on April 2, the Friday before the New York and Wisconsin primaries. As Carter's entourage flew across upstate New York, Carter sat in the forward compartment of his chartered jet and answered questions posed by Sam Roberts, chief political writer of the New York *Daily News.* As the plane approached Schenectady, Roberts asked Carter how he felt about construction of low-income, scatter-site housing in the suburbs. His own inclination, Carter said, was for a program "oriented primarily where the housing is needed most—downtown areas of deteriorating cities. There's a need to protect the family entity, the neighborhood," he said. "I don't think I would do anything to cause deterioration of neighborhoods. . . ."

Roberts then asked him: "Well, can a black central city survive surrounded by all-white neighborhoods?"

Carter said: "Yes. My next-door neighbor is black. It hasn't hurt us —provided you give people the freedom to decide for themselves where to live. But to artificially inject another racial group in a community? I see nothing wrong with ethnic purity being maintained. I would not force a racial integration of a neighborhood by government action. But I would not permit discrimination against a family moving into the neighborhood."

That was it. Roberts thought so little of Carter's reply that he did not use it until the sixteenth paragraph of his nineteen-paragraph story, and then without elaboration or comment. The quote ran on page 134 of the Sunday edition, and might have remained buried there for all time had it not been for Marty Plissner, the political editor of CBS News, who spied it and suggested to Ed Rabel, CBS's correspondent traveling with Carter, that he ask the candidate what he meant by the phrase. Rabel did so at his first opportunity, a press conference in Indianapolis on Tuesday, April 6, primary day in Wisconsin and New York. Carter, somewhat to Rabel's surprise, replied by using the phrase again: "I have nothing against a community that's made up of people who are Polish, Czechoslovakians, French Canadians, or blacks who are trying to maintain the ethnic purity of their neighborhood," he said. "This is a natural inclination on the part of people."[4]

Carter went on to say: "I would never, though, condone any sort of discrimination against, say, a black family or another family from moving into that neighborhood. But I don't think the government ought to . . . try to break down deliberately an ethnically oriented neighborhood by artificially injecting into it someone from another ethnic group just to create some sort of integration. I was the sponsor and passed, as Governor of Georgia," he continued, "an open-housing bill, which was unheard of in the South. . . . The Georgia legislature supported it, and I made sure we had no carry-over remnants of discrimination against blacks who wanted to move into white neighborhoods on their own volition. But I would not have supported a state program to inject black families into a white neighborhood just to create some sort of integration. So, the freedom of movement of families into and out of a neighborhood, I would maintain that, with my own influence as President, and with law. But to inject artificially another ethnic group into a community that was made up primarily of an ethnic group, I would not favor that."[5]

In all this, Carter had not yet said what he meant by "ethnic purity." En route to the next stop, South Bend, Indiana, reporters in the traveling party who had not read or heard of the *Daily News* interview began to play back their tapes of the Indianapolis press conference and to ask Rabel about the matter. Up front, in Carter's compartment, Greg Schneiders told Powell, "Jody, wee Jimmy stuck his foot in his mouth." But apparently they thought Carter could weather the squall.

When Carter made himself available to the press again at the airport terminal, the questioning continued—more intensely—to the candidate's obvious annoyance. Tired, agitated, perspiring, he offered a rare contrast to the alert, cool, at times almost icy demeanor he customarily displayed. Pressed on how he felt about federal or state low-income housing in subur-

4. Later Carter erroneously said he had made this statement in Milwaukee, "where there has been over a period of one hundred to one hundred and fifty years a compatibility among neighborhoods, where the churches, the private clubs, the newspapers, the restaurants are designed to accommodate the members of a particular ethnic group. I see nothing wrong with that as long as it is done freely." No one could remember Carter talking about ethnic purity in Milwaukee. The lapse was understandable, however, when one considered that after a down-to-the-wire campaign in Wisconsin, he had been up at 4:45 that morning to catch a shift change at an auto-body plant before flying on to Indianapolis.
5. Shortly after Carter made this statement, I received a phone call from Julian Bond, the Georgia state senator who was one of the few blacks in Georgia declining to support Carter. Bond insisted that no open-housing law had ever passed the Georgia legislature; all Carter could have been referring to, he said, was the establishment of a real-estate commission operating under an antidiscrimination regulation.

ban or middle-income urban neighborhoods, he again said he would defend the right of any family to live anywhere. But he also repeated his opposition to intentional disturbance of "the homogeneity" of established neighborhoods. "To create artificially within a community that is homogeneous in racial or economic status *a diametrically opposite kind of family,* I think is bad for both sides." Again, the choice of words was jarring. The questions continued, and Carter's pique intensified: "I did say I would not favor any resistance to integration of a neighborhood if it was voluntary on the part of the people who want to live there. That's the purpose of open-housing legislation, whether it applies to the South or the North. If you are trying to make something out of nothing, then I resent that effort. I'm not trying to say that I want to maintain with any sort of government interference the *ethnic purity* of neighborhoods. I do not say that at all. What I say is that the government ought not to take as a major purpose *the intrusion of alien groups* into a neighborhood simply to establish their *intrusion.*"

Carter became increasingly testy. "I think all of you were at the meeting when I was asked the question," he said, still laboring under the misconception that he had first used the phrase in Milwaukee. "At [that] time . . . none of you noticed it. There was nothing notable about it. Now, in retrospect, you are trying to make something out of it and there's nothing to be made out of it." Here was Jimmy Carter, suddenly cornered, seizing a lifeline he favored in those rare circumstances when he sensed political trouble but could not quite comprehend its dimensions: he blamed it on the press.

Still, the reporters persisted. "I'm a little confused," one of them said. "You say that ethnically pure neighborhoods are fine and it's fine for blacks to live where they want to live. If a black wants to move into another ethnic neighborhood, how do you protect the whites and all those people?"

Carter tried once more: "I'm not insisting on the phrase 'pure ethnic community.' That's not my phrase, that was a question asked of me, and *I'm not trying to keep any neighborhood pure.* . . . To try deliberately to tear down the *integrity* of those neighborhoods is not something that I am for."

Now the press corps had really caught the scent. Betty Rainwater, Carter's exasperatingly languid assistant press secretary, tried to stonewall the avalanche of reporters' inquiries and requests for clarification. Meanwhile, Carter went through the day—a visit to a Notre Dame football practice and another rally before returning to Milwaukee to await the returns.

The closeness of the Wisconsin primary and Carter's dramatic victory overshadowed the "ethnic purity" flap for a day (although *The New York Times* ran a page-one story on it, noting that while Carter defended the right of individuals to move into any neighborhood, "the emphasis of his remarks . . . was on the value of sameness in communities and on the costs of change and integration"). But when Carter moved into Pittsburgh to start campaigning for the Pennsylvania showdown, the matter inevitably came to the fore again. In another press conference in the office of Mayor Flaherty, Sam Donaldson, the brassy ABC correspondent who has never needed a road map to the jugular, minced no words: "Are such terms as 'ethnic purity' and 'alien group,' " he asked, "almost Hitlerian?" Carter's eyes blinked and his facial muscles tensed a bit. He ignored the thrust of this question at first, repeating his previous answers but avoiding any inflammatory phrases. Then he concluded: "If anyone derived from my statement the connotation that I have an inclination toward racism, then I would resent that because it's certainly not true."

Not only the pesky press was making an issue of Carter's language. Jackson and Udall predictably both jumped on him—though examination disclosed that their own positions, if not words, were not much different from Carter's. More seriously, Congressman Andrew Young of Atlanta, the former Martin Luther King, Jr., civil-rights lieutenant who had become Carter's stanchest black supporter, called the remarks "a disaster" and warned: "Either he'll be repentant of it or it will cost him the nomination." And to Carter's alibi that he had simply been answering questions, Young said: "He shouldn't have answered in those terms. I don't think he understood the loaded connotations of the words. They summoned up memories of Hitler and Nazi Germany. I can't defend him on this. It will be an issue in Pennsylvania." Young saw all of his missionary work for Carter going down the drain. "A lot of people who said 'You can't trust a Southerner' are going to say, 'See, I told you so,' " he complained. He joined sixteen other members of the Congressional Black Caucus in a telegram denouncing Carter's words.

Carter and his staff took an interminably long time to grasp the political import. "I never did feel badly about the statement," he told me a month later, "until I realized it hurt people's feelings." When Betty Rainwater, who was in South Bend, first phoned Hamilton Jordan in Atlanta about the statement, Jordan said to her: "So what?" Reflecting later, he said, "I suppose it showed maybe we were provincial or that we had a little bit of a cultural problem in not understanding the politics of big cities. It was just an unfortunate remark, but it took me several days to realize how serious a problem it was. There was no way to get around it; we just tried to plow through. We figured the best way to show it didn't hurt us was to put Jimmy in situations with black groups where he could explain his own feelings, and hopefully they would all come out and tell you guys [the press] that Governor Carter was still their man." Additional meetings with black groups were scheduled, and meanwhile Carter began to confer by phone with Andy Young and others.

But, as David Broder pointed out in an incisive analysis in *The Washington Post,* the problem was not simply with blacks for their own sake; black support had become a kind of badge of Carter's acceptability among white liberal activists. At just the time in the campaign Carter was beginning to make some converts among this hitherto wary constituency, his "ethnic purity" remarks fanned new suspicions. "I don't know who he is," a major union leader told Broder, "where he's going, or where he's been." And Young told him: "Blacks are much less disturbed than the white liberals. Blacks have a kind of radar about white folks and, somewhere along the line, Jimmy passed the test. But the Northern liberal who struggled through the holocaust period, and sees in the United States a potential for the same kind of demagoguery, found the words Jimmy used really frightening."

Still, Carter had important resources to tap in this sort of adversity. Leonard Woodcock, the president of the UAW who had signed on with him for Florida only but stayed aboard after he beat Wallace, phoned Jordan and offered to call Mayor Coleman Young of Detroit, a black. As a result, when Carter next visited Detroit, Woodcock and Young were both on hand to greet him, Young having already endorsed him, calling Carter's position on preserving ethnic neighborhoods "as American as apple pie."

The conversations with Andy Young and other blacks finally convinced Carter to apologize, after two days of stubbornly insisting he had said nothing to justify the accusation of racism.[6] At a press conference in Philadelphia on Thursday morning, April 8, he reported that he had talked the night before with black leaders around the country. "I think most of the problem has been caused by my ill-chosen *agreement* to use the words ethnic purity [as if someone else had suggested the phrase and he accepted it, which was not the case]. I think that was a very serious mistake on my part. I think it should have been the words ethnic character or ethnic heritage, and I think that unanimously my black supporters with whom I discussed this question agree that my position is the correct one. . . . I do want to apologize to all those who have been concerned about the unfortunate use of the term 'ethnic purity.' I don't think there are any ethnically pure neighborhoods in this country, but in response to a question and

6. Some very blatant countermeasures were tried in the first moments of concern. Carter headquarters disclosed that the candidate, who had resisted endorsing the so-called Humphrey-Hawkins Full-Employment Bill favored in the black political community, now saw virtues in an amended version and was supporting it.

without adequate thought on my part, I used a phrase that was unfortunate. . . . I was careless in the words I used. . . . I have apologized for it. It was an improper choice of words."

The other phrases he had used, Carter acknowledged, were "also unfortunate." As for maintaining the ethnic character of neighborhoods, he said, "blacks have taught us a great deal about pride in one's heritage, and I see nothing wrong with that concept being maintained." But what about the possibility that he had said these things in order to send a signal of sympathetic concern to Wallace supporters? Carter flatly denied it: "My support has been much more than from various minority and Spanish-speaking groups, and I would hope and believe their support is warranted, and I would never do anything to eliminate justification for their support. If I should ever take a racist or discriminatory attitude toward any ethnic group, I would prefer to drop out of the race. I would hope by my apologies I've eliminated that concern."

But for several more days, as Carter toured Northern cities with heavy ethnic and black populations, it was clear he had not. In Plains for the weekend, Carter and his aides met to figure out a way to end the controversy. They called in Jesse Hill, a prominent black businessman in Atlanta, who helped arrange a public show of black support highlighted by remarks by the Reverend Martin Luther King, Sr.—Daddy King. The rally, held on Tuesday, April 13, at noontime in a downtown Atlanta park, was a rousing success.

Carter talked, preached really, about a nation that grew up in slavery but threw it off, and blacks in the crowd shouted back "Amen." Then Daddy King took over. In strong, halting phrases reminiscent of his late son, he pulled out all the stops for Jimmy. "I've always been able to let my religion and politics work together." ("Yeah," someone shouted.) "And I've always fitted in somewhere a statement for this man who I love and believe in." ("That's right!") "I want to find that man who has lived so perfect that he's never made a mistake. I know I have; it may well be I'll make some mistakes before the day's out." ("We all do!") "But if there is a forgiving heart" ("Yes!"), "and one who stands to apologize, then this nation, this state and everyone else, has no choice but to accept. Further, and I preach it everywhere I go" ("Preach it!"), "I refuse to hate any man. I refuse to step low enough to have any envy or strife in my heart against anybody. I have a forgiving heart." ("Yeah!") "So, Governor, I'm with you all the way." The applause was deafening, and Carter beamed his appreciation, obligingly moving next to Daddy King as photographers captured them together. Jesse Hill then read an additional statement from Daddy King that said: "It is wrong to jump on a man for a slip of the tongue that everyone knows does not represent his thinking. I know where Jimmy Carter stands because I've been right here to watch him." The applause and cheers were even louder.

From the Atlanta rally, Carter and his party, now including a number of black state legislators and businessmen prepared to give testimony for him, departed for Philadelphia and another press conference. There, he tossed questions breezily aside, saying he had apologized for saying "purity" but he would stick by his basic position on the issue of preserving ethnic neighborhoods. The Atlanta rally apparently not only warmed his heart but also replenished his chutzpah; at one point, asked about the other offensive expressions like black "intrusion" and "alien groups," he blithely said "those phrases were taken completely out of context." Jimmy Carter, after a trying week, was again his supremely self-confident self, and he deftly managed to keep Jackson, his principal opponent, on the defensive through primary day.

As expected, labor was the key for Jackson, and it was clear almost at once on election night that for all of Jim Mahoney's boasting, labor could not deliver for him—whether as a candidate in his own right or as a stalking horse for Humphrey. I walked into the NBC election center shortly before eight o'clock and heard John Chancellor project Carter the winner. I was astounded, especially since NBC had been burned in Wisconsin for making a premature projection. I had thought for sure the network would wait until much later on, out of caution if nothing else. But so conclusive were the early raw votes and the precinct samplings that Scammon & Co. decided it would be just as foolhardy to wait now as it had been to jump the gun in Wisconsin.

Carter won impressively across the state and nearly held his own in Rizzo's Philadelphia. The final beauty contest percentages were Carter 37, Jackson 25, Udall 19, Wallace 11. In addition Carter ran away with the delegate race that was supposed to go to organization-backed Jackson. Carter wound up with sixty-four delegates, to twenty-two for Udall, nineteen for Jackson, seventeen for Shapp, three for Wallace, and forty-six uncommitted. (Ethnic purity had little real impact, though Carter's black vote fell off to "only" about 40 per cent.)

Carter, while saying "we still have a long way to go," claimed Pennsylvania had put his candidacy "in good shape to get a first-ballot victory." And with an eye on Humphrey, he warned that the party "might be committing political suicide" if it turned its back on the results of the primaries in picking a nominee. Humphrey, in Washington, conceded that Carter's victory was "significant" but, he noted, "it's a long time until July." As for Jackson, the Washington senator acknowledged that for one reason or another he had failed to get his message across. "We're eating exotic foods, riding elephants, playing basketball, and playing peanut farmer," he complained, and he for one would be "changing the nature of my campaign to eliminate a lot of the gimmickry." He insisted he was "going to go on fighting." But that was before reality could set in. By routing Jackson in a big-labor Northern industrial state whose major city was controlled by a machine pol solidly in Jackson's corner, Carter had knocked the remaining props out from under the senator. And in so doing, Carter had given Humphrey both encouragement to fill the regular-party void and pause about taking on such a formidable foe. As for Udall, he insisted he would continue to fight as the liberal standard-bearer, but he had been reduced to being a rallying point, not a contender.

Just how completely Carter had routed the opposition was not immediately apparent on primary night. Within three days, however, it would be so—but not without yet another controversy, one that once again raised suspicions on the Democratic left, clearly defeated but still far from ready or even willing to embrace the strange political evangelist from south Georgia.

21. A Breakthrough, and a Breach

There is often in politics a time when the confusion of the day is dispelled with such swiftness and clarity that, looking back on it later, one wonders how there could have been any confusion at all. Such a time was the three-day period immediately following the Pennsylvania primary. On Tuesday, April 27, the race for the Democratic presidential nomination was a struggle between Jimmy Carter and Henry Jackson, with Morris Udall still holding on and Hubert Humphrey waiting expectantly in the wings. By Friday night, April 30, Carter stood alone among the first wave of contenders, talking already of the task of unifying the party. He was only mildly distracted by the oncoming second wave—or ripple, as it was perceived then—from the late-starting challengers Frank Church and Jerry Brown.

It all started to come together, of course, with Carter's resounding Pennsylvania victory, but the effect of that victory was initially blurred by the old contenders' talk of continuing. Jackson and Udall had scheduled meetings for Wednesday, April 28, at which they were to decide how to persevere, and Humphrey, besieged by supporters urging him to get into the race, was cocking a more publicly attentive ear. But Carter, a man quicker to recognize political opportunity than his own missteps, moved with steely resolution to consolidate his gains.

Always an early riser, he was up at dawn and pressing his advantage in an interview on the CBS News morning show. An appearance on these network shows was an expectable prize for a primary winner, like a new car for the most valuable player in the World Series, and Carter used it to keep the heat on the opposition. Giving Jackson and Udall the back of his hand, he turned his determined gaze on Humphrey, all but daring him to enter the competition. "If Humphrey gets in," he said with that benign bludgeon of his, "I'll beat him. If he stays out, I'll be the nominee."

Carter claimed that Pennsylvania had enabled him to complete the first phase of his campaign, proving he had support among all segments of the electorate in all regions of the country. He called himself "the leading candidate now, and one who has no strong opponent among those who began the race a year and a half ago," and said it was time to gather the disparate elements of the Democratic Party behind him. It was clear already, he said, that he would have at least 1000 of the 1505 delegates he required for the nomination, and no one else in sight could come nearly so close. He was "perfectly at ease about any eventuality," he said, including a challenge from Humphrey, though he hoped the others could "move toward me" and get on with unifying the party.

But Wednesday morning, neither the declared opposition nor Humphrey indicated that they would start moving toward Carter. The luckless Udall, waving a copy of *The Washington Star* bearing an analysis that said "Mo Udall Got His Death Certificate," quipped: "I still refuse to go to the cemetery." He was "not going to allow this political party of mine to be stampeded," he said; it would be "outrageous" to leave the liberal wing without a candidate.

Jackson, however, had already begun to face the music. In a meeting in his Senate office on Tuesday, the hard realities of money had been confronted again. Though Jackson had raised a bundle, it had cost a bundle to raise it. Outside of Jackson's home state and California, Bob Keefe said later, "it cost a dollar to raise a dollar." And Jackson's fortunes were always tied directly to how much money he could spend. "When we could spend," Keefe said, "we did well. When we couldn't, we did lousy." If Jackson were to lose Pennsylvania, the prospects of raising money would be even grimmer. There were some potentially good primaries ahead for Jackson, as in Indiana only a week away, but without a victory in Pennsylvania, there might not be enough money. What it got down to, Keefe said, was whether a couple of extremely influential Democrats would throw Jackson a lifeline. "Scoop thought his only possibility of getting the nomination [if he lost Pennsylvania] would be the immediate endorsement of Meany and Humphrey, and that was not forthcoming," he said.

On Wednesday, April 28, his worst fears about Pennsylvania confirmed, Jackson met again in Washington with his aides and chief labor supporters, all of them chagrined at how the labor "machine" in Pennsylvania had fizzled. Once again the money situation was reviewed and the talk inevitably got down to whether Jackson would have to quit. The sentiments were mixed; a number of the labor people were Humphrey men, like those in Pennsylvania, or at least they were ready to switch over if the Minnesotan could be persuaded to run.

And indeed the pressure was mounting on Humphrey. On Tuesday, his old Minneapolis friend, Robert Short, the man who sold the Washington Senators to Texas, was in town pushing him to get into the race, or at least to sign a letter authorizing Short to establish an "exploratory" committee that could raise money. There was a deadline of sorts, inasmuch as the filing date for the New Jersey primary on June 8 was Thursday, April 29. Friends there, including Chairman Peter Rodino of the House Judiciary Committee, were ready to run on a Humphrey slate. A few days before, Humphrey had told Dave Broder he would not run in New Jersey: "If I wanted to run for President by running in the primaries, I'd have done it long ago. But there's no reason I should. I'm not hard up for exercise." But he would, he said, speak for an uncommitted slate headed by Rodino, Senator Harrison A. Williams, Jr., and State Party Chairman James Dugan "if they ask me."

Rodino, however, did not want to be associated with any halfway maneuvers. Unless Humphrey ran at the head of the slate, he would withdraw as a delegate candidate. With Short breathing down his neck, Humphrey told *The Washington Star*'s Martha Angle: "I'm going to listen very carefully to the possibility of establishing an exploratory committee. I may very well want to let some people look over the situation and report back to me. . . . I think there is a possibility that I might be the nominee, although it's not what I would call a big chance."

Short had planned a Wednesday-morning breakfast of Humphrey supporters at the Shoreham Hotel, but so many people wanted to attend that it got too cumbersome and was called off. "I didn't want a big meeting that would turn into a debate over New Jersey," Short said. "Humphrey told me he wouldn't go in there under any conditions, so what's the point of talking about it?" And some old friends, like Ted Van Dyk, an old congressional and campaign aide, were counseling Humphrey to stay out. Humphrey, he told Steve Isaacs of *The Washington Post*, "is not a negative, stop-anybody kind of man. He's too big a man to get involved at this late date in a negative exercise."

The fact was, Humphrey said later, he was tempted. "When I came out of the New Jersey area," he said, "I found there was an awful lot of support, and a good deal of pressure was brought on me to get in." To the old pro, it sounded good. "In all candor," he said long afterward, "I was giving it consideration."

Hubert Humphrey was clearly a man in the middle. Joe Crangle was pushing him particularly hard. "Joe was really gung-ho. He was all steamed up to really get going," Humphrey recalled. "He said, 'Whether you like it or not, we're going to put together an organization and be ready when we go to the convention.' " Wednesday afternoon, the Humphrey braintrust convened in his Senate office: Humphrey himself, Short, Crangle, Mondale, Richard Moe (Mondale's chief aide), Harry McPherson (a former Lyndon Johnson aide), Washington lawyers Max Kampelman and Neal Peterson, Tom Kelm (an aide to Governor Wendell Anderson of Minnesota), and David Gartner (Humphrey's administrative assistant). The burden of their message was that he would have to get into the New Jersey primary if he hoped to have a chance. Humphrey went around the room asking: "What should I do?" Most urged him to run. Then he asked them: "What if you were me?" Two changed their minds. The opposition argued that the move was too much of a long shot, or that Humphrey might in the end make a fool of himself, might become, as Humphrey pointedly said he did not want to be, "another Harold Stassen." Some used Carter's virtual dare to Humphrey to take him on as a lever to pry a positive response from their man. And from New Jersey came word not only from Rodino but from Williams and Mayor Kenneth Gibson of Newark: it was too late for exploratory committees and uncommitted slates; Hubert would have to get out front at once if he was to have any chance.

The meeting broke up with participants mixed in their judgment of what he would do. Humphrey phoned Paul Simon, poised to restart his draft-Humphrey group, and told him he was going home to discuss it with Muriel, his wife, but that he didn't think he'd become a candidate. Peterson called shortly afterward, telling Simon that an announcement statement was being prepared and that he should phone Humphrey at eight o'clock the next morning. "Just make sure if he doesn't go," Simon was told, "that he doesn't make a Sherman-like statement." Simon didn't know what to think.

At home, Humphrey reviewed the bidding with Muriel. He was both tempted and wary about New Jersey. The state's Democrats always had talked bigger than they were able to deliver, but Crangle had produced a poll by the Eagleton Institute at Rutgers that showed Humphrey leading Carter in the state by some outlandish figure like 61 per cent to 17. It would be a shame to pass up a good shot after all his labors to reach the presidency. He could always claim he was moving to preserve the concept of an open convention, now that Carter seemed on his way to reducing it to an empty exercise.

At about ten-thirty that evening, Humphrey talked to Mark Siegel, executive director of the Democratic National Committee and an old friend. Humphrey was in turmoil. He wanted to be President, all right, but he didn't want to be a spoiler, not at this late stage in his career. "There's something about this that's wrong," he told Siegel. "There's something in my gut that tells me: 'No.'"

However, somewhat to Humphrey's surprise, the family was reacting positively. "My wife, believe it or not, had made a hundred-and-sixty-degree turn, and by the time of the final meetings, she made a hundred-and eighty-degree turn. She said, 'You ought to do it. You can win.' Was I surprised? Would I be surprised," the old campaigner asked, grinning and looking up at the high ceiling of his office, "if she dropped out of the lamp up there and came floating down on an umbrella? I'm telling you, I couldn't believe what I was hearing."

It turned out, he said, that Mrs. Humphrey "was not very happy about Carter. I think Muriel felt that his pronouncements were more or less a repudiation of the things that I had stood for. And that he had said I was too old. But, whatever the reason was, she made a complete about-turn. And my wife is not a political activist. She'd had her stomachful of campaigning. But she was prepared to take on her share of the burden."

From all indications, Humphrey went to bed in the early hours of Thursday edging toward a decision to run. At eight in the morning, as he had been instructed to do, Paul Simon phoned Humphrey. "Well," the senator told him, according to Simon's clear recollection, "I talked to Muriel and the kids and I'm going to be a candidate." Humphrey, however, says he has no such recollection. Rather, he told Simon only that the situation "looks encouraging," he said. He told his wife he was going downtown "to think it out." Simon, though, heard what he heard, and was elated. He set about arranging a press conference for Humphrey to announce the momentous decision that afternoon.

Fifteen minutes later Bob Keefe of the Jackson campaign telephoned Humphrey. Jackson had already decided to pull back from Indiana and was now deliberating about whether he should hold on to what he had, throw in with Humphrey, and work for a brokered convention. There had been some crossed signals about what Jackson would do, and so Keefe had been asked to give Humphrey a direct report on what he could expect. It was likely, Keefe informed Humphrey, that Jackson was getting out of the race, and there were people in the Jackson campaign, including big labor support, who would help him. Then this conversation took place:

Humphrey: "Keefe, did you read the [*Washington*] *Post* this morning?"

Keefe: "No."

Humphrey: "Well, listen to this [reading an editorial on the aftermath of Pennsylvania]: '. . . This brings us to Hubert Humphrey. Should he or shouldn't he? God knows, we've never given anyone any advice in these columns and wouldn't dream of starting now. But we would venture to say that the message from Pennsylvania, as we read it, hardly argues for an early plunge into the arms of precisely those people to whom Senator Jackson reposed so much trust. A whole lot worse things could happen to the country than for Hubert Humphrey to be his party's nominee. But it matters how he gets there. For few worse things could happen to either Humphrey or his party than for there to be a recurrence of the fissuring of the Democrats and all the attendant bitterness that gave a grateful nation Richard Nixon two times running. . . .' What do you think of that?"

Keefe: "It sounds to me like they don't want you to run."

Humphrey: "That's what it sounds like."

Keefe: "Well, has the *Post* ever asked you to run?"

Humphrey: "No."

Humphrey said nothing to Keefe about having decided to run. Keefe postulated later that Muriel, herself having second thoughts, had hustled the paper in to her husband the moment he woke up, and the editorial had surfaced all the lingering doubts, the negative feelings about which he had spoken to Siegel the night before. "I kept asking people all day," Keefe said, "if they had read the *Post* editorial. I didn't find anyone who had. But since it was written for him, it apparently hit its mark."[1] (Humphrey later said that the editorial only reinforced his own thoughts.)

In spite of this conversation, Keefe, Jackson, and their associates gathered in Jackson's Senate office on Thursday afternoon and sat before a television set for Humphrey's press conference, in full expectation that he would announce his candidacy. "Scoop was prepared to jump in and help him," Keefe said, "but he wasn't going to ask him. He had decided in his own mind that he wasn't going to be the nominee of the party, and would just as soon it be Hubert. We had all gotten ourselves into the frame of mind that Hubert was going to be a candidate and we would do what we could to help him."

In the Senate Caucus Room, site of historic announcements of presidential candidacy by two Kennedys, by Eugene McCarthy in 1968, by Henry Jackson himself in 1972, the atmosphere was expectant. The television networks were giving the event their full treatment; special lighting bathed the room in unnatural brightness and heat for a late April afternoon. All the old and new Humphrey political associates were there, too numerous to name. In Trenton, meanwhile, Dugan and other New Jersey leaders were ready to file the necessary petitions to put the Minnesotan on the primary ballot just under the deadline. At the appointed hour, Humphrey came striding in with his family and closest friends, including his Minnesota colleague, Fritz Mondale. As always, he was beaming, waving, shaking hands. Others might have "worked" crowds; Humphrey consumed them, inhaled them, seemed to take sustenance from them. That was obvious to anyone who had ever seen him go into his act.

1. If the editorial was a factor, the episode would be the best refutation on record of my favorite definition of editorial writing, first conveyed to me by Bill Ringle of the Gannett Newspapers. "Editorial writing," he said memorably, "is like wetting your pants in a blue serge suit. It gives you a nice warm feeling all over, and nobody notices."

And so it was with ever-rising expectations among the packed audience that he walked to the microphone. He led up to his decision with all the drama his sympathetic presence and the guile of his speechwriter could muster. He had said he wouldn't enter the primaries, but he had also said that if at the time of the convention, "my party needs me and wants me, I would be prepared and honored to be the Democratic presidential nominee." He had remained, for all his inactive status, high in the polls; a host of friends were urging him to enter the New Jersey primary; he had discussed the whole matter with his wife and family and they "are prepared to support whatever decision I make."

But now he started to back off. He had no organization, no committee, no campaign funds, and he knew what a burden that could be. His name was also entered in the Nebraska, Idaho, and Oregon primaries (to be contested by Church and/or Brown), and he had no organization to cope with those contingencies. He blurted it out, tears seeming to well up in his eyes: "In light of all of these circumstances and others, I have arrived at a decision. I shall not enter the New Jersey primary, nor shall I authorize any committee or committees to solicit funds or work in my behalf." He intended to seek re-election to the Senate, to speak out on the issues, and, "if my party should need me or nominate me, I'm prepared to serve."

What had happened, Humphrey said later, was that he had gone up to his Senate office that morning, locked himself in, and reviewed the bidding. His integrity was at stake: he had told everybody he wasn't going to enter the primaries. If he ran in New Jersey and won, that would be only the start of a very hard grind. He would be forced to run in Nebraska, Oregon, and other states where his name would be on the ballot. He would have to raise money in small amounts in a short time, under a restrictive law. There was also the matter of illegal milk-fund contributions to past Humphrey campaigns. That certainly would be dredged up and he, and his family, didn't need it. And, finally, there was his health. Although his doctor had said he was okay, and his later cancer troubles were not anticipated at the time, he said that "in the back of my mind" he wondered whether his health would really permit another campaign.

"I picked up the telephone," he said, "called Muriel, and told her: 'I'm not going to do it, dear.' " Then he called in his braintrusters and told them the same, and more. "I said, 'All I gotta do is stumble just one place and the media will jump on me; old Humphrey lousing things up. There's no doubt in my mind there's a segment out there in that press corps that's just waiting to see whether I'll fall prey to the temptations that are being extended me. They're getting ready to just clobber me. Not that they're opposed to me, personally, but that I have given them assurance that I wasn't a candidate, and they're going to say, "He just couldn't resist. The old firebell rang and Humphrey came out of the barn." The first time we stumble, it isn't only going to be that I lost, but I'm going to be humiliated, and I don't need any more humiliation, I don't need any more knocks, and I'm not going to run. . . . Besides that, I do not want to be a spoiler. It is my judgment that this thing has gone so far that there is really no chance of me being nominated.' "

In Jackson's office, as in the Caucus Room, the impact was jolting. "There was sort of a shock wave," Keefe said. Jackson left the meeting uncertain about what to do, and Keefe and the others were groping. "If we were going to continue," Keefe said, "we had to do things, like scheduling the candidate. Every hour we were sitting there contemplating, we were losing options." It was too late to do any good in Indiana; there was, in fact, only more heartbreak ahead.

On Friday morning, Jackson met with his political lieutenants once more to review the prospects. The will to continue was there, but not the resources. To the end, Jackson nurtured the hope that the Supreme Court would free the federal matching funds due him once Congress and President Ford could agree on new campaign finance legislation, but the Court refused. "He was torn," Keefe said. "He had put a lot into it over the last few years, and he still wanted to be President. It was hard to cut that rope, but we sort of pushed him a little on it." Finally, reluctantly, Jackson decided to get out. He flew to Seattle that night with his wife and two staff aides and withdrew at a press conference there the next day.

"It was money," Jackson told me later. "There wasn't any question but that money was the overwhelming direct causal connection. And labor simply never got around to doing anything, except two or three unions, in Pennsylvania. It was because of Hubert. They just didn't get their materials out. I was to town after town and they failed, flat. They did not do the organizing job."

What about Humphrey? "He didn't help," Jackson said. "It was the confusion. He said he wasn't a candidate but he specifically addressed the state AFL-CIO and left the clear impression he was available, even though he told the press he wasn't. That just left labor saying, 'You know, Humphrey will be in it.' " Well, did Jackson ever talk to Humphrey and ask him to make a categorical statement? "Oh, he would tell me, 'They're all saying these things, but I've made it clear I'm not a candidate.' No, I never pressured him." Others were more pointed. An old congressional friend of Jackson's said Humphrey's timing "really screwed us. If he had made his withdrawal statement three weeks before, we would have had a clear shot at Carter in Pennsylvania."

But Jackson had problems that could not be hung on Humphrey. For one thing, as Keefe acknowledged later, his insistence on keeping up his attendance record in the Senate through 1974 and 1975 was a drag. "If you're going to run for President," Keefe said, "you have to have that as your first priority and drop everything else. Scoop had the Senate much on his mind. It was not a go-for-broke campaign."

In addition, Keefe said, Jackson's chemistry—"the charisma of competence," the ad men tried to label it—was not well suited for the stump. Even when he was doing respectably, in Massachusetts and to a degree in Florida and New York, "we were not making satisfactory progress in the polls. Scoop was getting enough coverage, but it wasn't helping. Carter's free media was winning votes, our free media was losing votes. Scoop was just not coming through as the kind of guy people were interested in. We didn't believe what you guys [the press] were telling us—that he was dull. Then we thought about trying to capitalize on it. One ad agency wanted to show him on TV saying: 'Hello, I'm Scoop Jackson. People say I'm boring. I don't think it's boring to have done—' and then tick off all he'd done. But it was no good. Should you run for President on the grounds you're boring? And he turned out to be too hot, too contentious. We had to be able to come in and outmaneuver the other guys with media money or organization, or something. When we had no support flying, when free media didn't carry our candidate, we did terrible."

Udall, in contrast to Jackson's withdrawal, professed to take heart in Humphrey's decision. "I just told some labor people they can either get on the [Carter] bandwagon or help me out," he said. "I'm the last horse to ride. It's me or Carter now, and I'm redoubling my efforts all the way." Udall's judgment conveniently overlooked the budding candidacies of Church and Brown, but it was not unusual to do so at that juncture.

Carter, campaigning in Texas the day Humphrey backed away, acted like a small boy who had just had a punching bag taken from him. He said he was "a little bit disappointed that [Humphrey] decided not to run. But I think he made the right decision. . . . I don't want to mislead you. We had mixed emotions about it. It would have been a much clearer choice if we had met head-on in New Jersey."

As it was, Humphrey's dramatic announcement—both the timing and setting, as well as the substance—proved to be yet another psychological boost for Carter. What Humphrey said he had said before, but this time he said it amid great expectations, and when they were not realized, Carter seemed all the more invincible. Also, the historic Caucus Room served to make a much bigger deal out of the decision than suited Humphrey's purpose, since he clearly was not taking himself out of the running completely, simply reiterating that he would not campaign. He remained available and ready if asked. Many of the headlines, however, said Humphrey was out, and Carter astutely accepted that interpretation.

Everything seemed rosy now for the Georgia peanut farmer as he campaigned in Texas, Indiana, Georgia, and Alabama for the next round of largely uncontested primaries. Of these, only a sympathy vote for Wallace in Alabama figured to interrupt the accumulation of delegates in Carter's inexorable run-everywhere strategy. But within the Carter campaign, known for solidarity and for fierce loyalty to the candidate, all was not rosy. An episode was unfolding that, while it had little political impact, is worth examining for the peek it afforded into an otherwise insular political operation. The allegations made in the course of the episode were dismissed as the gripes of an unsympathetic or misunderstanding outsider, but they were never specifically disputed by the candidate or staff.

On the day of the Pennsylvania primary, a new member of the Carter team, an experienced speechwriter named Robert Shrum, walked to the front desk of the Sheraton in Philadelphia. Shrum, little known if at all to the general public but fairly prominent in political circles as a former speechwriter for such liberals as John Lindsay, Ed Muskie, and George McGovern, handed the desk clerk two envelopes, asking that they be placed in the boxes of Pat Caddell and Jody Powell. They were copies of a letter of resignation to Carter. What made this gesture particularly strange was that the thirty-two-year-old Shrum had been recruited only two weeks earlier by Carter, on the recommendation of Caddell, one of Shrum's best friends.

The letter was relatively short and to the point. "Governor Carter," it began, "I have decided that in light of my own convictions and in fairness to you, I should leave the campaign without delay." Shrum then quoted what he interpreted to be backtrackings and contradictions in Carter's public positions on a range of issues of concern to liberals like himself, culled either from Carter's own private remarks reputedly in Shrum's presence or in conversations with key aides.

"I was disturbed," he wrote, for example, "to discover that you might favor a substantial increase in the defense budget in spite of your previous pledge to reduce that budget in the range of 5 to 7 per cent." Shrum later said he was told by Stu Eizenstat and Steve Stark of the Carter issues staff that Carter had ordered a moratorium on talk of defense cuts after Paul Nitze, an assistant secretary of defense in the Johnson administration, "told Jimmy that the military budget might have to go up maybe $20 or $30 billion dollars."

Shrum also referred to what he considered Carter's trimming or refusal to be specific on additional benefits for miners afflicted with "black lung," on diversion of highway funds for mass transit, on legislation for child-care centers, and on proposals for improvement of the economy. "You may wish to keep your options open," he wrote. "Within reason that is understandable. But an election is the only option the people have. After carefully reflecting on what I have seen and heard here, I do not know what you would do as President. I share the perception that simple measures will not answer our problems; but it seems to me that your issues strategy is not a response to that complexity, but an attempt to conceal your true positions. I am not sure what you truly believe in, other than yourself. I have examined my reactions closely. I have attempted to justify a different conclusion. But I cannot rationalize one. Therefore, I must resign."

The letter was not intended to be made public. Shrum, having dropped the copies off, took a train to Washington. He went underground, spending some time soul-searching with close friends. He then repaired to Boston, where he took refuge at the home of two others, the writers Doris Kearns and Richard Goodwin. He knew that his sudden departure, and the cause, would start tongues wagging and typewriter keys pounding. Except for Caddell, Shrum had been the only prominent outsider with ready access to Carter on a close-knit staff that had been with him since his days as governor, or before. The clique aspect of Carter's campaign had been a cause of concern to outsiders: particularly disturbed were Northern liberals who continued to look upon Carter as a breed apart, a politician on a different wave length, marching to a different drummer. Shrum represented a bridge to those people, and there was some evidence that this fact was one of the reasons Carter had taken him on.

Shrum had always wanted to be a presidential speechwriter, but his earlier choices had defeated that objective. Now, Carter appeared to be on the verge of a campaign breakthrough, and in fact Shrum's last act before writing the letter to Carter was to draft a Pennsylvania victory statement for him. Later Shrum observed about that statement: "I reread it when I finished it. I decided that it was good, and that I didn't believe it." Shrum's basic problem with Carter was, as his letter said, that he didn't believe *him,* either. After only nine days on the campaign, Shrum was convinced that for all Carter's avowals of truth-telling, he was—it could be put no softer way—a liar and a deceiver. "What made it hard," Shrum told me in an interview when he was still underground, "was to listen to the stump speech: 'I will never lie to you; I will never mislead you,' said with fervor and passion, and seeing people believe it."

Shrum's decision to quit did not come easily, in spite of its swiftness. He was, after all, very close to Caddell; Caddell had been instrumental in his recruitment and Shrum did not want to jeopardize what he knew to be Caddell's close relationship and high standing with Carter. Second, he was genuinely impressed with the quality of Carter's mind, his quickness and, especially, his political shrewdness. And third, Shrum was ambitious to work in the White House. But for all his own political smarts and pragmatism, he was an issues guy—the cynics would call him a bleeding heart— a writer who liked things spelled out, and therein was the rub.

The Shrum-Carter relationship, as Shrum later described it, began amicably enough. Through Caddell, Shrum had made some occasional suggestions for Carter speeches before the Florida primary, and had written a few speech drafts that Carter had liked. Shrum was lecturing at the Kennedy Institute of Politics at Harvard in early April when Carter asked him to become a traveling speechwriter. Shrum leaped at the chance. A week later he went to Atlanta to meet with Carter and acquaint himself with the issues people. Almost at once, he began to pick up troublesome vibes. During the meeting, he told me later, Carter learned that Mayor Maynard Jackson of Atlanta, who had hung back from endorsing him when he most needed it, during the "ethnic purity" flap, had passed the word he would endorse Carter now "for one last thing." Shrum said he heard Carter tell Eizenstat, "Jackson can kiss my ass, and you tell him that. I'm through calling him." This kind of exchange is not uncommon in private political meetings, and Shrum had been around long enough to have heard plenty like it. But Carter's out-front religiosity had prepared him for a somewhat less descriptive response.

Other remarks Carter made disturbed Shrum. On receiving a draft of an economic statement from Eizenstat, Shrum said Carter remarked: "I hope it doesn't commit me too much." And again: "We have to be cautious. We don't want to offend anybody. . . . I don't want any more statements on the Middle East or Lebanon. Jackson has all the Jews anyway. It doesn't matter how far I go. I don't get over four per cent of the Jewish vote anyway, so forget it. We get the Christians." Shrum later said he did not believe Carter intended this remark as anti-Semitic, but rather as politically pragmatic; it grated nonetheless.[2]

---

2. Later in the year, in Carter's controversial interview with *Playboy* magazine, he had this to say about Shrum's recollection: "Shrum dressed up eight or ten conversations that never took place and nobody in the press ever asked me if they had occurred. The press just assumed that they had. I never talked to Shrum in private, except for maybe a couple of minutes. If he had told the truth, if I had said all the things he claimed I had said, I wouldn't vote for *myself*. When a poll came out early in the primaries that said I had a small proportion of the Jewish vote, I said, 'Well, this is really a disappointment to me—we've worked so hard with the Jewish voters. But my pro-Israel stand won't change, even if we don't get a single Jewish vote; I guess we'll have to depend on non-Jews to put me in office.' But Shrum treated it as

Next, as Shrum reconstructed the meeting, Carter reported on a talk with a group of trucking executives who were potential contributors. They wanted reassurances that Carter wouldn't meddle with federal regulations affecting their industry, and Carter said, "I want to give them enough reassurance to satisfy them, but give them as little as I have to. . . . I'll tell them I oppose the diversion of the highway trust fund to mass transit."

Eizenstat (according to Shrum): "You can't do that. You're already on record as favoring it."

Carter: "All right, maybe that's what I've said, but I think all this mass transit isn't a good idea. I don't see why highway users should pay for subways. I think that money should be used for highways."

The whole meeting clearly unraveled Shrum. But there was more. "I had a hard time going to sleep the first night, but I didn't want to acknowledge my own feelings," Shrum wrote in a long memo later. "It had only been one day. I woke up the next morning trying not to think about the day before." He prepared a statement for Carter on mine health and safety that included support of legislation making miners automatically eligible for black-lung benefits after thirty years, a bill strongly backed by the United Mine Workers. Carter rejected the statement and that night on the plane, according to Shrum, told him, "I couldn't endorse these things. . . . They are too controversial and expensive. It would offend the operators. And why should I do this for Arnold Miller [president of the UMW] if he won't come and endorse me? . . . I don't think the benefits should be automatic. They *chose* to be miners."

By the Thursday night before the Pennsylvania primary—Shrum's fourth day with the campaign—he told Caddell he was thinking of quitting. They talked until three o'clock Friday morning on the steps of a Holiday Inn in Philadelphia; Shrum agreed to sleep on it. But on Friday Shrum found more to agitate him. On the campaign plane, he and Eizenstat discussed with Carter the possibility of urging Congress to override President Ford's veto of a pending child-care bill. Carter, according to Shrum, quickly said he would have vetoed it himself as too costly and restrictive on the states. "If I was Governor of Georgia I wouldn't accept the federal money under these standards. I'd close down the program first." He turned to Shrum, unsmiling. "I suppose your ex-boss [McGovern] thinks the bill is just great."

---

if it were some kind of racist disavowal of Jews. Well, that's a kind of sleazy twisting of a conversation."

Shrum, asked about Carter's reply, said: "I was pretty surprised at it. It's not true that the conversations never took place. I believe he doesn't believe he tells untruths about anything."

That cut it for Shrum. At the next stop he phoned Caddell and told him he was quitting. Caddell asked him to talk to Powell and Carter first; Caddell told him Ham Jordan had suggested it. (Jordan, according to Caddell, had remarked: "Look, I really don't agree with Bob, but when everyone is trying to jump on board, you really have to admire someone who would get off because of principle.")

En route to Memphis, Shrum sat with Powell, who tried to reassure him about Carter, taking pains to emphasize that "the McGovern crack" did not reflect Carter's true feelings about the man. On the next leg, indeed, Carter told Shrum how much he liked McGovern. Shrum asked some questions about Carter's positions but, by his own admission later, did not press very hard. "I didn't feel comfortable as a staff member interrogating a presidential candidate," he wrote in his personal memo—an excuse that does not seem to square with the intensity of his distress. In the end, Shrum decided to stay on. "I guess for a lot of reasons," he wrote, "I wanted to stay in the campaign. For the next two and a half days, I just didn't want to acknowledge the problems."

Caddell, meanwhile, was under the impression that all was resolved. He received a phone call from an excited Shrum in Memphis, after the Shrum-Powell conversation. It suggested Powell had done a better sales job than Shrum later admitted. "You've saved me from the worst mistake in my life," Caddell recalled Shrum saying. "I was really getting carried away."

But by the next Monday Shrum was coming unraveled again. At a lunch discussion with some Carter staffers in Philadelphia, the subject turned to the task forces Carter had assembled to work on various issues. One of the aides said, according to Shrum: "Jimmy doesn't take these guys seriously. He wants their names, but he doesn't like other stars around him. He's the star and he wants people to carry out his ideas." Shrum, brooding about such observations, went to his room to start writing the victory statement. When he had finished, he set it aside and started working on the letter of resignation, a task, he said later, that took him the next eighteen hours. He talked also to Paul Goodrich, another old friend in the campaign, who tried to dissuade him.

On Tuesday morning, primary day, Jack Germond, Bob Kaiser, Caddell, and I decided to observe a ritual of campaign off-days and go to the track over in New Jersey. Bob Healy, executive editor and political writer of the *Boston Globe*, was to join us when at the last minute he begged off to go to lunch with Shrum. I was aghast: "You mean you're going to miss an afternoon at the track just to have lunch with Shrum? You can have lunch with Shrum anytime." But he was adamant. He knew something I didn't. Caddell, busy picking losers with the rest of us all afternoon, said not a word.

When we got back from the track late in the afternoon and dropped Caddell off at the Sheraton, he ran into a frantic Betty Rainwater, Shrum's letter in hand, plucked from Powell's box. There then ensued a desperate effort by Caddell and Powell to contact Shrum, to bring him to his senses and get him back into the fold without either Carter or the press learning about his embarrassing defection. Shrum finally fled to the sanctuary of his friends in Massachusetts.

My colleague Dave Broder got the first inkling that Shrum was off the reservation the next morning at breakfast and passed it on to me. After a Carter press conference, I took Powell aside and asked him where Shrum was, and whether he had left the campaign. Powell stonewalled me, saying he didn't know. (He later said that response was technically correct because he had only skimmed Shrum's letter and efforts were going forward to get Shrum to reconsider, so he wasn't certain of his status. That, in the business of press agentry, is called protecting your credibility.) So I spent the next four days trying to track Shrum down. When I finally found him at Dick Goodwin's and we talked briefly on the phone, he was still extremely agitated, and uncertain whether he wanted to say publicly why he had quit so abruptly. He was aware, first of all, that going public would probably mean the end of his career as a political speechwriter. To "go public" is a direct violation of the unwritten code of political campaigns: whatever the problem internally, you keep it in the campaign. The press learns a lot about what goes on inside campaigns, that's true, but there is a lot it never learns. Some of the juiciest stories languish in the bosoms of campaign aides; that is the way it has to be if there is to be a free exchange of ideas about the development of issues, positions, and campaign strategies.

For all that, Shrum was ready to talk. "I really believe it would be bad for this person to be President," he finally blurted out. "I've decided I'll have to do it." We arranged to meet on Sunday morning at the office of Mark Shields, a block from the White House. I had never seen Shrum so emotionally unstrung. Thin to the edge of emaciation from long dieting pre-dating his stint with Carter, his hands shook as he talked, and he had to make a conscious effort to hold himself in control. Yet he was deliberate in his speech. He produced a ten-page personal recollection of his experience, from which much of the foregoing narrative has been culled. He said he had been told he was taken on "to make Carter more liberal," and to help combat the growing charges of "fuzziness." But the campaign and Carter wanted only "the minimum necessary appearance of specificity" conveyed. "The candidate and the campaign were the opposite of what they appeared to be," he told me, agitatedly. "Instead of being honest and straightforward, there was a degree of manipulation and deception I had not encountered in any other campaign." And he added about Carter's single-mindedness: "There were no private smiles." Finally, he said, there was no commitment to anything of value. "If someone asked George McGovern to be for the Vietnam war, he'd say 'No.' I think if somebody told Jimmy Carter there should be four thousand agencies [in the federal government] rather than two thousand, he'd say, 'Fine.' "

As I was concluding my long interview with Shrum, another invited reporter, Christopher Lydon of *The New York Times,* came in for his turn. I left, and in the next few hours managed to contact Jody Powell. He expressed chagrin that Shrum was going public. "I think what he's doing now is childish and hurtful," he said. "He's made a very hasty judgment about people he doesn't know and understand." A few nights earlier on the plane, Powell said he had explained Carter's positions on the defense budget, child care, and other matters. "Bob apologized and said he knew where Jimmy was coming from," Powell recalled. "He apologized for being childish about it." He said Shrum had misunderstood Carter's caution as opposition. "Jimmy wants to make damn sure he has all the answers before going with something." Powell also suggested that Shrum was under a great deal of pressure from liberals, including Alan Baron, who was in Philadelphia and saw Shrum during the crisis period.

By Sunday night, reporters traveling with Carter in Indiana were being asked by their editors to question the candidate about Shrum's disappearance. The inquiries, at an airport news conference in Terre Haute, caught Carter by surprise, because Powell and Caddell had held the letter of resignation from him, hoping to patch things up with Shrum. Actually, Carter had been asked about Shrum's departure on the previous Friday night at a press conference in Birmingham. He had seemed bewildered by the question, had praised Shrum and dismissed the rumor as erroneous. Now he said he had not seen Shrum's letter and declined comment. Nevertheless, to his growing irritation, further questions were posed. "I'm not going to make any kind of comment about Mr. Shrum," he said finally.

Charlie Mohr of *The New York Times,* a gentlemanly but persistent man who holds no one in awe, suggested that he would rephrase his question (concerning Shrum's charge that Carter had dissembled on advocating defense cuts) and delete any reference to Shrum.

"You can rephrase it any way you want to, but I'm not going to make any comment about Mr. Shrum," Carter shot back, bristling.

Mohr pressed on anyway: Had Carter said in private that defense spending would have to be increased?

Staring icily at Mohr, the candidate replied: "I'm not a liar. I don't make a statement in private contrary to what I make in public." The remark set his supporters to cheering and applauding, while he walked off, fuming.

By the next day Carter had been given the letter and a full briefing by his staff, and he apologized to the traveling press for his testiness the night before. Not having seen the letter at the time, he said, he felt he was being forced to answer questions about something he knew little of. Shrum had been "quite mistaken about two or three statements he made about me in the letter," but he did not go into detail. Shrum was "a superlative writer, and I think he felt when he came to work for us that because of his superlative writing ability I would just accept his speeches and parrot them to the public." Rather, Carter said, he liked to write his own speeches.

Before long, Bob Shrum was forgotten. Carter, by the next time he saw Caddell, had mellowed about it. "Hi, Pat," he said, grinning at his pollster when Caddell walked into the candidate's suite at the Hyatt Regency in Atlanta. "Did you bring me a new speechwriter?"

"No," Caddell said, relieved. "But Ham's going to make me director of personnel for the administration."

There was speculation that Carter's entourage would now become even more insular, that the candidate would be more cautious than ever about bringing in "outsiders." Soon, however, another McGovern speechwriter, a pliable functionary named Milton Gwirtzman, was brought aboard. Gwirtzman, no wavemaker, caused no trouble. The fierce loyalty to Carter among the staff remained unshaken by Shrum, though it did keep alive the skepticism many liberals still had about Carter, about any man who would promise never to lie or to mislead, and invite voters to reject him if they found him guilty of either.

Though the Shrum affair did not hurt Carter much, it was precisely the kind of incident that might have, for it challenged the core element of his candidacy—his own credibility. Carter's chief staff aides were always most concerned that the complaints about his lack of specificity might in time translate into a challenge to his honesty and integrity, qualities essential to his magic. Later, in the fall campaign, when Carter himself became *the* issue, an act of open rebellion or criticism from within the ranks about his trustworthiness might have been devastating. But it was Jimmy Carter's continuing good luck that for every knock there seemed to be a counteracting boost; Shrum's laments and warnings were all but lost in the glow of Carter's Pennsylvania breakthrough, Humphrey's retreat, and Jackson's capitulation. All that stood in the way of Carter's nomination now was what seemed to be a last-gasp round of eleventh-hour challenges from a pair of long shots—Frank Church and Jerry Brown.

22. The New Challengers: Church and Brown

The Democratic presidential race proceeded now on two very fast tracks. On the first, Jimmy Carter sprinted to accumulate enough delegates for a first-ballot nomination, trying to gather them up almost before the others realized they were out there for the taking, in state after state where he had prepared, and they hadn't. On the second track, the two late entries—Frank Church and Jerry Brown—tried somehow to underscore and feed on lingering doubts about Carter, and thereby to persuade the party to defer final judgment until the convention in July. The indefatigable Morris Udall, increasingly disenchanted with Carter as the prospective party standard-bearer, joined them, agreeing, in spite of his better instincts, to a negative campaign as the only way to "save" the party from Carter.

On the first track, Carter galloped virtually unchallenged through Texas on May 1 and Indiana, Georgia, and the District of Columbia three days later, suffering only a predictable setback at the hands of George Wallace in Alabama. In Texas, Lloyd Bentsen's favorite-son effort proved to be no more formidable than his inept bid as a national candidate; Carter walked off with ninety-two delegates out of ninety-eight at stake in the primary. In Indiana, with Jackson out, Carter got 68 per cent of the vote and most of the delegates, to 15 per cent for Wallace and 12 for Jackson. Birch Bayh, who had endorsed Muskie in 1972 when Muskie's star was falling,[1] this time came out for Carter the day before the primary, when he could still get aboard and not look bad. Bayh acknowledged he was "philosophically closer" to Udall, "but one thing I learned long ago is how to count." He was not particularly interested in becoming Carter's running mate, he said, but "I don't believe that anybody can turn down a request" to be Vice President—a bridge, as things turned out, he never had to cross. In Georgia, Carter breezed to an 84 per cent victory and got all fifty delegates; in the liberal District of Columbia, he surprisingly won 45 per

---

1. Which prompted Frank Mankiewicz, McGovern's strategist and quipster, to observe that it was "the first time a rat ever climbed aboard a sinking ship."

cent of the vote, to 26 for Udall and the rest split among local factions. According to some television and newspaper calculations, he now had six hundred solid delegates, more than twice as many as anyone else. Carter himself claimed nearly seven hundred.

Starting with Nebraska and Connecticut on May 11, however, both the opposition and the schedule would be tougher. Of the thirteen remaining primaries outside the South, eight would be in the Midwest or West, with Church, Brown, or Udall waiting, usually one-on-one, to take him on. Campaigning in Nebraska, at the foot of the Oregon Trail, Church told *The New York Times*' Johnny Apple of Carter's plight: "He's trying to lead a wagon through a series of mountain passes, and there's a different candidate waiting to ambush him at each one."

That circumstance, however, was not especially to Church's liking. "My hope had been that I might be the only late candidate," Church told me after the election. "I could have been the focal point of the last effort in the West against Carter and move to a climactic test in California. But there wasn't room for two late candidates, and Brown pre-empted California. My plan was based on the assumption he wouldn't run. Leo McCarthy, the Speaker of the California Assembly, was going to head up my committee in California if Brown didn't run. I thought if I could win in the late primaries I would not only create interest in my candidacy but beat Carter in California and attract a lot of those delegates chosen for other candidates. Once Brown entered the race, I had to be content with small victories, and I certainly didn't have the undivided attention of the press."

With Brown in and Udall somehow surviving, however, there was a chance of forcing Carter to spread himself thin by dividing up the primaries against him. According to John Gabusi, Udall's campaign manager, key figures in the Church, Brown, and Udall campaigns discussed the best allocation of resources after the Pennsylvania primary. Udall stayed out of Nebraska, Gabusi said later, "to give Church a shot at it," and Brown's Maryland plans inevitably led Udall to focus on Michigan. There, Carter charged that a "secret deal" had been made between Church and Udall that "they would kind of single-shot and concentrate all their efforts and all their money to beat Jimmy Carter." Furthermore, "this deal also explains why Governor Brown has been allowed a free hand in the state of Maryland to devote all his resources to opposing me there." All the Carter foes naturally denied any collusion.

In any event, Nebraska was all Church's. Ever since his announcement of candidacy in March, Church had focused on that state, emulating in his own fashion Carter's effort in Iowa a year before, building up a constituency by dint of hard work in the small towns across Nebraska. Until the last two weeks Church concentrated on rural Nebraska, finally switching his campaign to Omaha and Lincoln for a final blitz of the same kind of personalized campaigning that had made Carter famous. Carter, on the other hand, was in big-numbers politics now; his eye and his schedule were on major states that could add to his delegate total, like Michigan a week later. And so he did not go into Nebraska until the final week, and tried to get by on momentum, just as he had tried in Massachusetts, unsuccessfully.

Church was, to be sure, a bit of a stuffed shirt. He looked and dressed like the good kid who went to parochial school, always proper and tidy; and his gushy wife, Bethine, was always there to pluck lint from his jacket and to straighten his tie—even, embarrassingly, when he was on camera. Once, when I was interviewing him in the back seat of his car between campaign stops, she sat in the middle and answered the questions before "Frostie" (as she calls him) could. Yet he was a friendly sort, very intelligent, and he could be a tremendously effective speaker, especially on foreign affairs. He had been an early critic of the Vietnam war, and he spoke with ringing eloquence about the need to put the nation's foreign policy in step with its historic ideals. Carter too spoke of bringing America back to the teaching of its forebears, but he himself had gone along with Vietnam for a long time, and all too often still talked the language of the Cold War. Of all the candidates Carter had faced so far, Church was to be the most effective in blowing the liberal whistle on him.

Church also had the advantage in Nebraska of being a Westerner; he knew the issues of the West and could discuss them effectively: conservation, recreation, farming, hunting (including distinctly unliberal opposition to gun control). "I disagree with Jimmy Carter when he says the election is all sewed up," he would say. "The Midwest's not heard from; the West's not heard from." That there were eleven candidates listed on the Nebraska ballot, including Kennedy and Humphrey, was thought to be a factor working against Church because it would enable Carter to play his divide-and-conquer card again. But Church tackled that problem head-on, quoting Kennedy and Humphrey as assuring him they were not candidates and didn't want votes in Nebraska. "Had Ted Kennedy been interested in running," he would say, "I never would have entered. If Hubert Humphrey had decided to enter, I would have recognized the great following he has and I would never have entered the primaries." But, he would continue, "Humphrey said he hopes people will honor his wishes and not vote for him, and Kennedy has tried to get off the ballot here. Jackson has removed himself, and Udall does not intend to campaign in this state. The key by which we can pull off a tremendous upset that would bring the attention of the whole nation to Nebraska next Tuesday is to get behind one candidate. . . . We can begin to set the backfire that can change this whole campaign. It can start in Nebraska."

One who bought Church's message was the lieutenant-governor, Gerald Whelan. Originally a Jackson backer, he endorsed Church at the same Chautauqua pavilion in Hastings where William Jennings Bryan and Senator George W. Norris once spoke. In the end, the message to get behind somebody other than Carter jarred the Georgian's bandwagon in Nebraska. Despite the many liberal candidates on the ballot, on primary night the liberal and labor vote flowed to Church, especially in Omaha and Lincoln, giving him a narrow 39–38 per cent victory over Carter, with Humphrey drawing only 7 per cent and Kennedy 4. Church was jubilant. The result "launches my campaign and gives it legitimacy," he said.

Carter, for his part, treated the outcome as if it were a fleabite. "I can't win them all," he said. This response, though trite, underlined once again the strength of his run-everywhere strategy. For on the same night he was beaten in Nebraska, he was winning—though narrowly—in Connecticut's party-run primary, edging Udall by 33 to 31 per cent. Together, the two states brought him another 25 or so delegates, raising his delegate claim to 724. For Church, the night of May 11 meant psychological success; for Carter, it meant delegates: given each man's objective, they were both winners.

Still, generally speaking, the Carter luster had been somewhat tarnished, at a time when he could ill afford it. For one thing, the Nebraska result encouraged Joe Crangle and Paul Simon to start talking up a Humphrey draft again. Also, at precisely this juncture, a political phenomenon was taking place in Maryland that threatened to stop Carter's momentum dead in its tracks: a personality even more perplexing, hence interesting, than his own was being propelled into the nation's political consciousness.

Hamilton Jordan's pungent phrase for Jimmy Carter's differentness— "the weirdo factor"—was used in the assumption that an off-beat style of political evangelism, a Southern accent, and, above all, an out-front religiosity were detriments among most voters outside the South. In evaluating the candidacy of Governor Edmund Brown, Jr., of California, a weirdo factor also had to be considered, but an entirely different one, and in the main one that could be considered a plus.

Brown, like Carter, avoided the trappings of privilege. He rejected residence in the new "Taj Mahal" (as he called the mansion built for California governors by Ronald Reagan) and elected instead to sleep on a mattress on the floor of a rented apartment in Sacramento. Just as Carter carried his own clothing bag, Brown drove a 1974 Plymouth provided by the state car pool rather than be chauffeured in a limousine. Carter was a devout Baptist and lay preacher; Brown was a devout Catholic who dabbled in Zen Buddhism. Brown gave voters as many reasons to be cool to him as Carter did, yet the differentness in Brown seemed to turn people on, not away. Perhaps it was because he was so young—thirty-eight—and even younger-looking; perhaps it was because he was a bachelor, and women thought him handsome and sexy.

Carter, for all his pretensions otherwise, was a "promising" politician; he promised to cut the federal bureaucracy and defense waste, to name just two. And he not only promised; he asked the voters not to support him if they didn't want him to do it. He promised a leaner, more efficient government, and a more decent, honest, and praiseworthy one. Brown, however, promised only "no promises." While Carter preached the gospel of a government "as good as its people" (which I often feared might be a sentence as much as a deliverance), Brown preached the politics of lowered expectations; there were some things government could do and some it couldn't, and there was no sense in promising what couldn't be done. To many listeners it was wonderfully refreshing to hear a young politician, a liberal in most respects, who might have been full of the greatest expectations, saying no.

Brown, understanding this fully, used it to a fare-thee-well. He seemed to relish saying no, to the point of contempt for those, especially reporters, who might ask him how he would achieve this goal or that. A steady diet of Jerry Brown telling audiences what government *couldn't* do, and what he *couldn't* do, in the process of asking for support, got to be grating after a while. He seemed to toy with his audiences, to try to catch them with oratorical tricks designed always to prove that Jerry Brown was not what you thought he was, not what the press said he was. Being different came to be the essence of him, almost for its own sake. Yet, for all that, he *was* different, and he *was* interesting. And he wasn't always telling voters how much he loved them, the way the other strange one did.

For all his cleverness and brashness, Brown committed the same tactical error as all the other Carter foes. He waited too long, and then had to play catch-up. He had toyed with the idea of running for the presidency even in 1975 but he was inhibited, he told me later, by the fact that he had then been governor of California for only a year. In those twelve months he had not been out of the state once; that, too, was part of the Jerry Brown number. Other governors might have time to play at governors' conferences and on other junkets; he stayed at the job, giving the taxpayer his full dollar's worth. It was rather like Carter saying he would never lie or mislead the voters; he was letting the voters see he was not like all those other lying, misleading pols. But the fact was that Brown's decision to stay in California made it hard to take a preliminary reading on how he might fare around the country.

Two media events occurred, however, that whetted his appetite. One was a long article in *Playboy* magazine that had a phenomenal public response. Brown had recited to *Playboy* his litany of diminished expectations, and the favorable mail poured in on him. Also, there was an interview on the CBS show "Sixty Minutes" that was another ten-strike. Allard Lowenstein, the New Yorker credited with getting Senator McCarthy to run against Lyndon Johnson in 1968, was now on Brown's staff and talking to him about that experience. Pat Caddell, before signing on with Carter, talked to Brown's inner circle in California and came back convinced Brown was ready to go, possibly in time for the Massachusetts primary on March 2, but Brown could not make up his mind that early.

After that primary, where Carter ran fourth, Brown decided to try his luck. According to Mickey Kantor, his campaign manager, Brown told no one on the staff about his decision, had no polls taken, and simply dropped the news casually on four reporters interviewing him on March 12 in his Sacramento office. He didn't even tell his father, former California Governor Pat Brown, in advance. He phoned him when the old man was on his way to a political fund-raiser in Los Angeles hosted by the big-money contributor Max Palevsky for—Carter.

A premise of Brown's candidacy, Kantor said later, was that eventually Humphrey would get in and would freeze labor and party regulars from going to Carter; then, if Udall could beat Carter in Wisconsin, that would freeze the liberals as well. Along would come Brown, the fresh new face, sweep the big California primary, and be positioned to be tapped by the convention on about the third ballot. Originally, Kantor said, the plan was for Brown to run just as a favorite son in California, protecting his own turf and not getting too big for his britches—lest the California natives get restless about a green and overly ambitious freshman governor. But Carter's big victory in Pennsylvania forced him to change his plans.

"The weekend before," Kantor recalled, "it became absolutely clear Carter was going to win Pennsylvania and Humphrey might not get in. So we were going to have to change the chemistry of the election ourselves. We were on the ballot in California, New Jersey, Rhode Island, Maryland, but not Oregon. If Carter won in Pennsylvania he was well on his way, and we would have to perform a political miracle." And that miracle would have to start at the earliest possible moment: Maryland would be the place.

On the surface, Maryland looked bad: there was no Brown organization there; he was an unknown candidate; Carter was likely to ride in on the momentum of primaries in Pennsylvania, Texas, Indiana, and the

Southern states; the machine of friendly Governor Marvin Mandel was in disarray as a result of Mandel's legal troubles (he was under indictment on charges of mail fraud, bribery, falsifying federal income-tax returns, and a "pattern of racketeering activity"). Yet Brown had a few allies. Lowenstein knew a lot of people in Montgomery County, the high-income Washington suburbs, and Ted Venetoulis, the Baltimore county executive, was gung-ho for Brown. Venetoulis enumerated all the drawbacks, then told Kantor: "My gut tells me he can win." That was enough, inasmuch as Brown had no other option. "We almost *had* to go in," Kantor said, "we needed Maryland to go on to other states."

A week before the Pennsylvania primary Brown met with key political advisers at the Malibu home of Paul Ziffren, a former party national committeeman. Also there were Kantor; Lowenstein; Stephen Reinhardt, another former national committeeman; and Richard Silberman, the money man for the campaign. Kantor laid out the Maryland picture, and in a few days Brown said go. One important factor was the conviction that unless Brown established himself as a presidential candidate somewhere else, he could have trouble holding California against Carter.

One of the first things Brown did was to contact Humphrey. "He came to see me," Humphrey recalled. "He told me he wanted to run in Maryland first. He said, 'Who do you know? Who are the people over there?' And I told him. But I said, 'Jerry, I can't get involved.' " They talked several times on the phone. "He wanted to know if I thought he had any chance. I said, 'Well, it's pretty late, but you're a young man. You can't get hurt. You're new. You're not scarred up. You're not old-hat. It's a lot different for you running late in the primaries than for Hubert Humphrey. There's no mystique on Hubert Humphrey. They all know about me. You, you're brand-new. You'll most likely attract attention all over the country. You'll be a sensation all at once because there's nothing the press likes better than something that's new. You'll be a real asset to the media. They've been trailing these other candidates and listening to their speeches for months. They're tired. They want something new, Jerry. And you come into this ball game and you'll get the attention like nobody ever had it."

It was now only three weeks before the Maryland primary and too late to file delegate slates. Brown could run in the beauty contest only, and a major crash campaign in the media would be needed. "We had to hit people over the head with a two-by-four," Kantor said. "We had to make it a high-visibility thing. We bought practically everything we could get on radio and TV." And Brown would have to campaign personally, all-out, to stimulate press coverage, especially in Baltimore and Washington. In that effort, Brown was blessed, since all four major papers in the area—the

Baltimore Sun (morning and evening), *The Washington Post,* and *The Washington Star*—were primed to "discover" him. On the *Post,* as a result of jurisdictional prerogative, the coverage of his campaign fell to the metropolitan staff rather than the national staff, which was covering the rest of the campaign, and the metro staff treated his arrival and stay in Maryland as the Second Coming. Also, except for old face Udall running against Carter in Michigan the same week, Brown was the only interesting show around. "The press had to cover someone," Kantor said, "and there was nobody left but us."[2]

In three weeks, he said, Governor Brown's campaign raised more than $500,000 and volunteers came out of the woodwork in Maryland. The "weirdo factor" attracted the curious, and they liked what they saw and heard. He flew into the state for the first time on April 29, was greeted by Governor Mandel, and attended a wildly enthusiastic reception at the Baltimore-Hilton that drew about two thousand people. From then on it was a political roller coaster, a combination of saturation radio and television, extraordinary coverage by the Baltimore and Washington papers, and the peculiar appeal of this slight, intense young Californian with the distinctly predatory look. His responses in an interview in *The Washington Star* provided a sample of the Brown style: "The categories of politics are becoming increasingly irrelevant and so much verbal salamandering. I go to work early in the morning and I go home late. I put in twelve to fifteen hours a day, six days a week, and I try to live within limits and say things that make sense to me and, hopefully, to others. And whatever you want to call it, that's what it is. . . . I'm not going to overpromise or kid anybody, but times are tough and they may just get even tougher still. . . . I've lived a certain way and I've done that all my life and I don't see any reason why I should change. I just live the same way I always have. . . . I don't see why the governor ought to live any better than the people he represents. He's paid a good salary and it's quite adequate by anybody's standards. I don't think because you get elected you should live in some fancy or high style. . . . There's too much wining and dining and self-congratulation in the

2. The Washington area newspapers were not totally without other material. At this same time, a juicy politics- and sex-scandal was broken in *The Washington Post* and quickly picked up by all competitors. Representative Wayne Hays of Ohio, the autocratic, widely disliked but feared Democratic chairman of the House Administration Committee, was disclosed to have kept on his payroll at taxpayers' expense a vacant-looking blonde unskilled in the secretarial arts who openly confessed that her main duty was to sleep with Hays. The young woman, Elizabeth Ray, became an instant media celebrity and Hays, stripped of his chairmanship, eventually retired from Congress. Other confessions of congressional sex at public expense followed, and the Republicans sought, without much success, to equate these predominantly Democratic sins with the Watergate crimes. The furor, while adding some spice to the 1976 campaign season, had no measurable effect on the outcome.

political process. . . . I think that people in public life are not kings and they ought to live accordingly. . . . I have a certain unity in my life, whether it's sitting in my office talking to a group of people or running for President. I'm the same person. I have to get up in the morning and go to bed at night. That's about it. I go from one place to the next."

It was direct and it seemed candid, and whatever else it may have been, it was different. Maryland ate it up. A *Baltimore Sun* poll in early April had Carter ahead among 24 per cent of those polled, and Brown a distant fifth, behind Wallace, Jackson and Udall, with 7 per cent. By the final week of the primary, the same poll gave Carter 28 per cent, Brown 27 and coming on. The liberals, predictably, loved him; so did the Jews, suspicious of Carter; the blacks, surprisingly, preferred him to Carter; the party regulars, under the still-effective whip of Mandel and other Democratic pols, embraced him as a satisfactory anti-Carter horse to ride. (Mandel had never forgiven Carter for crossing him, in his view, on the chairmanship of the National Governors' Conference, nor had he forgotten a proposed Carter resolution to the governors to take it easy on Nixon for Watergate.)

All these factors helped Brown, but he was helped most by Carter himself. "Jimmy Carter made us important," Kantor said later. "He came in there and fought. If Carter had stayed in Michigan [holding its primary the same day] or Plains, and said he already had the delegates and wasn't worried about the beauty contest, if he had said Jerry Brown was a nice young man and let it go at that, we would have fallen flat. We were praying he would come in and try to beat us, and he did."

Assuming that with support from Mayor Coleman Young in Detroit and UAW President Leonard Woodcock he had the Michigan primary against Udall well in hand, Carter decided to go to Maryland and pin young Brown's ears back. During the last ten days he campaigned hard himself, brought in some 120 volunteers from Georgia and elsewhere, and poured money into radio and television. He labeled Brown the candidate of "powerful political bosses and machine politicians" (as usual declining to name them). Of course he meant his old rival Mandel, finally taking note that the governor had "expressed disapproval of my candidacy," and adding sarcastically: "So far I've been able to overcome that devastating blow in the primaries."

Carter did not dwell on Mandel's court problems; he didn't have to, because the local press was full of them. Brown, for his part, side-stepped them with all the aplomb of the clever pol he was beneath his novel trappings. Campaigning at Mandel's side, he was asked at one point whether he thought a Mandel endorsement would be a political liability. He was "not a citizen of Maryland and not as aware" of the extant political controversies there as others might be, he replied smoothly. Mandel insisted he was not endorsing anybody, but he didn't have to. His appearances with Brown got the message to the troops.

Carter also tried his patented lament that he was the underdog ganged up on by the politicians and overburdened by commitments elsewhere. Brown was ahead in the polls, he offered, because the Californian could focus on Maryland while Carter was running there and in a host of other primaries down the road. That was true, but the run-everywhere commitment was the strength of Carter's campaign. Equally damaging to Carter was the fact that this time he was the old face and Brown the new; he was the candidate on the defensive, and Brown on the attack. Brown lit into Carter about his promise of government reorganization. "It's not how the boxes are arranged but rather it's the people who are in them that count," he said. "It kind of reminds me of the secret plan that Nixon had about Vietnam." He noted that for all the supposed reorganization in the Georgia government under Carter, the number of state employees had increased. As for Carter's proposal for a zero-based budget—stripping federal budget requests down to zero each year and justifying all expenditures from there —Brown called it "a form of consumer fraud in the political arena." Zero-base budgeting, he said, "is a slogan that holds out the false promise that somehow there is an easy way to make the federal budget go down. There is no easy way." Rather, what was needed was "a rethinking of assumptions." This, after all, is the basic premise of zero-based budgeting, but Brown did not let himself get hung up on contradictions.

Carter was clearly knocked off stride. In his customary effort to bring all the sheep into the fold, he even went to Congress one day and, presumably for the benefit of federal government workers living in Maryland, temporarily put aside his anti-Washington pitch. "I'm not anti-Washington," he told an incredulous press conference on Capitol Hill. "I've never made an anti-Washington statement." It was a hard observation to swallow from the never-lie, never-mislead candidate who in a radio ad in Pennsylvania only two weeks earlier had been saying: "We know from bitter experience that we're not going to get the changes we need simply by shifting around the same group of Washington insiders. They sit up in Congress every year making the same political speeches and the same unkept promises." Brown commented: "I don't say I'm against Washington until I get there and then say I like Washington."

The result on primary night, May 18, was devastating: Brown 49 per cent, Carter 37 per cent. Brown whipped Carter in every corner of the state except for the conservative Eastern Shore and some rural pockets, routing him by 2–1 in wealthy Montgomery County outside of Washington, getting an estimated 70 per cent of the age eighteen-to-twenty-five voters, and even edging him among blacks. He jubilantly told a roaring crowd at his Baltimore hotel headquarters that he would go on to Oregon the next week as a write-in candidate. "The nomination is still open," he declared. Carter tried to brush off the result by observing again that "there's no way to win in all of them," but the dimensions of the defeat were sobering.

If that were not a bitter enough pill to swallow, the outcome in Michigan the same night, in a primary in which Carter was supposed to have no difficulty, was an embarrassment of nearly equal proportions. Despite Udall's winless record so far throughout the primaries, despite Carter's support from Woodcock, important segments of the UAW, and Coleman Young, Udall came within an ace of upsetting him. In addition to all these factors, the Carter camp had become complacent in the knowledge that George Wallace, who had received a whopping 809,000 votes or 51 per cent of the Democratic total in Michigan in 1972, was now a shell of his former self. The assumption was that a healthy share of these 1972 Wallace voters would go for Carter. But many of them, it turned out, were Republicans who had crossed over in the 1972 open primary to vote for Wallace. Now they were going back to their own party to support home-state candidate Jerry Ford in his desperate fight against Ronald Reagan. The Democratic vote dropped off to about 700,000 and in the process was returned to its traditional pattern in a traditionally moderate-to-liberal state—good news for Udall. Only continued support for Carter among blacks, heavily concentrated in Detroit and other industrial centers, gave Carter his narrow edge —306,301 votes or 44 per cent, to 304,297 or 43 per cent for hard-luck Udall. Once again, as in Wisconsin, the presence of already defeated Democratic candidates on the ballot may have cost Udall victory; Sargent Shriver got 6163 votes and Harris 4323 in an election Udall lost by a mere 2004.

The result in Michigan came close to confirming Udall's repeated insistence that if only he could get Carter "one-on-one" he could beat him. Udall had finally been convinced by his staff, and by his own growing conviction that Carter was a dissembler who ought not to be allowed a free ride to the nomination, to really go after Carter—even to the point of running a negative campaign that was contrary to his own instincts and personality. At a meeting in Washington after the Pennsylvania primary, John Gabusi had proposed the negative advertising campaign. Peter Hart, the pollster, objected, saying that it would clash with the public's favorable perception of Udall, lose what little base he had, and cost him more than he might gain. Udall himself also balked, but the staff showed him an animated cartoon prepared under the direction of Terry Bracy that had a Carter caricature alternately smiling and straight-faced as a narrator enumerated his switches of position on various issues. Walking back from the House recording studio, Udall mused, "It's good, but I just don't think we can use it." But Gabusi persuaded him that the message, if cute, was correct and legitimate and that Hart's data about Michigan indicated that this was the place to use it; the "fuzziness" issue against Carter was rising steadily in the public consciousness. Finally, Udall reluctantly agreed.

By now, Udall's direct-mail effort was paying off and, ironically, he was in passable financial shape to make a serious effort in Michigan. His best available troops were shipped into the state and Udall himself began to open up more on Carter, reminding labor people of the Georgian's coolness to repeal of right-to-work laws and shaping his own campaign carefully for coverage by television and radio. One day near the end, for example, he drove to Monroe, south of Detroit; outside an auto-equipment plant that had shifted some operations to Georgia, he attacked Carter on right-to-work and his late conversion to the Humphrey-Hawkins full-employment bill. Slowly—almost imperceptibly for those following him day by day—Udall was becoming a very effective, aggressive, stump speaker.

If he was reluctant to slash at Carter, much of that reluctance was dispelled by an impolitic attack made by Mayor Young, before a large number of black Baptist ministers, against Udall's former Mormonism: "I'm asking you to make a choice between a man from Georgia who fights to let you in his church, and a man from Arizona whose church won't even let you in the back door." The references were to Carter's opposition, in his church in Plains, to the barring of blacks from worship in 1965, and to long-standing discrimination against blacks in the Church of Jesus of Latter-day Saints, which Udall had left years earlier precisely because of its policies of racial exclusion. It was a double irony, inasmuch as Carter continued to attend his church, although the exclusionary ruling passed over his opposition remained on the books. Udall protested loudly about Young's attack but his aides later acknowledged that the remark probably helped him by creating a backlash of sympathy among white liberals in the big suburbs, which turned out strong for Udall. When Udall called on Carter to repudiate Young, Carter flatly refused. He would consider it, he said, only if Udall would "apologize for all the misleading statements he has made against me." Carter accused Udall of running an "almost entirely negative campaign" against him, including an attack "on religious grounds" in New Hampshire. Reporters who had covered that campaign were unable to recall any such attack and asked Powell about it. The press secretary offered lamely, "I'm not sure he [Udall] personally said anything about his [Carter's] religious beliefs, but it's been a fairly consistent theme" among Udall campaign workers.

Carter seemed all at once to be a candidate running scared, and Udall began to catch on. A Hart poll about ten days before the vote had Carter ahead by more than 30 percentage points, but it was soft support. With pressure on Carter mounting in Maryland, Udall and his exhausted staff extended themselves even further—and almost made it. Almost, but not quite. Carter was able to add on a victory in Michigan to offset the defeat in Maryland, pick up about a hundred more delegates in the two states and preserve his sense of inexorable progress. But Maryland and Michigan together gave the opposition the scent of Carter's blood. The two primaries confirmed that it was worth going after Carter's "fuzziness" on the issues, and the remaining foes wasted no time doing so.

The next Tuesday, May 25, was the single busiest primary day of the year—balloting in six states: Kentucky, Tennessee, Arkansas, Idaho, Nevada, and Oregon. Of these, the three border states were virtually uncontested shoo-ins for Carter; Idaho was Church's private preserve; and Brown had an easy shot in Nevada, where voters were within television range of southern California television stations and hence familiar with the massively popular freshman governor. That left Oregon, a state with a rich history in presidential primary politics: site of the first pure preferential test in 1910, Dewey's elimination of Stassen in 1948, and McCarthy's feat in 1968 of administering the first defeat to a Kennedy. Church, Carter, and Udall were all on the ballot, and although the Oregon secretary of state refused to list Brown, he decided to compete anyway, taking his chances on a very difficult write-in candidacy.

That difficulty was diminished, however slightly, by a decision by Udall a week before the primary to pull out of Oregon. The decision came after a fight between Gabusi, who wanted his candidate to take advantage of a good organization that had been building in the state for two years, and Stewart Udall, who said that Oregon should be left to Brown and Church against Carter. Twenty-four hours before the troops and $25,000 were to be shipped into Oregon, the whistle was blown. "It was the worst time of the campaign for me, in dealing with the people who worked with us," Gabusi said later.

Probably the most senseless idea in a campaign not overburdened with brilliance was now adopted: while the contenders did battle in Oregon, Udall killed several days in Kentucky, Tennessee, and Arkansas. The theory was that he might be able to pick up a few delegates there, and then be able to say at the convention that he had support from every region in the country, justifiably offering himself as the prime alternative to Carter. He could more profitably have gone ahead to Ohio, whose June 8 primary was vital and where in fact he finally did gear up.

Church moved into Oregon directly from Nebraska and was getting a jump among friendly Northwest neighbors while Brown was campaigning in Maryland, and Carter there and in Michigan. Still, Church did not seem to be doing very well, and when Brown and Carter arrived it appeared the contest would basically be between the two of them. Carter drew large and enthusiastic crowds during a seven-hour swing ending in Eugene; in Portland, two thousand Oregonians waited for more than an hour in a steady rain and chilly weather to greet the triumphant Brown. All three candidates focused on environmental issues, Brown particularly sounding his theme that "we're all on the same spaceship Earth, breathing the same air and drinking the same water." Church also discussed foreign policy, denouncing "the fraternity of compulsive interventionists" in Washington, and attacking both Carter and Brown as candidates of style rather than substance. "I'm up against two governors in this race," he would say. "One of them has been campaigning in generalities to avoid the issues. The other asks very good questions but has no answers." But Church seemed to be out of it. A Portland *Oregonian* poll taken before his success in Nebraska had given him only 8 per cent, to 32 for Carter, 15 for Humphrey, 10 for Kennedy, and 7 for Udall (Brown was not even listed). Since then, candidate polls showed some improvement, but not enough. One had Brown and Carter battling for first place with 25–30 per cent each, and Church third, just short of 20 per cent.

The live question was whether Governor Brown, the hot candidate, could pull off a political miracle on write-in ballots. "We had no media spillover from California, as in Nevada," Kantor said later, "but we thought Oregon's reputation for independent voting might make a write-in work. The state has a high educational level and a lot of young people." Hundreds of Californians, many of them state workers on "vacation," flooded into Oregon to help organize the educational process around-the-clock. Everything ever tried in a political campaign was tried here—1.2 million pieces of literature, door-to-door canvassing, phone banks, direct mail with computer cards instructing the recipient how to write in Jerry Brown on his or her county ballot. Radio advertisements told listeners that "on May 25, when you go to the polls, there will be a familiar name not on the ballot," and told them what to do about it. "Bring a Pencil to the Polls" was the slogan, and Brown carried a simple, direct message back and forth across the state: "Don't write me off, write me in."

The effort was about the most electrifying undertaking in the entire 1976 campaign, reminiscent as it was of the "kiddie korps" that had labored so tirelessly and brilliantly for McCarthy in New Hampshire in 1968. And Lowenstein, a leading force in that earlier effort, was in the thick of things in Oregon, speaking on campuses and rallying to Brown's side many of the Democrats who gave McCarthy his primary victory over Robert Kennedy there. It plainly shook up Carter. Chris Brown, engineer of Carter's New Hampshire victory and now his Western states' coordinator, was obliged to beef up a makeshift phone canvass. Carter's budget for television was sharply increased, and Carter himself canceled his planned return to Plains on the weekend before the vote. Carter treasured his weekends at home—they were a way to recharge his battery and put the campaign in perspective; every time his aides suggested he stay on the road, there was blood in his eye. But this time it had to be done. Carter complained at the Portland City Club on the Friday before primary day that circumstances had attached to the Oregon vote "an importance out of all proportion" to the state's thirty-four convention delegates, but he nonetheless campaigned all out, seeking the lion's share of what was said to be a large undecided vote.

As it turned out, he could have, as they say in Brooklyn, stood in bed. The undecideds broke predominantly for their neighbor Frank Church, and he won going away, with 35 per cent to only 28 for Carter and a remarkable 23 per cent for Brown, all on write-ins. Though Brown fell short of besting Carter, he did well enough to retain the magic he had first displayed in Maryland; he set off almost at once for Rhode Island, to try for another upset under the flag of a hitherto uncommitted slate that embraced him. Oregon was another disappointment for Carter, yet his run-everywhere strategy and the usual Carter luck enabled him to camouflage it. As expected, he had won easily in Kentucky, Tennessee, and Arkansas, adding more than a hundred delegates, before the bad news was delivered from the West Coast. (Church won in Idaho and Brown in Nevada, as expected.) Because the Brown write-in vote in Oregon was late in being tallied, many citizens went to bed in the East under the impression that the Brown drive had fizzled and Carter had beaten him soundly.

Among those in the East that night was Carter himself. He had flown back on May 25 and was spending the night at the New York-Sheraton. In his suite, in addition to the usual campaign aides, was David Nordan, a political reporter for the *Atlanta Journal.* Nordan asked Carter what he thought about a remark Senator Kennedy had made that day that Carter had been "intentionally imprecise" in testimony before the Democratic Platform Committee, and about speculation that Kennedy might be joining a stop-Carter movement. "I'm glad I don't have to depend on Kennedy or Humphrey or people like that to put me in office," Carter replied. He wondered why Kennedy had made such a statement, and added, "I don't have to kiss his ass." Nordan reported this private comment—to Carter's temporary embarrassment. The observation spoke worlds about Jimmy

Carter's sense of confidence, and his determination to become the Democratic nominee with no strings attached—even at this juncture, when his
magic seemed to be wearing off.

Three more primaries were held on June 1 with mixed results. Church
won handily in Montana. Udall focused on South Dakota, hoping with
endorsements from Senators George McGovern and James Abourezk to
win his first primary. Carter, however, denied him even that insignificant
state in what was a particularly humiliating setback after the high hopes
generated in Michigan. In the third primary, in Rhode Island, Brown pulled
off another mini-miracle. He sank a bundle of money into a heavy radio and
television campaign and used a hastily assembled but large volunteer organization to educate voters about which delegates, officially listed as uncommitted, were allied with him. Even another curtailed Plains weekend by
Carter, who marched in a Memorial Day parade in Rhode Island, failed to
blunt the rambunctious young Californian. The next day, thanks in part to
an abysmal turnout of 10 per cent that magnified the importance of Brown's
organization, the Brown-associated slates won 31 per cent of the vote, to
29 for Carter and 27 for Church.

All the candidates now pointed to June 8, dubbed Super-Bowl Tuesday
by the campaign intellectuals. On that one day, 540 delegates—more than
one-third the number needed for nomination—were to be selected in the
final primaries of 1976 in California, Ohio, and New Jersey. If Carter could
win 200 or so of them, his strategists figured, he probably could not be
denied. And if his late-primary setbacks suggested otherwise, if they hinted
that he did not wear well with the voters, well, that was something he could
worry about later, after he had captured the Democratic prize.

23. The Resistance Crumbles

The final, all-important round of presidential primaries in California, Ohio, and New Jersey turned out to be a game of musical chairs: Jerry Brown scared off the others in California, then himself concentrated on New Jersey; Frank Church tried his luck in Ohio, to the deep chagrin of Morris Udall, who hoped to have Jimmy Carter to himself there; Carter made a pass at California, hoping to pick up delegates, but focused on New Jersey and Ohio. As he had been all year, Carter was elusive to the end, closing in on a delegate majority as the others continued to seek psychological successes that would somehow slow him down.

For Frank Church, the final round was especially disheartening. He had now won four of six primaries, yet his candidacy was losing out to the glitter of Jerry Brown, who had parlayed his victories in Maryland, Nevada, and Rhode Island, and his surprising write-in vote in Oregon, into much greater media winnings. Church had a skeleton organization and little money for the large states, so he simply cast his net out for delegates and hoped that something would happen to keep the nomination open until the convention, where his solid credentials might yet recommend him.

But Church's candidacy was ill-starred. On the final weekend before the California primary, he contracted such a severe ear-and-throat infection that he was forced to bed in Los Angeles and had to cancel all his appearances. Then, after flying to Ohio to try to salvage something there, a natural disaster in Idaho—the bursting of a large dam on June 5, the final Saturday—obliged him to return home. Still ailing, he had to endure a flight on an expensive leased plane after his original charter had been damaged at the Cleveland airport when a luggage truck crashed into its propeller during preparation for take-off. Back in Cleveland late on Sunday, he arose on Monday and went to a television studio to tape a last-ditch nationwide fund appeal, only to be informed that the networks could not clear time for him.

On top of all this, Church's decision to campaign in Ohio had caused much bitterness in Udall's camp. Some of Udall's people believed they had a deal that Church would stay out, but Church felt he could not discontinue his campaigning after Rhode Island, having competed only in small states. With Brown pre-empting California, as Church said later, "I was forced into Ohio when I had nothing going." Until then, "it had served my purposes to choose states where Udall wasn't entered. I decided against entering Wisconsin, where I had no chance and he did; I didn't go into Connecticut for the same reason. Ohio was the first place I decided to try where Mo Udall also was deeply involved." But past favors didn't soothe the ruffled feelings.

For Udall, the Ohio primary was simply a case of completing the string. "We stayed in Ohio," John Gabusi said, "because we had had an extremely good month of cash flow, and it was the end of the road. It was almost a fatalism, an internal momentum that had nothing to do with the real life of the campaign. I wouldn't say it was surrealistic, but it had its own life." Ever hopeful, Udall's forces even planned a convention operation, complete with phone system; Rick Stearns, the McGovern delegate-counter in 1972, was to be Udall's convention manager. For Udall himself, Ohio became both an emotional and physical agony. He was now committed to hard, negative campaigning against Carter, whose slipperiness on the issues continued to infuriate Udall. "Who is Jimmy Carter?" he asked in a nationwide telecast. "You have the right to ask those questions of him, just as you have a right to ask them of me. That is what this campaign is all about, and that is why this campaign is not over." The "two faces of Jimmy Carter" cartoon having been so effective in Michigan, Udall approved new negative ads, one portraying Carter as a carnival barker employing the old shell game, noisy calliope music as background and a voice-over saying: "Voters are tired of presidential candidates who are playing the shell game with the issues."

Udall pushed himself through long days and nights on the stump, trying to ignore a severe pain in his leg that progressively worsened. "It was right below the left knee," he recounted later. "I'd been wearing long socks, over the calf, that pinch. I'm six-feet-five with long legs, and I used to tell the Secret Service, 'I'm going to die of cancer of the kneecap.' You're in planes, and in cars with little seats, and it's all day long. Well, I'm athletic and I like to use my legs, and I began to get a dull ache. I remember the night before the South Dakota primary, in Columbus, it hurt so bad I thought I had phlebitis or some damn thing. I couldn't concentrate on what I was saying because of the pain." He called a doctor friend who told him it was lack of use, so he began exercising in his room every morning "and running up stairs whenever I could."

But that was all the running Mo Udall was doing now. Though he could pump about $150,000 into Ohio, according to Gabusi, and Mark Shields agreed to come into the state to handle the campaign, Udall ended up splitting the anti-Carter vote with Church; neither of them was a match for Carter, making his biggest effort of the final round there.

Jerry Brown, meanwhile, was taking his chances on New Jersey, secure in his home base with a Field Poll showing him with 51 per cent of the California vote to only 20 for Carter and 9 for Church. He had most of the establishment Democrats, the liberals, and even the blacks. Carter made one of his best speeches of the year at the Martin Luther King Hospital in Los Angeles, telling about how he and King had grown up on opposite sides of the race barrier in the Deep South, but how events and King's leadership had brought them together in pursuit of a dream of equality in America. But Brown had nearly all the state's prominent blacks in his corner, from Mayor Thomas Bradley of Los Angeles to Lieutenant-Governor Mervyn Dymally and State Representative Willie Brown; the ingredients for the Carter chemistry were just not there. Jerry Brown challenged Carter to a debate, and Church joined him, but Carter dismissed the idea as "ridiculous" and went on his frontrunning way.

In New Jersey, Brown had to contend with sentiment for Humphrey that would not die. He was offering himself as a live alternative to Carter, but the uncommitted slate that had tried so hard to get Humphrey to file still held out the hope that if they could win, he would finally relent and become a candidate. Since early May, Brown had been pressing Humphrey directly to find out whether he was really out and, if so, why he wouldn't tell the Jerseyans so and urge them to back Brown. Humphrey would reply that what they did was up to them; they weren't his to release. "I think he was trying to hold on," Mickey Kantor said later. "In the back of his mind, he was still hoping that after June eighth it would still be uncertain and people would turn to him naturally."

In the absence of Humphrey's intercession, Brown's forces had to scramble for some way to horn in on the uncommitted delegates. Brown, Kantor, Lowenstein, others conferred with Senator Williams, Jim Dugan, the state party chairman, and Dan Horgan, the party executive director. About two weeks before the primary the uncommitted delegation met to decide what to do. "We were trying to hang very tough for a Brown delegation," Kantor said, but the delegation wouldn't buy it; a compromise was finally reached in which the uncommitteds would favor both Humphrey *and* Brown, surely one of the strangest hybrids ever in presidential primary politics. "We really agonized over the decision whether to go into New Jersey," Brown's manager said, "because it just was so incredibly tough. In Oregon, at least they could write in his name; in Rhode Island, you could say a vote for 'uncommitted' is a vote for Jerry Brown; here, we had to say, 'A vote for uncommitted is a vote, we think, for either Brown or Humphrey.' We were going from the sublime to the ridiculous; we were so far away from political reality and the way people were used to voting. But we had no choice; we were running for President."

Kantor insisted that Humphrey and Brown never talked out this arrangement. But, he said, "it was pretty obvious that just as we wanted Humphrey to stay in [to freeze regular party and labor support], he obviously thought Jerry Brown was the only hope he had of keeping the convention open. They never talked that way; it's interesting how people assume they did. Well, they never did. But it was clear it would serve each other's purposes. It was clear to Humphrey, it was clear to Brown."

Humphrey said later, however, that he and Brown did talk about New Jersey. "He called me about it," Humphrey said. "I told him that Jimmy Dugan was insisting he was going to run a slate that was uncommitted for Humphrey. I told him not to. I expressly told him I could not give that any encouragement or endorsement. 'Well,' Jerry said, 'what would you think if I went in?' I said, 'Go to it.' And he went up there."

Brown, unlike Udall, was not running out the string. "We hoped it would come down [at the convention] to a Humphrey-Brown decision; if Carter couldn't make it on the first or second ballot, Humphrey would make himself available and by the third ballot it would be Brown or Humphrey," Kantor said. "And we also hoped Udall would hold on in Ohio. We assumed if it was close in Ohio, and we could get forty per cent in New Jersey and a big win in California, that people would hold off. All we wanted was for people to remain neutral up to the first part of July, when we felt there would be national polls showing we were more popular than Jimmy Carter."

But Carter had other ideas. He kept the pressure on, shoring up his soft spots—as in a reassuring speech to Jewish leaders in Elizabeth, New Jersey, in which he said that a tenet of his Baptist faith was "an absolute and total separation of church and state." He reminded them that Harry Truman was a Baptist. And he kept telling the voters that the other candidates were ganging up on him; in Cleveland he charged unnamed critics with trying to stop his nomination "to maintain at all costs their own entrenched, unresponsive, bankrupt, irresponsible political power." The clear impression—in a speech to the Ohio AFL-CIO convention—was that he was alluding to his opponents for the nomination.[1] Later he denied it, telling reporters he really meant other (also unnamed) Democrats and Republicans Ford and Reagan—neither of them conspicuous in any stop-

---

1. It was appropriate that the Ohio AFL-CIO held its convention in Cleveland: a number of delegates came attired in what was known on the press bus as "a full Cleveland"—white polyester leisure suit, with white open-necked shirt, white belt, white socks, and white patent-leather shoes.

Carter effort. In such exercises, Carter was like a little boy who would steal all the cookies he could get away with, but when caught would insist he didn't even like cookies.

Another intemperate remark that came back at him in Ohio was his observation regarding Ted Kennedy that he wasn't obliged "to kiss his ass." Asked about it at a press conference, Carter at first said he didn't "remember the details" of the conversation. But when pressed on whether he had used exactly those words, he laughed and quipped: "That's the part I don't remember." Then he added: "I would have expressed it otherwise in the newspapers for attribution"—an implication that he had not expected to be quoted. He was just trying to say, he explained, that "I did not depend on particular people endorsing me to put me in office, that I didn't have to kowtow to anyone. It was no disrespect to Senator Kennedy, who is a good friend of mine."

Later, while Carter was speaking in a shopping mall in Steubenville, Ohio, ABC's Sam Donaldson and some other reporters rushed off and bought sweatshirts bearing the words "Kiss My——" with a sketch of a donkey as viewed from the rear. On the press bus, they presented one to Carter. He held it up, grinned, and said: "Don't give one to Ted Kennedy." Always the diplomat, he added, "Thank you. You've treated me well." To which a reporter called out: "Compared to what?" Carter grinned again. "Compared," he said, "to the way you treated Nixon the last year."

Carter was feeling good, and confident that he would come out ahead. But he kept his eye on Humphrey, who was now speaking in behalf of the Brown-Humphrey delegates in New Jersey and saying he might yet get in if Carter were three hundred votes short of nomination after the last round of primaries. "He's very close, but I have the sense that he's lost a lot of his zip," Humphrey told Johnny Apple. "If Carter does well Tuesday, fine, that's it. He'll go after the uncommitted votes pretty quickly, and I suspect that he'll get a lot of them. It would be futile to try to step in, and I would not do it. But if not, I'll try to get the answers to some questions: What is the true state of the uncommitteds? Are they really open, or have they made promises? How solid is Carter's support? What's the feeling toward me among the political leaders—the governors and the state chairmen?" But he added: "I have to be cautious and careful. I'm not interested in flights off the cliff." While Humphrey played this question-and-answer game with himself, Joe Crangle had his draft-Humphrey effort cranked up again, canvassing uncommitted delegates and even going so far as arranging for an airline charter to take Humphrey jetting around the country after the last of the primary voting.

Carter, however, was never idle. Between harangues against the bullies ganging up on him, he was on the phone to leading Democrats, telling them he was on the verge of another big primary day. It was the ship's-leaving-the-dock caper, and the message was the same coming from a political apostle of love as it would have been from Mark Hanna himself.

Carter returned to Atlanta on June 8, primary day, to thank the workers in his national headquarters and to await the returns before going on to Plains, where the townsfolk vowed to stay up until their first citizen got home from the last of the primary wars. He started the day in New Jersey, though, with a phone call to Mayor Daley. All through the campaign, Carter had assiduously maintained direct communications with Chicago's authentic boss, understanding full well that no other single Democrat, save Kennedy or perhaps Humphrey, had it within his power to tip the scales at the proper moment. "We would place a call to Daley every week or ten days," Greg Schneiders said. "Carter himself always talked to Daley. Nobody else in the campaign ever talked to him until after the convention. The calls were always the same, never specific, never that an endorsement at some point would be helpful. It was always, 'I just wanted to talk with you, let you know how the campaign is going.' "

This particular phone call, however, was specific, and urgent. Carter had somehow permitted himself to get involved in a fund-raising affair planned for Chicago in late June, and it appeared that it had become dominated by individuals allied with Governor Daniel Walker, Daley's bitter foe. About a week earlier, Peter Jones, a Montgomery Ward official and Carter enthusiast, had held a breakfast to plan the affair, and had invited among others Alex Seith, a prominent Chicago lawyer, chairman of the Cook County Zoning Board, and a prime adviser to Daley on national party affairs. When Seith saw all the Walker people there, he told Daley, who hit the roof. Later Seith phoned Carter, who was campaigning in New Jersey, and told him what was happening, including the group's intention simply to inform Daley after the affair was set, and invite him. That, emphatically, was not the way things were done in Chicago, and Carter didn't have to be told. Seith suggested that Carter might adjust the fund-raiser so as to include Walker people but not be dominated by them.

The next day Seith ran into Bob Abboud, the young chairman of the First National Bank in Chicago, and asked him whether he would be willing to chair the affair. Abboud declined, saying his position would not allow it. But beyond that, he didn't want any part of anything that so infuriated Daley. "He's so damned mad," he said, "I don't think he'll endorse Carter no matter how many delegates he has." Again Seith phoned Carter on the campaign trail, alerting him to Daley's mood. Carter needed to hear no more. He told Seith: "I'm going to cancel the thing. My friendship with

Mayor Daley is too important." By that time, Seith said later, the evening was expected to raise as much as $250,000 for the campaign. Carter said he would call Daley the first chance he had, and so inform him.

On Monday afternoon, June 7, Seith was on his way into Daley's office when he met Abboud coming out. "I'm staying a million miles away from that fund-raiser," the banker said. "He's still really mad." Seith went in and told Daley that he had talked to Carter, that Carter had had nothing to do with arranging the affair and was going to phone the mayor to "straighten this out."

Daley was noncommittal. For several years Carter had courted him: he supported the unsuccessful effort to seat Daley's Illinois delegation at the 1972 Democratic convention; and he had phoned Daley shortly after the mayor suffered a stroke in 1974, offering the use of a place at Sea Island to recuperate. But Daley was always very wary of being used: a single betrayal would reduce all the earlier gestures of friendship to a sham, and this latest incident had his defenses up. Daley would wait to hear what Carter had to say. Seith intentionally did not report Carter's plans to cancel the event and kick away a quarter of a million dollars; he felt that was up to Carter to say if he so chose.

Such was the background of Carter's Tuesday-morning call to Daley. According to Seith, Carter did indeed apologize to Daley for the mix-up and say he would cancel the fund-raiser, and the mayor was convinced that Carter had been an innocent party. He told Carter there was no need to cancel; they would just start from scratch and put a fund-raiser together Daley-style. (The $100-a-head affair was scrapped and a $500-a-head reception was substituted that ultimately netted the Carter campaign $300,000.)

Talk then turned to the day's big primaries. Carter laid it out cold: he was going to lose in California and New Jersey, but would win Ohio. Whether they cooked up together what happened next, or whether Daley acted strictly on his own, is not known; but the fact is that Daley took this prediction and used it in a way that would all but force an interpretation that what happened in Ohio was the important thing; that California and New Jersey were side shows.

Shortly after Carter hung up, Mayor Daley strode out of his office and held a press conference. He could have said that a candidate who lost two out of three primaries on the final day certainly had not proved his electability, and that the party should reserve judgment until the convention. He could have, but he didn't. Instead, he announced: "This man, Carter, has fought in every primary, and if he wins in Ohio, he'll walk in under his own power. . . . I've known him for years. He's got courage. I admire a man who's got courage. He started out months ago and entered into every contest in every state and he won 'em and he lost 'em and, by God, you have to admire a guy like that. . . . He's got a religious tone in what he says and maybe we should have a little more religion in our community. . . . The man talks about true values. Why shouldn't we be sold on him? All of us recognize the violent and filthy movies and the newspapers with all the mistresses on the first page stripped down to the waist. What are the kids going to do in the society that see that all around?"

It was pure Daleyese, and the message was loud and clear. He, for one, was not going to be left on the dock as the ship pulled out. In fact, he was going to provide the tug service. Just so there could be no doubt, the mayor added this about the possibility of a late Humphrey draft: "Who said that's the man now who should be knighted on a white horse to walk him into the convention? Our party isn't in bad enough shape to have to go to someone and demand him and draft him. I don't think anyone should be so honored, no matter who he is, and I don't think they will."

Even before most of the voters had gone to the polls in California, Ohio, and New Jersey, it was a shot heard 'round the political world. If Dick Daley said Ohio was the ball game, then Ohio was the ball game.

And so it proved to be. That night, Jerry Brown routed Carter in California, winning 59 per cent of the vote to 21 per cent, picking up 204 delegates to only 67 for the Georgian. In New Jersey, Brown was even more spectacular, booting home the makeshift uncommitted slate with 42 per cent to 28 per cent for Carter, 83 uncommitted delegates winning to only 25 Carterites. But all eyes now were on Ohio, and Carter, as he had predicted, came through impressively, especially in rural areas: 52 per cent to 21 per cent for Udall and 14 per cent for Church, and a whopping 126 delegates to 20 for Udall. The Ohio total gave Carter 218 delegates of the 540 selected that day; within hours, the walls of opposition to his candidacy, walls that somehow had stood through his early run of primary successes and seemed to be buttressed by the late victories of the second round of challengers, were crumbling. And Daley of Chicago, who had not even been permitted to be a delegate to his party's convention four years earlier, turned out to be the psychological demolition man.

By the time Carter arrived in Atlanta, word of Daley's statement had spread through the political community. Carter telephoned three of his remaining opponents—Church, Udall, and Wallace—and each indicated to him that they thought he had the nomination; Humphrey, according to Carter, was noncommittal. Carter did not telephone Brown because, he said later, the polls were still open in California and it would have been inappropriate. But, in light of Brown's behavior later that night and during the next few days, it probably would have been damned interesting. Brown seemed not to have heard Daley's dictum of what was important and what was not; he got the impression that his smashing victory in California and his surprisingly strong success with the confusing two-headed slate of uncommitteds in New Jersey were serious blows to Carter, and a big boost to his own chances. Others might be giving the nomination to the Georgian, but Brown emphatically was not. "The preliminary indications are that I've won overwhelmingly in both New Jersey and California," he said in Los Angeles, "which means that in every state I've entered, Carter has been defeated. I'm going to begin contacting uncommitted delegates tomorrow. . . . I'm going throughout the country and contest Mr. Carter for every delegate." At a private reception, Brown walked over to the actor Warren Beatty and said, "Listen, we've got to get Hubert off his ass. We've got to get him going. Tomorrow we'll start working on Hubert."

Carter finally went home to Plains for the postmidnight street party the folks had planned for him. While he was greeting well-wishers on the street, a local citizen handed him a slip of paper with a typewritten message. It said that George Wallace had called and left his private bedside number in the Governor's Mansion in Montgomery. It was important, and Carter was to call no matter how late. The candidate's mother, Miss Lillian, came over with the same message. Carter broke away, accompanied her into the railroad depot that served as his Plains headquarters, and placed the call. It was then 2:15 A.M. Wallace congratulated him on his success and said he had decided to announce his support the next morning. The feisty little Alabamian, who for more than a decade had run for President with the thinly veiled intent to blackmail the Democratic Party for concessions to his point of view, now, at the critical moment, asked Carter for nothing at all. "I told him," Wallace reported at a press conference in Montgomery the next morning, "all I asked of him is that he would promise, if elected President, he would use all the resources at his command to try to make all the people of this country one of the finest Presidents we've ever had." It must have been one of the most difficult conversations Wallace had ever had to conduct—this telephone call to the man who had dashed his own presidential hopes and replaced him as the South's political hero. If Carter didn't know his long quest for the Democratic nomination had reached a successful end before then, he knew it now.[2]

---

2. Skeptics had difficulty believing Wallace would not ask for something in return for releasing his delegates. After Carter took office as President, Wallace visited the White House with the nation's other governors. While there, he handed Jack Watson, secretary of the cabinet, a letter for the new President. In it, Wallace finally asked for something: that the Carter administration conduct research into a possible cure for paraplegics like himself, including twenty thousand veterans of America's wars.

The next morning, the floodgates opened. Mayor Daley held another press conference in Chicago. Beforehand, he called Senator Adlai Stevenson, told him what he planned to do, and together they agreed to release the eighty-six Illinois delegates pledged to Stevenson as a favorite son. "Carter's victory in Ohio is the ball game," Daley told reporters. "The man has such a strong amount of support throughout the country, there's no use in hesitating now. . . . I'll cast my vote for him, and there will be a Carter victory." Daley also put in a plug for Stevenson as Carter's running mate, but Stevenson did not push himself.

The Georgian, dressed in blue jeans and heavy work shoes, met reporters again at the Plains train depot. He had talked to both Daley and Wallace as well as Henry Jackson, he told them, and Jackson would soon be announcing his support—after clearing the matter with his delegates. Carter claimed that his delegate strength was up to 1260 and was certain to go over the 1505 mark with the commitments of these and other leaders.

Udall congratulated Carter, but said he would remain a candidate to fight for inclusion of liberal positions in the party platform. Church too acknowledged that the race seemed to be all over; only Humphrey and Brown were dragging their feet, and in Humphrey's case it was just a matter of hours. Joe Crangle, professing to be encouraged by Tuesday's results in New Jersey, claimed that *that* was the real battleground; Humphrey, far from being discouraged, should now get into the race. "People will have political blinders on," Crangle said, "if they don't look at the whole pattern. In the last fifteen primaries, Carter won only five, three in the South, and Michigan was a tie." He and Paul Simon made a date to see Humphrey that afternoon to urge him to run. Humphrey at first said he would confer with Carter and Brown before deciding, but Daley's words of the day before, extremely critical of a Humphrey draft, apparently weighed heavily on his mind. Humphrey said he was "a little unhappy but not too surprised" at Daley's reaction, and by late afternoon he was ready to put the whole business behind him. "The primaries now are over and Governor Carter has a commanding lead," he said. "He is virtually certain to be our party's nominee. I therefore will not authorize any presidential political activity on my behalf. And I will do all I can to help unite our party behind the candidate chosen by the delegates at the convention." It was not an endorsement, but neither did it bear the usual words about being available if his party needed and wanted him.

After that, there was only the meaningless last thrashing about by Jerry Brown. Why it took him so long to face reality was the final enigma of this most enigmatic of candidates. The reason, Kantor tried to explain later, was that he and his strategists were so focused on what they were trying to do, and thought they were succeeding so well at it, that they failed to grasp what was happening all around them. "We were surprised at how quickly it moved," he said. "We felt we had two weeks to four weeks before all that movement might start, two to four weeks to be able to affect all this. Things were moving so fast for us. We were concentrating on Oregon, Nevada, Rhode Island, New Jersey, California, and how the media was viewing this situation. And then the media turned on the Ohio victory so quickly, it was like being hit in the face with a bucket of cold water."

Also, Brown was committed to go to Louisiana to address the state legislature, and Governor Edwin Edwards, for reasons of his own, still wanted to endorse him, so Brown went ahead for the next few days. To be certain that Daley, Wallace, and Jackson were delivering on their promises, the Brown boiler room kept checking on whether their delegates were indeed going over to Carter. In short order, the checks confirmed that Carter had the nomination. Still, Brown remained a campaigning candidate, speaking before the National Press Club in Washington, attending a Robert Strauss birthday party in Texas, even making a costly nationwide telecast. Surely no other candidate would have behaved this way, after it was so clear he had lost. . . . Of course. That was it. "One of the things you've got to remember," Kantor said, "is that Jerry Brown's great strength is in not being the same, in being different, in not playing the game. We were concerned that if he just dropped out, he'd look like everybody else." Jerry Brown being Jerry Brown, there was not the remotest danger of that.

Jimmy Carter now had plenty of time, after a nonstop run of nearly two years, to sit back and savor the approach of his party's national convention. It would not be the final party battleground, after all, but a mere formality, a confirmation of the success he had engineered in winning eighteen out of thirty primaries entered. He could use the weeks until the mid-July convention to relax, to try to heal the wounds of the primary season, to deliberate on his choice of a running mate. His run-everywhere strategy had been brilliantly successful; if at times in the final weeks it had appeared to overtax him and his resources, it was his deliverance too. There had been fourteen primary election nights between the end of February and early June, and on every single one of them a Carter victory occurred somewhere. That fact, more than any other, kept the momentum going, enabled him to minimize setbacks and kept pressure on the opposition, which saw his delegate total mounting inexorably. The victory in Ohio, eclipsing his losses in California and New Jersey, was a fitting climax.

"I don't intend to lose," Carter had been saying ever since Iowa. At first, the words had seemed laughable in their audacity. Then, as success built upon success, they seemed to reflect his gritty determination; in time, that gave way in some minds to a kind of arrogance; until one realized that this was not a boast but a firm statement of purpose and conviction. From the start, Carter *had not intended to lose,* and by the time his opponents and his critics realized that, it was too late to stop him. On an incredibly long and ambitious journey, he was halfway to his destination. If he could put the party house in order, and select the proper person to run with him the rest of the way, the odds were very strong that Jimmy Carter would be the next President of the United States.

part VI

***THE
DEMOCRATIC
CONVENTION***

24. Unity, and Fritz Mondale

In the second week of July 1976, with the United States' Bicentennial celebration still fresh in memory, the Democratic National Convention opened in New York City. A year before, the expectation of a brokered convention had promised to make Madison Square Garden the scene of a typical Democratic donnybrook. Instead, the chances were that it was going to be a lovefest.

After his Ohio primary victory, while Carter busied himself attending fund-raising events to liquidate campaign debts, his associates had engineered agreement on a unity platform. By negotiating, cajoling, and occasionally strong-arming, Carter's forces under Stuart Eizenstat, his issues chief, brought an uncontroversial platform to the convention. They won black delegates' acquiescence in a limited welfare reform; labor acquiescence in a limited national health-insurance plan; Southern acquiescence in side-stepping the school-busing issue. Only on the question of amnesty for draft evaders and deserters was there a semblance of a dispute, and that too was resolved amicably. Sam Brown, the anti-Vietnam war activist who was state treasurer of Colorado, insisted that the platform committee support a "full and complete pardon" for all those in "legal or financial jeopardy" as a result of opposition to the war, a position more generous than Carter was espousing. After consultation with Eizenstat, Brown accepted an amendment permitting the President to consider pardons for deserters on a case-by-case basis, and the amendment carried. Brown explained that while he was not enthusiastic about the limitation, he would accept it so that "a much broader number of people" could support the platform. Eizenstat praised this concession as a "clear message to the country that the Democrats are prepared to unite in a way that we have not been united in a long time," and indeed it was. "You have to give up a bit," Brown said, "in order to take control of the presidency."

In this spirit the Democratic convention opened on July 12. Yet considerable apprehension about Carter remained in the party—among liberals particularly—about his lack of specificity on issues, his ability to seem all things to all men, his religiosity, his style. To those who for years had controlled the party and the convention mechanism, he was an unknown quantity, an outsider, a loner who had triumphed without them. The convention would be, in a real sense, a coming-out party for Jimmy Carter, an opportunity to show the party—and the country as well—what kind of a man, a leader, a Democrat he was.

The Carter luck continued to hold. New York City's Bicentennial festivities the week before, highlighted by the majestic visit of the Tall Ships of the world, had left this customary cauldron of ill temper, rudeness, and freneticism in an uncommon mood of cordiality. Cab drivers who on other occasions not only refused to stop for rush-hour passengers but also tossed epithets as they sped by now became ambassadors of good will. Waitresses, elevator operators, hotel clerks, shopkeepers were uncharacteristically courteous. Police put off their snarling and helped conventioneers find their way around. It was as if the city, besieged with financial woes and all too aware of the constant hostility to it in the great America beyond the Hudson River, had made up its mind to live down its reputation. The weather, too, shone on smiling Jimmy Carter. After a summer of oppressive heat and humidity, New York City, for six consecutive days, enjoyed the balminess of late spring, warm but comfortable, turning cool and even breezy at night.

Yet the convention was strangely overshadowed by the immensity of New York. At other conventions, a kind of fever holds the host city in its grip, excluding all other excitements and projecting a sense of carnival everywhere. But New York is New York, and there is nothing it hasn't seen. Even the spectacle of a peanut farmer from Georgia capturing the Democratic nomination, and the thousands of his sweet-talking fellow Georgians descending to watch it happen, did not seem to make a dent. Only the determination of New Yorkers to show their city at its best made one realize that something special was going on.

In this atmosphere, Carter quietly but resolutely set out to wield the convention as a tool in his first major job as presidential nominee: to convert resignation to his nomination into enthusiasm for it, to dispel doubts, and to make a positive impression on the millions of Americans who for the first time would be paying attention to him, drawn by the magnetism of the convention itself.

He started by attending a mammoth party for all delegates and alternates on a Hudson River pier, standing in line for hours shaking hands with all comers. He met also with women leaders to try to negotiate on the one outstanding controversial point facing the convention—their representation at the 1980 convention. The women were pressing hard for equality—50 per cent of all delegates. Carter, while opposing mandatory quotas, quickly softened up New York Congresswoman Bella Abzug with pledges to work for the Equal Rights Amendment in the fall campaign, and to appoint women to high posts in his administration. The women finally agreed to a platform compromise pledging the party to "promote," if not assure, equality in 1980.

That clearly was Carter's style, and an element that disturbed true-believing liberals. But the matter of women's representation was considered a minor one in the scheme of things. At this convention, the one piece of unfinished business that delegates, the press, and the public looked to for a reading on Jimmy Carter was the selection of his running mate.

The collapse of Carter's opposition on the day after Super-Bowl Tuesday had given him more time to contemplate his choice than any previous Democratic nonincumbent in memory had enjoyed. Throughout the primaries, Carter had listed his three criteria for a running mate: he would have to be the individual Carter felt was best qualified to become President if destiny required; he would have to be politically and personally compatible with Carter, to assure that as Vice President he could function as a loyal and effective lieutenant, and that in the event of ascendancy Carter's programs would go forward; and, of lesser importance, he should come from a region other than Carter's South.

Virtually every presidential candidate in every campaign has said he intends above all to select the individual who after himself would make the best President. The statement has become a cliché, to be mouthed and then ignored, shunted aside in the delegate-wooing, or in ticket-balancing in the wee hours in some room off the convention floor. Dwight Eisenhower took Richard Nixon in 1952 in order to win California; Adlai Stevenson took John Sparkman in 1952 and John Kennedy took Lyndon Johnson in 1960 to assuage the South; Nixon took Henry Cabot Lodge in 1960 for help in the industrial North and Spiro Agnew in 1968 to hold the critical border states; George McGovern in 1972 selected Thomas Eagleton and then Sargent Shriver as Catholics acceptable to big labor. All of them said they were choosing the best man available to be President, but the choices seldom could bear close scrutiny on those grounds. Barry Goldwater in 1964, in selecting Republican National Chairman William E. Miller of New York, a transparently flashy political con man and extreme partisan, at least had the decency not to try to varnish over his choice. He picked Miller, Goldwater said, "because he bugs Lyndon Johnson."

This kind of experience unfortunately had conditioned many voters to accepting mediocrity in vice-presidential candidates, to agreeing with John Nance Garner, Franklin D. Roosevelt's first Vice President, that the office was "not worth a bucket of warm spit." But several things had happened to change all that. First, there was the track record: since Truman's selection by Roosevelt in 1944, four of the last six presidents had been vice presidents—Truman, Johnson, Nixon, and Ford. Another Vice President, Humphrey in 1968, had barely missed the presidency. And had Agnew not been forced to resign in disgrace, he would have been a favorite to be his party's 1976 nominee. Also, the office had become functional within the executive branch—not, to be sure, to the satisfaction of the occupants, but nevertheless in ways that brought vice presidents considerable public attention and forums. The Eagleton affair too—dumping a running mate because a history of mental illness cast doubt on his ability to function as President —served in a negative way to underscore growing public concern about succession. Most important, there were the Agnew scandal, then Watergate and Nixon's resignation, which confronted the American people with their first unelected Vice President and then with the elevation of that man to become the nation's first unelected President. Selecting the No. 2 man was serious business, and deserved to be treated seriously.

Carter, whose canny sense of public opinion had already been amply demonstrated, was acutely aware of this growing concern. He also had a particular reason for wanting at his side an individual he could trust and depend on in the vice-presidency. As governor of Georgia, he had been plagued for four years by the presence as lieutenant-governor of his enemy Lester Maddox. Maddox had seldom missed an opportunity to harass Carter from his influential position as presiding officer of the State Senate, a number of whose members were Maddox men. The positions of lieutenant-governor and Vice President were not quite parallel, but there were enough similarities for Carter to know he wanted compatibility in his running mate.

Beyond all that, Carter took seriously for its own sake the possibility that the man he selected might be the next President, an attitude that soon became very clear. He also realized that in this choice on which some future administration might rest, the public would have its first view of him as a presidential decision-maker. He was determined to be thorough, careful, fair, and wise—as well as politically astute.

Actually Carter had started the procedure well in advance of his securing the nomination. In mid-April, even before he had won the Pennsylvania primary that drove Henry Jackson out of the race and made Carter the odds-on favorite, he had his staff draw up alternative methods on which he might proceed. Greg Schneiders and Ted Sorensen, among others, submitted memos. But Carter felt, and his aides concurred, that it was best to wait until he had clinched the nomination, lest he appear presumptuous. In early June, then, he had the staff compile a list of 300–400 prominent Democratic mayors, governors, members of the House and Senate, and other leaders, from which a short list of about two dozen prospects was culled. He also invited key staff aides to submit their recommendations.

Perhaps the memo that most helped to shape Carter's attitude was one marked "confidential" from Hamilton Jordan. Before Carter started talking to prospective running mates, Jordan wrote, "It is important that you have clear in your own mind the role that you would want the Vice President to play in the campaign and in a Carter administration. . . . Historically, the vice-presidency has not been a good job because the President has not allowed it to be. . . . There is always the campaign rhetoric about the Vice President playing an important role in the administration, but then, after the election, it turns into no more than a ceremonial job, frustrating to the people who have held it."

Jordan reviewed how Kennedy had picked Johnson "to balance the ticket," but Johnson "was viewed by the staff as a bumpkin not to be trusted," though Kennedy could have used Johnson's vast legislative skills to improve a "less-than-spectacular legislative record." And Johnson's "huge ego" in turn was threatened by the popularity of his Vice President, Humphrey. Jordan went on to talk about frictions that inevitably develop between staffs under these circumstances, and he told Carter he should pick someone whose abilities he really respected and whom he really intended to use, even bringing him directly into the White House.

In another memo, dated June 2, as part of a discussion of what Carter should do during the summer to firm up his image as a potential President, Jordan noted that the way he chose his running mate would be a critical component in the public perception of him. The vice-presidential decision would be the first "of presidential magnitude that you will make," and he observed that "in 1976 the best politics is to select a person who is accurately perceived by the American people as being qualified and able to serve as President if that became necessary." Jordan recommended most of the procedures Carter eventually followed, including a public demonstration of the care and thoroughness with which he approached the task.

As was his style, Jordan worked up a rating system for all Democratic U.S. senators, governors, and the most prominent mayors and members of the House, based on ability, integrity, and acceptance. He assigned a maximum of fifteen points for ability and integrity, and ten points for acceptance within the party and country, and then set about to learn what he could about each. The rating system produced five senators with the highest score: Alan Cranston of California, Abraham Ribicoff of Connecticut, Philip Hart of Michigan, Walter Mondale of Minnesota, and Mike Mansfield of Montana. Of these, only Mondale was a serious contender, although Carter also had particular regard for Ribicoff, who wasn't interested. Among the governors, Reubin Askew of Florida, Jerry Brown, Michael Dukakis of Massachusetts, and Patrick Lucey of Wisconsin led the list. From the House, Representative Thomas P. O'Neill, Jr., of Massachusetts, now the Speaker, Henry Reuss of Wisconsin, and Al Ullman of Oregon, now chairman of the House Ways and Means Committee, and among the mayors, Thomas Bradley of Los Angeles and Henry Maier of Milwaukee, had the highest ratings. But the listing of Governors, House members, and mayors was entirely cosmetic. Carter came to the conclusion at an early stage that he would probably have to select a senator, someone who knew his way around Washington and whose presence on the ticket could help counter the issue of inexperience in the national government that was sure to be raised by the Republicans if President Ford was to be their nominee, as Carter expected.

Along with these ratings, Jordan also made some very pointed observations about other prominent Democrats who did not scale as high, but were considered to be prospects. For obvious reasons of political diplomacy, Jordan later would not authorize my use of the names, but did agree to having some of the observations included here. They underscore the heavy public-relations aspect of listing certain people, either to make points with the prospects themselves or with a segment of the party. Putting names to the comments does not require a particularly vivid imagination. One said: "Might be a political advantage to be able to say he was under consideration. Otherwise, 'No' " Another: "Should only be considered for political advantage. Is not qualified to be President." And another: "Deserves public consideration because of early political support. Not qualified." And about one of Carter's competitors for the nomination: "Despite disgusting campaign tactics, he has a good record in Congress. Your public consideration of him would suggest you were not vindictive and would help with his supporters and with liberals." Needless to say, none of the recipients of these comments made the finals in Carter's deliberations.

In mid-June, Patrick Caddell and Hamilton Jordan decided that, without Carter's knowledge, a poll should be taken on obvious vice-presidential prospects. The *Boston Globe* got hold of it, to Carter's aggravation, and printed the results. It showed the best-known Democrats, like Kennedy and Muskie, running strongest, and was of little help.

Next, Carter started calling a list of about sixty prominent Americans in the Democratic Party, Congress, business, and labor for their views, meanwhile dispatching his most trusted friend, Charles Kirbo, to Washington to start asking questions. Soon Kirbo, a lanky, old-shoe lawyer, became a familiar if not readily recognized figure moving in and out of congressional and senatorial offices. He even contacted some of Washington's most knowledgeable reporters, like David Broder, for their views. Kirbo was becoming an object of considerable press attention, and he observed afterward that

"every time a reporter interviewed me, I interviewed him." Members of the
Georgia press specifically were asked to check with associates in the home
states of prospective candidates to find out what they could about their
"personal and political integrity."

Finally Kirbo set about interviewing personally, in the first week in
July, the seven men to whom Carter had decided he would talk himself:
Senators Muskie, Mondale, John Glenn, Church, Jackson, and Stevenson,
and Chairman Peter Rodino of the House Judiciary Committee. Congressman Brock Adams of Washington was another possibility whom many
people had suggested to Carter, but he was judged to be too little known.
Each was asked to fill out a questionnaire, drawn up by Kirbo and his law
partner, Griffin Bell, asking about past campaign contributions, marital
status, any arrest records, psychiatric treatment, tax audits, outside income,
and "anything in your personal life or that of a near relative which you feel,
if known, may be of embarrassment" in the election campaign. Also, each
was requested to furnish tax returns, complete financial statements, and
reports of physical examinations, which on receipt were turned over to tax
accountants and lawyers in Atlanta.

In all this, Greg Schneiders said later, Carter proceeded with a special
determination and seriousness "in light of the recent history" of the vice-
presidency. Carter was aware "that he was in an almost unique political
position: not needing to consider the best political choice so far as getting
the nomination was concerned, and being able to deal from a position of
strength going into the convention." For this reason, Schneiders said,
Carter recommended that in the future presidential nominees be given
thirty days in which to make their choice of a running mate. "He recognized
in his own case that sureness of nomination had made it possible for him
to make the best choice."

Carter's wide lead in the polls over President Ford, the expected Republican nominee, also affected his procedures, Schneiders said. "At that
time the feeling was that he *was* going to be President and he should start
acting like one in terms of a vice-presidential selection and any other major
decisions. In fact, acting in that way was the best politics."[1]

Carter's first inclination was to pick Church. "He thought Church was

1. In addition to those under consideration, some other candidates came forward on their own.
One day at the convention, Schneiders answered the phone and a man said he needed to see
Carter. Schneiders said he would take a message.
    "It's very important," the man said. "I have a suggestion on who he should choose for
Vice President."
    "Who?" Schneiders asked.
    "Me," the man said. "I'm unemployed." And then he added: "Look, I'm free all day. I
can see him at any time."

the most qualified, would add the most to the ticket, and also had the advantage of going through the primary system—a major consideration because Carter had made so much of going to the people in the primaries," Schneiders said. In fact, had Carter made the choice when he was vacationing at Sea Island right after the primaries, he probably would have gone ahead with Church. But he began to have reservations, not on the basis of any substantive information—none of the main prospects was eliminated as a result of derogatory information—but because of a lack of compatibility. Church was just not his kind of guy. As Carter thought about it, others came to the fore.

The first to be interviewed by Carter was Muskie. He impressed Carter with his independence. "He doesn't care if I like him or not," Carter told an aide later. But there was the Muskie temper, and a crankiness toward aides that bothered Carter. Carter said the fact that he was seeing Muskie first was of no importance, but he did observe that Muskie "has been willing to present himself to the American people"—a remark that seemed to be a crack at Mondale, who had folded his presidential campaign in November 1974 rather than face the ordeal Carter had so patiently endured.

Next it was Mondale's turn. His 1974 withdrawal of candidacy was, Schneiders said later, "the single most detrimental factor" working against him, and Carter himself acknowledged later that he at first "resented" Mondale's attitude. But everybody Carter or Kirbo asked was very favorable toward Mondale. Around the country he was held in great esteem, not only among fellow liberals but among all Democrats. And so Carter, though he said later he had feared Mondale was too liberal for the South and had been involved only in "peripheral issues" of national concern, decided to have a look for himself.

The two men had met only twice before, once in 1974 when Mondale was in Atlanta and dropped by to see the governor, and in early 1976, when Carter was on Capitol Hill and repaid the call very briefly. If Mondale had lost his interest in heading his party's ticket, the attraction in running for Vice President was strong. When it became clear that his mentor and fellow Minnesotan Hubert Humphrey was out of it, Mondale began to think he might be selected to give balance to Carter's ticket. And when Kirbo came around, Mondale and Richard Moe, his chief aide, gave serious thought to the matter. Mondale read all he could find about Carter, including his autobiography, *Why Not the Best?* He began, too, to map out how the vice-presidency might best function under Carter, considering what his special needs might be. "The more we learned about Carter," Moe said later, "the more we felt that that was what he would want to know from Fritz." Having been so close to Humphrey, one of recent history's more thoughtful (and frustrated) vice presidents, Mondale had a fairly firm concept of the office, and he thought it could be made into a useful one in the development of both foreign and domestic policy, especially for a President who had no Washington experience.

Mondale left for Plains with the book on Carter; he had boned up for the interview the way Carter himself predictably would have done had he been under consideration for the job. That made a distinct impression on Carter. "He found Mondale better prepared for the interview than anyone else, which was a funny, almost schoolboyish way of looking at it," Schneiders said. "But in fact Carter had a lot of respect for the thoroughness with which he came into it. He found Mondale very sure of himself, sure of who he was, of what he wanted, and what his ideas were about the vice-presidency. Mondale had studied Carter. Every question that came up on an issue, Mondale not only could spell out clearly and succinctly his own position but knew exactly what Carter's position was and where the two differed. He apparently had done a lot of homework."

Beyond that, the two men after an hour or so seemed simply to hit it off. "Carter kept emphasizing compatibility as a factor," Moe said later, "and we figured he meant not just personal but intellectual compatibility, and Fritz has a stimulating mind." The question of Mondale's pull-out in 1974 came up; Mondale explained that he wasn't adverse to campaigning so long as he thought he had a chance, but it had been clear he was going nowhere. Carter seemed to accept that. After the meeting, Carter was asked by reporters whether he was satisfied Mondale would be willing to undertake a vigorous campaign. "There is no doubt in my mind that he would be willing," Carter said.

Mondale broke in: "What I said at the time was that I did not want to spend most of my life in Holiday Inns. But I've checked and found they've all been redecorated. They're marvelous places to stay and I've thought it over and that's where I'd like to be."

Later the same day, Carter met with Glenn and pronounced him, too, "completely compatible." But from other reports, this personal encounter did not go nearly so smoothly or cordially as the Carter-Mondale meeting, and Glenn did not impress Carter as an intellect compared to the just-departed Mondale. Glenn would have to give an outstanding keynote address to the convention if he were to be a real contender. Still, his coming from the pivotal state of Ohio, and being so popular there, remained a strong point in Glenn's favor.

Once Carter got to New York, he met with the other four principal prospects—Jackson, Rodino, Stevenson, and Church—but by now aides were telling reporters that although Carter was continuing to keep his own counsel, he seemed to be focusing on the other three—Mondale, Muskie, and Glenn—and increasingly in that order. Labor wanted Mondale and was pointedly anti-Glenn. And even before Glenn delivered his keynote speech, the impression among insiders was that Carter had cooled on him. Then Glenn's bland and uninspired speech was largely ignored by the milling, chattering audience of delegates, and their tepid response seemed all the more so after Representative Barbara Jordan of Texas, the first black woman to give a Democratic keynote address and a heroine of the Nixon impeachment hearings, won a rousing reception immediately afterward, triggering a flow of telegrams to Carter to pick *her* as his running mate.

Carter, some aides said later, now was thinking more in terms of a Vice President who could step in and take over on Inauguration Day if necessary, and Glenn as a freshman senator with less than two years' Washington experience suffered by comparison with Mondale, who had nearly twelve years in the Senate, and Muskie, who had eighteen. Kirbo and Caddell were said to favor Muskie, but the younger members of the staff, including Jordan, reportedly wanted Mondale.[2]

With not much other real business to transact, the convention became a beehive of rumor about Carter's choice. Almost overshadowed by the hoopla was the fact that only four years after the divisive debacle of the McGovern nomination and campaign, the Democratic Party was together again. There was Humphrey, cheered on wildly, unleashing one of his patented partisan stem-winders: "The patriots of 1776 believed, and this party has always believed, that a democratic government must be an active force for the betterment of human life. But there are new Tories abroad in the land. And their words are newly fashionable. They appeal to cynicism. They cater to the people's mistrust of their own institutions. . . . They tell us our afflictions will be healed if we but leave them alone—if we seek private gain rather than public good. . . . There was no room for the Tories in Philadelphia in 1776. And I say there is no room for them in New York in 1976 or in Washington in 1977." Even more pointedly, there was McGovern, reminding his party of the cost of past division: "Eight years ago, some Democrats had doubts about Hubert Humphrey. And they gave us Nixon's first four years of war and domestic strife. Four years ago, some Democrats had doubts about me—and we got Nixon again. To repeat that sort of folly would be unconscionable. So let us unite around our candidate

---

2. David Broder told his colleagues at one point that he had learned exclusively how Carter would choose between Mondale and Muskie. Both would go to Carter's suite at the Americana Hotel, he said, and stand at opposite sides of the living room. Then Carter's young daughter, Amy, would come in and whomever she ran to first would be the nominee. This account could not be confirmed.

and retire the Republicans from the White House."

Four names were placed in nomination for President: Carter, Udall, Brown, and Ellen McCormack, the anti-abortion candidate. Udall promptly released his delegates and urged them to join him as "a soldier in the Carter campaign . . . Jimmy Carter is a good man who will make a strong President."

That was the mood in which the roll call for which Jimmy Carter had worked for four years finally came. The call of the states was anticlimactic, but the Carterites on the floor cheered anyway, as the majority was approached, and finally reached at 11:16 P.M. Ohio, the state whose primary hooked Dick Daley, George Wallace, and the Democratic Party for Carter, cast 132 votes for him and made him the nominee. Carter, sitting in his hotel suite, with television cameras watching him watch his own nomination on television, hugged his mother and said: "It has been a long time. I'm glad it's Ohio." As Amy and his grandson Jason scrambled onto his lap, the television cameras watched him watching his wife Rosalynn on the screen saying, "I miss Jimmy not being here with me," and he smiled. Then Governor Jerry Brown came on from the convention floor, announced California was going unanimously for Carter, and pledged his support. Brown had wanted to address the convention from the platform but had been refused, so he was taking what he could get. Finally a committee was appointed from the rostrum to call upon Carter and ask whether he would accept the nomination. Watching on television, he smiled again. "That's two decisions I'll have to make tonight," he said.

The original plan was for him to call the man he had chosen to be Vice President that night, but Carter decided to wait until morning. He instructed Schneiders to so inform all six finalists—Rodino had taken himself out because of eye trouble—and Carter went to bed, taking his decision with him: telling nobody, not Kirbo, not even his wife, or so the word went out later. Schneiders phoned all six to tell them Carter would be calling the next morning between eight-thirty and nine o'clock. Two hours before the appointed time, Mondale was up, working on an acceptance speech—just in case. When the phone rang at precisely eight-thirty, everybody in the room assumed it was Carter. Dick Moe answered and handed the phone to Mondale.

"Would you like to run with me?" Carter asked.

"Governor, I'm deeply honored and thrilled," Mondale said.

And that was it. Carter asked Mondale to tell no one. The Georgian said later he had informed his own wife of his choice only two minutes before the call to Mondale was placed. Even when the President of the United States phoned, shortly afterward, to congratulate him, Carter didn't tell Ford, either. And to keep the decision leakproof, when Carter phoned the five losers he merely told them they were not being picked, not who was —another remarkable demonstration of the Carter discipline.

His ability to keep a secret was not, however, the highlight of Carter's vice-presidential selection performance. The decision was, in a real sense, the most important he would be called upon to make as a presidential candidate. Beyond the popularity of his choice of Mondale within the party, the manner in which he arrived at the decision commended him for the presidency. His open and deliberative approach dramatically focused public attention on the importance of the vice-presidency, providing ample time and encouragement for information to surface about the aspirants. Thus, the chance of a repetition of the Eagleton affair was minimized. Also, his intense scrutiny of the prospects invited critical appraisal of his selection. He put himself under the gun by making so much of the whole business, and he clearly intended that the manner in which he reached it express his own executive ability.

As Carter himself noted, he had enjoyed the luxury of having time for a careful and leisurely approach to the problem; had he been engaged in a bitter fight for the nomination, he too might have dealt the vice-presidential nomination for delegates or, in the old tradition, dangled it before several individuals to gain their support with promises he could not keep. But he was able to take the high road, and he did: he treated the vice-presidential nomination with the respect and thought it warranted. Before the election of 1976 was over, he would have practical as well as aesthetic reasons to be satisfied that he had.

The final night of the convention was an unmitigated triumph. The conventioners, buoyed by their own display of party unity and by the overwhelming graciousness and good will of their host city, were in a celebrating mood. Cards that spelled out "Texas Loves New York City" flashed from the galleries; a huge bicentennial ball was sent bouncing sky-ward, from one delegation to another, volleyball style; there was community singing, and a rousing acceptance speech by the convention favorite, Fritz Mondale, featuring a frontal blast at the opposition: "We have just lived through the worst political scandal in our history and are now led by a President who pardoned the person who did it." The delegates erupted in noisy agreement. There was a sometimes poignant, sometimes hilarious film of Jimmy Carter's political rise, featuring cartoons of his now-famous grin (a row of glowing white teeth in the dark, with Rosalynn saying, "Jimmy, cut it out and go to sleep!"). And then, as Robert Strauss, the big, brassy, flamboyant riverboat gambler of a party chairman, introduced "the next President of the United States," Carter, his smile a mile wide, strode out from one side of the hall. Suddenly, unexpectedly, he was on the convention floor, walking through the cheering delegates, shaking hands on all sides, up from the people in a symbolic entry that seemed exactly right for the kind of campaign he had waged and won. He mounted the rostrum, walked directly to the microphone, and proclaimed exactly as he had done in hundreds of American towns and cities on his way to this place: "My name is Jimmy Carter, and I'm running for President."

The speech, and the delivery, were a tonic for this collection of Democrats who wanted something to cheer about. The film had softened them up; now Carter spoke dynamically, first to his own campaign warriors: "This has been a long and personal campaign—a humbling experience, reminding us that ultimate political influence rests not with power-brokers, but with the people. This has been a time for learning and exchange of ideas, a time of tough debate on the important issues facing our country. This kind of debate is part of our tradition, and as Democrats we are heirs to a great tradition." Next, he spoke to the party faithful: "I have never met a Democratic President, but I have always been a Democrat. . . ." And he ticked off his immediate predecessors: Franklin Roosevelt, "who inspired and restored this nation in its darkest hours"; Harry Truman, "who showed us that a common man could be an uncommon leader"; John Kennedy, "who called the young in heart of whatever age to seek a new frontier of national greatness"; Lyndon Johnson, "who took office in a tragic hour and who went on to do more than any other President in this century to advance the cause of human rights." He spoke to the "generations of immigrants" that had come into the party, and of the social and civil-rights legislation that marked its history. And then he turned his rhetoric on the opposition, calling for truth and justice in the administration of the government's affairs, spurring the convention to lusty cheers with a broadside at the whole sordid affair of Watergate and its aftermath: "It is time for our governmental leaders to respect the law no less than the humblest citizen, so that we can end the double standard of justice in America. I see no reason why big-shot crooks should go free while the poor ones go to jail."

Carter's speech was a lifting and all-embracing one and, for him, straighforwardly liberal. First Mondale, and now this; perhaps the liberals had been too hasty to judge. In any event, loyalists who were sure they knew Jimmy, and others who were not so sure, could come together in this moment in a spirit of hope and purpose.

Strauss, master of accommodation with all the subtlety of a nuclear explosive, orchestrated a grand finale that would have been comical had it not been for the good spirit of the moment. Suddenly he had *everyone* up on the rostrum with the triumphant, grinning Carter: Mo Udall and Scoop

Jackson and George Wallace and Abe Beame and Hubert Humphrey and Sarge Shriver and Brendan Byrne and Raul Castro and Moon Landrieu and even Strauss's wife, Helen. Like a drinker who has to have one more, and another, and one more after that, Strauss summoned literally dozens of the party's second- and third-string luminaries to the platform. Finally, unexpectedly, he introduced to give the benediction Daddy King, father of the civil-rights martyr, repository of a mountain of personal grief, friend and political benefactor of the new party standard-bearer. Before the convention knew what had hit it, Daddy King was preaching at the delegates, first jolting them into stunned silence. "I would like very much that we would cease walking, talking," he said. "In fact, not a word be uttered unless that word is uttered to God." Then he began coaxing murmurs and soon shouted responses of "Amen" from them, as if Madison Square Garden had in minutes been converted into a cavernous Baptist church. "Surely the Lord sent Jimmy Carter to come on out and bring America back where she belongs," he cried. ". . . As I close in prayer, let me tell you. We must close ranks now. If there's any misunderstanding anywhere, if you haven't got a forgiving heart, get on your knees. It's time for prayer." He preached and he flailed and he thundered; he worked up the audience to a Sunday-morning pitch, and when he had finished, he hugged his daughter-in-law, Coretta, Martin, Jr.'s, widow, as the conventioners joined hands and sang "We Shall Overcome," slowly and with conviction, somberly and with tears streaking down young and old faces alike. It was a fitting end to this greatest of nights for Jimmy Carter. If there were differences remaining in the Democratic Party, they were laid aside in this one emotional wave that swept over all reservations.

The fact was, however, that there *were* differences, and there *was* a lack of both conviction and commitment to Carter, especially among many of the liberals and the party regulars who had been beaten by this uncommon outsider. Still, there was plenty of time to bring them all under the tent. And the convention had made a start, a beginning successful beyond all expectations.

This optimistic outlook could be drawn especially in light of what had been happening in the other party. There, a fierce battle threatened to destroy what chance the minority Republicans had to retain the White House against Carter's challenge. To chart that battle, it is necessary now to return to New Hampshire in February; indeed, to go back even earlier, to the time, months before, when the essential elements of that initial and critical contest between Gerald Ford and Ronald Reagan first took shape.

part VII

**THE
DELEGATE
HUNT:
THE REPUBLICANS**

25. New Hampshire: Reagan's $90-Billion Problem

In August 1975 a package arrived at Ronald Reagan's Los Angeles office that was to be, perhaps more than any other single thing, the ultimate undoing of his political fortunes. It was the text of a speech written for him by Jeffrey Bell, an intense young conservative who came to Reagan's Washington staff with impeccable credentials from the Groton of the American right wing: he was a legislative representative and card-carrying member of the American Conservative Union.

Reagan for years had been offering up his same old speech, the anti-Washington diatribe about throwing the Democratic rascals out. But because the resident rascal was now a Republican, Jerry Ford, the old speech had no relevance. To use it intact against Ford would violate Reagan's Eleventh Commandment against attacking a fellow Republican, so a speech had to be concocted that would reshape the anti-Washington theme to be critical of the *status quo* under Ford, but not of him personally.

"Reagan had absolutely nothing to say," Bell recalled later, "so I hit on decentralization as his vision of the future. It was anti-Washington; he could talk about it without attacking Ford. People should have more control, and Washington less. You could get out of the old right-wing rut of calling for repeal of everything and saying that spending for things like education was bad. Instead, you could focus on programs being too remote. You didn't have to say, 'Abolish food stamps.' You could talk about controlling the program better at the local level."

And so Bell had gotten the assignment to write the new speech. He talked it out with other Reagan lieutenants—Californians Lyn Nofziger and Peter Hannaford, and David Keene, a former Agnew and James Buckley aide—but not much with John Sears, the campaign manager, and never with Reagan. "John was not keen about issues," Bell said. "Strictly speaking," Keene said, "everybody knew about the speech. I looked at it more from a rhetorical point of view, and assumed someone else was doing the analysis. My assumption later was that's what everyone did." When the text was finished, Bell shipped it off to California, where it was fielded by Hannaford and his side-kick, Mike Deaver.

Shortly after it arrived, Sears was talking to Hannaford on the phone. "Hey," Hannaford, a mild-mannered, unflappable, straight-shooting man, said, "the speech Bell sent out here is a helluva speech." Sears got a copy. "At first I thought it wasn't anything special," he recalled later. "It was very programmatic. It wasn't a cheer speech." He asked Nofziger what he thought. Now Nofziger was not one to look askance at some good, old-fashioned conservative rhetoric designed to make the Neanderthal heart beat faster. He was himself a galloping McKinleyite in political philosophy, and so he might have been expected to find Bell's speech a marvel of enlightenment. "I looked at the draft," he said, "and I saw that figure. It didn't seem realistic to me."

What Nofziger called "that figure" was a number that was soon to become a millstone around Ronald Reagan's neck—$90 billion, suggested as the saving that could be achieved by transferring a panoply of federal programs to the states for administration or quick death. It was, indisputably, a meat-ax figure that would win instant applause before a business audience—but also, if anybody was paying attention, serious scrutiny and questioning from Reagan's foes and the press. "It was bad stuff for anybody to be saying," Sears observed later, "but especially for a guy with Reagan's reputation"—that is, with a reputation for taking meat-ax approaches to complex problems.

Bell was well aware of the speech's potential to stir criticism. He produced page after page of questions likely to be raised, and answers to them—and shipped them out to Reagan along with the text so that Reagan would be prepared when inquiries came. But Bell had little confidence that Reagan would bother to read them. The governor's Washington campaign headquarters often prepared briefing books for him on issues, but Deaver and Hannaford would tell the Easterners they were wasting their time. "He won't read a briefing book," Bell was told. "He's a pro. He wings it." Such books had always been prepared for Richard Nixon, and Bell and Sears were believers in them. "John kept pushing them at Reagan," Bell said, "but it wouldn't take."

Sears, in reconstructing the genesis of Bell's speech later, said he had the idea that Reagan would put it in his file and save it for some special occasion. Therefore nothing was done at first to soften or refine it. In late September Reagan had a speech to give in Chicago, and Sears went to join him and the others there. Then and there Reagan "proceeded to give the damn thing before our very eyes," Sears recalled with bemused consternation.

Bell just as insistently contended that all of Reagan's key people, including Sears, had gone to Chicago to hear the speech because they knew how important it was. In any event, it was delivered, including the reference to a possible $90-billion savings in the federal budget.

"I don't know whether Reagan thoroughly read it himself beforehand or not," Sears said. "I rather think he jumped into his suit and went down to the airport and read it through on the way. By the time he delivered it, it was on the cards [Reagan's favorite three-by-five flip cards]."

Because the speech was to become so critical for months to both the fortunes and strategy of Reagan's and Ford's campaigns, it is instructive to study the pertinent section. After reviewing the federal dominance over states and localities in taxation against a background of high prices and low employment, Reagan said:

"This absorption of revenue by all levels of government, the alarming rate of inflation and the rising toll of unemployment all stem from a single source: the belief that government, particularly the federal government, has the answer to our ills, and that the proper method of dealing with social problems is to transfer power from the private to the public sector, and within the public sector from state and local governments to the ultimate power center in Washington. This collectivist, centralizing approach, whatever name or party label it wears, has created our economic problems. By taxing and consuming an ever-greater share of the national wealth, it has imposed an intolerable burden of taxation on American citizens. By spending above and beyond even this level of taxation, it has created the horrendous inflation of the past decade. And by saddling our economy with an ever-greater burden of controls and regulations, it has generated countless economic problems—from the raising of consumer prices to the destruction of jobs, to choking off vital supplies of food and energy.

"As if that were not enough," Reagan went on, moving now to his favorite culprit, "the crushing weight of central government has distorted our federal system and altered the relationship between the levels of government, threatening the freedom of individuals and families. The states and local communities have been demeaned into little more than administrative districts, bureaucratic subdivisions of Big Brother government in Washington, with programs, spending priorities, and tax policies badly warped or dictated by federal overseers. Thousands of towns and neighborhoods have seen their peace disturbed by bureaucrats and social planners—through busing, questionable education programs, and attacks on family unity. Even so liberal an observer as Richard Goodwin could identify what he correctly called the most troubling political fact of our age: that the growth in central power has been accompanied by a swift and continual diminution in the significance of the individual citizen, transforming him from a wielder into an object of authority."

Reagan was humming now, deeply into his view of the world of federal oppression. "It isn't good enough to approach this tangle of confusion," he continued, "by saying we will try to make it more efficient or 'responsive,' or modify an aspect here or there, or do a little less of all these objectionable things than will the Washington bureaucrats and those who support them. This may have worked in the past, but not any longer. The problem must be attacked at its source. All Americans must be rallied to preserve the good things that remain in our society and to restore those good things that have been lost. We can and we must reverse the flow of power to Washington; not simply slow it, or paper over the problem with attractive phrases or cosmetic tinkering. This would give the appearance of change but leave the basic machinery untouched. In fact, it reminds me of a short fable of Tolstoi's: 'I sit on a man's back, choking him and making him carry me, and yet assure myself and others that I am very sorry for him and wish to lighten his load by all possible means—except by getting off his back.' "

Now Reagan the clean broom was ready to offer his magic cleansing power: "What I propose is nothing less than a systematic transfer of authority and resources to the states—a program of creative federalism for America's third century." (One should note here that Reagan did specifically call for the transfer of "resources" along with functions—a fortuitous reference on which the whole later defense of the controversial proposal was to be constructed.)

"Federal authority has clearly failed to do the job. Indeed, it has created more problems in welfare, education, housing, food stamps, Medicaid, community and regional development, and revenue sharing, to name a few. The sums involved and the potential savings to the taxpayer arc large. *Transfer of authority in whole or part in all these areas would reduce the outlay of the federal government by more than ninety-billion dollars, using the spending levels of fiscal 1976. With such savings, it would be possible to balance the federal budget, make an initial five-billion-dollar payment on the national debt, and cut the federal personal income-tax burden of every American by an average of twenty-three per cent.* By taking such a step we could quickly liberate much of our economy and political system from the dead hand of federal interference, with beneficial impact on every aspect of our daily lives."

It was a whopping order, but the speech did not at first blush seem to be out of line with Reagan's general political philosophy. Nor did it fail to acknowledge there were some justifiable federal functions of national responsibility: "national defense and space, Social Security [attempts were made later to saddle Reagan with anti-Social Security Goldwaterite notions on this issue], Medicare and other old-age programs; enforcement of federal law, veterans affairs, some aspects of agriculture, energy, transportation, and environment; TVA [a second "Reagan is another Goldwater" problem later] and other multistate public-works projects; and certain types of research." But in sum it was a blueprint for a massive reduction in the federal bureaucracy and—though Reagan tried to deny it later—an open invitation to abandon many social-welfare programs at the state and local levels. "The decision as to whether programs are or are not worth while—and whether to continue or cancel—will be placed where it rightfully belongs: with the people of our states," Reagan said. "I think it likely . . . that some of the more worthwhile programs will be retained essentially as they are, many will be dropped, and others may be modified. But all the surviving programs will be run at much lower cost than is presently the case." And although he later tried to deny this, too, Reagan recognized as he spoke in Chicago that his proposal could mean the raising of more taxes locally to take up the slack. "As long as the system continues to function on this basis," he said, "we are going to see expenditures at every level of government soar out of sight. The object is to reverse this: to tie spending and taxing functions together wherever feasible, so that those who have the pleasure of giving away tax dollars will also have the pain of raising them."

Sears said later that he and the others listening to the speech recognized at once they were in the soup. That was what happened, this consummate pragmatist said, when ideologues got involved. "There's no question we'd have been better off if Reagan had never given it," Nofziger said. But Bell insisted that "Sears came back saying he thought it was good, and suggested we do a string of them on Reagan's 'vision.'" In any event, Reagan's camp had a temporary reprieve because the speech was largely overlooked by the press. Only one national, Washington-based reporter was present, Martin Schram of *Newsday*, and he focused on trying to discern whether Reagan really was going to run for President. As Reagan's party rode to the airport afterward with Schram in the car interviewing Reagan, Sears held his breath. Schram concentrated on strategy and never asked a question about the $90-billion proposal. Schram finally wrote a story quoting Reagan as saying only a "truly unforeseen" event such as the outbreak of war in the Middle East would stop him from challenging Ford. Schram did, however, alert *Newsday*'s desk about the $90-billion reference and three paragraphs were incorporated at the end of his story. The mention drew little attention. One local reporter, Joel Weisman, then reporting in the Midwest for *The Washington Post*, filed a story about the plan, but it ran inside the paper and also got little public attention. Reagan seemed home free on $90 billion.

What Reagan's camp did not know at the time, however, was that

Stuart Spencer, Ford's chief political strategist, having seen the *Post* story, recognized the potential for mischief at once. In Chicago for a Republican state chairmen's meeting a few weeks later, Spencer phoned Weisman, who was glad to discuss the speech at length. "He thought it was a page-one story," Spencer said later, laughing. "He was pissed off at the *Post.*"

Spencer got hold of a text of the speech and turned it over to Peter Kaye, Ford's campaign press secretary, who set to work to ambush Reagan with it in New Hampshire. Kaye put Fred Slight, the Ford committee's director of research, on the project and by November 19, the day before Reagan was formally to declare his candidacy, Slight sent Kaye an internal memorandum that seized on the vulnerabilities of the $90-billion plan and recommended ways to exploit them.

"Reagan's simplistic solution to what is obviously a complex area is a bit overwhelming to analyze," Slight wrote. Many of the programs Reagan was targeting were mandated by law, and only about 20 per cent were subject to a President's "discretionary authority." Reagan could be asked whether his proposals would require the federal government to renege on funds committed to states and localities, how he hoped to get it through a Democratic Congress, and how states and localities already under financial strain could be expected to take up the slack. Slight said that Reagan's plan could be attacked for being likely to lead to high unemployment, bankruptcy or fear of it for states and localities, increased local business taxes, and retardation of recovery in housing and other construction. The proposal, he concluded, "is completely out of touch with reality."

Slight also hoped to come up with a complete state-by-state breakdown of the effect of the $90-billion plan and had asked James Lynn, then director of the Government's Office of Management and Budget to provide it. But Lynn failed to do so—an indication of some of the committee's early troubles getting cooperation from the executive branch. Spencer and Kaye wanted to know first, of course, what the plan's effect would be on New Hampshire, which had no state sales or income tax and which clearly would have to institute one or the other, or both, if federal programs suddenly were dumped back on the states.

The day after Reagan entered the race, he was asked a general question about the $90-billion plan at a press conference in Bedford, New Hampshire, but he sloughed it off without incident. The next Sunday, however, on ABC News' "Issues and Answers," Frank Reynolds nailed him. Reynolds told Reagan that the federal government paid 62 per cent of New Hampshire's total outlay for welfare and observed, "That means New Hampshire has to either assume that or cut it down [under your plan]."

Reagan acknowledged that was true: "I think that you would have to have taxes increased at state and local levels to offset this, or to maintain some of these programs." If the federal government "stopped pre-empting so much of the tax dollar," the states and localities could take some taxes over, too.

But correspondent Bob Clark pointed out the special circumstances in New Hampshire. "In candor, wouldn't you have to tell the people of New Hampshire that you are going to have to increase your tax burden and that probably means either a sales tax or a state income tax?"

Reagan replied, "But isn't this a proper decision for the people of the state to make?"

Such responses were clearly inadequate in political terms. Bell was distressed, because Reynolds and Clark had not asked Reagan anything that hadn't been covered in the back-up Q-and-A he had prepared and sent to California with the original speech. "It worried me, it really did, that he couldn't come up with better answers," Bell lamented. "I guess people saw it as a plunge into right-wing fanaticism, but it didn't seem so at the time." And so he set about preparing more defenses. Meanwhile Sears, also concerned, persuaded Martin Anderson, his old friend and colleague from the early Nixon presidential years and a look-alike of David Eisenhower ("David without the Howdy Doody quality," somebody said), to deal with the hot potato.

From time to time the $90-billion plan would surface in the news community, as in a Washington breakfast Jimmy Carter held with political reporters, where he called it "ridiculous." But nobody wrote much about it. An early-warning signal came about two weeks after the "Issues and Answers" show in a column by Rowland Evans and Robert Novak that correctly reported that the $90-billion plan "has become the secret worry of [Reagan's] political managers" and "now threatens to be an albatross around his neck." The column told of the enlistment of Marty Anderson to help find a way out and concluded, "The Reagan campaign embraced, needlessly in hindsight, a proposal bearing high political risks. Even if the risks are ultimately avoided, Reagan must begin his campaign partly on the defensive—losing the nonincumbent's greatest advantage."

The issue sat there, like a time bomb, throughout December as Reagan, surging ahead in the national polls, got ready to blitz New Hampshire first thing after New Year's Day. And Peter Kaye was setting the timer. At the Ford campaign headquarters, he and Stu Spencer were running the project themselves, asking no questions about whether to do it or not, making sure nobody tried to shoot them down. Kaye went to New Hampshire to get the lay of the land and coordinate with his chief press aide there, John Breen, then went back home to California for Christmas and prepared some anti-

$90-billion press releases there. Two prominent New Hampshire Republicans, State Senate President Alf Jacobson and House Speaker George Roberts, were recruited to be the front men in the attack. On the day Reagan was to arrive in the state, January 5, Ford workers distributed press releases to reporters in New Hampshire and in Washington. And as Reagan was flying in from Los Angeles, Jacobson and Roberts held a press conference in Concord, raising the specter of new and higher state taxes as the price of Reagan's folly. The plan, Roberts said, "would cost the people of New Hampshire tens of millions of dollars just to maintain the existing mandated programs at their present level" and would force New Hampshire "to eliminate many necessary programs, to add to the local property-tax burden, or to institute a state sales tax, a state income tax, or both."

This last reference to the possibility of a sales or state income tax was political dynamite. Reagan's ally, Governor Meldrim Thomson, had won two terms largely on a no-new-taxes pledge; talk of imposing either tax on the voters was a red flag. Reagan, Roberts said, should "come down from the lofty peak of rhetoric and tell the people of New Hampshire in specific terms how he would implement his proposal."

Reagan, for his part, did not need to be briefed on Ford's strategy. The moment his plane touched down in Manchester—and awaiting Ford workers handed the anti–$90-billion press releases to the disembarking traveling press—he tried to lance the boil. "The people of New Hampshire, I understand, are worried that I have some devious plot to impose the sales or income tax on them," he told the reporters. "Believe me, I have no such intention and I don't think there is any danger that New Hampshire is getting one." And in Moultonboro, his first 1976 stop, he told two hundred people gathered in the Lions' Club hall: "I have no intention, with anything I have proposed, that New Hampshire should have either a sales or income tax." But the matter was not to be so easily banished. Spencer and Kaye had effectively injected it into the bloodstream of his campaign; the press took hold and was not going to let go for another seven weeks, until primary day, and not even then.

The tiny town of Moultonboro was a fitting place for a New Hampshire campaign to begin: a shivering horse with carriage and a team of three howling Eskimo dogs with sled awaited Ronald Reagan in the snow outside the hall. To keep the traveling television crews happy, Reagan was to ride in both carriage and sled. But the weather was so ferocious that the dogs were left barking and the horse was dismissed with a passing pat as the candidate went directly into the warm hall. Here he held the first of many "citizens' press conferences"—a few words of greeting, then the fielding of questions from the floor. This tactic was a risk, but a calculated one. Sears well knew that a heavy cloud of doubt hung over Reagan the Campaigner. In California, he had the reputation of being lazy and reluctant on the stump, a man who tired easily and was wont to fly off the handle or blurt out politically damaging remarks if he approached the ragged edge. But Sears knew also that Reagan, veteran of countless Hollywood sets and on-location sites, was a trooper in the old theatrical tradition. And so he charted a grueling schedule that at the very outset would lay to rest the old image, the speculation about the candidate's brittleness and his unwillingness to face interrogation. The schedule called for seventeen stops in less than three days, each of them featuring open Q-and-A sessions with the public—but, notably, not with the press.

Sears, as a veteran of the 1968 Nixon campaign in which the press was successfully held at bay for nearly a year, understood well the value of that tactic. But he understood also that the press once burned was twice cautious. And he knew that what had worked for Nixon in 1968 would not work for Reagan in 1976. First, reporters had come to understand, though belatedly, that Nixon's campaign in 1968 had faked them out: by being available but sparingly and only on his terms, Nixon had effectively neutralized them, had muffled their voice as the Greek chorus of the preconvention process. Reporters had been reduced to griping in print about their lack of access to him, when they might more profitably have been asking where Nixon stood on the issues, especially Vietnam. Much had been written between 1968 and 1976 about this failure; now, veteran political reporters were sensitive to the criticism and determined not to be similarly trapped. Second, Sears knew that in Nixon he had been dealing with a man almost paranoid in his concern about spontaneous exposure to press and public. But now, he had a man who could take such exposure in stride. Indeed, Reagan had learned as an actor to capitalize on the spontaneous; he had a feel for live audiences; he knew how to gauge an audience's mood, and how to play on it. Far from having to be concerned about public exposure, this was an element of Reagan's political strength.

There were, for all that, definite risks in giving Reagan his head in public, in letting him run on unmonitored, because Ford's strategists were determined, both in New Hampshire and in Florida, to paint him as another Barry Goldwater. It would not, after all, be hard to do: Reagan had built his early national reputation as a conservative political speaker largely on the basis of a fund-raising speech he had made for Goldwater on television in 1964. He was still a Goldwater man, he would tell anyone who asked, and he still believed Goldwater had preached the True Gospel in 1964; Barry had been unfairly treated by the press. And Goldwater himself might have proposed the $90-billion plan; it sounded like one of his schemes. Also,

Reagan's repeated criticism of the Social Security system reminded many of Goldwater's disastrous proposal in 1964 to make the system voluntary; the Ford forces were trying to hang that on him, too. Doubtless with that danger in mind, Reagan in Moultonboro assured the state's senior citizens that while he was not enamored of the Social Security system, they did not have to worry about having their benefit checks shut off by him. The federal budget had to be balanced, he said, but "changing benefits of any kind or reducing Social Security is not the way to go."

No matter how fond Reagan was of Goldwater, it was clear that he did not want to carry Barry's mad-bomber image. Goldwater-like controversies—the $90-billion flap and Social Security—had to be confronted head-on. And so, in a school gymnasium in Conway that first night, Reagan launched the defense of his $90-billion scheme. "Last fall," he said at a citizen's press conference, "I proposed that we take a good, hard look at programs run from Washington which add up to about one-quarter of what Washington spends. Very simply, it has concerned me that many programs that Washington administers aren't efficient and don't really help the people they were designed to help. I suggested that we consider them prime candidates for an orderly, phased transfer to state and local governments. This was not a budgetary proposal but one for transfer of control—authority and responsibility—from the federal government to those closer to the people. The people, through their state and local governments, would and should decide if they wanted to expand, modify, change, or replace these programs, and how best to do so."

His idea, Reagan said, wasn't new; presidents of both parties had embraced it in one form or another—Roosevelt, Kennedy, Eisenhower. Roosevelt "said the federal government should get out of the business of welfare," Reagan noted; Kennedy "protested against centralizing all authority in Washington"; Eisenhower established a commission of twenty-five distinguished Americans to study intergovernmental relations. Reagan quoted from its report: "Whenever possible, decisions to spend and decisions to tax should be made at the same governmental level, thus encouraging financial responsibility. Reserve national action for residual participation where state and local governments are not fully adequate, and for the continuing responsibilities that only the national government can undertake." Among the authors of this heresy, Reagan said, were Clark Kerr, his old nemesis as president of the University of California, the late Senator Wayne Morse of Oregon and—of all people—one of the big federal spenders of all time, Senator Hubert Humphrey. Reagan quoted Eisenhower in a 1957 speech to a National Governors' Conference, calling for "a task force to designate functions which the states were ready and willing to assume and that were being financed in whole or in part by the federal government in order to recommend those federal-state revenue adjustments required to enable the states to assume such functions." That was really all he was proposing, Reagan said, not some quickie, one-shot magic-wand budget cut and tax cut of $90 billion.

This new speech was the product of the hard-nosed rescue operation run chiefly by Marty Anderson. Riding back to our motel that snowy night after the Conway speech, Anderson began to grapple aloud with the major difficulty in Reagan's plan—how to finance the costly federal programs that were to be dumped in local and state governments' laps. Didn't Eisenhower at one time talk about relinquishing certain federal excise taxes to the states and localities, such as taxes on telephone use?

By the next day Reagan was beginning to tackle this major vulnerability. In a small church in the north-country town of Milan, he said some savings could be achieved by eliminating the "freight charge" incurred in collecting federal taxes locally, sending them to Washington, and having a portion returned under revenue-sharing and federal grants. Such taxes simply could "stay home" for local use. Also, he suggested, federal overhead could be reduced and states, when confronted with having to finance transferred programs, might "decide you didn't need them" and they would be dropped.

The Reagan defense did not halt the Ford team's attacks. Bo Callaway, Ford's campaign manager, told a breakfast meeting of reporters in Washington that Reagan was stuck with "a $90-billion boondoggle." He warned that "the American people will not tolerate going back to a system where you don't take care of people in need. The American people don't want elderly people thrown out in the snow." Also, he said, "they are not going to put up with a program that cuts back on Social Security." Despite Reagan's specific assurances that Social Security would not be affected, Callaway was slapping the old Goldwater label on him.

At every stop during a two-day tour of New Hampshire's sparsely populated north, Reagan worked to dispel any negative impressions his plan had fostered and to field voters' questions about it. The format enabled him to project an impression of openness and candor, with a modicum of risk. Questions from the crowd tended to be generalized and repetitive, such as, "Will you explain your 90-billion-dollar plan?" In response, he could serve up his stock answer, seldom being drawn into the kind of discussion and detail likely to be spawned by interrogation from experienced reporters who had heard the answer at previous stops and insisted on more specifics.

And soon Reagan *was* ready with specifics, courtesy of Marty Anderson. "He could pan-unscramble an egg," Nofziger said later in admiration of Anderson. In a speech at Keene Junior High School on his next trip to New Hampshire, Reagan suggested that $8 billion in federal liquor and cigarette taxes, plus unspecified other federal excise taxes, could be turned over to the states to help pay for his plan. The figure was a far cry from $90 billion, but he also said a portion of federal personal-income taxes "could be earmarked and kept in each state." The new Reagan strategy was evident: to try to convert the $90-billion sow's ear into a political silk purse.

In his car that afternoon, Reagan told me that his Los Angeles pollsters, Decision-Making Information (DMI), had found that New Hampshire voters were in agreement with the basic thrust of his plan—that Washington was too powerful, that it was involved in too many activities, and that everybody would be better off if many of the programs were handled closer to home. When I asked him whether the whole $90-billion flap hadn't thrown his campaign on the defensive when he needed to take the offensive against an incumbent President, Reagan said, "I'm not on the defensive at all, and in fact I'm going to do a little attacking. I haven't wavered one iota."

The polls, by Dick Wirthlin of DMI, did indeed seem to indicate support for what the Reagan people preferred to call the "transfer plan." For a time, Sears said later, "we were getting a little reverse English on it," because the suggestion from Ford's camp that Reagan would raise local taxes clashed with the public perception of him, and hence was not believed. But for all his denials Reagan *was* very definitely on the tactical defensive. Bell, for one, was frustrated by that posture. He knew about the favorable polls and thought Reagan could turn the matter around and make a plus of it, if he used the right approach. "I was going up the wall," he said. A major problem was the difference between how the campaign was seen from Washington and how it was viewed up close—and erroneously, in Bell's view—by the staffers traveling with the candidate in New Hampshire. "Reagan was on the defensive because we worried too much about the press," he said. "When the press kept writing about the ninety billion dollars, this bothered the traveling staff especially, and they were convinced it was really hurting Reagan, though the polls were refuting that." Sears and Jim Lake, Reagan's New Hampshire coordinator, told him, Bell said, that "we wanted to disguise the fact it was not hurting, so Ford wouldn't attack Reagan as an inexperienced warmonger, which was what we always feared would happen."

If the Reagan campaign in fact wanted to draw fire on the transfer plan to keep its man out of range on other, more vulnerable issues, it suceeded. Not only the press but President Ford began to unload on Reagan's $90 billion. Appearing before reporters at a briefing on his fiscal 1977 federal budget, Ford labeled Reagan's massive proposals "totally impractical" and said he could not "imagine fifty states having all of these programs dumped on them and then have to increase taxes if they want the programs continued." He ignored Reagan's explanation about paying for the transferred programs with simultaneously transferred tax authority. Finally campaigning in New Hampshire in early February, Ford kept hammering away in his deceptively folksy, nice-guy manner. In a speech at a Nashua Chamber of Commerce dinner (at which he inexplicably was obliged to give Nashua's Man of the Year award to one Sam Tamposi, Reagan's finance chairman in the state—an advance man's nightmare), the President pushed federal revenue-sharing as a way to help cities and states that "doesn't require you to raise local taxes."

It was not that Ford's people were unaware of what Sears called the "reverse English" on the transfer-plan idea. They knew the basic anti-Washington core of it was popular. But they were willing to risk that in order to gain a tactical advantage, to throw Reagan off-stride and make him spend valuable weeks explaining himself, when as the challenger it would have been more effective for him, and more trouble for them, if he had been on the attack. "We proved the benefit of some kind of attack in a campaign," Bob Teeter, Ford's pollster, said later. "If you don't point out the deficiencies in the other campaign, nobody will do it for you. You can create the issue, you can affect the perception of the individual, and you put that campaign under some pressure. They've got to spend time and effort figuring out how to react to what you're doing. And when they're under that pressure, you begin to see them making more mistakes."[1]

Stu Spencer thought that Reagan's strategists also erred in overexposing their candidate in New Hampshire, eroding what Spencer called Reagan's "star quality" and reducing him to just another politician on the make. The matter of candidate exposure was something very much in the minds of the Ford planners, because they had in the presidency a mixed blessing. They found that when Ford went out to campaign, he gained in the locality he visited but hurt himself elsewhere, spending too much of the incumbency's political currency and seeming to be less "presidential."

It was therefore prudent to use Ford sparingly on the stump and to attack Reagan, preferably with surrogates, thus keeping the President out

---

1. At one point in New Hampshire, the White House almost blew the $90-billion issue itself. In Ford's legislative proposals for the new Congress, word got out he was planning to suggest turning back portions of federal Medicaid and certain education programs to the states. Reagan immediately began to tell audiences that what he was proposing couldn't be all that bad if the President himself was suggesting the same basic approach. Such contradictions were maddening for those in the Ford political operation trying to keep Reagan on the defensive.

of the cross fire. In that regard, with Reagan shuttling between New Hampshire and Florida,[2] one other issue that had been pegged more for a Florida reaction than for New Hampshire—Social Security—began to bite against Reagan in the Granite State. The Ford operators got the ball rolling with an allegation distributed in a form press release by local Ford headquarters in New Hampshire and other primary states. A space was left blank to insert the name of the local committee spokesman and it read: "Over the last 12 years, _____ said, Reagan has at various times advocated voluntary Social Security, praised the present system and favorably called attention to a voluntary plan that would ruin it." When one of the press releases fell into enemy hands, Reagan charged Ford's campaign with tactics that "come under the heading of dirty tricks." In the post-Watergate era, that phrase had nasty overtones. Of the press release, Reagan said in Milford: "_____ is a liar. . . . To strike fear in the hearts of those who depend on Social Security is the cheapest kind of demagoguery. Nothing could be more despicable." Reagan said he believed "that Jerry Ford, the President, is a fair and honorable man. And I cannot make myself believe that he had a hand in some of the things his lieutenants are doing."

The press release should have alerted Reagan to the pitfalls of loose talk about Social Security. Still, being Ronald Reagan, he could not resist criticizing the system as poorly managed. He liked to tell listeners that it had an "imbalance of two and a quarter trillion dollars" and that while current recipients would get their monthly checks, there could be severe trouble down the road. It was true enough that if everyone in the Social Security program suddenly had to be paid off and workers suddenly stopped paying into the fund, a serious imbalance would exist. But such a circumstance was not a reality. The fund was lagging because high unemployment had reduced expected revenues from the tax on income.

In a speech in Florida, Reagan began to explain things that *could* be done—and got into more hot water. He quoted some economists as proposing that Social Security funds be invested in the "industrial might of the nation's economy." The Ford people jumped on this one with both feet. Secretary of Commerce-designate Elliot Richardson, campaigning in behalf

---

2. Of the two candidates, Reagan's travel schedule taxed his campaign treasury much more heavily, and the Supreme Court's ruling on January 30 that the composition of the FEC was unconstitutional aggravated his financial situation, by requiring a hiatus in the flow of the federal campaign subsidy. As with the Democratic candidates, the effect was not felt at once by either Reagan or Ford, because the Court allowed the FEC a grace period, and then an extension to March 22. In time, though, Reagan would definitely feel the squeeze—much more so than Ford. The President could simply have Uncle Sam bill him for the use of *Air Force One,* whereas Reagan had to pay cash to charter his campaign plane, as well as for other expenses.

of the President in New Hampshire, said of that approach: "You could be putting the United States government in controlling interest in every industry in the United States." He compared the scheme to a proposal in Britain that had been denounced as "wild-eyed socialism." The groundwork thus laid, President Ford picked up the issue. "Oh, it is easy to say that the Social Security trust fund upon which some thirty-two million Americans older and disabled in our society depend," he said, " . . . should be invested in the stock market, making the federal government a major stockholder in most American businesses. But that is the best blueprint for back-door socialism that I ever heard."

Again, Reagan was on the defensive. He had never wanted to invest the Social Security trust fund "in the stock market," he said. Besides, the idea wasn't his, only one he had heard some economists offer. He wasn't advocating that approach himself. He was not, he insisted, "a back-door, a front-door, or a through-the-window Socialist." But despite Reagan's denials, nice-guy Jerry Ford, who had been around politics a long time and knew how to use his elbows, kept repeating the allegation.

Spencer, viewing the maneuvering from the other side later said: "We had to get Reagan off-balance on that first trip in, and I think we succeeded. His trip was a floppo. He didn't take New Hampshire by storm. He was up there three days or so and he staggered around on that ninety-billion-dollar flap, and then immediately he went to Florida and we nailed him on Social Security. That kind of evened up the game in New Hampshire, and from there on it was a horse race."

Another time-honored barometer measured the dip in Reagan's fortunes. From the back of the press bus came the first home-made song of the 1976 campaign, to the tune of "Give Me the Simple Life":

> Cut 90 billion, make it a trillion,
> Just call me Ron the Knife;
> This old vaudevillian can save you a zillion,
> I'll give you the simple life.
>
> Aid to the old folks, it's good as gold, folks,
> I'll keep you free from strife;
> Barry's a cruel hoax, I won't play his jokes,
> I'll give you the simple life.
>
> And all those cheats who want a free ride,
> I'll guarantee to turn them loose;
> And all who break the law will be fried,
> Just watch me cook their goose.
>
> I may be crazy, but I'm not lazy,
> I campaign from dawn to night;

Fresh as a daisy, by keeping it hazy,
I'll give you the simple life.

Though Reagan was drawing some ridicule from the press, he remained a tremendous attraction in New Hampshire. It nearly always
seemed to be the movie-star quality that appealed to voters, that turned
them on. If his film career was a magnet for crowds, however, it also was
a reminder that he had spent much of his adult life play-acting. And
Reagan, for his own part, could not resist squeezing all he could out of a
role. Traveling with him on the campaign trail was a never-ending excursion
into fantasy. To illustrate the evils of excessive and inefficient bureaucracy,
and to justify his transfer plan that would substitute local and state vigilance
for federal gullibility in dispensing taxpayers' money, he liked to tell about
the man from New Jersey who stopped receiving his veteran's benefits check
because the VA notified him he was dead. When the man went down to the
VA office to protest, Reagan reported, they said the best they could do for
him was to give him the $700 that the law allowed for his burial. Or there
was the case of the lumber mill in Missouri that was ordered by the Environmental Protection Agency to reduce its smoke. It sent to Milwaukee for the
necessary antipollution devices and was told the delivery couldn't be made
because EPA had closed down the Milwaukee plant because it was too
noisy. Or the one about EPA having forty-one "lobbyists" on Capitol Hill,
which on examination turned out to be six.

Then there was Reagan's straight-faced report that small businessmen
and farmers are obliged to fill out ten thousand forms a year for various
federal programs, and that if all the federal paperwork were piled up, it
would fill four (sometimes five, he said) baseball stadiums. One could just
see the endless line of lower-echelon bureaucrats pushing wheelbarrows
crammed with government papers into Washington's Robert F. Kennedy
Stadium during the off-season just to provide that intriguing statistic.

Among the best were Reagan's stories about the "welfare queen" in
Chicago and Taino Towers in New York. "There's a woman in Chicago,"
he was fond of recounting, "who has eighty names, thirty addresses, and
twelve Social Security cards, and is collecting veterans' benefits on four
nonexistent deceased husbands." The woman, always unidentified, collected so much on her Social Security cards, Medicaid, food stamps, and
welfare, Reagan liked to say, that "her tax-free cash income alone is over
a hundred and fifty thousand dollars." In his never-ending diatribe against
"welfare chiselers," the woman in Chicago was the centerpiece. The trouble
was, though, that the woman, eventually identified by Chicago welfare
authorities as Linda Taylor, was actually convicted with using *two* aliases,

not eighty, and with receiving about $8000 fraudulently, not $150,000. Even after these facts were published—in an excellent article in *The Washington Star* by John Fialka—Reagan continued to tell the original story.

His other favorite was about New York's subsidized housing project, Taino Towers. "If you are a slum dweller you can get an apartment with eleven-foot ceilings, a twenty-foot balcony, a swimming pool and gymnasium, laundry room and play room, and the rent begins at a hundred and thirteen dollars and twenty cents and that includes utilities," he would say. The digs also had, according to Reagan, a doorman and indoor parking with twenty-four-hour security. But Fialka learned from the project's coordinator in East Harlem that only 92 of 656 units had high ceilings, and these were in six-bedroom units for large families that paid from $300 to $450 a month, depending on income. Also, the pool, gym, and other facilities were public, shared with the surrounding community of 200,000 Puerto Ricans and blacks.

It was ironic that during a primary in which one of the Democratic contenders, Jimmy Carter, was under extreme scrutiny for possible dissembling after having promised never to lie to or mislead the voters, Reagan could repeatedly get away with such incredible whoppers. But then he had never said, like Carter, that he would rather die than tell a lie or mislead. Ronald Reagan was, after all, an entertainer, and he certainly entertained.

By contrast, Ford on the stump was a sympathetic, but dull, plodder. When he did campaign in New Hampshire, less than three days in the state all told, he tried mainly to convey the idea that there were few ideological differences between himself and his challenger, and hence the voters would be wise to opt for experience in federal officeholding. "I've got a record," he told a news conference at the University of New Hampshire. "The public knows what my record is. If they want to compare it to the rhetoric and words of former Governor Reagan, I think that would be a very legitimate study for the American people to make. We can't say one thing and do another. We have to deal with reality, and we have. When the chips are down, I think the people will want a proven quality, rather than one who has never had to make those hard decisions. . . . We know some things about running the federal government."

Some hecklers from the People's Bicentennial Commission, an anti–big-business environmentalist group that had been trailing Reagan around the state, needled Ford, but he turned them aside by telling them that "blind criticism is no better than blind hate." The audience of about 3500 cheered and applauded. Subsequently Governor Thomson, while otherwise ignoring him, wrote the President a letter apologizing for "the rude, uncouth, and ill-mannered behavior of that small minority of malcontents" whose performance was "a stunning indictment of the time we live in." Ford wrote back acidly that the occasion was no such thing, but "rather, we witnessed a triumphant testimonial to the desire of free men and women to assert their rights to listen to a President whose views were unpopular with a noisy minority of the audience." (Among those who so asserted their rights that night was a student dressed as a gorilla who actually asked a question of a somewhat startled President of the United States, and got an answer. Presumably this was the same ape-clad student who had queried Reagan once before, perhaps as a reminder to Reagan of an old co-star in the movie *Bedtime for Bonzo.*)

Ford's first New Hampshire trip also was greeted by a front-page editorial in the notorious Manchester *Union-Leader,* in which its publisher, William Loeb, called the President "devious Gerald" (an improvement on an earlier Loeb nickname, "Jerry the Jerk"). The editorial might have been yet another page in the newspaper's long history of harassment of presidential candidates, but for some reason Loeb in 1976 pulled his punches. A reason may have been the publication at the time of an extremely critical book called *Who the Hell Is William Loeb?* by Kevin Cash, a one-time *Union-Leader* reporter, that became an immediate best-seller in New Hampshire.

Peter Kaye, however, inspired an attack from Loeb by saying at one point that "New Hampshire is a difficult state to organize. It's a hell of a state to walk in. Because if you go forty miles outside the city there's nothing but trees and bears." White House press secretary Ron Nessen also rubbed Loeb the wrong way by saying New Hampshire skiing was too icy. On the President's first visit, Nessen wore a large button that said: "Ski New Hampshire." But in dealing with these incidents, Loeb was mild compared to how he had been in the past with critics of his beloved state. (Loeb made his home, however, in Massachusetts.)

These and other incidents, taken together with Ford's unimpressive campaign style, and the consistently very large crowds for Reagan, all worked to create an impression as primary day approached that President Ford was in deep trouble in New Hampshire. Though it was true that his campaign had very deftly forced Reagan on to the defensive and kept him there, Reagan was running comfortably ahead in the polls. An indication that the Ford people realized there was a gap to close came in a press conference by the President about a week before the vote. Although he had suggested earlier that since there was not much to choose between himself and Reagan on ideological grounds, experience was the issue, he now insisted that Reagan was "to the right of me philosophically" and could not beat the Democratic nominee in November.

The charge gave Reagan a chance to play a big card he was holding, and he tossed it on the table with evident self-satisfaction at a press conference in Manchester the Friday night before the election. "I'm a little surprised by this statement about my so-called extremism," Reagan said, grinning. "It does come rather strange because he tried on two different occasions to persuade me to accept any of several cabinet positions in his administration, and did appoint me subsequently to his CIA investigating commission." Ford had personally talked to Reagan late in 1974, offering several posts including secretary of transportation, he disclosed, and through Donald Rumsfeld in the spring of 1975 had offered him the job of secretary of commerce. He rejected both offers, Reagan said.

Did he think Ford had made the proposals to keep him out of the presidential race?

"No," Reagan answered, laughing. "I just thought he recognized my administrative ability."

The White House quickly, if sheepishly, confirmed that the offers had been made. "The President has sought to unify the Republican Party and bring to the administration a wide range of views," a spokesman said, lamely.

For the Reagan camp, already optimistic, the disclosure of the cabinet offers seemed to be frosting on the cake. "We all chortled," Jim Lake said later, "and thought, 'Gee, we really clobbered him.' It was the lead on all the networks, and front page in all the major papers." But the fact was, the Reagan forces did not really seize the opening that Ford's *gaffe* had given them—an opportunity to undermine one of the President's strong suits, credibility. They thought they were safely ahead.

Still another political bonus seemed to have come Reagan's way with the news that Richard Nixon was going to China. In an act of callous disregard for the man who had pardoned him, Nixon had accepted an invitation to visit the People's Republic of China just three days before the New Hampshire vote. At Ford headquarters, Spencer and others discussed whether some attempts should be made to dissuade Nixon, or at least to have him make his connection outside the country. As it was, the Chinese sent a large jet plane for him and it landed at a military field near Los Angeles. The Ford strategists feared the effect of that scene on the voters in New Hampshire, and Callaway was particularly exercised. Before Nixon's departure date, Cheney, Morton, Callaway, Spencer, and Kaye met for breakfast at the White House. Callaway proposed that the Chinese be warned that their plane might be seized by federal marshals acting on behalf of American citizens whose property had been expropriated in China. That way, he suggested, the Chinese might tell Nixon to go to Vancouver or

Tokyo on his own and they would pick him up there. But Morton threw cold water on the idea. Finally it was decided that the whole Nixon trip was a dead cat; better to leave it alone all together than to risk picking up the odor.

This was Nixon's first major public foray since his resignation in disgrace in August 1974, and as voters prepared to go to the polls, they were confronted on the morning-television news shows and on the front pages of their newspapers with a stinging reminder that Ford had made it all possible. Nixon compounded his ingratitude by making remarks in a toast and speech in Peking that were immediately construed as a refutation of Ford's policy of détente toward the Soviet Union, which he had inherited from Nixon himself. In a question-and-answer session in Keene on his final campaign visit to New Hampshire, Ford soft-pedaled the whole business and described Nixon as a private citizen who could do what he wanted. Ford appeared to be about to pay a very high political price for Richard Nixon's constitutional rights, not to mention his incredible chutzpah.

Mary McGrory of *The Washington Star* summed up the situation best, as she often does, when she wrote: "Any other man might have delayed the many-squalored thing until Gerald Ford, under strong challenge from Ronald Reagan, could have had a clear run in the New England primary. But it was a question of disappointing the Chinese and disappointing Gerald Ford. Richard Nixon unerringly opted for the Chinese. They can do more for him. Sure, Gerald Ford had spared him indictment, trial, possible prison and even admission of anything graver than 'errors in judgment.' But what has he done for him lately? . . . Gerald Ford's problem here is that some members of his party who like him very much are not sure that he could run a two-car funeral. Richard Nixon's return to Peking has reinforced that sinking feeling. The memory of the pardon is like the smell of escaping gas over this first effort."

Despite such negative distractions, Ford's managers became more optimistic as the New Hampshire campaign drew to a close. For one thing, the economy seemed at last to be improving. The rates of inflation and unemployment were gradually dropping, and three days before the vote the Department of Labor reported that retail prices had gone up only 0.4 per cent in January, the smallest rise in five months. Food prices, most notable to the housewife, actually declined 0.4 percent. And politically in New Hampshire, the campaign seemed to be in hand. Batteries of phone banks were blanketing the state with calls reminding Republicans that their President needed their help. Bob Teeter's final polls indicated that Ford had closed the gap; the primary was a tossup.

On Reagan's side, though Wirthlin said later his polls provided about the same reading, expectations were sky-high. Not long before, Wirthlin said, Reagan had a lead approaching 8 per cent. Ford's limited but pinpointed campaigning in the areas of Reagan's greatest vulnerability—the heavily populated south bordering on Massachusetts and the seacoast—and similarly targeted tours by moderate surrogates like Elliot Richardson had wiped it all out and in fact had built a one-point lead for the President. Reagan came back to New Hampshire in the last week and, according to Wirthlin's figures, took over the lead again, but only by slightly more than one point. The trouble was, few really believed the race had become that close. The press, impressed by Reagan's continuing large and enthusiastic crowds and by earlier polling data, both from Reagan sources and from an independent survey in the *Boston Globe,* didn't believe it. Reagan aides, caught up in the upbeat mood of the campaign, didn't believe it, and reporters in turn noted the Reaganites' unrestrained optimism and believed it even less.

Hugh Gregg, the in-state campaign manager for Reagan, had said all along his man would do well to win 40 or 45 per cent of the vote. The judgment was sound politically and psychologically: Ford was the incumbent, and any candidate who ran close to him ought to have been able to claim a moral victory. McCarthy after all had lost to Johnson in 1968 by 6 per cent and was widely hailed as the "winner"; McGovern had lost to Muskie by 9.4 per cent in 1972 and he too was acclaimed for springing an upset. Reagan should have been able to expect the same treatment at the hands of the media, the self-anointed arbiters in the matter. "We tried to put out that coming close was good enough," Bell said later, but the attempt never took hold. One reason was that Meldrin Thomson was openly predicting a sizable victory; Thomson said on "Meet the Press" that Reagan would win by at least 5 percentage points. He also told reporters he had seen polls supporting that contention. Jim Lake ran into him shortly thereafter, when the gap had been closed, and told him: "Governor, I know you said that, but our data doesn't show it, and I wish you wouldn't say it. It's not helpful to our effort." Thomson replied, "Jim, I've seen it." Lake was mortified. "Well, we haven't seen it," he said. Others in the Reagan campaign said later that there *was* a Wirthlin poll showing Reagan ahead by 11 per cent going into the last week. "Pollsters have selective memory when it comes to their figures," one insider said.

In any event, there was confusion within the Reagan ranks, Wirthlin and Nofziger said later, because Sears liked to hold the poll results close to his vest. "He felt loss of the lead could have impacted negatively," Wirthlin said. But Sears thought the earlier expectations were what did Reagan in. "The *Boston Globe* was finding the same as us," he said. "You can't kid people: the press found out for themselves what we thought. We thought he was going to win, too."

Gregg for his part never budged, publicly or privately, from his estimate that Reagan could only come close; he never predicted victory. On the final weekend, Gregg said it wasn't necessary for Reagan to spend the last day in the state; he thought the candidate and the campaign had done all they could. The operation was geared to getting fifty thousand votes, which normally would have been enough to win. And so Reagan on the final Sunday afternoon went on to Illinois. Wirthlin, flying with Deaver from Los Angeles to join the party, said later, "I died a little when I got on the plane and found we weren't going to New Hampshire." Another day there could have made the difference, he thought. His poll data showed that New Hampshire voters were particularly influenced by Reagan's presence. But Reagan operatives in the state believed that having him there would only disrupt get-out-the-vote preparations that were so essential on the last day.

And so Reagan departed New Hampshire confident of victory, a confidence shared so visibly by those around him that he was ambushed not so much by Ford as by his own campaign's inability to poor-mouth. Cutting the incumbent down to size early was the essential ingredient in the whole Reagan strategy, and by now that meant winning, straight out. Dick Cheney, Ford's chief of staff, said later: "We were deeply concerned when we went into it that fifty-one per cent wasn't going to be enough for us. But in the end we were perceived as the underdog, and that bailed us out."

Winning was critical for Reagan because his campaign had contended that Ford was not a bona fide incumbent, being unelected; that as soon as the voters could, they would make clear they did not consider he had the assumed right of the usual incumbent to another term. Once Ford received a mandate from the electorate, anywhere and regardless of how small, it would bestow a legitimacy that would strip Reagan of that argument. Also, a Ford perceived as legitimate incumbent could grow stronger, and be much harder to defeat in succeeding primaries. In addition Wirthlin had polls that showed that only 29 per cent of New Hampshire Republicans thought Reagan would win the primary; that lack of confidence itself had to be a terrible drag on Reagan's chances, and could be lifted only by a victory. Reagan *had* to win New Hampshire.

By the same token, winning New Hampshire was critical to Ford, and Stu Spencer especially thought so. Since the summer of 1975, when he joined the campaign, Spencer had been warning everyone that if the President lost New Hampshire, he would probably lose the nomination; incumbency was his only real buffer against a candidate as popular as Ronald Reagan.

Primary day dawned clear and pleasant, ideal for a sizable vote—an early favorable sign for the President, the experts said, because zealous Reaganites voted in any weather. Reagan flew back to the state to await the returns and Ford stood by in the White House. But even before the polls closed, it was clear the election would be a cliff-hanger. "I figured we might have some trouble," Sears said later, "when at six o'clock it was still forty degrees out."

Early on, Reagan jumped to a lead of 52–48 per cent, and that margin held for several hours. The outlook appeared grim for the President. At his Washington headquarters, thanks to the determination of Bo Callaway and Peter Kaye that Ford's 1976 campaign would in no way resemble Nixon's of 1972, the doors were opened to the press. Reporters were free to wander about, talk and drink with high administration officials, campaign strategists, and general hangers-on. Bob Hartmann, speechwriter for the President, strode in and asked: "Has Callaway bounced for any booze tonight?" But the mood was more nervous than the remark suggested; it looked as though the President was going under, and there could be only one clearly identifiable culprit, at least in Stu Spencer's mind—Nixon.

"I was apoplectic," he said later. "It really burned me. I knew how any little thing could throw it off." Writing the story from New Hampshire that night, I phoned Spencer to get his response before my approaching deadline. He was livid. "If we lose, it will be because of Nixon," he said. "We knew where our standing was Sunday night. We were ahead. The only thing that could change it was that event. Look at the papers; look at the TV Monday morning—that toast from Peking. It reopened the pardon issue. Any time you have a close race, those changes have an effect." And it wasn't unintentional on Nixon's part, Spencer insisted. "He knew what he was doing. I think he's for John Connally."

Spencer said much the same thing in a loud conversation in a Ford committee hallway with Phil Jones of CBS. "The Secret Service better not let me get within thirty feet of Richard Nixon," he roared. Then he retreated to his office, drinking coffee and beer, receiving a steady stream of papers with vote returns, fielding phone calls from New Hampshire. Pinioned to the wall with a ball-point pen was a large *Washington Post* photo of Nixon in China, with the pen right through Nixon. Callaway meanwhile was trying to put the best face on things and to temper Spencer's irate outbursts—reportedly on instructions from the White House.

At the mansion, the President after a relaxed buffet supper watched the returns until past midnight. By this time, he was creeping up but while he was still trailing by fifteen hundred votes, he went to bed. (And, he told me much later, right to sleep. "I've always been able to put my head on the pillow and put the problems out of mind, and sleep fast and short," he said.)

In Concord, Reagan despite the narrowing margin remained confident. "He got himself up for it," Sears said later. "He was so high he could feel it." Despite cautions, Reagan went downstairs and spoke confidently to the press, while not claiming victory.

The early-morning watch continued. Finally, at 12:49 A.M., Spencer got a telephone call telling him Ford had just gone five votes ahead. He hung up the phone and said, smiling, to Jim Naughton of *The New York Times,* "Well, it's not a mandate." Soon the margin was up to 500. He summoned his secretary: "Bring me a scotch and soda, and light a cigar."

It had been a very, very close call. When the final results were in, they showed Ford had won by a mere 1317 votes—54,824 to 53,507 for Reagan. For all practical purposes, it was a tie. If only 659 more Republicans had switched to Reagan, the incumbent President would have been defeated and in Spencer's and Sears's opinion would have lost the nomination then and there. In the end, the critical factor was the larger than anticipated turnout. "We figured a hundred thousand and we knew we could deliver fifty thousand-plus for Reagan," Sears said. "We delivered almost fifty-four thousand, and we lost by thirteen hundred."

Reagan, asked at a postmidnight press conference whether the result wasn't "like kissing your sister," replied: "Not in this case. When you lose such a close race it just means that it was a moral victory instead of a victory." Well, then, somebody wanted to know, why didn't he look happier?

"I couldn't be happier," he said smiling. And he compared his vote percentage with those of McCarthy in 1968 and McGovern in 1972. "If those were victories for them," he said, "then this is a victory for me."

But his aides were unable to be so philosophical. "The optimism had been contagious," Dave Keene said later. "And then the way we lost, after being up there all night, made it much more disastrous. Our people were crestfallen."

Reagan's hopeful prediction of how the results would be interpreted was not borne out in the long run. True, at the outset some were willing to view the outcome as a tie. *The New York Times* reported a day later, for example, that "most analysts and most politicians said the results were so close that it provided no great advantage to either competitor. They are in the position of two blackjack players who will have to draw another card or two before the outcome of the game is clear." But Sears understood: "You're always faced, whether you like it or not, with what the perception of you is. The perception was that we were going to win, and we lost."

Reagan compared the defeat to losing a football game by an extra point. He intended, with the analogy, to minimize his loss, but it had the opposite effect. Ford twitted him, observing that "some of those who didn't do well seem to be satisfied with second. I never knew of a political campaign where finishing second was beneficial." The President, thanks to 1317 New Hampshirites, was off and running, and Reagan was still in the starting gate. Worse, he was running with a double handicap: his previously undefeated record as a candidate was blemished, and Ford's as an untested quantity was erased. ("They can't say I've never won any place outside Grand Rapids," the President told Spencer happily.) Reagan knew he would have to pay a big price for failing in New Hampshire, and he did not have to wait long to find out, in Florida, just how big. But even then, he would not appreciate the full dimensions of the New Hampshire setback in the long term.[3]

3. Actually, more Republicans may have cast ballots for Reagan than for Ford in the New Hampshire primary. It is possible in New Hampshire for persons not authorized by a candidate to run "favorable" to him for delegates. Three such individuals did so for Reagan, giving him three more delegates than there were delegate positions. Voters who cast ballots for more than the number of delegates to be chosen had their ballots thrown out. Governor Thomson later claimed that five thousand such ballots were invalidated, or more than enough to have given Reagan victory.

The New Hampshire secretary of state, William Gardner, said, however, that no count was ever made of invalidated ballots, and it was "unbelievable" to him that five or even two thousand were voided. Jim Lake said that everything possible was done to persuade the persons running as "favorable" to Reagan to bow out, but they refused. As a result of this experience, legislation was introduced in New Hampshire to have delegates selected directly on the basis of a presidential-preference vote instead of having separate delegate-selection balloting. At the Republican convention in Kansas City, Thomson startled Reagan by telling him, as the nomination slipped away: "The worst thing is, you really won New Hampshire!"

26. Ford Pours It On

        At five-thirty o'clock, on the morning after Ronald Reagan's defeat in New Hampshire, John Sears and his DMI pollster, Dick Wirthlin, sat in Sears's room at the New Hampshire Highway Hotel and reviewed the polling data on the next contested primary, in Florida two weeks hence.[1]

"I think we've got to go after Ford on the foreign-policy issue," Sears said. Wirthlin agreed. For one thing, it was a way to get the press' focus off his $90-billion plan, and perhaps Ford could be drawn into making a mistake himself. Reagan had made one major foreign-policy speech in New Hampshire and it had been very well received; also, time and again in his public Q-and-A sessions, responses to foreign-policy questions were heavily applauded. Republicans, Wirthlin's surveys showed, were not especially concerned about foreign policy; only 12 per cent of those asked said they were. But Reagan's hard-line approach offered a more clear-cut contrast with Ford's leadership style than did his handling of any domestic issue. Anyway, it was worth a try.

Sears went to see Reagan. "We didn't quite make it last night," he told his disappointed candidate. "We're going to have to start talking about foreign policy."

Reagan was agreeable.

Another aide, trying to ease the pain, put in, "I guess we did pretty well, in comparison to other challengers in the past."

Reagan looked at him, and smiled. "Well," he asked, "how come you guys look so bad?"

Reagan's resiliency surprised those who had never seen him lose before. "He probably had experienced more defeats than most people realized," Sears commented later. "Public office really wasn't the be-all and end-all for him, as it was for Nixon. I often wondered whether Reagan could really taste defeat, the way Nixon did. Nixon had no inner confidence. But this guy did. The frequency of ups and downs ran in his business, just as in politics. Actors are like ball players: you're good and then you're bad.

1. President Ford won the Massachusetts and Vermont primaries handily the next Tuesday, March 2, without active competition from Reagan.

And actors and politicians have something in common: you win and you lose. You could talk to Reagan. For one thing, he knows more about acting than politics, and he knew it. That made him a good listener."

After a couple of hours' sleep, Reagan and his entourage left New Hampshire for a day of campaigning in Illinois and then on to Florida that night. Reagan was cheerful on the plane, breaking out the "victory" champagne that had not been needed and drinking a toast to his near-miss with the traveling reporters. It was not bad, against an incumbent President, he rationalized.

In Florida, once again, the affliction of great expectations had already begun to plague Reagan. His in-state manager, an effervescent former state chairman named E. L. (Tommy) Thomas, proved to be even less a political diplomat than Meldrim Thomson. Early in the campaign he grandly predicted, without benefit of any polling data, that Reagan would score a 2–1 victory over the President. Actually, the best that Wirthlin's polls ever showed in the state was a 44–41 edge for Reagan in December, at a time when the Ford administration was in trouble over mishandling James Schlesinger's removal, and over the bad economic situation, and when the President's Florida campaign operation was in a shambles. By mid-February, ten days before the vote in New Hampshire, Wirthlin's polls showed the President moving ahead by 49–46, and then the figures soared to 51–34 a few days after his first primary victory. Reagan and Ford both figured there would be some linkage between New Hampshire and Florida, but neither expected that the momentum for Ford would be so great, giving him a 17-point lead.

Florida had started out as a potential disaster for the President. His lieutenants had selected a friend, Representative Louis Frey, Jr., to be his state campaign manager, but Frey, with his eye on either the governorship or the Senate, was a poor choice. He began by agreeing to be master of ceremonies at a dinner at which the principal speaker was going to be— Ronald Reagan. And the man he put in nominal charge of the campaign, a young fellow named Oscar Juarez, was obviously in over his head. Finally, after a White House strategy session, Stu Spencer contacted his old partner, Bill Roberts, in California and persuaded him to take over the Florida operation. From then on, the President's fortunes climbed.

Even before the New Hampshire results had taken their toll, Reagan also was hurt in Florida by the $90-billion controversy and by the efforts in the Ford camp to portray him as the new Barry Goldwater on Social Security. He found himself, in short, in the same defensive posture that had made it so difficult for him to get on track in New Hampshire. On top of that, when Ford began to bring to bear his now enhanced advantage of incumbency, his campaign began to take off. On the first weekend after the New Hampshire vote, Ford flew to West Palm Beach and, in a heavy, unremitting rain, motorcaded through fourteen towns and cities before large street crowds. He threw himself into it, riding with the top of his limousine down and sloshing his way to outstretched hands until his head and his clothes (including the now-visible bulletproof vest) were thoroughly soaked. The crowds loved it, and so, it seemed, did he. "There's a saying that aristocracy is a matter of the soul, not of the cloth," he told his greeters at Boca Raton at sunset, after his clothes had dried out but he still looked a mess. "I don't look very good, but I think I'm a darned good President."

What Ford was showing the Florida voters that day, in addition to his own fortitude, was the presidency itself—the impressive *Air Force One,* the big cars, the phalanxes of Secret Service agents, the stream of press buses and scurrying White House staff aides. Reagan, for all his movie-star celebrity, could not match the extravaganza of an American President in transit. Beyond that, Ford was able to demonstrate his incumbency by the old-fashioned device of the payoff—never referred to, of course, in such crass terms. On an earlier visit to Orlando, for example, he told the locals that their city would be the site of the 1978 International Chamber of Commerce Convention. And the next day, visiting a veterans' hospital at Bay Pines, he suggested strongly to men in wheelchairs lined up to greet him that they would get a new hospital.[2]

There were other plums: the award of a $33-million missile contract to the Martin-Marietta plant in Orlando; an $18-million mass-transit program announced in Miami by a cabinet member; a presidential announcement of a speed-up in naturalization of Cubans in Florida; the awarding by the President of the Congressional Medal of Honor to an Air Force ex-POW from Eglin Air Force base. Ford also promised to finish Interstate 75 to Fort Meyers, a project long a key issue in the state. He invited local television anchormen to Washington for Oval Office interviews that they duly reported as soon as they returned home—the weekend before the primary. As Bill Roberts said cheerfully: "When you've got it, use it!" And then there were the special advantages to the incumbent brought by good

2. In a memo to Bo Callaway in December, Ford's congressional troubleshooter Leo Thorsness reported that Florida Congressman C. W. Bill Young had advised him that "the way for the President to 'do good' in his district and the two adjoining districts [would be to] approve the VA hospital already studied and recommended by the VA at Bay Pines. . . . Bill says this is not for him, but for the President. Bill already has the veteran and military vote, about 100,000 in his area, and about a thousand per day are coming into Florida to retire—a very strong bloc and quite Republican. All the vet organizations in the state are solidly behind this hospital and it has been on the drawing board so long that it would not look political, according to Bill." Callaway replied that he had contacted the Office of Management and Budget, which told him there were eight other possible sites, and additional studies were being made.

economic news: unemployment down to "only" 7.6 per cent and the whole-sale price index off by 0.5 per cent, a sign of ebbing inflation.

All these things, plus Reagan's own problems, were causing even a supreme optimist like Tommy Thomas to have second thoughts. In late February he reduced his extravagant prediction to 55 per cent for Reagan but added, "I'd hate like the devil to do less than fifty per cent." Anything much lower, he conceded, would be "disastrous." This guy made Meldrim Thomson look like Doubting Thomas.

Of all the advantages of incumbency, perhaps the greatest was the ability to draw the public spotlight and media attention, and to overshadow the opposition. Reagan had come into Florida the first weekend after New Hampshire ready to launch a new attack on Ford's foreign policy. In a speech in Tampa, he struck hard at Ford on a number of such issues. But it so happened that Reagan's speech coincided with Ford's heavily reported motorcade through the rain on Florida's east coast. "When the President came in it really blew you out of the news there," Dave Keene said later. "It was a big thing, before and after. So the foreign-policy thing didn't take. Reagan went back to California thinking it had taken, and probably the guys on the plane thought it had. It took in *The Washington Post* and the New York *Daily News* and places like that, but it didn't take in Florida."

What happened was that national reporters traveling with Reagan, on the alert for anything new in Reagan's speech, zeroed in on his new foreign-policy material woven into the standard speech. But the local reporters, many of them hearing Reagan for the first time, plucked out his best, and oldest, cheer lines and wrote about them as if they had just come out of the cellophane. "They were covering the same old things," Keene said, "and what we wanted covered was not being covered. The impression one got of the campaign in reading the national press at that stage and in reading the local press was very different."

So, like an old Ronald Reagan movie in which the first take didn't quite work, the cast had to do the number over again, once Ford was back in Washington and Reagan could command the spotlight. "We had to get Reagan scheduled back in as soon as we could," Keene said, "and we had to hype the thing up with a television press conference."

The rerun took place at Rollins College, near Orlando. Reagan, break-ing with his Eleventh Commandment while piously insisting he was only attacking the President's policies, not his person, charged that Ford had shown "neither the vision nor the leadership necessary to halt and reverse the diplomatic and military decline of the United States." Ford and Secre-tary of State Henry Kissinger, he said, "ask us to trust their leadership. Well, I find that more and more difficult to do. Henry Kissinger's recent stewardship of U.S. foreign policy has coincided precisely with the loss of U.S. military supremacy. . . . Under Messrs. Kissinger and Ford this nation has become Number Two in military power in a world where it is dangerous —if not fatal—to be second best. . . . All I can see is what other nations the world over see: collapse of the American will and the retreat of American power. There is little doubt in my mind that the Soviet Union will not stop taking advantage of détente until it sees that the American people have elected a new President and appointed a new Secretary of State."

And then there was the Panama Canal. The issue of American rights over the canal, long in dispute between the Panamanian and American governments and long the subject of negotiation, was hardly a matter of primary concern to Americans in 1976. But it was a kind of litmus test for patriotism among conservatives, as Reagan knew, and certainly it was when it was discussed—as Reagan invariably did—in terms of America's inalienable rights. He had begun to weave into his speech a report from Latin America contending that the Ford administration had secretly accepted a compromise formula that would give Panama sovereignty over the canal. "If these reports are true," Reagan said in Winter Haven, "it means that the American people have been deceived by a State Department preoccupied by secrecy. They are due a full explanation. Presumably Mr. Ford has not been fully informed by the State Department, for if he were, I cannot imagine he would knowingly endorse such action. . . .

"State Department actions for several years now have suggested that they are intimidated by the propaganda of Panama's military dictator, Fidel Castro's good friend, General Omar Torrijos [Herrera]. Our State Department apparently believes the hints regularly dispensed by the leftist Torrijos regime that the Canal will be sabotaged if we don't hand it over. Our government has maintained a mouselike silence as criticisms of the giveaway have increased. I don't understand how the State Department can suggest we pay blackmail to this dictator, for blackmail is what it is. When it comes to the canal, we built it, we paid for it, it's ours, and we should tell Torrijos and company that we are going to keep it!"

For a while, the Panama Canal pitch was not much of an applause-getter. But then one day, before a retirement community in Sun City, near Tampa, Reagan cranked it out, and out of the blue, bedlam broke loose. "Reagan, who knows his audience very well, was so taken aback that he lost his place," Keene said. After that, references to the canal were sure-fire cheer lines. "The Panama Canal issue had nothing to do with the canal," Keene reasoned. "It said more about the American people's feelings about where the country was, and what it was powerless to do, and their frustration about the incomprehensibility of foreign policy over the last couple of decades." As such, it was quickly seized by Reagan as a vehicle to harness that frustration to his own cause.

Little by little now, the foreign-policy emphasis was bringing Reagan back from the 17-point deficit he faced after his New Hampshire defeat. So severe had the drop-off been that Sears could not bring himself to tell even Keene, his man in Florida. "Sears came to Florida essentially to hold my hand the last week," Keene said later. "The only poll I'd seen had shown us eight points down." Sears and Keene decided to collect some phone-bank data and feed it to Dick Wirthlin to gauge how Reagan was doing. "After a while John was on the phone with Wirthlin," Keene recalled, "and John is saying, 'We're up six points here,' and 'Ford dropped this many there,' and I'm sitting there getting ecstatic. So John hangs up and says: 'It shows we're going to lose, fifty-three to forty-seven.' I said, 'How in the hell can we be losing fifty-three to forty-seven if we came up all that way from eight points behind?' And he said, 'Well, there was one poll I forgot to tell you about.' "

The Ford campaign, under Bill Roberts, was not of course standing still. It hammered away at the $90-billion and Social Security issues and painted Reagan to the elderly Florida voter as someone who would upset the *status quo.* Reagan always polled poorly with the over-sixty-five set, and surveys found that these voters, resistant to change, were conditioned to vote for the incumbent. (Many were conservative, but ideology didn't mean as much to them as security.) Also, a majority of the retirees in Florida came from the Midwest, Ford Country; old people from the West, from Reagan Country, tended to go to Arizona or Nevada or California to retire. Roberts deftly used the experience that had made him and Spencer such an effective team in California to keep the President ahead, despite Reagan's steady comeback.

Even before the vote, Ford's camp was beginning to think that Florida could be the end of the road for Reagan. Flying back to Washington aboard *Air Force One* one night late in the campaign, the President told reporters: "Florida is really the key. If we win and win very well in Florida, they ought to know they can't win." And Rogers C. B. Morton, then the chief White House political consultant, said of Florida on election eve: "If it doesn't end it here, it will be ended in Illinois and North Carolina," the next two primaries. Reagan himself said on the final weekend he would be happy to finish a close second, but he vowed he would go on. A poll by the *St. Petersburg Times* telegraphed the result: Ford by 61–20 in Pinellas County, retirement country.

On election night, the results were not nearly that bad—Ford 53 per cent, Reagan 47 per cent—but the President got about 60 per cent of the over-sixty-five vote and approached a 2–1 margin in Pinellas. Reagan, campaigning in Illinois, again put up a brave front. "We're delighted with the outcome," he said. "We've challenged an incumbent. He has thrown all the heavy artillery at us, and we still got half the Republican vote." But Reagan was now 0–2, and the President's stature was further enhanced. Roberts had bailed out Frey and Juarez so effectively that Peter Kaye imagined the scene when the two Floridians drove the Californian to the airport after the primary: As Roberts walks to his plane, Frey turns to Juarez and asks: "Who was that masked man?"

In Illinois the next week, Reagan resumed his foreign-policy attack, which he now knew from Wirthlin's polls was clearly an effective strategy. And when Kissinger in a Boston speech aggressively counterattacked, Reagan immediately complained to the Federal Election Commission that Kissinger was violating the tradition of secretaries of state staying out of politics. "If an incumbent is to be able to use individuals like Dr. Kissinger, paid for by the public, for campaign purposes, while these individual expenses are not charged against the incumbent's campaign limits, then the limitations in the law are a mere mockery," Reagan's lawyer charged. Reagan said his first step to reshape American foreign policy would be to replace Kissinger. But Kissinger insisted that "I'm not engaging in political stumping and am not engaged in partisan activities. I explain the foreign policy of the United States. But when over a period of several weeks rather extreme charges are made, then I feel I have an obligation to put before the public what the foreign policy of this country is." Reagan's people, operating on the premise that Kissinger was becoming more and more unpopular, were succeeding in tying him ever closer to the campaigning President.

Ford, for his part, energetically endorsed his secretary of state. He would not, he said, "under any circumstances want Henry Kissinger to quit, period." And while defending his own foreign policy, he deplored its inclusion in the campaign debate. "I can assure you that when there are deep divisions within our country on foreign policy," he told the Chicago Council of Foreign Relations, "our allies begin to question what direction will America go, and . . . our adversaries are tempted to exploit or seek what they seem to think are weaknesses." This old lament, which is always made by every incumbent, in this case suggested that Reagan was scoring.

But the fact was that an Illinois victory was out of reach for Reagan. The President had the regular party organization locked up tight, from Senator Charles H. Percy and former Governor Richard B. Ogilvie on down. Reagan had spent a considerable amount of money—more than $700,000, according to one estimate—in Illinois, when the plan had been to knock out the President after beating him in New Hampshire and

Florida. But now the campaign was at least $500,000 in debt and could not match Ford's late infusions of cash. Well before primary night, Reagan was saying he would "be happy with forty per cent" of the vote, and the President was dancing deftly around suggestions that Illinois would be the end of his opponent's line. "We have to assume that my opponent will be in the ball game up until the end," he told Chicago broadcasters. "We're going to win, and what he does is a matter of judgment for him."

Reagan, in a last gasp on primary eve, accused Kissinger of being "almost hysterical" and Ford of using "the cheapest kind of political rhetoric" in promising pork-barrel benefits to localities. But the biggest wound inflicted on the President—and it was only a surface wound at that—came not from Reagan but from Ford's own campaign manager, Bo Callaway. Callaway, caught by allegations that he had used his position as secretary of the army to help develop a proposed ski resort, was forced to step aside three days before the Illinois vote.

It was, to many on the Ford committee, a blessing in disguise. Callaway as a campaign manager had been, to put it charitably, miscast. Inexperienced in running a national campaign, he was no match for the White House infighters—notably presidential aides Jerry Jones and David Gergen —and was treated like a second-class citizen at 1600 Pennsylvania Avenue. His request to sit in on senior staff meetings was turned down, and when he took his case to Ford he was rebuffed again, on the grounds that in the post-Watergate era the White House could not afford to be so overtly politicized. "I argued that politics is the essence of democracy," Callaway said later. "Politics is good, not bad. It should be open. It should be announced that I would sit in, and then I would just go ahead and do it." Again the answer was no.

Callaway boasted later that he had run the committee "the way I ran the army. I don't say I didn't make a lot of mistakes, but we had a discipline and we won every primary we were in." But Callaway's penchant for Knute Rockne–like pep talks and administration by memo drove the pros in the campaign bonkers. One memo dated March 8—the day before the Florida primary—to his senior staff read: "I have just received a letter from the Atlanta Area Council of the Boy Scouts of America pointing out that President Ford is the only President in our history to have earned the Eagle Scout badge. I was not aware of this and perhaps there are others who are not aware of it. It seems to me that it not only is important in itself, because there are so many Americans who believe in scouting, but also it tends to erode the myth that the President is not a leader." And he added, afraid no doubt of a leak: "This is just for your information."

On the Friday night before the Illinois primary the press first printed the allegation that Callaway had used improper influence with the U. S. Forest Service to get federal land cleared for a ski resort at Crested Butte, Colorado, in which he had an interest. When Peter Kaye got wind of the report he asked Callaway about it, and Callaway, traveling with the presidential party, tended to dismiss it. But when Kaye got details from press reports he advised Dick Cheney, the White House chief of staff. In his excitable way, Callaway kept insisting he was innocent, but Cheney just as insistently kept questioning him. Callaway finally told Kaye all the details, putting them in the best possible light, but by that time Cheney had decided that Callaway would have to go. He and Kaye discussed the best way to ease him out; it was decided Cheney would have breakfast with Callaway the next morning and just tell him.

At breakfast in Cheney's room, according to Kaye later: "Cheney played him like a guy landing a fish. Bo was flopping around, then lying there for a while, amid long, awkward silences, and then would start flopping around again. Finally, Bo asked, 'What should I do?' 'Better get a lawyer, Bo,' Cheney told him."

It was decided that Kaye would write a short statement saying that Callaway had volunteered to step aside "temporarily" until a congressional investigation was resolved. It would be given to the press pool while Callaway was safely sequestered on *Air Force One* en route to North Carolina, where Ford would be campaigning. Callaway left the room for a minute or two and Kaye pulled out a statement he had written the night before, in anticipation of the inevitable. When Callaway walked back in, Kaye handed it to him. Old Bo was incredulous. "Man," he said, "I always knew you could write fast. But I didn't realize you could write this fast!"

On *Air Force One,* Callaway needed some more persuading, but he finally agreed, was ushered into the President's presence, and came back to the rear of the plane, Kaye said later, "looking like death warmed over." Ford, arriving in North Carolina, announced that Callaway had "asked" to be relieved and that he had "acceded." He had "full faith" in Callaway's honesty and integrity, Ford said, but that was the end of Bo. He never rejoined the campaign, and Stu Spencer took over the committee's direction until a replacement could be found.[3]

Callaway's departure might have been the one memorable occurrence in an otherwise unmemorable primary except for an episode that took place late one night near the end of the campaign, in Peoria. The President had

3. In January 1977, after hearings by a Senate Interior subcommittee that voted on partisan lines that Calloway had used poor judgment, the Justice Department said that the "matter is no longer under active investigation" and that "no further action is contemplated."

been stumping among farmers in southern Illinois. In the course of the uneventful day, as members of the press corps gazed out from their buses on pastoral scenes, an inspiration struck Jim Naughton, a leprechaun who some years ago cast a spell over the personnel manager of *The New York Times.* Naughton was one of several White House reporters who never tired of kidding Tom DeFrank, the *Newsweek* correspondent, about his lonely days as a student at the then all-male Texas A&M, and about the reported dependence of Aggies on sheep for connubial satisfaction. In collusion with a White House advance man, a farmer just outside Peoria was persuaded to rent out a sheep, to be delivered to the Ford entourage's hotel that night. "It seemed appropriate," Naughton explained later with perfect reasonableness, "to have a reunion for Tom."

The sheep was to arrive at eleven-thirty. About a dozen reporters, advance men, and Secret Service agents anxiously milled about the lobby, their eyes on the front door. At one point, a middle-aged man and his wife, locals out for an adventurous night in Peoria, walked over to Naughton. "What are you doing?" the man asked.

"Waiting for a sheep," Naughton replied, as if the question were the height of folly.

At about midnight a pickup truck arrived—with nothing in the back. The assembled celebrants were dismayed. Just then the young farmer in work clothes sitting behind the wheel pushed open the door, revealing to them—on the seat beside him—the business end of a sheep.

Nobody seemed to know how to proceed. "Well," asked John Mashek of *U. S. News and World Report,* "do you have a sheep leash?"

The farmer did not, so everyone finally seized the sheep and began to waddle it toward the back of the hotel, with the local Good-Time Charlie and wife joining in. There, a Pinkerton guard who knew nothing of the caper obligingly held the door open, as if it were a nightly occurrence. Up the elevator the sheep contingent went, to the eleventh floor. Meanwhile, by previous arrangement, Ron Nessen was phoning DeFrank in his room, luring him down to the bar with the promise of a "Periscope" item, for which *Newsweek* regularly risks its solvency with a ten-dollar bonus for contributors. With a key previously acquired, the reporters let themselves and sheep into DeFrank's room. The sheep immediately registered its satisfaction with the accommodations by urinating on the floor. Amid much pushing, shoving, and shrieking, the shepherds sought refuge in closets and in the bathroom, and Good-Time Charlie's wife, climbing into the shower stall with several reporters, asked in all innocence: "Do you do this sort of thing all the time?"

For long minutes, DeFrank failed to return, the sheep meanwhile killing time by grazing on the carpet and defecating with abandon. Finally, one of the agents checked on his walkie-talkie and reported that the subject was on his way. DeFrank opened the door and was aghast at the sight. His benefactors quickly piled out, excusing themselves for intruding, with Naughton announcing that in deference to the situation, they would leave DeFrank alone with his sheep.

Later that night, after DeFrank had evacuated the sheep and cleaned up the mess, a hooker banged on his door looking for a friend. Irate, he chased her away and on his way, stepped into a puddle left by the sheep. It was quite a night, and things did not improve when, the next morning, the President of the United States, having received a full account, encountered him in the lobby and remarked: "I understand you had a visitor last night."

But for Naughton it was all in a night's work. To prove it, he listed on his next expense account, under "Miscellaneous," this notation: "Share of ewe rental—$5." "It went right through," Naughton reported later.

For Ronald Reagan, election night in Illinois seemed nearly as bad. The results barely kept him alive: Ford 59 per cent, Reagan 40 per cent, perennial Chicago candidate Lar Daly 1 per cent, with a large Republican turnout again benefiting the President. Dick Wirthlin thought that it might have been much worse, but Reagan's foreign-policy assaults continued to be effective, and in fact Ford's bandwagon effect from New Hampshire had been braked by it. Reagan was making a comeback, but it was hardly perceived, even among his own supporters, who were unreservedly glum. "I used to hate Mondays," John Sears told my colleague, Jim Dickenson. "Now I hate Wednesdays." *The Washington Post*'s cumulative delegate count after Illinois gave Ford 166, Reagan only 54, and 51 uncommitted.

Talk of Reagan throwing in the towel was heard everywhere, but not from the candidate. "We have met our goal in Illinois with something over forty per cent of the vote," he said from Los Angeles. "I have never been under any illusions that our grass-roots campaign could successfully buck the Illinois Republican organization and the promises being issued so bountifully by the White House. However, the fact that I have won something over forty per cent of the vote in this organization-dominated state indicates there is major dissatisfaction in our party with the kind of leadership it has been receiving." He vowed to go on and expressed confidence that "we will go to the national convention in August with at least a fifty-fifty chance of winning the nomination."

Sears bluntly looked past the next test, in North Carolina, and told Dave Broder: "He'll survive until Texas. But if he doesn't win there, he's out." And at Ford headquarters in Washington, Rogers Morton started to push. He said he had already asked Republican Senator John Tower of Texas, House Minority Leader John Rhodes of Arizona, and House Republican Whip Robert Michel of Illinois to "open a dialogue" with the Reagan people and try to persuade them to quit. It was time, he said, to start putting the party back together, and the Californian "can either throw his lot with the President . . . or he can continue to go around the country and articulate his cause. I think he's going to do what's in the best interest of the Republican Party."

It all sounded easy. But Ronald Reagan was not a man who liked to be pushed. The words from the Ford camp only stiffened his determination. "You have to recognize he made some pretty bad movies," Sears explained. "It must have been pretty embarrassing. But he knows that if you make a bad movie, you don't stop making movies." And so it was on to North Carolina, with no expectations of success, against an incumbent who was growing stronger with each primary victory—or so it seemed.

27. The Reagan Comeback

On March 17, the morning after the Illinois primary, John Sears took David Keene aside at the Marriott Motel near Chicago's O'Hare Airport. Maybe it was time, Sears said, to make contact with the Ford people and let them know that Reagan was ready to withdraw gracefully. What, if anything, would Keene want to do in the Ford operation? "Sears hadn't *decided,*" Keene recalled, "but he was *thinking.* Well, we decided we ought to fight it out a little bit longer, as long as we had some money, and ought at least to go through North Carolina. But things were tight then. Most people were off the payroll; I don't think John had taken any money since mid-January or early February."

If Reagan had known that Sears was even thinking about going to the Ford people about quitting, he doubtless would have been furious. Suggestions that he withdraw, Keene said, "got him feisty for the first time, and it forced a lot of our people to dig in." This feistiness surfaced at once on the campaign trail in North Carolina. Was it true, reporters in Greensboro asked Reagan, that a group of Republican mayors had asked him to get out? "For heaven's sakes, fellas, let's not be naïve," he shot back. "That pressure is engineered from the same place that they engineered the pressure for me not to run in the first place—the White House. . . . I'm not going to pay any attention to them now when they suggest that I should quit. Tell *him* to quit."

As Reagan toured North Carolina, the same, repeated questions triggered the same, repeated answers. Governor James Holshouser, Ford's North Carolina campaign chairman, and Governor Daniel Evans of Washington, another strong backer, simultaneously issued a statement they said was supported by seven other GOP governors calling on Reagan to withdraw "and with us and all other Republicans, work for the election of President Ford" (two of the seven later said they hadn't agreed to sign). Reagan brushed aside the gambit. "I have been averaging in the contested primaries better than forty-five per cent of the Republican vote," he said. "I am not going to take my advice from the campaign organization of Mr. Ford." The ball game, he said, was still "in the first inning" and at that stage "you don't take your bat and go home." Reagan kept hammering away at

Ford's foreign policy and, in an interview at Hickory several days before the primary vote, he insisted that "we have a chance of winning, and North Carolina is the first state where we've thought that." If anyone else in his operation believed it, though, he wasn't saying so.

Lyn Nofziger, who certainly didn't expect his boss to win in North Carolina, learned at firsthand the depth of Reagan's determination when he walked in on him in a motel room one day during that time. "I sat down and started very carefully to say . . . that he ought to stay in at least until Texas," Nofziger recalled. "Well, he misunderstood what I was starting to say. He thought I was beginning to say we ought to look to getting out, and he just interrupted me and said: 'Lyn, I'm not going to get out of this thing. I'm going to win this. I'm in this all the way.' He was feeling something out there."

The Ford camp's continuing pressure on Reagan was a compound error, because for the first time the President's campaign was substituting psychology for hard-hitting campaigning. Hoping that the time had come to permit Reagan to make a strategic withdrawal, the Ford team let up. "We thought we were going to win in North Carolina and sew up the whole thing," Dick Cheney said later. "As I look back on it now, it was our most serious mistake, easing off in North Carolina. You could make the case that if we were successful in forcing him out we would have had a lot more time to get our act together for the fall." Bob Teeter, the President's pollster, agreed: "We just didn't take North Carolina seriously enough. We should have sent the President there once or twice more. But the feeling was Reagan was beaten and there was no sense mauling him."

While the Ford campaign thus concentrated on trying to psych Reagan out, the Californian tore up the remaining vestiges of his Eleventh Commandment and waded into Ford. Discarding his file cards and speaking entirely off the cuff, he hit at Ford with every issue he could think of, from the Panama Canal and détente to the bloated Washington bureaucracy and excessive political use of his incumbency. "If he comes here with the same list of goodies as he did in Florida," Reagan said, "the band won't know whether to play 'Hail to the Chief' or 'Santa Claus Is Coming to Town.' " Yet Reagan was careful to hit above the belt. When the eager forces of Senator Jesse Helms, backing him in a North Carolina party struggle with Holshouser, started distributing a clearly racist flyer, Reagan blew the whistle on it promptly. (The flyer quoted Ford as suggesting that Senator Edward Brooke of Massachusetts, a black, "should be considered" for the vice-presidency, and failed to note that Brooke was only one of a number of prospects listed by the President.) The Helms faction would have injected similar themes into the campaign if the Reagan people had not threatened to shut off money. Still, in what the Helmsites saw as a holy war, their zealous support was critical.

One important function the Helms group fulfilled was that they continued to press for having Reagan on television all around North Carolina. Tom Ellis, Helms's chief political aide and state chairman for Reagan, nagged the Reagan strategists and even threatened to put a tape of an old Reagan speech on the air himself. The national campaign finally agreed, and Nofziger dug out a thirty-minute tape that had been made at no cost to the campaign at a Miami television studio the last week of the Florida primary. It was not of the most professional quality, but it was Reagan at his relaxed best. Nofziger dusted it off, cut out references to Florida, dubbed a "beggar" —a voice-over appeal for funds—on it, and shipped it off to fifteen of the state's seventeen television stations for prime-time viewing. The reaction was enthusiastic.

Use of this Florida tape climaxed an argument that had been going on within Reagan's campaign for months between Nofziger and other old California Reagan hands and Harry Treleaven, Nixon's 1968 television specialist, who had been hired as a media adviser. According to Nofziger, Treleaven had shied away from using Reagan straight-on because he feared it would look too rehearsed and would remind voters of Reagan's movie career. Instead, Treleaven had opted for a *cinema vérité* technique, filming Reagan on the stump in a more documentary style, to the chagrin of the old-timers. "Everybody always wants to do something their own way with Ronald Reagan," Nofziger said later, "and the best way is to just let him talk. Nobody ever figures it out. Each time you gotta go through this whole hassle." The thrust of the early ads, Dick Wirthlin said, was "to neutralize what they perceived to be the negatives of running an actor for President, which was done without reviewing it with us." His polls, Wirthlin said, indicated Reagan's movie connection was a plus with most voters, yet the early ads down-played it, even to the point of feigning poorer quality to avoid Hollywood slickness.

Meanwhile, Ford was having his worst days so far on the stump. In Charlotte, he gave a speech to several thousand teen-agers at a convention of the Future Homemakers of America that was so vapid as to be ludicrous. "I say with emphasis and conviction that homemaking is good for America," the President of the United States found himself proclaiming. "Never be ashamed to say, 'I am an American homemaker and I am proud of it. . . . Remember, it still takes a lot of living to make a home." Peter Kaye, never a mincer of words, proclaimed, "It was in North Carolina that Ford became a crashing bore."

Speechwriting wasn't the only problem. With Bo Callaway on the shelf, the job of both running the campaign committee and devising strategy fell to Stu Spencer, and he was the first to acknowledge that he was no administrator. In fact, he had turned down the offer to succeed Callaway, and Rogers Morton was moved over from the White House to head the committee.[1]

Even before Morton formally took the title of campaign manager, he received an unexpected and very private feeler from the Reagan camp. With former Nixon White House aide William Timmons acting as intermediary, Morton met at Timmons' downtown Washington office with John Sears on March 20, four days before the North Carolina primary. (Reagan, of course, knew nothing about the meeting. Sears was acting entirely on his own, in anticipation of another defeat in North Carolina.) The purpose, simply, was to discuss how the Reagan and Ford forces could best be brought together for the good of the party. It was not that Sears did not want to go on: he believed that once the primary calendar reached Texas on May 1, Reagan's fortunes could turn around. But it was the money. The Reagan campaign was nearly $2 million in the hole, far more of a debt than was publicly acknowledged. If a thoroughly defeated Reagan could be persuaded to give in amicably, perhaps arrangements could be made to have the Ford camp pick up some of the Reagan debt. Nothing was settled that day in Timmons' office; there was still, of course, the formality of the North Carolina primary to be disposed of.

Sears and Morton, confirming the meeting much later, both said it was mostly exploratory, with nothing specific said about Reagan getting out of the race. They talked of the need for party unity, they said. Morton acknowledged, however, that the subject of putting the Ford and Reagan campaigns together at a future time was discussed. With these two political pros, what *that* meant didn't have to be spelled out. It was left that if it were "appropriate" after the North Carolina primary, they would talk again. In the meantime, it wasn't constructive for Ford to speak of Reagan as an extremist, nor did it serve the cause of unity for his aides to keep suggesting that the time had come for Reagan to quit.

The very overture was a high-risk venture for Sears. If Morton had turned around and reported to the world that Sears had been in offering Reagan's sword, it probably would have been curtains for Sears, for Reagan's chances in North Carolina, and—it was not too much to suggest— for his chances for the Republican nomination itself. And Reagan without

1. Callaway was balking at a formal and complete severance, hoping to exonerate himself first. It was a week after the North Carolina primary before he finally agreed to step aside for good, with Ford himself presiding over the bloodless execution in the Oval Office and declaring Callaway "an absolutely honest person."

question would have been infuriated. That Sears was acting in what he saw to be Reagan's best interest, not to mention the party's, would probably have cut no ice with the candidate.

What made matters particularly sticky for Sears was that somehow Secretary of Agriculture Earl Butz learned about the meeting, and Morton so advised Sears. He now had Sears over a barrel, especially if Butz, who unlike Timmons had no moral obligation to keep his mouth shut, decided to let the secret out.

But Sears did not have time to sit back and worry. With this overwhelming debt, something drastic had to be done. On primary day in North Carolina, he flew to Wisconsin, to which the Reagan entourage had fled, with a radical proposal: that Reagan stop campaigning, concede Wisconsin, which he couldn't afford anyway, go back to Los Angeles and whip up a major fund-raising speech for nationwide television delivery. That, he reasoned, was the only way to survive until the Texas primary, when a string of primaries in the South and West could launch a "second phase." At least it could go a long way to liquidating the horrendous debt that was building with every passing day of active, jet-travel campaigning.

In Wisconsin, Sears met with no resistance from Reagan, who had been pushing to go on television in his old style for weeks. "All along," an insider said later, "Reagan was saying, 'God damn it, you guys, I ought to go on national TV. I can raise a lot of money.' But we all would put him down. We thought it was old stuff, that it wouldn't work. You know, 'You did it in 1964 but this is 1976.' It costs a hundred thousand dollars to put on a deal like that. But when we realized we were two million dollars in the red, a hundred thousand didn't look like so much." So Reagan embraced the idea, as well as Sears's counsel to get out if he didn't win in Texas. "Still," Sears said, "we weren't thinking about losing."

All this took place—and the traveling press was advised of the change in plans—before the results were in from North Carolina. Nofziger offered few details about the subject of Reagan's planned speech and some in the press corps assumed he might be preparing to drop out of the race. But it hardly made sense to spend $100,000 to do that. Meanwhile, Reagan fulfilled a speaking engagement that night at a hunters' club called Ducks Unlimited in La Crosse—where any foe of gun control like Reagan was bound to feel comfortable. While the assembled dinner guests finished eating, drinking, and raffling off a multitude of gifts, the first returns came in from North Carolina, showing him ahead. "They were dumbfounded," recalled Jim Naughton (who had been traded temporarily from the Ford to the Reagan press corps for three sheep and a low draft choice). "They didn't know how to handle it."

The press and television people, herded into a seedy hotel, clamored for a statement, but Reagan declined. Even he seemed to have trouble believing he really had won. "Lyn, I know you want me to go down [stairs]," he told Nofziger, "but I don't want to repeat what happened in New Hampshire." After much discussion, he proceeded directly to his plane, with reporters crowding around trying to get a victory statement— to no avail. Not until the plane was well on its way to Los Angeles, when the pilot reported over the public-address system that Reagan had won, 52 to 46 per cent, did he begin to celebrate. He tossed a football around to his wife and son Ron, Jr., a campaign worker, and aides drank champaigne and marched up and down the aisle singing: "Nothing could be finer than to give Ford a shiner, in the primary."

At Ford's headquarters in Washington, Morton was philosophical. "I don't think we've been dealt a very serious blow," he said. (Morton said not a word then or later about his earlier meeting with Sears.) And at the White House, Ron Nessen was candid: "The President had expected a close race, but he expected to win. So naturally he is disappointed. The point is we lost, and there are no excuses and no alibis." In the delegate race, however, Ford remained safely ahead, winning twenty-six of North Carolina's fifty-four, with Reagan getting the other twenty-eight—a net loss of only two.

Among the factors in the upset was the low turnout, less than 40 per cent, which worked to the advantage of Helms's disciplined and angry conservatives. Subsequent polls showed that 70 per cent of the Republicans who made up their minds in the last ten days decided for Reagan. Also, the Helms-Holshouser feud so badly split the state party that practically no one was neutral. That was one reason Reagan's victory surprised nearly everyone, including his own supporters: there were no detached party professionals not aligned with one faction or the other. The main reason for Reagan's success, however, was that his attack on Ford's foreign policy, which began in Florida, bore fruit in North Carolina.

After Reagan's North Carolina victory, his lieutenants had some second thoughts about bypassing Wisconsin on April 6, but there was really no choice. "We were broke," said Keene. "They were going to take our plane away from us. Our Wisconsin people faulted us, saying they could have won there. We got forty-five per cent, which was damned good, considering. I think we could have won some delegates, because we were close in three or four districts, but we couldn't afford a poll that would have told us which."

Further aggravating the problem was the fact that on March 22, the day before the primary, time had run out on the FEC, obliging it to stop paying federal campaign subsidies. "We were entitled to about a million dollars then," Sears said later. "That kicked us out of the Wisconsin primary." Considering Reagan's eventual showing of 45 per cent without campaigning, he said, "We probably would have gotten some delegates."

On the Ford side, Peter Kaye for one thought Reagan's decision to stay out of Wisconsin was his major mistake of the whole year. "Wisconsin was a crossover state [that is, with an open party primary] with a strong conservative voting streak in both parties, and the Wallace candidacy even that early was falling apart. Reagan was coming off North Carolina. Had he come back in there, had he not given up, he would have won a couple of congressional districts. As it was, we got forty-five–zero [in delegates] with a fifty-five-per-cent vote. We were damned lucky and it put us back on the rails after North Carolina."

In any case, the focus now became the Texas primary on May 1. Reagan bypassed the New York primary on the same day as Wisconsin, April 6, and Pennsylvania as well, on April 27. In both states, the prospect of having to spend a great deal of money on radio and television commercials, and the marginal chance of victory in slugfests against state and county organizations largely committed to Ford, persuaded Sears to skip them and hope to be able to go back in later and negotiate for delegates. The same was true in Ohio and New Jersey, though a last-minute effort was made before the filing deadline in Ohio to get the maximum number of Reagan delegates on the various ballots. On the flight to Los Angeles from Wisconsin, Reagan signed a slew of petitions, which Sears then brought back east on the red-eye flight and managed to file so that Reagan had delegates running in about fifteen of the twenty-five districts, plus a statewide slate.

Later there were allegations that Sears had seriously undermined Reagan's nomination chances by not competing in all these primaries more aggressively. But Sears defended his strategy. "It was our feeling that if we handled ourselves adroitly, we'd probably come out with as many delegates just by bargaining. It was often costing us much more money to try to do the same things as the Ford people because they were in control of the local organization in most places. What we'd usually have to do was go out and manufacture one. In many states, the local party headquarters also served as Ford headquarters. So the matter of running in a state as large as New York or Pennsylvania was not only a political decision but also an economic one." Sears said he was satisfied with the twenty delegates he finally got out of New York and although he hoped to have gotten more than the eventual ten for Reagan in Pennsylvania, "I don't know that we would have elected any more than we got if we'd run in the primary in April when we were losing everything." Sears conceded that if the financial situation had been better earlier, they might have made a stronger showing in New Jersey and Ohio in June, "but we were in a tremendous cash freeze." Charlie Black, one of Reagan's most astute field men assigned to Pennsylvania, said, "it would have cost half a million dollars to do a decent job and accomplish more than just making people mad and not electing any delegates. We just didn't have it, and John figured it was better to see who got elected and then go in to talk to them than to put up sacrificial lambs and let them get beat." And Keene said: "New York could have been our Vietnam. If we had gotten into a prestige fight there with Nelson Rockefeller you'd have to dump in everything you had. And if you lose, you're in an awfully tough position to talk to them later." Also, he said, delegates who had spent money to beat Reaganite opposition in order to get to the convention would not be prime candidates for conversion, if horse-trading became the order of the day.

Reagan's big television speech proved to be aesthetically a washout but financially a stroke of genius. It was no more than a rerun of what he had been saying in North Carolina, with emphasis on the anti-Washington theme and barbs at Henry Kissinger. (Kissinger complained he was being misrepresented, and the State Department issued a ten-page refutation of Reagan's points, but that succeeded only in focusing more attention on Reagan's hard-line position, popular with conservatives.) But most important, the speech was heard by a nationwide audience to whom it was new, and the undertaking raised a remarkable $1.5 million—enough to make a good dent in the debt and put Reagan in shape for Texas. And so, while the Democrats pre-empted the political spotlight through April with their show-down primary in Pennsylvania between Jimmy Carter and Scoop Jackson, both Reagan and Ford prepared for their own, on May 1, in the Lone Star State.

Sears got a lot of advice from kibitzers during this period, including one call from his old friend in San Clemente, Dick Nixon. "He was just sitting there with the phone," Sears said. "In a lot of ways he would have loved to be a political manager. He wasn't supporting Reagan, but he wasn't rooting against him. He was just more fascinated with the prospect of taking on an incumbent. He had some advice [for Reagan]; he certainly had been following the campaign." From time to time in the coming months, Nixon would have an aide phone Sears to ask a question about Reagan's strategy. Sears said he was sure Nixon was also talking to the other side, "but once he was out of office he didn't think Gerald Ford was your all-time best President. In fact he never intended to have him be President."

At the President Ford Committee, the staff was still trying to get itself straightened out after the Callaway flap. But Wisconsin raised their spirits, and they geared up in Texas for the knockout blow against Reagan they had let slip by in North Carolina. About half a million dollars of scarce campaign money was thrown into the race. "Our thesis in Texas was very simple," Spencer explained. "If we could stop him there, we had him. So we went after him. We didn't have to win. If we could pick twenty-four or thirty delegates out of Texas, that would have been a big hunk out of him. But Reagan's issues fit that state perfectly—Panama, Kissinger, oil, the farm problem." After the administration agreed to push a higher price ceiling on domestic oil, the President got support from independent oil producers, but Reagan countered by proposing a restoration of the oil-depletion allowances to their former high levels. The President charged Reagan more vehemently than was his custom with performing "a disservice to the American people" by saying the nation's military strength was insufficient, but Reagan continued to argue that the United States had fallen behind the Soviet Union. And he drove home the Panama Canal issue ever harder.

Flying into Texas by regularly scheduled airliner because he could no longer afford a chartered jet, Reagan found fertile ground in which to plant his suggestions that President Ford was involved in secret negotiations to give the Panama Canal away. As he campaigned, testimony was released by a congressional committee from Ambassador Ellsworth Bunker, head of the American team negotiating a new treaty with Panama. In it he said that he was acting directly on orders from Ford to negotiate a turnover of control of the Canal Zone to Panama "after a period of time" and the canal itself "over a longer period of time." The testimony seemed to contradict what Ford had declared a few days earlier in a Dallas press conference: "I can simply say, and say it emphatically, that the United States will never give up its defense right to the Panama Canal and will never give up its operational rights as far as Panama is concerned." Nessen tried to backtrack, a measure of Reagan's effectiveness. He said that Ford meant to indicate that "we are going to insist, during the period of [any new] treaty, that we have the right to operate, to maintain, and to defend" the canal. But what about *after* the term of the treaty? Reagan wanted to know. Ford called Reagan's stand "absolutely irresponsible" and warned that bloody riots, worse than those in 1964, "very likely" would result if Reagan's intransigent position were followed. But Reagan continued his simple formula: "We built it, we paid for it, and we're going to keep it." The proud, patriotic Texans seemed to love it.

Ford had other troubles too. For one, former Governor John Connally, playing coy perhaps in the hope he might get the vice-presidential nomination, finally closed the door on endorsing Ford—he did not want to be on the losing side in his home state. And, less substantively, there was Ford's attempt in San Antonio, as television cameras rolled, to eat a tamale without removing the husk. The "Bozo the Clown" syndrome was surfacing once more, and reporters joked that Ford was wooing "the klutz vote" again. Also, while Ford was drawing good crowds, he often lost them; in Lubbock, half the audience walked out on him before he had finished speaking.

Most important was the nature of the Texas primary itself—the first presidential primary ever held in that state. It was wide open for crossover voting, a circumstance that helped the Reagan strategists exploit Texas's conservative core. Two months earlier, the Ford field man for Texas, Al Zapanta, had sent a routine weekly report to Washington that noted that "Texas is moving well and is organized in such a manner that should bring us the maximum amount of delegates and votes in the May 1 primary." That was on March 5—four days before Governor George Wallace suffered his first stinging defeat at the hands of Jimmy Carter in Florida. That event changed everything in Texas. Tens of thousands of Wallace voters were gradually cut adrift during Wallace's subsequent slide in a series of additional primary defeats, and Reagan deftly moved in on them. A Wallaceite in Fort Worth named Rollie Millirons was recruited by Reagan media man Arthur Finkelstein to do radio and television spots that went something like this: "I've always been a Democrat, all my life. A conservative Democrat. As much as I hate to admit it, George Wallace can't be nominated. Ronald Reagan can. He's right on the issues. So for the first time in my life I'm gonna vote in the Republican primary. I'm gonna vote for Ronald Reagan." It was dynamite. And as the commercial went out over the Texas air waves, Reagan was campaigning in Wallace country, reciting Wallace's old conservative themes as his aides passed out fliers that said: "Democrats: you will *not* be committing a major indiscretion if you vote, this year, in the Republican primary." On the flier was a caricature of an elephant saying, "I'm for Reagan!" and a donkey adding, "Me too!" The real Wallace, meanwhile, was stumping across the state in a futile effort to hold back the inexorable Jimmy Carter.

On election day, a record turnout for a Republican statewide primary told the story—crossover Democrats had flooded into Republican booths to vote for Reagan, who completely swept all twenty-four congressional districts and all ninety-six delegates at stake. In one day's voting, Reagan was in the thick of the race again. *The Washington Post*'s delegate count put him behind Ford by only forty-nine—232–183—and he was also picking up delegates in various states selecting delegates by caucus or convention.

Three nights later, an even heavier blow fell on Ford: he was challenged by Reagan in three more primaries—Indiana, Alabama, and Georgia

—and was defeated in all three. Reagan swept the delegates in Alabama and Georgia—eighty-five in all—and captured forty-five of Indiana's fifty-four, putting him ahead of the President in the delegate count for the first time. If ever there was evidence of "momentum" in a campaign, the result in Indiana (which also permitted crossover voting) produced it. Two months earlier, in a poll commissioned by the state party committee, Ford had led Reagan by 24 percentage points; he had the governor, Otis Bowen, and the influential state chairman, Thomas Milligan, solidly in his corner in a notoriously organization-minded state. But Reagan's successes in North Carolina and Texas seemed to make voting against an incumbent more palatable, and the arguments he made against Ford's positions on issues were sinking in. Wherever Ford went and conducted Q-and-A sessions, Reagan's issues—the Panama Canal, détente, U.S. military strength—always seemed to come up. Reagan just got tougher, saying he'd go to war if necessary to protect and keep the canal. He was striking a responsive chord in the GOP electorate and, in states with open primaries, among Democrats. "He's going to drive us crazy for a while in these crossover states," Peter Kaye said. "Nothing's going to be easy from now on, anywhere." And he was right. "We may well lose Michigan if it's anything like Indiana," he said the night of the triple crossover setback. Down the road in two more weeks was the President's home state; a sure thing, ordinarily, but also a crossover state. And, if the President lost Michigan, everybody at the PFC knew, it would be curtains. Ford himself was described by his closest aides as "bewildered." He could not quite grasp why he, with such a conservative record, should be so vulnerable to Reagan's barbs and why, in fact, Reagan should be going after him so hard.

At PFC headquarters that night, Rogers Morton stuck his foot in his mouth clear up to the ankle. Of the triple loss, he blurted: "I'm not going to rearrange the furniture on the deck of the *Titanic.*" It had to be the most impolitic crack of the year. And to make matters worse, he was photographed, disheveled, sitting before a collection of empty liquor bottles. It was an unfair picture, inasmuch as the reporters had consumed much of the booze, but it seemed to say it all about the state of the Ford campaign.

One problem, some of the strategists thought, was that the President had been drawn once again into excessive campaigning, into running frantically around the country trying to put Reagan's fires out himself with ever more strident speeches. "He's still the President," Kaye argued. "He still has the trappings. He still has the office. He still has the power to use the office. He's got to get off the same level as Reagan." And so, in the next primaries, in Nebraska and West Virginia on May 11, Ford limited himself to two days on the stump in Nebraska, then returned to the White House to be "presidential" while his committee flooded the state with radio commercials that featured Goldwater defending his position, and attacking Reagan's, on the Panama Canal. (Reagan's statements, Goldwater charged in the radio spots, contained "gross factual errors" that could "needlessly lead this country into open military conflict.") Reagan, meanwhile, kept on attacking, the target now being administration farm policies, especially the previous summer's embargo on grain sales to the Soviet Union, which outraged Nebraskan farmers.

With the primaries coming so thick and fast now, neither man could spend more than two days in Nebraska the final week. Reagan also made a pass through West Virginia, but Ford was so confident there he didn't bother to go at all. Because both states held closed primaries, the expectation was that Ford could win both. He did win West Virginia, 57–43 per cent, but Reagan came through resoundingly in Nebraska, routing the President 55–45. "They certainly haven't stopped our momentum," Sears said, "and in a way we've increased it. We've shown we can win where there is no crossover vote."

The sensation of being front-runner for the Republican presidential nomination was a heady experience for Ronald Reagan, so heady that he now began to talk about the qualifications he would look for in a running mate. "I can't mention any names," he said, "but I believe that a Vice President should be compatible enough with the President to continue his policies if the duty fell to him, without a radical change in course." Those were words he might eventually rue, but nobody was paying much attention at this point—except to note such a comment in itself was a measure of the dramatic turnabout in events.

Now it was Gerald Ford who needed a comeback. He could not afford to lose in his home state; everything would surely fall apart if he did. Four years earlier, George Wallace had received a startling 51 per cent in the Democratic primary in Michigan, with many thousands of Republicans crossing over to back him. Would they now return, together with Democratic Wallaceites, to vote for Ronald Reagan? The question haunted Ford's campaign, and the President of the United States himself, all during the next long week.

28. The Ford Recovery

As soon as the pattern of Ronald Reagan's "second phase" strategy began to unfold—the winning of open primaries that permitted conservative Democrats to cross over and vote in the Republican contest —the Michigan primary on May 18 loomed as a potential disaster for President Ford. His home state's primary voting system was a particular invitation to crossovers: unlike some states where voters had to declare publicly in which party primary they wished to participate in order to obtain the proper ballot, Michiganders had complete anonymity. Once inside the booth, a voter merely had to pull a lever to reveal either the Democratic or the Republican ballot, whichever he chose. With Wallace no longer a serious contender on the Democratic side, and Jimmy Carter supposedly a shoo-in, the danger was real that great numbers of the 809,000 Wallace voters of 1972 would invade the Republican primary—or return to it—to vote for Reagan.

With just that objective in mind, Reagan moved into Michigan right after his Nebraska victory, saying all the sorts of things Wallaceites liked to hear. In an interview with the *Detroit Free Press,* he blasted school busing as a "failed social experiment" and said of the ban on school prayers: "I've told people if we got government out of the classroom, we might get God back in." He also sharply criticized Secretary of State Kissinger for his activities on a recent trip to Africa, which, he claimed, had inflamed racial tensions there. And speaking to a cocktail reception in Kalamazoo, he said: "I think the problems cross party lines and I think the people will cross party lines."

Meanwhile, a skeletal Reagan organization—small because the campaign was still in a tight financial bind and federal campaign matching funds were still held up—hoped to recruit Wallace leaders as it had in Texas. One supporter tried to spirit away from Wallace headquarters that campaign's list of twenty thousand Wallace voters, but he was caught; State Senator Jack Wellborn, the leading in-state Reagan backer, apologized for what he called "overzealousness." And as it had done in Texas, the American Conservative Union announced it was pumping $20,000 into Michigan for radio and newspaper advertising, independent of Reagan's campaign, to woo independents and Democrats (Translation: Wallace voters). The Reagan campaign itself budgeted about $80,000, mostly for television and mailings to foes of abortion and opponents of gun control—again likely Wallace voters. Wellborn said it might not be so much "crossovers" as "crossbacks"—Republicans returning to the party fold after their 1972 flirtation with Wallace—who would help Reagan upset Ford.

Ford's forces in Michigan—the regular state party organization led by the boyish-looking Republican governor, William Milliken—were determined to see that such an upset did not happen. A week before the primary, Milliken sat at his desk at the state capitol in Lansing and talked about the impending contest. Milliken is among the most amiable of the nation's state executives, and he greeted his caller with a gracious smile and a warm handshake. But when the pleasantries were over and the subject turned to the primary, his face took on an uncharacteristically hard, determined cast. "The President can't afford to lose Michigan," he said. "And he won't." Milliken was a governor who had seen Reagan up close at numerous conferences, and his determination was more than simple empathy for home-state boy Jerry Ford: he "deplored" Reagan's "divisive" candidacy, he said, and found the man's ideas asinine.

Milliken had mobilized one of the best state party organizations in Republican ranks to pull out all stops for Ford, down to the county and township level. In addition, the White House and the Ford committee dispatched some of their key people to Michigan. "Michigan was our Texas," Peter Kaye said later. "Everything we had went into Michigan." And Stu Spencer said, "It was the degree of victory we were after. We needed a big one, and we had to be concerned about that Wallace crossover." Milliken himself taped a radio commercial that said Reagan was talking "nonsense" with his $90-billion plan and blasted his "box-office diplomacy." Michigan, the governor told his radio listeners, was "the state where the celluloid candidacy of Ronald Reagan will be exposed."

For all the determination to beat Reagan back, there was some dispute about how to cope with the crossover problem. The party's astute and energetic state chairman, William McLaughlin, opted to treat it as the threat of invasion by Democrats into the sanctity of a decision that should be left to Republicans. He was, he said, "completely shocked at Governor Reagan's blatant appeal for Democrats to give him the presidential nomination of the Republican Party," and "stunned" to hear that Reagan had called on Wallace Democrats to cross party lines. "I urge the Governor to reconsider his tactics. By encouraging Democrats to create mischief in our primary, he severely damages our vital two-party system. It is and must remain the prerogative of a political party to choose its own candidates.

That prerogative no longer exists when one party has control of the decision-making process in both parties. . . . This tactic makes a mockery out of our party's nominating process and seriously threatens the destruction of the Republican Party."

All this was a rather strange pitch for someone in Bill McLaughlin's political position to be making. At least since the days of Governor George Romney, and certainly during Milliken's regime, the Republican Party had managed to hold office in one of the nation's most blue-collar states, seat of the auto industry, by down-playing party label and ideology. It had run precisely the kind of state government that made Michigan a state of ticket-splitters at election time.

Milliken and Senator Robert Griffin stepped in and the pitch was changed 180 degrees: they, and the President himself, began to appeal directly to Democrats and independents to cross over and vote—for Ford, not Reagan. (Independents were a particular target, in that they constituted perhaps 40 per cent of Michigan's 4.6 million registered voters.) "I want every person registered in this state to vote for me, whether they call themselves Democrats, Republicans, or independents," Ford pleaded at an airport speech in Detroit. And he appealed unabashedly for special treatment as a native son. In his home town of Grand Rapids, he recalled his beginnings as a congressman and said: "Now, some twenty-seven years later, I am asking for the help and assistance of all of the people of this part of Michigan and the great state of Michigan."

Also, on the final weekend and at considerable expense, Ford rode a whistlestop train from Flint in the east to Niles in the west on an overcast, wet Saturday, plaintively asking the home folks not to forget one of their own. This obvious publicity gimmick was perfect for television coverage, and it seemed to work, what with nearly two hundred reporters aboard, about twice the usual campaign contingent. The President strode through the spanking-new, seven-car Amtrak train greeting the press and assorted Republican hangers-on, even encountering the great Democratic trainmaster Dick Tuck. (It was Tuck who reportedly dressed as a trainman and waved a train out of a station in California in 1962 while Richard Nixon was in mid-speech on the rear platform, and who confessed to having infiltrated a female spy onto the Goldwater whistlestop train in 1964.) Tuck, who holds the record in sixteen states for longevity of unemployment while traveling first-class, was accredited as a writer for *Playboy*.

Of greater interest was an encounter Ford had with a heckler at the Battle Creek stop. "When I took office on August eighth of 1974," the President was saying, "it was not an easy job. We had some real tough jobs to handle and some very difficult and formidable obstacles ahead of us."

With that, in this state where 12.5 per cent of the work force was unemployed, a young man shouted from the audience: "You blew it!" Ford swung to his left, where the voice had come from, and shouted back: "We blew it in the right direction, young man, and those of you who don't agree —" (cheers interrupting him) "—if you would go out and look for a job, you'd get one."

Such distractions were minor, and the mood was upbeat, if at times a bit desperate, in this first whistlestop by a President since Harry Truman's famous "Give 'em hell" tour of 1948; that, in fact, was a bit of Americana to which the Republican Ford conveniently compared his own circumstance, as if he too were the underdog. Reagan, meanwhile, studiously played down his chances, repeatedly saying he had no reason to expect he could win in Michigan. His strategists resisted pressures to bring him into the state the final weekend, and he campaigned there only one day in the last week, while running radio and television commercials as his budget allowed.

In the end, the simple pull of the native son carried the day. Thousands of Democrats did cross over and vote for Reagan, but many more thousands of Republicans crossed back, not for him but for their fellow Michigander. In a massive turnout of about a million, which nearly doubled the previous high for a statewide Republican primary, the President overwhelmed Reagan by almost 2–1: Ford 65 per cent, Reagan 34 per cent, with fifty-five delegates for Ford and twenty-nine for Reagan. (On the same night, the President won in the uncontested Maryland primary and picked up all forty-three delegates, bringing him close to Reagan in the national count.)

For Ford, the night's work, and especially the Michigan landslide, was "just tremendous." Rogers Morton—whose office door was kept tightly shut all night after the unhappy memory of the whisky-bottle photo—crowed jubilantly, "We're swinging back." (Asked by a reporter whether he now wanted to "rechristen the *Titanic,*" he snapped: "I'm not going to christen anything.") John Sears, speaking for Reagan, said the obvious: "We weren't expecting to win in Michigan and we really didn't conduct an active campaign. When a man comes to his home state, he's bound to get an extra boost."

As true as that was, Michigan was in every sense, but especially in the psychological sense, a stopper for Ford. For the first time in weeks, Reagan's issues did not dominate; the issue was largely nice-guy Jerry Ford. It was easy, of course, to make a home-state primary into a personality and popularity contest. But winning so resoundingly was a tonic for everyone in Ford's campaign, and it provided Ford with a buffer against what was perceived as another possible multiple disaster: six primaries for a total of

176 delegates the next Tuesday, May 25, three in border states and three in the West, regarded as Reagan country.

Going into these six—the most on a single day in the 1976 campaign —the President received an additional boost when the New York delegation, until then formally uncommitted under the leadership of Vice President Rockefeller, agreed to give him 119 of its 154 delegates. Richard Rosenbaum, the ambitious state chairman, left no doubt as to why, and why then. "I have to think," he said, "that in all likelihood the President will be further down after Tuesday because of the states he is running in. I think it behooves us to exert leadership." Reagan had already chipped away nearly twenty delegates, and further Ford setbacks could erode the New York situation even more. "There's such a thing," Rosenbaum said, "as waiting too long." Reagan said the move "smacks of bossism" and suggested that Rockefeller was "interested in being Vice President again."

In Pennsylvania also, some 88 members of the formally uncommitted delegation of 103 backed a resolution supporting the President. Together with New York, that put Ford comfortably in the lead for delegates again: *The Washington Star,* for example, now had it Ford 732, Reagan 530, with 184 uncommitted.

Of the six primaries the next Tuesday, three were considered safe for Reagan—Arkansas, Nevada, and Idaho—and indeed they proved to be, for he easily won more than 60 per cent of the vote in each. He was also rated a slight edge in Tennessee, another crossover state. Only in Oregon was Ford considered a good bet. Though the President eventually did win there, flooding the state with surrogate candidates and conducting twenty-two phone centers capable of making twenty thousand calls a night, he campaigned poorly; Reagan, running well in rural areas, closed what had been a 13-point gap in a *Portland Oregonian* poll to 4. Though the state had a liberal reputation, Reagan was well known there and still had a full head of steam from his string of primary upsets. The vote was finally Ford 52 per cent, Reagan 48, with Ford getting sixteen delegates and Reagan fourteen. The sixth primary of the day, in Kentucky, was considered to be the real battleground, and it turned out to be—along with Tennessee, thanks to an eleventh-hour Reagan blunder.

In Kentucky, a peculiar procedure governed. In a fierce fight at a state party convention held before the primary, the Reagan forces led by former Governor Louie Nunn had captured twenty-seven of the state's thirty-seven delegates to the national convention. The primary was then held with no party crossovers allowed, to determine essentially how the delegates would vote at the convention *on the first ballot only.* This quirk gave Ford a second chance, and the President's strategists realized this could be of considerable importance if Ford were able to get to the convention with close to an absolute majority. Both candidates campaigned in Kentucky, and a late effort was made by Reagan's forces to create a school-busing issue. Ford, in an interview with Kentucky media representatives, left the impression that Louisville, a city that had suffered years before from a stormy busing controversy, might be considered by the Justice Department as a test case of the Supreme Court's controversial ruling on busing. The ACU made a strong effort in the Louisville area for Reagan, and he did carry the city and suburban Jefferson County, but Ford ran ahead in Lexington and rural areas, including those in the Tennessee Valley, winning the state, 51–47 per cent.

Some Ford strategists said that what happened in neighboring Tennessee on the final weekend had made the difference. What happened was that Ronald Reagan pulled another "Barry Goldwater," and he did it, incredibly, at the very scene of an earlier Goldwater faux pas, in the home country of the Tennessee Valley Authority. Even before Goldwater in 1964 had thrown away the border states with a suggestion that TVA be sold to private enterprise, those initials had been a red flag to Republican politicians. Reagan particularly should have been wary about saying anything at all about the popular and highly successful New Deal enterprise that had revitalized the whole area.

On the Friday before the primary, Reagan was doing a television taping in Knoxville to be used, ironically, in a paid commercial, when he nonchalantly dropped a bomb. Asked about TVA, he said: "Well, I have always believed that there is an example of the government starting out with what was supposed to be a more or less legitimate government operation, a flood-control project, that is suddenly becoming a great part of the power-producing combine of this country, competing with private enterprise but on a tax-free basis and with its own bonding power, able as an agency without the consent of the people to amass a debt against the people, to put the people into debt for hundreds of millions of dollars. And I still believe in the free marketplace, and that government, unless there's an absolute necessity, doesn't have a place in business."

All this sounded ominous, but surely Reagan wasn't going to fall into the same pit that trapped Goldwater. Now the questioner asked directly: "Barry Goldwater once suggested selling TVA, using that same argument: that it belongs in the private sector. If elected President, would you go along with that kind of argument?"

The warning flag was up and flying, but Reagan was undeterred.

"Well, if you look at it, that is the way TVA acquired its vast dominance in the power field. It actually outcompeted with privately owned utilities and bought them, and today, when the original concept is supposed to be produced by the impounded water . . . they actually produce the bulk of their power from steam-generating plants, not just from their hydroelectric projects. You're asking a question involving a gigantic combine and gigantic interests. I've told you what my philosophy is. . . . I don't think I can give you an answer. [Pause] It would be something to look at."

Reagan never should have added that last sentence.

Ford's forces immediately jumped in. Quickly they taped comments from Senator Howard Baker and the local Republican congressmen in both states and got them out to every radio station in southern Kentucky and Tennessee, together with a press release; Rogers Morton predicted "major political fall-out" among voters "who depend on TVA for jobs and lower power rates"; the President chimed in by telling a group of Tennessee reporters at the White House that he fully supported TVA; Senator Bill Brock called Reagan "unrealistic."

Reagan, realizing his mistake, tried to backtrack. "I don't have any plans to sell TVA to private enterprise," he insisted in Nashville. But he made clear he wished he could. "What I object to is government entering into competition with private enterprise." He didn't think, he said, "anybody's going to put a price tag on it and put it on the market. . . . You do have a monopoly situation involved, but I think that somebody jumped the gun and suggested I was going to destroy the Tennessee Valley Authority. . . . I cannot deny it, philosophically: I do not believe that the government should be involved in competition with the private sector. But it is there, a fact of life."

Ordinarily, on the final weekend of a primary in mid-spring, such remarks might be overlooked. But Ford made certain they were not, and Reagan's denials only served to give his original comments wider circulation. In the end, the flap probably cost Reagan Tennessee; he lost by only 2170 votes of nearly 250,000 cast. With delegates apportioned by congressional district, however, Reagan came out ahead, 22–21, but in the psychological battle—the one written about in the headlines and broadcast on television news—Ford was the winner. He had three of six primaries for the day, far better than anyone had expected. "It was the night that Reagan had to make a big comeback," Stu Spencer said, "and he didn't do it." And Peter Kaye noted: "Michigan stopped Reagan, and Tennessee and Kentucky turned it around. Then all we had to do was play out the string."

That was somewhat of an oversimplification, because three large primaries still lay ahead—California, Ohio, and New Jersey, all on June 8. On June 1, Ford picked up Rhode Island and South Dakota and Reagan won Montana, and the two candidates headed for the final day of primaries, both realizing they probably would emerge from the long ordeal of state elections short of a majority. Ford could clinch the nomination by winning California, still choosing its 167 delegates in the Republican primary on a winner-take-all basis, but that looked less and less likely; Reagan needed California simply to remain in contention, and he campaigned long and hard there—which suited Ford fine. When it became clear that Reagan was nearly unbeatable in his home state—he was 10 percentage points ahead in early May in the prestigious Mervin Field Poll—Ford campaigned in California only enough to keep Reagan occupied there. He concentrated instead on New Jersey, where sixty-seven delegates could be picked up and Reagan was not even on the ballot, and on Ohio, where ninety-seven delegates could be won against minor opposition. Reagan had managed back in April to file slates in fifteen of Ohio's twenty-five congressional districts plus a statewide slate, but he had done little groundwork, much to the chagrin of Ohio conservatives. "Our strategy was to keep Reagan pinned to California, to keep him the hell out of Ohio," Spencer said, "and we were pretty successful."

But there was only so much the Ford campaign could do to engage Reagan in California. Ford's operation, like Reagan's, was beginning to bump against the legal spending limit of $13.1 million for the preconvention period, and extensive delegate hunting would have to take place after the primaries were over. There was some hope that a media campaign in California could keep Reagan tied down, but that idea was fraught with difficulties. For one thing, Ford's national advertising operation had never seemed to get organized, and the chaos reached fiasco proportions in California. Peter Dailey of Los Angeles, who had masterminded Nixon's insulated but effective media campaign in 1972, was in charge until sometime in May, but he insisted on running it from California, creating great problems for the Washington headquarters. As the California primary approached, Dailey was fired and replaced by James J. Jordan, president of Batten, Barton, Durstine & Osborn, Inc., of New York. The result was a series of ads—production spots, they are called in the business—with actors and actresses extolling the virtues of Gerald Ford. But these so-called "slice-of-life dramatizations" bombed. Spencer and Kaye, both Californians who firmly believed that Reagan's own record as governor was vulnerable, pushed hard to have anti-Reagan ads made, but it was decided that nothing so divisive should undermine the President's chances to carry California in the fall. Still, an expenditure of about $600,000 by the Ford campaign there kept Reagan busy.[1]

Though by the last week of the primary the outcome was a foregone conclusion—the Field poll now had Reagan ahead, 56–32 per cent—California in the end proved to be beneficial for Ford, because its primary brought to the surface a mini-issue that caused Reagan difficulty in Ohio. The subject was one that at first glance seemed far removed from 1976 American presidential politics: the struggle of black guerrilla forces in Rhodesia to force Prime Minister Ian Smith to permit greater black participation in the government.

Taking questions before the Sacramento Press Club, Reagan was asked: "On the subject of Rhodesia, you said that we should guarantee that there is no bloodshed. How would we do that? With an occupation force, with military troops, observers, or what?"

Reagan replied: "They are fighting these guerrillas from across the border, and doing so very well. But whether it would be enough to have simply a show of strength, the promise that we would [supply troops], or whether you would have to go in with occupation forces or not, I don't know. But I believe in the interests of peace and avoiding bloodshed, and to achieve a democratic majority rule which we all, I think, subscribe to, I think would be worth this, for us to do it."

"You would consider sending U.S. troops if necessary?"

Reagan replied that if Rhodesia requested a "token" show of strength, he would provide it. "We discussed the same thing in the Middle East, doing the same thing there." He went on: "Possibly we could go in as we did in the Middle East under the U.N. Command. That was one of the most useful things that the U.N. has done in the last couple of decades."

Q: "You said a token force."

A: "I don't think you'd have to."

Q: "Would you, if you had to?"

A: "If we made such an arrangement, such a pledge, I assume we would. But I do not believe that this would be out of line with the policy that we followed in several other areas and the policy that we followed in the Middle East. And certainly it never involved us in war in the Middle East, nor do I believe it would involve us in war there."

Reagan's remarks immediately precipitated glaring headlines in Cali-

---

1. An effort was also made to deprive Reagan of the bundle of 167 California delegates by trying to engineer a last-minute legislative switch in Sacramento on the winner-take-all ground rules. The proposal, which would have permitted allocation of delegates in proportion to the popular vote, was slapped down unanimously by a caucus of the Republican State Senate.

fornia newspapers and wire-service dispatches across the country. President Ford called the idea of dispatching troops "irresponsible"; Morton said Reagan's suggestion "raises a serious question on his qualification to be President." Elliot Richardson, in Santa Barbara, accused Reagan of "shooting from the hip" and observed: "For a man who aspires to be President, this kind of thinking is frightening."

Reagan had talked himself into a tight spot, and he knew it. Defensively, he took out after what he called "the headline-hunting press" for misrepresenting a "hypothetical" answer, and he told a crowd in Santa Barbara the next day: "They tried first to say I wanted to have a war over the [Panama] Canal and now they're trying to say I want to have a war over Rhodesia. No, I don't." He didn't think troops would be required, and what he meant to say was that the United States should "go in and mediate a settlement. . . . The United States has agreements, guarantees to keep peace around the world. What I'm suggesting is nothing more than that. Eisenhower sent troops to Lebanon. They never fired a shot."

Once again, the Ford people leaped in. Swiftly shelving their new "soft" television advertisements, new spots were rushed into production featuring this narrative: "Last Wednesday, Ronald Reagan said he would send American troops to Rhodesia. On Thursday he clarified that. He said they could be observers, or advisers. What does he think happened in Vietnam? . . . When you vote Tuesday, remember: Governor Ronald Reagan couldn't start a war. President Ronald Reagan could."

Lyn Nofziger was worried about last-minute slippage of the Reagan vote, and he fired off a telegram to Ford charging "a dirty political trick beneath the dignity of a President" and demanded withdrawal of the ads. He was, of course, ignored.

By this time, Reagan's campaign advisers had decided their candidate was so far ahead that he could risk leaving California for a last-minute attempt to win some delegates in Ohio. But there he was met with more questions about Rhodesia—just what the Ford campaign was hoping for. "My God, if Ford had walked the length of the Sacramento River, we couldn't have won California," Kaye reflected. "But what the Rhodesia issue did do, by coming at Reagan so hard, it pinned him down and by the time he got to Ohio that weekend it was all anybody could talk about. That was the closest thing to the ninety-billion-dollar plan we had."

Reagan, irritated by the reporters' persistence about Rhodesia, tried to switch everyone's attention to his old, less controversial anti-Washington theme. But he could not resist his penchant for jingoism, even with this latest *gaffe* dogging him. At the airport in Canton, birthplace of President

William McKinley, he observed: "There have been people who suggest my ideas would take us back to the days of McKinley. Well, what's wrong with that? Under McKinley, we freed Cuba."

Charlie Black, sent into Ohio to generate what he could in the last week, acknowledged that Reagan couldn't win the state but emphasized the importance of simply cutting into Ford's delegate score. "We're in a situation where every delegate counts," he said. Reagan aides said privately their goal was to win six or eight of the fifteen congressional districts in which Reagan was slated, for eighteen to twenty-four delegates, but Reagan was more cautious. "Ten," he said, "is a nice round number."

The Ford effort in Ohio, however, was formidable. Governor James Rhodes and state party chairman Kent McGough committed the party machinery, and their own time; in both television and phone bank operations, the Ford effort outspent Reagan; and the special weapon of incumbency also was brought to bear. Administration officials poured into the state and the President himself endorsed expansion of a $2.7 billion nuclear fuel plant in southeastern Ohio that affected the economy of two districts where Reagan was pushing hard. "Our tax dollars are being used to buy votes," Reagan's state manager, Peter Voss of Canton, complained, but that was how the game was being played.

This final primary day proved to be a disappointment for Reagan. Though he routed Ford in California, 66–34 per cent, he was shut out in New Jersey, the President picking up all sixty-seven delegates without a challenge, and he fell short even of his own modest goal in Ohio, winning only three congressional districts, for nine delegates (though he received a somewhat surprising 45 per cent of the vote to 55 per cent for the President). In sum Ford collected 155 delegates to 176 for Reagan; the President had effectively blunted the California sweep.

Now, at last, the most widely publicized, and most costly, phase of the battle for the Republican nomination was over. Neither candidate, by mutual reckoning, had enough delegates to be nominated. Each claimed, though, that with what he would pick up in the remaining state conventions and in wooing uncommitted delegates around the country, he would win a first-ballot victory in Kansas City in August. Paul Laxalt, breakfasting with a group of Washington reporters, said the decision might well rest with a hundred or fewer uncommitted delegates. "They're going to get a lot of attention and free meals," the Reagan chairman observed. With two months to go to convention time, the hard persuading, arm-twisting, cajoling, and —eventually—even begging, began.

29. Loose Ends and Uncommitteds

On June 8, when the last of the primaries were over, eleven of the twenty-one states who chose delegates to the Republican National Convention through state conventions had completed that process. According to a *New York Times* tally, Reagan had won 178 delegates by this nonprimary route, to 114 for Ford and 64 uncommitted. Some 270 more delegates were still to be chosen in the other ten nonprimary states, and about 100 more had been elected as uncommitted in the states that had held primaries. Thus, at this late stage more than 400 delegates were still to be selected or to state a preference—more than enough to decide the outcome. President Ford, aiming at the required majority of 1130 delegates, was at least 170 delegates short, and Reagan needed about 270. So the two candidates and their campaign organizations set themselves the laborious job of winning the delegate slots that remained open—and sweet-talking the fence-sitters.

From the outset, Reagan's organization had been better prepared to do battle in the nonprimary states. This was unusual inasmuch as the President could count on the party structures to assist him in most states and provide leadership through important officeholders, from the governor on down. And in states selecting their delegates in convention, the key was turnout and commitment by the party activists. Among Republicans, one did not often find the off-the-street participation seen in Democratic ranks among cause-oriented enthusiasts; people involved in party affairs were mostly regular members of the establishment who did not entertain easily the idea of opposing an incumbent President.

But one central factor worked against Ford. His campaign had not thought it would have to struggle for every last delegate to win the nomination, and neither did most Republicans. The Ford committee's strategy was the strategy of the early knockout: beat Reagan in all the early primaries and force him to quit before the contest ever got down to serious delegate-counting. The Reagan campaign had also started with a knockout strategy, but had recognized after its New Hampshire defeat that it was in for a long haul. Stu Spencer started organizing for Ford in the caucus states early, but he found the going extremely hard, since few party regulars were taking

Reagan seriously. "There was just an attitude across the country that the President wouldn't have any problem," he said. "To get people excited at the precinct level was very, very difficult."

Also, the Ford campaign had no one person responsible for corraling delegates—a head-hunter, in political parlance—until just before the Michigan primary in mid-May, when it was reeling from six straight primary defeats. Jack Stiles, an old Michigan friend of the President, had been designated but had been killed in an auto accident, and the job was unfilled until James A. Baker, a Texan serving as under secretary of commerce, was asked by Rogers Morton to take it.

Jim Baker had been involved in Texas politics in Harris County (Houston), where he handled George Bush's losing campaign for the Senate in 1970 and carried the county for him by more than 60 per cent. Also, he had raised money for Nixon in 1972, but he had never been involved in national politics. He joined Ford's campaign strictly to keep track of delegates already selected, to make certain those supporting Ford stayed firm, and to try to bring uncommitted delegates over. Winning delegates in nonprimary states remained the task of Spencer's political division, which, until Baker came aboard, had been obliged to focus mainly on the primary competition. However, by the time Baker took hold and Spencer was able to address his operation to the convention states, Reagan's people were already hard at work. "We never thought we'd need the convention states," Baker said, "so we were woefully outorganized by the Reagan forces in them, most of which are the Western states, where their natural strength was anyway."

The deficiency of Ford's operation in the convention states—notably its dependence on local party leaders—became apparent as soon as the media's spotlight switched from the primaries to the state convention in Missouri on June 12. There, the President made a personal appeal for nineteen at-large delegates and was humiliated by a near-sweep by Reagan. In earlier congressional-district conventions, each selecting three delegates, Ford had won 5–4 over Reagan, and people had the idea that he would also have the upper hand at the statewide meeting in St. Louis. "I rode out on the plane," Baker recalled, "and I remember that the President was very confident that we were going to sweep the at-large delegates." But the local Ford forces, led by Governor Christopher (Kit) Bond, overlooked the fact that Reagan had won by a lopsided margin in one of the congressional districts he captured, and hence had many more delegates at the state convention than Ford from that district. "We just weren't counting right," one insider admitted. "It was a mistake to take the President in there. We were down ninety votes when he arrived. We should have been counting better." Ed Terrill, the campaign's regional manager, hadn't wanted Ford to come, Spencer said later, but come he did, and while he managed to cut into the deficit he was still snowed under. The Ford forces, led by Bond, contested about seventy or eighty Reagan delegates and for a time tried to push through a procedure whereby delegates could not vote on any challenge involving themselves. That rule would have permitted the Ford delegates to decide all challenges in their favor. Signs reading "Thou Shalt Not Steal" sprang up on the convention floor, and Ford's forces finally backed off, fearful of a serious party split that would extend to Bond's own bid for re-election in the fall. (He lost anyway.) All but one of the nineteen delegates went to Reagan, with the last spot given to Bond in a face-saving gesture to preserve some sort of unity.

The very next weekend there were three more conventions in Iowa, Washington, and Delaware, with Iowa the major battleground. (As expected, Reagan won handily in Washington, more handily in fact than anticipated, collecting thirty-one delegates to only seven for Ford; and the President picked up thirteen in Delaware, with four others going uncommitted.) A total of thirty-six delegates was at stake in congressional-district and state conventions in Iowa, and each side openly predicted it would win at least twenty. Though burned so badly and conspicuously in St. Louis, the President planned to put in another personal appearance in Des Moines, which would mean the first personal confrontation between Ford and Reagan since the start of the long campaign. But that very week, on June 16, three Americans, including U. S. Ambassador Francis E. Meloy, Jr., had been slain in Lebanon, the murders precipitating a crisis that led to the voluntary evacuation of all Americans from that country. At the last minute, Ford decided to stay in Washington to oversee the evacuation. Some politicians thought he was merely ducking out of Iowa, others that it was decided he would gain more at the state convention by demonstrating his on-the-job statesmanship. But the White House insisted there was no ulterior motive.

In any event, Ford's decision took some steam out of his political efforts in Des Moines. Governor Robert D. Ray, his chief backer in Iowa, said he was "terribly disappointed," but still predicted Ford would win twenty-three delegates. Peter Kaye, the eternal truth-teller, revealed the more ambivalent, and prevalent, response when he told Jim Naughton: "It might help by reminding people that he's President and he's in the business of having to live with tough decisions. . . . But Reagan is going to be there working on the delegates, and we're not."

Reagan was there all right, and his hard-nosed operatives led by John Sears, too. Again, Reagan made the argument that his strong showing in crossover primaries had proved his ability to attract Democrats and independents and thus win in a general election. "In primaries where Democrats can cross over, I have won without fail," he told the Iowans—ignoring the fact that he lost in two crossover states, Wisconsin and Michigan. Pinch-hitting for the President was Betty Ford, along with Senators Howard Baker, Robert Griffin and Robert Dole. But they were no substitute for the real thing in the kind of head-to-head politicking Reagan was able to carry out with many of the 3495 delegates in small caucuses. Many had already received "personal" letters from Ford, but without him there to follow up, his strategists were plainly nervous. Stu Spencer went to one of the district caucuses and listened to Reagan speak. "He turned some votes around, no doubt about it," he said.

In the six congressional-district caucuses, Ford won sixteen delegates to fourteen for Reagan, and the convention then settled in to vote for six remaining at-large delegates. The Ford forces had hoped to gain at least five of the six by running Governor Ray, Representative Charles Grassley, and four other well-known, high-ranking state party officials. But Reagan gained unexpected strength on a special nominating committee picking the six, and after much hassling won agreement for an even split. The central figure here was Dennis C. Bailey, a finance company owner who was thought to be committed to the party leadership on the at-large selections but turned out to be a closet Reaganite. Bailey was brought to see Sears and Clarence Werner, Reagan's field man in the state, in the early morning and they talked him into the split. The result was nineteen delegates for Ford and seventeen for Reagan. The Reagan people said afterward that had Ford's strategists elected to have a floor fight, the President could have swept the at-large bloc. "I'm just as glad they didn't gamble," Sears said. "We didn't have any good at-large candidates, so if they had gone for a slate, we would have been killed."

In all, counting the Washington and Delaware results, Reagan had added forty-eight delegates to his total for the weekend's activity, and Ford thirty-nine—not a very substantial gain or loss for either candidate. But that was the way the contest went now, nickel-and-diming each weekend through June and July. Because the race was so extremely tight, neither side could give an inch; in the combat of presidential politics, this was truly trench warfare.

No state convention better illustrated the point than Minnesota's, the weekend after the Iowa scramble. There, eighteen at-large delegates were at stake. Ford clearly had the upper hand in that progressive state, but the Reaganites were determined to squeeze what they could out of the situation, if only to gain some psychological mileage. Of the 1908 delegates who met in the old St. Paul Civic Center, a straw poll indicated Ford had at least

55 per cent. In a naked power play, a Ford-controlled rules committee voted by a 9–8 margin to require that each of the eighteen at-large delegates win by majority vote, rather than the top eighteen vote-getters being elected. This meant that in all probability only Ford delegates could make it and the President would sweep all eighteen.

The Reagan forces screamed bloody murder—or, in the more diplomatic language of 1976, "fairness." They argued that not only simple fairness but the interest of party unity would be served if the estimated 45 per cent favoring Reagan had some representation on the state delegation to Kansas City. David Keene and Sears pushed for six of the eighteen slots, but the proposal was rejected flatly by the Ford strategists, Bill Russo and Spencer.

The Reaganites raised this issue in part because they hoped that Minnesota's progressivism would be receptive to them. But they also wanted to establish clearly that the Ford people were not interested in "fairness" when they had the votes. The next day, in New Mexico, the Reaganites would be holding all the cards, and they wanted to be able to point to Minnesota as justification for rejecting any "fairness" plea from the Ford camp. They did so, and swept all twenty-one New Mexico delegates, in the process denying a slot to Senator Pete Domenici. Soon "fairness" became a friendly joke between the two sides, always raised by the candidate on the short end. In St. Paul, Spencer recalled later, "Sears and I saw each other. We were going for winner-take-all and Sears raised fairness. I said, 'We'll give it to you if you give it to us in Montana [which was holding a convention the same day to deal out twenty delegates after a nonbinding primary won overwhelmingly by Reagan].' And he answered, 'Hell, no.' And they took all twenty."

Anyway, the argument went back and forth in St. Paul and the Reaganites got nowhere. Balloting under the new rule produced an impossible vote-counting mess; more than thirty-five thousand individual votes had to be recorded. The Minnesota convention staggered on until three o'clock in the morning before any result was reached. Delegates got restless and then rambunctious, as all the concession stands closed, leaving the participants hungry and deprived of coffee. They resorted to such varied entertainments as community singing, a stickball game on the floor, a Japanese folk dance, and a reading from *Teahouse of the August Moon.* Finally the tally revealed that, as expected, Ford delegates alone had managed the required majority, but only seventeen of them. The eighteenth finisher, a Reaganite, fell short, so the hassling resumed over the eighteenth spot.

Keene moved into action to salvage something out of the bizarre night. The eighteenth and nineteenth finishers were both Reagan supporters, and

Keene had a brainstorm. "I went and cut a deal with Russo," he explained later. "One of our two agreed to step aside rather than have a runoff under the rules, so I went and told him: 'It's three o'clock in the morning. We're willing to drop one of our people. Let's give the last slot to him and we can all go home.' Russo agreed, and then, as the convention was voting on it, I told him that the rules called for a runoff among the top *four,* two of which were theirs, so they could have won it." Keene laughed. "There was no reason to tell him before," he said.

That was the climate of political hardball in which this last phase of delegate selecting was going forward: sometimes bitter, sometimes light-hearted, but always tenacious.[1]

The next week, the Ford forces pulled off an upset in North Dakota by having, for once, a state organization that came through for them. In what was represented to be a true unity slate, state party chairman Allan Young, a Ford ally, got the Reaganites, unsure of their numbers, to settle for a split that gave Ford at least twelve delegates and Reagan only four. But in Colorado the same weekend, a superior Reagan organization delivered the goods, giving their man twenty-six delegates to four for Ford, despite hard campaigning for his father by Jack Ford, who had spent a lot of time in the state.

The final set of convention states, on the weekend of July 16, was also a tradeoff. Ford took all of Connecticut's 35 delegates, despite still another go-around on "fairness"; Reagan got all 20 in Utah, even beating popular conservative Senator Jake Garn, siding with Ford. At the end of the long delegate-selection trail, neither candidate yet had a majority. *The New York Times* gave the President 1102 delegates, 28 short of the nomination; and Reagan 1063, or 67 short; with 94 uncommitted. News organizations differed on specific numbers, but none disagreed with the basic conclusion that Ford was ahead.

Now came the intensified psychological warfare, with each side trying to create the impression that the trend was breaking its way. An early gambit, even before the Connecticut and Utah finales, was a suggestion by Ford in an impromptu Oval Office press conference that he would accept Reagan as his running mate. Harry Dent, Ford's Southern regional coordinator, had been spreading word of a possible Ford-Reagan ticket as a way to pry loose some Dixie support, and the President seemed to encourage it. "I exclude nobody," Ford said. "I hope that individuals, meantime, will not

---

1. Among those at the Minnesota convention was Harold Stassen. As he stood unrecognized by many of the delegates, Jack Germond engaged him in conversation.

  "*You* know how tough primaries can be," Germond offered.

  "Yeah," Stassen replied, "but these guys don't have Tom Dewey running against them!"

exclude themselves, because we want the best ticket we can get to win in November." His prime consideration would be that the person selected "would make an excellent President," and when asked whether Reagan would qualify, he said pointedly, "That's a fair conclusion." Reagan meanwhile repeated that "I am not running for Vice President." Yet the speculation persisted, and that did his cause no good.

Other, more direct efforts at delegate persuasion were undertaken. Each side attempted to cloud the picture by inflating its delegate counts, with the Reagan camp predictably the greater offender simply because it was trailing. Jim Baker was the chief spokesman for Ford and John Sears for Reagan, and both men worked hard to give the impression that their candidates were moving inexorably toward a first-ballot nomination. As Baker's numbers, holding up fairly well under press scrutiny, crept closer to the magic number of 1130, Sears jumped in on July 19 with a flat claim that Reagan would have 1140. His numbers, he insisted, had "very little play" in them, whereas "there is a great degree of softness in Mr. Ford's strength." (Baker conceded later, after the election, that Reagan's support had tended to be firmer at that point.) "They were using the Trojan Horse argument," Baker said. "They were saying, 'There's softness in the Northeastern delegations.'" Baker countered four days later by disclosing 15 Hawaii delegates for Ford he said gave the President 1135—5 more than he needed. The President had certain tools to firm up his support, however, that Reagan did not, and the most impressive of these was 1600 Pennsylvania Avenue—the White House itself.

Unabashedly, Ford began to invite whole state delegations, especially those with large blocks of uncommitted delegates, to lunch, dine, or drink with him at America's most famous address. It got to the point where a minor local party official, Edwin Schwenk, the Suffolk County, New York, Republican chairman, had ten minutes with the President and reported afterward that Ford had agreed to take a closer look at the problems of a Suffolk sewer district facing cuts in federal aid! When Schwenk later announced that the Suffolk delegation was backing the President, Dick Rosenbaum, the party's state chairman and Ford's leader in New York, insisted angrily and defensively that "Schwenk got nothing."

The President also found himself having to field hard questions on more significant policy issues from the visiting delegates. Most of his meetings with them were held in the Cabinet Room (for smaller delegations) or the massive East Room, Blue Room, or State Dining Room (for the larger ones). Chairs were set up in a regular press-conference format. His usual approach was to mingle with the delegates for perhaps half an hour, speak for ten or fifteen minutes about the accomplishments of his administration, and then take questions for another hour or more. Ford committed himself, Dick Cheney said later, "willingly, because he knew the importance of it." No matter how long the questions would last, or how tough, he would hang in. When the New Jersey delegation of sixty-seven came, for example, a delegate asked him right off about his pardon of Nixon; others pressed him on abortion, offshore oil drilling, and the closing of military bases in New Jersey.

Mostly, the White House sessions were designed to cement support in a period when many of Ford's delegates were being pressured by Reagan's camp or by Reagan personally. "We had to make sure our Indians didn't leave the reservation," Baker said. Ford "did not want to be the first sitting President since Chester Arthur to be denied his party's nomination, and he worked extremely hard. He was tireless." When Ford was not meeting delegates personally, Baker said, he was talking to them on the phone, answering their questions.

The toughest delegation to deal with, Spencer and Baker agreed, was West Virginia's, formally uncommitted. Governor Arch Moore insisted throughout that he had at least twenty and probably twenty-two of the state's twenty-eight delegates locked up, but, Spencer said later, "you could never get him to do anything. You couldn't get him to sign a piece of paper, or hold a caucus," or in any other way demonstrate the delegates' firmness. They always seemed to be going off in all directions, telling inquiring reporters various stories of their loyalty and putting the Ford committee in a quandary. It was a policy on the committee not to contact state delegates directly if the head of the delegation was an individual of stature, such as a governor. But in the end, Baker and his operation were obliged to go in over Moore's head. The President finally had a lunch at the White House for the twenty-two whom Moore said were Ford people. Afterward, Moore insisted—despite some of them telling reporters they were uncommitted— that "there isn't any softness in our votes." No one knew whether to believe him or not.[2] Eventually, at the convention, Moore did deliver twenty delegates, but Spencer and others said later they doubted whether he really had them earlier, when he claimed he did.

Bringing delegates to the White House was only a last resort used in the delegate-wooing process. Baker, armed with books providing background on each delegate and aided by nine full-time aides working in

---

2. The West Virginia delegation lunched that day on breast of chicken, stewed tomatoes, and shrimp, which, a White House spokesman said, in answer to press inquiries, the President paid for "personally," and hence the cost did not come out of the committee's spending limit under the law.

various regions, invoked a kind of buddy system to persuade prospects. "What I tried to do was to find out whose judgment was most respected by a particular delegate," Baker said later. "Once we had determined who that was, we tried to get that person to work on that delegate. It may have been his neighbor, a cabinet member, a congressman. Ultimately, I'd say a hundred and fifty people were the ball game, and the President himself probably talked to or visited with practically every one of those uncommitted delegates." Often, repeated offers of help from cabinet members and congressmen were turned away. "We had to be careful," he said. "We wanted to make the approach to them the right approach. Most of the contacts were local. We tried to start with the local contacts and build up to the point where the President himself called. And we didn't want them pushed at all; we wanted them to feel they were making up their own minds and we weren't pressuring them."

When the President was not entertaining delegates he was phoning them, and key aides like Spencer and Baker were out around the country visiting others, trying to firm up "leaners" and win over uncommitteds. Various entertainments were offered; perhaps the most blatant was special seating on the flight deck of the U. S. S. *Forrestal,* an aircraft carrier, for about seven uncommitted New York delegates to view the great sailing ships in New York Harbor, marking the Bicentennial celebration on the July 4 weekend.

Reagan meanwhile was making his pitch, in person and by phone. In one well-publicized swing into the Northeast, he focused on Delaware, New Jersey, and Pennsylvania but came up more or less empty-handed. The typical exercise was for Reagan to set up shop in a hotel suite and then have uncommitted or wavering delegates shuttled in and out in groups of four and five. The kind of progress made was best illustrated during one such stand at the Penn-Harris Motor Inn in Harrisburg; a twenty-one-year-old college student named James Stein, who had been uncommitted but leaning to Ford, came out and announced he was now "unleaned."

The Northeast swing was made necessary, Sears acknowledged, because for all the supposed firmness among the Reagan delegates, some had been lost, especially in the South. Harry Dent was nibbling away at them in South Carolina, his home state, and also encouraging erosion in Mississippi, where the delegation had voted in April to go to the national convention uncommitted and there vote its thirty delegates as a bloc under the unit rule. Though the national party prohibited imposition of the unit rule, there was no way it could stop a state party from using it, and the rule had a long

and solid tradition in Mississippi. That tradition was now about to undergo
the greatest pressures in its history, as both Ford and Reagan zeroed in on
the Magnolia State—and on its colorful and eminently pressureable Republican party chairman, Clarke Reed.

30. *The Battle of Mississippi*

For the last ten years, when anybody in the Republican Party wanted anything done in Mississippi, there was one man and one man only to go to: Clarke Reed, the forty-eight-year-old state party chairman. Tall and wiry, with square, clean-cut features topped by an impressive silver-white mane that belied his otherwise youthful appearance, Reed was right out of some Hollywood casting director's dream of the political operator. He was slick and so fast-talking as to be almost incomprehensible. On top of that he was a whisperer; he liked to pull people aside and exchange confidences mouth-to-ear. He was Byzantine in style, and consumed with the intricacies of politics. He was consumed also, to his ultimate misfortune, with a desire to be always on the winning side, to hold on to power and influence—which after ten years had extended far beyond Mississippi in Republican ranks. He was chairman of the Southern Republican State Chairmen's Association and as such the Dixie GOP's leading *apparatchik* in the pulling-and-hauling to get a better deal for the South during the Nixon and Ford administrations. And a better deal to Clarke Reed got down primarily to having the feds get off the South's back—whether in the field of civil rights or education or any number of social-welfare impositions dictated from Washington.

At the White House, during the Nixon years particularly, it was customary in any major political decision affecting the Deep South to "clear it with Clarke," or at least to touch base with him. When you said "Clarke" you didn't have to provide any further identification; it was a sign of Reed's eminence that must have been particularly pleasing. But as the presidential election year opened in 1976, the assumption at the White House and in Republican circles generally was that Clarke Reed would be with Ronald Reagan and so, undoubtedly, would the Mississippi delegation. The Ford people did not have to know that he had been one of the earliest proponents of a Reagan candidacy back in the spring of 1975, when the nucleus of the embryo Reagan staff met in Los Angeles to lay the groundwork; they, and the world, knew enough about his ideology to guess he would be a Reagan man. He was and always had been a True Believer in conservative positions, foreign and domestic, and he liked to think and say that he acted out of ideological conviction. But the truth was that Clarke Reed's strongest ideological conviction was that the causes in which he believed were best served if he ran with a winner, if he could retain power.

Another motivation, however, beat strongly in Clarke Reed's breast. That was an instinct for self-preservation. After the 1975 gubernatorial election, in which the Republican candidate, Gil Carmichael, ran an unexpectedly strong race and emerged as a new power in the state party, people said Clarke's days were numbered as Mississippi's unchallenged Republican boss. And when he suddenly disclosed that he would not seek another term as state chairman but would only stay on as Mississippi's member of the Republican National Committee, some speculated that he was merely facing the inevitable. Reed himself insisted he could have been re-elected chairman unopposed, but that he had had enough. At any rate, Charles Pickering, a young state senator with his eye on the governorship, was elected Reed's successor. It was agreed that Pickering would not take over until after the national convention, where Reed would have his last hurrah.

The state convention was held unusually early, in April, to take advantage, Reed said later, of the enthusiasm brought to the party by Carmichael's close race. He wanted, he said, to enlist much of the new talent that had been recruited during that campaign. No thought at all was given to the question of whether those who wanted to be delegates to the national convention were for Ford or Reagan. And in that nonchalance lay the roots of all the turmoil that was to follow.

The new recruits tended on the whole to be younger and more moderate than the old group headed by Reed, and at the state convention many of them were elected as alternates, which in Mississippi was almost as good as being a principal delegate. The state convention continued a long-time policy whereby each of its thirty delegates and thirty alternates would have one-half a vote on issues before the delegation, with the unit rule—the majority getting all thirty votes—applying unless specifically rescinded by a majority vote of the sixty. So although no candidate preference was asked or stated at the time, the climate for the later blossoming of Ford support within this supposedly solid, conservative delegation was enhanced by the procedure that gave the more moderate alternates a vote.

In planning the state convention, Reed explained later, it was decided that party service would be rewarded and candidate preference at the national convention "would not be as important, because the nomination would be settled by the time we got there." If the Ford-Reagan competition were not decided in the primaries by April, everybody thought, it would be soon thereafter, and so Mississippi would have no real choice in determining the party standard-bearer anyway. With this prospect in mind, it was agreed also that the delegation would go to Kansas City uncommitted. There, the unit rule would be observed, casting Mississippi's thirty votes for whichever candidate had eliminated the other in the primaries. "The argument of who anybody was for really never came up because under the unit rule, we always felt we've come out reflecting the state position," Reed said. To keep peace, individuals favoring the President were placed on the delegation with known Reagan backers, who were in the clear majority.

Reagan's campaign in Mississippi, led rather casually at the beginning by Billy Mounger, an ace fund-raiser for the party, went along, Reed said, on the theory, "Don't worry about Mississippi, it's a Deep South state." David Keene, Reagan's Southern coordinator, said later, however, that while it was true his side was not concerned about Mississippi in the early stages, the reason was that Reed had pledged his own support and guaranteed the state would be with Reagan if he were at all in contention at the national convention. Keene had been recruited by John Sears at least in part because he was an old and good friend of Reed's. "I think one of the reasons John wanted me at the outset," Keene said, "was because he figured I could probably handle Clarke a little better than some people. Clarke committed to me early, but that was an easy commitment for him to make: he thought at the time that it was going to be over quickly one way or the other, and so did we. He said, 'I'll deliver Mississippi to you unless it's a joke, unless you've completely lost it by then.' I said, 'Look, I won't ask you then, but if I ask you, you've got to deliver.' He said, 'Fine.' "

Keene, as a one-time aide to Vice President Spiro Agnew and Senator James Buckley of New York, was one of the most effective young operatives in the conservative wing of the Republican Party. He had dealt closely with Reed for six or eight years and he knew his man. He knew that the idea of Reed as some latter-day Machiavelli was off-target, in fact exactly contrary to reality. "Clarke is not an evil guy," Keene said later. "He's weak. He's a guy whose reputation was made in part out of whole cloth. He's brighter than most of the people on the national committee; he's good copy, so the press like him; he's good at maneuvering to some extent, although not as good as he thinks he is. But his reputation was made fighting Nelson Rockefeller and Jacob Javits, and that doesn't take any courage, not if you're from Mississippi. You're rather expected to do that. He hadn't been in many battles where it was really tough. He had this feeling always that he should never lose, that you should never get into a thing where you're really tested because you might come out on the wrong side. So he took this assumption that this was going to be an easy one, because it was going to be over one way or the other. And when it came time to put together the delegation, he thought it didn't really matter. If it was going to be over, there wasn't going to be any trouble delivering it to whoever the winner was. And therefore they could remain neutral, and Clarke would get all the credit one way, or get the credit the other way for not coming out, and deliver his thirty votes to the guy who won. The worst thing that happened to Clarke Reed in his entire career was the fact that it wasn't over early. Because he then discovered that he put his delegation together in the sloppiest manner imaginable, that he had trouble on both sides, that he couldn't deliver it—at least to the extent that he thought he could. That was not a result of deviousness. That was a result of weakness, and a result of trying to please everybody."

Patching together a mixed delegation was a typical hedge for Reed, who felt he could always control it for Reagan by using the unit rule. "I kept badgering him, 'You know, Clarke, you'd better be sure of these people,'" Keene said. "And he'd say, 'Oh, don't worry about it.' Well, he eventually had as much to worry about as we did."

In the interest of having all segments of the state party leadership represented, the delegation that everyone assumed was for Reagan included Carmichael, who was very pro-Ford, and Douglas Shanks, a twenty-nine-year-old Jackson city commissioner, who was head of what passed for a Ford campaign in the state. It turned out to be, in due time, like boarding a couple of vampires at a blood bank. Carmichael and Shanks together would eventually start preying on the other members of the delegation in Ford's behalf, in direct challenge to Reed's leadership, and with telling effect.

Reed insisted later that from the time of the state convention at which he constructed this Trojan Horse delegation until late June or early July, there really was no Reagan organization in Mississippi. He said he warned the Reagan people in Washington and in the state that "this thing may get a little tight." But the Reagan camp denied that he had ever done so.

Meanwhile Shanks and Carmichael were having troubles of their own persuading the President Ford Committee in Washington that there was any constructive business to be done in Mississippi. Reagan had upset the President in North Carolina and was running his string of victories through Texas, Alabama, and Georgia, and the Ford strategists were wondering whether they were wasting time and money trying to win more delegates in the South. It was decided, in fact, to cut back the Southern field operations (run under the direction of Governor Holshouser of North Carolina), and in late May the Ford committee turned to that old Dixie political warhorse, Harry Dent, to be a kind of one-man overseer in the South.

Back in the lucrative practice of law in Columbia, South Carolina, after his somewhat frustrating years as Nixon's political adviser in the White

House, Dent resisted for a time but finally acceded. He was in the soup politically, anyway, having bucked the efforts of his own governor, James Edwards, to engineer a solid Reagan slate, and getting himself elected as an uncommitted delegate. His efforts for Ford really began one day after the closing down of the Ford field office, when he received a phone call that in a sense was the first, unheard shot in the 1976 battle of Mississippi.

Dent's caller was John Davis, a twenty-nine-year-old Ole Miss graduate who had worked in Carmichael's campaign and had just been laid off with the closing of the Ford Southern field office. Dent had asked that Davis be assigned to him but the Washington office said the campaign couldn't afford him. "Harry," Davis said, "I want to see this campaign through. I can go get a job but I'd rather do this. If you'll just feed me, I'll help you."

Dent, his hands more than full with his law practice and already working every night and weekend for Ford, readily agreed. "I took him into my home," Dent recounted, "and he just lived with me. He went to work with me every day and I set him up in my law office. He went everywhere with my family, just like another son."

And that was how Dent got onto the opportunity in Mississippi. "Harry," young Davis told him, "there's gold to be mined in Mississippi." Davis was aware of the inclinations of Carmichael and Shanks, and of the vulnerability of the delegation as constituted under Reed's misguided plan for party unity. Shanks was beginning to suggest that he for one would not go along with the unit rule, a position that provided the first crack in what had been expected to be unanimity for Reagan among Mississippi's thirty delegates. With the thirty delegates and thirty alternates each having one-half a vote on issues before the delegation, it would take a vote of 31–29 to break the unit rule. Shanks could be the tip of an iceberg that could sink Reagan's campaign.

Dent, who had been through all the civil-rights wars with Reed and had observed that since his own departure from the White House Reed had not gotten quite the same kid-glove treatment, knew how to approach him. He called his old friend and told him, half-joking, that he had wisely "put himself in the catbird seat." "I told him, 'Clarke, you're gonna be the kingmaker of this convention.'" Ford had taken a beating all over the South, except in Florida, and the die was cast for Reagan except among pockets of uncommitted delegates, the largest of which was in Mississippi. It was a golden opportunity for Clarke Reed to come to the rescue of the President, and put the South back into the front ranks of influence in the White House.

Dent was a great needler, and an entertaining storyteller and mimic. At an outing in mid-June held for the Southern state party chairmen by

Governor Holshouser at Atlantic Beach, North Carolina, he started working on Reed openly, half-kidding him about being "kingmaker" in front of the other state chairmen, most of whom had backed Ford and lost in their states.

"Now, Clarke," he would say in soothing, fatherly tones, "I want to tell you the updated version of the parable of the talents. Now, just imagine. After Ford's won this nomination, and we're sitting around the big table carving up the pie. There's Rosey Rosenbaum sitting up there at the head of the table, where he belongs. Boy, he's really been delivering, and holding every time he delivers. And the President's gonna turn to Rosey and say, 'Well done, thy good and faithful servant. Thou hast five talents and thou has increased them fivefold. Therefore, thou hast twenty-five votes at this table.'

"And, Clarke, then he's gonna look down there and he's gonna see me sitting at the other end, at the foot of the table. And he's gonna say, 'Well done, thy good and faithful servant Harry Dent. Thou wast entrusted with one talent and thou increased it onefold. Therefore, thou hast two votes at the table.'

"So there we are. Old Rosey Rosenbaum, the new king of the Republican Party. The new Northeastern strategy is gonna be put into effect. There's gonna be ol' Harry. Strom Thurmond [supporting Reagan] isn't gonna be there. Clarke Reed ain't gonna be there.

"But, Clarke, baby, you got thirty pieces of silver you can walk in there and throw on that table. Those thirty pieces of silver, in a timely fashion, would cover those twenty-five talents that Rosey had on the table. Then I could just see you coming in there, and the President could say, 'Well done, thy good and faithful servant Clarke.' And he could put you at the head of the table and put Rosey at the foot of the table. The Southern Strategy would prevail again. Long live the king!"

Reed protested that he didn't want to be a kingmaker, but he was listening. Dent started calling him "the reluctant kingmaker" in the presence of the other state chairmen and even sometimes before Dave Keene, who was keeping the heat on Reed from the other side. But it was Dent who had Reed's ear constantly. "I tried to explain to him this would be great for Mississippi, this would be great for the South; that the South had short-changed the President in those primaries and state conventions, and that Clarke would not only be the kingmaker for Ford but be the savior of the South and the Southern Strategy."

Luckily for Dent, also present at the Holshouser outing were the two heavies of the Ford campaign, Dick Cheney and Stu Spencer. Dent had known Cheney at the White House and took the opportunity to inform him at length about the possibilities for Ford in Mississippi. As an old White House political hand, Dent knew where the power lay. Up to now, according to Dent later, the PFC had been cool to spending much time or money on Mississippi, finding it hard to believe anything constructive could be achieved there, and generally brushing aside the efforts of Carmichael and Shanks. But Dent successfully got Cheney's ear, even flying back to Washington with him after the weekend to press his case.

Shortly thereafter, John Davis went by the White House to see Dr. Richard Brannon, formerly Dent's minister. Brannon had been taken on, Dent said, as "Mr. Southern Comfort," with Elliot Richardson at HEW, "to hold the South's hand while they desegregated the schools," and later was transferred to the White House. Davis showed Brannon a list of potential Ford delegates and alternates in Mississippi. Brannon was so impressed that he took him immediately to see Cheney, and one of his assistants, Jim Field. Cheney was interested, but the PFC continued to object, partly because Dent, Davis, and Carmichael were working with Cheney at the White House. A jurisdictional tug-of-war ensued.

Finally Rogers Morton at the PFC phoned Dent. "Look," he said firmly, according to Dent, "play this game right. Quit dealing with the White House. We're the ones responsible for Mississippi."

To which Dent replied: "If Cheney calls me, as long as the White House calls me, I'm gonna talk to them."

Dent told Cheney about all of this, and Cheney in turn advised Morton that he was taking a special interest in Mississippi. The Cheney-Dent conversations continued.

Meanwhile Dent and Davis were working the state through Carmichael and Shanks. As it became clearer and clearer that Ford would be crowding the 1130-delegate mark, they began agitating in mid-July for a big push to rally Ford support and possibly steal the state's 30 delegates out from under Reagan—and Reed. "We had goose egg in our column on Mississippi," Dent said, talking of the delegate count. "We'd been just sitting there all this time, just shy of enough votes for the newspapers and wire services to say Ford was over the top. It was all part of the psychological warfare thing, and Reagan had these thirty votes listed in his column. What I was trying to do was take the thirty out of the Reagan column and put them in the Ford column, which would mean a change of sixty votes. Whenever that was accomplished, it was going to be the end of Ronald Reagan. We were going to give them to the President and suggest he walk out to the Rose Garden and say, 'There it is.' "

The key to engineering this big switch, as Harry Dent believed all along, was "the reluctant kingmaker"—Clarke Reed. Dent continued working on him, enlisting even the President himself to try to shake him loose. One day in July, during a Republican party meeting, Reed and Charles Pickering, as the incoming state chairman, were among a group of party functionaries invited to a White House reception—a happenstance that Dent, the old White House operator, seized with alacrity. Knowing Reed's insecurity, Dent engaged him in conversation while awaiting the President's arrival, and meanwhile Cheney took Pickering into the Oval Office for a forty-five-minute conversation with Ford. "When it came time for the President to come in," Dent recalled later, "who comes walking in with him but Charles Pickering! He was about ten feet high. This was his first treatment like this.

"Well, Clarke's sitting in the big room there, and he sees Charles Pickering walk in. So, in the course of the reception, I grab Dick Cheney and I tell him, 'Now we take Clarke in.' And Cheney said, 'Okay.' The President was plugged in by Cheney and me. He knew what we were doing. So Cheney says, 'As soon as this is over, the President and I will be sitting in the Oval Office. You bring Clarke.' Well, Jim Field escorted us from the Lincoln Room, and Clarke says, 'Where we going, cat?' and I said, 'Oh, come on, cat, you gonna get the biggest stroking job you ever seen in your life. We're gonna *make* you the kingmaker whether you want to be or not.' Well, we take him in there, and we have an hour with him—the President, Dick and me."

Dent made all the arguments again for joining Ford, including of course the talents story. And the President, knowing Reed's feelings about ideological purity, assured him he would pick as a running mate somebody philosophically in tune with himself.[1]

Even after this presidential massage, though, Reed was hanging back. Dent stepped up the good-natured—but purposeful—ribbing. "The train's pulling out," he would say to Reed in front of his colleagues.

"Don't give me that," Reed would answer, "that's not gonna work."

Dent kept telling him anyway. But he was not eternally patient. "Doug Shanks kept saying to me, 'Man, you're never gonna get through to Pickering and Clarke. They're both committed.'" So Dent finally told Cheney that he was worn out cajoling Reed, listening to his gripes about the voting-rights act and such. "I'm going to the delegates and alternates now," he said, "and when I do, it's gonna make Clarke mad. But if we keep sticking

---

1. "The President asked Clarke who he wanted," Dent recalled, "and Clarke indicated that he was for Connally. But he really didn't drive home what he wanted. He said, 'That's your choice, Mr. President.'"

with Clarke and Pickering, in the end we're probably gonna end up with nothing."

Cheney was close to being convinced now that Mississippi could be fertile ground for Ford. Nose-counting in the delegation by Dent, Davis, Carmichael, and Shanks indicated that with Reagan's prospects for the nomination cloudy at best, there were more than twenty half-votes for Ford already of the thirty-one half-votes needed to gain control. But in light of the PFC's reluctance, something more was needed to trigger the kind of White House offensive they believed was required, and warranted. Dent pleaded that an energetic drive for Mississippi, if nothing else, made tactical sense. "If we don't do anything else but tie the Reagan forces down in Mississippi, in a place they've already got," Dent told Cheney, "then we will have accomplished a tremendous amount."

To strengthen Cheney's hand, and to persuade the PFC, Dent, Carmichael, and the others hit on a scheme that would also pressure the Mississippi delegates and alternates to climb aboard Ford's bandwagon. Without informing Reed, the four Ford men began calling delegates and alternates, with Carmichael telling them he had nearly enough votes to swing the delegation for Ford. Carmichael's pitch went like this: "I've got thirty votes committed to the President, and we just need yours to put him over. Yours will be the thirty-first. You can give the President the nomination." He then would ask the individual to send a telegram to the White House inviting the President to Mississippi, to prove that the Ford strength was there. The effort was surprisingly successful; Dent said later they had commitments from twenty-seven delegates or alternates and were pushing hard for the other four needed when Clarke Reed got wind of the maneuver.

"He went through the ceiling," Dent said later. "And so did Pickering, because we were going around them to their troops, and they wanted to be the brokers. They got on the phone and they stopped it."

Reed was, indeed, livid. "By God, Carmichael was not telling the truth [on having thirty half-votes]. But he had in the low twenties, and that scared the fool out of me." So Reed called Billy Mounger, the head of Reagan's delegation in the state, and told him, " 'Look, this guy's conning everybody.' But Billy told me, 'Well, I got a tennis tournament this week.' So help me."[2] Reed as delegation and state chairman was trying to stay neutral, but he was so outraged by Carmichael's telephone calls, and so frustrated by Mounger's tennis tournament, that he moved in. This effort by Reed to

---

2. Mounger confirmed that it was true he had been tied up during this critical week organizing a tennis tournament.

save the situation for Reagan was largely overlooked in the vitriol heaped upon him later. Together with Pickering, Reed called a meeting of the full delegation, at which he planned to confront the Carmichael gambit and remind the delegation of its vow to go to Kansas City uncommitted. He obviously hoped for a strong reaction against Carmichael's audacious move.

But there was some question later about Reed's motivation: Was it essentially an effort to save the delegation for Reagan? Or was it a reflexive reaction to a challenge against his already waning power in the state and party delegation? Some, including Keene, professed to have seen signs for weeks that Reed himself had been influenced by the over-all race after the primaries and final state conventions. "He began to hedge," Keene recalled. "I never counted more than twenty-five [full] votes [for Reagan], because I knew Doug Shanks and Gil Carmichael were going to break, and probably a couple of others were going to go with them, even under the unit rule. But I didn't realize that we had real trouble until Clarke started to waver personally. He concluded after the primaries that we weren't going to win. And at that point he couldn't go to Ford. He's a man of his word; he hates to give his word, but he isn't gonna just flat-out lie to you, or break it. So he began looking for a way out. And in the absence of that, he began giving out stories like, 'Yeah, most of our guys are for Reagan, but Reagan can't win,' which was hurting us not so much in the South but everywhere else. People began telling us, 'You can't even hold your own people.' "

And indeed this kind of slippage was causing great troubles in Reagan's campaign outside of Mississippi, and forcing the master strategist John Sears to cast about for a stopper. For the time being, though, whatever his motivation, Reed was undeniably helping Reagan's cause by blowing the whistle on the Carmichael telegram scheme.

As soon as Reed scheduled the delegation meeting, Dent asked for a chance to address the group. Reed readily agreed. Dent urged Cheney to come, too, so as to provide the strongest possible evidence of President Ford's own interest, and to do some person-to-person persuading. According to Dent, the PFC balked at even this show of White House clout, for fear that the delegation might in some way rebuff Ford—a risk to be avoided in the continuing psychological warfare. But Dent prevailed on Cheney and, together with Field, he flew to Jackson on Sunday afternoon, July 25, for the delegation meeting at the Ramada Inn, just minutes from the airport.

By now news stories had appeared about Carmichael's bold move to steal the delegation out from under Reagan, and television and newspaper reporters from around the country converged on the motel. Everybody knew that if Mississippi cracked for Ford, Reagan's candidacy would be finished. The Mississippi delegates and alternates, obscure folks leading normal lives, were besieged for interviews, which many of them granted on the run between being buttonholed by leaders of the Ford and Reagan campaigns. Into this maelstrom on Sunday afternoon came Clarke Reed, on a short flight from his home in Greenville. He was milling around the crowded lobby when Keene came up and said he had to talk to him privately. Reed figured Keene just wanted to bolster him in his determination not to let Carmichael get away with his ploy, or perhaps to go over the latest delegate count. But he figured wrong. The two went into Reed's room down the hall on the first floor, talked for a while, and then hurried out to attend the start of the meeting. Neither said anything to anybody about their talk, nor did they indicate that anything notable had been discussed.

At the delegation caucus, Dent, Cheney, and Keene all were allowed to make pitches for their candidates. First came Dent—Dr. Harold Hill incarnate. He told the assembled how "Mississippi is in the catbird seat" and Clarke had done a great job putting it there, but they ought to use the power now. He told them it was "the Battle of Mississippi" and he buttered them up some more in his inimitable style: "Now my good friend Clarke is probably a little peeved with us because we've been down here trying to lobby you good folks. But I told Clarke that you can't dress sixty beautiful women up in bikinis and put them on Broadway, and not expect Gerald Ford and Ronald Reagan to turn their heads and look at 'em. . . . Friends, we looking at you. My goodness, you're in the catbird seat if I've ever seen it. You know it took the whole South to do that in '68 in the convention. Now it's coming down to just Mississippi. Mississippi's got a chance to strike a real blow for the South." And he repeated his updated version of the parable of talents. "It's a question," he said, "of whether Clarke's gonna be the kingmaker or Rosey Rosenbaum's gonna be the kingmaker. That is, New York, or Mississippi. Don't let us down, friends. I'm not talking about Ford. I'm talking about the South. I'm in this thing because I'm for the South, and I feel what's good for the South is good for the country and good for the Republican Party. You know, we're all worried whether it's going to be a Northeastern strategy or a Southern strategy; it's gonna be a national strategy, and we better make sure it is. We haven't put anything on the table down here [for Ford] except Florida."

Cheney then took over, trying to reassure the delegation that Ford wasn't writing off the South. He answered some questions, then gave way to Keene, who reviewed the situation, unusually quickly it seemed, and also fielded some questions.

Neither side at this point thought it had the thirty-one votes needed to break the delegation's agreement to go to Kansas City uncommitted, or to put it on record for Ford or Reagan. And so the meeting adjourned with a decision only to remain uncommitted—a victory for Reed in that it nipped Carmichael's effort in the bud.

The delegation did, however, invite President Ford to Jackson to address it the next Friday, an invitation that would bring to a head the internal Ford campaign debate as to how aggressively Mississippi should be pursued. Cheney would say only that the trip was under serious consideration, and that tentative plans were being laid for Ford to come. That night, after talking to small groups of delegates, Cheney dined with Dent and some Ford delegates at LeFleurs, which passes for a good restaurant in Jackson. Reed and some Reagan people were dining there also, and after dinner Reed joined a table of reporters. He seemed unusually defensive and several times made the point that although he liked Reagan he had never been committed to him publicly. As he was holding forth, Dent came over too, and gave us yet another rendition of the parable of the talents. Reed smiled, but did not seem overly amused.

Later that evening, Cheney got together with Dent, Reed, and Pickering and sat around, talking and drinking, until nearly two o'clock. Reed said nothing special to influence him, but Cheney went to bed satisfied that it was politically safe to bring the President to the state later in the week. "I did not want to run the President into Mississippi and have the delegation caucus go for Reagan," Cheney said later—recalling that Ford the previous month had gone into Missouri blind and gotten burned. "It was clear that however you counted it, it was deadlocked, and there was not going to be a decision before Kansas City, and on that basis it made sense for the President to go in."

Reed could have told Cheney that a presidential trip would now make a great deal of sense for a special reason, but he did not. He did not because he had given David Keene his word that the information conveyed to him in the privacy of his room that afternoon would remain confidential. Reed, among the most loquacious of politicians, kept his mouth shut all through the caucus, through dinner with his colleagues and reporters, through the late-hour drinking with Cheney and Dent, and finally took the secret to bed with him.

What Keene had told Reed was a political bombshell.

"I told him our situation was tenuous," Keene recalled, "that we were in danger of losing some support, that the count wasn't there—all of which he agreed with, since he was out spreading the word that that's what the situation was. I told him there was only one way we could conceive of to change it, and it was to announce that Reagan was picking his V.P."

"Well," Reed remembers replying, "maybe that's all right."

"I'm not supposed to tell you who it is," Keene said, "but I will. It's Schweiker."

Reed didn't seem to be overly exercised by the news. He asked Keene: "Is it going to do it?"

Keene told him: "I think it will."

Reed said later that the news "gave me some bad vibes, but I didn't have time to think," what with the caucus about to start. It didn't really register on him at once. But at that interpretation, Keene just laughed and said: "When he tried to explain that to me, I said, 'Clarke, it was a conversation-stopper. If you weren't focusing, I might have thought it would attract your attention just a little bit.' "

It was not long, of course, before Clarke Reed the True Believer was able to focus on what had happened. Ronald Reagan, card-carrying conservative and apostle of the ideologically pure ticket, had picked Senator Richard S. Schweiker of Pennsylvania, a renegade liberal, as his running mate. In the Battle of Mississippi, that decision was about to change the order of combat significantly; and not only in Mississippi, but everywhere that conservative Republican hearts beat loyally for Ronald Reagan.

31. The Schweiker Affair

Ronald Reagan had never really cared for the traditional, midnight crash sessions to decide on a vice-presidential selection after the presidential nomination. He wanted to have his choice all ready to present to the convention if it gave him its nomination. Shortly after the last primaries in June, when neither he nor President Ford could claim enough delegates to be nominated, he asked John Sears, his campaign manager, and Paul Laxalt, his campaign chairman, to make a recommendation to him. He specified only that he wanted someone who would help to unite the party, someone he could trust and work with in office, someone who was not a member of the Washington buddy system, and whose family life and financial dealings would cause no embarrassment.

The assignment did not appear to be an excessively taxing one, or one that offered much room for imagination and innovation, because Reagan had been fairly explicit on the subject as a campaigner. "I do not believe you choose someone of an opposite philosophy in hopes he'll get you some votes you can't get yourself," he would say, "because that's being false with the people who vote for you and your philosophy."

The point was an important one to party conservatives, many of whom, like Clarke Reed in Mississippi, liked to say they had switched from the Democratic Party precisely because of its penchant for national tickets with a split political philosophy. When Reagan visited the Mississippi delegation in late June, in fact, he was asked about a running mate and, to the general approval of the audience, he repeated his answer.

But the two men he assigned to bring him a recommendation, and Sears especially, were not ideological purists. Sears was a political tactician who wanted to win; he did not want Reagan to emulate Barry Goldwater in 1964. They undertook the search at a stage when Sears professed to believe that Reagan still had a strong chance to be nominated. The South, including Mississippi, was holding, and he had hopes of making inroads in New York. He later contended rather cryptically that "there were some things going on in New York" involving Nelson Rockefeller's unhappiness with President Ford that might shake some delegates loose without Rockefeller himself breaking away. Because few Republican politicians in New

York expected that either Ford or Reagan could carry the state in the fall, Sears said, the situation was soft, and the lack of commitment might be exploitable. Sears would elaborate no further, then or even after the election, but obviously he was counting on some such breakthrough to get Reagan over the top.

In any case it seems clear that Sears embarked on the search for Reagan's ticket companion with mainly the general election in mind, because he first held a conversation on the subject with a man who could not notably help Reagan get the nomination—William D. Ruckelshaus. The former deputy attorney general, since resigning along with then Attorney General Elliot Richardson rather than fire Special Watergate Prosecutor Archibald Cox in Richard Nixon's notorious Saturday-Night Massacre of October 1973, had been practicing law in Washington. Ruckelshaus came from Indiana, most of whose delegates were already committed by law to Reagan on the first ballot as a result of his primary victory there, and he could probably be of most help in the fall election campaign, when he might offset liberal hostility to the GOP ticket. Also, as a Catholic, Ruckelshaus presumably could help exploit Carter's weakness among Catholic voters.

Sears and Ruckelshaus met in the first week in July at the Federal City Club in Washington with L. Keith Bulen, a former Republican national committeeman from Indiana. Ruckelshaus said later he considered that Sears had offered him a place on Reagan's ticket, telling Ruckelshaus he "had pretty much decided" on him. Apparently there was no follow-through, Ruckelshaus said later, because the Reagan camp eventually realized it did not have the nomination wrapped up and Reagan needed to choose somebody from the Northeast to help him win in Kansas City. Sears later denied he had ever made a firm offer to Ruckelshaus, and insisted that Richard Schweiker was the first and only choice he and Laxalt made.

"We took all the Republican senators and governors," Sears said, "and that didn't take very long. When you ruled out those who were too old, in our party you didn't have much left." There were no House members who were sufficiently well known, either. Also, as Laxalt noted, "if what we were going to do was purposeful, we had to expand the base; we somehow had to get the moderates and the liberals in the tent. And it was clear also from John's analysis that we had to develop additional strength in the Northeast, where there was a strong perception that Reagan was narrow-based and, in Goldwater fashion, was writing [the area] off. So we sort of backed into the situation. When you looked at the people who realistically fit into that slot, it was damned thin. Schweiker's name kept popping up."

Sears, continuing to insist that his prime concern was the general election, cited Schweiker's 100-per-cent COPE rating and his demonstrated appeal to both Catholic and Jewish voters, with whom Jimmy Carter had troubles. And, as a Northeasterner, Schweiker could carry much of the campaign there and free Reagan to contest Carter for the South. But others in the Reagan camp contended that the Schweiker selection was clearly aimed at securing the nomination. They said they were told Schweiker could break open the Pennsylvania delegation, with a spillover into New Jersey and other neighboring states, and bring twenty or twenty-five critical delegates into the Reagan fold—which was why it was necessary to have him disclosed as Reagan's choice in advance of the convention.

Sears, as was his style, rehearsed his reasoning with key aides like David Keene, Anderson Carter, the chief of field operations, Charlie Black, and Lyn Nofziger, first selling them on the idea of picking a running mate in advance as a way of squeezing delegates from Ford. If Reagan announced his choice, Sears said in an argument he continued to press until and during the convention, Ford would eventually have to do the same, because the pressure would mount from conservative supporters, fearful the President might select somebody like Chuck Percy, and from moderates afraid it would be John Connally. Not until *that* idea had gone over with his colleagues did Sears run down the actual list of prospective candidates, leading them inevitably to Schweiker. In all this, Sears talked about a candidate for the general election; if Dick Schweiker happened to be in a position to help crack the huge bloc of formally uncommitteds in Pennsylvania, well, that was a happy circumstance.

One member of the Reagan California group who did not always see eye to eye with Sears and certainly had no love for Schweiker said later of the move: "Frankly, I think it was a stroke of genius. There was really nothing else to do. We had to do something because we weren't getting delegates and Ford was." That was certainly true. Whether or not Sears and Laxalt started out looking for a running mate who could help swing delegates, they needed one by the time they were settling on Schweiker. In addition to the collapse of the mysterious New York deal Sears had hoped to bring off, Reagan's strength was ebbing away in a number of quarters. First, Buz Schwenk, of Suffolk County sewer-district notoriety, with at least seven uncommitted delegates in his pocket, took his woes directly to the Oval Office, apparently received some solace, and delivered his bloc to the President, despite efforts by Keene and other Reaganites to deter him. The White House was really playing its advantage now, and it was hurting. Then word came of cracks in the South Carolina and Mississippi delegations, and the possibility of others in Louisiana and Virginia. Clarke Reed was saying himself that Reagan was in trouble, and that kind of talk didn't help—in the North or the South. Sears's optimism turned around; the nomination was slipping away from Reagan unless something could be done at once.

Schweiker, if he would agree, was the answer. Sears was hopeful. "I knew he was a high roller," he said later. "He always took chances in Pennsylvania politics and that appealed to me. That quality would make it easy for him to do it."

On Friday, July 16, Laxalt placed a call to Schweiker at Ocean City, New Jersey, where the Schweiker family was enjoying the weekend. There was no phone in their cottage, but a neighbor took the message and Schweiker called Laxalt back from the boardwalk that night. They set up a meeting for Tuesday, July 20, in Laxalt's Capitol Hill office.

Schweiker said later he thought the meeting might have something to do with a list of Reagan's running mates, but he was not prepared to have the spot offered to him straight out. Yet that was what happened. "We did it rather crisply with him," Sears recalled, "and we didn't allow him a lot of time to think it over. But obviously he did feel what we said to him made a lot of sense."

What they said was that a Republican ticket could not hope to win in November unless it was broadly based, and that it was time the Republicans tried to bring its factions together in a true coalition. And, to Schweiker's even greater surprise, they told him they wanted to announce a Reagan-Schweiker ticket well in advance of the convention. "We explained to him," Sears said, "that we wanted to do this immediately because from a political standpoint it would change the dynamic of the campaign; people would stop saying how many delegates went for Ford that day." But they never mentioned any role for him in converting delegates in Pennsylvania or elsewhere to the Reagan cause, Schweiker recalled with certainty later. He asked them what they were expecting, "and they made clear they weren't expecting me to deliver delegates. Now, they also made it clear that part of their strategy was that by having a broad coalition and going to the Northeast, this would swing over some wavering delegates, but never once did they tie any *quid pro quo* into it. If they had, I would have rejected it, because getting into it this late, a month before the convention and after a twelve-month fight, I just wouldn't be in a position to guarantee anything. Polarization had pretty well set in." That there weren't such strings attached, Schweiker said, "was one of the things that attracted me to it." Schweiker noted that most of the delegates in Pennsylvania, though listed as uncommitted, were "preselected as Ford delegates" and hence not likely to be budged. "They knew it and I knew it," he said.

Though his name was not mentioned, a key individual in this whole move was Drew Lewis, a close friend of Schweiker's and former campaign manager, who was now head of Ford's campaign in Pennsylvania. If Lewis

could be brought around to Reagan, a split might be started in the delegation. Schweiker said he began thinking about Lewis, but decided it would
be improper to contact him too far in advance of an announcement. (He
also told the Reagan men that if he agreed to join Reagan he would have
to resign as a delegate-at-large in Pennsylvania, which would cost the
Reagan camp a delegate because the first alternate was, ironically, Lewis.)

It came as the final surprise to Schweiker to learn that Sears and Laxalt
had come to him without Reagan's knowing they were doing so! They
explained that while the last word would be Reagan's, "they had every
reason to believe he would accept it," having requested their recommendation. Schweiker asked for time to think about the offer, and the meeting
broke up, with Sears and Laxalt expecting it would be several days before
they would hear from the senator again. But the very next day Schweiker
telephoned and they met a second time. Schweiker had been up most of the
night discussing the offer with his wife, and she was in favor of it. By now,
it was clear he was on the hook. It was agreed he would go to Los Angeles
to talk directly with Reagan, after Sears had had a chance to brief the
governor on their conversations.

By Friday morning at nine-thirty, Sears was at Reagan's Pacific Palisades home. Reagan sat and listened quietly for nearly half an hour as his
aide made the case for Dick Schweiker, liberal. Not until he had to, did
Sears actually mention Schweiker by name. He ran through the list of
thirteen governors and noted that only two, Bill Milliken in Michigan and
Jim Rhodes in Ohio, came from major states and could really help Reagan;
he dismissed both, Milliken because it made no sense to run with somebody
from Ford's home state, and Rhodes because—because he was Rhodes; too
old, a terrible public speaker, and slightly unsavory.[1] Then he quickly
disposed of the House Republicans and ran through the Senate Republicans, "just to be thorough, slipping past Schweiker. Then I said, 'There is
a fellow in the Senate with a pretty liberal voting record, but he's against
gun control, he's a big man in the Captive Nations movement, and he's
against abortion, and basically on all the emotional issues he's got a pretty
defendable record. And he's absolutely clean.' I went through the whole
spiel of how we arrived at this fellow, and discussed how it would help us
in the election. I explained why we should go ahead and make the an-

1. A high official in Ford's campaign confessed later: "We were concerned they might do this
with a guy who did have control of a big bloc of delegates, just to get them, like Jim Rhodes,
who controlled about ninety." To which Keene said: "If you just cared about the convention,
you could have gone to Jim Rhodes, but who wanted to run in the general election with Jim
Rhodes?" And Sears remarked, "You've got to have some responsibility in this business."

nouncement quickly, and how that might contribute to our possible nomination."

Reagan's first question was not about any aspect of the political strategy, or about what kind of man or political creature Dick Schweiker was, but instead: "Do you think he'd do it?"

"Well, yes," Sears answered, "I think he'd do it. As a matter of fact, he's coming out here tomorrow to see you. Paul and I have discussed it with him, and he'll do it."

Reagan seemed pleased. A meeting was arranged at Reagan's for the next day. Schweiker, using the name of his press secretary, Troy Gustavson, as a cover, was waiting to hear at the Beverly Wilshire.

Late the next morning, July 24, Schweiker, Dave Newhall (his chief aide), Sears, and Laxalt arrived for lunch; Nancy Reagan was the hostess. For the next six and a half hours, Reagan and Schweiker talked. (Schweiker, before going in, had pronounced his host's name "Ree-gan" and had to be told it was "Ray-gan.") The first serious question on Reagan's mind was whether Schweiker would support his positions in the campaign and later in office. Schweiker replied that he knew what it was like to be the second man, since he had been brought up in a family business, under his father. "As long as I'm on the plane on the take-off, I'll be the first one out defending it after the crash," he told Reagan, who liked what he heard. Schweiker said he wanted only to be sure he could say his piece, and then he would line up behind the policy and defend it, whether he agreed or not. This, Sears said later, was the closest Schweiker ever came to laying down any kind of condition for his participation. As they talked, a kind of positive personal chemistry set in, both men said later. "You know," Reagan recalled telling Schweiker, "I have a strong feeling that I'm looking at myself some years ago" (presumably when he was easing out of his early liberalism).

Schweiker smiled and said, "Well, I'm no knee-jerk liberal."

And Reagan replied, "And I'm no knee-jerk extremist."

Then, about three hours into the discussion, as Schweiker remembers it, Reagan said, "I've made a decision, Senator, and I'd like you to be my running mate."

That was it. Most of the remaining three hours or so was devoted to planning how it would be done, how to make the most of the element of surprise. "During this whole eight-day period, we all stressed top secrecy," Schweiker said, "because we felt the only and the best way this had a chance of succeeding was to be a complete surprise to the Ford camp." Back in Washington, Schweiker managed to keep the secret by talking about it with his wife only in the evening or early morning hours, when their five children were asleep. (They were not told until the night before the announcement, and then were kept at home and forbidden to use the telephone.)

On Monday morning, July 26, before Reagan's press conference in Los Angeles (at noon, Eastern Daylight-Saving Time), while his top assistants started phoning conservatives around the country to break the news, Schweiker called Drew Lewis. Once Schweiker had decided to join Reagan, he suggested that it was possible Lewis, as a very old and good friend, might come over. Lewis had been having some differences with the President Ford Committee, and if he decided to desert the Ford camp, Schweiker estimated he might bring fifteen or twenty uncommitted or Ford-leaning delegates with him. If Lewis was to be gotten, however, it would have to be a quick strike, before the Ford forces could get to him. Some of the Reagan leaders had assumed Schweiker would contact Lewis at once, but Schweiker did not reach him until about two hours before Reagan's announcement.

Lewis was stunned at the news. "I pretty well told him I had crossed the bridge," Schweiker recalled. "I asked him not to hold a press conference until I could talk further with him, and to hold an open mind. I invited him to come down to Washington, or I would go up to Pennsylvania, but Drew wanted no part of it." Schweiker talked to Lewis about four times in all, for more than four hours, but Lewis would not budge.

The Reagan operatives who were phoning party conservatives encountered similar shock and negativism. After the Mississippi caucus had broken up in Jackson the night before, Dave Keene had flown back to Washington so that he could start phoning his people all over the South on Monday morning. He had asked Governor Jim Edwards of South Carolina, who had been trying to hold the South for Reagan, to come to Washington, too— but without telling him why. When Edwards appeared in Keene's office Monday morning, he was ready to pitch in for whatever needed doing. But "when I told him," Keene recalled later, "he sort of looked at his watch and said, 'Well, if I hurry I think I can get back to South Carolina.' And that was the end of his tour."

At the appointed hour in Los Angeles, Reagan went on television and made a brief, crisp announcement. He had selected as his running mate "a man of independent thought and action" who, while respected by his colleagues, "has not become a captive of what I call 'the Washington buddy system.' Since I now feel that the people and the delegates have a right to know in advance of the convention who a nominee's vice-presidential choice would be, I am today departing from tradition and announcing my selection. I have chosen the distinguished United States Senator, the Honorable Richard Schweiker. I am convinced that this is a ticket behind which all

Republicans can unite and one which will lead our party to victory in November." And then Reagan walked off, declining to field questions.

In Washington shortly afterward, Schweiker strode into a Senate Caucus Room full of television cameras with mastermind Sears close behind. "Governor Reagan's decisive stroke in one fell swoop has united the Republican Party for November by bringing together the conservative and moderate wings of our party," Schweiker said. "It instantly gives our party across-the-board appeal." Brushing aside reminders that Reagan had said he would run with a candidate who shared his conservative philosophy, Sears observed that Schweiker was "a very compatible running mate" whose choice would enable Reagan to run "a truly national campaign."

Problems surfaced almost at once. Asked what his position was on the Panama Canal, Schweiker engaged in an endless circumlocution, discussing détente and other foreign-policy issues, and finally acknowledging he had no position on the canal at all. The cries of protest from the conservative community were loud and immediate. Howard Phillips, the Nixon executioner of the antipoverty program and director of the Conservative Caucus, summed up the sentiment from the right wing by charging that Reagan had "betrayed the trust of those who look to him for leadership." And Stu Spencer at the PFC said with unveiled glee: "They stepped on old Oscar. Schweiker is one of the libs of all time."

Now that the bomb had been dropped, the strategy was simple: a speedy delegate breakthrough in the Northeast that would catch the White House off-guard and persuade would-be defectors in the South of the political wisdom of the Reagan-Schweiker ticket. And so while Schweiker belatedly tried to reason with Drew Lewis by phone, Keene was trying to hold the line with Clarke Reed and other influential Southern conservatives. "I told John [Sears] we would probably lose ten or fifteen delegates in the South," Keene said later, "and the move would be a disaster unless we picked up that and more in the Northeast in forty-eight hours. John was virtually certain that there would be quick movement for us in the Philadelphia area that would trigger switches in New Jersey and New York, and then we would move into Delaware and West Virginia, where he also saw softness."

But that did not happen. Drew Lewis not only rejected Schweiker's plea out of hand but immediately after his friend's first call he phoned President Ford at the White House. Ford had heard a rumor that Schweiker was going to join Reagan, but this was the first solid confirmation. "I want you to know," Lewis told him, "that I'm committed to you. I'm going to stick with you, and Pennsylvania will deliver you ninety delegates." (Ford eventually got ninety-three.) The Ford forces focused immediately on one group of uncommitted delegates known as "the Philadelphia Fifteen." The President phoned Billy Meehan, the Philadelphia party leader, and Meehan told him: "Mr. President, you don't have to worry about me. When I give my word, it's good." The Philadelphia Fifteen held for Ford, and a quick check showed no leakage to speak of anywhere in the Northeast. Ford called Lewis back to thank him again and tell him how much he appreciated his loyalty, especially in light of what good and close friends Lewis and Schweiker were. If there was any chance of Lewis wavering, and there seemed to be none, that second call certainly erased it. Lewis went to work immediately contacting the whole delegation. It was true that Lewis was very unhappy about the PFC in Washington, which kept changing representatives to Pennsylvania and interfering with his own efforts to keep the delegation in line. Lewis said later, in fact, that he had phoned Rogers Morton and had it out with him. But the Reagan people miscalculated if they believed that this unhappiness might persuade him to jump. "I tried to explain to Dick," he said later, "that the issue was not Dick Schweiker, it was Reagan and Ford. I felt Reagan could not win, and I told Dick I felt he was being used."

Even before Reagan's announcement, then, the White House had good reason to believe that the Schweiker ploy was not going to undercut the President's strength in Pennsylvania. That being the case, a counterattack could focus on the newly vulnerable Southern delegations. Inevitably, the focal point of that counterattack was Mississippi and "the reluctant king-maker"—the man with the thirty talents to throw on the big table to cover Rosey Rosenbaum's—the excitable Clarke Reed.

Dick Cheney and Harry Dent both headed home Monday morning after the meeting in Jackson. Cheney arrived in Washington first and learned of the Schweiker move as he arrived at his White House office. He immediately phoned Dent's office in South Carolina and left word. "The Schweiker thing was one more indication that Reagan was in trouble," Cheney said later. "We had a good hard delegate count, but Sears had floated a phony count that brought ours into question. They were looking for something to crack it, but the Schweiker thing gave us an opportunity to reach into the South and peel off Reagan support. For them, though, it was not that stupid a move. They had to do something. They could count as well as we could. We had to go like hell now to take advantage of it. We pulled out all the stops to pick up delegates, but they were coming in ones and twos. We knew Clarke was soft and we went after him."

Harry Dent was returning from Jackson to his home in Columbia by private plane. As soon as the plane landed, Dent's secretary rushed up and told him: "Call Dick Cheney immediately." He did.

"Guess what just happened," Cheney asked him.

"What?"

"Reagan just picked Schweiker for Vice President."

Dent was dumbfounded. He went directly to his office and put out a statement that called this decision "the most colossal political boner of the century." Then he picked up his phone and called Clarke Reed.

"And then began a three-day struggle," Dent said, "to get Clarke across the line. The Pennsylvania delegation was coming into the White House on Thursday, and there was a question whether we were going to be able to hold it. The reason they went to Schweiker was that John Sears saw what we were doing in Mississippi. So Cheney said, 'Get Clarke Reed across the line as fast as you can.' "

When Dent phoned Reed, he found him in an unusually agitated state. The relatively pacific mood in which Reed had first greeted the news had passed, and now he was irate. He had always opposed an ideologically split ticket and Reagan knew that. In 1968, after Nixon had pledged to the Southern chairmen he would not have one, the newspapers were pushing first John Lindsay and then Mark Hatfield, and Reed had told Nixon he would bolt in a minute if either of them were selected. "I'd probably made in the neighborhood of a hundred speeches in the South on the hypocrisy of the split ticket," he said later. Reagan had told the delegates in no uncertain terms he wouldn't do it. "Who is honorable in this thing?" Reed asked.

Dave Keene, who also was burning the telephone lines to Reed in Greenville now, realized too late what would happen. He had heard all of Reed's rhetoric on the split ticket many times but had believed he would accept Schweiker as a practical necessity. What Keene did not appreciate until this moment was that Reed had the very thing he was looking for: "An excuse to break his word."

Reed soon got all the excuses he needed. He took a call from Senator James McClure, the Idaho conservative, wanting to know what he thought.

"Hell, Jim, I don't know much about the guy." "Well, I'll tell you," McClure shot back, "I sit next to him [in the Senate]. This thing is horrible."

By the time Reagan himself phoned Reed to calm him, Clarke was well lathered. "He told me Schweiker was not a bad guy," Reed recalled, "and I said, 'Oh, come on, Governor, this is just what you said you wouldn't do.' He tried to tell me this guy wasn't different, that he was against abortion and all this, and I said, 'Well, there's no point in talking about all that. Governor, I'm sorry.' "

Reed sounded as if he were going to dash pell-mell across the line to

Ford without any coaxing. But that was not Clarke. Every time Dent talked to Reed that afternoon, Dent said, "he'd say, 'I'm coming later, I'm coming later.' And I said, 'Man, we need you now!' Later, later, always later. The way Billy Mounger and Keene were playing, it was later, later. And that's what we had to fight."

He was right. Keene, with one eye on Pennsylvania for the quick score Sears had been so confident would come, was working frantically to keep his finger in the Mississippi dike; word that Reed was deserting Reagan at this critical juncture could spoil what hope there was in Pennsylvania.

On that same Monday night, July 26, at Billy Mounger's house, the delegation leadership met—Mounger, Tommy Giordano, Haley Barbour (the state party executive director), Reed, and a few others. Reed told them he was going to switch to Ford because of Schweiker. They asked him to hold off while they tried to sort out what was happening and what the whole delegation should do. Reed was not the only one outraged by the Schweiker decision, but Keene was urging everyone to give it some time.

On Tuesday morning, Cheney and Dent talked again. "Harry," Cheney said, "we've got to have it today." John Connally, a holdout until now as he tried to play his own cards for the vice-presidential nomination, was coming in to endorse the President: he also was obviously seizing on Schweiker's selection as his justification to conservatives for the move. Ford gave Connally the full treatment, meeting first with him in the Oval Office and then taking him into the Rose Garden before reporters to disclose the endorsement. In the fall campaign, it would come to be called "the Rose Garden strategy"—campaigning from the White House—but Ford had been doing it for months, and especially since the end of the primaries.

"I think it's quite clear, between the two men, that the President is unmistakably the better choice, not only for the party but for the country," Connally said, as Ford beamed beside him. At Dent's urging, Cheney brought Connally back to his office immediately afterward and had him place a call to Reed in Mississippi.

"I'm coming, I'm coming," Clarke said again, but he still wouldn't say when.

One reason that Reed continued to stall was that Dave Keene was holding his feet to the fire, reminding him of the firm commitment he had made to him personally, not only to stick with Reagan but to deliver the delegation as well. "They're all going," Reed told Keene. "I'm going. This is it."

But Keene had checked and knew this wasn't so; many of the Reagan-ites in Mississippi were calming down. "If I were you I'd check with these people," Keene told him, "because you're going to be the only one going over the side, anywhere."

That night at about eleven-thirty, Reed telephoned Keene at home to tell him he was going to make the switch. "Look, Clarke," Keene said, still trying to buy time in the hope something would come through in Pennsylvania, "I've asked for a lot of things for Reagan. Now I'm asking for something for myself, because you owe it to me, because I've covered your ass plenty. I'm asking you personally to give me another twenty-four hours."

Reed said he couldn't. Keene reminded him he had promised personally. "You shouldn't make promises you can't keep."

"Well," Reed replied, according to Keene, "I've made some other promises."

"Well, screw them, not me," Keene said.

Reluctantly Reed agreed to a twenty-four-hour hold. On Wednesday, though, Cheney and Dent brought their heaviest artillery to bear on him. Dent told Cheney the first thing that morning: "Dick, you got to play the big card now. Put the President on the phone and tell him to tell Clarke to come—today. I've done all I can and we don't have him yet. He's coming, he's coming, but we don't know when he's coming. I'll bet he ain't gonna come until the convention, if he comes then."

Cheney did not like to put pressure on President Ford to make such calls because he knew it was not in Ford's nature to do so. Dent knew it too, having run in a string of uncommitted Southern delegates to the Oval Office, only to have the President fail to "close the sale" with the ultimate question. But they all knew Reed was the key; Cheney got Ford to agree.

According to Dent, Ford did indeed ask for Reed's endorsement, but Reed still held back, asking for forty-eight more hours. Ford uncharacteristically leaned on him, and Reed finally crumbled and agreed to endorse him that day. "If the President had not insisted," Dent said, "we never could have pulled Clarke across the line before the end of the day."

All afternoon Dent kept telephoning Reed, badgering him. "Where's your statement, Clarke? Man, you want me help you write it? I'll dictate it to your secretary."

"No, no, I need more time," Reed implored. "Man, I shouldn't have told the President."

Dent called Cheney again: "Dick, I don't believe Clarke's coming, in spite of what he told the President."

Then he was back at Reed another time: "Clarke, where's the statement?"

"Man," Reed said, "you cats don't let me off the phone long enough to write a statement. I just can't get this thing done today." Finally, with Dent pressing to make the approaching network-television news shows, Reed very reluctantly read a statement to him.

"Man, cat, that's a good statement," Dent told him. But Reed said he wasn't ready to release it. "All we need is for you to endorse us," Dent said. "Clarke Reed endorsing, man, that'll turn the world around."

Reed finally agreed to let it go at 7:00 P.M., Eastern time. He had promised Keene he would wait twenty-four hours, but at least, he told Keene apologetically later, he had waited until the "day" was over—until sundown! Next, Dent had to get it out to the press through Haley Barbour, who though ostensibly a paid party employee, was in fact defending Reagan ferociously. He called Barbour and held the line while Barbour at that moment was trying to talk Reed out of abandoning Reagan. Finally Barbour came on: "Mr. Dent, don't you make Mr. Reed do this."

"Haley, that's Clarke's statement. You don't have the right to throw it in the trash can."

"Well, Mr. Reed doesn't want it out until seven o'clock"—too late for the network news.

Dent, however, ran with what he knew. He tipped the television newscasters that Reed was about to switch, and that much did make the network shows. At seven o'clock, Barbour finally passed out the statement. "As I have expressed on hundreds of occasions," it said, "one of my reasons for leaving the Democratic Party was the cynicism of the philosophically split presidential ticket whereby we vote for a candidate of one philosophy and, if he is succeeded by his Vice President, the electorate has in effect been defrauded. . . . This kind of Vice President is too big a price to pay for the nomination." Reed said his decision to endorse Ford was "personal" and he would not try to persuade anyone else in the Mississippi delegation to follow suit. But everyone expected that Reed's move would mean that Reagan's stronghold in Mississippi would crumble. Reed himself said he considered "the nomination contest, for all practical purposes, over." Dent seemed to agree. "Mission accomplished!" he triumphed to Cheney.

But Dent was wrong. He should have learned by now not to count Clarke Reed as bagged.

Any lingering indecision in Washington about whether the President should visit Mississippi the next Friday, July 30, had of course been swept away. Dent came up to Washington so that he could make the trip with Ford on *Air Force One* and brief him en route on the volatile situation. As soon as the presidential party arrived in Jackson, Ford's principal lieutenants conferred as to whether the time was right to go for a vote, for a commitment to the President of all thirty delegates under the unit rule. According to Dent, after going over the delegate list, they believed they had twenty-nine sure votes and about ten potential ones. But thirty-one were needed to break the previous decision to go uncommitted to the convention, so they decided to wait rather than risk a rebuff. No vote was requested, and Ford simply spoke to the delegation about his accomplishments. He was so warmly received, however, that Dent went up to Giordano and asked whether they shouldn't ask for a vote anyway. Giordano again said no. In their hearts, after all, most of the Mississippians still were for Reagan. And Ford's continued support of Kissinger rankled a number of them.

Now it was the Reagan forces' inning. Schweiker had embarked on a swing through Reagan states in the South to demonstrate that he was not an ogre: South Carolina (to the home of Jim Edwards, now back on board), Virginia, Alabama, West Virginia, and—Mississippi. The Mississippi trip, by Reagan and Schweiker, would have been made much earlier but it was decided that it would be imprudent to go there right on the heels of the President, when tempers were still hot. It was on the following Wednesday, August 4, that The Odd Couple made it to Jackson.

By then, Schweiker said later, "the shock had worn off." Clarke Reed stayed on the periphery, joining Mounger, Charles Pickering, and a few others for a quick lunch with Schweiker, awaiting the separate arrival of Reagan. When Reagan got there, Reed received an icy, perfunctory greeting from him. The burden of Reagan's message was that Schweiker was not all that liberal. "If you simply abide by labels you ignore some basic facts," he told reporters. He had not gone back on his promise to pick somebody "philosophically compatible," he insisted.

The night before, Dent had been in Jackson armed with Schweiker's voting record, and he had briefed the Ford delegates on it. Now, when the time came to question Schweiker, the Reagan delegates themselves, and the uncommitteds, pressed him so hard about his views—and on whether he would be able to embrace Reagan's positions—that the Ford people were able to sit back and just listen. Later they returned to Dent's room and reported that Reagan and Schweiker were finished in Mississippi. Informal polls of the delegation indicated Ford remained ahead. "I pulled out of there later that night and headed back to South Carolina," Dent said, "convinced that it was definitely, absolutely on ice, and we would just have to wait until we got to the convention to get our votes." He phoned Cheney again before leaving and told him that.

After the meeting with Schweiker, Ford's Mississippi men let up a little. "The fire's out of Billy's belly," one of them told Dent concerning the Reaganites' state leader, Billy Mounger. But they were wrong. Mounger was aroused and fighting to hold on to every Reagan delegate he could. Even Giordano, who was meeting with the Ford leaders and would soon join them, was still saying he was uncommitted—in apparent deference to Mounger, who was the main Republican money-raiser in the state and had considerable clout. At one point in the psychological warfare Dent got twenty-nine names on a letter to Ford, but when Mounger made some calls, signatories began taking their names off. And when Dent, Reed, and Pickering all left Mississippi for a week of committee meetings in Kansas City in advance of the national convention, Mounger stepped up his pressure. "The further you got away from the Schweiker announcement," Dent said later, "the more the fire came back in Billy's belly." Reagan, too, was pitching in personally. From his ranch back in California, he burned the wires to Mississippi, telephoning every member of the delegation to pressure them —and to shoot down the recurring, Ford-inspired rumor that he would take second place on a ticket with the President.

And in the meantime, Schweiker and the campaign organization continued to try to stir some action in the Northeast, particularly in Pennsylvania. With the Mississippi delegation clinging to its decision to go to Kansas City uncommitted, the addition of Schweiker to the Reagan ticket had at least bought time. Reagan and Schweiker, touring New York, New Jersey, and Pennsylvania, succeeded in picking up a handful of delegates that at least gave them the argument that their marriage was working out. "We have great areas of philosophical compatibility," Reagan insisted in Newark. "Abortion, amnesty, capital punishment, forced busing, prayer in the schools, inflation—all these are areas of fundamental agreement." As Schweiker put it: "Only a coalition candidacy and a broad new stroke of drama can turn this thing around." Schweiker said later: "At one point in Pennsylvania we really did have a potential among people leaning or uncommitted of somewhere between fifteen and twenty delegates. But Drew Lewis was the key. The others were waiting for him. They didn't want to take the political risk if he didn't take it. He became the neck of the bottle. If he had resigned as Ford chairman, that fifteen or twenty would have been realized. But when he made the decision not to, he immediately chilled the waters. The whole nomination boiled down to Drew Lewis and Clarke Reed. It was that close a deal. We did succeed in fifty per cent of what we set out doing, because the Ford momentum was stopped. Mississippi was about to go, but it didn't. So, the shock wave, with all of its problems and complications, did succeed in putting the Mississippi delegation in a holding pattern."

That was the way matters stood as Republicans converged on Kansas City in early August. The Ford forces were now claiming enough delegates for their man to be nominated, but Sears had muddied the situation sufficiently so that nobody could be sure. Sears and Laxalt both insisted they had no tricks up their sleeves, that they just hoped everybody could vote their preferences and go home with a united party.

But anyone who knew John Sears knew there was about as much chance that he would go to Kansas City without some moves as there was that the sun would not rise the next day. It was a question of where he would strike. He was a man of surprises, and he would live up to his reputation.

part VIII

**THE
REPUBLICAN
CONVENTION**

32. A Surprise Strategy

Whenever the Republican Party meets in convention, it is as if a strict parochial school has decided to hold its annual picnic in Las Vegas. There is the same atmosphere of release, of discipline and propriety being set aside for a brief time, in an almost purposeful way. "Who Says Republicans Don't Have Fun?" The button and bumper-sticker question has become a kind of self-mockery. When the Grand Old Party invades a convention city, its delegates seem to work at having fun, if only to dispel the image that they, and Republicanism, are over the hill.

Yet the revelry is almost always country-club fun, Kiwanis fun; well-heeled and antiseptic, heavy on the posh cocktail party and the cold shrimp. The delegates are distinctly Wall Street and Yale if from the North, or Miami Beach and Ole Miss if from the South. The men have the look of successful business and new-car franchises, their women the aura of the beauty-parlor habit and the bridge table. They are mostly middle-aged or old, and the few young ones dress and act as if they are bucking for middle age. And they are white; they are so white that the occasional black face is enough to turn heads, except that the singular black can be counted on to be in proper Republican uniform, as if he too is bucking to get into the club.

For all its programed appearance, though, a Republican convention is often exceedingly emotional. Republicans, by and large conservative, tend to be very emotional when it comes to the issues or personalities they hold dear. There was never another scene to equal the breast-beating of the True Believers that night at the Cow Palace in San Francisco in 1964 when Ike Eisenhower excoriated the columnists and commentators, leading delegates to shake their fists and make obscene gestures toward the press section, or when Barry Goldwater let loose his ringing defense of extremism. Card-carrying liberals of the other party like to say that Republicans don't care, but they are wrong; Republicans care a great deal, and are very demonstrative about what they care about. It's just that they care about very different things.

This very emotionalism and the carnival atmosphere of stirred-up intensity in which it flourishes offered ample reason to expect that the showdown between Gerald Ford and Ronald Reagan would be a *Götter-dämmerung*. Reagan was the candidate of the Republican emotions and it seemed likely that his strategists would try somehow to confront this basically conservative party with some basic test of ideology that would set enough sparks flying to ignite an upset victory. The logical place to expect such fireworks was, of course, in the writing of the party platform. This rather purposeless recital of party objectives has often been the battleground of opposing forces in national conventions, and on several issues Reagan and Ford clearly differed: the future of Henry Kissinger for one, or of the Panama Canal for another.

Against this expectation, however, Reagan's chief strategist, Sears, insisted repeatedly that he saw no such fight in prospect, over either the platform or the party rules. All he wanted, he kept saying, was a fair Ford-Reagan test out of which a unified party, and hence one capable of winning the November election, could emerge. This objective, dismissed as a ploy, was actually a moderating element in Sears's strategy. In time, he found it necessary to force a confrontation on both rules and platform, but in such a narrow, almost noncombative way as to avoid any deep division in party ranks. Indeed the central controversy at the Republican convention became not one between the Ford and Reagan camps but between factions of Reagan's support over the wisdom of Sears's strategy—low-risk for a party nervous about divisiveness, but high-risk for Reagan as a candidate.

For weeks the Ford camp had worried that Reagan might get the upper hand on some procedural vote for which he would have more strength than he could muster on a presidential-nomination roll call. And by administering a series of procedural defeats to Ford, he might at last dispel the aura of incumbency that had been Ford's single strongest weapon all year. The delegates might become persuaded that they would be nominating a sure loser in Ford. By quirk of state laws, Reagan appeared to have about twenty more dependable votes on early procedural questions than on the first presidential roll call. In several states, primary-election regulations required allocation of delegates *on the first ballot for President only* in proportion to the primary results. For example, in North Carolina, when Reagan scored his first primary victory, his 52-per-cent margin entitled him to only twenty-eight delegates on the first ballot to twenty-five for Ford. But at a subsequent state convention, fifty-one Reagan supporters were elected delegates. Under the law, twenty-five of them had to vote for Ford on the first presidential roll call, but they were free to vote their own preference thereafter and also on any procedural or platform questions raised in advance of the first vote for President. The situation was comparable in Kentucky and a few other states. In Indiana, the situation was the reverse: Ford forces controlled the state party apparatus and hence named most of the delegates. But though they favored Ford, about thirty-five of them were bound by the results of the state primary—won overwhelmingly by Reagan—to vote for the Californian on the first ballot. With an over-all procedural-vote advantage of some twenty delegates, however, it made sense for the Reaganites to have a first test of strength in advance of the presidential roll call, where this edge could be voted.

The Ford camp, before the convention, feared the Reaganites would make a frontal assault on the state laws requiring strict adherence to the primary results. Paul Laxalt, Reagan's chairman, had raised the possibility that the first-ballot-only Ford delegates might simply abstain on the first ballot, thereby denying the President a majority. Then Reagan, with augmented strength, could win on the next roll call. Others had suggested that such "temporary" Ford delegates simply defy state law or regulations and vote for Reagan anyway. They argued that a national convention had no apparatus for enforcing state law or obliging a delegate to cast his vote in any manner against his personal wishes.

To guard against any such high jinks, the Republican National Committee adopted a resolution, unopposed by Reagan, that reinforced the integrity of state primary laws, and at hearings in Kansas City on convention rules in early August, the Ford camp pushed for its incorporation. There was much discussion that this "justice resolution" might become the focus for the major Ford-Reagan confrontation, but in fact the Reaganites never seriously considered contesting it. A typical reaction was that of stanch Reaganite Betty Lou Johnson of North Carolina. She was ready to go to the mat on any number of platform issues, and joined a rump group of conservatives that sought stiffer platform positions than the Reagan campaign was willing to fight for. But on defying state party law, for Ronald Reagan or anybody else, she was adamant: "It's just not right."

What Reagan needed was some other issue that would command the loyalty of all his supporters and at the same time reach out to uncommitteds and, if possible, some Ford backers as well. Though Sears came into the convention insisting that Reagan would have 1140 votes on the first roll call, he was blowing smoke; he knew he had to pry loose some Ford support if his candidate was to have a chance. The Schweiker gambit had been the first effort, and while it had not hurt Reagan as much as had been generally imagined—Mississippi had after all been shaky already—it hadn't produced any breakthrough either. A clear-cut ideological test seemed more promising.

Because Henry Kissinger had become the bogeyman of the True Believers, it seemed that the surest way to fire up the Reagan zealots would be to formulate some clearly anti-Kissinger platform plank to which *all* conservatives could rally. Sears, however, thought otherwise. He reasoned that any stands taken on ideological issues would be "easy to compromise one way or the other"—that is, the Ford forces would be able to water them down or simply swallow them.

On this basic Sears strategy—that the test should come on some kind of procedural rather than ideological matter—there was virtual unanimity within the Reagan camp, even among the ideologues. "The feeling was that we were not going to be able to structure a platform fight of any responsible kind," Dave Keene said later, "because the Ford people would cave in on anything of that sort; they weren't interested so much in the platform as in the nomination. Secondly, the available votes—those that were not bound by law and those that weren't very strongly committed—were not ideological votes; they were organizational votes. You had to show something other than simply an ideological position to get them. The contrary view was that you could have in some way stampeded them or so embarrassed the President that he couldn't run on the platform. Our feeling was that wouldn't happen, because the convention probably wouldn't accept something that was an outright insult to the President. And anything that was responsible he'd just cave in on."

Sears, notorious for keeping his counsel, had his own idea on how best to bring about a Ford-Reagan confrontation. But before he could air it, he had to deal with the True Believers who wanted to do battle with the Ford camp on the "blood issues." The leader of the True Believers was a nondelegate, Senator Jesse Helms of North Carolina, a Barry Goldwater of the 1970s who did not tolerate moderation in the pursuit of the conservative Holy Grail. He was against recognition of "Red" China and the "abandonment" of "The Republic of China" (Taiwan). He was against the Helsinki Pact with the Russians that sold "the captive nations" down the river. He was against unilateral concessions to the Soviet Union on nuclear testing. He deplored Ford's snub of Alexander Solzhenitsyn on his arrival in the United States in 1974. He was four-square behind Reagan against surrendering American "sovereignty" (which according to treaty did not exist) over the Panama Canal. He was, in short, a man with a mission, a man of principle, convinced that right was right, no matter what the nose count might be.

Helms sent telegrams to about fifty conservative delegates and alternates inviting them to attend a meeting on August 8, the Sunday evening of the preconvention week. (The meeting actually was a follow-on of a session in Atlanta on the final weekend in July, just before the Schweiker move, at which the matter of writing stanchly conservative planks had been discussed. Four Reagan aides had attended, but the Reagan camp did not pick up on the idea.) Helms, correctly assessing that Reagan's strategy did not focus on the platform, was determined to launch a sharply ideological debate on his own. Out of the Sunday meeting and later conversations came a list of twenty-two specific platform proposals, taking a strongly conservative position on every major issue. Helms's approach was a formula for intraparty warfare and one, Sears feared, the Reaganites could not win. Though the complexion of the convention was clearly conservative, Sears contended that to seem to repudiate the President outright would invite a backlash. In trying to erode the incumbent's strength, nothing must be done that might inadvertently add to it.

As the Helms conservatives were kicking up their heels on the platform, Sears asked permission to address the rules committee of the party, which was meeting to propose recommendations to the convention's rules committee. The expectation was that he would talk on the "justice amendment," but that was wrong. All through the preconvention week Sears had kept up a drumbeat of criticism against President Ford for declining to disclose his vice-presidential choice in advance. To most, it seemed an idle and somewhat naïve exercise: a sitting President would not be cajoled into naming his selection early, especially since such action might hurt him and alienate either the party's liberals or conservatives. But when Sears went before the party rules committee in the Continental Hotel ballroom on Monday, August 9, it became clear just why he had been harping for so long on the matter of vice-presidential selection. He had experienced at first hand what could happen when a presidential candidate picked his running mate and disclosed his choice early; now he was determined to see that Ford be made to name his own Schweiker and deal with the political repercussions. He proposed that advance announcement of a vice-presidential name be required of all presidential candidates.

Sears wrapped this blatantly political move in the trappings of altruistic reform, but he knew he wasn't kidding anybody. When Paul Haerle, the state chairman of California and a Ford backer on the committee, called his proposal a "misery-loves-company" rule, he was not far off the mark. But Sears with a straight face insisted that the party could jolt the public with its boldness in confronting a major problem. "I think most people worry about the vice-presidency and the way that it's done," he said, "simply because they wonder if someone isn't being paid off after the fact."

The proposal was immediately rejected by the party rules committee, dominated by Ford, but Sears had expected as much. By introducing the scheme there, he could now take it to the convention rules committee later in the week, and then on the convention floor for a vote by all the delegates.

As he rode down the hotel elevator, reporters jokingly called him a "troublemaker." He laughed. "And it's only Monday," he said. Then, walking out the lobby, he turned, grinning, and said: "See you fellas tomorrow."

Sears's proposal came to be known as Rule 16-C. All through the preconvention week he focused on it, saying at daily press conferences that the delegates had a right to know who Ford's running mate would be before balloting for President. Candidates for lower office in every state were going to have to run with the national ticket, he argued, and their chances might stand or fall on the identity of the full ticket, especially now that the public was so sensitive to the matter of vice-presidential succession. He even insisted somewhat implausibly that the issue was of such concern to the delegates that Ford could not be nominated unless he disclosed the name of his running mate. The Ford strategists quickly made it clear that under no circumstances would the President disclose his choice in advance, but rather would follow the "traditional" method of announcing the decision only after his own nomination had been secured. The Sears approach, they noted, would preclude the possibility of Ford's taking Reagan on as his running mate—a point they hoped would undermine support for 16-C within the Reagan camp.

At first Sears seemed to be banging his head against a wall. But by Thursday, August 12, the dynamics of the situation appeared to change in his favor, mainly because the Ford forces were trying to nail down more support by spreading the word that Ford was considering running mates from all factions in the party. In an involved process that had been initiated largely for public-relations reasons, the President several weeks earlier had asked all 4518 convention delegates and alternates, all Republican members of Congress, governors, members of the Republican National Committee, and other party leaders to submit to him five recommendations, in order of preference. The results, compiled for the President's consideration, were not made public and didn't have to be; just as Richard Nixon in 1968 had invited a similar expression of views and then ignored them, Ford gave Republicans a sense of participation in his decision without committing himself to anyone.

About a week after that call for advice had gone out—and obviously before all the replies could be compiled—Ford instructed Dick Cheney, White House counsel Philip Buchen, and his deputy, Ed Schmults, to contact about two dozen individuals. Those on the list were asked whether they were interested in being Ford's running mate, and whether they would agree if selected to release financial and other personal data requested in an accompanying questionnaire. In short order, most of those on the list let it be known they had been contacted. Ford, in the manner of an old-fashioned pol, had covered the waterfront: conservatives like Senator James Buckley[1] of New York and John Connally; liberals like Senators Mark Hatfield of Oregon and Charles Percy of Illinois; moderates like Governor Robert Ray of Iowa and William Ruckelshaus. There was somebody for everybody—and as Sears pointed out—somebody for everybody to be against.

As the list and the rumors grew and circulated, the inevitable happened: conservatives began to complain about the liberals on the list, and liberals about the conservatives. Each side threatened to withhold support unless reassured that Ford would not pick someone from the opposite party wing. To Sears's evident delight, nine Ford delegates in Maine, including State Chairman John Linnell, suggested they might abstain on the first ballot unless they were assured that Ford would not pick Connally. The Maine contingent feared that Connally so reeked of Watergate he would keep the Republican ticket on the defensive all fall. At the same time, Clarke Reed, agonizing over his earlier decision to abandon Reagan, issued an open warning to Ford not to pick a liberal, lest he lose the pivotal Mississippi delegation. Reports that Hatfield, Percy, Weicker, and Brooke were on the list "came as a shock," Reed said. Both Weicker and Brooke had said they weren't interested, and Hatfield and Percy were regarded as long shots at best, but their inclusion gave Reed the opportunity to demonstrate his independence at a time he was enduring heavy pressure from the Reaganites. "These people are not philosophically compatible with the President or the majority of Republicans," he complained—recalling that Ford had personally assured him during the last presidential visit to Jackson that he would select a compatible running mate. "I thought I could spook 'em off," Reed said later.

The protests from North and South were only brushfires, however, extinguished with swift assurances from the White House that the President would honor his commitment to select someone in tune with himself. Jim Baker, Ford's delegate head-hunter, phoned Linnell and told him not to worry about Connally. "Look," Baker said, "you're playing it exactly as they want it." Yet the Ford campaign could not eliminate Connally pub-

---

1. Buckley, in a surprise move initiated by the right-wing Illinois Congressman Phil Crane, suddenly made known that he would not "slam the door" on any attempt to place his name in nomination for the presidency. The idea had all the earmarks of being a Reagan attempt to force a second ballot by denying Ford a first-ballot majority, but the Reagan strategists denied having anything to do with it. Indeed, Reagan figured to lose more support than Ford by a Buckley candidacy. Richard Rosenbaum, the New York delegation and state party chairman, bluntly warned Buckley to withdraw or lose the New York Republican organization's support in his re-election campaign for the Senate. Buckley finally faced reality and bowed out.

licly, because he was the heavy choice of the Mississippi delegation. Linnell and his colleagues finally backed off. "The last thing we want to do," he said, "is to do John Sears's work for him." Reed, in a phone call to the White House, reminded Cheney of the President's personal assurances, and was told flatly that Ford intended to honor that commitment.

The fires were put out, yet the fact that they had been lighted at all said something important about this particular President. Though he was the incumbent, Ford was treated almost as if he were an interloper. The phenomenon of delegates openly threatening to withhold support from him if he chose a running mate not to their liking was a telling commentary on how shaky his hold on his party was. Not only was he an unelected President whose power had come not from the people but from the hands of the now-despised Nixon, whom he had favored by pardoning; his own conduct in office, especially in the last few months, suggested that he was somehow not a man of genuine presidential stature. The spectacle of his being obliged to entertain delegates in the White House, sometimes at gala state receptions and dinners for foreign royalty, was transparently demeaning; so were the hard questions that uncommitted delegates put to him. He was the President, yet too often he functioned like some Chicago alderman hustling to keep his job by old-fashioned ward-heeling.

All this was in striking contrast to the overbearing presidential aura that shone around Ford's two immediate predecessors, who came to their party conventions with the nomination in an iron grip, and lorded over every aspect of the proceedings. In 1964 Johnson ruled the Democratic convention in Atlantic City like an emperor, controlling the slightest details of platform-writing and procedure; in 1972 Nixon planned the Republican convention in Miami Beach so finely that a script was written and followed, complete with instructions to important participants about precisely where they should stand on the convention platform and how much time should be allowed for applause.

Had Ford been a man of strong personality like Johnson, he might have overcome the public perception of him as somehow unpresidential. Johnson, after all, had been unelected as President too when he directed the 1964 Democratic convention like a Toscanini. But Johnson's personality and bold political style so dominated his party's apparatus that after less than a year in office he was not challenged for the nomination, not even by Robert Kennedy. Ford, by contrast, came into his convention battered by primary setbacks, driven to indignities by the need to garner and keep delegates' support, and subjected to blunt warnings from potential deserters. In dealing with such threats, he only compounded the impression of softness. Part of the power of incumbency is the power to reward friends and punish enemies, but Ford was so conciliatory that he seemed always to be rewarding, never punishing. He seemed like one of those big dolls with the rounded base that when hit bobs back up for another punch. This only encouraged boldness in those who pressured him, a boldness that few would ever have expressed in dealing with Johnson, or even Nixon.[2]

Finally there was a conviction among many at the convention that Ford was merely a caretaker President keeping the seat warm between Nixon and the next choice of the people, Jimmy Carter. The polls seemed to substantiate this attitude, and further stripped from Ford the advantage that normal incumbency might have brought him.

As expected Sears's proposal for early disclosure of vice-presidential selections was defeated in the convention rules committee on the Saturday before the convention opened, by a vote of 59–44. But by receiving more than the required 25 per cent of the vote, a minority report could be filed. That meant the issue of Rule 16-C would come to the convention floor for a showdown vote by all delegates on Tuesday, August 17, the night before the roll call on the presidential nomination.

To many Reagan rank-and-file supporters, the choice of Rule 16-C to be the centerpiece of Reagan's convention strategy, seeking to force Ford's hand on choosing a running mate, was sheer madness. What was needed, they firmly believed, was the Helms battle plan—to hit Ford with one ideological challenge after another on the party platform, to confront him with alternatives he could not accept, and thereby to establish the real temper of the convention, which they all believed was Reaganite. What good was zealous support if it wasn't going to be tapped? The zealots were convinced that Reagan was a man of substance; what others saw as simplistic answers to complex problems they saw as powerful beacons of truth, knifing through the darkness of confused ambivalence with which party liberals and moderates had tried to smother the party for too long. Their own passions burned hot, and if some way could be found to fan them on the convention floor, Ford's chances might evaporate. Sure, Reagan was behind in the delegate count, but there were enough uncommitteds and enough "soft" Ford supporters to turn the convention around if their hearts and emotions could be aroused.

The existence of this potential, plus broad dissatisfaction with a very bland, noncommittal platform worked out essentially by the Ford camp, persuaded Sears finally to try some kind of foreign-policy challenge as well

---

2. Ford's very arrival in Kansas City on Sunday, August 15, was itself an expression of this weakness. A more secure President could have stayed in Washington until after his nomination was tendered by the party.

as 16-C. With the pressure continuing from Helms and the other ideologues, Sears moved to bring them more tightly within the Reagan councils so they could be watched and moderated, and, if possible, mollified.

"We were asking our troops to fight battles that were important, but were not the kind of battle they came to Kansas City to fight," Dave Keene said later. "You had to give them something to keep the blood warm in their veins." But the question was what to give them. In the platform committee, the Ford representatives, including Senators Hugh Scott of Pennsylvania and Roman Hruska of Nebraska, had already bent over backward to appease the Reaganites, especially the Helms people. On the Panama Canal, for example, the draft had first included a limp dishrag that said: ". . . as our discussions with the government of Panama necessarily continue, in no event will the United States surrender fundamental interests." The Reagan-Helms forces countered this phrase with a plank saying the United States should never agree in any way "to impair or relinquish United States sovereignty and control over the Panama Canal in perpetuity." Finally, after Senators Scott and Hruska had further tried to water it down, the plank noted that the 1903 treaty with Panama now under renegotiation gave the United States jurisdiction rights "as if it were sovereign." With the other side so willing to compromise, it was going to be hard to come up with something that would make them fight.

Yet there was no question the subject matter should be foreign policy. The turning point for Reagan's campaign in the primaries had been when he switched to foreign policy as the battleground. That was now his strong suit; a strategy was needed to show that it was on the convention floor.[3] With this in mind, Marty Anderson, Pete Hannaford, Ed Meese, and Sears set about drafting a comprehensive foreign-policy plank that was compatible with Reagan's position and party policy, but that would *have* to be contested by the Ford camp. The language had to make the challenge unmistakable, yet it had to be deftly worded so that it did not too crassly repudiate the incumbent Republican President.

Meanwhile Reagan plunged into a round of visits to delegations, including the unyielding Pennsylvanians under Drew Lewis, and then went

3. Sears saw the staging of an ideological fight as secondary in tumbling Ford. Only *after* 16-C had recruited Ford supporters and uncommitteds would the arithmetic and the mood be right for the bringing of a "raw-meat" issue to the floor. Ford had to be softened up with 16-C, then humbled by a proposed foreign-policy plank he would be obliged to oppose to erase the effect of his earlier loss.

Jim Baker, Ford's delegate head-hunter, challenged this logic later, however. A defeat for Ford on 16-C, he insisted, would have obliged him on the contrary to avoid at all costs any foreign-policy dispute that could not be won: it would have been better to accept a Reagan plank and a psychological setback than to risk a second straight roll-call defeat. The next night, he noted, Reagan would have some twenty less votes on the actual nomination roll call.

to the Alameda Plaza, his headquarters hotel, for a late-night session to chart the moves he hoped might yet bring him to victory. Present also were Nancy Reagan, the Schweikers, Dave Newhall, Sears, Anderson, Meese, Hannaford, Nofziger, Mike Deaver, and Jim Lake. During dinner in Reagan's suite, the broad strategic outlines were laid out to him: just the two tests—16-C and the foreign-policy plank; two rolls of the dice to take the whole pot. Sears outlined the 16-C fight and Anderson the foreign-policy plank. Reagan approved the plan, and Anderson, Meese, and Hannaford were dispatched to a midnight meeting with the Helms group to obtain its acquiescence on the foreign-policy test. For several hours they debated with the Helmsites pressing for tougher language.

The plank as it finally evolved was an only thinly veiled slap at Kissinger. It criticized directly or indirectly his policy of détente with the Soviet Union; Ford's snub of Alexander Solzhenitsyn; the Helsinki Pact; unilateral concessions in nuclear testing; the signing of "secret agreements"—a veiled reference to the Panama Canal Treaty. Called "Morality in Foreign Policy," it read:

"The goal of Republican foreign policy is the achievement of liberty under law and a just and lasting peace in the world. The principles by which we act to achieve peace and to protect the interests of the United States must merit the restored confidence of our people. We recognize and commend that great beacon of human courage and morality, Alexander Solzhenitsyn, for his compelling message that we must face the world with no illusions about the nature of tyranny. Ours will be a foreign policy that keeps this in mind.

"Ours will be a foreign policy which recognizes that in international negotiations we must make no undue concessions; that in pursuing détente we must not grant unilateral favors with only the hope of getting future favors in return.

"Agreements that are negotiated, such as the one signed in Helsinki, must not take from those who do not have freedom the hope of one day gaining it.

"Finally, we are firmly committed to a foreign policy in which secret agreements, hidden from our people, will have no part. Honestly, openly, and with firm conviction, we shall go forward as a united people to forge a lasting peace in the world based upon our deep belief in the rights of man, the rule of law and guidance by the hand of God."

Later, Helms's right-hand man and the manager of Reagan's North Carolina primary campaign, Tom Ellis, argued that specific references to the Panama Canal and Taiwan should have been inserted to make certain that the Ford camp could not swallow it. Such references were indeed in the draft when Helms signed it before submission to the convention, but according to the Reagan forces were subsequently deleted at a meeting at which Helms's aides were present. In any case, as Jim Lake, now Reagan's press secretary, later explained: "It was intentionally phrased carefully in terms so that it wasn't an outright sock in the jaw."

By introducing the proposed rules change and then challenging the foreign-policy plank, Sears managed to dominate the actual maneuvering at the convention and the headlines about it right up to Tuesday night, the time of the crucial roll calls.

16-C was not, as it turned out, washing well with Reaganites. Being conservatives, they did not look favorably on an upset to the *status quo* in any regard, even if it was to the benefit of their candidate. Just as many had balked at the idea of breaking state party law, so too did they object to "changing the rules in the middle of the game" on vice-presidential selection, as the Ford people put it, especially when such action was so clearly aimed at only one candidate—the President. And incredibly, many of them did not comprehend the very simple politics in 16-C. They took it simply as a reform of the system, the kind of thing "liberals" proposed, and turned their noses up at it.

Even one of the most outspoken and emotional supporters of Reagan at the convention, former Representative Thomas Curtis, head of the Missouri delegation and former chairman of the Federal Election Commission, insisted in a heated corridor conversation with me that 16-C was no political ploy but an altruistic reform. He told Reagan, he said, that he would not have spoken in its favor if it had been nothing more than a self-serving gambit. Other Reaganites were not so naïve or so pliable. They saw 16-C for what it was, and they didn't like it. Even in the Mississippi delegation, some saw it as a throw-away issue with little bearing on the convention's outcome, rather than the make-or-break test between Reagan and Ford that it was. This failure to convey the tactical importance of the 16-C test obviously hurt Reagan's cause; so did its essential "cuteness" among conservative delegates who were accustomed, indeed wedded, to doing things in the proper, orderly, traditional way.

The showdown on 16-C, and on the nomination itself, was about to come in the Mississippi delegation. Its steadfast decision to arrive at the convention with all thirty votes uncommitted, and with the unit rule governing, assured that Mississippi would be a rich and obvious prize, and who would get it would depend for a time on the firmness or vacillation of Clarke Reed. Considering how much blood, sweat, and tears had already been expended on both the delegation and Reed, it was a sort of cruel justice that it should be so.

33. Mississippi Again

In a contested national party convention, there is one essential ingredient for success: swift and sure communication. Unless the chief strategists and tacticians are aware of what is being said and done on the convention floor, in its corridors, and over the miles of telephone lines connecting all the delegations with the candidates' command posts, speedy response is frustrated. Anticipating all manner of problems in Kansas City, the forces of Gerald Ford and Ronald Reagan had laid out costly and complex networks of phones, television monitors, walkie-talkies, beepers, and various other devices of the communications age to keep a firm grip on unfolding events.

Each camp had a large mobile trailer parked immediately outside Kemper Arena—a bizarre new structure that has most of its supporting girders exposed outside the hall, to permit unobstructed view inside. Telephone lines went out from each trailer to the delegations and to floor leaders or whips in charge of dealing with problems as they arose in the various delegations. In Ford's trailer, the convention manager, Bill Timmons; the old Goldwater strategist F. Clifton White; and Jim Baker directed coordinators who were handling phones to the states and to twelve Ford whips (working for Senator Robert Griffin of Michigan, the floor manager, and Congressman Robert Michel of Illinois, the chief whip). In addition, ten "floaters" functioned on the floor—troubleshooters with walkie-talkies tuned in to the trailer. The whips wore red baseball caps, the floaters yellow. In addition, regional chairmen—Dick Rosenbaum for the Northeast, Harry Dent for the South, Ohio State Chairman Kent McGough for the Midwest, California State Chairman Paul Haerle for the West—had special telephone lines. The Ford trailer also had private lines into the anchor booths of NBC and ABC, high above the convention floor, in order to pass on information —and self-serving rumor, a service that CBS decided to do without.

In Reagan's trailer, John Sears presided over thirty-five direct lines to most of the states, with nine regional coordinators operating from small cubicles, as in a campaign boiler room. Paul Laxalt was floor manager, assisted by Helms, Congressman Crane, and Senator William Scott of Virginia.

All this electronic paraphernalia inevitably raised memories of Watergate, and so each campaign hired security men to guard the trailers and to sweep them daily for possible wiretaps or other bugs. Also, because the Ford trailer's telephone lines had to pass directly beneath Reagan's trailer, they were placed in a steel pipe to guard against sabotage or monitoring. For all this elaborate electronics to every corner of the convention hall, the lines that went from each trailer to one specific delegation—Mississippi—would prove to be the most vital, and most heavily used. And once again, the delegation's erratic chairman, Clarke Reed, would be a special target.

Reed, after having jumped the Reagan ranks weeks before, was having second thoughts. He confided to Lou Cannon of *The Washington Post* that he might have "overreacted" to Schweiker—an indication that he feared he might yet be on the losing side, dumped out of the "kingmaker" role and "the catbird seat" that the siren call of Harry Dent had promised him.

Because Reed was a member of the rules committees of both the Republican National Committee and the convention, he was watched closely by everyone in this preconvention week. He was like a cat on a hot tin roof, a description, if not a sensation, Reed probably would have liked. (He talked, incongruously for an Old South conservative, like a Motown hipster. Everyone was "that cat" to him; almost every sentence began with "Man, that cat——.") Dent continued his merciless needling of Reed, taking full advantage of his seemingly inexhaustible good humor. And Reed being so eminently flappable, a procrastinator in advance of a decision and an incurable worrier after the fact, Dent eyed him like a predatory animal, which some Mississippi delegates insisted Dent was, and disliked him intensely for it. The Reaganites were still at Reed, too. David Keene kept reminding him of his conservatism, of his recent "betrayal" of the cause. Knowing his indecisiveness, they did everything possible to make him feel even guiltier, telling him he owed the Reagan side something. Letters from right-wing organizations poured in, castigating him for his "defection," imploring him to come to his senses before it was too late.

There was, the Reaganites told him, one way he could partly redeem himself: side with them on 16-C. After all, it was in his interest for the President to be obliged to say in advance who he would pick as Vice President. And indeed the argument had some appeal for Reed. He knew that the sentiment back in Mississippi overwhelmingly favored Reagan. And even before the full Mississippi delegation had arrived in Kansas City, he had played his opening card—his blunt warning to Ford that he risked losing the Mississippi delegation unless he dropped several prominent liberals from his list of possible running mates. In the Haberdashery Bar of the Muehlebach Hotel, Reed told reporters he might back 16-C as a means of assuring that the President would not select a liberal. He was taking a good, hard look at 16-C.

The pressure on Reed continued. In the party rules committee where Sears introduced 16-C, Reed first tried to have the vote delayed, but then voted against it. "I may have to go with them on 16-C [in the convention rules committee]," Dent reported Reed had told him during this tense period. Dent followed him like a mother hen. "I kept getting messages: 'Better watch Clarke; he's flipping.'" On August 14, the Saturday morning before the convention rules committee vote on 16-C, Bill Timmons called Reed to join him for breakfast in his room at the Crown Center, the Ford headquarters hotel. Also invited were Dent, Bryce Harlow, and some others. Dent talked turkey to his old Mississippi friend and foil: "Clarke, baby, you're killing yourself here. You're here today, you're gone tomorrow. I'm talking to you as a friend. You're hurting yourself."

Reed, according to Dent, assured the group: "I'll be all right on 16-C." After breakfast, when Dent took Reed to the nerve center of Ford's campaign, they met Dick Cheney and Jim Baker outside the presidential office. "I'll be all right on 16-C," Reed assured them once more, but he added, again according to Dent: "If we don't need my vote and I see that, I might throw it away. But you'll get thirty votes on 16-C. I'm not going to flip. They ain't gonna get me." Then he went to the convention rules committee meeting and proceeded to vote *for* 16-C. It was easily defeated, so Reed could afford to give his vote to the Reagan side on this one. He was, as usual, trying to work both sides of the street—to placate everybody.

By now, the Ford forces believed they didn't actually need all of Mississippi's thirty votes. If they could dissolve the unit rule and get about half of those, according to Baker's nose count that would be enough to assure defeat of 16-C and crack Reagan's challenge. Just as important, Dent said later, "we would go over the top [1130 delegates] in all the national media counts. It would be a great psychological victory for us." And so Reed was pressed to help engineer a compromise dissolution of the Mississippi unit rule in advance of Tuesday night's critical floor vote on 16-C, or sooner if possible.

"Thus was born 'the Great Mississippi Compromise,'" Dent said later, in his penchant for dramatizing. "Clarke liked the idea. 'But I have to get back to you cats,' he said. 'I have to talk to Billy [Mounger].'" Dent deplored any consultation with Mounger, a rugged, stocky, combative man, small in stature but tough and determined, who still hoped to pull all thirty votes out for Reagan. To try to end-run Mounger, Cheney and Dent called in Charles Pickering, the incoming state chairman and a Reagan man. He was interested in the compromise for the sake of party harmony in the state, but did not want to be the instrument of Reagan's undoing. He too had to talk to Mounger. The answer came back to Cheney Saturday afternoon: Maybe, but get somebody neutral to propose it.

On Sunday morning, August 15, Dent called a meeting of the advance forces in the Mississippi delegation committed to Ford. For three hours they pored over the list of Mississippi delegates and alternates, trying to estimate how the delegation would vote on 16-C. "I told them the situation was eroding," Dent recalled, "that they'd been sitting back while Billy Mounger had been working. Billy was putting out stories and quoting local papers that it was being reversed [for Reagan], thirty votes the other way." The Ford leaders felt they had twenty-nine half-votes of the sixty delegates and alternates, not counting the unpredictable Reed, plus a number of leaners. "The question was, did we have the votes to move in that caucus Sunday night?" Dent said. He told them about the compromise idea and most bought it, although some wanted to push for all thirty. They were asked to come up with a suggestion about a neutral sponsor for the compromise.

A few hours later, Ford leaders Doug Shanks and Tommy Giordano met with the two most influential Reaganites in the delegation, Mounger and Victor Mavar, the state's national committeeman, to consider the compromise, in which each side would get fifteen votes on 16-C. Mounger and Mavar were not totally unwilling.

Still later on Sunday afternoon, most of the Mississippi delegates began to arrive at the Ramada East Motel in nearby Independence. Harry Dent was at another hotel, attending a caucus of his own state, South Carolina, but thinking of his assignment to bag a neutral from among the arriving Mississippians to sponsor the compromise. Suddenly the Ford team beeper he was wearing on his belt went off. It beeped about six times, piercing the stilled, heavily Reaganite caucus. Dent's vote was needed on an issue before the caucus, but he had to get up and leave, conspicuously, amid much snickering, for the Ramada East not far away.

Clarke Reed, meanwhile, was in Kemper Arena being interviewed by Mike Wallace of CBS. Standing within earshot was Jack Lee, the Ford camp's floor whip in the Mississippi delegation. To his surprise and dismay, he heard Reed tell Wallace that he planned to vote *for* 16-C on the floor, just as he had done in committee on Saturday. And not only that: Lee thought he heard Reed say he would help to *lead* the fight to deliver all thirty Mississippi votes for the proposal. Lee pushed the emergency button; the beeper call went out to Dent.

At the Ramada East, Dent again gathered the Mississippi Ford leaders in Doug Shanks's room. He had heard that the Reagan people were going to spring a surprise. They were going to try to amend the temporary rules with 16-C on Monday morning, when not everybody would be in the hall for what customarily were only formalities. It was going to be *the* battle, Dent told the group. "Clarke is now turned around on 16-C and he's going to deliver all thirty votes," he said. "We gotta stop that *tonight.*" Shanks, fresh from the meeting with Giordano, Mounger, and Mavar, whispered to Dent: "You may get fifteen to fifteen tonight." Dent was elated. Cheney had told Dent shortly before: "Harry, get that unit rule dissolved. We cannot have those thirty votes cast against us—Monday morning or any morning." So Dent pushed for a vote of 15–15 that Sunday night.

Dent dispatched his aide John Davis to find Reed. It took him more than an hour, because Reed was making himself scarce. Finally, minutes before the full delegation's caucus was to start, Davis came with Reed in tow.

Dent opened up on him immediately. "Clarke, my goodness, man, what in the world you doing to us?"

Reed was defensive. "Whattaya mean, whattaya mean, cat?"

"You just told Mike Wallace on CBS you gonna lead the fight and deliver thirty votes for Rule 16-C."

"Oh, my God!" Reed said, falling back flat on the bed in front of everybody. "What can I do? What can I do?"

Dent reminded him of his commitment to stick with the Ford people on 16-C.

"I gotta get out of this!" Reed answered. "I gotta get out of this!"

Dent had his man hooked, and now he began reeling him in. He told him about the reported Monday-morning gambit—"Pearl Harbor," Dent called it in his understated way—and said: "Clarke, they gonna use you tomorrow morning."

Reed was only too glad to have an out. "That would be a bunch of Mickey Mouse," he replied. "I don't put up with that kind of stuff."

"Why don't you tell your delegation that?"

"I'll tell the delegation that I ain't gonna put up with no Mickey Mouse and if that thing gonna be done Monday morning, to vote against it, all thirty votes against it."

Sure enough, Reed went into the caucus and told the delegation that he had heard the Reagan forces might try a sneak maneuver Monday morning. If they did, the whole delegation ought to vote against it. After much discussion, the delegation adjourned without taking any vote whatever on 16-C—which most of the arriving delegates still knew little about

—or on dissolving the unit rule. Dent had fallen short of his objective, but at least Reed had been persuaded to counter the reported Monday-morning surprise.

When the caucus broke up, Dent told a few reporters about the possible Pearl Harbor and Reed's reaction to it. Sitting just behind me as we talked was former Governor Louie Nunn of Kentucky, one of Reagan's Southern lieutenants. Nunn shortly afterward disappeared, presumably to phone the Reagan headquarters with what he had heard. If there was a sneak attack planned, it was abandoned right there.

But Dent and his allies in the Mississippi delegation prepared for the worst. Dent gathered nearly thirty of the Mississippians into two adjoining motel rooms for what he called "a prayer meeting" on 16-C. A fact sheet was prepared arguing that 16-C would preclude the option of Ford's selecting Reagan or of consulting with Reagan on a vice-presidential choice. "I started preaching," Dent recalled later, "about the lack of leadership in Mississippi, that these people were gonna have to take the leadership themselves. That there was a battle going on to retake Clarke Reed. We had Clarke's body but we didn't have his soul."

Dent also took the opportunity to make the dynamic Giordano head of Ford's campaign in the Mississippi delegation. By prearrangement, both Gil Carmichael and Shanks agreed to step back. Giordano had been working with the Ford leadership for some time, but had been dragging his feet on a public endorsement. Dent took care of that by telling this group that Giordano was now their leader. If Giordano had any qualms, this action removed them. For an hour the group again surveyed the delegate list, with everyone in the room assigned to lobby someone else on 16-C. Each was instructed to call John Davis by noon on Monday so that Ford's delegate count could be firmed up. "Tell John where you stand on your assignments to get these people squared away," Dent said, "so we know we got the votes. When we know we got the votes, we're gonna ask Clarke for a caucus." Dent is a great actor, and by his own recollection he "preached to them like a black Baptist preacher, but in a funny way," working the group into a lather. "There was a lot of laughter in that room," Dent recalled, "but boy, they were steamed up when we left there. They were ready to go hunt bear."[1]

---

1. One distraction rankled Dent. Shanks, a baseball fan, fiddled with the television dial looking for a ball game and instead got some news clips about the Mississippi delegation. Suddenly everybody stopped listening to Dent in order to watch themselves. "Look at Mississippi!" one of the delegates shouted, and they applauded themselves on the screen. The incident caused somebody to observe that if the delegation voted now, it would lose the spotlight. Dent,

Two members of the group went into the room of one of the uncommitteds, a man named Toxey Hall Smith, and sold him on sponsoring the 15–15 deal. ("It'll be known as the Toxey Hall Smith Compromise," Dent told him.) Either that, or a variation called "the Retzer Plan," after Mike Retzer, a twenty-year-old student and Reed protégé, who had been suggesting that the unit rule be dissolved and then the delegates apportioned on the basis of a vote of the full sixty delegates and alternates. Such an approach obviously would extricate Reed from his personal dilemma.

All this while, Governor Nunn was nosing around, picking up scuttlebutt about the Ford maneuverings and lobbying delegates himself in Reagan's behalf. Dent, for his part, had no interest in keeping the plans secret. In fact he wanted Clarke Reed to know that moves were being made without him, knowledge that would further shake his confidence. On the way back to their own delegations about one-thirty Monday morning, Dent and Governor Holshouser of North Carolina gave a ride to Billy Wilkins, former executive director of the Mississippi state party and another old Reed side-kick. "Now, Billy, we gonna win it with or without Clarke," Dent told him. "Clarke is really messing himself up. We gonna get a meeting tomorrow. These people want a meeting. They were unanimous in that room that they wanted a caucus, and they're ready to vote Monday. The 15-to-15 plan is going to be proposed, and there's gonna be a neutral, just like Clarke and Pickering asked for, to move for it. We're doing everything that they have suggested." Dent said later: "I guarantee you Billy was on the phone to Clarke immediately."

The next morning, August 16, as the Republican National Convention officially opened, Dent sought out Reed on the floor. "Clarke, baby," he said, "these people want to vote."

"Yeah, Giordano told me. But man, I'm busy, busy."

Dent pressed him: "Friend, you gonna lose control of your delegation."

But meanwhile, the Reagan people, Mounger and Pickering, were having second thoughts. Mounger particularly was irate over Dent's meddling. Shanks, Giordano, Dent, Reed, Pickering, and Mounger all gathered under the Mississippi placard on the convention floor and began openly to argue about whether to caucus or not. Press and television reporters saw something was up and crowded around, poking their noses, microphones,

---

recalling the moment later, said, "I could have choked Doug Shanks." But Dent moved in quickly to turn the point around. "What that proves," he told them, "is they're saying you can be the kingmaker. And it's time to be the kingmaker. If you fool around here, you're not gonna be the kingmaker."

and cameras into the midst of the stormy huddle.

Mounger lashed out at Dent: "You're not a member of this delegation! We don't want a vote!"

Dent snapped back: "I know why you don't want a vote. We got the votes and you don't." He was winning no popularity contests with the Reaganites by now.

Haley Barbour, the state party executive director, finally interceded and led the group toward the back of the hall, away from the press and television. The five men—Giordano, Shanks, Pickering, Mounger, and Dent—ducked behind the bunting into a tiny space and continued the argument. Reporters poked their microphones and tape recorders under the bunting to capture the dialogue. There was more stalling, but no decision on a Monday caucus.

All this pressuring made Reed and the delegation feel hemmed in by both sides. About ten uncommitted or wavering delegates went to the Crown Center to visit President Ford, by arrangement of Dent. But before going in they unloaded on Dent and Cheney. "The more pressure you put on Mississippi," a Reagan-leaning alternate, Daniel Jaber, told Cheney, "the more we'll buck you." Afterward, Jaber told reporters: "They understood. . . . We'll do in time what we want to do."

Cheney got the message; the Ford forces would not insist on a Mississippi caucus—so long as Reed lived up to his earlier commitment to oppose 16-C. Before the very man on whom he was lavishing such heavy attention, Dent reported to the uncommitted Mississippians what Reed had said to Mike Wallace. "This is a battle for the soul of Clarke Reed," he repeated. "If Clarke leads you people, thirty–zero, then you've ended up probably breaking our back. If Clarke will just do what he says [oppose 16-C] we don't need a meeting."

Finally, according to Dent, both Reed and Lillian Todd, the other Mississippi member of the convention rules committee, agreed to help the Ford forces beat 16-C on Tuesday night. The group was ushered in to see the President; Reed could not stay long but, according to Dent, who was present, personally told Ford before leaving that the trouble on 16-C in the delegation had been worked out. Moments after the meeting Dent told John Hart of NBC News in the Crown Center lobby that no caucus would be held that day, because Reed had agreed to go along with the Ford camp on 16-C. In minutes the word was on the airwaves and Reed was on the phone to Cheney, squawking: "Y'all put me on the spot." And, indeed, the Reagan forces who heard the report were on his heels again.

Cheney was firm. "Look, Clarke, we expect you to do what you told us." Clarke Reed's much-pursued soul was still up for grabs.

On the convention floor that night, both sides lobbied openly. Pat Boone, the singer, hustled for Reagan and switched a Mississippi minister; a black woman, Mrs. Jean Long, was brought to Reagan's suite and he turned her around. Nobody knew whose nose count was right by now.

On Tuesday morning, August 17, Holshouser had a breakfast meeting in his room at the Crown Center to plot President Ford's strategy on Mississippi for the day. Dent was present, and Shanks, Giordano, and other Ford men. As they ate and watched a group of Mississippi uncommitteds on the NBC "Today" show, Shanks brought word that two or three black delegates were being lobbied hard by Reagan personally and were wavering. He wanted Dent to arrange a meeting for these men with the President, but the best Dent could do was a tour of the seventeenth floor, the campaign command area. He told the shaky delegates as much. Still, all things are possible in a desperate situation: en route to the seventeenth floor they encountered Jim Baker, and Dent told him of the crisis. In a few minutes they were all in Ford's office for a half-hour chat, and they left placated.

Meanwhile, out at the Ramada East, the delegation was wooed without surcease. Governor Holshouser, Senator John Tower of Texas, Secretary of the Treasury William Simon, and other Ford supporters met with the Mississippians. Tower "disclosed" that he himself was on Ford's vice-presidential list but that Reagan people from the South would be excluded from participation in Ford's decision if 16-C passed, since he obviously couldn't ask Reagan or Reagan people for their advice if Reagan was still an active candidate at the time. Passage of 16-C meant, Tower said, that the South's voice would not be heard on the matter of a Ford running mate.

From the Reagan side, the delegation got the movie-star treatment. Efrem Zimbalist, Jr., reportedly wept as he related that "Iron Chancellor" Rosenbaum would not let Reagan advocates address New York's delegation. And in the early afternoon Reagan himself came by, lobbied for 16-C, and answered all the old questions about Schweiker for the nth time. (Schweiker was not brought along this time.) Reaganites in the delegation professed to be buoyed by their candidate's last-ditch plea, but both sides were plainly running scared. Baker had told Dent shortly before that the Ford camp had 1130 votes against 16-C and needed Mississippi's thirty as a cushion, so Dent told a meeting of the Ford leaders: "This is the ball game, friends. So let's don't us move to lift the unit rule." The Ford people decided they would go for the thirty, but if the other side moved to void the unit rule, they would go along. Dent was afraid that if the unit rule were lifted, a Reagan delegate on the floor would request the state delegation be polled, in which case only delegates on the floor—not alternates in the gallery, where the Ford strength was—would be counted. "Don't get outmaneuvered," Dent warned them, worried. Dent didn't know that anything less than the thirty wouldn't help Reagan, so desperate was Reagan on 16-C. "We needed it for insurance," Dent said later, "but for them it was vital."

At about three o'clock on Tuesday afternoon the critical caucus was called. Sliding doors were pulled tight, cutting the motel dining room in half and separating the press from the drama inside. Dent and Keene were excluded as the deliberations proceeded, with much debate again about 16-C but—surprisingly, no effort to lift the unit rule. Despite all the lobbying, there still seemed to be considerable confusion over the strategy of 16-C. "We were told by the Reagan people that 16-C wasn't the ball game," Reed insisted. "They told us the big test would be the roll call on the nomination, and they had to carry it then." But Keene insisted just as strongly that the strategy of going all-out on 16-C could not have been spelled out more clearly. "I told Mounger, 'You lose this thing and it's over; that's it. If Mississippi goes down the chute on 16-C, we lose it on the floor, we lose the nomination, it's all right there.' They knew the significance of it. Or they should have."

As the key vote approached in the delegation caucus, a limousine drove up to the motel and out stepped Ford's perhaps most influential voice with this pivotal delegation—John Connally. Tight-lipped, he was whisked into Haley Barbour's room. There, Dent quickly briefed him on 16-C and how the Mississippi vote seemed to be shaping up. A sensitive decision was at hand: should Connally, with his overpowering demeanor, go into the caucus in progress and use his muscle for the President before the vote was taken? Or was there a danger, considering the touchy mood of this already beleaguered, overlobbied, and weary delegation, that such a bold and heavy-handed move might backfire?

Barbour, for one, as a Reagan man was afraid of Connally's influence. "Governor, I don't think you ought to go in there," he said. "They're just getting ready to vote." Dent, fearful that the timing was wrong to play such an intimidating card, said to Connally: "I hate to see you get in this. Why not let them decide if they want you before or after [the vote]?"

Barbour was dispatched to get Pickering, who reported not surprisingly that the group preferred that Connally wait until after the vote was taken.

Dent was elated. "Governor," he whispered to Connally, "that means we got the vote"—meaning the Ford side needed no additional help.

Just then Barbour came running back in. "Okay, Governor," he said to Connally, "they just voted. You can get in there."

"They voted?" Dent asked. "How did they vote?"

"Thirty-one to twenty-eight," Barbour said. (One delegate abstained.)[2]
"Which way?"

Barbour, the Reagan man, was glum: "Y'all won," he said.

Dent recalling the scene later, said: "It was the shoot-out at the O.K. Corral. It was the crucial vote in the convention."

The delegates, the big decision off their chests at last, heard Connally patiently for a few minutes, then streamed out to the motel pool, where a beer party awaited them. Several cases of Coors beer had been sent to them from Joseph Coors, the right-wing Colorado brewer, who had hoped it would be used to celebrate a Reagan victory. Instead the Reaganites drowned their gloom in it.

The Ford camp thought the drawn-out "Battle of Mississippi" was at last over. But in fact another episode or two remained.

On Tuesday night Harry Dent was sitting in the Ford campaign's sky suite high in the side of Kemper Arena, awaiting the convention vote on 16-C. He was looking through a large plate-glass window down on the Mississippi delegation, up front and to the right of the platform, reflecting with satisfaction on the work he had done, when Jim Baker came in. Baker threw down a copy of the *Birmingham News* with a front-page headline that said: "Ford Would Write Off Cotton South?" The article, by Saul Kohler of the Newhouse Newspapers, was an account of a breakfast that reporters had had with Rogers Morton, where Morton had evidently said that Ford's campaign would concentrate on the big industrial states. Though Kohler quoted Morton as saying he thought Ford had a chance to carry "states of the peripheral South," the clear implication in his article was that the President intended to spend little time bucking Carter in Dixie.

Morton was on the floor at the time and Dan Rather of CBS collared him. He denied he had said Ford would write off the South. Whereupon Rather invited him to accompany him over to the Mississippi delegation to straighten the matter out—on live television. Someone in the Ford sky suite spotted Morton in Rather's grip and Morton was promptly ordered by walkie-talkie to get off the floor immediately. (Nice try, though, Dan.)

Copies of the newspaper, and word-of-mouth about the story, had

2. The vote at the end of the caucus roll call was actually 31–27, with Reed not voting until the end. Then, with the victory safely in the President's hands, Reed cast his ballot for Reagan —the "throw-away" vote he had threatened to cast all along. But he was true to his word: he had not hurt Ford, and the President had Mississippi's thirty votes on 16-C.

already spread to the convention floor and especially within the Mississippi delegation. Talk of defections from Ford, including another by Clarke Reed, floated up to the Ford sky suite.

By now, Dent had become entirely too visible to be useful, too much an outsider trying to steer the Mississippi delegation, and a perfect foil for Billy Mounger, striving desperately to restore an edge for Reagan. First Holshouser and then Tower were dispatched to give assurances to concerned Mississippians that Ford had no intention of writing off the South, that Morton—who had a record for putting his foot in his mouth—had been "misinterpreted" again.

But Mounger and Pickering were on the move, seizing the Morton story as a reason to call for another delegation caucus and another vote. Reagan had to have Mississippi—all thirty votes or any slice he could get—to have even a shot at 16-C. Sears, in Reagan's trailer just outside the hall, phoned the Mississippi delegation on the floor. Reed picked up the red Reagan phone. "Clarke," Sears said according to Reed, "we need every vote we can get. This is the ball game." He wanted Reed to caucus right away and try to get out from under the unit rule so that Reagan could get at least fourteen votes on 16-C. If he would help out on 16-C, Sears said he would understand if Reed felt he had to go with Ford the next night on the nomination.

Now Clarke Reed was utterly confused. Earlier Mounger had told him specifically that Reagan's strategists were holding to the unit rule on 16-C, even though it meant losing all thirty votes. The hope was that by the next night, on the nomination roll call itself, they could regain the upper hand in Mississippi and get all thirty votes then. Now, as Reed explained it later, "they were switching signals on us. First 16-C wasn't the whole ball game; then it was the whole ball game. That was what caused all the confusion, this changing in marching orders. And to get out from under the unit rule, we had to caucus."

Doug Shanks and Tommy Giordano, aware of the move, called Harry Dent in the sky suite: "Get somebody to the alternates. They're trying to get a caucus and Clarke's leading it." Charles Pickering had announced that the delegation was to meet in a room elsewhere in the hall, and pro-Reagan delegates and alternates had begun to file out. But Dent rushed down to the gallery section where the Mississippi alternates sat. "Keep your seats," he told them. Without the alternates, no vote could be reconsidered. To some of the wavering delegates and alternates, this move by the Reaganites to seek yet another vote after the delegation had decided in an above-board fashion to keep the unit rule and vote for Ford, was the final straw. One of the uncommitteds, Bob Rea, grabbed Dent's Ford badge and put it on his own lapel. "That does it," Rea said. But Pickering nonetheless pushed for a vote that might salvage a dozen or so votes for the beleaguered Reagan. Meanwhile, President Ford himself was on the phone telling Clarke Reed that the Morton story was not true. "We're not writing off the South," Ford told him. "We can't win without the South, you know that."

As the roll call on 16-C was proceeding, some of the Mississippians tried to commandeer a CBS trailer to caucus in, but then were thrown out by Mike Wallace when they refused to let their meeting be televised live. Dave Keene needed more time to find out whether John Sears indeed wanted the unit rule broken, and he asked Reed to pass when Mississippi's turn came. Reed agreed—to the jeers of the convention. Keene was most reluctant to ask the Reaganites in Mississippi to come out from under the unit rule. Billy Mounger for one had told him months before that he intended to honor it, no matter what, even if his vote was needed to break a tie for Reagan. "I didn't want to ask them to do that unless it made a difference," Keene said, "and because I knew some people like Billy wouldn't break." So he called Sears. "I told him, I have twelve to fifteen people who will break, but I'm not going to ask them to do it unless you tell me those twelve to fifteen votes are going to make a difference." Sears replied: "I can't tell you that." So Keene told Reed to vote all thirty for Ford. But by the time Reed did so, Florida, which had also passed, had already killed 16-C for the President on the second go-around. After all the pulling and hauling, after all the procrastinating, Clarke Reed, with his thirty talents, had missed his chance to be "the kingmaker."[3]

The only other notable disruption during the 16-C debate was a mild altercation in the New York delegation, when a Reagan delegate from Utah wrestled with Rockefeller over a "Reagan Country" placard and then irately ripped out the New York delegation's white phone, cutting Rosenbaum's communications with Ford's trailer. A security guard carted the man off, as a smiling Rockefeller gleefully held the dismantled phone high over his head. It was, unwittingly, a most symbolic gesture: as far as most Republicans were concerned, Rockefeller had been talking into a dead phone for years.

The evening was also marked by tumultuous cheering for the wives of the candidates, Nancy Reagan and Betty Ford, the latter dancing in her place in the gallery with entertainer Tony Orlando as the band played "Tie

---

3. On Wednesday, in the interest of state party harmony, the Ford people in Mississippi moved to dissolve the unit rule and to apportion votes on the nomination roll call according to the caucus vote. It came down to 32–28 to dissolve—or sixteen floor votes for Ford and fourteen for Reagan, with Reed voting for Ford. The sixteen were more than enough for the President, for the Reagan candidacy had collapsed.

a Yellow Ribbon 'Round the Old Oak Tree." Orlando, leering inanely, milked the opportunity for all he was worth. But this hardly was the emotionalism for which most of the delegates, the Reaganite True Believers especially, had come to Kansas City. Still, it would have to do, for this night anyway.

The Reagan "Morality in Foreign Policy" plank was up next. In the sky suite, a somewhat heated debate took place on how to deal with what clearly was a slap at the President's conduct of foreign affairs, and more pointedly at Kissinger. Rockefeller, Kissinger's old friend, wanted to take the Reaganites on, and he discussed the matter with Kissinger by phone. But the Ford forces had already won the critical victory, it was well past midnight, and delegates were leaving in droves. Baker argued for accepting the plank. "There were an awful lot of empty seats out there," he recalled. The 16-C vote had been too close for comfort; a loss would arrest Ford's momentum and lead to who-knew-what. The recommendation to the President was to accept the ambiguous plank, and in the end he gulped it down like a college sophomore of the fifties devouring a goldfish. "Ten per cent of the verbiage isn't worth fighting over," Bob Griffin said. "I'm not going to bleed and die over a few words." A converted Rockefeller added: "The whole thing is a tempest in a teapot. If you don't take it as criticism, why fight it?" Kissinger, meanwhile, who was under political house arrest all this time for fear his appearance at the convention would set off an uproar, kept his mouth shut. He prepared to make one of the least publicized and acclaimed visits to a hostile place in his much-traveled diplomatic career. His presence in the gallery the next night went virtually unnoticed.

With the convention's overwhelming approval of the foreign-policy plank, the last opportunity for a Ford-Reagan confrontation was finessed, and the convention recessed for the night knowing that on the following evening it would nominate Gerald Ford for the Presidency.

Jim Baker never was able to understand why Reagan's foreign-policy plank was written in language that was so easy to swallow. "I could see a two-word plank: 'Fire Kissinger,'" he said later, "and we would have had to fight it. And if we had been beaten, we could have lost the whole thing. We had eleven hundred and forty-five commitments and they were as strong as we could make them. But until that first vote was taken, how could we know we had them? Minds change. If there was going to be ballot momentum for Reagan, it would have had to be on some emotional issue." But Sears insisted such heavy-handedness would never have worked. "If we had won 16-C," he said afterward, "we would have moved immediately to have both tickets come before the convention and address the convention. That would have passed easily, and it would have raised the anxiety level on the other side. They were always afraid that if Reagan got before the convention, all hell would break loose. Ford would have been forced to make an all-night decision. If he had picked Dole, he would have lost some votes in the Northeast; he probably would have picked Baker, and he probably would have lost votes among those who were led to believe they might get a Scranton or a Richardson. Then it would have been time to go ahead with the platform fight on the foreign-policy plank, and they would have had to contest it."

All the next day, Wednesday, August 18, Sears tried to keep up a brave front as Reagan's strength slipped away. He retained to the last his droll sense of humor. Asked by a wiseacre at his daily press conference how long Reagan's acceptance speech would be, Sears said: "About twenty-five minutes."

"Does it have room for applause between sentences?"

"It would run about an hour with the applause. We clapped through it one night and timed it."

Reagan spent the day making meaningless rounds of friendly or nominally uncommitted delegations, pointedly turning aside suggestions that he agree after all to be Ford's running mate. He told the Missouri delegation he could not do so because "we have some basic disagreements" and he could not "defend causes in which I do not believe." Others, however, were still insisting he would change his mind. At one point Schweiker offered to step aside, but Reagan dismissed the idea at once, praising Schweiker for having taken the chance with him.

The nomination roll call that night proved to be anticlimactic. The Reaganites, faced with the reality of their defeat, cut up on the floor, chanting, yelling, horn-blowing, and otherwise interrupting a speech by Senator Jacob Javits, one of their pet adversaries. And already the long knives were out for Sears and his 16-C strategy. Tom Ellis, Reagan's campaign manager in North Carolina, said the strategy "stank," although he acknowledged there probably wasn't any way to force a battle, given the Ford camp's disinclination to fight. And Billy Mounger said of 16-C: "It was a terrible mistake. It was a lousy issue. It was just a bad rule. It was basically a political ploy and unless you were a hard Reaganite, you couldn't buy it."

Just before the roll call on the nomination that night, I walked back to the Reagan trailer to see Sears. He sat quietly, with his feet propped up on his desk, a battery of phones idle in front of him and a large monitor with four television screens playing out the inevitable on the floor just inside the hall. Political lieutenants sat in cubbyholes along the trailer's inside walls, each with a television monitor before him. The mood was relaxed and resigned.

"What have you got going here?" I asked.

Sears smiled wanly. "A loser," he said.

All the fight was gone. A day before, Sears had been the focal figure in the convention; now he was just another defeated campaign manager. His young son Jimmy came over and asked for money for a hot dog, and Sears shelled it out.

On the nomination roll call, West Virginia provided the winning delegates for the President, Governor Arch Moore finally delivering on his promise to produce 20 votes. That gave Ford 5 more than he needed to go over 1130. He wound up with 1187, to 1070 for Reagan.

On the winning side this night was Clarke Reed, but he could take little solace in it. He had been a card-carrying conservative for ten years as the Mississippi chairman and a leading voice for the South in the national party, but in the end he had contributed to the downfall of Mr. Conservative, Ronald Reagan. Later, when I encountered him in the lobby of the Muehlebach, he was forlorn. "I wanted to vote for Reagan," he told me. "I guess I didn't do much to help him." He paused, then added: "Politics used to be fun. Not now."

A few days after the convention, Reed telephoned me. The outcome was on his mind and conscience, and he wanted reassurance from a neutral source that other factors had undone Reagan, not just Clarke Reed. He just could not live with Schweiker, he said. That decision had hurt Reagan more than anything he, Reed, had done. Wasn't that so? And Reagan didn't go into Ohio early enough or file for all the delegates he could have won. That was more damaging than how Mississippi went, wasn't it? All spring, he insisted, the Reagan campaign had taken Mississippi for granted, had failed to really organize there, had left it all to him. And when the Ford forces began to peck away in the delegation, Billy Mounger was busy running some tennis tournament. He, Reed, had alone held the fortress against Carmichael and Shanks in that critical week before the Schweiker bomb was dropped. And finally, on 16-C, the Reagan campaign never sold the issue, never really let the Mississippi delegation know it was crucial for the whole convention until that Tuesday night on the floor when Sears phoned him and pressed him on it. His voice trailed off into a mumble. "You don't like to think you were at fault," he said finally. "I feel like I've wasted ten years in politics. But you've got to play."

Now all that remained was the selection of a running mate. All through the long year there were countless Republicans who wanted a Ford-Reagan ticket, and who wanted to believe it could happen—despite Reagan's pointed and repeated disavowals of interest. Even on this final night he had been obliged to send a handwritten note to his own California delegation that said: "There is no circumstance whatsoever under which I would accept the nomination for Vice President. That is absolutely final." Still, the speculation and the hope were fanned when Ford in his first postnomination act drove from the Crown Center to the Alameda Plaza to pay his respects to Reagan for a good fight waged, and to confer with him about the vice-presidency.

Many took that gesture to mean Ford would make an offer to Reagan, but Reagan had already taken steps to make sure that did not happen. Privately, Sears told the Ford managers that Reagan would meet with the President only on the understanding that he would not be embarrassed by having to turn down a President of the United States. Ronald Reagan really meant it: he did not want to be No. 2 on a ticket with a man he had criticized the length and breadth of the country for most of a year. He wanted to be free to say his own piece, as in the past. So, as Gerald Ford greeted the man he had just beaten, he knew there would be no awkward moment. They could get on with discussing other candidates, which is what they did.

Ford and Reagan held a unity press conference afterward and then the President returned to his hotel. He had successfully resisted all the pressure to name his own running mate early, and so now he was obliged to go into the traditional long night of deliberating. The last time a Republican nominee undertook it, the product was Spiro T. Agnew, who called his foes effete snobs and nattering nabobs. And before that, the same system had come forth with William E. Miller, selected by Barry Goldwater because he "bugs [Lyndon] Johnson." It did not seem possible the system could come up with a worthy successor to these premier slashers. But politics is, as they say, the art of the possible.

34. The Selection of Bob Dole

In the early crisis days of August 1974, when Gerald Ford had the presidency of the United States thrust upon him, one of his first and most important responsibilities had been to select the next Vice President. Not simply a vice-presidential candidate: *the Vice President.* It was a responsibility only one earlier President, Richard Nixon, had ever faced. Ford had been the first Vice President selected under the Twenty-fifth Amendment, and now he was picking his successor. In choosing Nelson Rockefeller, Ford with high purpose took the man he considered most qualified to be President: it was, in a sense, an easy choice, considering Rockefeller's broad governmental experience and Ford's own limitations.

It was an easy choice, but it proved to be, politically, a disastrous one. Still, even the right-wingers saw some merit in selecting Rockefeller over George Bush, the other finalist. Everyone knowledgeable in Republican politics considered Bush incompetent to be President; one of the best-kept secrets among conservatives was the way many of them, including Clarke Reed, lined up behind Rockefeller as the better alternative, for the sake of the country. Conservatives also held the view that Rockefeller's being Vice President enhanced the chances of nominating a true conservative in 1976, and in the meantime it would be convenient to have him to throw brickbats at. And for all of Rockefeller's fawning attempts to ingratiate himself to the right, that was what they did.

Small wonder that Gerald Ford, himself a conservative, was so susceptible to pressures from the right. Exposed to those pressures through the long months of presidential primaries and state conventions, the lesson was driven home to Ford in the national convention; only relentless pandering to individual delegates had saved the day for him. He had very nearly been denied the nomination of his party, the first President so severely threatened since Taft in 1912. Now he had to deal with the right wing once more in winning acceptance of his choice for a running mate. This obligation was emphatically expressed in the first step he took immediately after his own nomination—paying court to the barely defeated champion of the right wing, soliciting Ronald Reagan's views on who his running mate should be, on who would be acceptable to the right wing so emotionally frustrated by the lack of a real convention fight on the issues so dear to it. An unsatisfactory choice could trigger a runaway convention, demanding a draft of Reagan and repudiating the President who it had so narrowly, even niggardly, nominated the night before.

All this was facing Gerald Ford at a time when he, above all people, should have been thinking of the vice-presidential nomination in terms of what it could mean to the country. No other person, after all, had better reason to understand the fickleness and unpredictability of the American political system; what the political scientists talked about with concern, he had lived through. But now he was principally thinking of how to survive politically, and he reasoned he could not afford a split in his own ranks. When the right spoke, he had to listen.

The President laid the names of six prominent Republicans before Reagan—Senator Dole, Senator Howard Baker, former Governor John Connally, Secretary of the Treasury William Simon, former Deputy Attorney General William Ruckelshaus, and Secretary of Commerce Elliot Richardson. He knew that the latter two were, of course, unacceptable to Reagan, and the Californian now mentioned "drawbacks in some of the others, weaknesses they had in some part of the party," according to a Reagan insider later. But Dole, Reagan said, would be acceptable, as would one or two others.

It was not surprising that Reagan would mention Dole, a doctrinaire Republican conservative and an extremely hard and able campaigner, known for a biting wit and sarcasm that approached, and at times reached, insult. He was also ambitious: while toiling faithfully for Ford's nomination, Dole had taken time a few days earlier to phone Lyn Nofziger to solicit Reagan's backing for himself as Ford's running mate. Dole recalled telling Nofziger: " 'I don't know what's going to happen. I don't know if Reagan's interested in it. If he's not, and he talks to the President, and he doesn't have any preference—' it was just a shot in the dark. It wasn't any big deal. Lyn and I are friends. I didn't suggest Reagan raise it with the President. I said, 'You might at least let Reagan know of my interest.' "

Ironically Dole had originally thought of his chances to be the vice-presidential nominee more in terms of running with Reagan. "I thought if I was going to be on the ticket, it would be with Reagan," he said later, "a sort of Western-Midwest ticket based on his Sun Belt strategy. Then I was Schweikered. Not that I ever had any hint from Reagan, but just in my own little mind I thought, 'Well, if it's going to happen in '76, it's going to probably happen with Ronald Reagan.' I thought if they got down to the convention and Reagan won the nomination, they might be looking for someone in the Ford camp, someone with the moderate-conservative philosophy."

Though Reagan gave Dole a boost with Ford that night, the President made no commitment. Still, when he returned to the Crown Center to meet with the inevitable inner circle of his own counselors, he knew that Dole would pacify the most influential voice on the right.

Ford, before going to Kansas City, had already held three lengthy meetings to discuss his selection. At the first were Dick Cheney, Stu Spencer, Bob Teeter, Bryce Harlow, and White House aide Jack Marsh; at the second the same five plus Rockefeller; and at the third, the same six plus Melvin Laird, the former secretary of defense and old Ford crony from House days. Each of these meetings started with someone suggesting a spectacular choice that would grab the public's attention and possibly close the big gap in the polls: Anne Armstrong, or John Connally, or even Rockefeller. (Early in the procedure, Armstrong is said to have called to say she was not interested, but her name remained under discussion.) But the prime contenders who had emerged were William Ruckelshaus, Howard Baker, and Bob Dole.

Reagan and Connally were considered in a special category because of their elevated standing in the party, at least in the somewhat intimidated view of the Ford inner circle. But would Reagan in fact take the vice-presidential nomination, and should the ever-salivating Connally even be offered it? Few if any insiders doubted that Reagan would strengthen the ticket, but the signals were growing stronger that the Californian really didn't want to be on it. Those signals were categorically confirmed when Sears informed Cheney that Reagan would agree to meet with Ford after the presidential nomination roll call only on the firmest condition that he not be asked to join the ticket.

As for Connally, the view was widespread that he was soiled goods, regardless of his acquittal in the milk-fund bribery case. At a press conference in Kansas City, he had been so unmercifully and relentlessly peppered with questions about his finances and other dealings that it was clear to most of Ford's advisers that he was a high-risk proposition, and might smother the campaign with Watergate. "The press was sitting out there waiting for him," said Spencer, who had been one of his early boosters. "They had files on the milk-fund thing. We would have come out of Kansas City on the defensive, and we couldn't have that." Only the sycophantic John Tower pressed for his fellow Texan. Again for public-relations reasons, to mollify the Mississippi and other Dixie delegations, Connally's name continued to be floated, but he was not a serious prospect.

Of the others on the really serious prenomination list undergoing close scrutiny by Ford and the closest insiders, Baker at the outset seemed to have an edge, on paper, anyway. He was the "safe" choice, everyone agreed, but he had some drawbacks. (The disclosure that his wife had once had a drinking problem was apparently not a major one.) Polling data from Teeter indicated that he was not as well known or well regarded as assumed, and that the public perception of his performance as a Watergate committee interrogator was fuzzy and hence an uncertain political element. Lastly, Ford himself did not feel particularly comfortable with Baker. Ruckelshaus was pushed hard by Teeter and Rockefeller. But he was sure to upset the right wing, and like Baker might be a reminder of the Watergate issue by his very presence. Also, Ford did not know him well, nor was he particularly knowledgeable about Ford's campaign positions, and the lateness of the political hour required a person who could hit the campaign trail running. Ruckelshaus was an imaginative but risky choice, as was Anne Armstrong, advocated strongly by Spencer. And then there was Bob Dole. Not much was being said about him, but he was available. He could help win back the traditional GOP farm-belt base, and he knew the issues, having spoken for Ford in the convention states.

This unofficial, preliminary sorting out had already taken place when, shortly after three o'clock in the morning, the inner circle gathered around a long table in the President's suite at the Crown Center. It was the core group of Cheney, Spencer, Teeter, Harlow, Rockefeller, Marsh, and Laird. (Senators Bob Griffin and John Tower also joined the group during the discussion.) After reporting on his talk with Reagan, the President went around the table, asking the participants for their observations. The list quickly boiled down to the quartet of Baker, Ruckelshaus, Armstrong and, just barely, Dole. (Tower tried to keep Connally alive, but without success.) Through all this, Ford sat and mostly listened.

Considerable time was spent discussing whether the President should be influenced by the clearly conservative mood of the convention or whether he should look beyond it to the country at large and make a bold, provocative choice, such as Ruckelshaus or Armstrong. Baker was safe, all right, but he didn't turn anybody on. As a campaigner, he was judged as mediocre, and he could probably not make much of a dent in the South against Carter. Some Southern chairmen like Bob Shaw of North Carolina had passed the word (after being mildly lobbied by Dole) that they were not especially high on Baker. Armstrong's being a woman was clearly against her, Teeter's polls showed.

Ford seemed interested in Ruckelshaus, a demi-hero of Watergate who had stood up to Nixon. Ford was reminded, though, of the still-unleashed passions of the Reaganites on the convention floor. Party unity had to be preserved. "The mood of the convention figured prominently," one of those present said later. "It had been a tight vote and the convention was still very volatile. Most of us felt an important consideration was who the convention would back. In that climate, high-risk prospects seemed less likely."

The idea that a lovefest on the vice-presidential nomination was desirable at all costs was not universally accepted, however. In advance of the convention, Doug Bailey, a prominent political consultant soon to join the Ford campaign, had submitted a provocative memorandum in which he had explicitly suggested that it might be very desirable in terms of the general election actually to precipitate a battle over the vice-presidential nomination on the convention floor. Inasmuch as the public perceived Ford as a weak leader, Bailey argued, it would help to take a name to the convention that would start a fight; if it were rejected, Ford could simply tell the delegates that he would decline their nomination if they didn't go along with his choice. It being inconceivable that the convention would not back off when faced with such an ultimatum, Ford would leave Kansas City a strongman.

This basic idea, if not the memo and its extreme conclusions, was supportive of a Ruckelshaus nomination. A lively fight, the Ruckelshaus defenders were saying, would help Ford. But that notion ran counter to the general belief that Reagan and his supporters must be treated with kid gloves. And that consensus was, apparently, what did Ruckelshaus in. His name had been first on the list by the close of the meeting, when Ford, unable to make up his mind, decided to declare a recess and, as he told the group, have them all "sleep on it" and reconvene in a few hours. As they walked out, Harlow, who had urged a conservative choice, said to Teeter, Ruckelshaus's most outspoken backer, that it looked to him as though the President was going to decide on Ruckelshaus.

By the time the group reassembled about four hours later, though, it was clear to everyone that by some unexplained route Ford had dismissed Ruckelshaus and was now thinking, almost exclusively, about Dole. After going around the table one last time, Ford suddenly said, "Assume it's Bob Dole. I am not clear what happens next." Somebody piped up: "Mr. President, you had better call him." Everybody laughed. For the rest of the meeting of less than an hour, the discussion zeroed in on the Kansan—his merits as a campaigner, his record as a severely wounded World War II veteran, his sharp tongue as a blade to cut up Jimmy Carter, his popularity with the press, and how well he would work in a campaign strategy to keep Ford "presidential." Nobody had really been boosting Dole, but nobody had anything negative to say against him either. In the process of elimination, he was shaking out. (Afterward there was much conjecture that between the two meetings, somebody had gotten to Ford and made a very persuasive case for Dole. But Ford told me later that he didn't remember talking to anyone in that interim. "I went to bed," he said.) That Dole, like Ford, came from the Midwest, did not seem to matter: polls showed that farm and rural America would be a major trouble spot for Ford, and Dole could help there, as well as shore up the party faithful, keep the conservatives happy, and not overly exercise the moderates and liberals. Finally, and perhaps most important after all, Jerry Ford liked him. They had served together in the House; Ford enjoyed Dole's sense of humor, his freewheeling style; he agreed with his politics and was comfortable with him. Ford was weary; Dole was the line of least resistance. Hearing no objections, Ford finally said, "Okay, let's get Dole over here."

Dole was sitting in his room at the Muehlebach having breakfast with his wife, Liddy, and waiting. He was not exactly expecting a call, but he was hoping. A short time earlier Bob Clark of ABC News had tipped him that he was still in the running, which somewhat surprised him. And so, when the phone did ring and Ford said, "Bob, I want you on the ticket," Dole didn't hesitate: "Certainly," he replied. Secret Service agents were already on their way to pick up the Doles in a small rented car and bring them over to the Crown Center for a press conference. But before they could leave, Clark was on the phone again, saying he had heard the news from one of the losers. Dole didn't lie to his old friend; in minutes, ABC was airing Clark's clean beat on the story.

The selection of Dole came as a surprise, but went down well with that segment of the convention that Ford wanted to mollify, the unsatiated Reaganites. On the final night the President delivered what most thought was the best speech of his public life, containing no new theme but delivered flawlessly and highlighted by an unexpected challenge to Jimmy Carter to debate in the fall campaign. He was, Ford told the convention and millions watching on television, one of them. "You at home, listening tonight, you are the people who pay the taxes and obey the laws," he said. "You are the people who make our system work. You are the people who make America what it is. It is from your ranks that I come, and on your side I stand."

The President's distinctly upbeat speech was a tonic for a party that had come to Kansas City in a pessimistic mood. A measure of the importance his campaign chiefs placed on it was the fact he had practiced it for two weeks, including two trial runs that were video-taped and played back so he could assess his own performance.

The mood also was fed by a generous gesture in which Ford invited Ronald and Nancy Reagan to share the podium. The crowd, and especially the Reagan faithful, went wild, and the more so when their champion

extemporaneously delivered remarks that could have been his own acceptance speech. He laid particular emphasis on the party platform that now
included numerous right-wing shibboleths. Ford, of course, had no intention of touring the country in the fall on a platform that repudiated his own
foreign policy, but that truth could be overlooked for now in the aura of
conciliation that filled the hall. The Reagan delegates left disappointed but
somewhat assuaged, and Ford's people departed in a spirit of hope that
contradicted their knowledge of the reality of things: that theirs was still
the minority party, that they were running with an unelected incumbent
President who had barely won nomination, in a time of high inflation and
unemployment, and against a united opposition.

That reality called for political miracles that few imagined could be
achieved. Yet, with more astute use of the incumbency, and with luck, who
could tell? In selecting Bob Dole, the President had chosen a man he
thought could help. He would keep the party's conservatives happy; he
would stroke the farm vote; possibly his acid tongue might goad Carter into
error.

It is an old axiom of politics, however, that a vice-presidential candidate cannot really help a presidential nominee; the trick is to find one who
will not hurt him. Richard Nixon in 1968 had quipped to associates, in
advance of selecting Spiro Agnew, that he wished he could run alone. But
Gerald Ford seemed convinced that he had found in Bob Dole the refutation of that pessimistic axiom. It was a judgment to which he clung, publicly
anyway, through the fall campaign and beyond.

part IX

**GETTING
READY**

35. *The Carter Battle Plan*

When Jimmy Carter returned to Plains after his nomination, the warm welcome at the train depot was in one respect different from the homecomings of other successful politicians to the place of their origin. The difference was that Plains, Georgia, was not simply where Jimmy Carter had come from, but where he *lived.* Recognizing that simple fact was recognizing a core truth about the man: not merely did he trade on his humble and rural origins, in the best tradition of the American public man on the make, but he continued to be immersed in them. Carter was not an exemplar of the usual upward-mobility syndrome in which the young man in a hurry leaves home at an early age, makes good in the outside world, and then returns in a sort of pilgrimage to his own achievement. Carter continued to be an extremely involved citizen of Plains, Georgia; involved in its community, business, family, social, and church life. He was, obviously, the small town's first citizen, but there was nothing honorary about the position. During his swift political ascent from state senator to governor to Democratic presidential nominee, he continued to be an active participant in the life, the conflicts, and the responsibilities of his home town of 683 souls.

Well before Carter became his party's standard-bearer, Plains had felt the impact of his political success. The town did not in any sense try to hide from the limelight. As most other aspects of his personal life were, Carter's town was thrown into his drive for the presidency; the single most arresting object in this quiet hamlet was the large sign over a corner store on Main Street, the only commercial street, that said: "Plains, Georgia. Home of Jimmy Carter, Our Next President." The few stores and shops, all on one side of Main Street, wore new coats of paint, yellows and rusts and greens, making the block-long concentration of commercialism look for all the world like a Hollywood set. One almost expected, walking down the first side street, to see large beams holding the narrow façade upright, where the body of the shops and stores was supposed to be. But the shops were there, run by Carter kin and long-time friends, doing business as usual but also not beneath turning a buck on Jimmy's fame. They sold everything, from bronzed peanuts and small souvenir burlap sacks of the real thing, to

T-shirts and sweatshirts emblazoned with what was rapidly becoming the world's most famous set of grinning teeth.

For two dollars and fifty cents, one could take a thirty-minute tour in a small camper-bus to all the "historic points." It was an experience that did not have to take a back seat to a tour of the ruins of Pompeii. The visitor learned, first, that the town had once been located two miles away and had been called The Plains of Nebuchadnezzar, but was moved closer to the Seaboard Coast Line railroad tracks. The visitor learned also from the tour guide that the Carters had come "in 1830, right after the Indians left," and would see the Carter peanut fields; the swimming pool that Jimmy got the Plains Lions Club to build for underprivileged kids; the Plains Baptist Church, where all the Carters worshiped; the public-housing project, where Jimmy and Rosalynn lived when he left the navy; the Plains High School, "where Jimmy graduated in 1941 at the head of his class"; the home of brother Billy, his wife, Sybil, and their five children, "and they're expecting another at any time"; the Plains Convalescent Home, "where James Earl Carter, Jr., better known as Jimmy, was born, and where Miss Lillian also took her nurse's training; I'll bet you someday there'll be a marker by the window there where he was born."

Straight ahead was the Plains water tower, now painted in red, white, and blue, and beneath it "Television City, Plains, Georgia"—three network trailers. Across Main Street was "the Plains Men's Club, but it's hard to recognize because it's disguised as Billy Carter's Amoco station. There's an understanding there among the men that if someone's wife calls, she *just* missed him." Coming up on the left was the Plains Methodist Church, and behind it the home of Jimmy's aunt, "who Miss Lillian paid a nickel a day for their lunch" when Jimmy and his sister Gloria came over from school. And on the steps of that church "was where Jimmy asked Rosalynn for their first date. Little did she know that by saying yes, she was destined to become—a Baptist!" Down Woodland Drive, closed off by the Secret Service, "Amy's lemonade stand was on this side of the street." And farther down, you came to "the final resting place of many of the people of Plains. That is the graveyard. It used to be said that there were more people lying down than there were standing up. But that's not true any more." And up a red clay road to the right was another hamlet called Archery. "They say that's one of the most photographed roads in Georgia. That's the beginning of the Carter property. Picture if you will a little towheaded, freckle-faced boy jumping in the ditches, climbing the trees, running along the road, playing and doing his chores, and you'll have a picture of Jimmy Carter some forty or forty-five years ago."

Next was Jimmy's boyhood home, and the place "where Jimmy's

daddy, Mr. Earl Carter, built him a tennis court. He loved to play tennis, and even after Jimmy got grown, he could beat him in a game of tennis." There was Jimmy's treehouse, where he hid out one night when some of his folks' friends got too noisy, and wouldn't come down when called. "When he did come down, Mr. Earl was waiting on him with a switch, a peach-tree switch, and they say that's the worst kind. And that night, he got one of the six switchings he ever got in his life. He says he remembers them all." Next was the pond house, an old log cabin; "Miss Lillian says she likes to come out here to get away from the hustle and bustle of downtown Plains, Georgia. And right through there is the fishpond you probably saw on television."

The tour might have been a spoof, but it was not; it concluded back on Main Street, where Jimmy Carter himself might be found, in blue jeans and work boots, traipsing around his massive peanut warehouse or talking to his neighbors or reporters. Carter, being the astute and cunning politician he was, understood of course the public-relations advantage of having the public, through the press, see him dressed in that fashion in his natural surroundings. But the fact was that these *were* his natural surroundings, and this *was* the way he dressed when he was home, which was as often as he could manage it. And when, on Sunday morning, dressed in a suit and tie, he walked into the basement of the Plains First Baptist Church before the service and took his regular turn preaching the men's Bible class, he was doing what he had always done.

In such a setting, it was easy to accept that Jimmy Carter was what he said he was—a simple, straightforward common man of common tastes and virtues who had come out of the peanut fields of south Georgia to lead a nation back to its basic strength and goodness; who could not bear the thought of dissembling, or betraying a trust, of lying or misleading anyone. What this setting obscured, however, was that Jimmy Carter was also other things: a well-traveled and well-read man, urbane in many ways for all his folksy style and manner of speaking; a man at home in Plains, yes, but also at home in Atlanta, and in New York, and Concord, New Hampshire, and Tokyo: a man with homespun charity and love in his heart, yes; but also a tough, competitive, cold-eyed political professional with a steely determination to reach his lofty objective.

The people of Plains, it probably was fair to say, saw mostly, or almost exclusively, the first Jimmy Carter, and they romanticized his role in the larger world that was foreign to them. And it probably was equally fair to say that the people of politics in that larger world saw almost exclusively the other Jimmy Carter; they tended to denigrate his role, and his commitment, in that smaller world that was foreign to *them*. It was difficult to grasp that one man could be so simple and straightforward and so complex and conniving at the same time.

Some in the press corps, as well as some staff aides, seeing both Jimmy Carters, resisted the easy alternative of dismissing one or the other as phony, or both. Instead, they looked upon him as he really was: an exceptionally purposeful and disciplined man, trying to remain the first, simpler Jimmy Carter, in the face of the pressures and the demands that he be the second, more sophisticated and complex Jimmy Carter; trying to apply the precepts that guided the first Jimmy to the more callous, suspicious world in which the second Jimmy pursued his burning ambitions—and not always succeeding.

Above all else, Carter seemed to want, and need, to be accepted and sought after in both worlds; he had a penchant, in fact, for saying what certain people wanted to hear when he was with them, adjusting his positions a degree or more to accommodate a particular audience. He did not contradict himself exactly, but intentionally or not he often fudged; he blurred the perception of where he stood. When critics said he was fuzzy, he would answer, often with some heat, that he was specific. Or, more often, he would argue that complex subjects could not be reduced to simple either-or equations, and those who pretended they could be were the dissemblers. Still, living in the worlds of both the simpler past and the more complex, urbane, and skeptical present posed problems for him. He spoke, to give another example, of the simple virtues of love and compassion, yet on occasion he lashed out at individuals in bursts of seeming pettiness. Or, as the self-styled outsider, he castigated the establishment, only to woo and openly praise prime establishmentarians like Mayor Daley of Chicago. Such conduct raised questions about who Jimmy Carter really was, and whether he was any more trustworthy than his less-pious-sounding party brethren.

At the Democratic convention in New York, Carter's choice of Fritz Mondale as his running mate, and his generous and all-embracing acceptance speech, had placated many of the doubters. And in his appearance before the Democratic National Committee on the morning after the convention adjourned, a forgive-and-forget attitude about preconvention opposition to him encouraged others that he would not simply assume command of the party but would extend and enhance its unity. "I realize," he said then, "many of you had other choices. There is no distinction in my mind between those who came to support me late, after supporting superb other candidates, and those who supported me from the start." Calling Bob Strauss "the greatest party chairman I have ever known," he asked him to remain in the job, observing that contrary to rumors "there never was any doubt about who I wanted to lead the party." He kept on the rest of the

DNC leadership as well and reiterated an earlier pledge that he would help raise money for Democratic candidates in the fall campaign, since acceptance of the $21.8 million federal subsidy eliminated the need for him to raise money for his own campaign.

No one expected, of course, that Bob Strauss would run Carter's campaign against Gerald Ford. Hamilton Jordan, Carter's campaign manager through the convention, would continue in that capacity, and it was decided even before the convention that his campaign headquarters would remain in Atlanta. That decision was partly done for public-relations reasons, serving to underscore the "outsider" aspect of Carter's candidacy, but partly also to keep the campaign firmly in the hands of the people who had engineered Carter's nomination. To launch a presidential campaign from Georgia on behalf of a former one-term governor took a healthy dose of self-confidence in the first place; the success of that effort could not but reinforce the self-confidence and breed a concomitant lack of awe in the political prowess of all those who had contested Carter and then succumbed to him. "We're not going to turn our campaign over to anybody in any state," Jordan told me in July. "Heavies" from previous presidential campaigns, who many kibitzers were saying would have to be brought in to take over in the fall, would not be offered top staff jobs, he said; they would be invited to take "advisory" roles. Tim Kraft, the young architect of Carter's victories in Iowa and Pennsylvania, was selected to be national field coordinator for the fall—which meant he would assemble the coordinators who would go into each region and state to run Carter's campaign. As in the primaries, outside leadership would be provided, in the hope of avoiding disputes among local Democrats.

In the media campaign as well, the decision was to plan and operate from Atlanta. Jerry Rafshoon would expand his own advertising operation, recruiting volunteers from others in Atlanta, and, as he had in the caucuses and primaries, Rafshoon would get an early start to establish the image of Carter as a national candidate. (He would get Carter out of the peanut fields more often in the commercials and into settings suggesting his experience in government.)

The decision to keep the campaign's direction in Atlanta meant that the team that won the nomination would move to the task of winning the election with no basic changes. In addition to Jordan and Rafshoon, Jody Powell would continue as press secretary and traveling political adviser, Charles Kirbo as the unofficial senior adviser and troubleshooter, Robert Lipshutz as campaign treasurer, Pat Caddell as pollster, Morris Dees as fund-raiser, and Landon Butler as political director. In addition, Richard Harden, an Atlanta accountant who was Carter's first director of the Department of Human Resources in Georgia, would become budget chairman, with primary responsibility for overseeing allocation and dispersal of the federal subsidy.

All these basic decisions were made before the national convention, together with a determination that the DNC would oversee an extensive voter-registration drive, and would be asked to raise the funds for it, plus $3.1 million for Carter permitted under the new funding law. For all the talk of unity and of bringing everyone into the campaign, the Atlantans meant to keep a tight rein; a certain hostility toward the party regulars, in fact, went beyond Carter's rhetoric about the establishment. Congressmen who expected help in fund-raising from Carter would have to pitch in for the DNC—*or else.* "We've got financial leverage over these people," Jordan said bluntly. "Instead of Jimmy going in to compete with them for money, we've got him coming in to help them raise money. We can tell them, 'If you don't help us and the DNC on voter registration, we're not going to raise money for you.'"

Also well in advance of the convention, Jordan had busied himself with a long staff memorandum that was a parallel to his early memos to Carter on how to capture the party nomination. The memo, dated June 2—a week before Carter clinched the nomination—meticulously rated each of the fifty states in terms of how much time, money, and effort should be allocated by candidate and campaign. The determining factors were the size of a state and its electoral vote, its normal Democratic preference and hence potential, and the need to make a campaign effort there, based among other things on how well or poorly Carter had done in each state in the preconvention period.

The memo, updated in August to factor in Walter Mondale's selection and the latest polling data, included Jordan's basic contention that the size of a state was as important as the Democratic potential and the need to campaign combined. Therefore he started by assigning each state 1 point for each electoral vote it had, for a total of 538 points. Next he assigned half that amount for Democratic potential, and the same for need to campaign.

The potential was determined by another rating system giving each state 1 point for each Democratic governor or U.S. senator; 1 point if its congressional (House) delegation had a Democratic majority; 1 point if both houses of the state legislature were Democratic; 2 points if the state gave more than 40 per cent of its vote to George McGovern in the 1972 presidential race, and 1 point if it gave 35 per cent. Under this formula, five states—California, Minnesota, Montana, Rhode Island, and Wisconsin— received the maximum of 7 points, and hence were said to have the greatest potential. Seven others—Connecticut, Delaware, Illinois, Iowa, Kentucky,

Massachusetts, and Nevada—plus the District of Columbia were next; all were placed in Group A. (The allocation of credits for support of McGovern somewhat skewed the conclusions, in that clearly safe states for Carter in the South that had rejected McGovern in 1972, like Georgia and Alabama, got lower ratings, though they were solidly Democratic otherwise.)

The allocation of resources according to need involved a more complicated and arbitrary set of judgments. Eleven states where there was "the greatest need to campaign" were put in another group: states where Carter had lost in the preconvention period—California, Maryland, Missouri, New York, New Jersey, Washington; states Carter had won in narrowly—Wisconsin, Michigan, Connecticut; states in which Carter spent little time or resources—Missouri, Washington, and Connecticut; states where Caddell's polls showed Carter running close to or behind Ford—Maryland, Washington, Illinois, Indiana, Michigan, and Connecticut. Another group included Texas and Florida, where a heavy challenge was expected; Ohio and Pennsylvania, rated critical but where Carter's lead seemed solid; and nine Plains, Mountain, and Western states.

When all the formulae were applied, Jordan computed the "per cent of effort" of the whole campaign to be assigned to each state. California warranted the largest, 5.9 per cent, Wyoming and Alaska the least, 0.6 per cent each. Next, the statistics were applied to a master scheduling formula for Carter, Mondale, and their families. Jordan arbitrarily put a numerical value on a day's campaigning for each: Carter, 7; Mondale, 5; Rosalynn Carter, 4; Joan Mondale, 3; each Carter child, 1. The figure was multiplied by the planned number of campaigning days starting on Labor Day to arrive at the total of "scheduling points." Carter, for example, planned to campaign 43 days, so he had 43 times 7, or 301 scheduling points; Rosalynn planned 35 days, so had 35 times 4, or 140 scheduling points. Next, using the "per cent of effort" formula, the number of scheduling points for each state was calculated. Oregon, for example, rated 1.7 per cent of the total campaign effort, or 16 scheduling points. Jordan meticulously calculated that Carter could spend half a day there (3.5 points), Mondale, a full day (5 points); Rosalynn Carter, a full day (4 points); Joan Mondale, half a day (1.5 points); and Jack and Judy Carter a full day (2 points). "These five trips, spread over an eight-week period, would give the ticket good exposure in the state of Oregon," Jordan wrote.

As in the primaries, the plan was for Carter to run everywhere, but with ten border and Southern states as a solid base of 96 electoral votes: Virginia, North and South Carolina, Kentucky, Tennessee, Georgia, Alabama, Mississippi, Lousiana, and Arkansas. Jordan also projected Florida and Texas as Carter states, though only after a serious challenge from Ford, for 43 more electoral votes. Next he factored in Massachusetts and the District of Columbia, won by McGovern in 1972, plus Minnesota and Wisconsin as recently strongly Democratic, for 38 more, plus two other winnable border states, Maryland and Missouri, for 22. These, Jordan calculated, would give Carter 199, or 74 per cent, of the 270 electoral votes needed. (Eventually, he got 187 of the 199, losing out, narrowly, only for Virginia's 12.) Thus, Carter could nail down the election by carrying only California (45 electoral votes) and New York (41) of the remaining seven largest industrial states, or any three, such as Pennsylvania (27), Illinois (26), and Ohio (25).

The first version of Jordan's memo, in June, had drawn some conclusions that still held up well:

"The Southern states provide us a base of support that cannot be taken for granted or jeopardized. The Republicans cannot win if they write off the South. Consequently, we have to assume that they will challenge us in the South. I believe that they will challenge us in those larger Southern and border states that they view as contestable—Texas, Florida, Maryland, and Missouri. I believe we can win each of those four states. . . .[1]

"Based on the analysis of Democratic potential in each state, we should not publicly concede a single state to the Republicans. This should be our public posture, which will result in their having to worry and spend time and resources defending states that are likely to vote Republican. . . .

"Although the Southern states provide us with a rich base of support, it would be a mistake to appear to be overly dependent on the South for victory in November. It would be harmful nationally if we were perceived as having a 'Southern strategy.' The strength of the South in the electoral college is quite obvious to the media. But to the extent that regional bias exists in this country—and it does—there would be a negative reaction to a candidacy that was perceived as being a captive of the Southern states and/or people. Sad but true. Southern regional pride can be used to great advantage without unnecessarily alienating potential anti-Southern voters."

The August version of the memo also discussed a matter that proved later to be difficult—the use of other Democrats, and especially the greater and lesser stars, including Carter's defeated primary rivals, some of whom grumbled about not being contacted until very late if at all. But the ceiling on spending imposed by the campaign law was clearly a limiting factor here. "As most of the surrogates we will want to use are elected officials," Jordan wrote, "they will require expenses for travel and a certain amount of staff support. We simply do not have the money and will not have the staff to

1. Carter did.

try to utilize hundreds or even dozens of surrogates." Jordan supplied Carter with the names and phone numbers of only fourteen such persons, with a special admonition to Carter that he ought to call them himself. "Senator Mondale has offered to help with this project," he wrote, "but I think it is important that you personally make these requests, as it will give you a good excuse to get to know these people better." And he added pointedly: "Most of them feel like you should have already called them anyway."

Not only was the list short but the time requested from each was surprisingly brief: Mo Udall, four days (in liberal areas); George Wallace, two days (in Florida and Mississippi, early); Frank Church, four days; Hubert Humphrey, four days (across the Northern industrial tier—barely enough time for him to get his motor running); Jerry Brown, six days (in California and his winning primary states); Peter Rodino, four days; Ted Kennedy, four days (for help with Catholic ethnics, suburban liberals, blacks, and chicanos); Henry Jackson, five days (among Jewish voters); Barbara Jordan, five days; Birch Bayh, four days; John Glenn, four days; Senator Joseph Biden of Delaware, six days; Governor Rafael Hernandez Colon of Puerto Rico, four days (in New York and Chicago); Governor Jerry Apodaca of New Mexico, four days.

In the seven weeks between the convention and Labor Day, while Jordan refined his elaborate battle plan, other hopeful Democrats imagined that this luxurious free time would be used to bring all the disparate elements of the party into the fold; that other orthodox sources of political power, beyond a few conspicuous stars, would be invited to participate in the planning of the campaign. Instead, many of these important political figures who had either opposed Carter actively or had remained neutral, after a perfunctory phone call or two from Carter, sat and waited: nothing happened. The Atlantans went about the business of expanding their organization, but in the same go-it-alone way that had marked their drive for the nomination.

Some, like Governor Patrick Lucey of Wisconsin, warned that Carter would not have an easy time getting elected, no matter what the polls said. He called for more specificity on the issues. But Jody Powell said his candidate was determined to campaign just as he had done in the primaries: "There'll be no surprises. He just told people what he believed and what he meant to do, and he isn't going to fool around with any other approach."

But that was before Carter had really faced the challenge of running as the majority party's standard-bearer. No longer could he rail against the establishment; he was now the leader of it. It was a dilemma. Powell insisted later that the Carter campaign *did* reach out to the regular party people.

"Had we not," he said, "we might well have lost the election." But he acknowledged that leading Democrats were seldom brought to Plains; overt conciliation would have clashed with Carter's preconvention image as an outsider. "It was hard to judge where the balance was," Powell said, "between getting the support of Democratic organizations on the one hand and not appearing to be their captive on the other." Also, he said, Carter spent a great deal of time during the summer in reading, studying, and attending briefing sessions—an exercise that led some to suggest that Carter was preoccupied with thoughts of what he would do when he got to the White House, to the short-changing of plans to get there. Though Powell did not say that himself, he acknowledged that "we could have spent a little more time on politics and a little less time on issues."

But the limit of $21.8 million on spending was perhaps more significant. Media advertising was budgeted for about $10 million—a modest figure compared to earlier campaigns if one took inflation into account. So there was precious little money for state organizations with neighborhood store fronts and all the paraphernalia that went with them in the past. Kraft's field operation was budgeted for only $3.1 million for the whole country; grumbling and griping from the provinces was inevitable. Also, there was less inclination to engage local political leaders, for their less manageable activities might drain the treasury. Tight money required tight control; centralization and hard feelings were the inescapable result.

In some ways, for all that, traditional Democratic backing seemed to fall in place easily. Four days after the close of the party convention, for example, George Meany announced the AFL-CIO's endorsement of Carter, pledging "all-out support" of labor's extensive political organization, which had sat out the 1972 McGovern campaign. Yet within the labor movement gripes could be heard that the Carter staff didn't know the political players and were not getting in touch with them. There was some friction, too, between the AFL-CIO's COPE and the new coalition of liberal, reformist-minded unions concerning their involvement in Carter's campaign.

While Democratic activists around the country waited to be called, the Carter staff moved forward with its own preparations. Kraft interviewed more than two hundred persons and selected political organizers—some of whom had been involved in the primary campaigns of Carter's rivals—for conferences in Atlanta and elsewhere on how to run the campaign in various states. This approach precipitated the customary complaints that the outsiders sent in didn't know the political geography or the influential political movers. At the same time, in one of the more astute decisions, the very able Jim King, formerly Ted Kennedy's advance man, was recruited as chief of scheduling and advance. In August, he scoured the country for the most experienced advance men and women, brought a hundred of them to Atlanta for a training exercise, and wove together an effective team. About seventy-five were asked to be on call, especially for the final weeks of the campaign. King himself came to be an essential member of Carter's traveling party, overseeing the work of the advance corps and taking charge of the care and feeding of the traveling press. A big, jolly man with the map of Ireland all over his baby face, King offered the Carter entourage efficiency, humanity, and a healthy sense of the absurd in political campaigning, in about equal doses; he made himself the closest thing the campaign had to the indispensable man.

These were weeks that tried the souls of the accompanying press corps. Now bedded down in the Best Western Motel in nearby Americus, they were reduced to the kind of crumb-gathering that marks the journalistic baby-sitting of Presidents. Carter helped out occasionally by draining his fishpond, a muddy "photo opportunity," or playing softball with the reporters and Secret Service agents—and demonstrating anew his passion for winning. Wearing a jersey bearing the words "Big News," he served up his soft underhanded pitches to reporters wearing "Newstwisters" shirts, as if it were the seventh game of the World Series. When his third baseman extended himself plunging after a twisting foul ball but failed to get it, *The Washington Post*'s Helen Dewar reported that some other players called out, "Good try," but pitcher Jimmy Carter snapped: "Ya shoulda had it."

Such divertisements were not sufficient, however, to occupy a man who had been running for President so hard for so long. He was plainly thrown out of synch by the idleness; in early August, before the Republican convention, he went to New Hampshire for some fund-raising, and to make a carefully prepared speech on the nation's need to cope with the deterioration of family life. But he upstaged his own speech by tearing into President Ford, ridiculing his pursuit of delegates and linking him with the Republican albatross, Nixon. "We've seen an almost unbelievable spectacle in Washington," he said, "the President of the United States deeply concerned about an ex-movie actor, traveling all over the nation to get a handful of delegates here, a handful of delegates there, [while] neglecting the basic responsibilities of leadership." He talked of the failures of "the Nixon-Ford administration," and predicted darkly that after the Republican convention the GOP would mount "an almost unprecedented vicious personal attack on me" and on Mondale, out of desperation. It was not the sort of performance likely to enhance Carter's reputation as the politician of compassion and love, or to elevate the campaign.

Jordan, for one, did not like the tack Carter was taking. In the August update of his strategy memo, he told his boss straight out: "I thought the tone of your remarks last week in New Hampshire were highly partisan and unpresidential. I feel that you should re-examine the manner in which you publicly discuss Ford's relationship with Richard Nixon. The American people perceive Gerald Ford as being an honest, well-intentioned man who inherited a job bigger than he can handle. They see many of the same attractive personal qualities in you, but have made the tentative judgment that you are more capable of leading the country than Ford. I do not worry in the weeks and months ahead that we can clearly demonstrate that you are a better-qualified person to lead the country and manage the government. I do worry that our campaign rhetoric might undermine the favorable personal image you have with the American voters. Any statements which are perceived . . . directly or indirectly, by the American people as being personal attacks on Gerald Ford will hurt us and help him."

Jordan was specific: "I feel strongly that you should discontinue using the phrase 'Nixon-Ford administration,' " he wrote. "I believe that the Republican Party generally and Gerald Ford specifically can be held responsible for many of the problems facing our country today. The American people are ready to hold them accountable at the polls in November for the past eight years, but the phrase 'Nixon-Ford administration' suggests a very conscious effort on your part to equate Ford, the man, with Nixon, the man. This does not and will not wash with the American people and I believe that it will be generally interpreted as a personal attack on the integrity of Gerald Ford. When I watched you say that on the news recently," Jordan concluded, "it sounded harsh and out of character for you. It certainly did not sound like a man who wanted to put Watergate behind us and unite the country."

That Jordan felt free to pose such pointed criticism at the Democratic presidential nominee, a man old enough to be his father, said something about Carter. If he did not like criticism, it was nevertheless indisputable that he had created a climate among his closest aides, young as they were, in which they did not hesitate to be bluntly critical. That side of Carter was not fully appreciated; perhaps it was obscured by his own seeming rigidity and righteousness, but others on the staff attested to it. Even Greg Schneiders, younger than Jordan, much less experienced politically, and a relative newcomer, came to feel comfortable telling his rather strait-laced boss when he thought he had screwed up. There was plenty of blind idolatry around Carter, but the healthy degree of candor was refreshing after the Nixon years of wall-to-wall yes men.

Just because Carter permitted his aides to chew him out, though, did not mean he always paid attention to them. A few days after the Republican convention he was at it again, in a somewhat muted form, from Plains. In a press conference, he defended the phrase "Nixon-Ford administration" on grounds there had been, he said, "almost complete continuity" in policy under the two Republicans. He certainly did not mean there was any Ford link to the "crimes" of the Nixon administration. Well, didn't the phrase nevertheless link Ford to a man who was "fairly unsavory"? Carter replied, mildly but devastatingly: "It's not my fault that Nixon is unsavory."

Jordan said later: "He didn't accept it [my criticism] because he kept doing it. I could have written that memo four or five times in the campaign. Gerald Ford is too nice a man to attack without it hurting you. But Jimmy was getting mixed advice. He had a year and a half to figure out his themes for the primary, but in the general election, he didn't have that. None of us ever quite figured out the dynamics of dealing with Ford as President."

Carter was drawing increasing criticism from outside the campaign as well. On a trip to California, he was taken to task for attending a party given by Warren Beatty, the actor, and attended by about fifty Hollywood stars. But Carter's talk to them was among his most memorable:

"If *we* make a mistake, the chances are we won't actually go to prison, and if we don't like the public-school system, we put our kids in private schools. When the tax structure is modified, which Congress does almost every year, you can rest assured that powerful people who are well organized, who have good lawyers, who have lobbyists in the Capitol in Washington—they don't get cheated. But there are millions of people in this country who do get cheated, and they are the very ones who can't afford it. . . . I can go a mile from my house, two hundred yards from my house, and there are people there who are very poor, and when they get sick it's almost impossible for them to get a doctor. In the county where I am from, we don't have a doctor, a dentist, a pharmacist, a registered nurse, and people who live there who are very poor have no access to preventive health care. We found in Georgia that poor women, who are mostly black, in rural areas have twenty times more cervical cancer than white women in urban counties, just because they haven't seen a doctor, because the disease has gone so far that it can't go further. . . . So, I say, public servants like me and Jerry Brown and others have a special responsibility to bypass the big shots, *including you and people like you,* and make a concerted effort to understand people who are poor, black, speak a foreign language, who are not well educated, who are inarticulate, who are stymied, who have some monumental problem, and at the same time to run the government in a competent way, well organized, efficient, manageable, so that those services that are so badly needed can be delivered."

This Jimmy Carter, who was moving out from the quiet summer of Plains toward the formal Labor Day kickoff of his campaign, seemed to be like a fighter trained to a fine edge, with the championship bout still weeks away. In a speech before the American Legion's convention in Seattle, he chose intentionally to reiterate his stated determination to grant a "blanket pardon" to all Vietnam draft resisters. "I do not favor a blanket amnesty," he said, making this special distinction, "but for those who violated Selective Service laws I intend to grant a blanket pardon." The audience of more than fifteen thousand legionnaires and their wives reacted violently. "No! No!" men cried out, and Carter was engulfed in a flood of booing that ended only when the Legion's national commander, Harry Wiles, gaveled for silence. Through it all, Carter stood quietly, eyes down at first, and then flashing his smile. The reaction was expected; Carter obviously had chosen to throw his plan in the teeth of the Legion as a means of demonstrating to the wider national audience his courage as a campaigner. It was a pointed refutation of the allegation that he always tailored his speeches to please his audiences. But the question here was, which audience was the prime one, the Legion or the country beyond? Carter's remarks on a pardon were counterbalanced by support for a strong national defense, but the latter was lost in the public outcry against the pardon proposal. Some regular Democrats began to worry that Carter was playing to liberal sentiment too much.

In Des Moines the next day, Carter continued to link Ford with Nixon, and at the Iowa State Fair, he attacked the farm and export policies of "Nixon, Ford, and Butz," and especially the unpopular grain embargo of 1975. He pledged that if elected he would "stop embargoes once and for all." But then, when pressed in an interview with the *Des Moines Register,* he said that in times of national emergency, which he did not foresee, he might have to resort to an embargo—a position that Republican vice-presidential nominee Bob Dole seized on at once to demonstrate that Carter flip-flopped on the issues.

The trip to the West, acknowledged to be a shakedown cruise for the September campaign, displayed an aggressive, hard-hitting Carter, but also one who committed *gaffes.* His meeting with the Hollywood set, no matter how pointed (and sparsely reported) his lecture on poverty had been, was criticized as unbecoming a populist candidate—especially because the guests included Armand Hammer, president of the Occidental Petroleum Company, convicted of making an illegal contribution to Nixon in 1972. Then, in a slap at John Connally, Carter observed that only George Wallace ranked lower in the polls as trustworthy, and he had to apologize to Wallace. And, at a time he was being briefed by George Bush, director of the CIA, Carter's staff released an internal memo citing Bush among defeated Republicans rewarded with high appointments, and he had to apologize for that too. But Powell dismissed these incidents as minor, as part of a candidate getting used to the closer scrutiny he would undergo as the Democratic nominee.

That Carter would be facing closer examination certainly should not have come as a surprise to him or his staff. One might have expected him to be more on his guard. But the summer of 1976 was an odd time, a lull after the intense pursuit of the nomination. It was a time for planning and reflection, and for catching up on a lot of things that were put off—like interviews with various elements of the press. Reporters and writers were pressing Powell for interviews, and he and Carter did their best to comply. Carter, always reaching out to new audiences, always being the Good Shepherd in search of the one strayed member of the herd, talked to *The New York Times,* and *The Washington Post,* and the network correspondents, and a host of magazine writers. Even *Playboy,* which ran extensive interviews with public figures and earlier in the year had done one on Jerry Brown that had received wide interest and acclaim, got to talk to the candidate, not once but several times. Robert Scheer, a free-lancer who wrote for *Playboy,* was a persistent sort, and so were his editors, and when they did not quite have all they felt they needed, Carter gave Scheer and Barry Golson, a *Playboy* editor, one more interview in his home in Plains, in late July. It was an unusually probing interview, and Carter pressed his points on Scheer and Golson after its formal conclusion as he walked them to the front door. So arresting were his observations that Scheer kept the tape recorder running to capture Carter's final observations. Scheer was enthused enough to call Powell afterward and suggest that he listen to the tape. But Powell said he would rather wait until the whole piece was put together and would review it then—or so he recalled later. Monthly magazines have interminably long lead times, however, and it would be weeks before the article could be published. So Powell thought no more of it, and moved on to more immediate matters.

By now Jordan had refined his strategy for the fall campaign. In a situation room in the Atlanta headquarters, Rick Hutcheson, Carter's young preconvention head-hunter and now the national campaign coordinator, presided over the nerve center, a place for centralizing candidate travel, field work, polling data, research, and other vital functions. Large maps of the country charted the itineraries of each family member: Carter, of course, in his campaign color, green; Mondale in red; Rosalynn Carter in blue; Joan Mondale in yellow; the children in purple. The lines crisscrossed from coast to coast, indicating that every week everywhere, a Carter or a Mondale would be out.

Meanwhile Pat Caddell had been polling the states, determining where Carter was strongest and weakest, where he needed to campaign earliest and most often. The state-by-state priority was secret for two reasons: to keep it from the Ford camp, and to avoid ruffling the feathers of Democratic leaders in states getting short shrift. Before Jordan would permit Hutcheson to show me the maps, he ordered that segments touching on the priority rating be covered over with large sheets of wrapping paper. Politics, like war itself, could be hell.

At the same time, a large issues staff under Stuart Eizenstat was busy turning out position papers, working with some fifteen task forces of experts in fields ranging from economics to national defense. The staff was instructed by Carter to present him with options, rather than selecting positions for him, and to avoid any ideological rigidity, inasmuch as the candidate notoriously defied ideological categorization. Once the fall campaign began, however, quite a few members of the Carter camp complained that for all the experts, Carter, in consultation with Powell, was given to deciding on policy positions off the top of his head; to responding to issues crises in the same arbitrary—and politically risky—manner.

As Labor Day approached, though, all seemed in readiness. Jordan's priority system for the allocation of candidate and money was now squarely anchored: maintenance and reinforcement of Carter's Southern base; securing traditionally strong Democratic states; and a run-everywhere strategy that would keep the heat on Ford. "Assuming we win in the South," Caddell said at the time, "the math is compelling. They can't really run everywhere. They're behind and can't try to catch up everywhere."

Jordan, in his strategy memo, had made the same point—while holding the South, Carter could give Ford fits by flirting with Republican areas of strength. "We should spend a small amount of time early in the campaign challenging Ford in states that are traditionally Republican in a presidential election," he wrote. "Ford lacks a base of support; there is not a region of the country or a political grouping of states that he can count on in November. Consequently, he lacks the mathematical base on which to build a majority of the electoral votes. Without a base, he lacks a strategy. By making a trip early in the campaign into several traditionally Republican states, I believe that we can effectively put Ford on the defensive, making him spend time and money in states he should carry. Perhaps even more importantly, we can prevent the Republicans from ever developing a clear strategy for winning." But the South could never be counted as in the bag. "The Southern and border states are our base of support that cannot be taken for granted or jeopardized," Jordan went on. "The only way we can lose in November is to have this base fragmented. We need to spend early time campaigning in the South and several key border states. If our solid lead here holds, we can probably cut back on time here in October and simply show the flag regularly."

Jordan cautioned that it would be dangerous to get cocky and gear the campaign for a large victory, rather than just victory itself. *"Our clear and single goal must be to simply win 270 electoral votes,"* he wrote, underlining this sentence. "To expend our limited resources trying to win 400 electoral votes, we could very easily fall short of the 270 we need to win the election. . . . We must never forget that in 1968 in six weeks Hubert Humphrey closed 20 points on Richard Nixon and almost won the presidency. We will probably not know until mid-October if the election is going to be close or if there is a potential for a big victory. . . . If by mid-October we have a commanding lead and have the flexibility previously advocated, the goals and objectives of the campaign can be appropriately broadened. If our projected lead in the electoral college is commanding and our survey results solid in mid-October, we can begin to spend an appropriate amount of time and resources trying to win the mandate we will need to bring real and meaningful change to this country."

But Jimmy Carter was never one to minimize his own potential. While Jordan, Caddell, and others played the electoral-college numbers game and plotted as scientifically as they could where the limited resources might best be expended, Carter, the supreme optimist, prepared for the climactic eight weeks with bolder conceptual thinking: the thinking of a man who expected to be the next President. In an interview with some reporters in Plains two days before starting out, he displayed a determination not only to win but to rout the opposition. "I think it is important to win with a broad base of support," he said. "I would rather have a six-per-cent victory in all the states than a fifteen-per-cent victory in fifteen states and lose the rest of them." He underlined that "the mandate that's crucial to me" to carry out his campaign pledges could come only "from a wide-ranging success among the electorate" that would impress a recalcitrant Congress. He would not narrow his campaign focus, he said, "unless it becomes mandatory that we do so in order to avoid a defeat."

Such talk made it clear that Jimmy Carter was not thinking, on the eve of Labor Day, of an election that was close enough to court defeat. He had always run flat-out and he would continue to do so. After nearly three months of contemplation in Plains, he was raring to go. "I can hardly wait," he told the reporters. Nobody doubted it.

36. The Ford Battle Plan

About two weeks before the Republican convention, Stuart Spencer went over to the White House one day to see President Ford. He took with him a black loose-leaf notebook of 120 pages plus appendices written by a number of campaign strategists. In the company of Dick Cheney, Spencer walked into the Oval Office. The book, of which there were only four copies, was the battle plan for the fall campaign against Carter, and it was not easy reading for the President. It was some hard-nosed politicians' assessment of an uphill challenge against a majority-party nominee who had an immense lead in the polls, by a minority-party incumbent with serious shortcomings, not the least of which was his weakness as a speechmaker. Bob Teeter had taken polls showing that when Ford had personally stumped in the primaries, he had lost ground nationally.

Spencer, a man with all the directness of a well-hit line drive, wasted neither words nor sensibilities: "Mr. President," he said, observing protocol in his form of address, "as a campaigner, you're no fucking good!"

Ford winced, then managed a laugh. He had been a campaigner all his life, and there was a combative partisanship in him that belied his easygoing nature. In 1974, first as Vice President and then as President, he had beat the bushes for Republican congressional candidates, with great relish but with little effect except to win the gratitude of those candidates—and to diminish his own very limited luster. Spencer was firm: the only way Ford could hope to beat Carter was to fall back into the sanctuary of the White House, to be "presidential," marshaling resources and Ford's own time for a final blitz on the road at the very end. The President, reluctantly, kept a copy of the strategy book and told Spencer and Cheney he would let them know what he thought.

What Ford read was not easy to take: a situation, and an analysis of himself as perceived by the public and confirmed by the polls, that were both depressing and embarrassing.

"You face an unique challenge [it said]. No President has ever overcome the obstacles to election which you will face following our convention this August. For example, President Truman trailed Dewey in August, 1948, by 11 points, whereas we expect to be trailing Carter by about 20 points after our convention. Of course, the Ford-Carter gap will begin to close . . . on its own almost irrespective of what we do. However, although the point-spread may close over time fairly easily, down to a point where Carter is 5 to 10 points ahead, the remaining distance to victory will be very difficult."

Then the battle plan laid Ford's deficiencies on the line. "These [public] perceptions do not necessarily reflect your true character or style as President," the book said, obviously by way of letting him down easily. "They are a reflection of how the TV viewer and newspaper reader 'sees' you." But there was no minimizing their importance: "We have presented this with the bark off because we must solve this perception problem in order to successfully communicate your leadership qualities. This obstacle must be overcome or there is no chance of victory."

First the positives in public attitudes were stated: "I like him [Ford]: he is a good man who tried hard. I hope he succeeds. . . . He is safe and will do the right thing. . . . He came in under horrible circumstances and the situation in the country has gotten better under him. . . . An honest man who will try to do the right thing; he has restored honesty in government. . . . He will keep the activists from taking over and springing another Great Society on us." But then the bad news: "Not decisive. . . . Not really on top of the job. . . . Doesn't seem to have a clear view of where he is going and why; doesn't seem to understand our problems or have solutions for them. . . . Spends too much time on politics, too worried about election; doesn't seem to spend enough time on the people's business, too much of an old politician. . . . Seen as part of the old-time, do-nothing Washington establishment. . . . He is politically expedient; he seems inconsistent— swings one way and then another. . . . Not strong enough to lay Reagan away; does this reflect on his abilities? . . . Not in control of government. Henry Kissinger and others seem to be able to control him; he is their puppet. He doesn't seem to want to use his power and authority. . . . Makes errors; may not be smart enough to do the job. . . . Fights with Congress while problems remain unsolved. . . . Boring, not exciting. . . . Appointed by Nixon, whom he pardoned."

For page after page, Ford's political advisers served up this sort of appraisal, but concluded: "One positive thing is that we are not working against a hard, anti-President Ford feeling. Even the disapproval in the Gallup Poll [although high] is not firm. . . . It is just that not enough voters have a strong, positive feeling about the Ford personality and character."

The book warned Ford that he was a gone goose if he made any serious mistake along the way. "Because you must come from behind," it said, "and are subject to many constraints, no strategy can be developed which allows for any substantial error." But it was not pessimistic. "We firmly believe that you can win in November. During times when you and your administration pulled together and projected a positive image of action and accomplishments, your standing in the national polls rose accordingly. Furthermore, your national support has solidified somewhat. However, although you have been able to positively influence the voters, efforts to do this in the past have resulted in very limited and temporary increases. Most importantly, your national-approval rating declined during the periods when you were perceived as a partisan, particularly when we campaigned."

Spencer, Teeter, and others who put the strategy book together were impressively prescient in assessing Carter's position: "Notwithstanding Carter's enormous popularity at the present, it must not be forgotten that he never got more than 54 per cent of the vote in any of the contested primaries, and never won in a head-to-head race. Furthermore, Carter was beaten in eight out of the last eleven contested primary fights. There is ample historical precedent for the proposition that such a rapid rise in national popularity . . . is generally followed by a decline. We believe that much of Carter's rise in the polls is due to his 'media' image as a winner. However, between now and the election, he will not be able to rely on these 'victories.' "[1]

The book was blunt in stating that Ford was in a sense at Carter's mercy, that only blunders by Carter could keep Ford in the White House. "If past is indeed prologue," it said, "you will lose on November 2—because to win you must do what has never been done: close a gap of about 20 points in seventy-three days from the base of a minority party while spending approximately the same amount of money as your opponent. You cannot overcome the Carter lead on your own, no matter what you do. Of course, your 'offensive' campaign is a crucial element, but to win, Carter's position must be changed by a strong attack launched by the vice-presidential nominee and others."

Carter would have to stumble, but at the same time Ford would have to do something about his own image. First of all he had to clean up the mess in his own campaign, adopt a firm strategy, and stick to it. No names were mentioned, but the implication was clear: Rogers Morton, who was popping in and out of the campaign but never really taking hold of the PFC, had to go. Also, the sniping at the PFC from the White House—from Jerry Jones, Dave Gergen, and Ron Nessen—had to stop. And, most important,

---

1. As noted, Carter's run-everywhere strategy in the primaries enabled him to post a counteracting victory somewhere on every primary day when he lost somewhere, thus maintaining an impression of momentum despite the setbacks.

a skillful, innovative advertising team had to be used. Peter Dailey, the holdover advertising expert from the Nixon campaign of 1972, was trying to run things with one hand, staying on the West Coast and delegating authority and direction to Bruce Wagner of New York, regarded by the ranking PFC operatives as bullheaded and inept. Spencer and Teeter wanted the advertising to be taken over by the best young campaign team in Republicanism—Doug Bailey and John Deardourff. In 1974 these two had pulled off the neatest trick of the political year, working successfully to elect the liberal-leaning Governor William Milliken to another term in Michigan and at the same time, with a masterful negative television campaign against unpopular Democratic Governor John Gilligan in Ohio, returning one of the great rogues of the era, James Rhodes, to the Governor's Mansion in Columbus. Ford had to have them for the fall effort.

To win, the strategy blueprint said, "we must persuade over 15 per cent (or about 10 million people) to change their opinions. This will require very aggressive media-oriented efforts." But, the book said, Ford could "run hard without relying on the traditional campaign 'hoopla' "; he could be "an active candidate and yet be perceived as a working President."

There was nothing written explicitly of what came later to be known as "the Rose Garden strategy"—the President "campaigning" from the sheltered confines of the White House lawn, making "presidential" announcements against backdrops conducive to television coverage, while Carter plunged on in the pit of complete public exposure at the mercy of the wolves of the press. But it was always what Spencer had in mind, as his point-blank description of the President as a campaigner had suggested.

Knowing that Ford liked to compare himself to Harry Truman, who upset the odds in 1948 and beat Dewey with a whirlwind whistlestop train campaign, the book pointedly tried to deflate that approach. "If Truman had to implement his '48 campaign today," it said, "he would probably lose because of TV. Truman was *not* that good on the stump (his speeches were awful!) and, while his 'Give 'Em Hell, Harry' style was pleasing to relatively small crowds—who would only see it once—it probably would have quickly worn thin if seen nightly by millions in living color."

As a prelude to the Rose Garden strategy, the book urged Ford to make a public declaration about his intended style of campaigning right after the convention, along these lines: "Presidential campaigning has become a circus which no longer fully serves the needs of the American people and the political process established by the Constitution. The President can appropriately use this bicentennial year to demonstrate how the process can be improved. He can contribute by campaigning on the issues and thus assisting the people in making one of the most serious choices they must to preserve democracy and freedom." This was, of course, an elaborate euphemism that, coarsely translated, said: "Pull a Nixon, Jerry. Get inside the White House, stay there, keep your head down, and your mouth shut. Use the trappings of your office to remind voters of your incumbency, while we rev up a solid media effort for you. Meanwhile, let Carter go out on the firing line and make the mistakes that will do him in."

Because Ford always seemed to inflict wounds on himself, political as well as physical, when he took to the stump, and because he tended to overkill when he got heated up in talking about his opponent, the book emphasized that Ford had to take care not to make sharp personal attacks on Carter. And, to counter Ford's own high appraisal of himself as a campaigner, the book argued: "It is true that some of the President's primary campaigning did result in an increase in his local popularity in the area campaigned in, but these examples would be very misleading if applied to the general election. There is no question that people who actually see the President are influenced by that event, and local press has its beneficial impact. However, for the general election, presidential-campaign events are not significant in terms of their impact on the people who attend. These people are mainly important as backdrops for the television viewer. During the general election, all presidential travel must be planned for its impact on those who learn about it through the media."[2]

To this end, the blueprint said in another page right out of the Nixon book for 1968 and 1972, it was important to "carefully plan, prepare, and execute *all* on-camera appearances. The President should be seen on television as in control, decisive, open, and candid. . . . Prep time (fifteen to thirty minutes) should be built into the President's schedule [with Bill Carruthers, a television adviser], immediately preceding on-camera events." For example, the campaign Bible said, Ford "should rehearse his acceptance speech before departing for Kansas City, using a Teleprompter and videotape"— a piece of advice that was followed to the letter.

While Ford was astutely and privately emulating Nixon the programed campaigner, Ford's campaign would set about trying to paint Carter as another Nixon. "Carter's campaign must be linked [in the public mind] to Nixon's '68 and '72 campaigns—very slick, media-oriented. A candidate that takes positions based on polls, not principles. . . . The following similarities should be pointed out: A candidate who tried to be all things to all people. Avoids specifics on issues. Driven by personal ambition—

2. The report estimated that only about a million people would actually see Ford, including Carter supporters, if he campaigned three days a week from mid-September on.

harsh and manipulative. Secretive and surrounded by a protective and fiercely loyal staff."

To cut into Carter's lead, the book said, "he must be seen as: An unknown. A man whose thirst for power dominates. Who doesn't know why he wants the presidency or what he will do with it. Inexperienced. Arrogant (deceitful). Devious and highly partisan (a function of uncontrolled ambition). As one who uses religion for political purposes; an evangelic. As liberal, well to the left of center and a part of the old-line Democratic Party." Carter, Ford was told in one of the few bad pieces of advice in the book, would be vulnerable in the South because of his selection of Mondale and the Democrats' liberal platform. "We must mount an attack on him on conservative issues, both economic and social. If we can succeed, we can keep him busy holding the South, which at present he takes for granted. By occupying him there, we can free the President and his advocates to concentrate on the swing states." But again the caution: "The attack in the South must be on issues. We should not attack him personally there since this would cause a backlash of regional pride. It must be a respectful disagreement on a high plane." In referring to the importance of not hitting Carter personally in Dixie, a footnote said: "An example of how *not* to attack Carter is Senator Dole's line on "Face the Nation" (July 18): 'He is Southern-fried McGovern.' "[3] The book emphasized elsewhere that the vice-presidential nominee should be an "aggressive campaigner who can take the lead in implementing the Attack Carter Plan," but added he should be "a man who is perceived as an Independent, or at least moderate Republican, without strong party identification. [He] must have a strong image of freshness and non-Washington establishment. Honest. A man who has good credibility with the press." Also, it said in another context: "We cannot dwell on the unification problem, nor spend resources working on Republicans. The fact is that if we're 15 or 20 points behind, party unity will be a function of Ford's perceived winnability. If Republicans think he's going to win, they'll pull behind him; if they think he's going to lose (as they perceived, correctly, Goldwater would in 1964), the party will remain divided no matter what we do." Yet Dole was selected by Ford in large part to help hold Republicans.

The strategy book, for all its sharp criticisms of Ford, repeatedly expressed confidence that he could beat Carter. It offered a state-by-state

---

3. The author of this line, Cheney aide Mike Duval, was watching Dole on the television panel as he was editing the campaign-strategy book, and inserted the footnote. Later, en route from Kansas City after the convention, he mused: "We better get that page out."

assessment and assigned priorities for the campaign's limited resources. The plan started out assuming a Ford base of 83 electoral votes—the Plains and Mountain states, three New England states, and Indiana. It gave Carter 87 —six states in the South, Minnesota, Massachusetts, Rhode Island, Hawaii, and the District of Columbia—and rated the remaining 368 to be possible for either. It allocated the least resources to safe Republican and Democratic states and assigned "maximum resources" to the nine largest states —the industrial belt from New York to Illinois (excluding Indiana), plus Florida, Texas, and California. And it urged that Ford keep his Republicanism under wraps. "The President must not campaign for GOP candidates," it said flatly. "This will seriously erode his support among Independents and ticket-splitters. The President should not attend any party fund-raisers. Any support given to a GOP candidate must be done in a manner to avoid national-media attention. For example, the President can make telephone calls, sign mailers, do video endorsements for fund-raisers, etc." Also, he was to make special efforts among Catholics, Jews, farmers, and other "constituency groups." Above all else, he was to hammer home one theme: that he offered both trust and accomplishment, and that the shifty, inexperienced Carter offered neither.

The strategy book was a heavy dose of reality—and, some might even say, impertinence—to administer to a President. But a short time later the word came back: Okay; Ford would buy it, including the distasteful requirement that he stay off the stump until the later stages of the campaign. "Telling Ford he was a bad campaigner never was a problem," Teeter said later, "because of the kind of guy he was. He was always great to work with."

Spencer's only regret was that his friend and the PFC's able if outspoken press aide, Peter Kaye, was being eased out after the convention. Kaye was considered too cozy with the press, since he operated on a premise foreign to most Republican politicians—that it served both candidate and public to be open and candid at all times. Kaye was to be replaced by William Greener, a veteran government flack who had worked under Nessen before going over to the Pentagon with Donald Rumsfeld. Greener was Rumsfeld's protégé, a gregarious sort, a kind of press groupie, in fact, who looked like Bert Lahr and constantly clowned in Lahr-like fashion. But unlike Kaye, Greener did not have a close relationship with Spencer, and his value to the reporters was limited. Royston Hughes, the treasurer of the Ford campaign, had once said to Kaye: "You're not one of us! You're one of them!" That was never said of Greener.

Spencer, who considered Kaye the best press secretary he had ever worked with, seriously weighed the possibility of quitting the campaign when Kaye was moved aside. Had the President declined to follow the basic plan of staying off the firing line in the early going, he told Jim Naughton, he would have. Spencer and Greener kept their distance through the fall, and with Kaye's departure the Ford campaign lost one of its best-working duos.

Ford's campaign strategy actually was late in being formulated, so engrossed were Cheney and Spencer in winning the nomination. But informal plans had been laid in May by Cheney, Spencer, and Teeter. At the core of their talks, usually in Cheney's office at the White House in the late afternoons, was the basic idea of achieving maximum mileage from the incumbency. Spencer set to work writing a broad campaign plan, refining it in time with detailed recommendations for budget and staffing, down to the state level.

In the second week in June, three second-level aides to Cheney had lunch at the Szechuan East, two blocks from the White House, and began to talk about the fall campaign. The three were Mike Duval, a holdover from the Nixon days, Foster Channock, and James Connor. They discussed the advantages of incumbency and the President's shortcomings as a stump speaker, and Duval later went to Cheney with their conclusion—that Ford would be better off with what they called a "no-campaign campaign" strategy. At Cheney's suggestion, Duval wrote a memo that said in essence that the President ought, after securing the nomination, to announce at the convention that he would not actively campaign, but stick to his job and let the people decide on the basis of his performance in the White House. He would pointedly reject the $21.8 million in federal funds available to him as his party's nominee and offer to debate Carter on a series of substantive issues.

The group's idea dovetailed with the thoughts of Cheney, Spencer, and Teeter. Jerry Jones, who had been a thorn in the PFC's side all along, joined the White House group along with Teeter, who thereby became a kind of bridge between this group of political greenhorns and the veteran Spencer. Duval was assigned to pull together all the ideas, including Spencer's work on staff and budget planning, into the basic document that was presented to Ford.

By rights, Rogers Morton as the campaign manager would have been a key figure in this advance planning. But Morton was ailing and he had no stomach for administration anyway. Then the "writing off the Cotton South" episode at the convention finished him if he wasn't finished before. When Ford's strategists met at the President's vacation retreat in Vail, Colorado, after the convention, the first order of business was a shakedown of the campaign leadership. Ford needed vastly improved management at the PFC over the operation that had struggled and stumbled to his narrow nomination victory. Morton was eased out and, when John Connally declined the job, Jim Baker, who had done a superb job as delegate hunter, was asked to take over. At the strong urging of Teeter and Spencer, the team of Bailey and Deardourff was hired to handle media advertising—a decision that in the end came exceedingly close to keeping Gerald Ford in the White House. With Cheney continuing to operate as White House overseer and chief liaison with the President, this was the team that would undertake what they knew the situation required—a highly professional, error-free effort from Labor Day to Election Day. Greener was also involved and, later, Elly Peterson, a veteran Michigan Republican pro.

The influence of Bailey and Deardourff was felt at once. The first phase of their two-pronged plan involved simply conveying information about this accidental President's personal and family life, and about his concept of the presidency, which was dramatically less imperial than either Nixon's or Johnson's. Most importantly, the voters would be reminded about how things were at the end of Nixon's regime, the better to appreciate Ford. "We felt in many respects that part of Ford's problem was that he was sort of a victim of his own success," Bailey explained. "In two years, the country had returned to a kind of normalcy, and Ford was likely to be measured by normal measurements of the President, whereas the fact was in those two years we had really come an extraordinary distance. It was necessary to remind people of the conditions under which he assumed the presidency, in order to get them to focus on how far the country had come."

More difficult for Bailey and Deardourff was the final essential ingredient of the positive side of the campaign—what Ford saw for the future. "He had not communicated what he wanted the country to be moving toward," Bailey said. "He used to talk about his 'vision.' I don't think he ever really understood what we were talking about when we used the term 'vision.' He's not a conceptual thinker. He doesn't think in broad strokes of history. So there was never a full meeting of minds on that subject." Deardourff agreed. "I never was sure," he said, "that the President or anybody else that he had around him had a clear sense of what you did for an encore after you got things back on an even keel."

As for the second phase of the campaign, cutting Carter down to size, only the broadest outlines were discussed in Vail. Teeter's polling data carefully exposed Carter's vulnerabilities: his lack of experience, especially in foreign affairs, no clear public perception of his record of accomplishments, and his failure to be specific enough on the issues. All had to be exploited.

Bailey and Deardourff insisted on complete control over media advertising, and they were given it. The President approved specifically of the use of so-called negative advertising against Carter, after assurances that it would be in good taste and within the bounds of responsible political discourse, which it turned out to be.

The role of Senator Dole was also planned by the new campaign executive committee and presented at daily meetings with the President. The farm states, the traditional Republican base, would be Dole's first priority, along with the Reaganites. And he would carry the brunt of the campaigning in September and into October, enabling Ford to stay home being presidential. "They said they wanted somebody who could go out and mix it up a little, and hit the ground running," Dole said later.

The meetings succeeded in pulling together an effective team for the fall campaign and in mapping the over-all strategy, but there was one major omission: Nobody invited Ronald Reagan. A swift roundup of key Reagan aides was achieved: Lyn Nofziger, David Keene, Charlie Black, and Jim Lake all were quickly signed up, but Reagan was never asked to attend nor was there any attempt to integrate his campaign organization (which had nearly engineered the President's defeat) into Ford's. Not only Reagan but Paul Laxalt and John Sears, his chief strategists, were ignored. According to Nofziger, who joined Dole, Laxalt called a meeting of Reagan's national organization about two weeks after the convention to consider the ways it could be used, yet nothing was heard from the Ford people. The President finally phoned Reagan in September and asked for his help, and Reagan suggested that Cheney work out a schedule with his aide Mike Deaver. About two more weeks passed and Deaver heard nothing, until Nofziger finally talked to Spencer. A schedule was prepared for Reagan and sent to him; the Ford people contended later that Reagan never responded.[4]

One final bit of business at Vail concerned how the debates with Carter should be set up. Cheney assigned Duval to represent the White House in the negotiations with Carter, to be supervised by the sponsoring League of Women Voters' Education Fund. Ford, who had seized the initiative in challenging Carter, now tried to keep it by unilaterally declaring the ground rules he wanted. He proposed that the debates start within four days of Labor Day, that each of them last ninety minutes, and that foreign policy, national security, and defense be the first topic. "It is my very strong

---

4. Reagan eventually did campaign, but not until October with Dole, and he talked more about the conservative platform than about the virtues of Gerald Ford. "He was effective in the South," Dole said later. "I think perhaps a little more emphasis on the ticket and a little less on the platform would have been helpful. But we carried California, and that's his home base. He was always very cooperative when I was with him. It's got to take a while when you lose in a hard-fought contest to saddle up another horse and ride off somewhere."

conviction," he told reporters outside his rented Swiss-style chalet, "that the American people have a right to know where I stand on the issues and where my opponent stands on the issues. I look forward to the first one and each of the next three, and the sooner we get started the better."

The people's right to know was not, of course, Ford's principal reason for wanting an early start, or for wanting national defense and foreign policy to be the first subject. The Ford team wanted to get going as soon as possible, Bailey and Deardourff said later, because Ford was steamed up after his convention victory and because there was little enough time to engage Carter, considering his lead in the polls. Everyone agreed that it would be best if Ford could lead with his strong suit in terms of experience, although they rightly expected that the Carter forces would object. The Carter negotiators preferred that all three debates be open-ended in terms of subject matter; and although they eventually agreed that two of them be on national security and domestic matters, they held firm on *not* having foreign policy first.

Duval, with the clear vision of hindsight, later tried to suggest that he went into the negotiations with Ford's proposal for an early start with a national-security debate as no more than a negotiating ploy. The strategy really favored a later debate to counter the anticipated early media surge on Carter's part. "We wanted to discount everything Carter did in September," Duval said, "in essence to force the public mind into neutral through September." But if that was Duval's idea going into the negotiations, rather than an assessment after the fact, he apparently did not share it with the others at Vail. Both Bailey and Deardourff said that they and the rest of the braintrust would have been delighted if Carter had accepted the President's proposal to debate early. As for proposing national security as the opening topic, Duval said later, Ford knew Carter would never buy it. Actually, Duval insisted, there was concern that Ford might "lose" the foreign-policy debate in viewers' eyes unless he outpointed Carter by a wide margin, and therefore it was risky to start off with that subject. That, however, was another point on which Duval and others had sharply different recollections.

Though Ford was not to start campaigning until well past Labor Day, Dole was dispatched at once to start cutting Carter down to size. While the strategy meetings were still going on at Vail, he flew to Seattle and spoke soon after Carter's unpopular Vietnam war-pardon advocacy to the American Legion. Dole told the cheering legionnaires that Ford's position on

Vietnam draft evaders was "unequivocal." There would be, he said, "no blanket pardon, no blanket amnesty, no blanket clemency." The next day he flew to Des Moines, again on Carter's heels, attacking him as inconsistent on the critical farm-belt issue of grain embargoes.

On the following day, he was back in Vail to take part in a press conference in which Ford and Connally launched a pointed "fear" campaign against the Democratic nominee. Connally contended that the American people were going to elect Ford because they "frankly, know this President." Then he added: "On the other side, frankly, everywhere I have gone throughout the country, in every strata of society, I have detected a note of fear about Governor Carter, an uncertainty about Governor Carter." Connally went on in that vein until he was interrupted by the President, who observed that Carter's inexperience in foreign policy reflected "fear and apprehension of the American people." He seconded Connally's observation that the American people "don't want a person whose name they didn't know a year and a half ago running American foreign policy."

That was just the beginning. It demonstrated that the advice put forward by Spencer, Teeter, Bailey, and Deardourff was already being taken: to have any hope of winning, Ford and his supporters had to prey on the public doubts about Jimmy Carter.

The meetings in Vail broke up more optimistically than might have been imagined even a week earlier. And that optimism was encouraged by the latest Gallup Poll showing that Ford, who had trailed Carter by 33 percentage points in late July in the same survey, and 23 points just before the Republican convention, had dramatically cut the lead to only 10 points, 39–49. The poll further showed that outside Carter's South, the two nominees were running virtually even: Carter 44 per cent, Ford 43. Pat Caddell, Carter's pollster, professed relief. "I'm not worried," he said. "I'm glad to see it happen because it's been out of whack so badly. It's good that it happened sooner rather than later." And Carter attributed the results to "the healing of strong division" in Republican ranks after the GOP convention. His own earlier lead, he said, had been exaggerated by "the general euphoria that always sets into a nation as they observe the conclusion of any harmonious convention." A week later Carter's Gallup lead was up to 15 per cent again, 52–37—apparently as some of the positive feeling for Ford after his convention success wore off. But still, the gap was not so wide as to mire the Ford camp in the doldrums.

Five days before Labor Day, the two sides reached agreement on the debates. The first would be held on September 23, and the subject would be domestic and economic issues. According to Duval, Ford had achieved both his objectives—a late start and a subject area in which he would not be so heavy a favorite as to run a high risk of being perceived as the debate's loser. On the Carter side, the negotiators had wanted all open-ended debates so that Ford could not be "programed," but they believed they had won by moving foreign policy and defense back to second place, in October, and by achieving agreement—not really contested—on complete parity with the President in all facilities (no trappings of the presidential office would be seen on the set). When Jody Powell inquired about this matter at one point, William Ruckelshaus, acting as a Ford negotiator, reassured him. But, Ruckelshaus asked Jim Karayn, the former public-broadcasting official handling the debates for the League, "I wonder how you're going to handle 'Hail to the Chief.' " Karayn replied: "We're going to play it with a Dixie melody." There was also some question about the panelists being required to address the President as "Mr. Ford," but Karayn refused to ask the reporters to do that. Carter would find out in short order that the major "trapping"—that Gerald Ford *was* the President—could not be removed, especially in Jimmy Carter's own consciousness.

One possible obstacle remained—court challenges by the independent candidate Eugene McCarthy and a third-party candidate, Carter's old friend Lester Maddox, on the grounds that they should be included, or at least should be granted equal television time. But the League of Women Voters' Education Fund proceeded on the assumption that these challenges would be rejected, as they eventually were.

Now, at last, the excruciatingly long preliminaries and the complex, exhausting sorting out were over. It was coming down to eight weeks of campaigning across fifty diverse states and, through television, into millions of American living rooms. Already the electorate seemed weary, and the customary complaints about the excessive length of the presidential campaign were heard. But after all that had gone before, eight weeks—fifty-seven days, actually, from Labor Day to Election Day on November 2— were really not so long. It seemed, in fact, an intimidatingly short time to the masterminds of the Ford campaign, as they studied their polling data and computer charts, their ofttimes uninspired candidate, and their beleaguered minority party. They knew it would take a near-perfect campaign, and some missteps by the usually sure-footed Carter, to keep Gerald Ford in the White House.

part X

**THE
FALL
CAMPAIGN**

37. Carter's Shaky Start

On Labor Day morning, Jimmy Carter, standing on the front porch of Franklin Delano Roosevelt's summer retreat at Warm Springs, Georgia, speaking from a lectern bearing the famous Yalta portrait of FDR, launched his final drive for the presidency. The selection of Roosevelt's "Little White House," where he had come often as President for treatment of legs crippled by polio, was a sharp break from Democratic Party tradition. For decades it had been customary for the Democratic standard-bearer to begin his fall campaign in Detroit's Cadillac Square, in symbolic salute to the American workingman in the automobile capital of the nation and the world. But Carter and his strategists didn't want to open in Ford's home state of Michigan; they wanted to take special note of, and capitalize on, Carter's own Southern origins, his aspiration to become the first man of the Deep South to be elected President since Zachary Taylor of Louisiana in 1848. At the same time, they needed to tie him to the progressive traditions of his party. That connection was extremely important too: for all the talk of unity and solidarity at the nominating convention in July, Carter remained an enigmatic, suspect figure—especially among Democratic liberals who traced their social-consciousness to the New Deal innovations of FDR.

The Carter image-enhancers left nothing undone to evoke the memory of Roosevelt. Two of his sons, Franklin, Jr., and James, were on the platform; Graham Jackson, a black accordionist who had been a favorite of FDR's and the subject of a famous photo showing him weeping at the news of Roosevelt's passing, played "Happy Days Are Here Again," which still means FDR to millions of Americans; patients in wheelchairs were up front to hear Carter's speech.

Emulating Roosevelt, Carter said his purpose too was to restore "strength and hope to an afflicted nation," and he cast his opponent as a latter-day Herbert Hoover, a good man stymied in inaction at a time crying out for forceful change. "This year, as in 1932, our nation is divided," Carter said. "Our people are out of work and our national leaders do not lead." Roosevelt's opponent forty-four years earlier, he said, "was an incumbent President, a decent and well-intentioned man who sincerely believed that our government could not or should not with bold action attack the terrible economic and social ills of our nation. He was leading a Republican Party which lacked the strength and vision to bring us out of those dark days."

Carter also invoked Harry Truman and John F. Kennedy, but he was careful at the same time to set himself apart from the policy of wholesale federal spending to cope with national ills that was a favorite Republican target. "We should decentralize power," he said. "When there is a choice between government responsibility and private responsibility, we should always go with private responsibility if it is adequate. . . . When there is a choice between welfare and work, let's go to work." And he took pains as well to be the different, the unbought candidate: "As a political candidate, I owe the special interests nothing. I owe the people everything."

Carter's nationally televised speech began a sixteen-hour day on the campaign trail that took him to a stock-car championship in Darlington, South Carolina, a rally in Norfolk, Virginia, two fund-raisers, and on to New York City. For his first week, stops in twenty cities in eleven states were scheduled. Meanwhile, President Ford spent the holiday, the world was told, working at the White House. A statement was issued in his name castigating the Democratic-controlled Congress for failing to enact a comprehensive tax-revision bill, and ABC News aired an interview with him at the White House in which he talked about how his election in November would give him more power over Congress.

On the next day, Ford launched his Rose Garden strategy, using a bill-signing ceremony in the Rose Garden to defend an earlier veto. "Without this constitutional check and balance," he said, "the original bill [on standards in day-care centers] might now be law and making day-care services more costly to the taxpayer and increasing the federal intrusion into family life." He had vetoed an earlier version, and had vetoed fifty-four other bills in twenty-five months in office, he said, "with one concern in mind—to protect the American people from unrealistic responses to their very real needs, to see that the federal government does not merely serve the people but serve the people well." It was better than any campaign speech, what with the White House as a backdrop for the whirring television cameras. And later in the day he suddenly showed up in the press-briefing room of the West Wing to read before the television cameras a statement denouncing the government of Vietnam—which the day before had released the names of twelve dead American airmen, previously listed as Missing in Action—as "callous and cruel." He demanded an immediate account of all American military men listed as missing in Southeast Asia. Here was the President of the United States on the job, not gallivanting around the country like Jimmy Carter. And here, his campaign plotters well knew, was the President speaking from the most advantageous forum in the land, and saving precious campaign funds, to boot.

The Rose Garden and the White House were not, unfortunately for Ford, politically snag proof. Incumbency had its drawbacks, foremost of which was that it carried a huge bureaucracy for whose conduct the President was ultimately responsible. A week earlier it had come to light that Clarence Kelley, director of the FBI, had been the beneficiary of some $335 worth of carpentry, mainly the construction of two window valances in his apartment, done by the FBI's carpentry shop. Amid much hoopla, Attorney General Edward Levi asked for a report that he turned over to Ford, recommending that Kelley be asked to pay for the work but be retained in office. Ford accepted the recommendation, and that would have been the end of the matter except that Carter, campaigning in New York, seized on this innocuous incident almost as if it were the second coming of Watergate. He overreacted in a way that blunted his impressive start and ushered in a campaign tone that was to demean both candidates and the electoral process itself.

Carter came down on Kelley like a cat on an unwary mouse, and before the episode was over, he and Ford seemed to try to outdo each other in tastelessness. It started with Carter telling an audience at Brooklyn College that law-enforcement officials should set an example in fighting crime, and that "the director of the FBI ought to be purer than Caesar's wife." He didn't blame the Republicans for all the increased crime, "but there's been a great contribution to the crime rate in this country because of Watergate, because of the CIA revelations, and because of the disgraceful actions in the FBI."

Jim Wooten of *The New York Times*, acting as pool reporter at a smaller meeting between Carter and some local black political leaders, asked Carter as they walked through a corridor whether, if he were President, he would have fired Kelley. "Knowing what I know now, yes, I would have fired him," Carter replied. But when Wooten asked whether, if he did become President, he would then fire Kelley, Carter said, "I will cross that bridge when I come to it." Wooten that day wrote an article calling Carter's second answer an "apparent contradiction," which provoked vigorous objections from Jody Powell, who said he saw no inconsistency in the two remarks.

At any rate, Carter warmed to the subject as the day progressed. In North Philadelphia, he observed that Kelley had been "caught with government employees using my and your tax money decorating his apartment. So President Ford had the Attorney General investigate it, and the Attorney General said he did it and President Ford said, 'Well, let's let him stay where he is.' " It was just a short hop to Watergate, which of course Carter had steadfastly insisted he would not inject into the campaign because the American people had heard enough about it. "When people throughout the country, particularly young people, see Richard Nixon cheating, lying, and leaving the highest office in disgrace, when they see the previous Attorney General violating the law and admitting it," Carter said, warming to his subject, "when you see the head of the FBI break a little law and stay there, it gives everybody the sense that crime must be okay. If the big shots in Washington can get away with it, well, so can I."

Now it was Ford's turn to overreact. The next day he called reporters to the south lawn of the White House and accused Carter of flip-flopping. Not only that; Ford shamelessly invoked Kelley's late wife, who had died ten months earlier of cancer, as evidence that Carter was guilty of "a lack of compassion" toward Kelley. "I hope that Governor Carter understood," Ford said with all the unctuousness he could muster, "that Mrs. Kelley at that time [when the valances were installed and other gifts given] was suffering terminal cancer and that was a very sad and difficult time for the director of the FBI."

Carter by now was thoroughly irritated by the entire matter; by the press coverage of his own remarks, which he did not consider flip-flopping at all, and by the ability of the White House to take his remarks and breathe new life into what was essentially an extraneous issue. He and Powell discussed the whole business between themselves. "He was kind of bitching and I was kind of bitching, and we were consoling each other," Powell said later, "and I said, 'Well, he's [Kelley] about to get married again. He's obviously not in too bad shape over it all.' " To Powell's surprise and dismay, Carter told reporters: "Obviously I sympathize with anybody whose wife is dying of cancer, but that doesn't have anything to do with it," and besides, Ford had brought up the matter "after Director Kelley announced that he was remarrying." And with that, the Kelley affair hit rock bottom.

Carter's extraordinary churlishness, and Ford's sickening display of the maudlin, were not encouraging signs. Beyond that, the whole episode also obscured what potentially was a much more potent issue to be posed against the Republican ticket: a report of illegal campaign contributions to Robert Dole. *The New York Times* reported that Claude Wild, long-time chief lobbyist for the Gulf Oil Corporation and distributor of an illegal Gulf political slush fund, had told a grand jury he gave $5000 to Dole's administrative assistant, William Kats, in 1973 for Dole's re-election campaign of 1974. Kats said he had no recollection of the gift. Wild subsequently told reporters he had given $2000 in cash directly to Dole in 1970 for other

Republican senatorial candidates. But when Dole denied receiving it, Wild contended he had been "in error" and had done "a serious disservice" to Dole, and he declined comment on the alleged $5000 payment. On television panel shows and in interviews, Dole stonewalled and tried to turn the discussion to Carter's admittedly legal use of a $41,702 investment tax credit in his peanut business in 1975. Dole said he favored the credit as a way to stimulate the economy and didn't quarrel with Carter's use of it, but wondered aloud about a man making "a nice little saving" for himself while advocating tax reform. Bob Dole repeatedly rebelled against the claim that he was a hatchet man. He was right; sometimes he only wielded a penknife.

Carter's gross mishandling of the Kelley incident was only one indication of a bad start. On the same day that he took out after Kelley, he ran head-on into the abortion issue, which he had been finessing with considerable success. A neighborhood meeting in North Philadelphia, intended to demonstrate that Carter would continue his "intimate personal relationship" with the voters, had to be moved from a Catholic to a nearby Lutheran church when the Catholics insisted that the agenda include abortion. Carter's position—he personally opposed abortion and would do all he could as President to restrict its use, but would not back a constitutional amendment barring it—already had him in trouble with the Catholic hierarchy. A group of Catholic bishops had labeled his stand "disappointing," and on this particular issue, his "fuzziness" was causing him grief on both sides—from the anti-abortionists and from women's rights groups. On a walking tour to the Lutheran church, he repeatedly told women along the way he would not back an anti-abortion amendment, "even in an election year." A small group of picketeers, including two nuns, confronted him with a small white coffin: it was the kind of demonstration that would dog him through most of the campaign. And at a hotel in Scranton that night, several hundred more demonstrators waved anti-abortion signs and chanted, "Life! Life! Life!" as television cameras and microphones recorded the scene.

It had been a carefully planned day in which Carter was supposed to demonstrate his concern about housing, joblessness and street crime by walking and talking in urban slums and poor neighborhoods. Now it had been clouded by the media's attention to the abortion flare-up and the Kelley incident. Carter's staff was irritated; the press cared only for the sensational, contentious issue. But the staff had planned the whole day specifically to manipulate the media's coverage to Carter's advantage; his own ineptness in the Kelley matter, and that of his staff in the church-switch snafu, had sabotaged their own designs to use the media mechanism to their advantage.

Press critics never tire of accusing television and newspapers of being distracted from substantive discussion of issues, from the "real" story, by trivial and frivolous incidents. But the fact was, the campaign more times than not was a pitched battle between the candidates' staff aides, laboring to stage events for their own ends, and the media, trying to cut through the propaganda to record the reality. In this instance, Carter's attack on Kelley may have been irrelevant, but it happened, and it told the public something about the candidate that was at least as revealing as a carefully programed walk through a North Philadelphia neighborhood. The candidates played hardball, and so did most of the accompanying press; that was what running for President was about. The agenda was always in the hands of the candidates, not the press; if the reporting on the campaign seemed frivolous or irrelevant in comparison to the great problems facing the country, it was usually because the candidates were frivolous or irrelevant in what they said.

Reporting, for all the advancement and sophistication in the business, remains first of all the telling of what happens, of what is said and done. Many reporters, their skepticism about politicians strained over the years and stretched to cynicism, mistakenly pay lip service to the old axiom that the only way to look at a politician is down. That is a serious shortcoming. The way to look at a politician is searchingly—to hold him to reasonable standards, but without assuming from the start that he is incapable of maintaining them. If he is incapable, or if he has momentary lapses, that becomes evident soon enough.

Some candidates, like Carter, invited the application of higher standards to their conduct by proclaiming higher standards for themselves. A man was asking for closer scrutiny if he said he would never lie to the voters or even mislead them, if he said he didn't want their support if they ever caught him lying or misleading; the very pledge was a self-imposed yardstick of integrity. When reporters seemed to hound Carter or nit-pick about the self-serving exaggerations that are characteristic to most politicians, they were holding him to his own measure. I'm different, he was telling the American electorate. I'm *really* honest, not like all the others. Okay, the media was saying back to him, we're listening.

Carter and some of his aides complained on occasion that the same yardsticks were not being applied to Ford, and in a sense they were right. The presidency, and the press' much more limited access to the President, did give Ford a free ride at times. Just because Ford never said he'd never lie was no justification for not scrutinizing his campaign statements and deeds. Yet a human element entered into the equation: Carter's righteous boast of purity was taken as a challenge by men and women whose professional work was to record what politicians did and said and, in the journalism of the 1970s, to record whether they spoke the truth. Perhaps unintentionally, Carter had thrown down the gauntlet. His was a different, attention-catching pledge, and it doubtless helped to set him off from the pack. But the price he paid was a particularly tenacious press corps that had been lied to by experts for years and that tried its damnedest, day after day, not to get burned.

In a sense, Richard Nixon's lies made life more difficult for Jimmy Carter, precisely because he promised never, never to lie. And the voters, too, their confidence in all politicians diminished by their experience with Nixon, were particularly wary. Ironically Jimmy Carter had advanced to his place as the presidential nominee of the Democratic Party in part at least because Americans hungered for somebody new, and honest, in government. Yet voters had trouble believing that anybody could be as honest as Carter insisted he was, and they reserved judgment on him. In a way, the longer Jimmy Carter proclaimed his differentness and his integrity, the longer the doubts clung.

Luck in scheduling during that first week enabled Carter to recover somewhat from his troublesome beginning with the Catholics and the anti-abortionists. Jim King brought him the next day to Pittsburgh's Polish Hill, where a friendly priest, Father John Jendzura of the Immaculate Heart of Mary Catholic Church, turned out the kids from his school in force, kissed Carter on both cheeks, and produced the "media event" the Carter campaign needed. Carter donned a red-and-white T-shirt that said "Polish Hill" and enjoyed the kind of close-in contact in the ethnic, Catholic neighborhood that he had sought. Dave Broder wrote in *The Washington Post* that "next to having Carter carried on the shoulders of the Notre Dame football team into St. Peter's for a private audience with the Pope, it was the best the campaign could do." The objective of this first week's trip—to New York, Philadelphia, Pittsburgh, Cleveland, and the traditional torchlight parade in Chicago—was obviously to shore up Carter's strength among relatively conservative blue-collar ethnic—and heavily Catholic—voters, and it seemed at least partially successful. Meanwhile Ford did his best to make trouble. He told a group of prominent Catholic bishops at the White House that he would support a constitutional amendment permitting regulation of abortion by the states, and while this was not all the bishops wanted, they expressed their preference for his position over Carter's.

If the church hierarchy and the anti-abortionists were cool to Carter, one group distinctly was not: the big-city Democratic pols, who now scampered to seize a share of the limelight he basked in. "In at least two of every three stops," Jack Germond wrote, "they attach themselves to him like leeches, trying to use his celebrity to strengthen their own positions." This was a happenstance that most politicians welcomed, but it posed a particular problem for Carter, the antiestablishment politician. He had to tap the resources of the majority party to his own ends, but he did not seem to be at all comfortable around the old pols, nor they with him.

An exception was Mayor Daley, the epitome of all that Carter professed to abhor in bossism politics. Daley had delivered for him, though, on the important last primary day in June and promised to deliver for him in November, and it was hard, going to Chicago, not to believe he could do it. A visiting Democratic candidate could always count on a Daley welcome that rivaled the days of the pharaohs. Even if the arrival occurred in the crush of the city's horrendous rush-hour traffic, Daley managed in minutes to empty the expressways from O'Hare Airport all the way to downtown Chicago, making them look like *On the Beach* after the nuclear holocaust. The telltale presence of Chicago police at every single intersection for miles stamped the miracle as a Daley operation. This year's torchlight parade did not disturb the tradition, either. Fireworks, block after block of waving ward-organization banners and thousands upon thousands of the Cook County faithful attested to their love of Hizzoner, and the jobs he gave them.

It was, as Dave Broder wrote in *The Washington Post,* a dazzling and even unsettling evening. With tongue in cheek, Broder observed that Carter later, in speaking about preventive health care to a bunch of precinct captains, began "for no apparent reason" to call out the names of childhood diseases, observing that his doctors in Georgia had "tried to immunize me against those diseases, and quite often succeeded." Carter, Broder suggested, was probably suffering from overexposure to the Daley treatment. A measure of the growing paranoia about Carter in Washington was the fact that Broder's humorous story launched a whispering campaign among otherwise sane though liberal Democrats that Carter might be snapping under the strain. Checks were made into his medical history for any evidence of psychiatric trouble or treatment, and although none was found, the rumors persisted well into the fall. Such was the potency of a night's heavy exposure to Daleyism.

Carter returned to Plains after that first week confident that he had blunted the picture of him painted at the Republican convention as a typical Democratic free-spender, and a liberal in conservative trappings. He had eschewed the black audiences that risked unsettling blue-collar white voters, and focused instead on middle-class, white, big-city America. The anti-abortionists were pesky, but the polls suggested that their noise exceeded their political influence. If he had made a mistake, Carter acknowledged to reporters, it was in raising and holding on to the business about Clarence Kelley. "It may have been better had I not got involved in [it] at all," he confessed. The whole go-around "took up about a day and a half of news-media attention and kind of interrupted our week's main themes" —his appreciation of blue-collar concerns.

All this time, Gerald Ford remained in the White House. "It suits me fine for him to stay in the White House," Carter said, but the strategy already was getting under his skin. "President Ford can walk out in the Rose Garden and make a minute-and-a-half statement and that's his only confrontation with the American people on the evening news," he lamented. "I make a hundred different statements a day."

There could be no quarreling with Carter on that score, and the Ford camp didn't bother. The Rose Garden strategy was working completely according to plan. The sentiment had now settled in among the Ford strategists, in fact, that not having the first debate until September 23 could contribute mightily to their chances, by persuading the public to suspend judgment on the two candidates at least until after the first debate. Partly for this reason, it was decided that Ford's television commercials would not be aired until a few days after the first debate, thus saving money and telescoping their effect into a shorter period closer to Election Day.

Actually, the rather late start for the commercials was dictated as much by Bailey's and Deardourff's inability to get them ready earlier. They decided that most of the television ads prepared by their predecessors would not do because, among other reasons, they focused too much on the incumbency and not enough on Ford the man. Still, there was a heavy dose of rationalization in the late start. "We were trying to convince ourselves," Doug Bailey said later, "that this not only was necessary but was the right thing to do. And it became clearer and clearer that it would have been a waste of money to put on much advertising before the first debate."

Not until September 15 did Ford venture out into the country, and then only to the politically safe confines of his alma mater, the University of Michigan. In a scene straight out of a college movie musical of the 1930s, Jerry and Betty Ford paraded into Crisler Arena to the cheers of fourteen thousand extras and walked onto a stage draped with a huge M, as the Michigan Fight Song rolled over the happy throng of middle-class whites. Ford served up promises of lower federal home-mortgage loans and new tax breaks for parents sending their children to parochial schools—direct pitches to middle-income and Catholic voters. Then he went directly at Carter on the issue of credibility. "It is not enough for anyone to say, 'Trust me,' " Ford said. "Trust must be earned. Trust is not having to guess what a candidate means. Trust is leveling with the people before the election about what you're going to do after the election. Trust is not being all things to all people, but being the same thing to all people. Trust is not cleverly shading words so that each separate audience can hear what it wants to hear, but saying plainly and simply what you mean, and meaning what you say."

The night was not without its disturbances. A group of hecklers booed and catcalled, and once, while Ford was in mid-sentence, a cherry bomb exploded, causing him to flinch and pause for a second as the audience gasped. But he recovered and resumed his speech. As he did, however, demonstrators toted a banner through the arena saying "Don't Pardon Ford for Letting Nixon Off." Such unpleasantries were never visited upon Ford in the Rose Garden, nor were they bait for the television cameras there. It was with a sense of security, no doubt, that the President returned to the more predictable confines of the White House, there to await and prepare for the first televised debate.

Ford's Rose Garden strategy posed a vexing problem for the press corps. It was, after all, an exact replay of the dodge used to such practical, self-serving effect by Nixon four years earlier. Carter, like McGovern in 1972, protested bitterly and long that the media was playing directly into the incumbent's hands; permitting themselves to be spoon-fed daily at the White House from a menu of ersatz news events that was passed on undigested to the public on the nightly television news. The press corps was thus reduced for all practical purposes to covering a one-candidate campaign, and it was all but inevitable that it magnified unimportant disputes within the open and accessible Carter campaign, just as it had done to McGovern in 1972.

The media, at the same time, could not ignore Ford's antics in the White House, no matter how trivial or trumped-up. The trick was to make certain that the staged Rose Garden events were identified *as such,* in print or on television. Most reporters covering the White House came to do just that, usually referring to "the Ford campaign at the White House," or some variation. Still, on television, the important thing for the President, portraying himself as an on-the-job incumbent, was simply to be seen with the White House as a backdrop, and there was not much the visual-oriented medium could do to minimize that effect. Mike Duval, the Nixonite holdover who had the look, manner, and style of a Haldeman intern, perhaps inadvertently laid it out when he said: "We didn't mind the network correspondents saying he was using the White House. People aren't going to remember the voice-over; they're going to remember the visual."

One "visual" that was destined to be long-remembered did not help the President. It occurred in Binghamton, New York, the day after Ford's visit to Ann Arbor, when Vice President Rockefeller, trying to help Dole get his disorganized campaign on track, encountered a group of hecklers. Dole had first tried to quell the protesters with wit and then had turned angry: "I hope you're on his [Carter's] side," he snapped. "We don't want you on our side. If you'll just shut up and be quiet, we'll go on with the rally." Rockefeller broke in, exchanged jibes with the hecklers, and finally extended the middle finger of his right hand to them in the ultimate gesture of contempt—as cameras snapped the put-down for posterity. (The photo of the broadly grinning Vice President thus occupied, with a smiling Dole in the background, made the front page of *The Washington Star* and an inside page of *The Washington Post* the next day, but neither the picture nor any reference to the gesture appeared in *The New York Times*. Instead, the *Times* ran a page-one photo of Dole and Rockefeller standing unsmiling before microphones at party headquarters in Manhattan the same day. This is known as press responsibility.)

Rockefeller's gesture was in a sense a fine commentary on the attitude in both camps toward the voters' intelligence and sensitivities in this early phase of the fall campaign. The exchange between Carter and Ford over Clarence Kelley's perquisites and his late wife; Dole's rather cavalier treatment of serious allegations against him concerning campaign money; Ford's blatant use of the White House as a television prop—all these were ways of giving the finger to the American electorate. Perhaps they were only unfortunate lapses in an otherwise conscientious effort to conduct a thoughtful dialogue on the issues, and perhaps the media were too ready and willing to seize on them. But again, the press did not introduce these tasteless elements into the campaign; the candidates did. What if the press had "saved" Ford and Carter from their own cheap remarks about the late and the future Mrs. Kelleys and not reported them? One can only imagine the outcry about censorship when the public eventually learned of them, as was inevitable in an open society. And did *The New York Times* better serve the sensibilities of the public interest by ignoring in both text and photography the obscene gesture made by the Vice President of the United States in a public appearance? Similar questions about the proper role of the press continued to be raised throughout the presidential campaign, but only because the candidates by their own words or actions introduced themes and incidents that the media could not responsibly ignore.

The more probing question would have been whether it was necessary for the press to pursue some of these matters until the very last embers died, to the neglect of more substantive issues, rather than reporting them fully in a day or two and then being done with them. It must be remembered, however, that a present-day presidential campaign is a moveable feast as long as a candidate is touring the country; in each city or town there is a fresh batch of reporters and television teams waiting a turn to ask questions that may be old to the traveling press corps and the candidate, but new to *them.* There is a dynamic of repetition built into campaigning in a country that gets its information not just from NBC, CBS, ABC, *The New York Times,* and *Newsweek* but also from the *Boston Globe,* the *Cleveland Plain Dealer,* KMOX in St. Louis, and KLZ-TV in Denver. And if a candidate changes his position or moves from it, it is inevitable that the story will be kept alive for another news cycle or two. That is the price candidates must pay in a decentralized news-gathering and news-distributing system, often overlooked because of the prominence of the major national networks, newspapers, and newsmagazines.

Many stories that are ultimately circulated nationwide have their genesis in questions posed by little-known local reporters, sometimes on a subject that has been examined to a fare-thee-well by the press corps accompanying the candidate. A candidate on the stump is not unlike a traveling salesman going door-to-door, trying to sell his established line but never knowing, when the next door is opened, whether he will make a sale or get a glass of cold water in his face. That is why candidates and their campaign managers work hard to curb the spontaneous and the unexpected and to channel exposure to public and press into controlled, predictable appearances. Nixon and his communications henchmen were ruthlessly effective at the exercise, until events—largely revealed by the press—broke through the barriers. Carter, to his credit, like McGovern in 1972, adopted a more open approach and in some ways suffered for his openness—while Ford, as Nixon in 1972, operated from the sanctuary of the White House.

It was unrealistic, however, to expect that experienced reporters, knowing how all politicians—Jimmy Carter certainly not excluded—tried to play the media to their own best advantage, would not become suspicious and tenacious, sometimes to excess. The best reporters, though, never thought of themselves as being in anybody's pocket, certainly not the candidate's, not even their own employer's—as anyone can attest who has ever been in a campaign press room at deadline time and heard reporters arguing vehemently with their editors on the lead or play of their stories. The problem was, of course, that on presidential campaigns, as in coverage of a local alderman's race, there are excellent, good, mediocre, and poor reporters; most deplorably, there are stupid or shameless reporters who are not restrained even by the direct denigration of their colleagues from asking the most asinine and self-serving questions, thereby embarrassing all others who ply the reporters' trade. Some few in the press seem to think that candidates should suffer fools gladly if the fools have press cards—just as some officeseekers think the press should do likewise, as long as the candidate possesses a public forum. The result is a highly charged adversary relationship—oftentimes tempered by personal cordiality, good will, and good sense on both sides, but always there. Since a political candidate is in the business of putting his best foot forward to get elected, and the press is in the business of holding that foot to the fire, the adversary relationship is inevitable.

For Carter, the relationship was tested daily. On the day Rockefeller was demonstrating his digital dexterity in Binghamton, the Georgian granted an interview to some Associated Press reporters and editors in Washington that illustrated the risk of being available. Carter was asked about his oft-repeated but never specific pledge that if elected he would bring about a comprehensive reform of the nation's income-tax burden. He said, in part, that he would seek "to shift a substantial increase toward those who have the higher incomes and reduce the income [tax] on the lower-income and middle-income taxpayers."

Q: "What do you mean when you say 'shift the burden'?"

A: "That means people who have a higher income would pay more taxes at a certain level."

Q: "In dollar figures, what are you thinking of as higher?"

A: "I don't know. I would take the mean or median level of income, and anything above that would be higher and anything below that would be lower."

Q: "The median family income today is somewhere around twelve thousand dollars. Somebody earning fifteen thousand dollars a year is not what people commonly think of as rich—"

A: "I understand. I can't answer that question because I haven't gone into it. I don't know how to write the tax code in specific terms. It is just not possible to do that on a campaign trail. But I am committed to do it, and I have already talked to congressional leaders in the House and the Senate about the need and have found an agreement among them. As far as telling you specifically what the tax code would be, there is no way I can do that."

Among the reporters who took part in the questioning was Walter Mears, a veteran political writer for the Associated Press who was very familiar with Carter's proposal for sweeping tax reform, and with Carter's as-frequently stated disinclination to be pinned down on specifics about it. The latest answers, Mears said afterward, came across to him not as any change in policy by Carter but simply as another exercise in his practiced penchant for dodging specifics that could get him into trouble. "There was never any question in my mind," Mears said, "that Carter was doing what he always did when anybody tried to pin him down. He wanted to avoid saying anything." Consequently Mears in his story written Friday (for an agreed-upon Sunday release) mentioned the answers on tax reform only secondarily and focused on another aspect of the interview. Mears and Jody Powell had agreed beforehand, however, that Carter could correct any errors in the transcript in which he clearly misspoke himself. When nothing was heard from the Carter campaign by Friday night, the pertinent excerpts from the transcript were transmitted on the AP wire.

It so happened that in the transcript, prepared by a private firm, the words "and middle-income" were dropped from Carter's first answer, leaving the clear impression that only lower-income taxpayers would get relief under his plan and, therefore, the implication that middle-income taxpayers would pay more. The transcript was corrected the next afternoon, but among the places to which the AP ticker transmitted the original transcript was 1600 Pennsylvania Avenue—the semipermanent address of the Ford campaign. By noon the next day, Saturday, the Ford operation had quickly revved up a broadside against Carter. Dole, after a meeting with the President, strode out to the front lawn and, brandishing the wire copy, told reporters: "I'm astounded to read here that he's [Carter] going to raise taxes for half the American families—anyone above the median income. . . . I'm talking about families making between twelve thousand and fourteen thousand dollars. . . . Their taxes would go up, and I guess he intends for the other taxes to go down. Anybody who is below that median income would be fearful to get above it, and anybody above it, according to Mr. Carter, would have their taxes increased. I hope that's not what he calls tax reform."

It should be noted that Dole's criticism did not make reference at all to Carter's answer in which the words "and middle-income" were inadvertently dropped from the transcript, but rather focused on his response using the term "median level of income"—which was correctly quoted and never disputed.

In short order, the White House had mobilized a platoon of soldiers to take off after Carter. Ron Nessen called Carter's answers a "major blunder" comparable to George McGovern's call for $1000 for everybody. Others who weighed in included Secretary of the Treasury William Simon and James Lynn, the OMB director. "Governor Carter has finally become specific," Simon said. "In the first major announcement of his tax plan, he calls for increased taxes on all families earning more than fourteen thousand dollars a year. I think that is absolutely incredible." Lynn agreed.

Meanwhile Stu Eizenstat had been trying to reach Walter Mears. Eizenstat had spotted the omission in the original transcript, apparently before hearing about Dole's attack, and Mears, after listening to a tape of the interview again, had a correction sent. Mears then called Bill Greener, the Ford campaign's press spokesman, who said the administration statements would stand, since the correction did not touch on the argument Dole, Simon, and Lynn were raising. Now Mears wrote a new lead on the story, citing the AP's inadvertent omission but noting that Dole and other critics stood by their attacks on Carter. In this instance it was the alertness of political operatives at the White House, not the press, which at first downplayed the tax-reform answer, that forged the issue.

Carter plainly was disturbed over the whole incident. Powell described the Republican attacks as "typical political distortion and misrepresentation." Using a bulky copy of the U.S. income-tax code as a prop, Carter the next day waved it with difficulty at an audience in Kansas City and asked: "When you start to prepare your returns, how many of you have a battery of lawyers or CPA's to make sure that you get all of the advantages of the windfalls that have been put in these regulations? . . . I would never increase taxes on the working people of our country in the lower- and middle–income groups, but we will shift the burden of taxes to where the Republicans have always protected—onto the rich, the big corporations, and the special-interest groups." And later, at the airport in St. Louis, he told reporters the AP story was "very accurate" but the interpretation placed on it by the Republicans "completely distorted. . . . I'm not going to add a tax burden onto working families and the middle-income categories—fifteen thousand-dollar income. What I'm going to do is try to eliminate the loopholes and privileges that have been put in the tax code like the income-tax shelters for large corporations. . . . The average working family that doesn't benefit now from the special loopholes will certainly not have their income taxes increased under my administration."

The Republicans, however, were confident they had a winning issue. Dole, campaigning in Panama City and Orlando, Florida, exulted: Carter "is on the hook now and he's trying to wiggle off." He warned that "a vote for Carter is a vote to raise taxes," and insisted that Carter had not simply misspoken: "If he doesn't know after three years of campaigning what the median income of a family in America is, I suggest he ought to get out of the race."

Yet the Carter strategists thought they might be able to turn the issue to Carter's advantage. Powell said the Kansas City speech was "the beginning of an effort to make them sorry they ever brought the subject up." The Democratic Party was proud, after all, of its self-assigned label as the party of the people, meaning the working people. The issue opened the whole matter of special treatment and tax loopholes on which the Republicans were vulnerable. And the timing was propitious, because Carter was heading East to take part early the next morning in a campaign tradition that would of itself evoke the memory of the workingman's hero, Harry Truman. The Democratic National Committee, in the Truman tradition, was staging a gala whistlestop train ride from New York's Pennsylvania Station, under the Hudson River and across New Jersey, Pennsylvania, Ohio, Indiana, and Illinois into Chicago. Carter would be the featured passenger on the first day, as far as Pittsburgh, and Mondale would take over for the second day, into Chicago. It was a natural means for Carter to reinforce his posture as a loyal Democrat, concerned about gut Democratic issues that blue-collar, lower- and middle-income voters cared about.

That night, as the Carter entourage pulled into the Statler-Hilton, just across Seventh Avenue from Penn Station, Powell opened an envelope that had been left at the desk for him by *Playboy* magazine. It contained something that instantly drove all else from his mind and confronted him with another, totally unexpected side of his candidate; something that was to focus the attention of blue-collar America, and of white-collar and white and black and Catholic and Protestant America as well, on the haunting question: what kind of bird was this Jimmy Carter?

38. Playboy, *and the First Debate*

The last time Jody Powell had talked to Robert Scheer, a free-lance writer completing an interview with Jimmy Carter for *Playboy* magazine, had been about a week after the Democratic National Convention, in Plains. Late on the afternoon of July 21 Scheer had phoned Powell and, as Scheer remembered it, told him: "I just had a dynamite interview. Do you want to listen to it?"

Powell declined the offer. "I said, 'No, when we get the whole thing put together, we'll do it then.' " And that was the last he heard from or about Scheer and his *Playboy* interview until the third Saturday in September. "I didn't keep track over the summer of the publication date," Powell recalled, "and all of a sudden I get a call saying the thing is out." Barry Golson, the *Playboy* editor who had accompanied Scheer on that last interview at Carter's home, phoned to say he and Scheer were going to be on the "Today" show on Monday morning to talk about it.

That was not Powell's understanding of the way the matter was supposed to be handled. Powell said later Scheer and Golson had agreed to show him the interview—culled from five hours of questions and answers—*before* it went to press, and they never had. Nor would Golson read it to him now over the phone. "I said, 'You promised to get this to me,' " Powell recalled. "And he said, 'Well, we never could work out a time to get with you.' I said, 'What's to get with me? All you do is put the thing in the mail.' And he said, 'No, we didn't want to do it that way.' " (A later story that the interview had been sent, and was sitting unscanned for weeks on Powell's desk, was not true, both Powell and Scheer agreed.)

Scheer acknowledged later that he had told Powell he would let him look at the transcript; he insisted he had tried repeatedly to reach the press secretary and left numerous telephone messages. But he was not about to send him the transcript because that procedure had proved to be disastrous in a previous *Playboy* interview with Jerry Brown. "I got burned by Brown. He sat down and tried to rewrite the questions and answers." Even if he *had* shown the material to Powell, Scheer said, he never would have permitted editing. He had learned his lesson. And so, because Powell was such a hard man to reach, constantly on the move in the campaign, nothing could be done.

Rex Granum, a young deputy to Powell who had sat in on Carter's final interview with Scheer and Golson and had helped to arrange most of the several sessions Scheer had had with the candidate, insisted that Scheer knew he could always reach Powell through him, and never once tried. "Every other time Scheer wanted to get hold of Jody, he'd track me down and I'd go get him," Granum said. "There was never any question in my mind that we would have a shot at looking at the transcript. We got an absolute promise from Scheer that we were going to look at it before it went into galleys."

But all that was wheel-spinning now. With the appearance on the "Today" show set—"Golson and Scheer told me the reason they were going on was they wanted to make sure it wasn't oversensationalized," Powell recalled, grinning—there wasn't anything anybody could do anyway. Powell phoned Scheer at his home in Brooklyn and arranged to have a copy of the interview sent to him in time for his arrival at New York's Statler-Hilton on Sunday. As soon as he read it, Powell said later in a marvel of understatement, "I figured we were going to catch some shit." He talked to Greg Schneiders about it that night and alerted Carter to watch the "Today" show the next morning.

What went out to the millions of early-morning television buffs, and shortly thereafter to the Associated Press, were the most arresting and eyebrow-raising highlights of a long and probing interview. As printed in the magazine, it was, for all the later fanfare, an interview touching mostly on questions that had been raised repeatedly by other interviewers, with one notable exception: an examination of the relationship between Carter's religious beliefs and his responsibilities as a public official. It had all begun, Scheer explained later, with a speech Carter had given in San Francisco in which he had said that according to the precepts of his church homosexuality was a sin. Scheer pursued the question of whether Carter as President would, in appointing judges, be influenced by their attitude toward perpetrators of victimless crime, including drug use, adultery, sodomy, and homosexuality. Carter replied:

"Committing adultery, according to the Bible which I believe in, is a sin. For us to hate one another, for us to have sexual intercourse outside marriage, for us to engage in homosexual activities, for us to steal, for us to lie, all these are sins. But Jesus teaches us not to judge other people. We don't assume the role of judge and say to another human being, 'You're condemned because you commit sins.' All Christians, all of us, acknowledge that we are sinful and the judgment comes from God, not from another human being.

"As Governor of Georgia, I tried to shift the emphasis of law enforcement away from victimless crimes. We lessened the penalties on the use of marijuana. We removed alcoholism as a crime, and so forth. Victimless crimes, in my opinion, should have a very low priority in terms of enforcing the laws on the books. But as to appointing judges, that would not be the basis on which I'd appoint them. I would choose people who were competent, whose judgment and integrity were sound. I think it would be inappropriate to ask them how they were going to rule on a particular question before I appointed them."

Well, he was asked, should those laws on the books governing personal behavior be enforced? Carter noted that nearly every state had such laws, but that police often decided they were not worth enforcing "to the extent of disturbing consenting adults or breaking into a person's private home." Still, he said, he didn't mind that the laws stay on the books as a standard, if individual states wanted to keep them. But he acknowledged that "you can't legislate morality."

So far, so good. Nothing very controversial in that. Now his observation that homosexuality was a sin was raised: How would he deal with it in a political context? "The issue of homosexuality always makes me nervous," he said. "It's obviously one of the major issues in San Francisco. I don't have any, you know, personal knowledge about homosexuality, and I guess being a Baptist, that would contribute to a sense of being uneasy. . . . It's political, it's moral, and it's strange territory for me. At home, in Plains, we've had homosexuals in our community, our church. There's never been any sort of discrimination; some embarrassment, but no animosity, no harassment. But to inject it into a public discussion on politics and how it conflicts with morality is a new experience for me. I've thought about it a lot, but I don't see how to handle it differently from the way I look on other sexual acts outside marriage."

Carter seemed to be having trouble getting through. He noted that Harry Truman was a Baptist. "The main thing is that we don't think we're better than anyone else. We are taught not to judge other people. But as to some of the behavior you've mentioned, I can't change the teachings of Christ. . . . I believe in them, and a lot of people in this country do as well."

Then, he was asked, as President, in appointing justices to the Supreme Court— Carter broke in, impatient now with the line of questions. "I think we've pursued this conversation long enough. If you have another question . . . Look, I'll try to express my views. It's not a matter of condemnation, it's not a matter of persecution. I've been a governor for four years. Anybody can come and look at my record. I didn't run around breaking down people's doors to see if they were fornicating. This is something that's ridiculous."

This interview, as the others, went on to other matters. Mostly they were between Carter and Scheer, the Berkeley-educated, self-styled radical, with no one else present. Scheer said later that Carter seemed to enjoy being engaged on subjects a bit more challenging and philosophical than the routine inquiries about political tactics and strategies that were a customary fare from most reporters. Powell, too, thought the interview was going well, and that was one reason he permitted Scheer to see Carter so many times. "The thing kind of perked along," the press secretary said later, "and it seemed to me it was a pretty damn good interview, and that Scheer was a good interviewer, which I still think. Jimmy was being pushed in some areas that probably did him good to be pushed in. It seemed to me to be shaping up into the kind of long look at this guy that really hadn't been done. I thought it would probably be good to have that sort of interview available and on the record. My thoughts as we got into it were, it's too bad it's not being done for some other magazine than *Playboy*, that it's too good for *Playboy*, frankly, that it deserved a magazine of a little better literary reputation." But there was no concern, then or later, that it might be a bad idea for a man of Carter's proclaimed religiosity to appear at all in a glorified girlie magazine like *Playboy*. Carter himself, asked about it by Scheer, replied: "I don't object to that at all. I don't believe I'll be criticized." After all, Jerry Brown had undergone the same routine and the heavily favorable public reaction to his interview in *Playboy* was considered in retrospect one of the prime catalysts for his own candidacy.

For all of Carter's patient replies, Scheer and Golson decided that *Playboy* still had not captured the essence of his views on the relationship between the religious tenets that governed his personal life, and how he saw his role as a political man called upon to make political as opposed to moral judgments. They met with Powell and said so. "We said Carter wasn't coming across on the subject," Scheer recalled, "and we needed to have more time with him." Powell agreed, and told them after the convention to come down to Plains. Carter was being inundated with interview requests but Powell would squeeze them in.

The final question of the final interview, according to Scheer, was again in the sticky area of religion and politics. Carter's position was that abortion was "wrong" and that he would do all he could as President to minimize the need for it—within the framework of the Supreme Court decision that held it was within the prerogative of a woman and her doctor to terminate a pregnancy in the first three months. It was the sort of seeming ambivalence that made him so difficult to understand; that, and his overt, almost dominating religiosity. And so, as the interview was ending and Scheer and Golson said good-by and moved toward the door, Carter was asked: "Do you feel you've reassured people with this interview, people who are uneasy about your religious belief, who wonder if you're going to make a rigid, unbending President?"

Carter, speaking softly, made one final attempt to get through to these two men who were not Southern Baptists. As he spoke, Scheer held up his microphone and signaled to Carter that the tape was still running, and Carter nodded; he seemed to the interviewers to understand.

". . . One thing the Baptists believe in is complete autonomy. I don't accept any domination of my life by the Baptist Church, none. Every Baptist church is individual and autonomous. . . . The reason the Baptist Church was formed in this country was because of our belief in absolute and total separation of church and state. . . . What Christ taught about most was pride; that one person should never think he was any better than anybody else. One of the most vivid stories Christ told in one of his parables was about two people who went into a church. One was an official of the church, a Pharisee, and he said, 'Lord, I thank you that I'm not like all those other people. I keep all your commandments, I give a tenth of everything I own. I'm here to give thanks for making me more acceptable in your sight.' The other guy was despised by the nation, and he went in, prostrated himself on the floor and said, 'Lord, have mercy on me, a sinner. I'm not worthy to lift my eyes to heaven.' Christ asked the disciples which of the two had justified his life. The answer was obviously the one who was humble. The thing that is drummed into us all the time is not to be proud, not to be better than anyone else, not to look down on people but to make ourselves acceptable in God's eyes through our own actions and recognize the simple truth that we're saved by grace. It's just a free gift through faith in Christ. This gives us a mechanism by which we can relate permanently to God. I'm not speaking for other people, but it gives me a sense of peace and equanimity and assurance."

It was standard Bible teaching, but Carter was warming to his sermon, just as he did on Sunday mornings in the basement of the Plains First Baptist Church. Now, though, his audience was a pair of hard-bitten journalists from a hip cosmopolitan magazine. He personalized the sermon a bit, perhaps the better to drive home his point:

"I try not to commit a deliberate sin. I recognize that I'm going to do it anyhow, because I'm human and I'm tempted. And Christ set some almost impossible standards for us. Christ said, 'I tell you that anyone who looks on a woman with lust has in his heart already committed adultery.' I've looked on a lot of women with lust. I've committed adultery in my heart many times. This is something that God recognizes I will do—and I have done it—and God forgives me for it. But that doesn't mean that I condemn someone who not only looks on a woman with lust but leaves his wife and shacks up with somebody out of wedlock."

If any of those present—Scheer, Golson, Granum, and Carter himself —was surprised by the bluntness of this confession, he gave no outward indication. Carter went on:

"Christ says don't consider yourself better than someone else because one guy screws a whole bunch of women while the other guy is loyal to his wife. The guy who's loyal to his wife ought not to be condescending or proud because of the relative degree of sinfulness. One thing that Paul Tillich said was that religion is a search for the truth about man's existence and his relationship with God and his fellow man, and that once you stop searching and think you've got it made—at that point, you lose your religion. Constant reassessment, searching in one's heart—it gives me a feeling of confidence. I don't inject these beliefs in my answers to your secular questions."

It was a return to the same recurring theme: a man lives his own life and adheres to God's standards for himself, and does not think himself better or judge others as worse for their transgressions, be he a private or a public man. But having said that, Carter wanted to emphasize that, for himself, his religious precepts would govern his own public as well as private life. Clenching his fist and gesturing as he spoke, he concluded:

"But I don't think I would *ever* take on the same frame of mind that Nixon or Johnson did, lying, cheating, and distorting the truth. Not taking into consideration my hope for strength of character, I think that my religious beliefs alone would prevent that from happening to me. I have that confidence. I hope it's justified."

That was the way it ended. Scheer insisted later he was not particularly titillated by Carter's language. "I guess he gave me a Sunday-school lesson," he said. Yet Granum observed that Scheer seemed very excited as they left the house and drove into town. But then, to Granum, he always seemed that way: "a guy of almost indiscriminate excitement." "You're not going to tell anybody about this conversation, are you?" Granum said Scheer asked him. "You know this was a private interview." For his own part, Granum said, he had listened "without a sense of great distress" and in fact had found Carter's remarks that he would not pass judgment on others "refreshing."

The *Playboy* editors did not have to be told they had a live one. The interview was scheduled for the magazine's November issue, to be published

October 14, but *Playboy* decided it had better not sit on it. First Golson called Jim Wooten of *The New York Times* with it the week before the "Today" show appearance, but when the *Times* showed no interest, "Today" was contacted.

In New York City, Carter watched the "Today" show and then immediately crossed the street to Pennsylvania Station and, after a kickoff ceremony, boarded the Democratic Whistlestop. By then, news desks around the country were signaling their correspondents on the train, as it moved through New Jersey and into Pennsylvania, to get Carter's comment. As the candidate walked through the thirteen cars, greeting Democratic hacks and reporters, he was asked about his remarks in *Playboy*. "I'm not concerned about it, I've not read it," he said. Asked specifically by a reporter from *The Christian Science Monitor* about his use of the word "screw," Carter replied: "I don't remember saying that. I guess I'll have to read it." Later Powell told reporters Carter did remember, after all.

Powell, meanwhile, had the pertinent parts of the interview reproduced and made available to reporters on the train who wanted them; he drew attention to the theology and played down the words used to convey it. He quoted some scripture of his own—"judge not lest you be judged," and, as he put it, "not worrying about the mote in your brother's eye until you've dealt with the beam in your own eye." As for the likely political effect of Carter's statements, "I suspect there will be some attempt, if past history is any indication, for our Republican opposition to attempt to take the thing out of context. I wouldn't be surprised if there might be some committee-woman somewhere who would rise up and declare that anybody who says 'screw' ought not to be President. But I don't think that's going to sell." The interview itself, he insisted—always trying to see the silver lining in the cloud as any self-respecting flack will do—"furnishes a very worthwhile picture of him as a human being, and particularly of the intersection of those two aspects of his life, his religious faith and his public policies."

Carter left the whistlestop in Pittsburgh that night upset at himself, and returned to Plains to prepare for the first of his three televised debates with Ford, in Philadelphia on Thursday night, September 23. As he did, adverse reaction to the *Playboy* interview began to spread, especially through the religious community. The Reverend W. A. Criswell, pastor of the nation's largest Baptist church, the First Baptist Church of Dallas, was typical: "I am highly offended by this. I think he's mixed up in his moral values, and I think the entire church membership will feel the same way. The whole thing is highly distasteful." Carter's own pastor, Bruce Edwards, remarked plaintively, "I do wish he would have used different words."

Rosalynn Carter, meanwhile, professed not to be concerned at all by any of it. But some, like Dr. Jerry Vines of Mobile, Alabama, a former president of the pastors' conference of the Southern Baptist Convention, wondered why Carter had given an interview to *Playboy* in the first place. "*Playboy* is known for its gutter approach to life," he said, "and its whole philosophy comes right from the barnyard. . . . A lot of us are not convinced that Mr. Carter is truly in the evangelical Christian camp." Another minister, in New York, even challenged Carter's view that it was not up to him to criticize others. "It is not holier than thou," he said, "to condemn another man for shacking down with another man's wife." (To which William Safire, a Nixon speechwriter and publicist who is considered somewhat of an expert on the political vocabulary, remarked in his *New York Times* column: "If you are going to use sexual slang, Reverend, get it right. One does not shack down. One beds down. One shacks up.")

Finally, and probably inevitably, the *Playboy* incident inspired the frustrated Rodgers- and-Hammersteins on the press bus to make a contribution, which was sung privately to Carter and his wife at a party for him on his fifty-second birthday at a Pittsburgh hotel later on in the campaign. Through the excellent offices of Jim King, who called ahead, an advance man met the party in Pittsburgh with straw boaters for a quintet of reporters to wear, and doff at appropriate times, as the song was rendered, to the tune of "Heart of My Heart":

> Lust in my heart, how I love adultery;
> Lust in my heart, that's my theology.
> When I was young, at the Plains First Baptist Church,
> I would preach and sermonize—
> But oh, how I would fantasize.
> Lust in my heart, who cares if it's a sin?
> Leching's a noble art.
> It's okay if you shack up,
> I won't get my back up;
> 'Cause I've got mine, I've got lust in my heart.
>
> Lust in my heart, oh, it's bad politically;
> Lust in my heart, but it brings publicity.
> When I grew up, and ran for President,
> A bunch of women I did screw—
> But in my head, so no one knew.
> Lust in my heart, I said I'd never lie,
> I guess I wasn't smart.
> But I'm no gay deceiver,
> I'm a Christian eager-beaver;
> As *Playboy* said, I've got lust in my heart.

Carter laughed heartily and, it seemed, genuinely at the lyrics and the routine. The purveyors assured him that the ribbing was traditional and told him about the most famous of recent parodies, for George Romney in 1968, which went: "And then I went and spoiled it all by saying something stupid, like 'I'm brainwashed.' " Carter grinned and asked: "Have you ever written one for a winner?"

At the time, though, the *Playboy* matter was nothing for Carter to laugh about. His campaign had gotten off to a shaky start, and now this incident—over which cartoonists and gagsters could and would have a field day—cast doubts on the political commodities he had been selling as his worthiest traits: his sincerity and piety. How could a man who proclaimed himself to be so religious use that kind of language, especially knowing it would be published, and especially knowing it would be published in *Playboy?* Maybe that was it. Maybe the language was meant intentionally, the amateur mind readers began to suggest, to signal to *Playboy*'s readers that he wasn't all that square after all.

At least one insider, Greg Schneiders, entertained that idea. "He's a politician and a good one," Schneiders said, "and within the bounds of truth he speaks to people in the language they're most comfortable with, and about the things they're most concerned about. He tries to reach people on their own level and on their own terms, and I think he was doing that, perhaps to an extreme, with the *Playboy* thing. Because of the diversity of his background, he can reach all kinds of people in a very natural way, on their own terms. But he was reaching a little bit, and also probably misreading the nature of the *Playboy* reader." Jody Powell put it a little differently: "I really do think he was talking more to [the two of] them than to anybody else. In Jimmy's mind, it was, 'This is my last chance to try to make these two turkeys understand what I've been trying to say.' He was putting it as bluntly as he could."

Carter himself, after he became President, told me there was no ulterior motive in the language he had used, but he insisted he had not expected to be quoted. "The only word that I used that I know of that was at all off-color," he said, "was the word 'screw,' and this is not a word that was used by me for the first time, in that interview. I did not consider myself being quoted directly at that stage of the interview. The interview was over." He knew there was a tape recorder there, he said, "but I'm not sure I knew it was running. The guy was just standing there with it, but they had agreed with us to go over the text of the interview before it was printed and submit the interview to Jody."[1]

The interview had already been too much of a burden to him, Carter said. "I was furious at Jody for giving *Playboy* so much of my time. This

1. Golson, in a subsequent *Playboy* article, said Carter definitely understood that the tape was running. He quoted from the tape itself as having Scheer say, as he pointed to the recorder, "I'm taking *real* notes," to which Carter is represented as saying "Good."

was the last [session]. I was relieved to get through with it. The guy said, 'I really don't understand how you, a strait-laced Baptist, could hope to go to Washington and preach to other people and tell them how to run their lives, in sex matters and so forth.' And I said, 'Well, that's not part of the Christian religion. We feel that we're all sinners and that we don't have the right to preach to other people; Christ teaches us to judge not lest we be judged.' And I gave him the example of adultery, which is part of the Sermon on the Mount.

"If in fact I or Jody had gotten the text [of the interview], which we never did, and had gone over it, we would have obviously eliminated that word. It's not a very bad word. . . . I'm not trying to be coy or holier than thou, but on occasion I use a word like 'screw' when I'm talking to customers in my warehouse, or around Billy's service station, or when I was in the Navy. I'm not so pure that I never have used language of that kind. I don't have any reason to mislead anyone. At the time, I thought the interview had already been over. I was not aware that any of that would be in the article."

Carter said the press' intensive coverage of the episode "was very surprising to me," but "I can't blame anybody, for that article or for the way the press covered it, except myself. I don't think the press made a mistake, and I can't blame *Playboy.* They had a hot item on their hands and they saw fit not to submit it to Jody for approval, and to go on the "Today" show. It wasn't their fault, I guess they probably sold more *Playboy* magazines than they ever sold before, and I was the one who gave them the story, so I can't really blame them. If I had been in their shoes, I would have probably done the same thing."

Whatever the circumstances, the interview had the press bloodhounds after Carter again. "It increased the weirdo factor," Ham Jordan said later, using his favorite expression for Carter's "differentness" that nagged at those who didn't know him. The morning after Carter returned to Plains, he went over early to the peanut warehouse, as he often did, where a host of reporters awaited him. He told them that he had no regrets about granting the interview, and that was that; he walked quickly off, mistakenly tried to get into a newsman's car, and was redirected by a Secret Service agent. In retrospect, Powell said that stonewalling the matter was probably a mistake, but the first debate was coming up, and Carter wanted to do well, with no unnecessary distractions.

Ever since the 1960 presidential campaign debates between John Kennedy and Richard Nixon, a mythology had grown about their importance:

Kennedy had made mincemeat of Nixon and the debates had made the difference in the campaign—the one-half of one vote per precinct that gave Kennedy the presidency. Actually, the first of the four debates was the only one for which most observers gave Kennedy anything approaching a clear "victory." Those who heard the debate on radio did not have this impression, but most of those who watched on television concluded that Kennedy had won. Kennedy, trailing by 47 per cent to 46 in the Gallup Poll going in, took a lead of 49–46 after the first debate. During the subsequent debates, Nixon nearly erased that lead.

In an election as close as the 1960 one, no one factor could be singled out as the cause of victory or defeat. Yet it was the firm view of Kennedy insiders that the debates had at least established that their candidate, regarded before the debates as too young and too inexperienced to be President, was the equal of Nixon. Theodore Sorensen said later the first debate "shored up Southern and Stevenson Democrats" who had been doubtful about Kennedy for many of the reasons voters were later indicating doubts about Carter. "They saw Kennedy before the debate as a new and untested face, and people were uneasy about his religion and his accent." Also, old-line politicians "felt he was a hard-nosed politician with a small group around him who had made it without them," Sorensen said—another concern expressed about Carter.

Hardly anyone, however, could remember what Kennedy and Nixon had actually said in that first debate. What they remembered was Kennedy's vigorous, confident demeanor, his often bemused attitude toward his opponent, compared to the patronizing, haggard, and harried Nixon, who was in a sweat. Kennedy "won" that debate because he went into it better prepared, less tired, and above all with a clear idea of what he intended to do. He executed flawlessly his plan to stay on the offensive. He arrived in Chicago, site of that debate, in time to rest and go through a dry run in his hotel suite, with aides tossing anticipated questions at him. The exercise gave him a feel not only for possible questions but also for the combative atmosphere in which he would soon be thrust. At the studio, he required little make-up because he was, as always, well tanned. Nixon by contrast arrived late, exhausted from a crushing schedule. He underwent no Q-and-A warm-up, and to boot, en route to the studio, he struck on a car door the same knee he had injured seven weeks earlier. Learning that Kennedy had foregone heavy make-up, he foolishly settled for an inadequate application of a shaving stick, which was no match for his five-o'clock shadow. In the debate, he seemed intimidated, not only by the rich and self-confident young Kennedy but by his own image as a gut fighter, which he appeared determined to diffuse by being deferential to Kennedy to a fault. In a sense, while Kennedy was psyching himself up to win, Nixon was psyching himself down simply to be acceptable. The result was disastrous.

However questionable the conclusion that the Kennedy-Nixon debates had decided the 1960 election, it endured over the next twelve years. In 1964 Lyndon Johnson, far ahead of Barry Goldwater in the polls, took no chances and declined to debate. Nixon—a politician with a long memory and a passion for self-preservation—ruled out the possibility of debating Hubert Humphrey in 1968 and cavalierly dismissed a confrontation with George McGovern in 1972. But in 1976 the conditions were better: candidates had been nominated by the major parties who had never faced a national electorate, and, beyond that, the incumbent President was the underdog. He had to debate in hopes of closing the gap.

From the start, Carter's aides were supremely confident that if they could isolate Gerald Ford from his august office, Jimmy Carter—tougher, more intelligent, quick-witted, better prepared—would take him to the cleaners. In fact, some of them privately expressed *concern* about that possibility. Jimmy, they said, might administer such a pasting to Ford as to cause a public backlash against a man who showed so little deference to the President. Cool it, one adviser after another counseled Carter. Some, like Jordan, said he expected neither man clearly to outclass the other. But in the corridors of the Carter headquarters in Atlanta, the talk was optimistic. Many of the Carterites accepted the stereotype of Ford as dull-witted, oafish, an automaton who was programed for set responses and not very well programed at that. The dream of a 1976 version of the 1960 Kennedy "knockout" of Nixon wafted through their reveries.

One psychological factor they could not properly gauge, and hence could not cope with in advance: what would be the effect on millions of Americans when a challenger directly took on, disagreed with, contradicted, the President? For all the damage done to the office by Watergate and Nixon, the presidency remained a special object of respect, even reverence, for the American people. Carter himself was uncertain what the chemistry would be at that moment when he finally stood on the stage with President Ford and matched wits, statistics, and barbs with him. He had no sense of awe toward Gerald Ford the man, the dogmatic Republican, the pardoner of Nixon, the ineffectual leader. But separating that man from the presidency was vexing.

When the debates were first agreed to, it was expected the pressure would be on Ford. He was trailing badly in the Gallup Poll, and he appeared to be staking all on the debates. Carter merely had to hold his own, with the clear opportunity of scoring a breakthrough if he did better than that. But Carter's differences with the Catholic bishops on abortion, his argument with Ford over Clarence Kelley, his misspeaking in the AP interview on tax reform, and now his freewheeling *Playboy* interview had thrown him on the defensive. The time he had set aside to shore up party loyalty, to harden soft spots among Jewish, Catholic, and ethnic voters, and to dissipate his reputation for evasiveness on the issues had instead been consumed explaining away these diversions. Now the objective had changed: he had to do well enough to draw attention away from his September troubles. The issue was Jimmy Carter, and whether he was a man of good judgment.

Carter approached the debate not like a fighter training for a championship bout but like a student accustomed to receiving A's who brushes up on his subjects before a final examination. He studied the thick briefing books that had been prepared for him, and he watched film of the first Kennedy-Nixon debate. But he would not permit his aides to rehearse him on likely questions, as Kennedy had done. He had in a sense been cramming all summer long, while Ford was still engaged in his struggle with Ronald Reagan for the Republican nomination; if Carter wasn't prepared now, he would never be. On the afternoon of the debate, he examined the set on the stage of the Walnut Street Theater—after 167 years the oldest in continuous use in the nation. He toted in a clothing bag the dark-blue suit he would wear, slipping it on in a theater dressing room, to make sure it looked right under the brilliant television lights. Then he returned to his suite at the Benjamin Franklin Hotel, took a nap, looked through his briefing books again, and spent the final three hours dining alone with Rosalynn. (Schneiders said later it probably was a mistake for the two of them to be sealed off like that, though Carter had told him that nothing was healthier for him psychologically than to be with her. "That was a very low-key, quiet atmosphere he was in, and then from that he went right into this highly combative atmosphere.")

Ford, meanwhile, had played—to the hilt—the role of boxer training for the big championship fight. As far as was humanly possible, nothing was left to chance; the President was subjected to what Doug Bailey later called "extraordinarily rigorous training." Under the direction of Mike Duval, at least a week before the first debate the family theater at the White House was converted into a rough mock-up of the actual set to be used in Philadelphia. The podium was identical, down to the same television camera angles, so that Bill Carruthers, Ford's television adviser, could recommend the most attractive position for the President to assume. As Ford stood at his lectern, cardboard cards were held up by hand indicating "one minute," "thirty seconds," and "cut"—similar to the electric timing devices that would be used in the actual studio to monitor the time of his answers.

Various aides—Duval, Carruthers, Bob Teeter, Alan Greenspan, his chairman of the Council of Economic Advisers, Agnes Waldron of the White House press section, William Hyland, a deputy to National Security Adviser Brent Scowcroft, Doug Bailey, Dick Cheney—took turns at the reporters' panel and threw questions at him by the hour. Then a complete videotape was played back so they could all study what he said, and how he looked and sounded as he said it.

At one session, a television set was even brought in and set up on Carter's lectern. On a closed-circuit arrangement, old tapes of Carter answering reporters' questions on panel shows like "Meet the Press" were run off in Ford's presence, to familiarize him with Carter's style. Ford would be asked and would answer a question, and then Carter, on tape, would have his "turn." The intent was, one who was present said later, for the President to give his own spontaneous rebuttal to each taped Carter answer. But that wrinkle was just a bit too much for Ford; he wouldn't do it. Nor did he want a stand-in for Carter.

The questioning of Ford was tough and dogged, particularly on subjects on which he was considered vulnerable, and he did not always like it. "The one thing that always seemed to get him on edge," one insider recalled, "was any time a question would come that would seem to imply he lacked compassion. But Duval had a strong feeling, and correctly so, that this was a whole area where he was bound to get a bunch of questions." Once, the aide said, "he got about three of them in a row and he simply said, 'I'm sorry, I'm not going to answer that, because I think it's just a plain dumb question.' He was obviously perturbed." On other occasions, when he got off a good and forceful answer, he would grin with open self-satisfaction, or when he made a poor start he would stop in mid-answer and start again, knowing that for all the attempts to make it "real," this was still practice. Mostly, he was a pliant and obedient student in this crash course on how to debate for the presidency of the United States.

The "teachers," for their part, never forgot that for all the play-acting, it was the President standing up there. "Even this President," the same insider said, "suffered from all the stories you hear about staff people never telling him anything but what he wanted to hear. There never was hard discussion of difficult questions in difficult areas. He would get *asked* the questions, but if his answer was off target, nobody seemed to want to say so. Of course, his answers were never totally wrong. But it was clear that his mind does not work in a way as to take political advantage of every opportunity." For this reason, the aide said, "his debate preparation was nowhere near what it should have been. He received mountains and mountains and mountains of paper but very, very seldom was there any discussion with him as to strategy; it was all left to him. It's part and parcel of the problem: if you don't think in conceptual terms, you don't think in strategic terms either; it isn't clear what you're setting out to do."

On the day of the first debate, Ford like Carter arrived early in Philadelphia. He went to the stylish home of an official on the Walnut Street Theater's board and also checked the theater set, wearing the dark-blue suit in which he would debate several hours later. Then he returned to his temporary residence and had dinner with Dick Cheney and other aides. Before returning to the theater, Cheney, Teeter, and Bailey took him aside and reviewed in general terms the political situation then existing, and what it suggested in terms of the style and purpose he should pursue during the debate. (This exercise was repeated before the third debate, but not, notably, before the second, according to Bailey.)

As for the other participants in the debate—the questioners—they had done no consultation or rehearsal at all. The moderator, Edwin Newman of NBC, and the three panelists, Elizabeth Drew of *The New Yorker,* Frank Reynolds of ABC News, and James Gannon of *The Wall Street Journal,* steadfastly declined to get their heads together, for fear they might be accused of collaboration or collusion. But there had been plenty of discussion about their being chosen for the panel. The League of Women Voters' Education Fund did the selecting, although each of the candidates was invited to nominate up to fifteen prospects for each debate. According to Jim Karayn, a list of 131 newspaper, magazine, and television persons went to the six-member League committee that made the final choices. Of the sixteen chosen for the four debates, perhaps four had been nominated by the Carter or Ford campaigns. In 1960 the networks had used their own reporters exclusively in the first debate to try to build up their reputations as reporters rather than television celebrities; this time, the League was running the debates and the networks were supposedly just covering them as news events, thereby avoiding a challenge under the FCC's equal-time provisions. In 1960 the panels for the last three debates were selected by lottery from among the reporters traveling with the candidates; this time, Karayn determined to downplay the traveling press, which, he said later in a misplaced generalization, "pretty well have their minds set on tomorrow's headline."

As Karayn and the League officials sorted out names and deliberated, considerable lobbying went on behind the scenes, both by news organizations and reporters who for the sake of ego, history, or their own careers wanted to share with Ford and Carter the anticipated television audience of about 100 million viewers. Some of the networks and newspapers, Karayn said later, tried to say which of their reporters would go on if selected; some charged that their aces had been blackballed when they weren't picked. An aide came into Karayn one day and told him: "*Time* magazine is livid. They want to know, 'Who vetoed Hugh Sidey?' " Karayn insisted that the candidates had no veto power and did not attempt to assert any, that well-known political reporters were bypassed because they traveled with the candidates too frequently to suit the new criterion; or somebody else from the same news organization was asked; or each panel had to have a geographical mix; or lesser-known panelists were preferred. Among those who lobbied him directly, Karayn said, some of them delivering letters of recommendation by hand somewhat apologetically, were three of Washington's best-known reporters. Karayn would not identify the three but said that "most of the people who lobbied hardest were already on the list."

The intense interest among reporters in being named to the debate panel inspired tireless Jim Naughton to another of his patented capers. He drafted a very official-sounding telegram notifying the recipient he had been selected as a panelist for the first debate and dispatched one to Phil Jones of CBS News and the other to Tom DeFrank of *Newsweek,* he who earlier in the year, thanks to Naughton, had shared his room in Peoria with a sheep. Both went for the gag—hook, line, and sinker. Their bosses didn't think it was so funny, though, and for a time made threatening noises in Naughton's direction.[2]

The first debate attracted tremendous public interest. Outside the Walnut Street Theater, political protesters and the just-plain curious packed in behind police barriers as the candidates entered. The wall behind the panelists was constructed in such a way that the orchestra seats provided no view of the stage. Selected League guests, party bigwigs, and reporters therefore

---

2. After the election, DeFrank struck back. Three days after Ford's defeat, Naughton got a phone call from Dick Cheney. Naughton, who had been updating an obituary on Ford of the sort that newspapers keep in their files for famous people, had requested an interview and Ford had agreed. "The President is going up to Camp David before going out to California," Cheney advised the reporter. "Be at the main gate tomorrow morning at nine o'clock."

Was it going to be an exclusive interview, Naughton asked?

"You're the only one now," Cheney told him.

Naughton stayed up until nearly 2 A.M. preparing questions. Then he went to bed, got up three hours later, and drove to the presidential retreat in the Catoctin Mountains of Maryland. He checked into a hotel to have a place to write after the interview, and met George Tames, a *Times* photographer assigned to accompany him. Together they approached the Marine at the Camp David gate, who was not expecting them. Naughton phoned Cheney at the White House. "George Tames and I are at the main gate and they have no record of our appointment," he said.

"Is that a fact?" Cheney replied.

The next thing Naughton knew, Tom DeFrank's voice was on the phone. "Oh, gee, Jim, they didn't cancel your interview, too, did they?"

Naughton hung up and told the guard: "I've been had."

"I assumed as much, sir," the Marine said. Naughton took the caper like the professional practical joker he is, with a tinge of admiration for DeFrank—and a vow to get even with co-conspirator Cheney, sometime, somewhere.

huddled into the small balcony; they were admonished against cheering, applauding, or even laughing lest they distract the debaters or, more importantly, affect the judgment of the millions watching in their homes.

Carter was the first candidate to arrive on the set. He stood quietly at his waist-high lectern, licking his lips from time to time. An aide plugged in a floor wire to a connection taped to the heel of his shoe, from which another wire ran up his pants leg and around his waist to a small microphone at his chest, under his tie. When Ford strode in, he went quickly over to Carter, offering him his hand. Carter took it and smiled, but there was no conversation as Ford moved at once to his lectern and had his own microphone connected.

In the balcony, the atmosphere was electric—a feeling that we were about to witness some momentous historic event of uncertain outcome. Aides of Ford and Carter could be seen standing in the wings, outside camera range and therefore not visible on the color-television sets placed conveniently for simultaneous viewing. For all the advance promotion of Carter as a supercool operator, he seemed notably more unsettled than Ford. At one point, when a young director named Nancy Kaplan asked the President for a voice-level, he quipped: "You're a very attractive stage manager." Carter smiled at the remark but said nothing.

By prearrangement, Carter drew the first question, from Frank Reynolds, about how, specifically, he would cut unemployment. Carter gave a lengthy and stilted reply calling for cooperation between the government and the private sector in housing and inner-city problems, increased production, and shifting of the tax burden onto the rich. The response was adequate enough, but Carter recited it in an almost schoolboyish way, as if he were determined to dispel by the sheer volume of words and statistics any doubts that he was vague and indecisive. He was the one who sounded programed.

Ford, with a look of steely determination in his eye and speaking through tight lips, jumped on him at once: "I don't believe that Mr. Carter has been any more specific in this case than he has been in many other instances," Ford began, then launched into the standard Republican solution of expanding the private sector through tax incentives and cutting federal taxes. Carter still seemed unnerved. He was standing before millions of Americans on the same platform with the President of the United States; something inside him, he acknowledged later, said it would not do to go after the President as if he were a Chicago alderman. Jody Powell, back in Plains in August, had suggested that "once you sit down eyeball to eyeball, all the pomp and circumstance of office which Ford used so effectively against Ronald Reagan won't mean anything at all." But one had to wonder, watching there in the theater, whether Jody had bothered to tell that to Jimmy. And it was a fighting Jerry Ford that Carter now faced; Ford gripped the rounded edge of his lectern as he listened to Carter, staring—even at times glaring—at his opponent, like some big menacing bear straining to leap at his adversary. Carter in contrast seemed somewhat disoriented, tentative, and deferential.

It went on like that, Ford attacking, Carter slow in counterpunching at first, but gradually coming around as he became accustomed to being in the ring. Ford's aggressiveness seemed to encourage Carter to be less cautious; in a sense, the President's heavy-handed tactics served to solve Carter's problem of how to cope. Soon the two men were trading barbs; once Carter began to feel comfortable exchanging accusations with Ford, he became more forceful, more confident. Both were giving stock, familiar answers to the range of domestic issues raised—the economy, taxes, balancing the federal budget, government reorganization, amnesty, public-service employment. On this last, Carter accused Ford of being insensitive to the human side of unemployment; and when Ford charged that Carter had said he would "raise taxes on about half the working people in this country," Carter countered that the President had deliberately misquoted his views in the AP interview.

As the debate approached its conclusion, with some eight minutes of the scheduled ninety minutes to go, Carter seemed to be taking the upper hand. Ford's attacking seemed to snap Carter out of his early trance. But then, as Carter was in mid-sentence in a response deploring CIA and FBI abuses, technical disaster struck. The sound system, inexplicably, quit. In the theater, Carter continued speaking for a moment or two, unaware that his words were not being amplified. Edwin Newman at last broke in, telling both debaters that they were not being heard. As technicians scurried around backstage and the theater audience of 450 in the balcony buzzed in disbelief, the two candidates stood mute, like supporting characters in a Buster Keaton movie.

For the next twenty-seven incredible minutes, these two men at the very center of American politics in 1976 stood in silence, not talking to each other, seldom even looking at each other, as the mightily embarrassed television crews sought the difficulty. It turned out to be the result of a short circuit in something called an electronic capacitor, about the size of a cigarette filter, but the trouble couldn't be located and sound was not restored until a separate line was rigged to a television truck outside.

Everything, it seemed, had been anticipated and prepared for except this. The networks kept their cameras focused on the two candidates. They in turn stood frozen, neither one willing to be the first to sit down on one of the high metal stools behind them. The stage manager, seeing both men perspiring, took mercy on them. She directed the cameras to focus away, then signaled to Ford and Carter. Each reached into his pocket quickly, wiped his brow with a handkerchief, and replaced the handkerchief. Then the cameras were swung back on them. Finally, after twenty minutes or so, Carter did sit down, but Ford still declined.

After the sound was restored and the two candidates had delivered their closing statements, Carter's assistants were rueful; their man had begun to hit his stride and was hurt by the technical failure, they thought. To many observers, Ford had had the edge, although not by much. He had committed no mental or physical faux pas and he conveyed the image of a knowledgeable and capable man. For Carter, after his shaky start, the debate had served to demonstrate his grasp of domestic issues and his commitment to Democratic Party goals. But there was no knockout. The first debate's principal achievement was catching the American public's attention, reminding voters that they had only six weeks to make a choice.

In the Gallup Poll just before the debate, Carter had led Ford by 18 per cent, 54–36. After it, the poll found the lead had dropped to 8 points: 50–42. Other factors had to be counted in to explain this result, of course, but at any rate the race was getting tighter, and there was trouble ahead for the Democratic challenger.

Somewhat surprisingly, neither the three members of the debate panel nor Ford had mentioned *Playboy* to Carter. It would have been hard for Ford to introduce the subject and the panelists apparently considered, as Powell expected they would, that the matter was not serious enough to be dealt with in this august forum.

But the morning after the Philadelphia debate, Hamilton Jordan discussed with some reporters another potential magazine crisis. It was an interview Carter had given to Norman Mailer for *The New York Times Magazine,* about to be published, in which Carter emphasized again that as President he did not intend to judge how people lived their personal lives. Mailer wrote: " 'I don't care,' he [Carter] said in his quiet decent voice, as if the next words, while not wholly comfortable, had nonetheless to be said, 'I don't care if people say ____,' and he actually said the famous four-letter word that the *Times* has not printed in the 125 years of its publishing life. [That was how Mailer agreed to put it, after negotiating with the *Times'* editors.] He got it out without a backing up of phlegm or a hitch in his rhythm (it was, after all, not the easiest word to say to a stranger), but it was said from duty, from the quiet decent demands of duty, as if he, too, had to present his credentials to that part of the 20th century personified by his interviewer."

Jordan was fearful that the quoted remark could add to Carter's woes, and his reporter-companions did nothing to ease his mind. They reminded him of Romney's "brainwashing" crack and how that had hurt him when the press began describing it as part of a pattern of misspeaking. The next day, on an inside page, the *Times* made a brief mention of Carter's latest reported use of an obscenity. When nothing came of it, Jordan phoned me at home the following night to ask whether I thought the Mailer thing had blown over. I told him *The Washington Post* had decided it didn't warrant the kind of coverage given to the *Playboy* remarks, and he seemed considerably relieved.

On the morning after the first debate, Carter made campaign stops in Houston and Dallas before going on to California that night. Although Americans were talking about the first televised confrontation, a subject of continuing interest in the Lone Star State was still the *Playboy* interview —but not because of anything Carter had said about lust, or any profanity he had used. What bothered Texans was Carter's very last remark in which he had forcefully insisted, "But I don't think I would *ever* take on the same frame of mind that Nixon or Johnson did, lying, cheating, and distorting the truth." Invoking the hallowed name of Lyndon Johnson in the same breath with that of Richard Nixon was not a prudent action to be taken by a presidential candidate, even one from the South. Earlier Carter had phoned Lady Bird Johnson and told her he regretted "the implications that might be drawn" from linking Johnson with Nixon, but the Republicans in Texas were riding him hard on it.

Among the unhappy Texans was Bob Strauss, the national party chairman, who feared the remark might lose Texas for the Democrats. Strauss told Carter as much, warning that the issue was sure to be exploited by Strauss's old friend and now political adversary John Connally. It was, as the loquacious Strauss later observed in the rear of the plane, "like giving Heifetz a Stradivarius. John knows how to play it."

Carter apparently agreed that he would have to do something before the matter went further. As he got off his plane in Houston, he walked over to a group of Texas reporters in a roped-off area on the runway tarmac. First he answered a question about the debate the night before, and then a general question on whether he had any regrets about the *Playboy* interview. Seeing his opportunity, Carter volunteered that the only thing he regretted was the complete misunderstanding over his feelings about Lyndon Johnson. The traveling press corps, getting off behind Carter, came scurrying over quickly enough to hear—and capture on their tape recorders—the candidate telling the locals:

"After the interview was over, there was a summary made that unfortunately equated what I had said about President Johnson and President Nixon. . . . If any misrepresentation of what I feel about President Johnson caused Mrs. Johnson any discomfort or embarrassment, for that I am truly sorry. . . . I realize that, if you read it, it says that after the final session was over, there was an analysis that was made after the completion of the interview. My reference to Johnson was about the misleading of the American people; the lying and cheating part referred to President Nixon. And the unfortunate juxtaposition of these two names in the *Playboy* article grossly misrepresents the way I feel about him."

The clear suggestion was that it had been *Playboy* that had taken the dig at Johnson, not the candidate. As Carter finished, Sam Donaldson of ABC News, a reporter as unobtrusive as the bubonic plague, pulled a copy of the article out of his pocket and went after Carter right there. "He saw me pull it out," Donaldson said later. "I commenced to read and I asked him if those were his own words." Another reporter, Larry Knutson of the Associated Press, joined in. "He ended the press conference," Donaldson said, "and he came back thirty seconds later to me, and said, 'I want to make it very clear: I said that. I have not said I didn't say that.' "

A Carter aide told Donaldson later that by catching Carter up at this point, "we'd saved him in a sense. . . . If he had left that press conference, apparently having gotten away with planting with those Texas reporters the belief that somehow it was *Playboy*'s summary, we all would probably have devoured the son of a bitch. I think he thought at first he might be able to get away with it. He was not actually lying. He said 'a summary.' He didn't say '*Playboy*'s summary.' He tried to get away with it; he was caught, and fortunately he recognized it and had to come clean. He could not leave the scene maintaining that somehow it was someone else's fault."

Among those in the press corps that day was Robert Scheer, the perpetrator of it all. When he heard Carter talking to the Texas press, he said, "I panicked. I ran back to the plane to get the tape of the interview. I put it on and listened to it as I was running back. It was clear. He *had* said it." Curiously, no reporter in the party ever asked Scheer to play the pertinent part of the tape, and Powell assured him that Carter was not denying the accuracy of the quotation. Scheer at his first opportunity phoned the *Playboy* editors in Chicago and got their approval to release the tape if Carter attempted to deny its contents. But the candidate did not make that step necessary.

Carter's entourage went on to Dallas for another speech—by all reports one of Carter's better efforts—but it got little coverage outside of Dallas because the reporters were huddled in the hotel press room by this time, either writing stories about the flap at the Houston airport, or comparing notes and tapes on what Carter did or didn't say about the "summary" and the "unfortunate juxtaposition."[3] By the time the party trooped back aboard the plane for the flight to California, Powell had a clear idea of what was going on. Donaldson, Carl Leubsdorf of *The Baltimore Sun,* and others got into a discussion, then an argument, and then a shouting match with Powell, who accused them of "nit-shitting," while they in turn accused Carter of trying to wing one past the provincials, and themselves. One highly respected reporter who was present but not a party to the argument said later he considered Carter's use of language on the Houston tarmac "one of the most intellectually dishonest things I'd ever heard a politician say." Powell said, "It was Jimmy at his worst and the press at their worst; Jimmy's tendency to say too much when just a flat statement would do. If there had been nothing said before about it, and you read exactly what he said, that is a very legitimate interpretation. And as soon as it became clear that his remarks were being misinterpreted, he immediately clarified them."

Back on the plane later, Powell told some reporters they were getting on shaky ground when they tried to determine his boss' motivations. But, he said later, "I was dealing with a brushfire." Finally he and Schneiders went forward and told Carter what all the commotion was about. "We've been doing battle back there," Schneiders told him. Powell suggested it would probably be a good idea to sit down with some of the reporters to explain his position, and to hear theirs.

In San Diego early that evening, Carter, Powell, and Schneiders sat in Carter's room at the Harbor Inn and decided to ask several newspaper reporters who had been traveling with them to come in for an off-the-record talk. Powell rounded up about a dozen of them. Carter in his shirtsleeves straddled a bench, and Powell sat off in a corner. Beer was served and Carter started out saying how much he liked and respected everyone in the room. He said he knew they were concerned about what had happened in Houston and so was he. He regretted any misunderstanding, because after all, they were all in the campaign together and they all wanted what was best for the country. And so, he said, he wanted to get their "advice" on how the campaign coverage could be improved.

That was the wrong word to use; some of the reporters already were uneasy about coming into an off-the-record session with a presidential candidate in the heat of the campaign; they were not in the business of advising candidates. One of the group, Marty Schram of *Newsday*, told Carter as much, and others agreed. Carter backed off, and then proceeded

---

3. In the *Dallas Times Herald* account of the press conference, Carter was reported as saying the reference in the *Playboy* interview "was a distortion of his true feeling about Johnson."

to the matter at hand. He discussed what he had said in Houston, and expressed bewilderment at some of the coverage. His complaint, he said, was not with the print media, but "The television coverage is destroying us." In the chat about his use of words, Carter denied that he played any particular games with nuances. Charlie Mohr of *The New York Times* respectfully disagreed, and started to quote Carter from memory to make his point; Leubsdorf took out his notebook and read verbatim quotations to Carter on the "summary" and the "unfortunate juxtaposition." Carter acknowledged that he could see how his language might be misconstrued, but it had never been his intent to confuse.

The group turned to a comparison between the way the traveling press was covering Carter and the way the White House press was covering Ford. Carter, and Powell especially, began to complain. Anyone who looked at the campaign of 1976, Powell said, could conclude that the way to get elected was to shut out the press. And if that was the lesson, it would be the third time in a row it had happened. Any candidate who tried to be reasonable got his brains beat out. "Maybe we'll have to close the campaign [to the press]," he suggested. Carter was reminded that he had said earlier it would "suit me fine" if Ford decided to stay in the White House; now he had changed his mind. Mohr told him that what he and his campaign did was entirely up to him, but if he decided to run a closed campaign, "then of course the press would write about it."

After maybe half an hour of this kind of exchange, Carter left, perhaps because he thought the conversation was getting nowhere. Powell said he thought the meeting was "helpful" and that "things got better, but probably for other reasons."

One of the other reasons was that the President, for all the sanctity of the White House, was starting to get some heat from the press too. For Hamilton Jordan, any turn could not come soon enough. "First the Kelley thing, then *Playboy* and the first debate," he said later. "They all killed time and we couldn't get untracked. It was like the Chinese water treatment in September."

But now Gerald Ford began to undergo the treatment.

39. Trouble for Ford

When the tide of trouble began to shift toward Gerald Ford, the movement was hardly noticed, in the furor over the *Playboy* interview. On September 21, United Press International reported that William Whyte, the vice president of U.S. Steel who had hosted the 1974 secret meetings planning for Ford's takeover of the presidency, admitted that he and U.S. Steel had paid for three Ford golfing holidays at a New Jersey country club. (Later it was disclosed that U.S. Steel also financed two Ford trips to Disney World in Orlando, Florida.) Ford quickly acknowledged through Ron Nessen that as a congressman he had played golf with his old friend at the club. It was a minor matter, but it was the first pebble in a rockslide.

On the same day, *The Wall Street Journal* reported that the Watergate special prosecutor, Charles Ruff, was investigating campaign contributions that might "involve" Ford's campaigns while he was a congressman. Paul Henry, the Republican chairman in Kent County, Michigan, Ford's home area, acknowledged that records had been subpoenaed. "We honestly don't know what the prosecutor is looking for," he told *The New York Times*. The *Journal* article also said a subpoena had been issued for the financial records of the Marine Engineers Beneficial Association, a maritime union that was Ford's largest contributor in his 1972 House race.

This allegation brought down an avalanche of questions on Nessen in the White House daily briefing. Nessen insisted that the President did not have to be defended because "nobody has said there has been any wrongdoing." He reminded the reporters that the President had undergone an extensive background check by four hundred FBI agents and twenty-five special investigators when he was before the House Judiciary Committee for confirmation as Vice President in 1973; nothing untoward had been uncovered then.

At the same time, still another allegation surfaced—an old charge but potentially a severely damaging one. John W. Dean III, the former White House counsel for Nixon who had first exposed the Watergate cover-up, was about to publish his personal account in a book entitled *Blind Ambition*. In the book, Dean said he had been told that Ford, in contradiction of his public sworn testimony, had discussed with the White House ways to block plans for hearings into Watergate before the 1972 election. If the allegation were true, it would mean that Ford was implicated in the sinister events that led directly to his own assumption of the presidency.

At his vice-presidential confirmation hearings in 1973, Ford acknowledged that in the fall of 1972, in advance of the election, he had met twice with Republican members of the House Banking and Currency Committee, whose chairman, Wright Patman of Texas, wanted to investigate the laundering of Nixon campaign money and its possible relation to Watergate. Ford insisted that he had done so at the Republicans' request, simply to ascertain their position, and not under any White House directive to kill the investigation. However, in the spring of 1974, White House tapes dated September 15, 1972, were released on which Nixon was heard specifically ordering that Ford be pressed to help curb the hearings.

"Jerry Ford is not really taking an active interest in this matter that is developing," Dean explained to Nixon, "so [Campaign Finance Chairman Maurice] Stans is going to see Jerry Ford and try to brief him and explain to him the problems he has. . . ."

Nixon replied, "What about Ford? Do you think so? [John] Connally can't [get involved] because of the way he is set up. If anybody can do it, Connally could, but if Ford can get the minority members . . . [New Jersey Representative William] Widnall, et cetera. Jerry should talk to Widnall. After all, if we ever win the House, Jerry will be Speaker, and he could tell him if he did not get off—he will not be chairman, ever."

Dean agreed. "That would be very helpful to get all of these people at least pulling together," he said, "if Jerry could get a little action on this."

Haldeman broke in: "Damn it, Jerry should."

And later on the tape:

Dean: "I think Maury [Stans] could talk to Ford if that would do any good. I think Maury ought to brief Ford on exactly what his whole side of the story is. Maury understands the law."

Haldeman: "I will talk to [Richard] Cook [a deputy in the congressional liaison office]."

Nixon: "Maybe Ehrlichman should talk to him. Ehrlichman understands the law."

Haldeman: "Is that a good idea? Maybe it is."

Nixon: "I think maybe that is the thing. This is a big play. He has to know that it comes from the top. While I can't talk to him myself, he has to get at this and screw the thing up."

Dean told Nixon that Representative Garry Brown of Michigan, a

Republican on the Patman committee, had already taken the lead to block the investigation on the grounds that it would impair the rights of the Watergate suspects to a fair trial.

"Right," Nixon said. ". . . Tell Ehrlichman to get Brown in and Ford in together, and then they can work out something. They ought to get off their asses and push it. No use to let Patman have a free ride here."

Eighteen days later the committee killed the planned hearings by a 20–15 vote, with all fourteen Republicans voting against them. Brown, in an interview with *The Washington Post* after the vote, said he had worked with Ford and the Justice Department to block the hearings, but that he had never discussed the matter with the White House. Ford testified in 1973 that he had never talked to Nixon, Ehrlichman, Dean, or Haldeman about it either. Although as House Minority Leader he conversed almost daily with William Timmons, Nixon's chief congressional liaison, Ford said, "even in this case I do not recall any conversations concerning this particular matter."

At the time Ford testified, the 1972 tapes had not yet been made public. When they were, in 1974, the obvious question to ask was: Did Ehrlichman or anyone else follow through on Nixon's order to lean on Ford? And if so, what did Ford do?

Now in his book, Dean wrote that Timmons told him he had indeed discussed scuttling the Patman hearings with Ford by raising, at Dean's suggestion, the possibility of blackmailing Patman. (John Connally had told Dean he had heard in Texas that Patman might have "received some contributions from an oil lobbyist" that he had not reported as required by the law. Dean said he asked the lawyer for CREEP, Kenneth Parkinson, to check into campaign contributions to Patman and other members of his committee, and he passed the idea on to Timmons.) "Timmons, who met regularly with Jerry Ford, had explored with him Connally's suggestions about Patman. 'What do you think?' I asked Timmons. 'Do you think we ought to dig into this stuff? Parkinson sent me a file on which contributions these guys have reported.' 'Well, John, you know this is kind of sensitive,' said Timmons, 'and I talked to Jerry about it. Jerry doesn't think it would be such a good idea. And, frankly, I'll tell you the problem is that, uh, Jerry himself might have some problems in this area, and so might some of our guys on the committee. I don't think we ought to open this up.' "

The suggestion that Ford himself might have received illegal campaign contributions dovetailed with the report of the special prosecutor's investigation of the campaign files in Michigan. Just as important, Dean's account suggested that Ford had perjured himself before the congressional committees in saying he had never talked to anyone at the White House about killing the Patman hearings. This was a very, very serious allegation for a President, or for a presidential candidate.

When the Nixon tapes were first released in May 1974, Patman had seen this potential at once, and he had written to Chairman Peter Rodino of the House Judiciary Committee during Ford's vice-presidential confirmation hearings, urging him to obtain the tapes from September 15 (the day Nixon ordered that Ford be enlisted) to October 3, 1972 (the day the Patman hearings were voted down by the committee). "Obviously," he said, "either the President's orders were not carried out by his trusted aides or Mr. Ford's testimony before the Senate committee is untruthful." But those tapes were never made public.

Now, in 1976, apprised of Dean's story, Timmons angrily denied it. He acknowledged that he had talked to Dean about using a report of an alleged illegal campaign contribution as a way to deter Patman. But he insisted he had rejected the notion out of hand and had never discussed it or any other tactic for sidetracking the hearings with Ford. "Dean asked me what was my view on whether it [pressure] should be used," Timmons said. "I said I didn't [think so]. If you opened that door, you'd never know who you'd touch."

Ford's aides, asked about Dean's account, chose to fall back on President Ford's previous congressional testimony—given before release of the Nixon tapes—that to "the best of my recollection" he had never talked to anyone at the White House about killing the Patman hearings. This had all the earmarks of old-fashioned, Nixon-era stonewalling, but the press did not seem exercised. For weeks, little more was made of the matter.

While these several clouds were gathering over the President's head, he took to the campaign trail, this time going into the Deep South, fulfilling a pledge he had made at the Republican convention that he would not concede a single state. Bob Teeter's polls suggested that Ford had a chance in Louisiana and an outside shot at Mississippi. Also, influential Republicans like Harry Dent had been pushing for a Southern swing to keep the pressure on Carter. The Republicans hired a steamboat, the *Natchez*, and Ford campaigned down the Mississippi to New Orleans to the strains of a Dixieland band. Here was another pure "media event," and it worked: two press planes were required to handle the herd of reporters and television technicians it attracted. In his speeches, the President attacked Mondale as "the biggest spender in the United States Senate," in the clear hope that he would prove to be the weak link on the Carter ticket in the South.

Carter, meanwhile, having had his little talk with his traveling companions of the press, labored hard to resume the offensive. In Portland, Oregon, he alluded for the first time to the accounts of Ford's free golfing vacations, courtesy of U.S. Steel and, the White House now admitted, several other firms. "The American people are fair, our government is not fair," Carter said. "You can't expect any better from political leadership that has been bogged down in Washington the last twenty-five or thirty years, deriving their advice, their counsel, their financial support from lobbyists and special-interest groups. They belong to the same clubs, they play golf on the same golf courses, they communicate with one another in the absence of participation, understanding, control by the people. We can't run this government or this administration or this campaign from those private clubs or from the White House Rose Garden."

In this sermonizing, Carter was somewhat handicapped by the disclosure that he, too, as governor of Georgia, had made three trips in 1972 and 1973 to hunting lodges owned by timber companies that did business with Georgia. On one of them, he said, he took several members of his family and went hunting, but the main purpose was to discuss state government reorganization. The difference between his trips and Ford's, he said at a press conference in Pittsburgh on October 2, was that he went less frequently, and the trips were all reported publicly, at the time and since then. "I don't intend to do it in the next four years as President," he went on. "The standards for that sort of exchange of friendship and favors has been substantially raised since the Watergate revelations."

Other Democrats, too, now began to go to the attack. Strauss accused Senator Dole of trying to undermine Charles Ruff, the Watergate special prosecutor, when he said that Ruff's investigation into Michigan Republican campaign records was "nothing but election-year politics." "While Democrats generally have kept their silence with respect to this investigation," Strauss observed, Dole's remark "is the very same response Americans got from Nixon, Agnew—and Dole—in 1972, covering up the Watergate scandal until after the election."

In Plains the next day, Carter called on Ford "to have a frank discussion with the American people through the news media" on the matter of his Michigan campaign contributions. He had no way of knowing whether there was any case to be made against the President, Carter acknowledged, but, he said, "the easiest way to resolve it is for Mr. Ford to face the news media for a change, answer tough cross-examination questions, and let the American people know the facts." He said it was up to Ruff to decide if and when to make any public report.

Finally yielding to public pressure, Ford held an impromptu press conference in the Oval Office. He had never diverted campaign money for his personal use, he insisted, and he expressed confidence that Ruff would conclude the same. He hoped this would be cleared up quickly, for "justice delayed is justice denied."

Carter was caustic about this informal press announcement, at which tape recorders were barred. "As far as I'm concerned Mr. Ford's statement ends the matter. . . . I do feel that Mr. Ford took a step in the right direction, at least by having an unannounced, silent press conference. . . . Later, when he has his open preannounced press conference with sound, there might be even more opportunity for the public to know what went on."

As the final month of the campaign began, *The New York Times* and the Associated Press reported that both the FBI and Ruff were about to close their investigations and give the President a clean bill of health. But the matter instead dragged on for another two weeks.

Carter meanwhile appeared to be working his way out of his slump. He was regaining his old form, hitting the anti-Washington theme, bringing the attack to the Republicans and Ford, and touching the rhetorical bases expected of Democratic candidates by the party regulars. At one point, in Boston, he labeled Ford as "even worse" than Nixon in lack of concern for unemployed workers, and, despite Ham Jordan's warning, continued to link the two men. "The spirit of this country," he said, "has been damaged by Richard Nixon and Gerald Ford. We don't like their betrayal of what our country is, and we don't like their vision of what this country ought to be."

Still, out among the pols, uncertainty about Carter persisted. Joe Crangle, the Buffalo Democratic leader who had tried to draft Humphrey, showed up at a Carter rally and told reporters that the race in this usually Democratic area seemed about even. "We've got our work cut out for us," he said. "I think we can turn it around by Election Day." And at the airport in Boston, while Carter consorted with Senator Ted Kennedy and other state party leaders, Mayor Kevin White stood alone and told reporters how he had not yet been contacted by Carter's coordinator in Massachusetts. White said he was picking up bad signals. "It's not that he's a Southerner," he said. "It's him: he's a very strange guy, and people out there seem to sense it, too." (Mayor White, like all good politicians, was always listening for signals. Mike Barnicle, the *Boston Globe* columnist, wrote that when White was born and the doctor picked him up by his feet and slapped him, White didn't cry: he said, "Whaddaya hear?")

As White talked, Carter was awkwardly going through the ritual of meeting Boston pols, with Kennedy as his sponsor. Kennedy did not look as if he was enjoying it much. A ball-and-a-beer clubhouse pol Jimmy Carter was not. He was cordial, but no backslapper; there were no discernible sparks of enthusiasm. It would not have mattered, except for the new campaign law: Carter needed these people, since the limitation on funds and the drain of paying for television commercials made it impossible to build an organization from scratch without them. Carter had to use the existing political structure if he could, but as he toured the country, reporters heard more and more often that the locals felt they were being ignored, or snubbed. Still, for all this, Carter was the Democratic nominee and the Democrats wanted the White House back.

Carter, as the challenger, tried hard to get the focus of the press and television off himself and on Ford and the Republicans. But the *Playboy* matter died slowly: at Boston College, a large banner hung from the balcony proclaiming: "Jimmy Carter for Playmate of the Year." And at a rally in an airport hangar in Nashville, Vanderbilt students held out a sign that said to Carter: "Smile If You're Horny." Then, at last, another development occurred that countered the *Playboy* interview. Ford all at once was ambushed by something that had been said a month before by a member of his cabinet to a magazine writer, the very same John Dean whose book contained such dangerous allegations.

In an account of the Republican National Convention written for *Rolling Stone* magazine, Dean told of a conversation between himself, the singers Pat Boone and Sonny Bono, and a cabinet officer whom Dean declined to identify:

"Pat posed a question [to the cabinet member]: 'John and I were just discussing the appeal of the Republican Party. It seems to me that the party of Abraham Lincoln could and should attract more black people. Why can't that be done?' This was a fair question for the Secretary, who is also a very capable politician.

" 'I'll tell you why you can't attract coloreds,' the Secretary proclaimed as his mischievous smile returned. 'Because colored only want three things. You know what they want?' he asked Pat. Pat shook his head no; so did I. 'I'll tell you what coloreds want. It's three things: first, a tight pussy; second, loose shoes; and third, a warm place to shit.' "

This remarkable conversation at first attracted little attention, until *New Times* magazine decided to fill the blank: the name of the cabinet member. First, according to George Hirsch, publisher of *New Times,* Dean was pressed to identify him, but declined. Next, each cabinet member's office was checked to determine who might have flown from Kansas City to California on that particular day. The answer: Secretary of Agriculture Earl Butz. Boone then confirmed that Butz indeed was the man.

The White House learned who the culprit was when a network reporter heard about the *New Times* sleuthing and informed Senator Edward Brooke of Massachusetts. Brooke telephoned Butz and told him simply that he was not fit to serve in the cabinet. Butz alerted Dick Cheney that a storm was brewing, and Cheney told Ford late on Thursday afternoon, September 30, in the course of a campaign-strategy meeting attended also by Jim Baker and John Deardourff. The President, Deardourff said later, "sat and shook his head in sorrow and increasing agitation. He said he wanted a strong statement of his own to make it very clear he did not approve of that sort of thing, and intended to talk to Butz at once and then decide what to do." Deardourff volunteered that Butz "ought to be fired," but Ford only repeated he would talk to him.

The President moved quickly—though inconclusively. On Friday morning he had Butz into the Oval Office—the second time Ford had been obliged to call Butz in for shooting off his mouth. The first had been in November 1974, when Butz, at what he thought was an off-the-record press breakfast, told of an Italian woman's supposed comment on Pope Paul VI's opposition to birth control: "He no playa the game, he no maka the rules." Then Ford had insisted on and had gotten a public apology, and he was demanding the same this time.

"The President informed the Secretary," Nessen told the White House press corps late in the day, long after Butz's visit, "that such language and attitudes were not acceptable from a member of his administration. The President told the Secretary the remarks were highly offensive to him and to the American people. The President's statement to Secretary Butz amounted to a severe reprimand. Secretary Butz expressed his regret and informed the President that he was issuing a public apology."

A spokesman for Butz said the secretary "regretted any offense which may have been given to any person or group, and issued a complete apology." Although it was no excuse, the spokesman said, "he was merely repeating a comment made decades ago by a ward politician in a large Midwestern city."

That was not enough for blacks, and certainly not for Democrats. Brooke, publicly labeling Butz's remarks "vulgar and offensive," repeated: "No man who harbors such thoughts is fit to serve in the Cabinet of the United States." Two Republican colleagues, Senators Charles Mathias of Maryland and Jacob Javits of New York, joined him in demanding Butz's resignation. The spokesman for the President Ford Committee, Bill Greener, conceded that Butz's remarks were "shocking and outrageous" and "obviously hurt us." Even Ford's running mate, Dole, was critical: campaigning in Burlington, Vermont, and in Portland, Maine, where protesters toted signs that said "Jerry: Allow Us Some Earl Depletion" and "Butz Is Ford's Agnew," Dole called the remarks "stupid" and "totally tasteless."

Still, for all that, it was an election year and there were some cold political facts to be considered. First, Butz was extremely popular in the farm states Ford needed to win. Second, Ford's hopes of winning any substantial share of the black vote, or gaining the support of white liberals offended by what Butz had said, were minuscule in any case. And so, although members of his own party were demanding Butz's resignation, and though Carter called Butz's remarks "disgraceful" and said he "should have been fired long ago," Ford held off, and pointedly stayed beyond the range of reporters at the White House.

Butz, all this time, was agonizing about what to do. He sought Dole's advice. "I said it was something he would have to work out with the President," Dole said. Others in critical positions were more forthcoming. Paul Findlay of Illinois, the ranking Republican on the House Agriculture Committee, while calling Butz "the greatest Agriculture Secretary in history," added: "The racial slur which he voiced is so revolting that [he] would render a great service to the President if he would offer to resign."

Still, Ford procrastinated. Signals were sent out to Butz through the press that the President would not be ungrateful for his resignation; they were an open invitation for him to put his head on the block. But Ford, so often pictured in cartoons as the flat-footed heavyweight slugger, would not apply the finisher. Like Nixon before him, he disliked personal confrontations, and especially having to fire anyone. And so he fumed and waited for Butz to fall on his own sword. And waited.

It was turning out to be one hell of a lofty campaign, what with lust, profanity, and now racism dominating the headlines. The press gave the Butz story its full spotlight, but it was hard not to, what with Jimmy Carter and Fritz Mondale riding it for all they were worth, and even Bob Dole in characteristic candor deploring it. Another day passed; Butz huddled with his Agriculture Department aides, told them that he thought the reaction was "overblown"; he was inclined to ride out the storm. But the storm would not blow over.

On October 4, a full three days after his first reprimand from Ford, Earl Butz finally resigned. Ashen-faced, he appeared in the White House press-briefing room and told reporters: "This is the price I pay for a gross indiscretion in a private conversation. The use of a bad racial commentary in no way reflects my real attitude. By taking this action, I hope to remove even the appearance of racism as an issue in the Ford campaign." After Butz had left the room, the President came in, looking doleful. He said accepting the resignation "of this good and decent man" was "one of the saddest decisions of my presidency." He praised Butz as "a close personal friend, and a man who loves his country and all that it represents. . . . Yet

Earl Butz is also wise enough and courageous enough to recognize that no single individual, no matter how distinguished his past public service, should cast a shadow over the integrity and good will of American government by his comments."

In the three days it had taken to come to this inevitable conclusion, the Democrats were able to reap the maximum political harvest from the incident; three days in which the Ford campaign was stalled while the President delayed. Butz's remarks were bad enough, but Ford's procrastination was almost worse, raising again the question of how firm his leadership was, of whether he was capable of making hard decisions in a job overburdened with them.

What hurt, John Deardourff said later, was "the failure to see quickly that the Butz matter had to be resolved one way or the other in a very short period of time; that in the glare of the publicity surrounding a presidential campaign the decision-making time has to be truncated substantially. A year before, both the timing and the decision would have been regarded as appropriate. The fact is, he accomplished precisely what I believe he wanted from the outset to accomplish: to have Butz leave, but leave under his own propulsion in a fairly short period of time. . . . You don't immediately kick an old friend and ally in the face. You do what you have to do."

There was little time, though, for post-mortem judgments. The second televised debate between the two contenders was at hand. In this one, they would consider national defense and foreign policy, which everyone said was Gerald Ford's strong suit. More than two years in the White House, and before that many years on the House Appropriations Committee, had prepared him for this encounter with a man whose experience of foreign affairs was largely limited to drumming up business for Georgia in his one term as governor. The second debate was Ford's opportunity, after the recent unpleasantness, to get his campaign on the tracks again.

40. The Second Debate: Eastern Europe

On October 7, the day of the second Ford-Carter debate in San Francisco, Stu Spencer had breakfast with a group of reporters in Washington before getting on the plane for California. As usual, he talked straight: if his candidate were to have any chance to be elected, he would have to win at least five and maybe six of the eight largest states: New York, New Jersey, Pennsylvania, Ohio, Michigan, Illinois, Texas, and California. The first six would clearly be the battleground—industrial, big-city, blue-collar, ethnic, heavily Catholic. Carter had underscored his own vulnerability with Catholic voters by working the New York-to-Chicago ethnic belt so diligently.

The President did not require the extensive dress rehearsals in the White House family theater that had preceded the first debate. But he did review his first performance, and Carter's, on a videotape on which an audience response had been superimposed by Bob Teeter. Teeter had measured studio reaction by having a selected group of viewers press a button to indicate their degree of favorable or unfavorable response to each answer. Then the reactions were scored and a number was superimposed on the tape so that the President could tell at once how the sample audience had received everything he said. He also underwent dry runs with Secretary of State Henry Kissinger, retired General Brent Scowcroft, his White House national security adviser, and Mike Duval, his coordinator for the debate. In addition, background material was given to him in large doses. Ford, one associate said later, "was convinced he'd get questioned on the Helsinki Agreement and its relationship to Eastern Europe and Soviet domination, and/or about the Sonnenfeldt Doctrine." The Sonnenfeldt Doctrine was a reported position enunciated by one of Kissinger's deputies, Helmut Sonnenfeldt, to the effect that the Soviet sphere of control in Eastern Europe was a fact of life; that American policy ought to proceed from an acceptance of it. The Ford administration steadfastly insisted that no such doctrine existed and was certainly not a part of official American policy. These matters were brought up now with Ford, and the President seemed clear about both the facts and the policy. "He knew that subject very well," one participant said.

Ford also went into the second debate with at least one briefing paper, Doug Bailey said, "that suggested his strength would emanate from two incontrovertible facts: the country was at peace, and Jimmy Carter had no practical experience in formulating or conducting either foreign or defense policy." No matter what questions were asked and no matter what Carter said, Ford was advised to reiterate those two facts. This technique is a familiar one to anyone who has ever appeared on television to sell a product, or himself. Experienced book authors, for example, are asked all kinds of questions that have nothing to do with their books; they soon become masters of the trick of ignoring the question and answering in a way that brings the discussion back to their product. This is known as the As-I-say-in-my-book technique; Ford was primed to employ the politicians' variation of it.

One tactic suggested by Bailey was to have the President urge Carter to name the individual he would select as his secretary of state during the debate or at least before the election. Carter, after all, had no experience in the field; Americans should know who would be the brains behind his foreign policy. If Carter refused to say on grounds that such disclosure went against tradition, Ford could point out that it wasn't traditional, either, for a man to run for President without foreign-policy experience. "He understood the problems this would create for Carter," Bailey said, "and he liked that."

Despite all the careful preparation, though, Ford went into the second debate disturbed and distracted by all the speculation about his campaign finances as a congressman. "It had a numbing effect, especially because of Watergate," one of his aides said. "You couldn't throw it off easily. In his bedroom before the debate, he seemed somehow unfocused."

Another aide was more specific. He said Ford was just plain angry. "He developed a very strong dislike of Jimmy Carter. More than anything he was absolutely incensed at two things. One was Butz: he was incensed at the insensitivity of Carter, not to allow Ford and Butz some kind of time to work out the problem. I'm not sure he ever saw it as a legitimate argument that Butz should have been fired thirty seconds after the President heard of the remark. In his mind the only way to approach a problem like that is to give the man time to realize his own mistake and let him take his own initiative; that was the only humane thing to do. The second thing that angered him were the questions that were coming from Carter and others about his own integrity. It absolutely infuriated him. That had him just boiling inside."

Carter, for his part, was suffering too: he had disappointed many people in the first debate by his disinclination to take the argument to the

President, and he had plainly disappointed himself. But he was raring to go now, and this time he agreed as a warm-up to field some questions from aides. For less than an hour, Ham Jordan, Jody Powell, Jerry Rafshoon, Stu Eizenstat, Pat Caddell, Representative Les Aspin of Wisconsin and foreign-policy advisers Zbigniew Brzezinski and Richard Holbrooke went through the exercise with him. Also, he was shown a videotape of the first debate.

The scene of the second debate, San Francisco's Palace of Fine Arts, had a set almost identical to the one used in Philadelphia. The moderator was Pauline Frederick of National Public Radio, and the panelists were Max Frankel, an associate editor of *The New York Times,* Henry Trewhitt, diplomatic correspondent of *The Baltimore Sun,* and Richard Valeriani of NBC News.

From his very first response, Carter went on the attack. Asked by Frankel whether he really differed with the Republican record on foreign policy, Carter replied: "I think this Republican administration has been almost all style and spectacular and not substance. . . . Our country is not strong anymore; we're not respected anymore. . . . We've lost in our foreign policy the character of the American people. . . . We've tried to buy success from our enemies, and at the same time we've excluded from the process the normal friendship of our allies. . . . We've become fearful to compete with the Soviet Union on an equal basis. We talk about détente. The Soviet Union knows what they want in détente, and they've been getting it. We have not known what we wanted and we've been out-traded in almost every instance. . . . As far as foreign policy goes, Mr. Kissinger has been the President of this country. Mr. Ford has shown an absence of leadership, and an absence of a grasp of what this country is and what it ought to be. That's got to be changed."

Ford immediately counterattacked, charging that Carter in 1975 had called for a defense-budget cut of $15 billion and later reduced it to a $5–$7 billion cut. "The kind of defense program that Mr. Carter wants," he said, "will mean a weaker defense and a poor negotiating position."

The battle was joined. For the next 90 minutes the two candidates had at each other, and this time the aura of the presidency was no shield for Ford. Carter aggressively bored in at every turn. When Ford alleged that "Mr. Carter has indicated he would look with sympathy to a Communist government in NATO," Carter shot back: "Mr. Ford, unfortunately, just made a statement that's not true. I have never advocated a Communist government for Italy. That would obviously be a ridiculous thing for anyone to do who wanted to be President of this country. I think that this is an instance of deliberate distortion." So, too, he said, was the charge he had ever advocated a $15-billion defense cut (though a Georgia newspaper did quote him to that effect in 1975).

Doug Bailey, watching the debate on television back in Washington, was pleased to hear Valeriani ask Carter next whether, considering his limited experience in foreign affairs, he ought not to name his secretaries of state and defense and his national-security adviser before the election. Surely Ford would nail Carter now, as Bailey's briefing paper had urged. But when Carter simply declined, Ford let the whole matter go by.

Now the questioner was Frankel, a former Moscow correspondent for the *Times*. He reminded the President of certain facts: "Our allies in France and Italy are now flirting with communism. We've recognized the permanent Communist regime in East Germany. We've virtually signed in Helsinki an agreement that the Russians have dominance in Eastern Europe. We've bailed out Soviet agriculture with our huge grain sales. We've given them large loans, access to our best technology, and if the Senate hadn't interfered with the Jackson Amendment [tying trade to freer emigration of Soviet Jews], maybe you would have given them even larger loans. Is that what you call a two-way street of traffic in Europe?"

Ford proceeded to justify American policy toward the Soviet Union—citing limitations on nuclear weapons and the benefits of grain sales to American farmers—and then he came to the Helsinki Agreement. "I'm glad you raise it, Mr. Frankel," the President said.

But he wouldn't be glad for long. What came next surprised millions of viewing Americans, astonished his foreign-policy advisers, and elated Carter and his supporters. At first the response seemed routine: "In the case of Helsinki, thirty-five nations signed an agreement, including the Secretary of State for the Vatican. I can't under any circumstances believe that His Holiness the Pope would agree, by signing that agreement, that the thirty-five nations have turned over to the Warsaw Pact nations the domination of Eastern Europe. It just isn't true. And if Mr. Carter alleges that His Holiness by signing that has done [so], he is totally inaccurate."

But then Ford added: "And what has been accomplished by the Helsinki Agreement? Number one, we have an agreement where they notify us and we notify them of any military maneuvers that are to be undertaken. They have done it. And in both cases where they've done so, there is no Soviet domination of Eastern Europe, and there never will be under a Ford administration."

Pauline Frederick turned to Carter, but Frankel broke in: "I'm sorry, could I just follow?" he asked. "Did I understand you to say, sir, that the Russians are not using Eastern Europe as their own sphere of influence in occupying most of the countries there, and making sure with their troops that it's a Communist zone, whereas on our side of the line the Italians and the French are still flirting with—"

This time Ford interrupted—surely because he had misspoken in saying there was no Soviet domination of Eastern Europe. Perhaps he wanted to correct himself before matters got out of hand? But no: "I don't believe, Mr. Frankel, that the Yugoslavians consider themselves dominated by the Soviet Union. I don't believe that the Rumanians consider themselves dominated by the Soviet Union. I don't believe that the Poles consider themselves dominated by the Soviet Union. As a matter of fact, I visited Poland, Yugoslavia, and Rumania to make certain that the people of the United States are dedicated to their independence, their autonomy, and their freedom."

In the theater, Jim Naughton recalled later, "there was an audible intake of air. I kept thinking of the Alliance of Poles Hall in Cleveland, and how they might be throwing beer bottles at the screen by then." Stu Spencer, watching with Brent Scowcroft from a room just off the stage, said later of that moment: "Scowcroft went white. Right then I knew we had problems."

Carter handled the moment with aplomb. He calmly picked his targets, one at a time. First, there was Ford's suggestion that Carter was somehow criticizing the Pope. "Well, in the first place," he said curtly, "I'm not criticizing His Holiness the Pope. I was talking about Mr. Ford." (Catholic voters, are you listening?) Then he accused the President of endorsing the Sonnenfeldt Doctrine. And lastly he observed: "I would like to see Mr. Ford convince the Polish-Americans and the Czech-Americans and the Hungarian-Americans in this country that those countries don't live under the domination and the supervision of the Soviet Union behind the Iron Curtain."

The Carter insiders were beside themselves. Pat Caddell turned to Stu Eizenstat. "Oh, my God! I can't believe it!" Eisenstat replied: "That is the dumbest thing I ever heard!" After the debate Caddell went to Carter's dressing room and told his candidate: "That's probably the most decisive presidential debate in history."

Carter, on the scent now, replied happily, "Wait until you see the next one."

Frankel was as surprised as anyone else at the response he had gotten from the President. Only later did he recognize that the framework of the answer—excluding, of course, the incredible argument that there was no Soviet domination of Eastern Europe—was identical to a response Kissinger had given him months earlier in a discussion of the same matter. Kissinger had defended the Helsinki Agreement by saying the United States would not agree to anything that was not already a fact of life, observing —twice—that the Pope certainly would not have agreed unless that was so. It was clear to him, Frankel said, that Ford's answer had come from a Kissinger briefing or briefing paper. Except, of course, the President did not quite get it right.

Months later, I asked President Ford why he had said what he did. "Subjectively," he said, "the East European countries still consider themselves as a people independent. Governmentally they are not, particularly those countries that are actually occupied in part by Soviet forces. In the momentum to answer the question, I thought of it in the first sense, and not in the latter, and I still believe individual Poles consider themselves independent of the Soviet Union. Now, they recognize as I do that governmentally they're not. It was just a little careless on my part in not being more definitive. But it certainly came out the wrong way."

At the time, the seriousness of Ford's error was not apparent to everyone in the Ford camp, certainly not to the President. Riding away from the theater, he and Dick Cheney compared impressions and both agreed that he had performed better than he had in the first debate. A television reporter had run up to the car and tried to ask a question about Eastern Europe, but Cheney and Ford apparently thought nothing of it at the time.

The President returned to the private home where he was staying, talked to his wife by phone, and was just leaving to go to a rally downtown when Kissinger called. According to one insider later, Kissinger "told the President he'd done a great job and he never mentioned Eastern Europe. Then he called Scowcroft just yelling and screaming about it." Scowcroft acknowledged later that the secretary of state had phoned. "He called me and said, 'How did it go?' And I said, 'Well, we've got a problem with Eastern Europe.'" Kissinger and Scowcroft agreed that the national-security adviser had better do what he could to straighten out the matter with the press.

Ford went to the rally at the St. Francis Hotel, but nothing was said about the debate. He returned to his temporary residence and went to bed. Scowcroft, Spencer, Jim Baker, Ron Nessen, and Cheney meanwhile rode from the rally on the press bus. In the lobby of the Holiday Inn, John Carlson, Nessen's deputy, who had been picking up the gist of the press corps' chatter, informed Nessen: "Hey, you've got a real problem on Eastern Europe."

The Ford team huddled and Scowcroft told the rest of them straight out: "Look, let's face it. It was a mistake. The President was wrong."

But nobody thought of calling Ford and getting him to deal with the problem head-on—"I don't know why," Nessen said later. Instead, it was decided that Cheney, Scowcroft, Spencer, and Mike Duval would face the music. And it took only a moment for the first discordant note to be struck.

"Are there Soviet troops in Poland?" was the very first question from the press.

"Yes," Scowcroft replied.

Reporter: "How many, would you say?"

Scowcroft: "Offhand, I don't recall. There are four divisions. I am not sure, but a substantial number."

Reporter: "Do you think that would imply some Soviet dominance to Poland?"

Scowcroft: "I think what the President was trying to say is that we do not recognize Soviet dominance of Europe and that he took his trip to Eastern Europe—to Poland, to Rumania, to Yugoslavia—to demonstrate, to symbolize their independence, and their freedom of maneuver."

Reporter: "Do you think he succeeded in saying what you just said he said? He said Poland was free at one point during that answer."

Cheney: "I think the point was the President was focusing on the fact we want separate independent relationships with each of those nations, and that was the purpose of his travels. I think you would get a similar statement, I would assume, from some of those governments, and that the policy of his administration is that we are interested in separate, independent, autonomous relationships with governments like Yugoslavia, Rumania, and Poland."

Reporter: "Did he misspeak himself? Is that what you are saying?"

Cheney: "I would have to go back and check the transcript, but I think you have to look at it within the context of the allegation that was made, that somehow this administration recognizes or has sanctioned the change or wants a relationship based on the assumption of dominance, and we don't assume that. We want a separate independent relationship with each of those countries."

Reporter: "But he did misspeak himself. That is fair enough to say, isn't it?"

Scowcroft: "I think you have to look at the transcript."

Reporter: "We got his quote."

Scowcroft: "That is clearly what he was getting at. . . . He does not concede the domination of Eastern Europe. That is what he took the trip for—to demonstrate, to symbolize the independence of those countries. He did not concede—"

Reporter: "Are there Soviet troops in Rumania, too?"

Scowcroft: "No."

Reporter: "If we have this many questions about it, do you think

President Ford got his point across to the audience? Why wasn't he able to make this clear?"

Cheney: "I felt it was very clear as I watched it. I understood exactly what he was saying, and I think the American people will understand exactly what he was saying, too."

And a few minutes later:

Reporter: "Let me read you the White House transcript: 'There is no Soviet domination of Eastern Europe and there never will be, under the Ford administration.' Does domination now exist?"

Scowcroft: "I think the point is, he was trying to say that we do not concede the domination of Eastern Europe. That is the whole context within which he made that answer."

Reporter: "He said, 'I don't believe the Poles consider themselves dominated by the Soviet Union.' Is that a valid statement?"

Scowcroft: "I think that is another element of it. In the sense of the acquiescence of the people of Eastern Europe there is no domination at all. Not that we don't concede it. There is none."

Scowcroft was doing his best, and Spencer too tried to be just as positive as possible. "I don't view it as a political problem at all," he said blandly. "I think the President answered the question very forthrightly, and in the manner most people understand. . . . As far as the debate goes generally, I look at it more from the standpoint of perception and style; I think the President was forceful tonight."

As for Cheney, asked to give his "fight card" on the fourteen questions posed to the two candidates, he said he scored it 9–5 for the President. Duval, who previously had said Ford had hit a triple in the first debate and a home run in the second, offered that in his view it was 14–0—and in so doing only made it clearer why he had such a galloping credibility problem with the more discerning members of the press corps. Some were already writing that Ford had committed a "major political blunder."

That quick press reaction, in fact, was blamed later by a number of Ford's key aides for shaping public opinion about Ford's remarks. According to Nessen and Duval, a Teeter poll taken right after the debate had the President "winning" by 11 percentage points; but in successive polls through the next day as the press and television reaction spread, he fell progressively behind, until finally the surveys had him "losing" the debate by an incredible 45 points! "What that meant to me," Nessen said afterward, "was that the average guy in his living room watching the debate did not perceive it to be a monumental mistake. After twenty-four hours of being told it was a bad mistake, the public changed their minds."

Teeter's evidence suggested that the press and television had been inordinately influential in shaping public opinion. Yet would it have been better had they not emphasized Ford's *gaffe*? Should that job have been left to Carter, who after all had done a fair job on his own of pointing out the President's error? The fact was, the media could hardly stand aside. Almost as soon as the President's words were spoken, Republicans were busy trying to minimize or even reconstruct their meaning, and Democrats were trying to maximize their clear message. The press as usual had the task, while conveying both the Republican and the Democratic responses, of putting the whole matter into clear focus and appropriate perspective, and largely did so.

Up to now the Ford strategists had run essentially an error-free campaign, and except for elements outside their control, like the investigations of Ford's finances and the Butz affair, had done a masterful job, bringing their candidate from nowhere in the polls into contention. But now they had a self-inflicted wound to close, and the surgery had to be done fast; there was not that much blood in the patient to start with.

Teeter, who had watched the debate at home in Ann Arbor, phoned Cheney the next morning and told him: "Boy, this is beginning to hurt us."

Cheney replied: "Look, we've been trying. We're working on it." What he meant was that he and Spencer were doing their best to get Ford to admit cleanly he had misspoken, and thereby cut his losses. But the President was just not going to do that. On a flight from San Francisco to Los Angeles that morning, Cheney spoke first to him, alone in his forward cabin, then came back and told Spencer and Nessen the President wouldn't budge. Spencer still wouldn't take no for an answer; he was getting negative signals from all around the country and he knew something had to be done. He and Cheney went forward to work on Ford together. They came back rebuffed again. "His feet were in concrete on this one," Spencer said of the President later. "And he was sore at us for putting the heat on him." Cheney and Spencer huddled with Scowcroft anyway and worked up a draft statement.

At the University of Southern California, Ford said: "Last night in the debate I spoke of America's firm support for the aspirations for independence of the nations of Eastern Europe." The United States, he said, "has never conceded and never will concede their domination by the Soviet Union"—what he probably meant to say, but didn't quite, the night before. "I admire the courage of the Polish people and have always supported the hopes of Polish-Americans for freedom for their ancestral homeland," he said. "It is our policy to use every peaceful means to assist countries in Eastern Europe in their efforts to become less dependent on the Soviet Union, and to establish ties with the West."

The President mouthed the words, but he was still insisting privately to his aides that no clarification was necessary; that he hadn't said anything that required restating. Others, however, saw the matter differently. Carter, in Salt Lake City, said Ford had committed "a very serious blunder" and had "disgraced our country by claiming Eastern Europe is free of the domination of the Soviet Union. . . . It either indicates ignorance on Mr. Ford's part or he stated something he knew not to be true." Carter gave his listeners their choice: the President of the United States was either stupid or a liar. "The Soviet Union has tank divisions and hundreds of thousands of troops" in Eastern Europe; "did Mr. Ford not see those tanks when he visited those countries?"

The response of Aloysius Mazewski, president of the Polish-American Congress, was typical of the ethnic groups' sentiment: "Our people do usually vote Democratic, but we were aware that many of them were not enthusiastic about Carter and were going to vote for President Ford. I think many of them will go back to the Democratic side now." And Victor Viksnins, chairman of the Captive Nations Committee, added: "There are no free countries in Eastern Europe and the President should be the first to know that." Jody Powell, who had just learned about the life-span of a campaign *gaffe,* observed: "It will take him a few days to explain his way out of this one."

But Ford, it turned out, was not all the way *in* yet. The next morning, at a breakfast with a group of friendly businessmen in Burbank, he repeated his statement that the United States did not concede that the Russians should dominate Eastern Europe. Then he added: "It has been alleged by some that I was not as precise as I should have been the other day. But let me explain what I really meant. I was in Poland a year ago and I had the opportunity to talk with a number of citizens of Poland, and believe me they're courageous, they are strong people. They don't believe that they are going to be forever dominated, *if they are,* by the Soviet Union." Incredibly, he had done it again!

The breakfast was held in a small room, with only a group of "pool" reporters admitted, but the program was piped into a nearby press center where most of the traveling press party was able to listen. Very shortly, Ron Nessen got a phone call from John Carlson. "I wouldn't say John was in a panic, but very close to it," Nessen related later. "He was saying, 'This is unbelievable! I can't believe it! The press is going wild! People are yelling and screaming, racing around filing bulletins and laughing!' He made it sound like the place had just blown up in his face." For Ford's staff, the report of a press corps in fits of laughter had to be disheartening. "The East European thing resurrected our worst negative," Bob Teeter said later.

Another aide was more pointed: "It was the 'dumb' issue all over again."

President Ford's campaign entourage proceeded, in emotional disarray, to the next stop, the Glendale City Hall, for a rally. There, as Nessen and Cheney arrived, Carlson came out of the press center across the street. "Ron, don't go in the press center," his deputy told him. "You're going to be bombarded." But there was no alternative. In short order Nessen was surrounded, and so was Cheney when he arrived. Still more "clarifications" were needed.

After the President's rally speech, he was taken to the City Hall, where Cheney and Spencer informed him of the situation. He was plainly irritated, but something had to be done, and fast. After a while, Cheney came out and told Nessen: "I think we're going to have to make another clarification. You make the arrangements."

But that was not so easy. Some of the press corps had already boarded buses about three blocks away, behind a barracks building. Others were in the press center filing copy or phoning. And it was now about two o'clock in the afternoon—five in the east, and very close to the deadline for the evening television shows that Nessen wanted to reach. So a makeshift arrangement was rigged up in a parking lot behind the City Hall. Ford spoke into a hand-held microphone plugged into a speaker system built into the side of his black limousine. Other mikes were then held up to the speaker and piped into the public-address system on the press buses. He realized, the President said, that there were four divisions of Russian troops in Poland and some in other East European countries. But, he said, "that's not what President Ford wants and that's not what the American people want." He reminded his listeners of his support for the so-called captive nations and concluded (a bit sarcastically, Nessen thought): "I trust that my observations will put an end to this misunderstanding."

"Well," Cheney said to Nessen, as the reporters raced to file their stories, "now they have their pound of flesh."

Nessen said later: "Once a thing like that happens, there is a certain mechanism in the press that has to do with pack journalism partly, that requires a person in public life, whoever it may be, to publicly confess his error before the matter is dropped. Once a public figure makes a mistake, he must cleanse himself by publicly admitting his error to get off the hook."

But Carter, for one, would not let his opponent up, even then. In Albuquerque, the Georgian let his instinct for the political kill go unchecked. "Apparently when Mr. Ford went to Poland," he said with obvious malice aforethought, "as happened to Mr. Romney last time, he was brainwashed." That, of course, was the accepted political code word for stupidity and gullibility. "Jimmy has an instinct for the jugular," one of his assistants said, "and he felt somehow he could finish him off." The Romney reference had come up in a staff meeting, and Carter obviously had tucked it away for future use, Powell said later.

In addition to the East European *gaffe,* Ford now was being plagued anew on the matter of his campaign and personal finances. *The Wall Street Journal* reported that a 1973 Internal Revenue Service audit of his tax returns from 1967 to 1972 found that he had violated no laws but that he and his wife must have gotten along with from $5 to $13 a week in pocket money. Also, the audit showed, four times in 1972 clothes for the couple were bought with checks written on a political funds account Ford maintained, and that the IRS had docked the Fords $435 in tax on the income. Also in 1972, the report said, Ford had paid $1167 for a family ski vacation at Vail out of the same political account, later reimbursed with a personal check. Finally, the report found Ford had written the latter check on an already overdrawn bank account, bringing his balance to roughly a minus $3000 at the time. His accountant's secretary explained he had covered the deficit in a few days.

Carter, going for the knockout again, seized on this report too: "I call on the American people to force Mr. Ford to tell the truth, the whole truth, and nothing but the truth." I call on the American news media to insist that Mr. Ford be cross-examined in a carefully prepared, open, previously announced news conference with sound. And I call on Mr. Ford to make sure that these discrepancies are eliminated so the American people will know who he is, what he stands for, and what he means when he makes these conflicting statements."

While he was at it, Carter attacked Ford for another statement he had made in the second debate—his claim that he had supported legislation to penalize American companies cooperating with the Arab boycott of firms employing Jews and doing business with Israel. "He and his administration officials did everything possible to block antiboycott legislation," Carter said, quite rightly. He also ridiculed Ford's debate promise that the Commerce Department would make public the names of companies cooperating with the boycott, noting that the next day the White House said only the names of firms cooperating in the future would be disclosed.

To his aides on the campaign plane, Carter's turnabout to the offense may have seemed warranted and vote-getting, but to his major advisers back in Atlanta, including Hamilton Jordan, Jerry Rafshoon, and Pat Caddell, it was self-destructive overkill. "What we saw was really what was affecting the electorate," Rafshoon said later. "[But] the people on the plane, sometimes you thought they were smoking something. After the second debate, when Jimmy got so aggressive, I got sick. *They* all thought the name of the game was to drive home the breakthrough. But you know how it came over on the tube. It looked bad, it really did. Hamilton sent a Telex to lay off."[1]

Part of Carter's vehemence, Powell told me later, had to do with something he had told the candidate the night after the second debate. More than a week before, Powell had begun to get inquiries through the press about reports that Carter had been involved with other women, some of them specifically named. Powell was certain these rumors came from Republican sources, and he did not want to concern his candidate with them, particularly because the names included that of a woman who, together with her husband, was an old friend of Jimmy and Rosalynn Carter. "I got steadily madder about the whole damn thing," Powell recalled, "and he could tell. He asked me several times before the debate what was the matter with me." After the debate was over, he told Carter. "He was pissed. Even though there was certainly no indication that Ford knew about or had anything to do with all this, it made him mad as hell. And that was one of the reasons I didn't restrain him, didn't say, 'Look, those remarks are a little intemperate.' "

During all this furor, much was written and said about how Ford's remarks on Eastern Europe were going to do him in with the ethnic voters he needed across the Northern industrial belt if he was to win. But Bob Teeter insisted his surveys showed the loss was not in any segment of the electorate so much as in momentum and time. The controversy used up valuable campaign days when there were all too few left, and the campaign leveled off when a steady climb had to be sustained.

The President, flying from California to Oklahoma, finally took steps. He phoned Mazewski, the Polish-American Congress leader, from *Air Force One* and apologized directly for "the misunderstanding." Plans were laid for a meeting with ethnic-group leaders at the White House early the next week. But Carter was campaigning hard in Cleveland, Indianapolis, and Chicago, cities with large East European populations, and he was making the most of the issue, though in a less harsh, more chiding manner than he had in the West. At a meeting in a church in the heart of Cleveland's black community, Representative Louis Stokes, the Democratic power-wielder there, played straight man for Carter by saying, "It doesn't surprise me that Mr. Ford didn't know the condition of relatives of Americans in Eastern Europe. Mr. Ford doesn't know anything about Americans in America. Ask him [at the next debate], 'Where's 88th and Quincy [a nearby

---

1. Carter himself assiduously monitored the campaign as covered by the television networks. Each week, Rafshoon would video tape all three networks' evening-news shows and send them to Plains for Carter's weekend viewing.

intersection]?' " Carter replied that after the election, "There'll be one President in the White House who'll know where 88th and Quincy is." Ford, he said, "is on shaky ground when he talks about experience. If we had wanted experience, we would have kept Richard Nixon. At least other Presidents knew whose tanks were in Poland." And at a dinner of Polish-American leaders in Chicago the next night, he pledged that he would do nothing as President "that suggests we would ever accept permanent Soviet domination" over Eastern Europe. . . . "It's time we had a President who understands the facts about Eastern Europe and who will speak up for freedom throughout the world."

In heavily Polish-American Buffalo, meanwhile, Fritz Mondale marched joyfully in the city's annual parade honoring General Casimir Pulaski, the Polish hero who died fighting for the American Revolution. Some in the crowd happily wore what were to become collectors' items— buttons proclaiming "Poles for Ford." Joe Crangle, who only a week earlier had been talking about needing to "turn it around" for Carter, now said: "We were losing the ethnics: there was no negative on Ford, and there were reservations on Carter. Now there's a big negative on Ford and they're getting to know Carter better." And Mayor Stanley Makowsky said: "Many were undecided. Sometimes it takes one thing that pushes them over the brink. This looks like it."

Even Bob Dole had to admit that the Republican campaign was hurting. The President's statement "presents some problems," he said, especially because Carter and Mondale "are on the trail trying to stoke the fires." He understood that, he said. As one of the great fire-stokers in the business, he most certainly should have.

On his way back to Washington, the President made a swing through Oklahoma and Texas, still probing for the Carter soft spot in the South. He kept hammering at the reports that Carter in 1975 had advocated a $15-billion defense cut, but Jody Powell said he didn't remember it, and even if Carter had made the statement once or twice, "it's immaterial." (This rather remarkable denial seemed to get lost.) And with John Connally at his side, Ford tried to make something of Carter's *Playboy* remarks, saying that "although we had our differences, Lyndon Johnson never distorted the truth when discussing the tough issues affecting America's strength." Attending Sunday services in Dallas at the nation's largest Baptist church, he listened approvingly while the pastor, the Reverend W. A. Criswell, stuck it to Carter from the pulpit: "There are other public media through which we can discuss the moral issues of life and government than the pages of a salacious, pornographic magazine," Criswell intoned.

Back in Washington, Ford finally—five days after the second debate

—admitted on October 12 that he had made a mistake. After a forty-five-minute meeting at the White House with ethnic leaders, he said: "The original mistake was mine. I did not express myself clearly; I admit it." He said he recognized that the Soviet Union through its military power did dominate Eastern Europe, but he would never "accept or acquiesce in this Soviet domination," and "any man who seeks to persuade you that I think otherwise is engaging in deceit and distortion."

Gerald Ford was only saying the obvious, but because it had taken him so long to say it, a campaign that had been on the move had been arrested. Not reversed, however, because Carter's own behavior, and continuing public unease about him, prevented him from taking full advantage of Ford's rhetorical blunder. Yet there was no doubt that the engines of the President's comeback drive had stalled, and there were only three weeks to go until Election Day.

41. Accentuating the Negative

It had not been what one could call an uplifting campaign for the highest elective office in the land. The political horizon had been cluttered with superficial matters: the valances in Clarence Kelley's apartment built by FBI carpenters; artful dodging by both Ford and Carter on the abortion issue, in blatant courtship of the Catholic vote; reports of Ford's free golfing trips and Carter's hunting trips; Carter's dissembling on a tax-reform statement and Ford's dissembling on Carter's dissembling; disclosure that Carter lusted in his heart, and pious denunciation from presumably lustless Republicans; a sick racist joke from a cabinet member who was dismissed but called "good and decent" by his boss; an incredible boner from Ford denying Soviet domination in Eastern Europe. Herblock, *The Washington Post*'s personally gentle but professionally surgical cartoonist, summed up the mess by depicting the two presidential candidates as boxers punching themselves in the jaw as the ringside announcer reported: "Ford is rocked by a left to the jaw—Carter takes a hard right to the mouth—both men are hurting—"

And so was the country. After the long months of sparring and occasional slugging during the primaries and the nearly six weeks of general-election campaigning, there had been little of an elevating nature to mark the 1976 competition for the presidency. One night I went knocking on doors in a low-income neighborhood of Pittsburgh and came upon a middle-aged woman, her hair in curlers, looking at television. "Have you been watching the presidential debates?" I asked her.

"Oh, I watched a few minutes of the first one and then I turned it off," she said. "I don't want either of them influencing my vote. I want to make up my own mind." And there was the woman in California who told Don Oliver of NBC: "I think I'm going to vote for Ford. I voted for him the last time." It was frustrating to anyone who earned his livelihood following candidates around and trying to convey the substance of what they had to say to the electorate. So many Americans were not listening, and so many were listening but not believing.

It was not that the candidates always dealt in superficialities, probed for vulnerabilities in their opponent, succumbed to exaggeration and oratorical bombast. But they performed these public sins often enough to distract attention from their more serious, substantive statements. Perhaps the press should have been more discriminating in what it conveyed. But a political campaign has never been a clean exchange on issues; it has always been, and remains, a dynamic testing ground of a candidate's ability to function—yes, and survive—under extreme pressure, much of it unpredictable, just as a President must function and survive under extreme pressure in the White House. And so, the campaign was not uplifting, or enlightening on a whole range of important issues, but, as Captain Flagg said in *What Price Glory?*, it was the only war we had.

As the final three weeks began, there was more of the same. The President, having vetoed farm price-support increases a year before, suddenly raised wheat price supports by 50 per cent and corn and other grain supports by smaller amounts as a prelude to a campaign swing through the farm belt. Only twenty-four hours earlier, the senior economist at the Department of Agriculture, J. Dawson Ahalt, had told reporters there was "no economic justification" for such aid. Acting Secretary John Knebel conceded that "some people may question the timing" of the increases, but that didn't stop a President who knew he needed the farm vote to be elected and who needed all the help he could get, especially now that he had lost the services of Earl Butz, the farmer's hero.

Having thus done his part to elevate the tone and level of the campaign, the President held a televised press conference and began it this way:

"For too many days this campaign has been mired in questions that have little bearing upon the future of this nation. The people of this country deserve better than that. They deserve a campaign that focuses on the most serious issues of our time, on the purposes of government, on the heavy burdens of taxation, on the cost of living, and on the quality of our lives and on the way to keep America strong, at peace and free. Governor Carter and I have profound differences of opinion on these matters. I hope that in the twenty days remaining in this campaign we can talk seriously and honestly about these differences so that on November second the American people can make a clear choice and give us, one of us, a mandate to govern wisely and well during the next four years."

The background for these remarks had been provided earlier in the day by a statement from Watergate Special Prosecutor Charles Ruff that no evidence had been found to support an allegation that Ford as a congressman had diverted campaign contributions to his personal use. Feeling thus assured that the inquiry had reaffirmed "my personal reputation for integrity," Ford proceeded immediately to turn his back on his own suggestion for a more serious tone in the campaign. He attacked Carter for having "slander[ed] the good name of the United States" by saying in the second debate that the country was slipping militarily and in the eyes of the world. To pointed questions about John Dean's allegation that he helped kill the first proposed Watergate hearings on orders from the Nixon White House, he continued to refuse to reply.

Dean, appearing on NBC's "Today" show a few days earlier, had said that Richard Cook, the congressional lobbyist for Nixon, had discussed killing the Patman hearings several times with Ford, then House Minority Leader. But Cook—though he acknowledged he had met with Dean because Dean was frantic about the possibility of the hearings being held—denied ever having talked to Ford about the matter. Ford, for his part, said: "I have reviewed the testimony that I gave before both the House and the Senate committees, and those questions were asked. I responded fully. A majority of the members of the House committee and the Senate committee, after full investigation, came to the conclusion that there was no substance to the allegations. I do not believe they are any more pertinent today than they were then, and my record was fully cleared at that time."

A reporter tried again: "Mr. President . . . I don't think you quite answered the question. The question is not about your testimony at the time specifically. It is about the new allegations from John Dean that, in fact, you did discuss six times with Mr. Cook the matter of blocking the investigation by the House of Watergate, and at the time you said . . . you did not recollect such discussions. Do you now recollect discussions with Mr. Cook on that subject?"

More stonewalling: "I will give you exactly the same answer I gave to the House committee and the Senate committee. That answer was satisfactory to the House committee by a vote of twenty-nine to eight, and I think a unanimous vote in the Senate committee. The matter was fully investigated by those two committees, and I think that is a satisfactory answer."

The fact was, of course, that when Ford gave his congressional testimony, the tapes of Nixon ordering that Ford be pressed to kill the Patman hearings had not been disclosed; hence he had never been asked about the incident, let alone about specific conversations with Cook. There was one obvious solution: Ruff could check the White House tapes to determine whether anyone ever reported back to Nixon that conversations were, or were not, held with Ford. At issue was whether the present President of the United States might have perjured himself before congressional committees. Representatives Elizabeth Holtzman of New York and John Conyers, Jr., of Michigan asked Ruff to listen to the tapes in question. But he refused, and the election went forward with this allegation—in ways more serious than any other—unchecked.

Later, I talked to President Ford about the matter. "That's all on the record," he said. "I don't want to get in the position today of saying something even slightly different from what I testified to under oath."

Recalling that in the past he had limited his denials to his best recollection and "I do not recall any conversations," I then asked him: "You don't care to make it stronger than 'the best of my recollection'?"

He answered: "That was in 1973, and my recollection today wouldn't be any better than it was then, so I'll leave it just the way I testified."

At any rate, Ruff, in clearing Ford of allegations of impropriety in his campaign finances and doing nothing about Dean's charges, gave the President a breathing spell of sorts, an opportunity to start again after several difficult weeks. In the interlude, the public was treated to a selected short subject, in the form of the first televised debate between vice-presidential nominees.

The idea of a debate between second-echelon running mates had been the League of Women Voters', and Dole and Mondale had readily agreed (though Mondale's camp contended later that Dole tried everything he could think of to delay and get out of the commitment). As was usually the case with vice-presidential candidates, they had not been getting much public attention. Dole's early troubles with reports that he did—and then that he did not—receive illegal corporate contributions from a Gulf Oil lobbyist, and his performance as the overtly campaigning half of the Republican ticket throughout most of September, had earned him more publicity than Mondale. But the Rose Garden strategy brought media coverage to the White House, and as far as the television-watching public was concerned Dole was not really carrying the brunt of the Republican campaign. What he, and Mondale too, did was to provide a presence in the secondary markets of political campaigning—the Camdens and Toledos and Salinas of America—that often don't rate a presidential candidate. They worked the regular-party clubs and the ethnic and church groups; the labor skates, for Mondale, and the Kiwanis set, for Dole. And they tried, in the great tradition of would-be vice presidents, to keep their noses clean. Their constant concern, and unwritten or even unspoken orders, were: Don't screw up.

Mondale had demonstrated an unusual amount of independence from Carter in that he determined from the outset that Watergate was a legitimately exploitable issue; he did not hesitate to castigate the Republicans about it. Mondale also publicly parted company with Carter in evaluating certain civil-liberties decisions of the Supreme Court under Chief Justice Warren Burger—Carter defending the Court's rollback of strictures against the powers of law-enforcement officials, Mondale deploring it. But by and large they made a harmonious team.

Dole, after solving some organizational problems, had proceeded diligently to work the regular Republican lodes, especially in the farm belt. If his barbs sounded harsh to the opposition, the Republican faithful loved them. Only once did he hear anything from his boss, the President, about his campaigning. That was early on, when he was dispatched to a huge farmfest in Mankato, Minnesota, and made a hopeful semiprediction that Ford would raise price supports on wheat and corn, as Dole expected he would. It turned out, though, that the President was not quite ready to do so, and he mildly admonished his running mate for jumping the gun. (After Secretary Butz was dismissed, though, Ford did boost the supports.) Though the Democrats griped about Dole's slashing style, most Republicans in the Ford campaign, even the few liberals, thought he was doing a good job holding the farm states and other Republican loyalists. There was some disagreement about whether this indeed was what the Republican running mate should be doing, when the ticket had to win in major industrial states of the North. But that was another argument, and it had been lost in Kansas City. Dole was pretty much left to his own devices—"an unguided missile," said Lyn Nofziger, assigned to his campaign plane.

Both Mondale and Dole broke off campaigning several days before the debate to pore over briefing books that included their party positions and the voting records of the opposition. Mondale alternated between cramming and playing tennis; Dole, more casually, also studied. The day before the debate, two young aides, Kim Wells and Peter Wallison, posed questions to Dole in his Houston hotel room. But Wells said later: "He resented the debate. He'd been campaigning since August twentieth and didn't have much time to prepare. He was concerned, but, around the Tuesday before the debate, the concern just evaporated. He was very much at ease: cracking jokes, very offhand. He felt confident."

That offhand attitude was noticeable when Dole and Mondale walked onto the set. "I think tonight may be sort of a fun evening," Dole said in his opening remarks. ". . . I've known my counterpart for some time. We've been friends and we'll be friends when this debate is over. And we'll be friends when this election is over—and he'll still be in the Senate." That was vintage Dole. Then he proceeded to make a very rambling introductory statement, lauding Ford in general terms, taking a dig at Carter as ambitious, calling Mondale "the most liberal Senator in the United States Senate." Mondale, by contrast, focused on the national situation as he saw it: high unemployment, "raging inflation," slipping purchasing power, lack of an energy policy, and lack of leadership. He was serious, unsmiling, determined, and, it seemed, just the slightest bit nervous.

Over the next seventy-five minutes, Dole moved from his light vein, in which he repeated his gag description of the vice-presidency as "indoor work with no heavy lifting," to bitter and cutting sarcasm, delivered unsmilingly. Between suggesting that George Meany, president of the AFL-CIO, "was probably Senator Mondale's make-up man" and even denigrating the host League of Women Voters after Mondale had cited the League's high approval rate of his voting record, Dole managed in effect to lay all twentieth-century wars at the feet of the Democratic Party. Asked about his 1974 comment that Ford's pardon of Nixon was "prematurely granted and mistaken,"[1] Dole shot back that the issue of Watergate wasn't a very good campaign issue, "any more than the Vietnam war would be, or World War One or World War Two or the Korean War—all Democrat wars, all in this century." (He used, of course, the abbreviated name of the opposition party that has long been an expression of contempt from the mouths of many Republicans.) And then, noting that he himself still carried the wounds of World War II, he added: "I figured up the other day if we added up the killed and wounded in Democrat wars in this century, it would be about 1.6 million Americans, enough to fill the city of Detroit."

Mondale, who had shaken off his early nervousness and was crisp and aggressive, was incredulous but calm. "I think that Senator Dole has richly earned his reputation as a hatchet man tonight. Does he really mean that there was a partisan difference over our involvement in the fight against Nazi Germany?"

Dole, in sum, behaved like a kid who, when forced to play a game he doesn't like, proceeds to spoil the fun for everyone else. His initial whimsy, disconcerting enough in this serious setting, soon degenerated into standard partisan barbs interspersed with wisecracks. Watergate was "a Republican problem," he acknowledged at one point, but on the night of the break-in, he said, though he was then the Republican National Chairman, it was "my night off." As for Carter, he has "three positions on everything: that's why they have three debates." From start to finish, Dole played stand-up comic and partisan hit man.

President Ford, who watched the debate with Senator Charles Percy in Joliet, Illinois, phoned Dole and told him: "You did great. Your perform-

---

1. Dole might never have been asked the question that got him in hot water if his own staff had not objected to an agreement between two of the panelists, Marilyn Berger of NBC News and Walter Mears of the Associated Press, to switch places and, hence, the order in which they asked questions. As a result Mears got to ask Dole two questions instead of one, and this was the second.

ance was superb." (Percy was less enthusiastic. He told the President, "I thought Mondale scored heavily." And he observed later, "Things that go over well at a hundred-dollar-a-plate Republican dinner don't go over on television.") Two former Reagan campaign aides had even more interesting observations: Charlie Black thought Dole had been "warm" and "conversational . . . [although] a lot of people expected him to come across as a real heavy," and Lyn Nofziger's opinion was that Dole had "lightened the thing up but still got his jibes in." Oh, well. "Every man to his own taste," said the farmer as he kissed the cow.

Carter, from a Kansas City hotel room where he had watched the debate with Senator Thomas Eagleton at his side, phoned Mondale. "You're a great man," he told him. "You showed you're completely qualified to be President. I'm just glad I'm not running against you." But although Mondale had indeed acquitted himself well, the talk in political circles for the next several days was all about Dole. People who had anticipated that he would be a real hatchet man on the campaign trail had until now been disappointed; he had wisecracked, and poked fun at the opposition, but no more than at himself. In his big moment in the living rooms of America, however, he had lived up to his earlier billing: dark, brooding, sarcastic, even mean. I confess that as I sat at my typewriter at *The Washington Post,* watching the debate on television and writing the article about it against a late deadline, I thought of Richard Nixon. It was reminiscent of Nixon's seesaw performance at his famous "last press conference" of 1962, after having lost his bid for the governorship of California. There was a nervous, erratic quality about Dole, a carelessness. He spun off snide remarks almost as if he were unaware of the huge television audience or, perhaps more accurately, as if he were intentionally disdainful of it.

As strongly negative editorial comments rolled in against Dole in the next few days,[2] the Kansas senator picked up on the campaign trail where he had left off. "I thought I was very friendly," he said. "I called him Fritz a couple of times. He called me 'hatchet man.' " If it seemed strange that he would refer to himself using one of the worst labels a politician can have, those who thought so simply did not know Bob Dole. Personally he was one of the most open, good-humored, and straightforward politicians in Washington, so candid that he seemed not to realize sometimes when he was damaging himself. And perhaps because he was so willing to put himself down, he showed no reluctance to put others down, too, and hard.

---

2. George Will, the thinking conservative's columnist, wrote: "On the equitable principle that you should praise those most in need of praise, let us now praise Robert Dole. Until Dole took wing in his debate with Walter Mondale, it was unclear when this campaign would hit bottom."

When he talked about his campaign style, he was not apologetic. Asked why he thought Ford chose him as his running mate, he had said that among other things, "They wanted somebody who could mix it up a little." Obviously, he considered his crack about "Democrat wars"—which he repeated later in the campaign—as no more than mixing it up a little.

Also, Dole saw his job more to keep Republicans in the fold, in the farm states and elsewhere, than to win converts. He pointed to a Teeter poll taken after his debate that showed Republican defections from the Ford-Dole ticket had declined by 8 or 9 per cent. Ford, in paying court to the conservative and Reaganite elements in his party by choosing Dole, ignored the advice in his strategy book to pick "a man who is perceived as an Independent, or at least moderate Republican, without strong party identification," and not to "dwell on the unification problem." Yet just what Dole's performance meant at the election polls on November 2 is difficult to gauge. Teeter contended that it had little negative effect, that Dole had helped to shore up support for the ticket wherever he campaigned. Pat Caddell said that *his* polls showed a slightly negative effect against Dole, with nearly half of his respondents saying they thought Dole was unqualified to be President. In contrast, his surveys indicated Mondale made such a favorable impression that he helped voters gain a more positive attitude toward Carter because Carter had selected him.

At any rate the Carter camp now viewed Mondale as such a plus that a commercial was prepared, for use everywhere but in the South, that showed Mondale and Dole and said: "What kind of men are they? When you know that four out of the last six vice presidents have wound up as presidents,[3] who would you like to see a heartbeat away from the presidency?" "I called it our Mondole ad," Jerry Rafshoon said later.

On only one other occasion did the Carter campaign use any blatantly negative advertising. In Texas, commercials were aired quoting Ronald Reagan criticizing Ford on foreign policy and juxtaposing Carter's voice on the same subject—to show the similarity between Reagan's and Carter's attitudes. These ads were run in the South only.

The Ford campaign, by contrast, was deep into negative advertising, but internal Republican polls suggested that the public did not recognize it. The centerpiece was the man-in-the-street ad masterminded by Doug Bailey. The day after the first Ford-Carter debate, Bailey took a film crew to downtown Chicago and randomly began to film interviews of people who said they intended to vote for Ford. In six subsequent days of filming—there

---

3. Actually, it was four out of the last seven: Ford, Nixon, Johnson, and Truman. Agnew, Humphrey, and Alben Barkley didn't make it.

and in Los Angeles, Houston, Pittsburgh, and Atlanta—some 230 people were interviewed, of whom 50 or 60 were actually used in one or another television or radio ad. The best-known one, eventually, was an interview with an Atlanta woman who said: "My friends here in Georgia don't understand when I tell them I'm going to vote for President Ford. It would be nice to have a president from Georgia—but not Carter." The ads were believed to be effective in the job the Ford campaign now focused on in the final two weeks—fanning public doubts about Jimmy Carter.

Another purpose of the negative advertising was to try to goad the Carter campaign to respond in kind, in the belief that such action would be disapproved of. "One of the reasons that we started the man-in-the-street advertising, which we felt we could get away with because we were the underdog," Bailey said, "was that we hoped they would see that as an excuse to start their own negative advertising." Tony Schwartz, a New York advertising expert known for negative advertising (the famous little-girl-with-a-daisy anti-Goldwater ad in 1964) was hired by Carter in mid-fall, and Bailey and John Deardourff expected that their surmise was correct. Schwartz was responsible for the "Mondole" ad, but other negative ads he prepared were never used—in part at least because Rafshoon developed a deep dislike for him and his work. "He came up with such crap," Rafshoon said later. "He had these Jewish characters in New York on-camera talking about why they were against Gerald Ford and were going to vote for Jimmy Carter. [The technique, of course, was the same as Bailey's highly effective use of an Atlantan putting Carter down, except—according to Rafshoon—actors were used.] And he had this one he called 'The Résumé.' It was like an employment manager sitting there with his finger on a résumé of Gerald Ford. It said: 'Against Medicare,' 'Against This,' 'Against That.' It ended up with a cute line that said, 'Mr. Ford, you'll be hearing from us on November second.' The problem was, he had Ford being against all these things. Probably the American people favored that, all these big-spending bills he vetoed. I looked at it, and I said, 'The effect of looking at that on television was to say, "You're god-damned right. I'm going to vote for him!" ' They were just so heavy-handed. If you're going to do negative advertising on Ford, you can't do anything heavy-handed." Another unused Schwartz ad had a man saying he was out of a job and knew what it meant, but that Ford didn't, because Republicans talked about "necessary unemployment." Still another showed Ford's long congressional record in opposition to social-welfare legislation.

Schwartz wrote off most of Rafshoon's complaints to sour grapes: Schwartz had been featured in a *New York Times* article in mid-October that gave people the impression Rafshoon had been shunted aside. Rafshoon's trouble, Schwartz said later, was that he reacted to negative television advertising "in terms of a print ethic" rather than as something the viewer sees, hears, and feels: *reading* about Ford's rejection of costly programs might make the reader favor Ford, but *hearing* about them was different. "In sound," he said, "you feel what you hear."

At any rate, when technicians and editors in New York film labs told Bailey that Schwartz was working for Carter, "we assumed that meant tough stuff. We waited on tenterhooks for Tony Schwartz's stuff to appear, and it was a great disappointment when it didn't." (Around the country, Bailey had paid workers monitoring local television, primarily to make sure that Ford ads purchased actually ran, but also to make copies of new Carter commercials.)

With three weeks to go, the Ford man-in-the-street ads were aired, and Bailey held his breath for the Schwartz counterattack. "Suddenly," he recalled, "we got a call from a friend at an Indianapolis television station saying the Carter anti-Ford ads had arrived. It got some of us quite excited. We thought they had really overstepped the bounds and were about to make the big mistake. We were told they were scheduled to run about ten days before the election. We assumed that the negative ads would focus in on Nixon, which was clearly the weakest link in our chain, but also the one where we felt Carter could most easily be offensive. Every time he had talked about the Nixon-Ford administration, that was the kind of linkage the public did not like."

Bailey arranged for a copy of this first anti-Ford ad to be shipped to him at once. "Without announcing it in advance," Bailey said, "we arranged for a major press conference in Washington the next day to show that these ads were now running. At one point the idea was for it to be conducted by Richardson and Ruckelshaus, which we felt would be a classic way to turn a Nixon ad against Carter." But when the ad came on, it was not paid for by the Carter committee; it carried a disclaimer saying it had been produced and paid for by the Marion County Democratic Committee. And it was only a single-shot buy in the one city.

"It was a classic," Bailey said in admiration. "Frankly, it was so good we decided not to go ahead with the press conference. It opened with a picture of the White House and a very nonprofessional announcer saying, 'Here's a message from the man who picked Gerald Ford to be President of the United States.' On comes Nixon with a super that says 'Checkers Speech, 1952,' and he does his bit, about how Truman had produced all these problems, yet it was Harry Truman who went out and picked Adlai Stevenson. And he says, 'You wouldn't elect the man who created the problems. Why should you turn around and elect the man he picked to solve the problems?' Then the announcer comes back on and says, 'We couldn't have said it better ourselves.'

"It was very painful. There's no question that the ad was truly ingenious. There was no sophistication to it, in the sense of quality production work. My guess was that it was purely locally produced."

Bailey said that if he had been able to tie the ad to Carter directly, "Carter probably would have lost the election. It would have been considered unfair, and it would have created an issue—Carter trying to run against Nixon—that would have done him in. What we were left with was the problem of whether to try to make a gigantic issue out of one thirty-second ad that was in fact paid for by the Marion County Committee and ran on one station in Indianapolis one time. So we dropped it."

If Carter was careful not to become too negative toward Ford in his advertising, he showed no such prudence in his own campaigning. He continued to say that Ford was "even worse than his predecessor" in dealing with the country's economic woes. At the same time, he complained frequently about Ford's insistence on repeating Carter's slip about raising income taxes for those above the median income, and his reported early pledge to cut the defense budget by $15 billion. On October 16, from the Midwest, Carter sent Ford a telegram about his "erroneous statements about my position on several important issues. . . . I am sure that after these corrections you as a man of integrity will refrain from making these misleading and erroneous statements to the American people." But Ford, whistlestopping through Illinois, brushed the telegram aside, saying he would be "delighted to help [Carter] clarify his position" on any issue. To punctuate the response, at Joliet the President repeated that Carter twice had said he would cut the defense budget by $15 billion, and at Pontiac he reiterated the line about higher taxes over the median income. Carter, Ford proclaimed, would say "anything anywhere to be President of the United States," sounding "like Bella Abzug" in New York and like "a little old peanut farmer" in rural Illinois. "He wavers, he wanders, he wiggles, and he waffles, and he shouldn't be President of the United States."

The campaign seemed destined for a bitter climax. The President and his television ads were pushing relentlessly at Carter; the Georgian, in turn, went to his strength—running heavy advertising in the Southern states that hammered away at Southern pride among whites and blacks, making personal pleas to Democrats at every campaign stop, and whining about Ford's attacks on him.

The Democrats, as usual, had the numbers on their side; getting the bodies warmed up and propelled toward the voting booth was always the principal problem, and Carter addressed himself to it avidly. In Tampa, he told a very friendly crowd that the easy way would be to stay home, to say, "I'm a coward, I'm afraid of the future. I give up on my nation. I'm not going to try to control my own destiny." But he warned them: "We've only got two weeks. If you don't participate and the Republicans do, they'll be in the White House for four more years." And in New York the next night, at a large party fund-raiser, the plea was even more urgent: "To these people who may not take the trouble to come out on November second, I say, please don't be disgusted, please don't give up; our system of government will work."

Out around the country, though, unless one of the candidates made a personal appearance, there wasn't much going on to generate enthusiasm and voter turnout. The campaign spending limitation, and the decisions of both Republican and Democratic campaigns to devote half the available funds to media advertising, was starving local organizations. State campaign managers accustomed to hustling the vote had to hoard the money allocated to them for a push in the final weeks. Old pols, used to doing things in the old way, were miffed—a condition more hurtful to outsider Carter than to Ford, a good old boy among Republican regulars from 'way back. Gerald Doherty, running things for Carter in New York, was accused of merely baby-sitting the Carter campaign there, to which he explained defensively to *The Washington Post*'s Bill Claiborne: "No matter what people in the party may want you to do right now, come October twentieth you have to have a certain amount of money in the till, or by the end of the campaign you'll find yourself over the [federal] spending limit." Grumbling continued, too, about "outsiders" running state campaigns on the Democratic side. Governor Milton Shapp said bluntly that bringing State Senator Joe Timilty in from Massachusetts "has set back the momentum of the campaign tremendously" in Pennsylvania.

On the plus side for Carter, however, was the work of organized labor. COPE, having sat on its hands in 1972, was manning phone banks, sending out voluminous mailings, and otherwise stirring up the troops. All this activity compounded Ford's difficulties, especially in those critical Northern states where the election would be decided. Of the six major ones, Ford was ahead only in Michigan. Polls on both sides indicated that he was in hailing distance of Carter in the other five—New York, New Jersey, Pennsylvania, Ohio, and Illinois. If the President could just make a dent in the South, he might win by taking three of them. California was looking better for him, and the mounting unpopularity of Democratic Governor Brendan Byrne in New Jersey and of Richard Daley's hand-picked gubernatorial candidate, Michael Howlett, in Illinois, gave cause for Republican hopes in those two states. Also, registration was down for the Democrats in New

York, though the party still had a lead of more than 800,000 and would probably come through for Carter. That left Pennsylvania and Ohio as the places where the election might well be decided.[4]

Now, with two weeks to go, Ford was hitting his stride again. He laid plans to make one final Southern swing and then, after the third debate, to stay on the road for the last ten days. Distracting problems, however, continued to bother him. This time it was the wagging tongue of General George Brown, chairman of the Joint Chiefs of Staff, on his favorite subject of Israel and Jews. Two years earlier, at Duke University, Brown had told an audience that Israel had too much influence in the American Congress and that Jews "own . . . the banks in this country, the newspapers." For that, he was rebuked by Ford and he apologized. This time, Brown was quoted in an interview with Israeli cartoonist Ranan Lurie as saying that Israel and its armed forces have "got to be considered a burden" to the United States. And of Great Britain as a power he observed: "It's pathetic now, it just makes you want to cry. They're no longer a world power. All they've got are generals and admirals and bands. They do things in great style, grand style. God, they do it well—on the protocol side. But it makes you sick to see their forces. . . ." This time Ford did not reprimand Brown, and Carter said he thought he should.[5] It was a minor matter, but a distracting one.

As the third Ford-Carter debate approached, the Gallup Poll showed that for all the campaigning and all the millions of dollars spent on radio and television, each candidate had slipped since the previous survey in early October, when Carter had led Ford 48–42 per cent; now he was ahead 47–41, with 2 per cent for Eugene McCarthy and 10 per cent for other candidates or undecided. It was a sobering statistic. Caddell's own polls were bringing in ever more somber signals. "We were seeing serious slides in all the big states, and we were virtually even everywhere—Pennsylvania, Texas, Illinois, Ohio, New Jersey; Florida, Mississippi, and Oklahoma were

4. In Pennsylvania, Carter may have benefited from some kind words he had said more than a year earlier at a wildlife federation meeting in Pittsburgh at which he shared the platform with H. John Heinz III, the Republican senatorial candidate in 1976: "If every member of Congress had the same understanding, sensitivity, capability, and motivation as Congressman Heinz, you would not have to be concerned about the future of our nation." Carter's praise of the locally popular Heinz was actually used in a Carter flier in the Pennsylvania primary. Later, in the general election, with Carter now supporting Heinz's Democratic opponent, Representative William Green, Heinz's media mastermind, David Garth of New York, used the flier and Carter's praise in a one-minute television commercial. Some key figures in the PFC suggested later that Heinz, a big winner, and Carter had entered into a deal to help each other, but the charge was denied.
5. Ford, in a press conference, said Brown's remark was imprudent—but it came out "impudent." Also, as he tried to walk into the East Room, a doorknob came off. "It's easier to get in the Rose Garden," he said. "I guess we had better go back to it."

tightening up, there was slippage in South Carolina and we were losing Louisiana." And if the polling data was predicated on extremely low voter turnout, he said, then Carter ran behind. Also, most notably, Carter was continuing to do very poorly among women. "Particularly housewives," Caddell said. "They were essentially close to us on the issues, but on personality questions they felt far safer with Ford. We had to break through that concern on the risk-safety question and get them to vote on issues."

It was thus not surprising that Carter's campaign, that third weekend in October, sank into a deep funk. Even the usually cocky Hamilton Jordan was depressed. A crisis meeting of all key staff people was called in Atlanta on Monday morning, October 18, in the office of Bob Lipshutz. The situation was reviewed and plans for the last two weeks were mapped out. Then the original braintrust—Jordan, Kirbo, Powell, Rafshoon, Caddell, and Lipshutz—stayed behind to discuss the seriousness of the situation. It was decided that Carter's television advertising had to be refocused before it was too late. It had to take dead aim on Carter's major weakness—that voters, and women especially, continued to be nervous or even fearful about him. "We had to address these attitudes directly," Caddell said, "and in a way that would reassure women."

On the campaign trail, Carter's strident attacks on Ford were being received very badly; their deleterious effect had to be corrected at once—in new commercials, and in the approaching third debate. Powell, Rafshoon, and his writers set to work, along with Caddell armed with his polling data. They labored in Rafshoon's Atlanta office until two o'clock the next morning to produce new copy for the ads. Fearing that Powell's return to Atlanta might lead the press to guess how bad things were, a cover story was put out that he had a bad cold, which happened to be true but was not the reason for his departure from the campaign trail. "We didn't want to tell Jimmy how bad things were," Caddell said, "but when Jody came back he said, 'We don't have to worry. He knows how bad it is. I can tell: When I talk to him, he isn't arguing back.'"

On that Monday, Carter was campaigning in Florida. On Tuesday, he flew to New York for a Democratic fund-raising dinner and that night, at nearly nine o'clock (a strange hour to be doing commercials with a tired candidate, I thought at the time), he was zipped to Schwartz's studio to cut the new tapes. The last copy for the ads was polished by Powell in Atlanta and phoned to Rafshoon, who had flown to New York to prepare for the late-night taping. There was neither time nor inclination to do anything fancy. Carter looked and talked right into the camera (the simple "talking-head" technique) in a calm and benign way, reminiscent of the Jimmy Carter of the early primaries, speaking of his aspirations for the country—

soothingly and reassuringly, his strategists fervently hoped.

Meanwhile the organizational effort was reoriented to aim directly at the electoral soft spots. For example, daytime phone calls were stepped up to reach housewives. Also, Carter was primed to continue the same subdued, benign style in the third debate, for which he and Ford flew to Williamsburg, Virginia. The morning of the debate, October 22, at a preparatory meeting in Carter's suite, he told his insiders that he intended to introduce the matter of the *Playboy* interview himself because of, among other things, the need to reassure women. He indicated what he intended to say, and Kirbo sharpened and smoothed out the language for him.

For this final debate, at the College of William and Mary, each man was for the most part cautious and even-tempered. Ford too had been counseled by his advisers that stridency was inadvisable, and he was reminded not to let Carter get under his skin as he had before and during the second debate. "He just didn't have the capacity for subtlety," one aide said of the President. But neither could Carter entirely curb his tendency to go for his opponent's throat. He accused Ford at one point of a "callous indifference" to the plight of poorer families hard-hit by inflation and unemployment. And when the President contended that under his leadership "the United States is leading the free world out of the recession," Carter said: "With all due respect to President Ford, you ought to be ashamed of making that statement." Carter's aides, in the wings, winced.

Through most of the debate, the President found himself defending his record. Once again he was questioned, this time by Jack Nelson of the *Los Angeles Times*, about the allegations that he had cooperated knowingly with the Nixon White House to help stop Wright Patman's investigation into Watergate. Again Ford stonewalled, and when Nelson raised the question of release of the Nixon tapes that might shed light on the situation, Ford said the tapes weren't under his control and that he believed "the matter is closed once and for all." Carter, notably, declined an opportunity to comment at this point, deftly leaving Ford to stew in his own juice.

Carter, when asked to comment on the low level of the campaign, seized the chance to discuss the *Playboy* interview. He acknowledged that "in the heat of the campaign . . . I've made some mistakes. And I think this is part of just being a human being. I have to say that my campaign has been an open one and the *Playboy* interview has been of very great concern to me. I don't know how to deal with it exactly." Other public figures, including Jerry Brown, Walter Cronkite, and Albert Schweitzer, had given interviews to the magazine, he noted, as well as Ford's own secretary of the treasury, William Simon, and conservative columnist William Buckley. "But they weren't running for President," he said, "and in retrospect, from hindsight, I would not have given that interview had I to do it over again. If I should ever decide in the future to discuss my deep Christian beliefs and condemnation and sinfulness, I'll use another forum besides *Playboy.*" And then, being Jimmy Carter, he added: "But I can say this: I'm doing the best I can to get away from that and during the next ten days, the American people will not see the Carter campaign running television advertisements and newspaper advertisements based on a personal attack on President Ford's character. I believe that the opposite is true with President Ford's campaign and I hope that we can leave those issues in this next ten days about personalities and mistakes of the past. We've both made some mistakes. . . ."

Ford, on the same question, alluded to Wayne Hays and other powerful Washingtonians plagued by sex scandals: "We have seen on Capitol Hill, in the Congress, a great many allegations of wrongdoing, of alleged immorality. Those are very disturbing to the American people." The country was turned off, too, he acknowledged, "by the revelations of Watergate, a very, very bad period of time in American political history," and by the Vietnam war. But he cited the nation's bicentennial celebration as evidence of a new spirit in the country, and he too pledged to conduct his campaign on a high plane during the last days.[6]

Ten days to go. For those who had been involved in the marathon from the beginning, it was hard to realize that the hour of decision—the great national electorate finally choosing between the two survivors—was at last so close. Now it was time to sprint to the wire, to throw all remaining resources of money, wit, energy, and human endurance into the run. Whatever kick the runners had left in them was called for, and had to be expended, now.

6.The candidates might have had a chance, then and there, to demonstrate their commitment to a heightened level of campaigning, had the third debate's panelists carried through with a plan they had hatched beforehand. They agreed that when they got to the time for the last questions, they would waive their time and request each candidate to ask his opponent one question. The moderator, Barbara Walters, was so informed just before air time, but the timing at the end got confused and the idea was not carried out.

42. Down to the Wire

One morning in mid-October, Bob Teeter and John Deardourff were talking about having President Ford campaign in major cities via the format of a television talk show, so as to reach the largest possible audience. Who, they asked themselves, would be the ideal host? Deardourff started ticking off names. "I wonder where Hugh Downs is? Or Frank Blair?" And then he said: "Joe Garagiola." Teeter replied at once: "That's the guy." They tried the idea out on Ford later in the day, and his response, too, was instantaneous: "That would be terrific." And so was born "The Joe and Jerry Show"—the centerpiece of Ford's last desperate dash for an upset victory.

The last ten days of Ford's 1976 campaign seemed a blur, a mad race around the country—the President, the presidency, *Air Force One,* all the trappings of executive power, and Joe Garagiola were on constant display. Ford, encouraged by Teeter's polls and driven by his own determination, threw himself into the effort wholeheartedly. He used one set speech, positive and upbeat, over and over. And in California, Deardourff unveiled his secret weapon: Garagiola, the former St. Louis Cardinal player turned television personality, a disarmingly open, unassuming, regular guy. He had met Ford in July, flying with him to an All-Star game in Philadelphia, and now he was signed on to host six "talk show" commercials of half an hour each.

Garagiola, who had retired with a mediocre .257 lifetime-batting average as a hard-ball catcher, proved himself more adept as a softball pitcher, tossing up easy questions to Ford and then marveling as the President belted them effortlessly into the bleachers. Garagiola, with prominent local Republicans sitting in, would ask toughies like: "Gosh, Mr. President, there sure are a lot of people worried about taxes, and just what are you going to do to help them out?" Or:

Q: "How many world leaders have you dealt with?"

A: "One hundred twenty-four leaders of countries around the world, Joe."

Upward of a million viewers looked at "The Joe and Jerry Show" in each of the major industrial states. At a cost of $60,000 apiece, they constituted one of the prime bargains of the campaign. In the final week, Ford even used the format to deal head-on with "the Nixon problem"—the concern that his pardon of his predecessor, or indeed any association of him with Nixon in the public mind, might be his undoing. In Chicago, Garagiola was programed to ask him about the differences between the Ford and Nixon administrations. "Joe," the President obligingly replied, "there's one very fundamental difference. Under President Ford there's not any imperial White House, which means there's no pomp, there's no ceremony, there's no dictatorial authority. We've tried to run the White House as the people's White House, where individuals have an opportunity to come individually or in groups and express to me their views and recommendations." To hear him tell it, it sounded like Andy Jackson revisited. And in Philadelphia, Garagiola underhanded one about references to the "Nixon-Ford adminis-tration." Ford swung effortlessly into it: "We don't get much of that because I think the average guy in the street knows that on August 9 [1974] there was a distinct break between the previous administration and between my administration."

It was all very relaxed, and the same mood seemed to be catching on outside the television studios too. In San Diego, on the next-to-last Sunday night of the campaign, there began one of those cherished side-shows that keep campaign junkies going. This one could have been called "President Meets Chicken" and, as was often the case in such epics, a featured per-former was Wee Jimmy Naughton of *The New York Times.* It so happened that among a galaxy of movie stars, entertainers, and other celebrities on hand for a Ford rally that night was a personage known only—and widely in the San Diego area—as "The KGB Chicken." He was a young fellow, reputedly paid about $18,000 a year to attend parades, football games, and, if necessary, bar mitzvahs, costumed as a chicken, complete with a huge chicken head, to publicize the local radio station. The moment Naughton saw the chicken, it was love at first sight.

"He was a very good chicken," the reporter said in admiration, recall-ing the episode later. "He was very enthusiastic. When the band played 'The Star-Spangled Banner,' the chicken's beak synched it. And when the invoca-tion was given, the chicken bowed his head. He was a great chicken."

After the President arrived, he thanked all the movie stars and enter-tainers, who included the Serendipity Singers ("Those supersingers—Serebinity," he called them), and then he saw it. He stared, then guffawed, in his thoroughly open way. "The chicken! I love it!" he yelled into the microphones. And with that, the chicken came strutting across the stage, arms flapping, and, as if he were Sammy Davis, Jr., himself, embraced the President of the United States. Ford, delighted, hugged the chicken back.

Naughton, standing to the side in the press section, said half to himself: "I've got to have that chicken head." Ron Nessen overheard him. As the program proceeded, he led Naughton through the Secret Service to the edge of the stage, where he introduced him to the chicken.

"I'd really like to take that head along," quoth Naughton to the oversized barnyard visage before him.

"I can't let you have this one," replied the chicken, "but I have another one at home that I paid a hundred and twenty dollars for."

"How about a hundred dollars for a used chicken?" Naughton offered.

A deal was struck. The chicken gave the reporter his card—it said "KGB Chicken," of course—and they shook hands. The chicken promised to deliver the goods to the Town and Country Motel that night, and Naughton, returning to his room after a cocktail party, found it on his bed. This magnificent object was nearly three feet high, with a large red comb on top. Naughton loved it dearly.

On the press plane the next day, Chicken Jim Naughton modeled his new acquisition for his colleagues, and cameras snapped up and down the aisles. That night, the President elected to hold a late press conference at the airport in Portland, Oregon. Chicken Jim, working as he did for an Eastern daily, could not hope to make his last edition at that hour, so was at loose ends.

"I said, the hell with it, and went back on the plane, got the chicken head, put it on, and stood on the tarmac to the rear of the press conference." Other reporters and Dick Cheney egged him on—so to speak—saying he was chicken if he didn't ask Ford a question. At one point a Secret Service agent came up and grabbed him by the upper arms. But motivated only by duty, not curiosity, the agent simply asked: "Do you have a credential?" When the chicken showed one, the agent said, "Oh. Okay," and went about his business.

As the press conference proceeded, two CBS film crewmen suddenly hoisted Naughton to their shoulders. As seen later in a CBS film clip taken from over Ford's shoulder, there unexpectedly emerged from the crowd of sober-faced reporters this huge chicken head. The President played it cool and said nothing. Later, in a reception line, the chicken again greeted a laughing Ford. Naughton was primed to say to him: "Mr. President, your campaign puts me in a fowl mood." But he forgot his lines (fortunately, some would say) as Ford hugged him and asked: "Are you going to put this on your expense account?"

"Sure," Chicken Jim told him.

"How can you do that?"

"I'm going to put it down," Naughton explained patiently, "as

'Chicken for the President.' " And he did, to the tune of $100. (The night after the election, at a cocktail party, Naughton informed Arthur Ochs Sulzberger, publisher of the *Times,* that since the caper had been so widely publicized, he was indeed going to put the cost of the chicken's head on expenses. Sulzberger said by all means, and even told Naughton to send the bill directly to him. The reporter did so, noting for anyone who might think $100 for a chicken for the President a strange item: "Approved by Mr. Sulzberger, 11/3/76." It sailed right through.)

The chicken caper captured well the cheerful optimism that now pervaded Ford's campaign. Serious *gaffes* had been forgotten, along with the Rose Garden strategy, and he was running full tilt toward the finish line. Yet he still had some troubles, to be sure. One was the lack of help from Ronald Reagan. Reagan continued to campaign, but essentially for Republican congressional candidates, talking about the conservative platform shaped to his liking at the convention. Jim Baker, Ford's campaign manager, tried again to get Reagan to make a swing for Ford through pivotal Southern states but Reagan by now had a full schedule that he said he could not change.

Then there was the economy. The statistics continued to haunt Ford: on October 28, five days before the election, the Commerce Department's index of leading economic indicators fell for the second straight month, by seven-tenths of 1 per cent, with farm prices dipping 5 per cent from mid-September to mid-October. Carter, campaigning in Philadelphia, argued that they made "a mockery of Ford administration predictions" of economic recovery. The prospect, he warned his urban audience, was for "a further decline in the standard of living for the average worker." The country "simply cannot depend on those who created this economic mess to clean it up," he said.

Finally, there was Bob Dole. In Providence a week before Election Day, he reiterated his line about "Democrat wars." Already thoroughly censured for the observation in his debate with Fritz Mondale, Dole nevertheless observed: "Four times in this century we have gone to war. Each time the harsh light of history reveals that war rarely began for reasons that were self-justifying—but, rather, because of weakness, wishful thinking, and bad leadership." Asked how a Republican President would have handled the Nazi and Japanese threats in World War II, he said, lamely, "I don't know about that." Of that war, and his crippling injuries in it, he said: "I've had a lot of reservations—not about fighting it—but every time I get dressed in the morning, I think about it. . . . Without sounding like flag-waving, I have to struggle to button my shirt. I don't have any feeling in my left hand.

I can't use my right. You begin to think how it happened. I guess I'm fair testimony that I did my bit for my country."

The next day, in Troy, Ohio, Dole pulled back. He read a statement conceding that Vietnam and World War II "were not partisan wars in the sense that a clear division of political philosophy separated the party in power from the other party when the fighting broke out. They were fought for what was perceived to be in the national interest. No, I don't believe World War II was a Democrat war and I don't believe Vietnam was. But I do know that no country is likely to attack us or attack our allies if we are strong, and through strength Gerald Ford has given us a world at peace." But a day later, asked at a news conference whether he was still calling the last four wars "Democrat wars," Dole blandly replied: "I never did, never did."

By now, so certain was Carter that Dole had become a detriment to the Republican ticket, he took to running on the coattails of his own running mate. "Remember," Carter told a crowd in Pittsburgh on October 27, "you're voting for a ticket, not just one man. . . . Carter-Mondale, that's our ticket. Ford-Dole, that's the other ticket." (Mondale, meanwhile, continued to tie the Nixon can to Ford's tail. "Nixon and Ford say you can't put people back to work," he said in Akron, "but Carter and Mondale will.")

This invocation of Mondale was more than icing on an expected victory cake. In Illinois, the *Chicago Sun-Times'* poll indicated Carter's lead had shrunk in a week from 10 percentage points to 1; in New York, the *Daily News* had Carter slipping from 9 points to 6; elsewhere, in critical states, Bob Teeter's surveys, taken nightly, showed the gap closing. On October 30, the Harris Survey, in conjunction with ABC News, indicated what the electricity of the campaign trail was already communicating: it was now a horserace—Carter 45 per cent, Ford 44 per cent, as of a week before the election.

Ford's television advertising campaign was now in full swing, reaching millions more people than the voices of Jimmy Carter warning of economic disaster, of Fritz Mondale reminding of the Nixon connection, or of Bob Dole and those "Democrat wars." And Ford, the grinning Garagiola always at his side, was pushing himself hard; his voice was starting to go under the strain of long hours of exhorting the large crowds that came out for him. He seemed more and more confident, and his staff was exuberant. "We've got our number together," Ron Nessen said on the Thursday before the voting. ". . . It's going to be a landslide. We're going to gloat for four years." (The next night, incredibly, the Ford party spent several valuable hours going thirty miles by motorcade from Houston to Baytown, Texas, so the President could watch a high-school football game. "A little bit of a break for the President," Nessen called it. And if it reminded a nation of football freaks that Jerry Ford was one then, well, so be it.)

As Carter worked the Northern industrial belt, he hinted at but pointedly did not promise a tax cut, drew good but not exceptional crowds, and expressed confidence—yet there was growing tension among his staff. In New York, he assured a crowd he would never tell New York City to "drop dead"—as a headline in the New York *Daily News* had once characterized Ford's refusal to provide federal aid to the impoverished city. Ford himself had never uttered that phrase, and earlier, when Tony Schwartz, the political advertising expert, had prepared an ad for Carter using the same words, it had been rejected as too harsh. But previous expressions of high standards were not always remembered in the final heated days.

Carter got last-minute help from the U. S. Supreme Court when it rejected a request from Eugene McCarthy to set aside an order by New York state's highest court keeping his name off the presidential ballot. McCarthy's candidacy, the subject of much ridicule all year long as the brilliant but acerbic former senator pursued his independent course, was not dismissed cavalierly by the Carter strategists. They had been concerned that McCarthy might drain off significant segments of New York's liberal Democratic vote, possibly tilting the state and, with it, the whole election to Ford. Carter's supporters had been in the forefront of the legal battle in New York to bar McCarthy from the ballot. Also, Sam Brown, state treasurer of Colorado, the youth coordinator for McCarthy's 1968 presidential campaign and later a leader of the 1969 Vietnam moratorium demonstration in Washington, was persuaded to write to former McCarthy backers, urging them to support Carter. For his troubles, Brown received a visit later from a McCarthy coordinator in Colorado, who gave him a present—thirty pieces of "silver"—three dollars in dimes—and a note that said: "In case Carter forgot." Jimmy Carter was not the only candidate who turned to the Bible to get a message across.

Carter, for all his self-confidence, was showing some signs of strain. At a breakfast for senior citizens in Pittsburgh on the final Thursday morning, he walked up to Ed Bradley, the CBS correspondent covering him. Carter had seen CBS's report of a parade and rally in New York's garment center the day before (coverage of which, in Carter's view, had been botched because of poor positioning of the camera truck). What did he think of it, Bradley asked warily, noting Carter's icy mien. "I thought it was crummy," Carter snapped.

On the last weekend, Ford swung up from Texas to a suburb of

Philadelphia; across upstate New York in the rain, to Long Island for a massive rally at the Nassau Coliseum; west to Pittsburgh, and on to his home town of Grand Rapids for a stirring and emotional wind-up on Election Eve. By now he was so hoarse he could hardly speak, but at each stop he rasped out his plea for support. He was excited, revved up; as he mounted the platform at each rally and the band played the Michigan Fight Song, he would raise his fist, wave it in time, and shout "Let's go! Let's go! Let's go!" like a cheerleader. At his side at every stop, introduced as "your friend and my friend," was Garagiola, looking for all the world like a kid at the World Series. The old ballplayer told the crowds, "Unless you vote, it's like loading the bases and then praying for rain," and the audiences loved it. "What you see is what you get," Teeter said later approvingly of Garagiola. It was a comment he could have made about his candidate as well, which may have been why Garagiola proved to be such a valuable and effective home-stretch resource. Not even the patented Ford goofs could quell the rising enthusiasm. In a Philadelphia suburb, under a huge lighted sign on a high-rise building directly in front of him that read "One Oxford Valley," the President said how glad he was to be "right here in Orchard Valley, Bucks County." After the laughter died down, he added: "We were in the right county, anyway."

In town after town, Ford's campaign was like a floating football rally. In Syracuse, after greeting Ben Schwartzwalder, the old Syracuse football coach, and Dolph Schayes, the all-time Syracuse basketball star, and introducing his friend Joe, Ford told the crowd: "You know, we're in the last quarter and the ninth inning. That's when you win. That's when Dolph Schayes used to win for you in Syracuse, that's when Joe Garagiola used to pull it through, and that's when Jerry Ford is going to win!" It was all so informal, so chummy, that folks seemed to forget that Jerry Ford was the President of the United States; they slapped him on the back and they hugged him; the fact was, they *liked* him, because he *was* a regular guy.

The mood was getting absolutely buoyant now; Ron Nessen sat in the rear of a press bus and talked about how he was going to take Jody Powell on a tour of the White House after the campaign was over—as a visitor to the press secretary's office, not as a future occupant. And who could argue with him? The Gallup Poll in its final survey had the President edging into the lead for the first time, 47 per cent to 46 for Carter, and 4 per cent undecided. It was, of course, too close to call: a margin of error had to be allowed in the science of polltaking. But the fact that Ford in the summer had been 33 points behind made the final figures, and the comeback, remarkable, no matter what the final outcome might be.

On the last campaign day, Monday, November 1, Ford spoke at an airport rally in Akron-Canton, a noon rally on the steps of the Ohio state capitol in Columbus, at a shopping mall rally in Livonia, Michigan, and then on to a massive, teary homecoming in Grand Rapids. Under a banner over the main street that read "Welcome Jerry and Betty, GR Loves You," he motored to a giant rally on the steps of the Pantlind Hotel. His voice choked with emotion and tears welling in his eyes, he urged his fellow Michiganders to support him one more time, and then, with his arm around his wife, joined them in singing the Michigan Fight Song a final time. It had been an extraordinary odyssey, this campaign that led Gerald Ford back to the constituency that had made him its congressman in twelve consecutive elections. He ended with greater hope and expectations than he could have dreamed—only two months earlier—would be his.

For Carter, the final weekend was one of more than customary eleventh-hour campaign trepidation. As he made his own last swing, through Louisiana and Texas, out to California, and back to Michigan in a last-minute effort to grasp Ford's home state from him, an incident back home in Plains threatened suddenly to undo him. On Sunday, October 31, the Plains First Baptist Church—of which he was the most celebrated member —without prior notice canceled its regular services when a black minister seeking membership presented himself to worship there.

The minister, the Reverend Clennon King of the nondenominational Divine Mission Church in Albany, Georgia, about forty miles away, came to the door of the small country church with two black women and a child. He was turned away by the pastor, the Reverend Bruce Edwards. Edwards, himself an advocate of full integration in the church, informed King that the church's board of deacons on the previous Tuesday night had voted, over his opposition, to deny King, who was not a Baptist, membership and to call off the Sunday services if he showed up.

King's effort to gain membership had all the earmarks of a partisan effort to embarrass Carter, who eleven years earlier had opposed the policy of exclusion when it was originally approved by the deacons. King insisted that politics had nothing to do with it. "There's no timing at all," he said, "but God times things. I don't know why God timed it this way." To some more skeptical observers, however, the idea leaped out that it was not God doing the timing, but enterprising Republicans. Since the 1965 policy was set, Carter had brought a number of blacks into the church to worship— state troopers when he was governor and later, when he was a presidential candidate, Secret Service agents. But there were no black members, and so far as could be determined no black had ever tried to become a member until now, the Sunday before the presidential election.

Carter had learned about the deacons' decision three days earlier, in a phone conversation with Edwards' wife, but had decided to say nothing. Told about the confrontation that Sunday afternoon while campaigning in Fort Worth, Carter said: "The only thing I know is that our church for many years has accepted any worshipers who came there, and my own deep belief is that anyone who lives in our community and who wants to be a member of our church, regardless of race, ought to be admitted. And I know that the pastor agrees with me. I hope this will be the outcome of the problem in Plains." And later, on the way to San Francisco, he added: "For several years, the Plains Baptist Church has admitted worshipers without discrimination. I will seek church action to continue worship opportunities and also offer membership to those who live in our community and who share our religious faith."

The reference to "those who live in our community" was purposeful, of course. King—well known in south Georgia as a political maverick and windmill-tilter, a minister of his own church forty miles from Plains—was immediately suspect. He had run for President in 1960 on an Afro-American Party ticket; in 1962 he had sought and failed to receive political asylum in Jamaica on grounds of "insidious persecution in the United States"; in 1966 he was arrested in Chicago and jailed on a California charge of failing to provide support payments for his six children. He spent four years in California prisons before the law under which he was imprisoned was overturned by the state Supreme Court. And in 1970 he had threatened to run as a Republican against Carter for governor, but eventually did not. If this *was* a put-up job, the Republicans might have come up with a more credible figure.

The incident nevertheless shook the Carter campaign, coming as it did in the final forty-eight hours and threatening the very heart of Carter's support, the black vote—especially in the South. One prominent black leader in Philadelphia, a former Udall backer named Charles Bowser, said: "I don't know if I can go on campaigning for Carter. The news discouraged me and if it is widely disseminated, it could discourage a lot of black people about Jimmy Carter. The question in my mind is, How could the man justify staying with a church that passed such a rule?" And Walter Fauntroy, the District of Columbia's delegate to Congress and a black minister, said it was "incredible that a Christian church could have such a policy." But he said he hoped "the nation's future doesn't turn on what a few hypocritical people in a church in south Georgia do."

Once again, as in earlier controversies, Congressman Andy Young took the lead in mobilizing support for Carter in the black community, which was already rising to his side, so fishy did the whole incident seem. "We orchestrated quite a response," Ham Jordan said later of an effort coordinated in Atlanta on Sunday night by Landon Butler. "All the things that happened to us, and then all of a sudden out of the blue *that* happens —and it backfired. Southern conservative whites resented it because they saw it as an improper use of Carter's church and private life to embarrass him. And then it was a kind of rallying point for blacks who were embarrassed by Clennon King. . . . We got Jesse Jackson to make a speech up in Boston and we recorded some stuff, and Andy, with Daddy King, coordinated a black response. I called Jimmy, we had been working on it all night, and Andy was somewhere else and he was plugged in on a telephone patch. He said to Jimmy, 'We got a problem, but you don't need to dodge it or resign from your church.' We had no way of knowing what the reaction would be, but it turned out to be a plus, mostly because of the way Carter handled himself. A lot of people in the country felt sorry for him. Here's a guy running for President and he's got this guy trying to embarrass him in his home town."

Jody Powell, in Sacramento with Carter and having learned only shortly before of the final Gallup Poll showing Ford edging ahead by one percentage point, thought it was important enough to awaken the candidate. "The only time in the whole two years when I actually almost thought we were beat was that Sunday night," he said later. "It was five o'clock in the East, but I called my wife, I felt so bad. With that and the Gallup Poll, that was a very bad night."

Two things, he said, bailed Carter out. One was a decision to face the matter directly on television the next morning. After Carter had talked with Young, Powell said, "we decided the best thing we could do, based on the *Playboy* experience frankly, was to address the damn thing."

Early the next morning, a press conference was held in Sacramento at which a grim-faced Carter said, in line with Young's advice, that "I can't resign from the human race because there's discrimination . . . and I don't intend to resign from my own church because there's discrimination. I think my best possible approach is to stay with the church to try to change the attitude which I abhor." Coretta King, who went on to Los Angeles with Carter, added that "the raising of this issue at this time has been instigated and is consistent with the low level on which the campaign against Governor Carter has been run."

The other saving development was a timely reaction to yet another occurrence on the part of Powell's assistant, Betty Rainwater, back in Atlanta on Monday. The word got out that the President Ford Committee had begun to send out telegrams to four hundred black ministers around the country, signed by campaign manager Jim Baker. The telegrams asked:

"If the former Georgia Governor and life-long member of the Plains Baptist Church cannot influence the decisions and opinions of his own church, can we expect him to influence the issues and opinions of the United States Congress?"

The head of the PFC's "black desk" told UPI the telegrams were sent in response "to a number of calls we got about why the church was closed" —a transparent alibi. "The prevalence of such a telegram to so many black ministers seems to be conclusive evidence that this whole episode is designed to embarrass Mr. Carter," said one recipient, the Reverend Alfred Waller, pastor of the Shiloh Baptist Church in Cleveland.

On Monday afternoon, the office of Democratic Representative William Clay, a Carter supporter in St. Louis, got hold of one of the telegrams from a black constituent and notified Betty Rainwater. A copy was telecopied to Atlanta and, according to Rainwater later, the Carter people noticed it was stamped with a time only minutes after the story of the Plains incident had moved on the news wires Sunday. It was now late Monday afternoon, shortly before the network television evening-news shows were to start. Rainwater phoned the three major networks, pointing out the apparently almost simultaneous release of the telegrams with the episode itself. That night, Walter Cronkite on CBS reported the allegation on his show, watched by millions. "If the thing had broken as hard the other way as it eventually did for us," Powell said, "we could have lost the election. But in a way it invigorated and gave our black supporters something to do, something to talk about, a renewed incentive for the last two days."

Baker said later that it was a mistake to have sent the telegrams, which he said were cleared through Elly Peterson, a deputy chairman for voter groups, and Spencer. As for having anything to do with the Reverend King applying for membership in the church on the Sunday before the election, Baker said that "as far as I know" the Ford committee was innocent.[1]

Carter's campaign, in any event, had great expectations about the black vote. Some of the most prominent black leaders—Jesse Jackson, Coretta King, Representative Barbara Jordan, Mayor Richard Hatcher of Gary, Indiana, and others—in special programs financed by the Democratic National Committee called "Wake Up, Black America" and "Operation Big Vote," had been speaking all over the country, urging blacks to register and

---

1. Baker acknowledged that as a result of extreme prudence in accounting procedures to make sure the federal ceiling of $21.8 million on spending was not exceeded, the Ford campaign left about $1 million unspent. The money could have been used for more media advertising at the end or for any number of neglected needs. In pursuit of the black vote, for instance, the PFC allocated only $270,000, Baker said. Dole, for one, made much of this neglect later.

vote. Claims were made that a million new black voters had been registered, and John Lewis, director of the Voter Education Project in Atlanta, said half of them were in the South.

Still, Carter and his aides had no way of knowing how this eleventh-hour controversy would cut with the voters, white and black. That uncertainty, plus the Gallup and Harris polls differing on who was ahead but agreeing that the election was too close to call, kept the Carter entourage bound in tension. But very large crowds in southern California boosted the candidate's spirits; he was able to sleep on most of the four-hour flight to Flint, Michigan, where he made his last-ditch effort to deny Ford his home state. Mondale joined him in Flint for an enthusiastic and emotional finale, and then the two men parted and each headed for home, to vote on Tuesday and await the judgment of the nation.

For millions of Americans, the last act of the campaign was the viewing of two carefully prepared television appeals, each thirty minutes long, run on each of the three major networks on a rotating basis, from eight o'clock Monday night to eleven o'clock in each of the time zones. First, half an hour on Ford was shown on ABC, then half an hour on Carter, and then the taped shows were repeated in sequence, first on NBC, from nine to ten o'clock, and on CBS, from ten to eleven.

The Ford presentation, by Bailey and Deardourff, featured a laudatory introduction from aboard *Air Force One* by Garagiola, an endorsement from the singer Pearl Bailey, then biographical film clips, many of them repeated from the film shown at the Republican convention in August. Finally the President was shown, in vest and shirtsleeves, speaking hoarsely from the airborne plane. (The tape had been made the previous Saturday as Ford flew from Houston to Philadelphia.) He repeated all his customary campaign themes and concluded by reminding his audience that two years earlier, on taking the oath, he had asked the American people as their first unelected chief executive "to confirm me as your President with your prayers." Now he said: "I want your prayers as you gave them to me two years ago, but I would hope that you would confirm me this time by your ballots."

Carter's presentation, by Bob Squier, a Democratic television consultant and producer, had him speaking from behind a desk in his home in Plains. Carter answered questions from citizens whose queries had been filmed weeks earlier by Squier and his crew on street corners, farms, and homes around the country—a candid effort to deal one final time with the "fuzziness" issue. Though he described Ford's record on the economy at one juncture as "absolutely terrible," Carter was generally restrained and relaxed in this final bid for votes, this last event on his long campaign odyssey.

The campaign that had begun for Ford nearly two years earlier and for Carter two years before that ended quietly and, no doubt for millions of weary voters, mercifully. Neither one of the final telecasts provided anything to jar the voters or make late converts.

The Ford media team, however, chose to forgo the use of some film that would have shaken the viewing electorate. After the second debate, President Ford had campaigned in Dallas from a limousine with an open top, in what was a particularly harrowing day for the Secret Service, though it passed without incident. Doug Bailey was there, filming for television spot commercials to use in Texas, and it occurred to him at once how things had changed for the better—one of the basic Ford campaign themes—in the thirteen years since John Kennedy had been shot there. "I really was very struck by the historic fact that this was not just a president in an open limousine in Dallas," Bailey recalled. "This was a preannounced parade route, and it wasn't just a matter of the President popping up every once in a while and waving to the crowd. He was like that the whole bloody way, twenty or twenty-five minutes."

As Bailey thought of the circumstance, his mind went back at once to the opening of Ford's campaign at the University of Michigan, to the explosion of the cherry bomb in the midst of his speech, and how it had caused Ford to flinch for just a second and many in the crowd to gasp. What if the two incidents were brought together on film: to dramatize on one hand the continuing, largely unspoken threat of violence in the political environment of the country, and on the other the progress in restoring normalcy to the point where this President, who already had been the target of two assassination attempts, felt he could campaign from an open car in Dallas?

Bailey set to work preparing a five-minute film—worried from the start, he said, that the loudest opposition would come from the Secret Service, who "would interpret this as some sort of invitation [to an assassin]," and that they might be right. But, he said, "I had no doubt, from the moment the thought struck me, that we were going to have powerful film."

He was right. It began with a marching band playing the campaign theme, "I'm Feeling Good about America," full of lines about hope and the restoration of normalcy. Then faces and voices of citizens came on attesting to "the change that has come over America." The film showed placid and happy faces, with the announcer saying: "You see it with our elderly, you see it with our young, you see it in our factories, you see it on our farms." And then, amid the cheering students at the Ford rally at Ann Arbor: "And how long has it been since we've seen it on our college campuses?" The camera cut to Ford speaking: "Trust is not cleverly shading words so that each separate audience can hear what it wants to hear, but saying plainly and simply what you mean, and meaning what you say!" And then he went on: "Trust is not having to guess what a candidate means—"

Abruptly, the sharp shot was heard: the President half-ducked, a startled look on his face, and in the stunned crowd women could be heard shrieking. He recovered quickly and pressed on with his speech. The theme was sung again, and the scene switched to Ford's motorcade through the streets of Dallas. The announcer said: "Neither the cherry bombs of a misguided prankster nor all the memories of recent years can keep people and their President apart. . . . When a limousine can parade openly through the streets of Dallas, there's a change that's come over America. The people and their President are back together again."

The effect was devastating. When I heard and watched the film for the first time in Bailey's office after the election, it literally sent chills up my back. But just what that effect would have been on voters in the last days of the campaign nobody could tell. When the film was shown to the members of the Ford campaign's executive committee on the morning of the third debate, argument immediately broke out.

"There was agreement on only two things," Bailey said; "that it was extremely powerful, and that it had to be tested." Jim Baker, a Texan, "made a strong argument that there was no question that if the ad ran in the state of Texas, we'd lose the state," Bailey said, and Dick Cheney felt the ad "could backfire, that people would resent all those memories being brought back." Teeter's polls at the time showed Ford slightly ahead in Texas, and, besides, everything was now going so well that nobody wanted to risk all on a high roll. "Everybody in the campaign felt it was pretty much on target," Bailey said. "We were closing a half a point a day and were within striking distance in every one of the big states. We knew it would be very close."

It was decided, therefore, that Teeter would have to screen the film before a panel of voters. A Teeter aide ran the test in Cleveland on the night of the third debate before a group of voters (selected from the phone book) with a history of splitting their tickets. "It was shocking to them," Teeter said later. "It was just too emotional. It wasn't seen as a bad commercial or a good commercial. It was just frightening." Also, Bailey said, "this film forced you to go back, not to the conditions two years ago, but to the conditions that have existed over the last thirteen years. You couldn't escape those memories coming back to you. It is entirely possible that out of all that, the over-all reaction would be a negative one to Ford for having seemed to trade on past tragedies, or anger that the campaign forced them to think about things they preferred not to think about. Or even to focus in on their memories of Jack Kennedy, with the result that they would find Carter more akin to those memories than Ford. But the thesis was, if you're behind, then what do you do? Just stick to the game plan, not ever rock the boat, not ever throw the bomb? Or do you try to change people's minds by reaching them as emotionally as you can?"

If the campaign had not been so close, Bailey said later, "I think we would have used it, if we were five points behind and really needed it." But it *was* close, and so it was decided that the film simply could not be shown. Ironically, concern over Texas—which Ford lost anyway—was a major factor. "Even if there had been no worry about shaking up the emotions," Bailey said, "even if the panel had liked it, everybody agreed we couldn't run it in Texas. And frankly, I don't believe there was anybody in the campaign at any stage who was prepared to deal with John Connally if in fact we had written Texas off. You could deal with Jim Baker, but neither Jim Baker nor anybody else could deal with Connally."

Though the cherry-bomb commercial thus never had the opportunity to keep the voters awake on Election Eve, some of the Ford insiders spent a restless night anyway. Bob Teeter, for one, went to bed with one nagging fear: "I could just see myself waking up in the morning, turning on my television set, and there would be Nixon voting early in San Clemente. And some network reporter would go up to him, stick a microphone in his face, and ask him who he voted for. And Nixon would say: 'Who do you think? I put him in, didn't I?' "

part XI

CONCLUSION

43. New President, Old System

In the early morning of Tuesday, November 2, Gerald and Betty Ford in East Grand Rapids, Michigan, and Jimmy and Rosalynn Carter in Plains, Georgia, were up and casting their ballots. Political wisdom dictated that photographs of them in the act of voting, shown later on television and in the afternoon newspapers, could be a stimulus to the lazy or otherwise occupied electorate. It was the last bit of permissible politicking for Ford and Carter on Election Day. Later the President returned to Washington and Carter went up to Atlanta to await their fate as depicted that night in the maps and the charts, the graphics, and the famous voices of the network news giants.

Bob Teeter's fears were unfounded. Richard Nixon did not show up at his regular polling place, Concordia Elementary School, in San Clemente. An aide reported that he and Mrs. Nixon had voted earlier by absentee ballot in anticipation of a trip to the desert that, he claimed, was subsequently canceled. But afterward, in the post-mortems, many argued that in this very close election "the Nixon issue"—meaning his pardon by Ford—though not extensively discussed in the campaign had been a prime factor. Among those who thought so was Ford himself. "Some of the Democratic candidates directly or indirectly alluded to it and refreshed memories," he told me after the election. "So there's no doubt, without any concrete proof, that it had an impact." At the time he pardoned Nixon, in his own first month in office, he had not decided to run for President in 1976, Ford said. Had he so decided at the time, I asked him, would he have gone ahead with the pardon anyway? "Whether I would or wouldn't have, if I had known I was going to be a candidate—" He paused for a moment, then went on: "I still think I would have."

In an election as close as this one was, though, it was fool's play to try to single out one reason for the way it turned out. And close it was: approximately 40.8 million votes or 49.9 per cent for Carter to 39.1 million or 47.9 per cent for Ford, a margin of only 2 per cent. In the electoral college, the outcome was even more sobering: 297 votes for Carter, 241 for Ford, the narrowest victory since 1916, when President Woodrow Wilson defeated Charles Evans Hughes by 23 electoral votes.

Furthermore, despite clear skies and pleasant weather over most of the nation, the turnout was the poorest in twenty-eight years—only 54.4 per cent of all Americans over the age of eighteen. It was calculated that of all voting-age citizens, only 27.2 per cent cast ballots for Carter and only 26.1 per cent for Ford. Put more starkly: for every American over the age of eighteen who voted, roughly speaking one did not; for every one who voted for Carter, three did not. And had Carter not been from the South, the turnout probably would have been even lower; voters in eleven Southern and border states went to the polls at rates higher than the national average.

Jimmy Carter was elected, but the result was hardly a rousing endorsement and certainly not the "wide-ranging success among the electorate" that he had said before Labor Day was crucial to him to deal effectively as President with Congress. Blacks, Protestants, Southerners of both races bailed him out. In the American system, however, a mandate can be a single vote if it satisfies the constitutional requirements that trigger the peaceful transference of power. Once the victor assumes the office of President—and with it the immense influence and all the prerogatives—the margin by which he has seized that office fades quickly. The American people by tradition and desire set their chief executive apart, no matter how large or small a winner he has been; even the unelected President had found that out. Ford's incumbency proved to be his most potent weapon in seeking the office on his own. In itself, it was a substantial reason for the closeness of an election that a unified majority party should have won handily in a time of high inflation and unemployment.

Carter isolated another obvious reason for the close result. "President Ford campaigned on the fear of change and the future, and he told people, 'You know I've been a good President but you don't know about Jimmy Carter,'" he said in a press briefing in Plains after the election. "His charge that I was waffling and that I would eliminate military bases, things like that, was effective in a negative way. But it was a correct and proper political decision. Our polls confirmed this. [Lack of] confidence was the reason for our shrinking lead. There was uneasiness and uncertainty in the twenty-thousand-dollar-and-above income bracket about taking a chance on a man they didn't know."

Carter also charged that television coverage of his campaign, and what he called "excessive deference to the President on the evening news shows," had a "crippling" effect on his own efforts. But he said at the same time that "if it hadn't been for the debates, I would have lost. They established me as competent on foreign and domestic affairs and gave the viewers reason to think that Jimmy Carter has something to offer."

What he did not say was that his insistence on making himself the issue in the general election, as he had done advantageously in the primaries, also narrowed the race. It had the effect of destroying his position as challenger, made it easier for Ford to defend his own record, and kept Carter himself on the defensive. Only Ford's blunder about Eastern Europe temporarily relieved the pressure, and even in that instance Carter helped Ford by attacking him excessively for it. "If I had let him just stew in the misstatement on Eastern Europe, rather than push the issue," Carter said, "I would have been better off. The polls showed that the people thought I was being strident."

Carter was also hurt by the fact that he ran as an outsider in the primaries and then found himself in the general election having to embrace, and being embraced by, all the old Democratic Party hacks. Whenever a candidate appears to be inconsistent with the image he sets for himself he is in trouble. Carter, by invoking the names of all the old party greats, while the Mayor Daleys and lesser Democratic lights were sidling up to him on one public platform after another, compromised his self-description as an outsider going it alone.

"That caused me horrible trouble," Carter said in our Oval Office conversation. "That was the biggest problem we had. . . . I finally made the difficult decision to be completely loyal to the Democratic nominees wherever I went; not to try to avoid them; to be on the platform with them; to share news coverage. It really hurt us in two or three states. . . . In almost every instance, an incumbent governor, or incumbent U.S. Senator or state party chairman, even though they may be quite popular, my association with them in an overt way was damaging. . . . I had run a kind of lonely campaign up to the convention; that's my nature and that's part of my political strength. To go into the position as the titular head of the Democratic Party, the head of the ticket, compelled by fairness to campaign with local and state congressional candidates, not only removed the lonely, independent candidate image depending on the voter only but it was also a reversal of what I had been during the primary season. It contributed to the claim that I was a person of mystery and that I was fuzzy on things, that I changed my positions. I never could resolve that question. But I think that my demonstration of loyalty to those Democratic candidates was the proper thing to do." Proper, and probably beneficial in the long run. Though voter registration dropped 3 per cent nationally, the Democrats registered significant numbers of new voters in two critical states that eventually went to Carter: Texas and Ohio. Together they provided 51 of his winning margin of 56 electoral votes.

But why the poor turnout nationally? In 1976, there had been prolonged primary competition for the nominations of *both* parties for the first time in more than fifty years. Also, the election marked the first time in twenty-four years that neither of the candidates had run for national office before. These factors might have been expected to whet the voters' appetites, but they did not. It may have been that the wounds of Watergate were burned more deeply and lastingly into the political consciousness of the electorate than generally realized, and were kept raw by the subsequent scandals that continued to afflict Congress, state and local governments.

In Peter Hart's July 1976 survey of nonvoters for the Committee for the Study of the American Electorate, 87 per cent of those asked agreed with the statement that "what this country needs most, more than laws and political programs, is a few courageous, tireless, devoted leaders in whom the people can put their faith." In the 1976 election, they seemed—by staying home—to be saying that they did not think they had found such leaders in Carter or Ford.

Yet both candidates, ironically, focused essentially on the matter of trust. "In our mind," Ford's advertising man Doug Bailey said, "the election was always going to turn on the question of trust." Ford's positive advertising tried to emphasize how far he had brought the country to believing in its President again, after Nixon; his negative advertising simultaneously labored with great success to keep alive the public doubts about Carter's trustworthiness. And Carter, as he had done all year, tried to sell himself first and foremost as a different, unstained kind of politician of unshakable integrity and trustworthiness, the candidate who promised never to lie or mislead.

Both Ford and Carter knew from their own polling data that the electorate was interested in character in 1976—not surprising, in light of the fact that the voters had bought experience at the expense of character in 1968 and 1972, in Nixon. The press, too, no doubt in large measure because it had been burned so badly by Nixon, was taking an extra-close look at character. Carter often squealed like a stuck pig at the constant probing, especially when the reporters were not satisfied with his vague proposals for tax reform, government reorganization, and the like, things he said he could not be specific about until he was elected. After Nixon, though, the press was in no mood to buy a pig in a poke, no matter how much he squealed. Carter sometimes had difficulty understanding that.

The press' concentration on character, sometimes to the point of psychoanalysis, inevitably extended the life of such controversies as Carter's use of the phrase "ethnic purity," Ford's long delay in firing Earl Butz, Carter's *Playboy* interview, and Ford's payola golfing vacations. Inevitably, the press and television were blamed for undue focus on such matters at the expense of what are always called "the substantive issues." But Ford's and

Carter's positions on everything from abortion to zero-based budgeting were reported repeatedly through the year. For the voter to make a judgment on Carter's character, it was just as important to know whether he had been dishonestly trying at a press conference in Houston to put off on *Playboy* his insult to Lyndon Johnson, as it was to know where he stood on a "substantive issue" like school busing. So, too, inquiries about Ford's role in blocking Wright Patman's investigation were as important in gauging the character of the man, as questions about his position on prayer in the schools.

Because the dialogue in a presidential campaign often seems to be reduced to bickering over what one of the candidates meant when he said this or that, or used this word instead of that one, it is frequently dismissed as demeaning or purposeless. But if the candidates choose to compete for votes over such nuances and shadings, it is both natural and necessary that the media and the public try to pin them down; this is especially so if the overriding question in the public mind is whether the candidates can be believed, and trusted.

Also, because American presidential campaigns almost inevitably are dominated by less than cosmic controversies and issues, it is said that the system doesn't "work." But if a prime purpose of the political system is to give all contenders an equal chance to achieve leadership, then the system worked without question in 1976. Jimmy Carter embarked on his bid for the presidency without fame, without established political support, and without much money. By deft use of the resources he had—himself, his family, time and a superb sense of timing, incredible determination, a high order of general and political intelligence, and the ability to attract other able people—he achieved his goal. That others were not as diligent, clever, or even lucky as he was, and hence failed, is not a commentary on the system, but on them.

Having said that, it can justifiably be asked whether it takes a Jimmy Carter—a man of such uncommon drive, ambition, self-discipline, and singlemindedness—to become President of the United States today, and whether it should. Indisputably, a political system that extracts such a price from presidential candidates—not just the ultimate winner but all those who enter the lists with high hopes and leave in disillusionment and often bitterness—cries out for improvement, and can be improved. The chaos of the system and incredible length of the campaign may well be prime reasons for voter disenchantment.

First, obviously, something must be done about the confusing and debilitating primary obstacle course. It is perhaps inevitable, and commendable as well, that more and more states have elected to use the popular primary to select national-convention delegates. In addition to being more democratic than the activist-oriented state caucuses and conventions, the allocation of delegates according to primary results is as a rule less vulnerable to challenge. But as the number of primaries has increased, and candidates have felt obliged to compete in them, the burden—financial and physical—has become oppressive. In 1976 most candidates entered the primaries selectively, except for Carter, who ran everywhere. In 1980 it seems likely that Carter's run-everywhere strategy will be emulated if there is a large field in either party, if only because it worked in 1976.

The most prevalent suggestion to deal with the proliferation of primaries—and one with some support in both parties—is to establish a series of regional primaries. In 1976 several states did coordinate their primary dates —Massachusetts and Vermont on March 2; Oregon, Idaho and Nevada, and Kentucky, Tennessee, and Arkansas, all on May 25. Such groupings permit a concentration of candidates' time and resources, and media attention, on a particular area of the country, and also cut down on costly and wearying cross-country travel. But unless there is some kind of national coordination, the positive effect is diminished.

One approach, originally sponsored by Walter Mondale, would create six regional-primary dates, each about a month apart; a state would have to hold its primary on the appropriate date if it had a primary at all. Another plan would create five regions. Each four years, the time sequence of the regions' primary elections would be picked by lot, so that no one region would be perpetually dominant by being first.

Some concern has been expressed in smaller states that their absorption into any regional-primary scheme would yield them much less candidate and media attention than received by the largest state or states in the group. But this argument does not recognize that most smaller states are already given short shrift by campaigners.

An exception to the regional concept that, in my opinion, could and should be made, is the New Hampshire primary, for both traditional and practical reasons. New Hampshire has for years jealously fended off all attempts to be replaced as host to the nation's first primary or, as in 1976, to be pulled into a New England regional grouping. It would be a mistake to end the tradition of New Hampshire as the kickoff state, not so much because of its reluctance to forego the honor but because, as already noted, only in such a small-state early primary can many underpublicized and underfinanced candidates hope to compete. In such a low-budget state, a candidate with little notoriety or money can gain a toe hold with a good showing and thus survive for the more costly later primary tests. As in 1976, New Hampshire could hold its primary one week before the regional primary for the rest of New England, thus preserving its own special purpose and at the same time not overly taxing candidates who might choose to run in the other New England states.

An alternative proposed by Morris Udall would be a series of four primary-election days, stretched out through the usual primary season. But in order to overcome the inordinate impact a candidate might have in his home region, they would not be grouped by region. Under this scheme, single states in New England, the South, the Midwest, Rockies, and West Coast might all hold their primaries on a single day, providing a better sense of nationwide strength for the competing candidates. But this approach would do nothing to alleviate heavy travel costs, and might well increase them. Candidates almost certainly would concentrate on the largest state in the group.

The national primary, likewise, would be extremely expensive for any contender and would rule out the candidacies of the little known and the underfinanced. Jimmy Carter, for example, probably would not have been able to run under such a scheme. The national primary as usually proposed would have a runoff of the two highest votegetters if no one received 40 per cent of the total; a safeguard against an extremist or regional candidate— a George Wallace—capturing his party's nomination in an overcrowded field. This idea, however, has fallen into wide disfavor among reformers, and should. It amounts to two, or maybe three, national elections instead of one.

A danger of the regional primary is that the winner of the first region might get such a jump on the rest of the field—might develop such "momentum"—that the voting in the other regions would become meaningless. But that possibility already exists for the candidate who does well in the early-primary states of New Hampshire, Massachusetts, or Florida. California's late primary, though it was the largest of 1976, had no influence on the Democratic nomination and merely prolonged the agony for Ronald Reagan on the Republican side.

For the sake of media and public perspective, some breathing space is needed between primary dates, so that the previous results can be properly digested and placed in the context of the full primary calendar. Otherwise, "momentum" becomes everything. Udall, perhaps the prime victim of Carter's momentum in the early 1976 primaries, put it this way later: "We had thirty primaries, presumably all of them equal. After three of those primaries, I'm convinced, it was all over. The die was cast. Just imagine the whole process being completed by Carter who wins New Hampshire by twenty-nine [per cent] to my twenty-four, he comes in fourth in Massachusetts, and then he beats Wallace by three percentage points in Florida. In the ensuing two weeks he shot up twenty-five points in the Gallup Poll, almost without precedent, by winning two primaries and coming in fourth in another one.[1]

"If there was a state in America where I was entitled to relax and feel confident, it was Wisconsin. I'd been there thirty times and I had organization, newspaper endorsement, and all the congressmen and state legislators. Well, I take a poll two weeks before the primary and he's ahead of me, two to one, and has never been in the state except for a few quick visits. That was purely and solely and only the product of that narrow win in New Hampshire and the startling win in Florida. And he won there only because everybody wanted to get rid of George Wallace.

"It's like a football game, in which you say to the first team that makes a first down with ten yards, 'Hereafter your team has a special rule. Your first downs are five yards. And if you make three of those you get a two-yard first down. And we're going to let your first touchdown count twenty-one points. Now the rest of you bastards play catch-up under the regular rules.' "

The combination of an opening New Hampshire primary (and earlier precinct caucuses in states like Iowa) plus regional primaries a month apart would bring desired order and rationality out of the present chaos—and still provide a chance for future Jimmy Carters to come from nowhere into serious contention.

It would be helpful at the same time if a way could be found to assure uniform rules for the primaries. The maze of different kinds of primaries —presidential preference ("beauty contest"), delegate-selection statewide, by congressional or state senatorial district, with or without proportional representation—has made presidential politics an insiders' game that even many of the insiders cannot follow. Small wonder that the average voter throws up his hands. But the chances of achieving such uniformity are slim. The Democratic National Convention in 1976 passed a resolution urging Congress to keep its hands off the conduct of primaries, and it is not likely that Congress, populated for the most part by obedient party members, will seek to intrude further.

Another troublesome area is the electoral college, and the continuing possibility of the election of a President who has not won the popular vote, as has happened three times. That possibility was raised anew in 1976, critics noting that had some 9245 votes shifted in Hawaii and Ohio, Ford would have lost the popular vote but won in the electoral college. In 1970

---

1. Actually Carter went up from 5 per cent in the Gallup Poll before the New Hampshire primary to 26 per cent after the Florida primary.

a constitutional amendment proposed by Birch Bayh abolishing the electoral college and substituting election directly by popular vote passed the House handily but was filibustered in the Senate by small-state senators, mainly from the South. This year Bayh has been trying again, with the help of Senate rules making it somewhat easier to force a vote, and the endorsement of President Carter. Bayh's amendment provides for a runoff between the two highest finishers in the event no candidate receives 40 per cent of the total vote.

An alternative would be to retain the electoral vote and, in the event a candidate wins the electoral vote but loses the popular vote, to have an immediate runoff between the two highest popular-vote finishers. This would also presumably require a constitutional amendment, since the Constitution provides for selection of the President by electors from the states only, with no reference whatever to the popular vote. Short of complete abolition of the system, Carter earlier had suggested that the electoral college itself—that is, the procedure whereby electors are chosen who actually cast each state's ballots through the "college"—be discarded, while retaining the allocation of electoral votes by states. This step would eliminate the problem of the so-called "faithless elector," who at the time of voting ignores the electoral vote of his state and casts his ballot independently, as one Washington state elector did in 1976, voting for Reagan rather than Ford, the winner of Washington's electoral votes. Under this revision, as soon as all electoral votes were tallied and certified—on Election Night or soon thereafter—the winner would be declared, rather than going through the drawn-out procedure of each state's electors meeting and reporting their votes to Congress in mid-December for official declaration of a winner. Carter later abandoned this more limited change and agreed to Bayh's plan to get rid of both the electoral college and the electoral vote entirely.

Two senators, Republican Strom Thurmond of South Carolina and Democrat Howard W. Cannon of Nevada, still favor this more limited approach. They would also have electoral votes in each state distributed in proportion to the popular vote, rather than the present winner-take-all method, as a means of retaining the concept of federalism in presidential elections.

Also needed before the next presidential election are revisions in the federal campaign-finance law. The law, the target of much abuse during 1976, in my opinion functioned reasonably well for its first trial, except that the Federal Election Commission let the President Ford Committee commit daylight thievery on accountability for presidential travel and use of White House staff for campaign purposes. The major problem, and it was a most serious one, was the failure of Congress and the President to reconstitute the FEC swiftly after the Supreme Court ruled, in late January 1976, that it could not exercise both legislative and executive functions. The uncertainty of the future, and the hiatus and subsequent delays in providing federal subsidies, worked unnecessary hardships on the campaigns of all Democratic candidates surviving into the April primaries, and on Ronald Reagan. Ford's delay in signing the law when it was revised, thereby hamstringing Reagan, was one of the more shameful episodes of the campaign. "The most difficult aspect of it for us," Carter said later, "was the on-again, off-again type of commitment to the basic law. It made for a great deal of uncertainty when I didn't have time to deal with uncertainties, and I think it was perhaps even more devastating to some of the other candidates." He was right. Udall particularly was sent reeling by the uncertainty, just as he thought he might be getting into contention with strong showings in Wisconsin and New York. But that problem presumably will not recur. Still, some way is needed to get the losers out of the competition cleanly rather than having them hanging around like walking corpses, just to earn a final few bucks from the federal-subsidy arrangement.

One simple and valid revision would make it considerably easier for candidates to qualify for federal matching funds: raise the individual-contribution limit to a single candidate from $1000 to $5000. The prime target of the legislation was supposed to be the fat cat who can buy elections, or try, like Nixon's multimillion-dollar benefactor of 1972, W. Clement Stone. If $1000 will not buy a candidate's soul, though, neither is $5000 likely to.

In the 1976 general election, there was much complaining that the $21.8 million ceiling for the major-party candidates did not provide enough money for the staffing and supplying of local and state campaign organizations, thus drying up local involvement and enthusiasm. There is no doubt that grass-roots politics took a back seat to media politics—and was shortchanged in the allocation of resources. It is not realistic to expect future presidential candidates to cut back on television advertising, especially when voters tell pollsters they take more of their information on the candidates from advertising than from the news media (a jolting acknowledgment that can only serve to spur the hucksters to new heights of televisual legerdemain).

Therefore, more money should be made available before 1980 to enable the candidates to tap the talents and the energies of willing workers at the neighborhood level. Providing campaign paraphernalia is elemental, and essential. When a campaign button becomes a status symbol in this country, to be hoarded rather than worn and passed around, something is wrong. (In Pittsburgh, at the end of the campaign, I saw a grown man and woman actually fighting over a Carter button.) People who give their time to political candidates usually are motivated by an old-fashioned team spirit. As ridiculous and even juvenile as it may seem, buttons and bumper stickers are the fix of many a political campaign junkie. Since neither customarily leads to the use of more addictive political drugs, such as personally seeking after high office, why shut off the supply?

The simple way to deal with the problem is to raise the level of the federal subsidy to the major-party candidates to perhaps $30 million, with a proviso that a reasonable limit be placed on spending for media advertising. If Congress is unwilling, an alternative would be to oblige the television networks to provide a certain amount of free time to each of the candidates, with the savings to go into grass-roots politicking. The networks certainly would squawk, but they always do when a suggestion comes along to reduce their gigantic profits to merely colossal.

Somewhat surprisingly, Ford, supposedly of the party of the fat cats, said after the election that he would not favor raising either the $1000 individual contribution limit or the $21.8 million limit for each major-party candidate in the fall. As for drying up grass-roots politics, he said: "It puts a greater burden on local organizations to go out and raise their own money instead of getting fed out of the Washington operation. They still have the opportunity under the law to raise their own money and I think that is fair, particularly since the Washington headquarters of a presidential candidate is not drawing money out of their local potential." Carter said he thought the $21.8 million was adequate, but he would favor legislation requiring the networks to provide free time "if I were sure it would be fair to third-party and lesser candidates." But he said he would prefer debate-like use of the time, rather than turning the time over to the candidates for spot commercials of their choice.

Later, as President, Carter proposed that candidates be given an unspecified additional amount of federal money to cover the costs of complying with the complex campaign-finance laws, and that they should not be required to report funds spent by congressional candidates to include their party's presidential nominee on joint campaign buttons, bumper stickers, and the like.

Improvement should be made in other areas as well. The assistance to responsible independent and third-party candidates should be liberalized, to increase the already woefully slim chances for new political movements to survive—an idea totally consonant with the Constitution, which, as Eugene McCarthy never tired of pointing out in 1976, makes no mention of Democrats or Republicans. "The American Revolution was not financed with matching funds from the Crown," McCarthy liked to observe, flailing against the whole public-financing scheme, which shut him out, and the limit on individual private contributions, which thwarted his favorite fat cats. He imagined the signers of the Declaration of Independence suggesting to Jefferson that he change the language to read: "We pledge our lives, our sacred honor and up to a thousand dollars." McCarthy needed 5 per cent of the total vote to qualify retroactively for federal reimbursement of his campaign expenses. He didn't come close; he polled 745,042 votes, or 0.9 per cent.

Finally, Carter has sponsored a new, simplified system of voter registration enabling qualified citizens to sign up at the polls on Election Day on presentation of proof of identity and residency. Democrats, and some Republicans, have voiced strong support for the measure as a way to boost voter participation, but most Republicans have opposed the idea as too prone to fraud and—though they don't say it—too prone to registering more Democrats, who usually fare better in open registration.

Taken as a whole, it is, beyond a doubt, an imperfect system. But it is a durable and malleable one, and it works. The evidence was seen dramatically and emotionally at noon on January 20, 1977, when the two ultimate protagonists of 1976 stood together on the steps of the United States Capitol: Gerald Ford, the President soon to be private citizen; Jimmy Carter, the private citizen soon to be President. Four years earlier they had also stood on these steps, honored but unnoticed guests as another President and his Vice President, both since banished from power, vowed to uphold the Constitution. The turmoil that ensued between that 1973 scene and this one still affected the national climate, and may indeed have affected the outcome of the drama that was now ending. In that intervening time, Ford and Carter had battled relentlessly and sometimes bitterly for the exercise of national power. But now, in good will, the one was benignly relinquishing that power and the other assuming it in a ceremony of tasteful simplicity.

First the young Vice President-elect, Walter Mondale, took his oath of office, with his predecessor, the beleaguered and hapless Nelson Rockefeller, at his side. Next the President-elect, his hand on a family Bible given to him by his mother, repeated the oath after the Chief Justice. Then he awaited the quieting of the applauding crowd and spoke as the President of the United States for the first time. In a gesture of conciliation, he began by saying to Ford: "For myself and for our nation, I want to thank my predecessor for all he has done to heal our land." Then he reached over and shook Ford's hand. It was a simple and generous thing to do, but a welcome one after the long months of deep partisanship, and it seemed to take the retiring President by surprise.

That gesture, in fact, was more remembered afterward than anything specific the new President said in an unusually low-key inaugural address that set a tone of confident but limited expectations. It was, altogether, a day more for the symbolic than the concrete. More stirring than all of the new President's words, spoken in his curious Georgia lilt, was the powerful, deep-voiced rendition of the "Battle Hymn of the Republic" by the Atlanta University Center Chorus, standing on a long platform below him. The singing of it, by this brilliant body of black young men and women, at the inauguration of the first President from the Deep South in 127 years, seemed itself to say something about how far the nation had come in the last four years.

After the traditional lunch for the new President in the Capitol, he and his wife and daughter got in the presidential limousine for the ride at the head of the Inaugural Parade to the reviewing stand outside the White House. But scarcely had the motorcade begun to roll down toward Pennsylvania Avenue when the Carters—Jimmy, Rosalynn, and Amy—climbed out and proceeded to walk the full distance to their new home. This symbol too was obvious but welcome: the man from Georgia who had gone directly to the American people to win the presidency was telling them that even now, presumably at greater personal peril, he was with them still. A wave of warmth and approval flowed through the crowds that lined the avenue as the First Family stepped smartly by, smiling and waving.

For four long years, as Jimmy Carter campaigned first in solitude and later in the glare of the mass media's focus, he had not taken—indeed had pointedly resisted—the easy way to get where he was going. He had campaigned longer hours in more distant places before fewer people than had any of the others, and he had campaigned always at the same purposeful but unhurried pace he exhibited now as he marched to the White House. As a campaigner, he had a fetish for punctuality but he always managed time to talk with and to listen to the people he met along the way. "I don't consider it a sacrifice," he would say repeatedly, as he ticked off the numbers of towns he had visited in a particular state. Others would complain about the ordeal of the campaign trail, about the excessive number of primaries, about the time away from home and the steady diet of nondescript food in nondescript motels. But Carter endlessly insisted that the experience was a great privilege and opportunity.

In the skeptical, even cynical world of politics such observations went down hard. His perseverance was chalked up to ambition; he simply wanted the presidency more than the others, the consensus held, and was willing to work harder to get it. No one could argue with that premise, but it became clear in time that Carter also meant what he said: he looked upon campaigning, as with nearly everything else he did, as a learning experience —for him, and for the voters.

He went to the people, he said in the Oval Office later, because they could not make themselves heard on their own. "The average quiet, some-what reticent, timid, and inarticulate person has to be sought out by the candidate," Carter said. "When I was campaigning the first year, with very little news coverage and without Secret Service protection, I felt that I was completely compatible with the average worker in a factory who would stop and chat with me in the early-morning hours, or among farmers; I could go out in the fields with them and talk to them." But it was not possible to do that in quite the same way after a while, as he became successful, and certainly not now, now that he was President.

As he embarked on his presidency, however, Jimmy Carter vowed to keep in touch with the American people. After four years of almost constant, daily, direct communication with them, it seemed to have become a way of life for him. In his first weeks in the White House, he made repeated gestures to the people—visiting them in their government offices, talking to them in a relaxed televised fireside chat, fielding their questions phoned directly to him in the Oval Office, sending his daughter to public school, dropping in on their entertainments in his new home town of Washington, going out into the country to answer their questions in an old-fashioned town meeting. He was, after four years of campaigning for the presidency, in a real sense still campaigning.

There was no telling how long Carter would want, or be able, to keep it up. Perhaps he was, after all, only like the marathon runner who, when finally crossing the finish line, simply runs on for a while, gradually slowing his pace to a walk, so as not to jar his system with abrupt change. But perhaps he did believe, as he so often said, that he drew his strength from an intimate contact with the American people, and did not want to lose that contact.

If Jimmy Carter, the thirty-ninth President of the United States, did so believe, and continued to act on that belief in substance as well as in symbolism, only good could come of it, for the country, and for him.

Index

Atlantic City, New Jersey, 482
Attack Carter Plan, 535
Austin, Mimi, 78, 79
Ayres, B. Drummond, Jr., 273

Bailey, Dennis C., 436
Bailey, Doug: 508, 533, 538,
    540, 541, 553, 573, 574, 575,
    595, 597, 619, 636, 646;
    Dallas-Ann Arbor film of,
    637-39; films man-in-the-street
    commercials, 616-17, 618
Bailey, Pearl, 3, 13, 636
Baker, Sen. Howard H., Jr., 85,
    428, 436, 501, 505, 506, 507
Baker, James A.: 484n, 487,
    489, 495, 497, 500; and Ford
    delegate hunt, 434, 439-41,
    481; manages Ford campaign,
    3, 538, 591, 599, 628, 638,
    639; signs telegrams to black
    clergymen, 634, 635
Baltimore, Maryland, 155, 164,
    333, 334, 337
Baltimore Sun, The, 334, 335,
    582, 596
Baptist Church, 270, 272, 330,
    338, 346, 370, 492, 563, 565,
    567, 568, 570, 632; *see also*
    Plains First Baptist Church
Barbour, Haley, 466, 468, 494,
    496-97
Barkan, Alexander, 129, 130,
    133
Barkley, Alben, 616n
Barnicle, Mike, 589
Baron, Alan, 106, 107n, 241,
    325
Bartlett, Gov. Dewey F., 145
Baseball, color line in, 95-96
Bass, Robert, 64
Batten, Barton, Durstine &
    Osborn, Inc., 429
Battle Creek, Michigan, 424
"Battle Hymn of the
    Republic," 655
Bay Pines, Florida, 400
Bayh, Senator Birch: 128,
    152-54, 156, 179, 188, 212,
    228, 234-35, 241-42, 260, 290,
    521; endorses Carter, 327;
    and Iowa contest, 200-206,
    212, 213, 214, 236, 240; and
    Massachusetts primary,
    241-42, 246, 247, 249-50; and
    NDC endorsement, 187-89; in
    New Hampshire primary,
    177-78, 244, 231, 234-35, 236,
    237, 240; 1971 presidential
    candidacy of, 153, 158;
    proposes abolition of electoral
    college, 651; supporters back
    Udall, 280, 291, 292; as

vice-presidential possibility,
    362; on Wisconsin ballot, 276;
    withdraws, 250, 278
Bayh, Marvella, 153, 154
Baytown, Texas, 630
Beame, Abraham D., 9, 370
Beatty, Warren, 351, 525
Becker, Benton, 43
Bedford, New Hampshire, 237,
    378
Bedtime for Bonzo, 390
Belgium, 115, 170
Bell, Griffin, 363
Bell, Jeffrey, 373-74, 377, 379,
    384, 393
Bell, John, ix
Bentsen, Sen. Lloyd M., Jr.:
    120, 128, 142, 156, 162-63,
    215, 216, 218-19, 260, 276;
    Carter on, 219n; Carter
    swamps in Texas, 327; as
    vice-presidential possibility,
    156, 163
Berger, Marilyn, 614n
Bergland, Bob, 297
Berkeley, California, 564
Berlin, New Hampshire, 232
Bernstein, Carl, 44n, 89-90
Beverly Hills, California, 66
Bicentennial celebration, 357,
    358, 441, 624
Biden, Sen. Joseph, R., Jr., 521
Billings, Lemoyne, 123
Binghamton, New York, 554,
    557
Birmingham, Alabama, 265,
    268, 325
Birmingham News, 497
Birth control, 591
Black, Charlie, 417, 432, 458,
    539, 615
"Black lung" benefits, Carter
    and, 320, 322
Blacks: 293-94, 307-308, 338,
    430, 619; and Brown, 335,
    337, 345; and Butz incident,
    590-92; and Carter campaign,
    7, 133, 193, 265, 303n,
    305-308, 335, 337, 338, 345,
    366, 370, 521, 525, 547, 552,
    606, 619, 633-36, 644; and
    Carter housing program,
    302-303; and Democratic
    party, 129, 130, 357; and
    "ethnic purity" remarks, 305,
    306, 308, 321; and Ford
    candidacy, 592, 634-35; and
    Harris, 145, 215; and
    Michigan primary, 337; in
    Mississippi Republican
    delegation, 495; and New
    Hampshire, 222; and Plains
    Baptist Church, 338, 632-35;

Reagan and, 95, 411; at
    Republican conventions, 475;
    and Shriver, 215; voter
    registration of, 635-636
Blaine, James G., 25
Bleicher, Michael, 281, 282,
    283, 284, 287
Blind Ambition (Dean), 584
Blue-collar vote; *see* Ethnic
    vote
"Blues in the Night," 234
Boca Raton, Florida, 400
Bode, Ken, 204, 281
Bond, Gov. Christopher (Kit),
    434-35
Bond, Julian, 127n, 303n
Bono, Sonny, 590
Boone, Pat, 495, 590
Boren, Gov. David, 216
Bossism: 229; ally of Jackson,
    260, 300; Carter opposes, 260,
    290, 300, 335, 552; Carter
    woos, 348, 516, 552; of
    Clarke Reed, 443-44;
    primaries compete with, 26,
    27, 28; Reagan victim of, 426
Boston, Massachusetts: 85, 86,
    124, 248, 249, 253, 257, 276,
    320, 404, 634; busing issue in,
    243, 244; Carter in, 240,
    245-47, 589; television in,
    222-23, 231; Wallace carries,
    250
Boston College, 590
Boston Globe, 245, 246, 248n,
    323, 362, 393, 394, 556, 589
Bourne, Sen. Jonathan, 26
Bourne, Dr. Peter: 115, 143n,
    208; memo to Carter by,
    107-108, 109, 110
Bowen, Gov. Otis, R., 420
Bowser, Charles, 633
Boy Scouts of America, 405
Bracy, Terry, 204, 276, 337
Bradlee, Ben, 123-24
Bradley, Ed, 630
Bradley, Thomas, 345, 362
Brady, Msgr. Frank, 207
Brady, Harold, 194
Brannon, Dr. Richard, 449
Brattleboro, Vermont, 226
Brazil, 115
Breckinridge, John C., ix, 24
Breen, John, 379
Bregman, Stan, 126
Bremer, Arthur, 60, 273, 279
Brill, Steven, 225-26
Brinkley, David, 5, 11, 237
Brock, Sen. W. E. (Bill), 428
Broder, David, 113, 118, 132,
    133, 235, 236, 306, 312, 324,
    362, 366n, 408, 551, 552
Brokaw, Tom, 5